SECURING AND CONTROLLING CISCO ROUTERS

SECURING AND CONTROLLING CISCO ROUTERS

PETER T. DAVIS

CRC Press
Taylor & Francis Group
Boca Raton London New York

CRC Press is an imprint of the
Taylor & Francis Group, an **informa** business

AN AUERBACH BOOK

CRC Press
Taylor & Francis Group
6000 Broken Sound Parkway NW, Suite 300
Boca Raton, FL 33487-2742

First issued in hardback 2017

© 2002 by Taylor & Francis Group, LLC
CRC Press is an imprint of Taylor & Francis Group, an Informa business

No claim to original U.S. Government works

ISBN-13: 978-0-8493-1290-8 (pbk)
ISBN-13: 978-1-138-43699-2 (hbk)

Library of Congress Cataloging-in-Publication Data

Davis, Peter T.
    Securing and controlling Cisco routers / Peter T. Davis.
        p. cm.
    Includes bibliographical references and index.
    ISBN 0-8493-1290-6 (alk. paper)
    1. Routers (Computer networks) 2. Computer networks--Security measures. I. Title.

TK5105.543 .D38 2002
004.6--dc21

2002019683

Library of Congress Card Number 2002019683

Visit the Taylor & Francis Web site at
http://www.taylorandfrancis.com

and the CRC Press Web site at
http://www.crcpress.com

Dedication

To Thomas Finlay Brick,
welcome to the world,
with all its frailties.

Peter T. Davis

Contents at a Glance

Contents

SECTION III: PREVENTING UNAUTHORIZED ACCESS: NETWORKING

SECTION IV: PREVENTING NETWORK DATA INTERCEPTION

19 Using Encryption and IKE 437

APPENDICES

Acknowledgments

Writing and publishing a book requires a great deal of dedication and hard work by many people. This book is no different. For his part, the author would like to thank the following people:

Christian Kirkpatrick, who got me involved in the project. Thanks for your help and patience.

Rich O'Hanley, who suggested the topic.

Andrea Demby, whose excellent editing is evident in the final product.

Michael Walther, because he kept me honest and gave me his valuable insight and technical advice.

Ben Udkow, who has generously agreed to provide time on SimRouter to every book purchaser.

Everyone at CRC Press and Auerbach who worked on this book and who I have not mentioned by name.

Everyone who contributes to Internet user forums. I found some useful, helpful information about Cisco routers.

Everybody who is seeking ways to improve their networks and systems.

Everybody who encouraged me to write this book.

Janet and Kelly for their understanding. Sorry about hiding in the basement when you and Jack went on your walks.

Introduction

If you are reading this introduction, you obviously want to learn about securing and controlling Cisco routers. You recognize that Cisco has captured a very large share of the internetworking market, and that knowledge of their products makes you more valuable to your present and future employers.

Regardless of your purpose for wanting to learn about router security and control, this book is for you. It is intended primarily for individuals who do not want to learn how to configure and maintain routers, but want to become familiar with tasks, the relationship between tasks, or the commands necessary to perform a security review or audit. However, it is an excellent resource for network operators or administrators tasked with securing their perimeter and networks.

In the book, you will find the things you need to know to operate the Cisco IOS efficiently, effectively, and economically — but chiefly securely. Completing the Practice Sessions included with most chapters will provide you with a solid base for embarking on the *Cisco Certified Network Administrator (CCNA)* accreditation programs, if you desire to do so.

You will build on tasks in each lesson and progressively move to more complex tasks. At the end of the book, you will have a firm grounding in Cisco routers. Following is a look at how the remainder of the book is organized.

Organizing the Job of Learning Cisco Security and Control

Material in this book has been organized to lead you through a logical step-by-step approach to learning the Cisco IOS easily and quickly. Obviously, your speed of progression depends on your skills and background knowledge. Although this is the case, you are encouraged to read the book in sequential order. Chapters tend to build on each other; for example, the concept of networking is introduced early in the book so that you will think about it throughout the remainder of the book.

The following sections give an idea of what can be expected in each chapter.

Chapter 1: The Need for Security

Chapter 1 discusses the threats and risks facing your organization and your network. Included in the chapter are descriptions of basic Cisco security features.

Chapter 2: Understanding OSI and TCP/IP

This chapter explores introductory networking concepts. It begins with the ISO's OSI seven-layer model and compares and contrasts it to the TCP/IP protocol suite. Included in the chapter's lessons are descriptions of network components and options.

Chapter 3: Routed and Routing Protocols

Chapter 3 introduces routed and routing protocols. You will learn how routers move packets from one network to another. Included in the chapter is a discussion of the various routing protocols and the differences between them.

Chapter 4: Understanding Router Basics

Chapter 4 provides you with the tools to navigate your way around the router. You will learn about the various modes of the router and how to move from one to the other.

   You will also learn about the router components: RAM, NVRAM, Flash, ROM, and interfaces.

Chapter 5: Managing Your Router

This chapter begins with how to set up your router. In addition, you will learn how to update the IOS. If your updates are not successful, then you will need to study the material on troubleshooting your router included in this chapter. You can use the log you learn how to set up as well. If that does not work, use a Simple Network Management Protocol agent or the Cisco Discovery Protocol that you learn about here.

Chapter 6: Introducing Security Services

By the end of Chapter 6, you will have learned how to implement non-AAA authentication, including enable, enable secret, console, auxiliary, virtual terminal, and line passwords. You will also learn about TACACS, the username database, CHAP, and PAP.

Chapter 7: Implementing AAA Security Services

Chapter 7 provides a basic knowledge of AAA security services. Discover the benefits and uses for AAA security services. You also learn how to enable AAA and use security servers.

Chapter 8: Implementing AAA Authentication

In Chapter 8, the pace quickens. First, you will learn how to create method lists. Then you will find out how to configure AAA for login, PPP, ARA, and NASI authentication. You will also learn how to set up banners and log-in messages.

Chapter 9: Implementing AAA Authorization

Chapter 9 demonstrates how to implement AAA authorization. You will learn about TACACS+, If-Authenticated, None, Local, RADIUS, and Kerberos authorization.

Chapter 10: Implementing AAA Accounting

In Chapter 10, you will see how to configure AAA accounting and learn about Command, Connection, EXEC, Network, and System accounting.

Chapter 11: Configuring TACACS and XTACACS

Chapter 11 introduces the first AAA security servers: TACACS and XTACACS. You will learn how to configure these protocols for authentication.

Chapter 12: Configuring TACACS+

In Chapter 12, you will learn about TACACS+, another security server. You will learn to implement the protocol for your router, and how to set up authentication, authorization, and accounting.

Chapter 13: Configuring RADIUS

In this chapter, you will discover RADIUS and learn how to configure authentication, authorization, and accounting.

Chapter 14: Configuring Kerberos

This chapter leads you through a discussion of Kerberos. Learn how to define a Kerberos realm, copy SRVTAB files, retrieve a SRVTAB file from the KDC, specify Kerberos authentication, and enable credentials forwarding.

Chapter 15: Basic Traffic Filtering, Part 1

In Chapter 15, the beginning of traffic filtering, you will learn to create standard and extended static access lists, and how to apply the access list to an interface.

Chapter 16: Basic Traffic Filtering, Part 2

In this chapter you will learn about additional ways to filter traffic. You will find out about named access lists and prefix lists. Finally, you will learn how to monitor and verify access and prefix lists.

Chapter 17: Advanced Traffic Filtering, Part 1

Chapter 17 starts you on some advanced filtering tools. Learn how to use time ranges in time-based access lists and see how to configure lock-and-key by creating dynamic access lists.

Chapter 18: Advanced Traffic Filtering, Part 2

In this chapter, you will discover reflexive access lists. In addition, you will learn about Context-Based Access Control (CBAC).

Chapter 19: Using Encryption and IKE

In Chapter 19, you will learn all about the differences between IPSec and Cisco Encryption. This chapter will lead you through configuring Certification Authority interoperability and how to use IKE and set up ISAKMP.

Chapter 20: Configuring IPSec

Chapter 20 provides an explanation of IPSec. It shows the correct way to create crypto maps (manual, IKE-established, and dynamic) and how to apply them to an interface.

Chapter 21: Configuring Denial-of-Service Security Features

In Chapter 21, you will find out about protecting yourself against denial-of-service attacks. Learn how to control directed broadcasts, IP source routing, ICMP redirects, and unreachable messages and SYN floods.

You will also learn how Network Address Translation might help, and about queuing and traffic policing to aid in your fight.

Chapter 22: Configuring Neighbor Authentication and Other Security Features

Finally, you will find out about preventing fraudulent route updates. This chapter finishes with some security controls not covered elsewhere.

Appendix A: IP Addressing

Appendix A provides a useful starting point for addressing. If you forget about classful addressing and CIDR, this is the place to start.

Appendix B: Subnetting

Appendix B helps you work your way through the complex subject of subnetting. Learn how to calculate various subnet masks based on your organization's requirements.

Appendix C: IP Protocol Numbers

Appendix C provides a reference as to what numbers ICANN under the auspices of the IANA assigned to the various protocols.

Appendix D: Well-Known Ports and Services

Appendix D provides a list of well-known and registered ports for handy reference.

Appendix E: Hacker, Cracker, Malware, and Trojan Horse Ports

Appendix E provides a list of some port numbers that you must watch carefully because they are often associated with lax security and security breaches.

Appendix F: ICMP Types and Codes

This appendix lists possible ICMP type and code combinations you might find and might want to filter or block.

Appendix G: Determining Wildcard Mask Ranges

This appendix describes how to calculate the correct wildcard mask range when attempting to summarize an arbitrary range of IP addresses.

Appendix H: Logical Operations

Appendix H provides a primer on binary mathematics.

Appendix I: Helpful Resources

Appendix I provides useful Usenet Newsgroups, mailing lists, and RFCs for further research on this subject.

Appendix J: Bibliography

Because this book is really the beginning of your journey, this bibliography provides additional reading. Do not forget my other eight books!

Appendix K: Acronyms and Abbreviations

Appendix K provides help on decoding all those TLAs: three-letter acronyms.

Appendix L: Glossary

This glossary contains definitions of the major networking and information processing terms used throughout the book.

Conventions

The presentation of Cisco routers is best accomplished by providing commands as you will enter them and see the output. You will make choices by working through these commands.

Icons in this book will draw your attention to information considered interesting or important. The icons are used as explained here:

Tip: The Tip offers advice, teaches an easier way to do something, or explains an undocumented feature.

Note: The Note presents interesting tidbits of information related to the surrounding discussion.

Caution: The Caution helps you steer clear of disaster, alerts you to potential problems, or warns you when you should not skip a task.

In addition, most chapters end with a Practice Session that includes a review of key concepts by providing tasks that you can try on a real router network. SimRouter has made available one hour of time on their networks. The majority of chapters come with a checklist so you can start the process of reviewing your systems.

In the text, terms are treated in the following manner:

- Menu names are separated from menu options by a | symbol. For example, |Select | File | Close| indicates that you need to select the File menu and choose the Close option.
- Keyboard keys, information that appears onscreen, and Cisco commands appear in `computer font`.
- User-typed entries appear in **`boldface computer font`**.
- New terms introduced to the reader appear in regular *italics*.
- ^ or **Ctrl** represents the Control key. For example, should you see ^**D** or **Ctrl+D**, you should hold down the Control key while you press the D key.

- Nonprinting characters, such as passwords, are italicized and appear in angled brackets < >.
- ! or exclamation points at the beginning of a line indicate a comment line. They are also displayed by the Cisco IOS software for certain processes.
- Default responses to system prompts appear in square brackets [ ].
- *Italics* within the command syntax indicate arguments where you supply values; in contexts that do not allow italics, arguments are enclosed in angled brackets (< >).
- Keywords or arguments appearing within square brackets [x] are optional.
- A choice of required keywords (represented by x, y, and z) appears in braces separated by vertical bars, for example {x | y | z}. You must select one.

Use and abuse this book. Mark it up. Make notes in the margin. Highlight significant sections. Tear out the commands and use them. Learn from it. Finally, enjoy using this book as much as I enjoyed writing it for you.

If you have questions or comments about the book, you can send e-mail to Peter T. Davis at ptdavis@pdaconsulting.com.

About This Book

This book starts where you are likely to start — at the beginning. Its design ensures that you learn concepts when you need them, as you start your exploration of Cisco router security and control. By following the book, with its orientation and examples, you will learn simple tasks that build on each other until you have mastered the basics of the IOS. If you faithfully follow the book, you can perform a simple Cisco IOS review or audit.

Anyone with a working knowledge of computers can learn how to gather information, set passwords, backup the IOS, add and delete users, create access lists, and generally maintain security.

Who Should Read This Book

Anyone interested in learning to use Cisco security and control will find something of value in this book. The thrust of the book, however, is toward those people who will secure or audit a Cisco router and therefore must grasp the key tasks.

For both, this book covers Cisco routers from the basics to tasks and ideas that you are sure to find interesting and useful as you progress beyond those basics.

This book is for you if one or more of the following statements applies to you:

- You have the task of securing network security.
- You have to review the implementation of Cisco security measures.
- You are interested in becoming Cisco certified.
- You just found out that you will be taking over administration of existing routers.
- You have been told that your organization will install a Cisco router next month.

- You applied for a job at an organization that uses Cisco routers exclusively and you want to get the job.
- You just want to learn about a widely used internetworking product.

THE BASICS

I

Chapter 1

The Need for Security

In this chapter, you will learn about:

- Router risks
- Existing threats
- Recommended controls
- Specific exposures

The New Reality

In the good old days, network threats were fewer and far between. A teenager sitting in his room might try to discover your backdoor modems using a war dialer inspired by the movie of the same name. Another dogged hacker might try to leave a message on your console saying, "Kilroy was here." A disaffected employee might try to read the salaries of the executive staff to start trouble. However, attacks from crackers, hackers, phreakers, and phrackers are no longer benign. War has been declared. Make no mistake; there is a war going on. Your organization's infrastructure is at risk. As a network and security professional, you are on the front line in defending your enterprise.

If the chilling events of September 11, 2001, did not convince you, then perhaps nothing will. But check out the archives at http://www.2600.com, http://www.attrition.org, or http://www.alldas.de.

New break-ins illustrate the next likely major battleground for terrorist organizations: the realm of cyberspace. Within days of the first U.S. airstrikes on Afghanistan, a group of pro-Taliban crackers in Pakistan penetrated several Indian government computers, including one in the atomic energy agency, and posted messages of support for Osama bin Laden and his al Qaeda terrorism network. The group, which calls itself the al Qaeda Alliance and opposes the U.S. effort in Afghanistan, downloaded internal files and vandalized three major Web sites. On October 22, 2001, attrition.org reported that another group known as the

3

Pakistan Hackers Club (PHC) broke into sites in India, the United States, and the United Kingdom, and left predictable venomous messages. At various times during the previous year, they reported that G-Force, another Pakistani hacker group, had broken into numerous sites in India. Not to be outdone, Indian crackers struck back at Pakistani Web sites. The American Muslim Council reported that someone broke into its servers on November 2, 2001, and sent out explicit messages with attached viruses to their subscribers. One subscriber in Saudi Arabia complained about the 3000 messages flooding his mailbox. And so the war escalates.

Note: The Council claims that this was a deliberate attack, while others feel it was just a coincidence. They got the Snow White or Hybris virus and passed it on. Nothing more, nothing less; no big deal. Either way, you will want to block messages from them.

And the attackers are sending out scouting parties to perform reconnaissance. According to DShield.org (http://www.dshield.org/topports.html), which collects statistics on online attacks, the "most-probed" ports in late 2001 were: 80 (http); 138 (netbios); 6346 (gnutella); 53 (domain); 21 (ftp); 111 (sunrpc: U/Linux remote procedure call); 22 (ssh); 123 (ntp); 27374 (subseven Trojan); 69 (tftp); and 25 (smtp). However, these probes are only about 40 percent of the attacks and probes; the other 60 percent of the probes and attacks are distributed across all the remaining ports.

At the beginning of November 2001, the CERT/CC, the government-funded security watchdog group, warned that routers may become a major point of attack. As of that date, router hacking had not become widespread, but the CERT/CC saw the beginning of a new trend. The CERT/CC representative felt that attacks targeting routers, which largely help drive network traffic, could substantially impact Internet performance. They advised that there were reports of router compromise because of weak and default passwords. Also mentioned was the availability of public resources instructing novices how to exploit router security weaknesses. The representative further stated that they expected to see automated exploit tools surface in the future. (In November 2001, there were 71 router exploits available at http://www.antionline.com. Some of them were specific to the Cisco IOS.) Finally, the CERT official cautioned that routers might become a primary target in future attacks, potentially choking network traffic. They suggested administrators turn off any unneeded functions or services, select difficult-to-guess passwords, and encrypt communications used to manage or change router settings over the Internet.

Armed with a plethora of cracking and denial-of-service tools, the cyberterrorists might start unleashing attacks, crippling networks that support critical infrastructures. The FBI's National Information Protection Center (NIPC) issued a warning in November 2001 advising companies responsible for infrastructure support systems to become extra-vigilant. The NIPC advised that the potential "for future DoS (denial-of-service) attacks is high."

So the attackers are going to start targeting your routers. Not that you do not have enough problems already. If you are a network or security administrator, your environment might seem chaotic. While fighting the external war, you are fighting minor skirmishes within your organization as you try to bring some order to your networks. People complain that you are a blocker, not a facilitator. They pronounce that your security requirements will delay or kill a much-needed project, application, or system. Your wire closet and network operations center might look peaceful at night when everyone else has gone home but they are sitting in the middle of a war zone. Before you dismiss these statements as trite or melodramatic, think about it.

You are a soldier enlisted in the war to protect your organization. Your network monitoring station is the distant early warning system alerting you to logic bombs lobbed at your network and the viral terrorism unleashed to infect your systems. Your routers are on the front line and sometimes in no-man's-land. Many organizations are oblivious to these threats and unaware of the scuds aimed at them. Perhaps because the attackers do not normally attack you head-on, but rather attack stealthily in the middle of the night when your defenses are down. Perhaps because the action is similar to guerrilla warfare. And had you heeded U.S. President Bush after the wanton destruction of the World Trade Center buildings, you know this is a different war. You are being hit from all directions and your attempt to fight back is ineffectual. They pop up from nowhere, hit you with a freely available software tool, and disappear behind a network quagmire in the "dark address space" of the Internet. Defending against these cyberterrorists means trying to hit thousands of moving targets. To compound the problem, they camouflage themselves to pose as allies (i.e., customers, suppliers, and clients).

The fact that you purchased this book means you at least acknowledge the need to protect your networks. Crackers know the material in this book. (If they did not before, suffice it to say, they do now.) That is their edge. They know that there are weaknesses in the applications that Cisco includes on their routers. They know they can easily defeat some forms of Cisco password encryption by downloading a small program from the Internet. They know they can use this password-cracking program on their PalmOS. So, turn the tables on your enemies and read and implement the security controls in this book.

As more people access the Internet and companies expand their networks, the challenge to provide security for networks becomes increasingly difficult. You must expend more effort on shoring up your electronic defenses. Organizations must determine what parts of their internal networks they must protect, learn how to restrict user access to these areas, and determine what network services they should filter to prevent potential security breaches. The attackers are seeking or compromising your most vital assets after your employees: your data. Your organization depends on information systems to conduct its business and to meet its contractual and regulatory obligations. This dependence poses a compelling responsibility to protect your networks.

You can address network security at the data-link, or media, layer (where packet snooping and encryption problems can occur); at the network, or protocol, layer (where Internet Protocol (IP) packets and routing updates are controlled); and at the application layer (where, for example, host-level bugs become issues). This book focuses primarily on the network and transport layer, but this does not mean that you should not consider other security measures. Physical security is still a required and cost-effective measure. If you cannot physically protect your router, then you cannot logically protect your network. Any oaf with physical access could easily send a BREAK signal on the console port, modify the system configuration, and reboot the modified system. (In fact, you will learn how to do this in Chapter 5.)

Over the past few years, Internet-enabled business, or E-business, has drastically improved organizations' efficiency and revenue growth. E-business applications such as E-commerce, supply-chain management, and remote access allow companies to streamline processes and lower operating costs, while increasing customer satisfaction. These applications require mission-critical networks accommodating voice, video, and data traffic; thus, the networks must scale to support more clients and provide greater capacity and performance. However, as networks enable more and more applications and are available to more and more users, they become more and more vulnerable to more and more security threats. To combat those threats and ensure that crackers do not compromise your business, security technology must play a major role in your network.

Without proper protection, any part of any network is susceptible to attacks or unauthorized activity. Professional crackers, company competitors, cyberterrorists, or even employees can violate your routers, switches, and hosts.

Cost of Intrusions

Network attacks cause organizations several hours or days of downtime annually as well as serious breaches in data confidentiality and integrity. Depending on the level of the attack and the type of information the attackers compromised, the consequences of network attacks vary in degree from mildly irritating to completely debilitating, and the cost of recovery from attacks can range anywhere from hundreds to millions of dollars.

When crackers compromise the availability of your applications, you could easily lose millions of dollars per hour. For example, organizations running E-commerce Web sites lose revenue as customers shop elsewhere for their products and services; informational Web sites can lose precious advertising time; and manufacturing organizations might shut down their lines because they do not have access to information regarding their raw materials.

When someone compromises data confidentiality, the consequences to an enterprise are not always immediately felt, but it is never the less costly. For example, when a cracker gains access to an organization's e-mail system, he might steal proprietary information that provides competitive advantage resulting in a loss to your organization of the time and money spent on research and development to gain that advantage.

When a cracker compromises data integrity, an organization must often incur prohibitive costs to correct the consequences of such an attack. For example, a malicious cracker might modify your Web site and replace relevant information with digital graffiti or offensive content. Your organization would have to spend money not only to fix the site, but also to counter the resulting negative publicity.

The legal ramifications of breaches in data confidentiality and integrity are also extremely costly for organizations. Existing and pending laws and regulations generally stipulate that organizations in violation could face a range of penalties. You also face possible civil action.

Even when an external hacker perpetrates the attack, the courts may potentially find the company storing that information negligent because the organization did not adequately safeguard the information. Furthermore, companies suffering breaches in data integrity might face litigation initiated by clients who are negatively affected by the incorrect or offensive data and seek monetary or punitive damages. For example, should you choose not to do any egress filtering on outbound traffic and your systems act as zombies to deny service to another organization, that organization might successfully sue you for damages.

Designing the Security Infrastructure

Obviously, an organization cannot adopt the approach of the ostrich — putting its head in the sand. An organization must adopt a proactive stance on network security. A good place to start is with an architecture. Should a builder attempt to build a house without plans, who knows what might result. You might find that the plumbing was omitted and the builder would need to add it in after finishing the house. This means that the builder would need to demolish some finished walls to rough in the plumbing. The net result is that costs would increase and the delays would prevent the homeowners from moving in on time. Well, it seems pretty obvious, but perhaps it would surprise you to find out that many organizations develop their security infrastructure in this manner. They are constantly in firefighting mode; when they discover problems, they fix them without any regard to an overall architecture. Their security programs grow like coral: each new control is added to the existing infrastructure until the weight causes a part to snap off. Some controls conflict with other controls, other controls are implemented needlessly, while still others go missing. The objective of any network security program is to protect networks and their applications against attacks, ensuring information confidentiality, integrity, and availability. When designing an organization's network security architecture to meet this objective, you must consider several factors. Your networks and their associated applications do not all have the same risks from attacks or possible costs of repairing damages after an attack. Therefore, you must perform cost-benefit analyses (i.e., risk analyses) to evaluate the potential returns on investment for various network security technologies and components versus the opportunity costs of not implementing those items.

Security Policy

The best place to start is to develop a security policy. Make your security policy a formal statement, supported by your organization's highest levels of management, regarding the business rules for information protection and the implementation guidelines for the available technology. You must ensure that you determine your security policies according to business needs. Business needs should dictate the security policy; a security policy should not determine how a business operates. The policy should flow down from the corporate goals and out of the information technology (IT) plans.

To develop an effective security policy, consider the following steps:

1. *Identify your network assets.* Identify both your network's assets and the protection they require.
2. *Determine risks, threats, and threat agents.* Understand how potential intruders can enter your organization's network or sabotage network operations.
3. *Limit the scope of access.* Create multiple barriers within your networks so that unlawful entry to a part of your network does not automatically grant entry to the entire infrastructure.
4. *Identify assumptions in your risk analysis.* Identify, examine, and justify your assumptions, as any hidden assumption is a potential security hole.
5. *Determine the cost of security measures.* Understand costs in terms of increased connection times, inconveniences to legitimate clients accessing the assets, increased network management requirements, and actual dollars spent on equipment or software upgrades, and weigh these against potential benefits.
6. *Consider human factors and their effect on the controls.* To ensure compliance with your security measures, ensure clients can get their work done as well as understand and accept the need for security.
7. *Implement pervasive and scalable security.* Use a systematic approach to security that includes multiple, overlapping security methods.
8. *Remember physical security.* Do not neglect the physical security of your network devices and hosts.

Security policies represent trade-offs. With all security policies, there is usually a trade-off between user productivity and security measures perceived as restrictive and time-consuming. Your policy should strive to provide maximum security with minimum impact on user access and productivity. Some security measures, such as network data encryption, do not restrict access and productivity. But encryption consumes lots of cycles. Consequently, you have a trade-off.

Because business requirements and security technologies are always evolving, you should consider the security policy a living document requiring, at a minimum, an annual review. You must systematically update it to reflect new business directions, technological changes, and resource allocations.

Security Plan

Next, you need to integrate your security policy into the existing enterprise network. You should define the access and security requirements for every service so you can divide the network into security zones with clearly identified trust levels. You can deal with each security zone separately and you can assign a different security model to each. You should aim to contain security breaches to a particular zone or part of your network. Just as the bulkhead in a ship contains a leak so that the ship does not sink, your layered security limits the damage a security breach has on the entire network. In addition, your network security architecture should define common security services that you will implement across the network. You should consider these typical services:

- Password authentication, command authorization, and accounting (AAA)
- Confidentiality provided by virtual private networks (VPNs)
- Access control

You will want to implement varying levels of control in your security zones to identify clients, protect your perimeter, protect confidential information from eavesdropping or tampering during transmission, and ensure the integrity of your system and applications. After you make the tough decisions, deploy the security architecture in phases, addressing the most critical areas first.

Phases of Securing a Network

Security is not a place you arrive at; rather, it is a continuous process. To maintain a high level of network security, you need to cycle through these three main phases:

1. Establish a security policy that defines the security goals of the enterprise.
2. Implement network security technologies in a comprehensive and layered approach so that the organization does not rely entirely on only one type of technology to solve all its security issues.
3. Audit the network on a recurring, periodic basis to ensure that the organization is compliant with the security policy and that you find no irregularities. You should use the results of the audit to modify the security policy and the technology implementation as required or to develop a security awareness or training program.

Identifying Security Risks and Threats

The above discussion introduced some simple security concepts. There are many good books on this subject, which is really beyond the scope of this book. Part of the discussion above focused on identifying risks. To determine the best ways to protect against attacks, network and security administrators should understand the many types of attacks and the damage that these attacks can cause to their infrastructures.

Cisco IOS software provides a comprehensive set of security features to guard against specific security risks. This section describes a few common security risks that you might find in your network. You will also find a known vulnerability associated with each risk. The risks that this book focuses on include:

- Preventing unauthorized access into networking devices
- Preventing unauthorized access into networks
- Preventing network data interception
- Preventing denial-of-service attacks
- Preventing fraudulent route updates
- Preventing unauthorized changes

Preventing Unauthorized Access into Networking Devices

If someone were to gain console or terminal access into a networking device (e.g., a router, switch, or network access server), that person could do significant damage to your network. They might reconfigure the device, or they even might view the device's configuration information.

Historically, password attacks, attacks where a perpetrator gains unauthorized access to network passwords in order penetrate confidential information, have been the most prevalent type of attacks. When someone cracks the password of a legitimate user, that person has access to that user's network resources and typically a launching pad for getting access to the remainder of that network and others. Often, crackers can easily obtain passwords because users typically choose common words or numbers for passwords, enabling the crackers to use programs that methodically determine those passwords. Crackers also deploy social engineering techniques to gain access to passwords.

Typically, you want administrators to have access to your networking device but you do not want other users on your local area network or those dialing in to the network to have access to the router. Administrators can access Cisco networking devices by dialing in from outside the network through an asynchronous port, connecting from outside the network through a serial port, or connecting via a terminal or workstation from within the local network.

To prevent unauthorized access into a networking device, you should configure one or more of these security features:

1. You can configure passwords and privileges at each networking device for all device lines and ports, as described in Chapter 6, "Implementing Non-AAA Authentication." The router stores these passwords. You can configure up to 16 different privilege levels and assign each level to a password. For each privilege level, you define a subset of Cisco IOS commands that the user can execute. You can use these different levels to allow some users the ability to execute all Cisco IOS commands, and to restrict other users to a defined subset of commands. When users attempt to access the device through a particular line or port, they must enter the correct password applied to the line or port before they can access the device.
2. For an additional layer of security, you can configure username and password pairs, stored in a database on the networking device, as described in Chapter 6, "Implementing Non-AAA Authentication." You assign these pairs to lines or interfaces and authenticate each user before that user can access the device.
3. If you want to use username and password pairs but you want to store them centrally instead of locally on each individual networking device, you can store them in a database on a security server. Multiple networking devices can then use the same database to obtain user authentication and, when necessary, authorization information. Cisco supports a variety of security server protocols, such as RADIUS, TACACS+, and Kerberos. Should you decide to use the database on a security server to store log-in username and password pairs, you must configure your router or access server to support the applicable protocol. In addition, because you must administer most supported security protocols through the AAA security services, you

will need to enable AAA (see Chapter 7). For more information about security protocols and AAA, refer to Chapters 7 through 14.

Note: Cisco recommends that, whenever possible, you use AAA to implement authentication.

---

4. If you want to authorize individual users for specific rights and privileges, you can implement AAA's authorization feature, using a security protocol such as TACACS+ or RADIUS. For more information about security protocol features and AAA, refer to Chapter 12, "Configuring TACACS+" and 13, "Configuring RADIUS."
5. If you want to have a backup authentication method, you can configure AAA to specify the primary method for authenticating users (e.g., a username and password database stored on a TACACS+ server) and then specify backup methods (e.g., a locally stored username and password database). You use the backup method when the networking device cannot access the primary method's database. To configure AAA, refer to Chapter 7, "Implementing AAA Security Services." You can configure up to four sequential backup methods.

Caution: Should you not have backup methods configured, the router will deny you access to the device when it cannot access the username and password database for whatever reason.

---

6. If you want to keep an audit trail of user access, you can configure AAA accounting as described in Chapter 10, "Implementing AAA Accounting."

In many circumstances, AAA uses security protocols to administer its security functions. If your router or access server is acting as a network access server, AAA is the means through which you establish communication between your network access server and your RADIUS, TACACS+, or Kerberos security server.

Cisco IOS Password Vulnerability

Numerous organizations have reported on the weak encryption that allows programming code to take an encrypted Cisco IOS type 7 password and compute the plaintext password. (You will learn about password types in Chapter 6, "Implementing Non-AAA Authentication.") Crackers can get a copy of the encrypted password through one of the following methods:

- Polling Cisco IOS configuration file through SNMP. So, you should disable SNMP unless absolutely necessary.
- Attacking a TFTP server where the backup file exists. Harden the OS of the TFTP server and ensure you have installed all patches. In addition, do a port scan periodically to ensure that only services you support are running.

In Chapter 6, you will see an example of GetPass!, a Windows-based program that exploits this weakness, and learn the names of some others.

Buffer Overflow Vulnerability

In June 2000, CERT reported that MIT Kerberos had multiple buffer overflow vulnerabilities that attackers could use to gain root access. Ensure you have installed all patches.

Leap Year Vulnerability

When you configure the Kerberos Client functionality to provide access control on Cisco products, it will fail in a deny state when the expiration of the credentials falls in January or February of leap years, thus denying any Kerberos-authenticated access.

There is an error in how the Kerberos Client calculates timestamps in replies from the Key Distribution Center (KDC) during the first two months of a leap year. As a result, the authentication request fails. This problem will not occur in months after February and only in a leap year.

Request Authenticator Vulnerability

If an attacker can sniff the traffic between the RADIUS client and the RADIUS server, he can passively produce a dictionary of Request Authenticators and the associated (protected) User-Password attributes. If the attacker observes a repeated Request Authenticator, he can remove any influence of the Shared Secret from the first 16 octets of the passwords by XORing the first 16 octets of the protected passwords together. This yields the first 16 octets of the two (now unprotected) user passwords XORed together. The impact of this attack varies according to the strength of the user passwords.

Preventing Unauthorized Access into Networks

If someone were to gain unauthorized access to your organization's internal network, that person could cause damage in many ways. Conceivably, that person could access sensitive files on a host, delete files, plant a virus, leave a Trojan sniffer program, or hinder network performance by flooding your network with illegitimate packets.

Your employees on the inside network also pose a security risk. They could attempt to access another internal network, such as the Research and Development subnetwork, with sensitive and critical data. They could intentionally or inadvertently cause damage; for example, they might access confidential files, change important data, or tie up scarce resources.

To prevent unauthorized access through a networking device into a network, you should configure access lists to filter traffic at networking devices. Basic access lists allow only specified traffic through the device; the router will simply drop other traffic. You can specify individual hosts or subnets that you allow into the network and you can specify what type of traffic you allow into the network. Basic access lists generally filter traffic based on source and destination addresses, and protocol type of each packet. Advanced traffic filtering is also available, providing additional filtering capabilities; for example, the Lock-and-Key Security feature requires the authentication of each user with a username and password before allowing that user's traffic into the network. All the Cisco IOS traffic filtering capabilities are described in Chapters 15 through 18.

You can require the authentication of users before they gain access into a network. When users attempt to access a service or host (such as a Web site or file server) within the protected network, they must first enter certain data such as a username and password, and possibly additional information such as their date of birth or mother's maiden name. After successful authentication, the router can assign users specific privileges, allowing them to access specific network assets. In most cases, you would facilitate this type of authentication using CHAP or PAP over a serial PPP connection with a specific security protocol, such as TACACS+ or RADIUS. Just as in preventing unauthorized access to specific network devices, you need to decide whether or not you want the authentication database to reside locally or on a separate security server. As before, a local security database is useful when you have very few routers providing network access. A local security database does not require a separate and costly security server. A remote, centralized security database is convenient when you have a large number of routers providing network access because it prevents you from having to update each router with new or changed username authentication and authorization information for potentially hundreds or thousands of dial-in users. A centralized security database also helps establish consistent remote access policies throughout your organization. Cisco IOS software supports a variety of authentication methods. Although AAA is the primary (and recommended) method for access control, Cisco IOS software provides additional features for simple access control outside the scope of AAA. For more information, refer to Chapters 6 ("Implementing Non-AAA Authentication") and 8 ("Implementing AAA Authentication").

ACL Vulnerability

Access lists are a great tool for preventing unauthorized network traffic; that is, when they work! There are six known vulnerabilities involving Access Control Lists (ACL) in multiple releases of Cisco IOS Software Release for Cisco 12000 Series Internet Routers. You will not find all vulnerabilities present in all IOS releases, and they affect only line cards based on Engine 2. The six vulnerabilities are as follows:

1. ACL will not block non-initial fragments of a packet. This means the router will not block all traffic. By sending an offending traffic in packet fragments, it is possible to circumvent the protection offered by the ACL.
2. The router ignores the keyword `fragment` in the compiled ACL (Turbo ACL) when someone sends a packet destined to the router itself. It is possible to cause a denial-of-service on the router itself when you send enough packet fragment traffic to the router.

3. The router ignores the implicit deny ip any any rule at the end of an ACL when you apply an ACL of exactly 448 entries to an interface as an outgoing ACL. This vulnerability does not affect an ACL with any other number of rules, greater or less than 448. Should an outgoing ACL contain exactly 448 entries and an explicit rule deny ip any any is not present as the last statement, the ACL will fail to drop packets. This may allow some undesired traffic to pass into the protected network, thus violating your security policy.

4. The router adds support for the fragment keyword in an outgoing ACL. Previously, only an incoming ACL supported this keyword and the router was ignoring it on an outgoing ACL. This vulnerability may allow fragmented packets into the protected network when you apply the keyword fragment to an outgoing ACL.

5. An outbound Access Control List (ACL) may not block all intended traffic on a router when you configure an input ACL on some, but not all, interfaces of a multi-port Engine 2 line card. The vulnerability applies to traffic that the router does not filter on an inbound ACL on the ingress port. Any ACL you apply at the ingress point will work as expected and block the desired traffic. This vulnerability can cause unwanted traffic in and out of the protected network.

6. The ACL does not filter packet fragments despite using the fragment keyword. Someone could exploit this vulnerability to attack systems supposedly protected by an ACL on the router.

Cisco has fixes for most software versions, so you should check their site. In addition, you could filter packet fragments (see Chapter 16 for packet filtering).

Preventing Network Data Interception

When packets travel across a network, they are susceptible to being read, altered, or hijacked. (Hijacking occurs when a hostile party intercepts a network traffic session and poses as one of the session endpoints.)

When you send your data across an open network such as the Internet, you expose your data to a fairly significant risk. Unauthorized individuals might read sensitive or confidential data, modify critical data, and disrupt communications by altering or replaying packets.

To protect data as it travels across a network, you can configure network data encryption, as described in Chapter 19, "Using Encryption and IKE." Cisco Encryption Technology (CET) prevents people from examining or tampering with routed traffic while it travels across a network.

Typically, you do not use CET for traffic routed through networks that you consider secure. Consider using CET for traffic routed across unsecured networks, such as the Internet, when your organization could suffer damage should unauthorized individuals examine or tamper with the traffic.

CET, however, is older proprietary software, so you might want to configure IPSec network security. IPSec provides security for the transmission of sensitive information over unprotected networks such as the Internet and provides a more robust security solution than CET. IPSec also provides data authentication and anti-replay services in addition to data confidentiality services, while CET provides only data confidentiality services. Refer to Chapter 20, which describes how to configure IPSec.

Should you configure IPSec, you also might want to configure Certification Authority (CA) interoperability. CA interoperability permits Cisco IOS devices and CAs to communicate so that your Cisco IOS device can obtain and use digital certificates from the CA. Refer to Chapter 19, "Using Encryption and IKE," to learn about CA interoperability.

Finally, when using IPSec, you might configure the Internet Key Exchange security protocol. IKE is a key management protocol standard used with the IPSec standard. You can configure IPSec without IKE, but IKE enhances IPSec by providing additional features, flexibility, and ease of configuration for the IPSec standard. Refer to Chapter 19, "Using Encryption and IKE," to learn about IKE and the ISAKMP feature.

ISAKMP Vulnerability

ISAKMP provides end-to-end IP-layer security without the burden of manually pre-keying Security Associations. It is, however, susceptible to well-known attacks. Because the daemon only uses host-oriented keying, it is susceptible to attacks.

Also, the router keeps the authentication keys in flat files and there is no concept of indirect trust. An unscrupulous individual who can acquire root privilege could mangle a key file, thereby making authentication impossible, or add any public keys of his choosing to the public key ring.

Refer to Chapter 5, "Managing Your Router," for a discussion of logging and how you might use its capabilities to warn you of this.

Preventing Denial-of-Service Attacks

A common type of attack is denial-of-service (DoS). DoS attacks are particularly nasty because although they do not provide intruders with access to specific data, they tie up valuable resources, preventing legitimate users from accessing the network, systems, or applications. Crackers can send large amounts of fragmented, jumbled, or otherwise unmanageable data to machines connected to corporate networks or the Internet, thereby denying service to your clients.

Even more malicious are distributed denial-of-service (DDoS) attacks, in which an attacker compromises multiple machines or hosts. According to the 2001 Computer Security Institute (CSI) and FBI "Computer Crime and Security Survey," 38 percent of respondents detected DoS attacks, compared with 11 percent in 2000.

You can configure your router to intercept one known DoS attack: a SYN flood. In addition, you can configure the router to remove or control some services frequently used in denial-of-service attacks. You will learn how to do this in Chapter 21, "Configuring Denial-of-Service Security Features."

CDP Vulnerability

There is a vulnerability in how Cisco routers (generally IOS v 12.1 and 2) handle the Cisco Discovery Protocol (CDP). You can consume all the router's available memory by sending a large amount of CDP neighbor announcements. Should you do so, you can cause a crash or some other abnormal behavior.

To trigger this vulnerability, the attacker must live on the same segment as the target router. You cannot exploit this vulnerability over the Internet unless an attacker has a helper program already planted on the internal network.

Cisco has fixes for this vulnerability, so check out their site. You also could disable CDP as a workaround for this vulnerability (see Chapter 21 to disable CDP or limit to an interface).

ARP Vulnerability

It is possible to send an Address Resolution Protocol (ARP) packet on a local broadcast interface (e.g., Ethernet, cable, Token Ring, or FDDI) that could cause Cisco routers in the AGS/MGS/CGS/AGS+, IGS, RSM, 800, ubr900, 1000, 1400, 1500, 1600, 1700, 2500, 2600, 3000, 3600, 3800, 4000, 4500, 4700, AS5200, AS5300, AS5800, 6400, 7000, 7200, ubr7200, 7500, and 12000 series to stop sending and receiving ARP packets on the local router interface. Rapidly, the router and local hosts cannot send packets to each other.

ARP packets received by the router for the router's own interface address but a different Media Access Control (MAC) address will overwrite the router's MAC address in the ARP table with the one from the received ARP packet. This vulnerability can result in a denial-of-service attack against the router, once the ARP table entries timeout. This attack only works when the attacker is on the local segment.

Cisco recommends that you upgrade your software.

NAT Vulnerability

Software bugs in the Cisco 1700, 2600, 3600, AS5800, RSP7000, 7200, and 7500 family of routers can cause packet leakage between network address translation (NAT) and input access filters. This causes input access lists to "leak" packets in certain NAT configurations. This means that all those addresses you were protecting are getting out.

Check the Cisco Web site for the availability of patches. You should also refer to the chapters on packet filtering.

Scanning Vulnerability

Later in the book, you will learn how attackers can use the Internet Control Message Protocol (ICMP) to perform a denial-of-service on a third party. An interesting twist to this attack happens on the Cisco 12000 series routers with line cards based on the Engines 0, 1, and 2. You can degrade the performance of these routers by having them send a large number of ICMP Unreachable packets. In some cases, the router will stop forwarding packets. When someone sends a high volume of traffic to the router that requires ICMP Unreachable replies, the processing of the replies can saturate the CPU. You could do this by doing a heavy network scan.

Cisco has an available patch. You can also prevent the router from sending ICMP Unreachable messages at all (see Chapter 16 for denying unreachable messages) or you can rate-limit them (see Chapter 21 for rate limiting).

TCP Sequence Guessing Vulnerability

Cisco IOS software on the following routers may contain a flaw that permits the successful prediction of TCP initial sequence numbers:

800, 1000, 1005, 1400, 1600, 1700, 2500, 2600, 3600, MC3810, 4000, 4500, 4700, 6200, 6400 NRP, 6400 NSP series, RSM, 7000, 7010, 7100, 7200, ubr7200, 7500, 10000 ESR, 12000 GSR, ubr900, and ubr920

To provide reliable delivery, the Transmission Control Protocol (TCP) makes use of a sequence number in each packet to provide orderly re-assembly of data after arrival, and to notify the sending host of the successful arrival of the data in each packet. TCP sequence numbers are 32-bit integers in the circular range of 0 to 4,294,967,295. The host devices at both ends of a TCP connection exchange an initial sequence number (ISN) selected at random from that range as part of the setup of a new TCP connection.

After the devices establish a session and data transfer begins, the router regularly augments the sequence number by the number of octets transferred and transmitted to the other host. To prevent the receipt and re-assembly of duplicate or late packets in a TCP stream, each host maintains a window, a range of values close to the expected sequence number, within which the sequence number in an arriving packet must fall. Assuming a packet arrives with the correct source and destination IP addresses, source and destination port numbers, and a sequence number within the allowable window, the receiving host will accept the packet as genuine.

This method provides reasonably good protection against accidental receipt of unintended data. However, to guard against malicious use, the router should generate a number that an attacker cannot infer from a particular number in the sequence.

Should the router not randomly choose the initial sequence number or the router not randomly increment the ISN between the initialization of successive TCP sessions, then someone could forge one half of a TCP connection with another host to gain access to that host or to hijack an existing connection.

This vulnerability only affects the security of TCP connections that originate or terminate on the affected Cisco device itself; it does not apply to TCP traffic forwarded through the affected device in transit between two other hosts.

To remove this vulnerability, Cisco offers free software upgrades for all affected platforms. Workarounds are available that limit or deny successful exploitation of the vulnerability by filtering traffic containing forged IP source addresses at the perimeter of a network or directly on individual devices. To prevent malicious use of this vulnerability from inside your network, you can use IPSec or SSH to the Cisco device for interactive session, MD5 authentication to protect BGP sessions, strong authentication for access control, etc. To prevent malicious use of this vulnerability from outside your network, you can use ACLs to prevent the injection of packets with forged source or destination IP addresses.

Preventing Fraudulent Route Updates

All routing devices determine where to route individual packets by using information stored in route tables. The router creates this route table information using route updates obtained from neighboring routers.

If an attacker sends the router a fraudulent update, she could trick the router into forwarding traffic to the wrong destination. This could cause the exposure of sensitive data or the interruption of network communications.

To ensure that the router receives route updates only from known, trusted neighbor routers, you can configure neighbor router authentication as described in Chapter 22, "Configuring Neighbor Authentication and Other Security Features." This chapter describes the security benefits and operation of neighbor router authentication. When you configure neighbor authentication on a router, the router authenticates its neighbor router before accepting any route updates from that neighbor. This ensures that a router always receives reliable routing update information from a trusted source.

BGP Vulnerability

You could send bogus router advertisements to the router. The router has no way of verifying the routes. This means it accepts any route it receives although it is not cost-effective or fraudulent. These problems were, in large part, the basis for L0pht's claims before Congress that it could take down the Internet in about 30 minutes.

Preventing Unauthorized Changes

An unauthorized individual might gain access to your router and start making unauthorized changes. These changes might affect the operation of the router; for example, they configure IGMP after you have removed it. The changes might affect the traffic you allow into your network and the applications that people can access. The changes might involve the resetting of passwords on the router, thereby causing a denial-of-service for your legitimate clients. Your imagination limits you when thinking of what someone might do given the ability to make unauthorized changes.

Less insidious, but just as challenging, are changes made by authorized individuals in an unauthorized way. For example, your network administrator decides to change one of the existing access lists without proper documentation or without telling anyone else.

You can learn how to detect authorized and unauthorized changes in Chapter 21, "Configuring Denial-of-Service Security Features." Chapter 22, "Configuring Neighbor Authentication and Other Security Features," shows you how to remove problem applications that crackers might exploit to get authority or run arbitrary commands on the router.

Exhibit 1   Cisco IOS Security Features

Feature	Description
Authenticating proxy (cut-through user authentication)	Allows you to apply user-based access policies, as opposed to group- or IP-based ones
Context-Based Access Control (CBAC)	Allows the router to examine application layer data to determine the state and context of TCP and UDP connections to dynamically open or close connections as necessary
Dynamic access lists	Allows the router to open a port for temporary access to authenticated users
Failover/hot standby option	Allows you to create a redundant, hot spare
Network address translation (NAT)	Allows you to hide private IP addresses from public networks
Port to application mapping (PAM)	Allows context-based access controls to work on nonregistered, nonstandard, or custom ports
Reflexive access lists	Allows incoming TCP and UDP packets only when they belong to a session initiated from behind the firewall
Standard and extended access lists	Allows you to perform traffic filtering by evaluating all packets at the network layer. Some extended access lists can evaluate information at the transport layer.
TCP Intercept	Allows you to intercept a SYN flood, preventing denial-of-service attempts
User authentication and authorization	Allows the verification of identities and the assignment of permissions based on user accounts

HTTP Vulnerability

A remote attacker can execute arbitrary commands at the highest privilege level using the HTTP server. Cisco introduced the HTTP server to allow router management using a Web browser. The problem affects the HTTP server in Cisco IOS v11.3 and higher when linked to a local authentication database. This bug can allow an attacker using a particularly formatted URL to bypass authentication and control the router. You should disable the HTTP server on your router. You can use TACACS+ or RADIUS for authentication when needed. See Chapter 22 to remove HTTP, Chapter 12 to configure TACACS+, and Chapter 13 to configure RADIUS.

Looks pretty gloomy, does it not. Do not despair; Cisco provides help. Exhibit 1 provides a snapshot of Cisco IOS security features.

So, it is obvious you have lots to look at and do for the remainder of this book. Let us begin with a discussion of the Practice Session.

Practice Session

At the end of each chapter (except this one), you will find a Practice Session to reinforce the material covered in the chapter. Because there were no commands to learn in this chapter there really is nothing to practice. In the next chapter, you will learn how to set up your account with SimRouter and try various commands. Should you follow the Practice Sessions conscientiously, you should have a good start on a secure configuration for your routers.

Security and Audit Checklist

There is also a Security and Audit Checklist at the end of each chapter. These checklists should help focus your thinking on the contents of the chapter. If you are a security or network administrator, you should attempt to answer each question for your organization. If you are an internal or external auditor, you might want to use these questions as the basis for your control evaluation.

1. Does your organization understand the business requirements for the network?
   - Yes
   - No
2. Has your organization appointed someone with the responsibility for defining security policy?
   - Yes
   - No
3. Does this person report to someone in your organization who can effect change?
   - Yes
   - No
4. Has your organization performed a network risk assessment?
   - Yes
   - No
5. Was the makeup of the risk assessment team appropriate?
   - Yes
   - No
6. Does your organization know what an hour of downtime costs?
   - Yes
   - No
7. Does your organization have a plan for keeping up-to-date on all network vulnerabilities?
   - Yes
   - No
8. Has your organization appointed someone to track these vulnerabilities?
   - Yes
   - No
9. Is this assignment appropriate?
   - Yes
   - No
10. Has your organization developed a network security policy?
    - Yes
    - No

11. Is the network security policy approved at the appropriate level in your organization?
    - Yes
    - No
12. Does anyone in your organization monitor compliance with the network security policy?
    - Yes
    - No
13. Has your organization ever performed or had someone do a penetration test?
    - Yes
    - No
14. Does your organization periodically perform network security testing?
    - Yes
    - No
15. Was the period between network security tests determined by your risk analysis?
    - Yes
    - No
16. Does your organization have a physical security program that includes the protection of all interconnectivity devices?
    - Yes
    - No

Conclusion

Cisco IOS software has many security-specific features, such as packet filtering access lists, TCP Intercept, AAA services, packet logging, and encryption. This is neither an exhaustive list, nor can you substitute it for an understanding on your part; it is simply a reminder of some of the things that are sometimes forgotten.

Think of these features as ways to keep your network running. When faced with security threats, you can deal with them by controlling:

- Access to the router
- Access to the network
- Access to transmitted data
- Denial-of-service attacks
- Route updates
- Router changes

Cisco offers a comprehensive array of market-leading, enterprise network security features to make implementation and maintenance of good network security easier and more cost-effective. These features are the subject of the remainder of this book. However, regardless of how many good security features Cisco provides, Cisco cannot install them and take control of your router. The onus is on you.

Enough aggrandizement of Cisco. Let us begin our journey together, starting with the obligatory overview of the OSI model and the TCP/IP protocol suite.

Chapter 2

Understanding OSI and TCP/IP

In this chapter, you will learn about:

- The OSI model
- Encapsulation
- Protocol data units
- The TCP/IP protocol suite
- Internet layer
- Transport layer

In addition, you will get an initial taste for using SimRouter to practice what you learn in the chapter. You will see how to get started with SimRouter by logging in and scheduling yourself a practice session.

The OSI Model

The Open Systems Interconnection (OSI) model has been around for a long time in computing years. Adopted in 1983 by the International Organization for Standardization (ISO), the OSI model describes the method for transmitting data between two systems. By defining a standard, the OSI model allows you to select multiple vendors in your organization. Thus, you can have Cisco routers and 3Com hubs connecting IBM mainframes and Compaq computers. Manufacturers that develop products that meet the standard can, in theory, connect their products to any other manufacturer whose products meet the standard. While most of you are probably familiar with the model, different people define the seven layers differently. Thus, the OSI model is offered here in review.

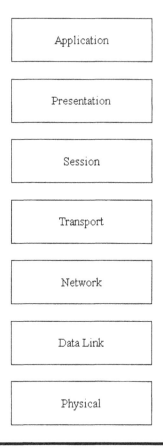

Exhibit 1   The OSI Model

Note: Only Apple uses all seven layers in their protocol stack. Other developers/manufacturers have fewer layers and provide most or all of the functionality of the seven layers.

The standard developers knew that sending data from one system to another was a fairly complicated process and that they required a model as a reference for discussion. The first thing they did was to break the process into manageable tasks. The Open Systems Interconnection (OSI) model consists of seven layers. Each of these layers has a distinct function and interacts and communicates with the layers directly above and below it. Exhibit 1 depicts the seven layers of the OSI model.

Starting from the top, the following mnemonic will help you remember the OSI layers:

All People Seem To Need Data Processing

The people in Detroit will tell you that it really should be:

All People Seem To Need Domino's Pizza

Staying with the pizza theme, there is another mnemonic you can use to remember the layers from the bottom up:

Please Do Not Throw Sausage Pizza Away

Whichever you use to remember the layers, let us look at each layer in turn.

Application Layer

The application layer is the highest layer of the OSI model. This is responsible for supporting the communication components of an application. This is an important concept. The application layer is not Microsoft Word, but communication components that support word processing, if any. Word does not reside at layer seven, but would interface with the application layer when it needs network services such as file transfer. Programs that use the application layer are known as application processes. It is possible for a user program to interface directly with the presentation layer; however, to do this, the program must initialize communication with peer application processes, establish appropriate presentation contexts, and transfer files or messages itself. Alternately, user-level processes may include available modules that support commonly required application-related services, such as file transfer, e-mail, or file and print services. These modules provide a standard method of passing data to the presentation layer. User-level processes are actually gateways to the presentation layer. Using these available modules constitutes using the application layer of the OSI model. It is typically easier to use these modules than to worry about interfacing properly with the presentation layer.

Presentation Layer

Originally, the presentation layer was conceived to allow ASCII machines to talk to EBCDIC machines. It was later seen as a way to let visually oriented programs, such as text editors, work with different terminal types. However, the standard developers have significantly expanded the role of the presentation layer. It now has responsibility for handling all issues related to the representation of transmitted data. These issues include compression, conversion, and encryption.

Note: At one time, IBM mainframes supported both ASCII and EBCDIC character sets. IBM decided to drop support for one data format. Although many other vendors supported ASCII at the time, IBM decided to go with its proprietary EBCDIC. So, if using IBM technology you want to send a file to someone else, you may need to convert it.

Different machines have different ways of representing data internally, so conversions are necessary to ensure that different computers can understand each other. The job of the presentation layer is to take the internally formatted data from the sending machine, convert it into a suitable bitstream for transmission, and then decode it to a format the receiving machine can understand at the other end. That is, the presentation layer acts as an interpreter that understands both formats and is responsible for making sure both computers get information in a format each can understand. This is true whether one is talking about compression, conversion, or encryption.

Session Layer

The primary function of the session layer is to allow users to establish connections or sessions, and to transfer data over those connections (or sessions) in a controlled manner. There are two types of services provided by the session layer: administrative and dialog.

The administrative service handles the establishment and teardown of a connection between two presentation entities. The administrative service also determines the type of connection established. For example, the connection might be full-duplex or half-duplex. Sessions are established when one application process requests access to another application process. After the session is established, dialog services are used to control and supervise the actual data transfer.

Example session layer protocols include:

- AppleTalk Session Protocol (ASP)
- Digital Network Architecture Session Control Protocol (DNA SCP)
- Network File System (NFS)
- Remote Procedure Call (RPC)
- Structured Query Language (SQL)

Transport Layer

The transport layer is the highest layer directly associated with the transport of data through the network. This layer defines end-to-end connectivity between host applications. The basic functions of the transport layer are to:

- *Establish end-to-end operations*: provides end-to-end transport services, which constitute logical connections between the sending and receiving hosts
- *Segment upper-layer applications*: allows multiple applications to use the network simultaneously, as it segments data from multiple upper-layer applications into the same data streams for transport on the network
- *Send segments from one host to another*: uses checksum calculations and built-in flow control to ensure the integrity of segmented data
- *Ensure data reliability*: can optionally request that the receiving host acknowledge that it is actually receiving the data

There are three network types associated with the transport layer:

- Flawless error-free delivery
- Perfect packet delivery
- Unreliable service, lost and duplicate packets

These basically translate as connection-oriented or non-connection-oriented protocols. In the TCP/IP overview, you will learn about connection-oriented and connectionless (or non-connection-oriented) protocols.

Network Layer

The primary concern of the network layer is getting data all the way from the source to the destination. The network layer is the first layer you have looked at that actually has any real effect on the physical network. This layer is in a unique position because it provides the interface between user machines and the actual network. The layers above the network layer (i.e., transport, session, presentation, and application) typically run on the user's machine. Meanwhile, the network layer and the two layers below it (data-link and physical) have actual responsibility for controlling the network.

The functions implemented at the network layer include routing, switching, flow control, data sequencing, and error recovery. Some of these functions might appear to duplicate those of the transport layer, but, in fact, they do not. The network layer's functions are concerned with end-to-end connections, possibly spanning multiple network links. The transport layer does not concern itself with the intermediary links and devices as does the network layer.

Flow control at the network layer is concerned not with the two end stations, but instead with the links and devices that the conversation crosses. If too many packets are present at any one link at any given time, those packets will interfere with each other, causing congestion errors and bottlenecks. Communicating systems use flow control at the network layer to prevent those types of conditions from occurring by trying to provide fair, orderly, and efficient access to network links.

The most important function of the network layer is route determination. Without route determination, everything else the network layer does is moot. The network layer determines the path that data will take to travel between a node on one network to a node on another network. What path is actually used depends on what routing protocols are used within the network. In Chapter 3 you will learn the various methods used to accomplish this.

Data-Link Layer

The data-link layer is the layer responsible for moving data in and out across the physical network. There are two sublayers in the data-link layer:

- The Logical Link Control (LLC) sublayer
- The Media Access Control (MAC) sublayer

The data-link layer is divided this way so that the LLC sublayer need not concern itself with the specific access method. The MAC sublayer deals with interfacing the physical media, while the LLC sublayer handles the interface to the network layer. The LLC sublayer is responsible for assembly and disassembly of frames, addressing, address recognition, and cyclical redundancy check (CRC) calculations and validation. The MAC sublayer is responsible for defining how access is gained to the shared network media. This is dependent on the type of network, while the LLC is media independent.

Together, the two sublayers divide output data into frames for transmission on the physical link. The data-link layer provides framing, flow control, and error detection and correction.

Physical Layer

The bottom layer of the OSI model is the physical layer. By the time the data arrives at the physical layer, it has been fully packaged, all the control and data fields have been set, and all the physical layer needs to do is place the data on the wire or send it out over the air. At the physical layer, bits are transformed into signals (for analog lines) on the transmission medium. It is the physical layer that defines what signals on the line constitute 1s and 0s, and which are just noise. Physical layer specifications define things such as allowable cable lengths, maximum capacities, and the physical wiring of the network.

While it is important to understand the physical layer, someone concerned with auditing or securing routers need not delve too deeply into the subject. You just need to know that the wiring sets limits on the network.

It is worth noting that the application, presentation, and session layers provide communication. The communication layers set up the interactions for user-level applications. This book focuses on the connection layers: transport, network, data link, and physical. The difference is simply shown. For example, you do not speak Russian. You take your phone off-hook and dial a number in Chernovtsy, Moldavia. The phone in Chernovtsy rings and someone picks it up. Ah, you have a connection. Now, unless the other person speaks English, you do not have communication. That is the difference between those layers concerning themselves with connection and communication.

Caution: You might have heard of Moldavia and are wondering why. Well, there was a famous hostile ActiveX control involving this former Soviet Socialist Republic. If you visited a particular Web site advertising "Russian Girls, Girls, Girls," then you would have had the opportunity to see more free pictures when you downloaded its special viewer. So you download the viewer, which is an ActiveX control, that runs and turns off the volume on your modem, disconnects you, and dials an ISP in Moldavia unbeknownst to you. You sit looking at free pictures for several hours, thinking nothing of it. Then the end of the month comes; you get your telephone bill and there is a $1000 charge to a number in Moldavia. Moldavia? Never heard of it. Stupid phone company. No. Sorry; here are the records and you must pay. Oops! Perhaps this is an opportunity for context-based access control.

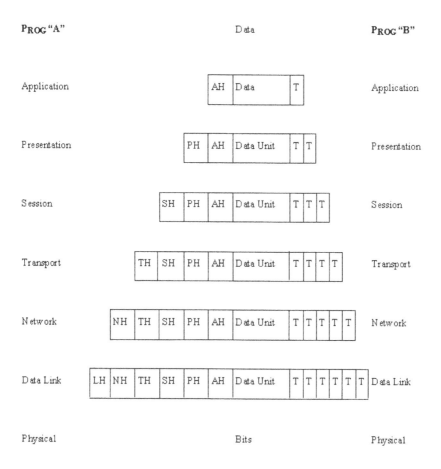

PROG "A"	Data	PROG "B"

Exhibit 2   Encapsulation at Work

Encapsulation

Another concept implicit in the foregoing discussion is encapsulation. As data travels down the stack, each of the various layers encapsulates (or envelops) the data from above with its own header and trailer (when applicable). Exhibit 2 depicts this concept of encapsulation.

The receiver passes the data up its stack and the various layers read and strip off their headers and deliver the data to the next layer based on the contents of the header. When discussing layers, note that there are different names associated with the payload at different points in the protocol stack.

Protocol Data Units

The data and control information transmitted through internetworks takes a wide variety of forms. Unfortunately, not everyone uses these terms consistently in the internetworking industry to refer to these information formats. Sometimes, networking people use them interchangeably. Common information formats or protocol data units include:

- Frame
- Packet
- Datagram
- Segment
- Message
- Cell
- Data unit

Frame

A frame is an information unit whose source and destination are data-link layer entities. A frame is composed of two components:

- *Data-link layer header (and possibly a trailer)*. The header and trailer contain control information intended for the data-link layer entity in the destination system.
- *Upper-layer data*. Data from upper-layer entities is encapsulated in the data-link layer header and trailer.

Packet

A packet is an information unit whose source and destination are network layer entities. A packet is composed of two components:

- *Network layer header (and possibly a trailer)*. The header and trailer contain control information intended for the network layer entity in the destination system.
- *Upper-layer data*. Data from upper-layer entities is encapsulated in the network layer header and trailer.

Datagram

The term "datagram" usually refers to an information unit whose source or destination is a network layer entity using a connectionless network service.

Segment

The term "segment" usually refers to an information unit whose source and destination are transport layer entities.

Message

A message is an information unit whose source and destination entities exist above the network layer (often the application layer).

Cell

A cell is an information unit of fixed size whose source and destination are data-link layer entities. Switched environments, such as Asynchronous Transfer Mode (ATM) and Switched Multimegabit Data Service (SMDS) networks, use cells. A cell is composed of two components:

- *Header.* The header contains control information intended for the destination data-link layer entity. A cell header is typically 5 bytes in length.
- *Payload.* The payload contains upper-layer data that is encapsulated in the cell header. The cell payload is typically 48 bytes in length.

The lengths of the header and payload fields are always exactly the same for each cell.

Data Unit

Data unit is a generic term referring to a variety of information units. Some examples of common data units include:

- *Service data unit (SDU).* SDUs are information units from upper-layer protocols that define a service request to a lower-layer protocol.
- *Protocol data unit (PDU).* PDU is OSI terminology for packet.
- *Bridge protocol data unit (BPDU).* The spanning-tree algorithm uses BPDUs as hello messages.

That terminates the discussion of the OSI model. Now turn to the focus of this book: the TCP/IP protocol suite.

TCP/IP Overview

Several years ago, there was a shootout to see what protocol suite would win as the enterprisewide solution. NetBIOS with NetBEUI, a likely contender because it was widely deployed in Windows platforms, was unacceptable because it was not a routable protocol. IPX/SPX only worked with NetWare and was proprietary. Bang! Apple was pushing AppleTalk, but you know how that one went. That left, in effect, SNA and TCP/IP. SNA was popular with large IBM customers who might already have had a mainframe (MVS) and minicomputers (OS/400) in place. But SNA was proprietary and you paid a premium for it. Bang! Bang! On the other hand, in the early 1970s, the U.S. Department of Defense Advanced Research Projects Agency (DARPA) funded the development of the TCP/IP protocol suite, making the protocols publicly available. Because the protocols are in the public domain, they have become the *de facto* standard for open-system data communication and interoperability.

In contrast to the OSI model, the TCP/IP protocol suite has only four layers. The suite was developed long before the OSI model and is built around the DoD (U.S. Department of Defense) or DARPA model. Exhibit 3 contrasts the OSI and DoD models.

OSI Model   DoD Model

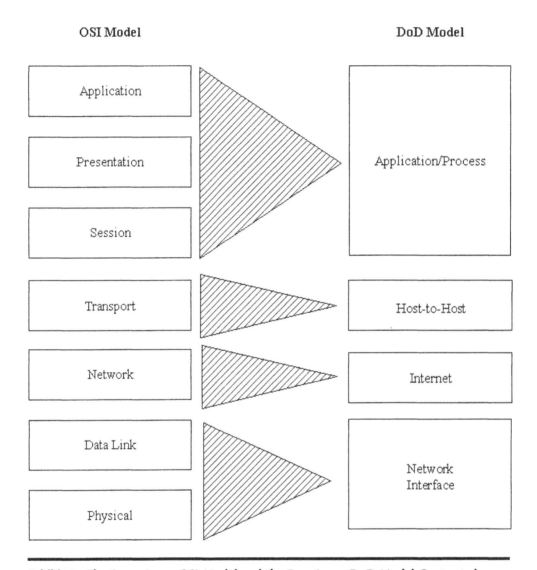

Exhibit 3   The Seven Layer OSI Model and the Four Layer DoD Model Contrasted

Exhibit 3 can be used to explain the various layers of the DoD model. The application/process layer defines the upper-layer functionality included within the application, presentation, and session layers of the OSI model. Support is provided for application communications, code formatting, session establishment, and maintenance functions between applications.

The DoD host-to-host layer maps directly to the transport layer of the OSI model. The host-to-host layer defines connectionless and connection-oriented transport functionality. Host-to-host is the DoD layer where TCP and UDP work.

The DoD Internet layer maps directly to the network layer of the OSI model. The Internet layer defines internetworking functionality for routing protocols. This layer is responsible for the routing of packets between hosts and networks. The Internet layer is where IP, ARP, RARP, and ICMP work in the DoD model.

The DoD network interface layer maps to the data-link and physical layers of the OSI model. Data-link properties, media access methods, and physical connections are defined at this layer.

The TCP/IP protocol suite follows a conceptual model that is similar (if not identical) to the DoD model. It also has four layers, as illustrated in Exhibit 4.

Let us focus on the Internet and transport layers for the remainder of this chapter.

Internet Layer

The Internet layer includes the following protocols:

- Internet protocol (IP)
- Internet Control Message Protocol (ICMP)
- Address Resolution Protocol (ARP)
- Reverse Address Resolution Protocol (RARP)

At the internet layer, TCP/IP uses the Internet Protocol (IP) for logical addressing and path determination. The Internet Control Message Protocol (ICMP) provides messaging that can help troubleshoot a network. The Address Resolution Protocol (ARP) provides the service to match a known IP address for a destination address to a MAC or physical address. The Reverse Address Resolution Protocol (RARP) provides the reverse service of ARP; that is, it translates known MAC addresses to IP addresses. You will learn about IP, ARP/RARP, and ICMP in this chapter.

Internet Protocol

The IP concerns itself with routing functions — getting packets from network A to network B. IP is used by all other protocols except the Address Resolution Protocol (ARP) and the Reverse Address Resolution Protocol (RARP) to transfer packets from host to host over an internetwork.

In the IP packet header, there are fields that communicate things such as logical addressing, path determination, and limited quality-of-service features. The IP header contains several fields that are of interest to anybody concerned with security, audit, and control. Exhibit 5 illustrates the IP datagram header format.

The fields of the IP datagram header include:

- *Version:* 4-bit field that specifies the IP version used. The current standard is IPv4. Everything learned in this book is based on IPv4.
- *IP header length (IHL):* 4-bit field representing the length of the IP packet minus any upper-layer data.
- *Type of service (ToS):* 8-bit field used to establish precedence for certain packets. It is a very simplistic form of quality of service. This field specifies how hosts and intermediate devices should handle the packet. You can break the field further into precedence (3 bits), type of service (4 bits), and MBZ (1 bit). ToS has 1-bit delay, throughput, reliability, and cost subfields.

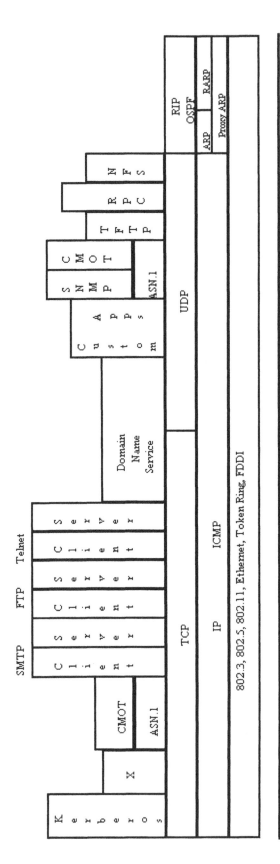

Exhibit 4   TCP/IP Protocol Suite

Version	IHL	Type of Service	Total Length
Identification		Flags	Fragment Offset
Time-To-Live		Protocol	Header Checksum
Source Address			
Destination Address			
Options			
Data			

Exhibit 5   IP Header Datagram

- *Total length:* 16-bit field giving the total length of the packet. The maximum total length of the packet is 65,535 bytes.
- *Identification:* 16 bits for use when a router must fragment a packet. The router uses the field and the two following when it must fragment a packet. A router must fragment a packet when it exceeds the maximum transmission unit (MTU) of the receiver. It breaks up the packet to meet the MTU limitations. The Identification field is a simple, unique sequence number for fragments. The destination system uses the Identification field when reassembling the packet into its original form.
- *Flags:* 3-bit field used to connote the following fragmentation information:
  - *Bit 0:* Reserved.
  - *Bit 1:* Don't Fragment (DF) bit. Set on packets that the router should not fragment. When it is 1, it indicates Don't Fragment the packet.
  - *Bit 2:* Last Fragment (LF) bit. Set for the Last Fragment in a series. When it is 1, it means there are more fragments to follow.
- *Fragment Offset:* 13-bit field identifies the offset of this portion of the original packet before fragmentation.
- *Offset Time-To-Live (TTL):* 8-bit field holding a value representing hops per second. Conceivably, network instabilities could cause a packet to get stuck in a routing loop, going around and around forever. Think of the denial-of-service attack you could do! For this reason, the developers

thought of placing a maximum life on a packet. A router has the respon-sibility to decrement the value by one, and to discard the packet (i.e., copy the packet to the bit bucket) when the value hits zero. When TTL is greater than 1, the router forwards the packet to the next hop router or the destination network (where the router directly connects to the destination network).

Note: Traceroute makes use of the TTL feature by sending out a packet the first time with a value of 1, and then 2, and then 3, etc., until it reaches the specified destination, all the while reporting back to the program and displaying it for you.

- *Protocol:* 8-bit field specifying the protocol number of the upper-layer protocol that should receive the data in the packet. The protocol number for TCP is 6; for UDP, it is 17. Refer to Appendix C, "IP Protocol Numbers," for a complete listing of the potential 256 values.
- *Header checksum:* 16-bit field that holds a value representing the calculated checksum of the IP header only.
- *Source address:* 32-bit field that normally identifies the source (or sender's) address.
- *Destination address:* 32-bit field that normally identifies the destination (or receiver's) address.
- *Options:* optional 32-bit field for vendor-specific data. If used, the field might hold data for security, timestamping, or special routing.
- *Padding:* field used to pad out the length of the header to a multiple of 32 bits. The field contains zeros.

An IP packet header is 20 to 24 bytes in length.

Address Resolution Protocol and Reverse Address Resolution Protocol

In Chapter 3, you will learn how a node resolves software addresses to hardware addresses, and vice versa. Underneath this process are the ARP and RARP. Basically, the sender broadcasts the ARP packet. The receiver responds with its hardware address, while all others ignore it after copying the sender's software and hardware address mapping to its response cache.

Note: ARP is not a routable protocol, so your router does not need to worry about it. ARP requests do not leave the local network.

RARP allows a node to broadcast its hardware address expecting a server daemon to respond with an available IP address. For example, diskless worksta-tions use RARP to acquire an IP address.

Type of Hardware		Type of Protocol
Hardware Length	Protocol Length	Operation Field
ARP Sender's Hardware Address (0-3 octets)		
ARP Sender's Hardware Address (4-5 octets)		ARP Sender's IP Address (0-1 octets)
ARP Sender's IP Address (2-3 octets)		RARP Target's Hardware Address (0-1 octets)
RARP Target's Hardware Address (2-5 octets)		
RARP Target's IP Address (0-3 octets)		

Exhibit 6   ARP/RARP Packet

Exhibit 6 shows you the ARP/RARP packet.
The packet components are as follows:

- *Type of hardware:* 16-bit field specifying the target host's hardware interface type. Ethernet uses 1.
- *Type of protocol:* 16-bit field defines the protocol type the sender supplied. An IP address is 0800.
- *Hardware length:* field that specifies the length of the hardware address.
- *Protocol length:* field that specifies the length of the protocol address.
- *Operation:* field that specifies whether an ARP request/response or an RARP request/response is required.
- *ARP sender's hardware address:* field that specifies the sender's hardware address.
- *ARP sender's IP address:* field that specifies the sender's IP address.
- *RARP target's hardware address:* field that specifies the target's hardware address.
- *RARP target's IP address:* field that specifies the target's IP address.

Internet Control Message Protocol

IP packets encapsulate Internet Control Message Protocol (ICMP) messages. Using a connectionless, unreliable transfer protocol, ICMP reports on errors in the network. Routers usually generate ICMP messages as they receive and route the IP packet. The most common ICMP messages include:

- Destination unreachable
- Time exceeded
- Echo request
- Echo reply

Caution: ICMP does not include flow control or error recovery, so a cracker can easily duplicate the message. If a machine sends ICMP redirect messages to another machine in the network, it could cause the other machine to have invalid routing tables.

Exhibit 7 shows the ICMP message format. Although ICMP formats vary based on the type of service requested, all messages have the following header format:

- *Type:* 8-bit field identifying the message. Appendix F, "ICMP Types and Codes," provides details on the various ICMP types.
- *Code:* 8-bit field that further explains the Type field. Appendix F, "ICMP Types and Codes," provides details on the various ICMP codes.
- *Header checksum:* 16-bit field that holds a value representing the calculated checksum of the ICMP message. The router uses the same algorithm for calculating this value as it does for the IP checksum.

Transport Layer

There are two protocols at the transport layer: Transmission Control Program (TCP) and User Datagram Protocol (UDP). TCP is a connection-oriented transport while UDP is a connectionless transport.

Transmission Control Protocol

TCP, defined in RFC 761, is the connection-oriented transport layer protocol for the TCP/IP suite. Many TCP/IP applications use TCP for transport, including FTP, HTTP, SMTP, and Telnet. TCP as a transport is commonly used by an application when reliability is necessary at the transport layer. Refer to Appendix D, "Well-Known Ports and Services," for a list of applications or services that use TCP.

A TCP segment header provides a number of services, including guaranteed delivery, sequencing, acknowledgments, windowing, and session control.

Exhibit 8 illustrates the TCP header format.

The TCP header is 20 to 24 bytes in length. The fields of the TCP segment header are:

- *Source port:* 16-bit field that identifies the port the source (or sender) opened on the computer to connect to the destination computer. Refer to Appendix D, "Well-Known Ports and Services," for a list of valid source ports. Generally, this is a port greater than 1023.

Exhibit 7   ICMP Message

0	8	15 16	24	31

```
0                  8               15 16              24             31
┌───────────────────────────────────┬───────────────────────────────┐
│           Source Port             │        Destination Port       │
├───────────────────────────────────┴───────────────────────────────┤
│                          Sequence Number                           │
├────────────────────────────────────────────────────────────────────┤
│                      Acknowledgement Number                        │
├──────────┬──────────┬─┬─┬─┬─┬─┬─┬──────────────────────────────────┤
│Data Offset│ Reserved │U│A│P│R│S│F│          Window Size           │
├──────────┴──────────┴─┴─┴─┴─┴─┴─┴──┬──────────────────────────────┤
│             Checksum               │        Urgent Pointer         │
├────────────────────────────────────┴──────────────────────────────┤
│                             Options                                │
├────────────────────────────────────────────────────────────────────┤
│                              Data                                  │
└────────────────────────────────────────────────────────────────────┘
```

Exhibit 8   TCP Header

- *Destination port:* 16-bit field that allows the TCP segment to identify the application that is communicating with the source port. Refer to Appendix D, "Well-Known Ports and Services," for a list of valid destination ports.
- *Sequence number:* 32-bit field specifying the sequence number of the first byte sent in the data portion of the segment. The value of this field is the sequence number of the first data octet within this segment when the SYN bit is not set. When the SYN bit is set, the value of this field is the initial sequence number (ISN), and the first offset is set to ISN + 1.
- *Acknowledgment number:* 32-bit field identifying the next byte expected from the sender. TCP uses an expectational acknowledgment scheme in which the receiver sends the sequence number of the next byte it is waiting for in the series of transferred bytes. The systems assume an established connection when the ACK bit is set.
- *Data offset or Header length:* 4-bit field representing the length of the TCP segment minus any upper layer data. The protocol represents the value as a number of 32-bit words in total. The TCP header will always be some multiple of 32.
- *Reserved:* 6-bit reserved, unused field. Always set to zero.
- *Flags or Code bits:* 6-bit field that allows the header to communicate any control-related functions affecting connection-oriented sessions, such as setup and teardown. There are six control functions:

■ *URG:* This bit makes the Urgent field in the segment significant. When the URG bit is set, the contents of the Urgent field become meaningful; otherwise, the field is ignored. It is typically set when the segment is part of the urgent data.

■ *ACK:* This bit communicates to a receiving host that, among other things, this segment is *acknowledging* receipt of a segment that has been sent. Cisco uses the keyword `established` to check whether the RST or ACK flags are set.

■ *PSH:* This bit is set to signify a *push*. It basically tells TCP to send any received data to the application even when it has not received the entire data stream.

■ *RST:* This bit signifies that a host is terminating a transport session.

■ *SYN:* This bit is used to communicate that a transport session should be initiated. It signifies to a receiving host that the sender wishes the receiver to *synchronize* with the sender's sequence number.

■ *FIN:* This bit is set by an application to signify that it has *finished* sending a data stream and the data can be sent to the destined application.

■ *Window size:* 16-bit field for the receiver to communicate to the sender how much buffer space is available to receive additional segments.

■ *Checksum:* 16-bit field that holds a value representing the calculated checksum of the TCP segment. The receiver uses to validate a segment.

■ *Urgent Pointer:* 16-bit field used when the URG code bit is set. It holds the value of the end of the urgent data; that is, it indicates the end of the urgent data.

■ *Options:* optional 32-bit field for vendor-specific data. It will commonly hold the maximum TCP segment size negotiated between the two hosts.

■ *Maximum segment size:* optional 16-bit field used to specify the maximum segment size for packets with the SYN bit set.

■ *Padding:* optional field used to pad out the length of the header to a multiple of 32 bits. The field contains zeros.

TCP Connection

In the discussion above regarding code bits, there was an allusion to the three-way handshake. Exhibit 9 shows how a client establishes a TCP session with a server. Looking at Exhibit 9, you can see that a connection requires a three-way handshake as follows:

1. To initiate the connection, the source host (Host A) sends a SYN segment (the SYN bit is On or set) and an initial sequence number (ISN) in the Sequence Number field to the destination port and host address (Host B). In Exhibit 9, the ISN is 300.

2. The destination host (Host B) responds with a segment containing its initial Sequence number and both the SYN and ACK flags set. Host B generates an ISN (900 in Exhibit 9). Host B leaves the SYN flag on because they are still trying to synchronize, and sets the ACK bit on to show this is an acknowledgment of the segment sent by Host B. The last thing Host B needs to do is create the acknowledgment number by adding one to the original ISN. Hence, in this example, this is 301 (300 + 1).

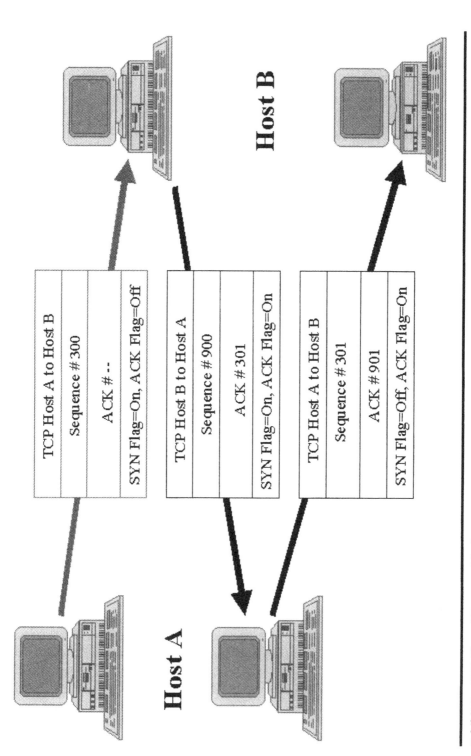

Exhibit 9 TCP Three-Way Handshake

3. The source host (Host A) acknowledges the SYN from the destination by turning off the SYN flag and leaving the ACK flag set. Host A creates an acknowledgment number by adding one to the destination's original ISN, or 900. Hence, the acknowledgment number is 901. One last thing; Host A uses the acknowledgment number (301) from Host B as the sequence number.

Once the two systems establish a session, they can transfer data. As they send data, the sender increments the sequence number to track the number of bytes. The destination host will increment the acknowledgment numbers to acknowledge segments sent and received.

The states that TCP goes through in establishing its connection allows firewall devices to easily recognize new connections versus existing connections. As stated, access lists on routers allow the use of these flags in the TCP header to determine whether or not it is an established session.

Socket

A socket is the combination of the IP address and TCP port. The socket is a logical concept just like a port. A socket is similar to an address in memory because you can write to sockets or read from them. You can send data to a socket and, in turn, another system can send data to a socket on your system. A local and remote socket pair (quadruplet) determines a connection between two hosts uniquely:

- The source IP address
- The source TCP port
- The destination IP address
- The destination TCP port

Your firewall can use this quadruplet to track the many connections on which they are making forwarding decisions at a very granular level. During the establishment of the connection, the firewall will learn the dynamic port assigned to the client for a particular connection. For the period of time that the connection exists, the firewall allows the dynamic port through. Once the connection is finished, the firewall will close the client port. By tracking the state of a particular connection in this manner, security policy rules do not need to compensate for dynamic port assignments.

User Datagram Protocol

UDP, defined in RFC761, is sometimes euphemistically called the Unreliable Data Protocol. It is, as previously stated, a connectionless protocol and delivery is on a best-effort basis. It is a very simple transport protocol with a minimal amount of overhead. There is no sequencing, acknowledgments, flow control, or windowing, so there is no guarantee that the packets will arrive. The receiving host validates the UDP header checksum, and where there is a difference, the device drops the packet without reporting the error back to the sending host. Applications using UDP may implement reliability features within the application itself where required.

Caution: UDP, like ICMP, does not include flow control or error recovery, so a cracker can easily duplicate the message.

Generally, UDP applications are time based — just send it and forget it. The timer starts, and when there is no response, it times out and an appropriate message is sent. A prime example of this is your browser. When you enter a URL, your browser tries to resolve the address, and when it cannot, it makes a DNS query. If the DNS server is unavailable, you get a message back after a short period of time. The Trivial File Transfer Protocol (TFTP) and DNS are good examples of UDP applications. Network administrators frequently use TFTP to upgrade their routers. Refer to Appendix D, "Well-Known Ports and Services," for a list of applications or services that use UDP.

Exhibit 10 shows you the UDP header format:

- *Source port:* 16-bit field that identifies the port the source (or sender) opened on the computer to connect to the destination computer.
- *Destination port:* 16-bit field that allows the UDP segment to identify the application that is communicating with the source port.
- *Header length:* 16-bit field representing the length of the UDP segment.
- *Checksum:* 16-bit field that holds a value representing the calculated checksum of the UDP segment. The receiver uses to validate a segment.

The UDP header is always 8 bytes in length.

That is enough terms and theory for now. You might want to review Appendices B, "IP Addressing," and C, "Subnetting," before moving on to the following practice session.

Practice Session

At the end of each chapter from here on, there will be a Practice Session where you can apply what you have learned in the chapter. To do the Practice Session, you will need to set up a SimRouter account and schedule some time.

SimRouter is an integral part of this book. You can find SimRouter at www.simrouter.com or toll-free 877-7SimRouter. SimRouter is a complete Cisco network accessible through the Internet. The SimRouter network is not a simulation, but a live network.

Everyone who purchases this book will find a Special Access Code inside the front cover of the book. You can schedule your time in advance by making a reservation once you have signed up. To schedule time, you must log in and reserve your time 15 minutes in advance. When you sign in to SimRouter, you will be able to schedule your session for any available time.

	Source Port		Destination Port	
	Header Length		Checksum	
		Data		

Exhibit 10   UDP Header

Tip: If you are using SimRouter to do the practice sessions, you might want to familiarize yourself with today's exercises and wait until you have enough to do to schedule your first one-hour session.

To log in to SimRouter, follow these steps:

1. Go to the www.simrouter.com site.
2. If you are currently a member of SimRouter, enter your `username` and `password` in the log-in area. If you are a new member, select Become a Member and complete the form. Enter your Special Access Code at the bottom of the Member ID signup page.

Note: Should you lose your member name or password, send an e-mail to support@SimRouter.com with your first and last name (and member name, if known).

3. You will see the Welcome Web page shown in Exhibit 11. You can see whether you currently have any personal or group sessions scheduled. Click Schedule from any page once you log into SimRouter. Should you not have sessions available, you will see a Purchase Sessions button; otherwise, you will see a Schedule Session button. Click on the Schedule Session button.
4. You can click on the calendars to find available time and then simply select the desired session time, as shown in Exhibit 12.
5. Return to www.SimRouter.com at the time you just scheduled. Once you log in, you will have an active link to enter the SimRouter Network, as shown in Exhibit 13.
6. When you click on the Enter the SimRouter Network button, you will see the configuration in Exhibit 14. Double-click on any router to telnet to the router.
7. Exit your telnet session by selecting the Disconnect option from the Connect menu in the Telnet window.
8. When you finish your session, click on Log Out.

At the time of this writing, the current configuration is as shown in Exhibit 14. Once you sign in, you have full console access to all the following equipment:

- Cisco 4500 with 8 MB Flash and 32 MB DRAM
  - NP-2T Dual Serial Port Module
  - NP-2R Dual Token Ring Module
- Cisco 2501 with 16 MB Flash and 8 MB DRAM
  - Two Serial Ports
  - One Ethernet Port

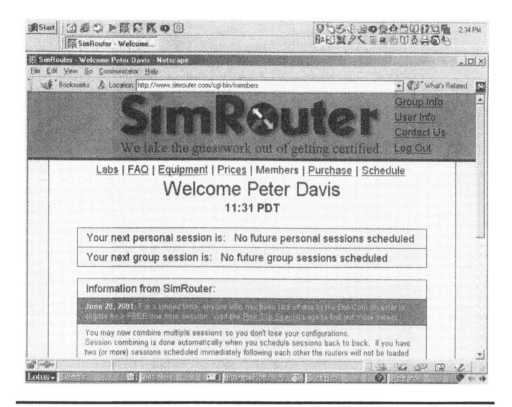

Exhibit 11   Welcome Web Page

- Cisco 2501 with 8 MB Flash and 16 MB DRAM
  - Two Serial Ports
  - One Ethernet Port
- Cisco 2502 with 8 MB Flash and 4 MB DRAM
  - Two Serial Ports
  - One Token Ring Port
- Cisco 2524 with 8 MB Flash and 8 MB DRAM
  - ISDN BRI with Integrated NT1 WAN Module
  - Fractional/Full T-1 DSU/CSU Interface Module
- Cisco 2524 with 8 MB Flash and 4 MB DRAM
  - ISDN BRI with Integrated NT1 WAN Module
  - Fractional/Full T-1 DSU/CSU Interface Module
- Teltone ISDN Demonstrator

Note: Not configurable or accessible by console.

Note: All equipment can be remotely power cycled; that is, you can reboot the machines anytime you want.

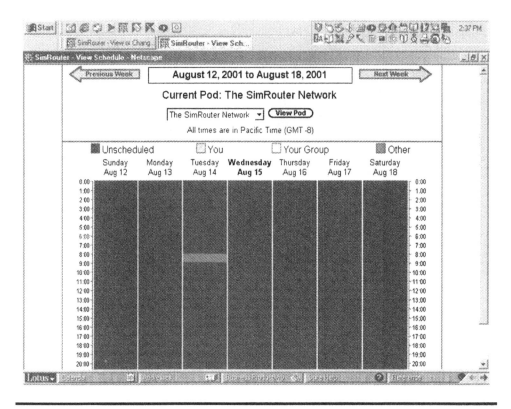

Exhibit 12   Schedule Web Page

Security and Audit Checklist

1. Does your organization support TCP/IP?
   - Yes, go to question 2
   - No, most of this book applies to TCP/IP
2. What version of IP do you use?
   - IPv4, go to question 3
   - IPv6, wait for the updated version of this book
3. Does your organization have a network architecture that enumerates supported protocols?
   - Yes
   - No
4. Does your organization have a network architecture that enumerates supported applications?
   - Yes
   - No
5. Does the architecture document the purpose of each protocol and application?
   - Yes
   - No
6. Do you support encryption?
   - Yes
   - No

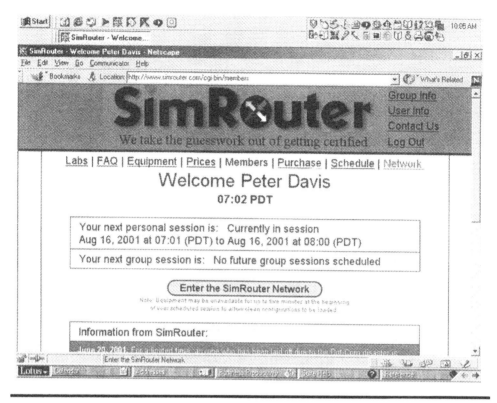

Exhibit 13   Entering the SimRouter Network

7. At what layer is encryption supported?
   - Application
   - Session
   - Transport
   - Network
   - Data-link
8. Do you support UDP applications?
   - Yes
   - No
9. Do you develop RPC-based applications in-house?
   - Yes
   - No
10. Do you know the network address(es) for your organization?
    - Yes
    - No
11. Does your organization support subnetting?
    - Yes
    - No
12. If you answered yes to the previous question, do you know the subnet masks for all networks?
    - Yes
    - No

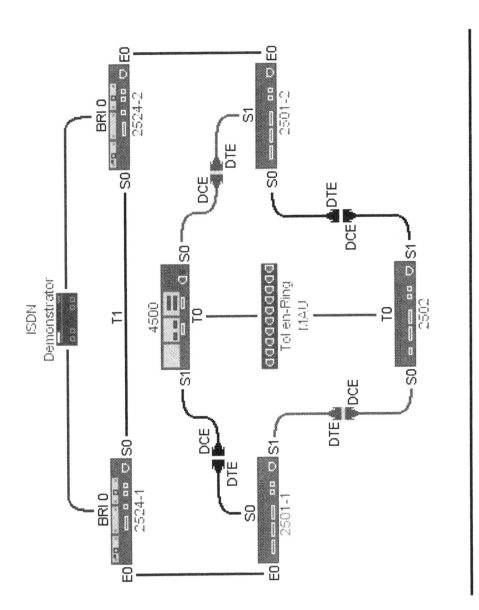

Exhibit 14   The SimRouter Network

13. Does your organization support supernetting?
    - Yes
    - No
14. If you answered yes to the previous question, do you know the subnet masks for all networks?
    - Yes
    - No
15. Is the ARP cache protected on all systems?
    - Yes
    - No

Conclusion

In this chapter, you learned about the OSI and DoD models. The OSI model has seven layers and the DoD model provides all the functionality of the OSI's seven layers but does it in four layers. In addition, you saw the various components of the TCP/IP protocol suite. In the next chapter, you will learn about some more layer 3 protocols — the routing protocols.

You should have a good understanding of the TCP/IP protocols, IP addressing, and subnetting at this point. These topics are all necessary when you start to write access lists and try to prevent unauthorized access to your network.

Hopefully, you took the time to set up your account and to familiarize yourself with SimRouter.

Chapter 3

Routed and Routing Protocols

In this chapter, you will learn about:

- Path determination
- Logical and hardware addresses
- Routing algorithms and protocols
- Distance-vector, link-state, and hybrid routing protocols

You also will have an opportunity to practice what you learn in the Practice Session and use the information by following the Security and Audit Checklist.

Routing Activities

When you need to move data between two networks, an internetworking device called a router is responsible for the movement of this data. Routing data on an internetwork requires that a couple different events take place: an appropriate path for the packets must be determined, and then the packets must be moved toward their final destination. That is, routers perform two basic activities: path determination and packet switching.

Both path determination and routing of packets (or switching as it is also referred to; packets are switched from an incoming interface to an outgoing interface on the router) take place at layer 3 (network layer) of the OSI Model. Another important layer 3 event is the resolution of logical addresses (such as IP addresses when TCP/IP is the routed protocol) to actual hardware addresses.

Path Determination

Routers enable you to divide a large network into logical subnets; doing so keeps network traffic local on each subnet, enabling you to take better advantage of the available bandwidth. It is then the job of the router to move data packets

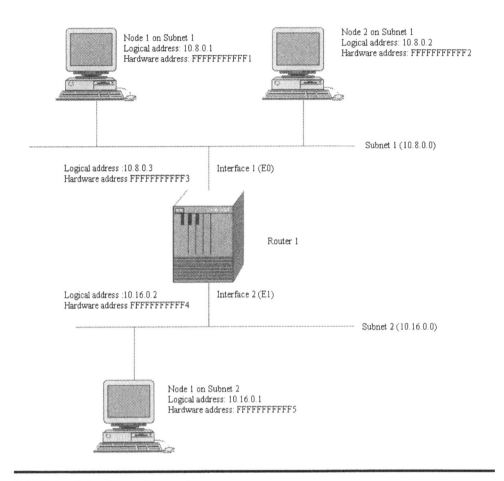

Exhibit 1   Subnetting a Network

between different subnets when required. Routers can also serve as a connection device between your networks (all your subnets are viewed by other enterprise networks as a single network although you have divided them into logical parts). Routers can also serve as the connective device to other networks to which your network is attached. The best example of many different networks connected for communication purposes is the Internet.

For the purposes of discussion, let us create a network that contains subnets connected by a router. You will also create a logical addressing scheme. Exhibit 1 shows a network that has been divided into two subnets using a router. The types of connections between the subnets (Ethernet, Token Ring, FDDI, etc.) and the router are not important at this time, so just suppose that the appropriate protocols and interface connections will be used to connect these subnets to the router.

In this example, the router has two network interfaces — Interface 1 and Interface 2 — that are connected to Subnet 1 and Subnet 2, respectively. The logical addressing scheme used to address the various nodes on the network (logical addresses must be assigned to each interface on the router as well) is set by you, based on addresses either assigned or available to you. So, the first node on Subnet 1 (or alternatively, 10.8) is assigned the logical address 1 (or 10.8.0.1). The first node on Subnet 2 (or 10.16) is assigned the logical address 10.16.0.1.

Exhibit 2   Common MAC Addresses

First Three Bytes of the MAC Address	Assigned Manufacturer
00-00-00	Xerox
00-00-1D	Cabletron
00-00-#D	AT&T
00-00-48	Epson
00-00-A2	Bay Networks
00-80-D3	Shiva
00-AA-00	Intel
02-60-8C	3Com
08-00-09	Hewlett-Packard
08-00-20	Sun
08-00-5A	IBM

Note: Should you need help with the concept of subnets and subnet masks, refer to Appendix B, "Subnetting."

Each node on the network will also have a unique hardware address. For the sake of this discussion, the hardware addresses for the nodes start with FF-FF-FF-FF-FF-F1 and are consecutively numbered. Remember that the hardware addresses are unique; that is how they are made.

Note: Hardware addresses are 48 bits in length. The IEEE assigns unique 24-bit identifiers to NIC manufacturers. The manufacturers then assign unique 24-bit sequence numbers. The 48 bits become the hardware address and is burned-in to every NIC when they are made at the factory. Cisco also assigns router interfaces a burned-in hardware address when manufacturing a router. Cisco's MAC addresses start with 00-00-0C. Other common MAC addresses are shown in Exhibit 2.

If you want to find out what codes the IEEE has assigned to the various hardware manufacturers, go to http://standards.ieee.org/regauth/oui/oui.txt.

One noteworthy hardware address is FF-FF-FF-FF-FF-FF. This MAC address is the broadcast address.

Logical and Hardware Addresses

When you connect networks using a router, you end up with two different types of traffic: (1) local traffic, in which nodes on the same subnet communicate with each other; and remote or network traffic, in which nodes on different subnets are communicating with each other. The latter type of traffic must pass through the router. The next two subsections explain how communications within a subnet and between subnets take place.

Communication on the Same Subnet

First, take a look at the situation where two computers on the same subnet communicate. Node 1 on Subnet 10.8 must send data to Node 2 on Subnet 10.8. Node 1 knows that the packets must go to the logical address 10.8.0.2 and Node 1 knows that 10.8.0.2 resides on the same subnet (so, in this case, the router will not be actively involved in the movement of packets). However, the sending station must resolve the logical address of 10.8.0.2 to an actual hardware address.

Now, Node 1 might already know that the logical address of Node 2 actually refers to the hardware address FF-FF-FF-FF-FF-F2. Computers actually maintain small memory caches where they keep this type of logical-to-hardware address resolution information (ARP cache). If Node 1 has no idea what the hardware address is for Node 2, then Node 1 will send a broadcast message requesting the resolution of the logical address of Node 2 to its hardware address. When it receives the hardware address, Node 1 will use the address to send the packets to Node 2, which copies the packets into memory because they are tagged with its hardware address — FF-FF-FF-FF-FF-F2.

Communication between Different Subnets

Now take a look at a different scenario, one in which a computer on a subnet wants to send data to a computer on another subnet.

Node 1 on Subnet 10.8 wants to send data to Node 1 on subnet 10.16. So, Node 1 on Subnet 10.8 wants to send data to logical address 10.16.0.1. Node 1 on Subnet 10.8 knows that address 10.16.0.1 is not on the local subnet, so it will pass the packets to the default gateway, which is the router interface connected to Subnet 10.8. In this case, the logical address of the gateway for Node 1 on Subnet 10.8 is 10.8.0.3. However, again this logical address must be resolved to a hardware address — the actual address of Router Interface 1.

Again, using broadcast messages, Node 1 on Subnet 10.8 receives the hardware address of FF-FF-FF-FF-FF-F3 related to logical address 10.8.0.3 and sends the packet on to Router 1 via Router Interface 1. Now that the router has the packets, it must determine how to forward the packets so that they end up at the destination node. It will take a look at its routing tables and then switch the packets to the interface connected to the destination subnet.

Packet Switching

After the router has the packets, packet switching comes into play. This means that the router will move the packets from the router interface that they came in on and switch them over to the router interface connected to the subnet they

Exhibit 3   Routing Tables for Router 1

Subnet Logical Destination	Router Interface
10.8	1
10.16	2

must go out on. However, in some cases, the packets might have to pass through more than one router to reach the final destination. In our example, there is only one router. Router 1 knows that the logical address 10.16.0.1 is on Subnet 10.16. So, the router will switch packets from Router Interface 1 to Router Interface 2.

Again, the router uses broadcast messages to resolve logical address 10.16.0.1 to the actual hardware address of FF-FF-FF-FF-FF-F5. The router addresses the packets correctly and then forwards them to Subnet 10.16. When Node 1 on Subnet 10.16 sees the packets for itself (hardware address FF-FF-FF-FF-FF-F5), it copies the messages into its memory space.

You can see that routing involves the use of logical addresses and hardware addresses to get packets from the source (i.e., the sender) to the destination. Each routable protocol (e.g., IP and IPX) uses a slightly different method for resolving logical addresses to hardware addresses, but the overall theory is pretty much the same as outlined here.

Routing Tables

From above, you have learned that the router switches the packet from one interface to another. How does the router know where to switch the message? By the use of routing tables. Routers use software to create these routing tables. The routing tables have hardware interface information that provides the router with the beginning route (for the router) to move the packet to the destination address.

Routers are not concerned with individual node addresses when building routing tables; they only concern themselves with getting the packets to the appropriate network. Rather than computing the entire path to a destination, the router merely selects the next hop leading to that destination, and relies on the next hop machine to select a further hop that gets the packet closer to its ultimate destination. For example, using the logical addressing scheme of Exhibit 1, the router's routing table would appear as shown in Exhibit 3. Notice that every router interface is mapped to a particular subnet. That way, the router knows that when it examines the logical address of a packet, it can determine the subnet to which to forward the packet.

Basically, this router table means that packets destined for any node on Subnet 10.8 would be routed to Router Interface 1. Any packets destined for Subnet 10.16 would be switched to Router Interface 2. In the real world, the router interface would be designated by the type of network technology it supports, such as E0 for the primary Ethernet interface, or S0 for the primary serial interface on the router.

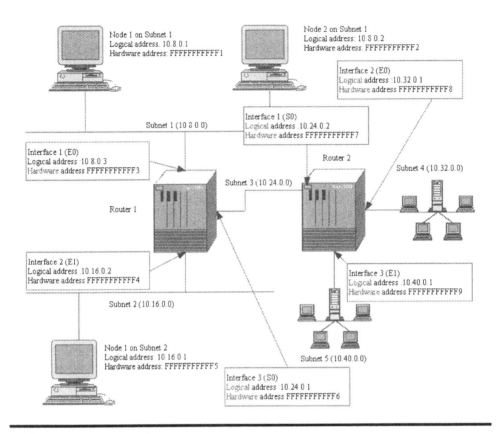

Exhibit 4   The New Topology

Note: You use a letter and a number to identify ports. With Cisco routers, you identify the serial port — the port used to connect to your wide area network or your ISP — by an S and the Ethernet port by an E. When you have multiple ports of each type, you usually label the first port on the router as 0. Thus, you would identify the first Ethernet interface as E0.

When multiple routers are involved — on large networks — the routing tables become populated with more information. For example, expand the one-router, two-subnet network to five subnets deploying two routers. Exhibit 4 shows the new topology. Now you might look at Exhibit 4 and think that there only are four subnets, but the serial connection between the two routers is a separate subnet and must have its own network address.

With the expansion of the network and the increase in the number of subnets, Router 1 will have a different routing table. It now must have information to pass packets to nodes on Subnets 4 and 5. But as you just learned, the router does not have to worry about getting the packets to the actual nodes; it just has to worry about forwarding the packets to the correct router so that they can get to the correct subnet.

Exhibit 5   Routing Tables for Router 1

Subnet Logical Destination	Router Interface
10.8	1
10.16	2
10.24	3
10.32	3
10.40	3

Independent hop-by-hop routing requires that all machines have a consistent view of how to reach all destinations in the network. When consistency is lost, two or more routers may form a routing loop, and the packet never makes it to its destination.

Exhibit 5 provides the routing table for Router 1 using the addressing scheme previously used for numbering subnets. Notice that Router 1 forwards packets for Subnets 4 and 5 through the same interface — Interface 3. So, Router 1 is happy to forward packets for Subnets 4 and 5 to Router 2. Router 2, in turn, has responsibility to switch the packets to the correct interface connected to the appropriate subnet.

Router 2 would have a similar routing table to forward all packets for Subnets 1 and 2 to Interface 1 destined for Router 1. Router 1, in turn, would handle the switching of the packets to the appropriate subnet.

All these routing decisions require software. The router will have software for network transport (such as *routable protocols*; for example, TCP/IP or IPX/SPX) as well as software for determining the best or optimal path for packets to travel to reach their final destination. The latter software is a *routing protocol*. Routable and routing protocols are discussed in the next sections.

Routable Protocols

In Chapter 2, "Understanding OSI and TCP/IP," you learned about routable or *routed* protocols. This book concentrates on TCP/IP, but there are other routable protocols, such as IPX and AppleTalk. These three protocol suites provide sufficient information in the network layer header to allow the router to forward packets from the source node to the destination node even when the router has to forward packets across various networks.

Routing Protocols

Whereas routable protocols provide the logical addressing system that makes routing possible, routing protocols provide the mechanisms for maintaining router routing tables. Routing protocols facilitate inter-router communication, which allows them to share route information used to build and maintain routing tables.

Several different routing protocols exist, including Routing Information Protocol (RIP), Open Shortest Path First (OSPF), and Enhanced Interior Gateway Routing Protocol (EIGRP). And while these different routing protocols use different methods for determining the best path for packets routed from one network to another, each basically serves the same purpose. They help accumulate routing information related to a specific routed protocol such as the Internet Protocol.

It is not uncommon to find host and server machines running more than one network protocol to communicate. For example, a Windows 2000 (W2K) Server in a domain might be using TCP/IP to communicate with its clients, while at the same time using IPX/SPX to support file and print servers.

Routing protocols also embrace this concept of simultaneously but independently running protocols. Multiple independent routing protocols can run on the same router, building and updating routing tables for several different routed protocols. This means that the same media can actually support different types of networking (e.g., peer-to-peer and client/server).

Routing Protocol Basics

Routing protocols not only provide information for router routing tables, but also have responsibility for determining the best route through an internetwork for packets as they move from the source station to the destination station. Designers have refined routing protocols to optimize routes on an internetwork and also to remain stable and show flexibility. They also designed routing protocols to use as little processing overhead as they determine and provide route information. This means that the router itself does not have to have a large multi-processor device to handle the routing of packets.

The next section discusses the mechanisms that routing protocols use to determine paths.

Routing Algorithms

An algorithm is a mathematical process used to arrive at a particular solution. It is repeatable; that is, using the same input, one will get the same output. With respect to routing protocols, the algorithm can be thought of as the set of rules or process that the routing protocol uses to determine the desirability of paths on the internetwork for the movement of packets. The router uses the routing algorithm to build the routing table the router uses as it forwards packets.

Note: Everyone knows that, despite his statements to the contrary, Al Gore did not invent the Internet. However, he may have invented, and hence be in tune with, routing processes, and that may be why they call them Al-Gore-rhythms.

Routing algorithms come in two basic flavors, based on how they calculate routes: *static* and *dynamic*. Static algorithms consist of internetwork mapping information that a network administrator enters into the router's routing table. This table dictates how packets are moved from one point to another on the network. All routes on the network are static; that is, unchanging. Static routes are preferable for routes coming into and out of a router used as part of a firewall configuration.

To add a static route to a router, use the following syntax:

```
route interface_name ip_address netmask gateway_ip [metric]
```

where:
interface_name is the internal or external interface name
ip_address is the internal or external IP address; you use 0.0.0.0 to specify a
    default route

Note: You can abbreviate 0.0.0.0 to just plain 0.

---

netmask specifies a network mask (see Appendices C and G) to apply to the
    ip_address; you can use 0.0.0.0 (abbreviated to 0) as the default route
gateway_ip is the IP address of the gateway router (next hop address for this
    route)
metric specifies the administrative distance applied to this route when comparing
    it with other routes to gateway_ip

Static routes are obviously predictable. Because the network administrator computes the routing table in advance, the path a packet takes between two nodes is always precisely known, and you can control it exactly. With dynamic routing, the path taken depends on what devices and links are functional, and how the routers interpret updates from other routers.

In addition, with static routing, there is no overhead. When you have a high-speed link such as FDDI or Fast Ethernet, the overhead is negligible; but when you have a low-speed, dial-up link, the overhead is significant. How significant is it? Well, suppose you have a network with ten network segments (or subnets). Every 30 seconds, your routers will broadcast an update for each segment. Each route takes 16 octets (or bytes, should you prefer), plus a marginal amount of overhead; the minimum size for an update in this network is 160 bytes. Each router must then send a 160-byte update on each of its interfaces every 30 seconds. This might not seem like a lot, but increase it to 100 segments and you are sending approximately 1.5 kB every 30 seconds. As you can see, you give over a lot of your bandwidth to send RIP updates.

Finally, static routes are easy to configure for small networks. Your network administrator simply calculates the paths and inserts them in the router.

The principal problem with static routes is that you must maintain them. Alas, the price of simplicity is its impact on scalability. Imagine that you have a network with 200 subnets or segments. To implement static routing, you would need to compute the next hop for each network segment for each router — approximately 2400 routes. That should keep you busy in your spare time! Forget the time consumed in this Herculean effort, and think of how error-prone the process might become. Yes, you might only need to do this once; but move or add any segment, and away you go again.

Also, static routes cannot adapt to changes in network topology (an attribute admired in a firewall device); they are, after all, static. Should a certain route become unusable for any reason whatsoever, there is no process for the routers on the network to recognize this event, update the routing tables, and adopt a new route to move the data packets to their final destination. This inability to adapt to network changes — even when redundant paths are available — and the problems associated with scaling are the primary reasons for using dynamic routing.

Dynamic routes are scalable and adaptable because the router builds and maintains them through routing update messages. Routers learn about the network topology by communicating with other routers. Each router announces its presence, and the routes it provides, to the other routers on the network. Messages providing route information on changes in the status of routers or links prompt the routing software algorithm to recalculate routes and update the router's routing tables accordingly. So when you add a new router, or add additional subnets to an existing router, the other routers will hear about the addition and adjust their routing tables correspondingly. Unlike static routing, you do not have to reconfigure the routers to tell them that you changed the network. This takes some of the random errors out of the process — errors that humans might have introduced.

Note: Although your impression may be that dynamic routing is highly preferable to static routing, dynamic routing requires more overhead (with respect to processing and bandwidth requirements) due to the broadcast messages and table updating. In many cases, static routes provide a more secure and efficient network. In addition, dynamic routing tends to be more complex; the routers have to send the correct information to the correct interfaces at the correct time.

If this does not help you choose between static or dynamic routing protocols, there is a middle ground. There is a hybrid scheme in which some parts of the network use static routing (e.g., your perimeter or the *access* networks) and some parts of the network use dynamic routing (e.g., your *core* and *distribution* networks). Static routing works well on the *access* networks because there are few paths or a limited number of connections. On the other hand, *core* and *distribution* networks have many router connections and change more often.

Note: The core network is basically the heart of the network. Most of the data on networks will pass through core routers, so you should configure your network so that when a core router goes down, you do not lose everything. Distribution routers typically provide access into the core and are responsible for quality of service to network applications trying to cross the core. Access routers are the routers where users gain access to your network. Access routers limit broadcasts and stop unwarranted traffic from entering your network; that is, where you apply your access lists.

Core routers are commonly Cisco 7000 and 12000 series routers; distribution routers are commonly Cisco 3600 and 4000 series routers; and access routers are commonly Cisco 1000, 2500, or 2600 series routers. Of course, which router you use at what level is less a function of the model and more a function of its purpose. You could use a series 2500 router as a core router for a small network. Just remember that you might want to expand the network in the future; so what you design now needs to be flexible enough to grow with your organization.

You can further subclassify dynamic routing algorithms (and the routing algorithms that employ a certain algorithm) by how they provide update information to the various routers on the internetwork. *Distance-vector* routing algorithms send out update information at predetermined intervals (such as every 30 seconds with RIP). The router sends two basic types of information: (1) it tells its neighbors how far away it thinks the destination is; and (2) it tells its neighbors what direction (or vector) to use to get to the destination. The router provides the distance using some metric (which you will learn about a little later in this chapter). Routers using distance-vector algorithms pass their entire routing table to their nearest router neighbor (i.e., routers directly connected to them). This basically sets up a domino effect as each router reacts to a change in the network. Every router, in turn, informs its nearest neighbor of changes in the network.

Look at the diagram in Exhibit 6. As Router 1 realizes that the connection to Network 1 is no longer up, it sends an update message (sent at 30-second intervals) to Router 2 letting Router 2 know that the connection is no longer available. At its next message interval, Router 2 will update Router 3 with the information that Router 2 is no longer a path to Subnet 10.8. This updating continues until all routers know that Subnet 10.8 is no longer available via the link to Router 1. By the time Router 4 finds out, the link could be operational again! Of course, you could improve the resiliency of this network by providing some alternate paths, such as connecting Subnet 10.8 to Router 2 and providing a link from Router 1 to Routers 3 and 4, from Router 2 to Routers 3 and 4, etc.

The downside of distance-vector routing is that routers are basically using hearsay information to build their routing tables; they are not privy to an actual view of a particular router's interfaces. They must rely on information from a particular router as to the status of its connections. This is obviously a situation that opens itself up to spoofing. In Chapter 22, you will learn about Neighbor Router Authentication to help mitigate spoofing. Because of the reliance on hearsay information, it is possible for a router to set up inaccurate routes and end up with an unstable period. To compensate for these problems, most protocol developers added the *split-horizon* concept. When a router is updating its tables, it omits any reference to routes it has learned about from other routers for that interface. Others also have implemented a feature called *poison reverse*. With poison reverse, the router includes the route and does not omit it, but marks it

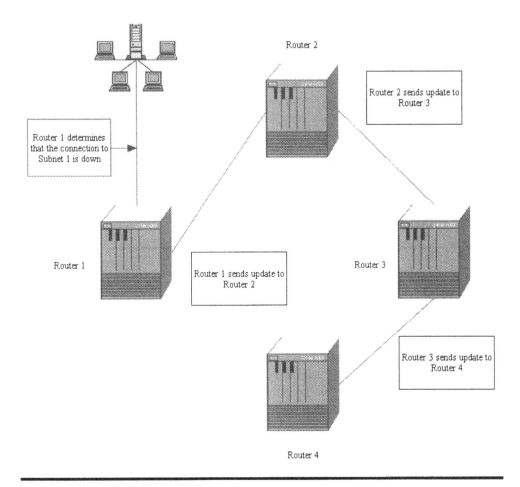

Exhibit 6   Distance-Vector Algorithm Updating Its Neighbors

as unreachable. This causes any receiver depending on the route to remove the destination from its routing table.

There are other features that prevent routers from going into an infinite loop. One solution is the *hold-down* interval. When a router learns that a route is no longer reachable along the path it previously used, it starts a timer during which time it will ignore any other routing information it might receive about this path. This allows other routers to learn about a failure before it starts depending on a route. The difficulty is in setting the timer interval. It obviously needs to be of sufficient length for other routers to receive another update where the first one was lost.

Another strategy for updating routing tables on an internetwork is the *link-state* routing algorithm. Link-state routing protocols not only identify their nearest neighbor, but also exchange link-state packets that inform all routers on the internetwork about the status of their various interfaces. This means that the router sends only information on its direct connections, not the entire routing table as is done with distance-vector routing. This means that link-state routers can build a more comprehensive picture of the entire internetwork and make more intelligent decisions when choosing paths for routing packets. Convergence also takes place more quickly on an internetwork using link-state routing protocols.

While link-state protocols avoid loop-forming behaviors, long convergence times, and stable-state resource consumption, they have some important disadvantages. Distance-vector protocols are easier to configure than link-state protocols. Link-state protocols are complex because they need to generate a topology map and compute the best path to all destinations. While there are algorithms and methods for doing these, it is up to the network planners and operators to select a way and to implement it properly. Distance-vector protocols are less processor-intensive; it takes time and resources to generate a topology map and calculate the best paths.

The final strategy for updating routing tables is a hybrid of the previous two. An excellent example of a hybrid routing protocol is Cisco's proprietary Enhanced Interior Gateway Routing Protocol (EIGRP). EIGRP exhibits the characteristics of distance-vector and link-state protocols as follows:

- Converges much faster than distance-vector routing protocols
- Provides incremental updates
- Supports multiple routed protocols and VLSM
- Scales well
- Uses the same composite metric as IGRP
- Sends multicast updates, not broadcasts

Routing Metrics

So far, you have learned the different types of routing algorithms (static versus dynamic) and the three ways that they update their routing tables (distance-vector, link-state, and hybrid). To complete the discussion on routing protocols, you need to understand one more topic: how routing protocols actually determine the best path between a sending and a receiving node when more than one route is available.

Routing algorithms use *metrics* to determine the benefits of one path over another. An algorithm can use several metrics to make this determination, including path length, quality-of-service, and cost-of-service. Regardless of how your routing protocol calculates it, the metric allows a router that hears about a destination from multiple routers to select the best path by comparing the "distance" of the various alternatives. How the router makes the comparison depends heavily on how the metric is computed.

For example, RIP, a distance-vector routing protocol, uses the concept of *hop count* for its metric. A hop is the movement of packets from one router to another router. A router destination with a hop count of 16 is considered unreachable. When two paths are available, the router will select the route based on the path with the fewest hops; that is, the router that announces the lowest metric. With RIP, when a router announces information it has learned, it adds one hop to the metric for each of these destinations. In this manner, the farther you get from the destination, the higher the metric.

The problem with routing protocols that use only one metric (such as hop count) is that they become very single-minded in their pursuit of the best route for a particular set of packets. RIP, for example, does not take the speed or reliability of the link into account when it selects the best path, just the number of hops. So you may select a path that has the fewest number of hops but force the packets over a 56K leased line, which costs you money, rather than use Fast Ethernet within your company. When you choose a protocol that uses hop count as its only metric, this can happen.

To overcome the lack of flexibility provided by hop count as a metric, several other routing protocols use more sophisticated metrics. For example, the Interior Gateway Routing Protocol, a distance-vector protocol, can actually have up to 255 hops as a metric. These metrics might include bandwidth (line capacity), load (the amount of traffic already being handled by a particular router on a particular interface), communications cost (you can send packets along the least cost alternative), or any other measure of desirability of a route. When you use several routing metrics to choose the path, you get a much more sophisticated determination. For example, when a routing protocol uses metrics other than just hop count, you might choose a path with more hops because it costs less.

Metrics are either dynamically or administratively set. Hop count is an example of a dynamically set metric because the routing protocol determines this value by communicating with other routers. When the number of hops changes, the router will automatically update this metric. The reliability of a circuit is an example of an administratively set metric because a network administrator would set the metric based on some external metric, such as observation or statistical analysis.

In contrast, a link-state protocol does not provide information about destinations that it knows how to reach. Instead, it provides information about the topology of the network in its immediate vicinity. This information consists of a list of network segments (or links) attached, and the state of those links (functioning or nonfunctioning). The router then floods this information throughout the network. Each router can then build its view of the current state of all the links in the network. From this view, every router can compute its best path to all destinations and populate its routing table with this information. In the simplest case, this computation may be the path with the fewest hops. Again, this link-state information might include the bandwidth of the link, current load on the link, administrative weights, or even policy restricting certain traffic across the link. You may not want classified data to leave your organization.

Types of Routing Protocols

Real-world enterprise networks consist of several routers that move packets between the various subnets found on the network. To move packets efficiently, it is not uncommon to divide several connected routers into subsets of the internetwork. A subset of the network containing several member routers is referred to as an *area*. When grouping several areas into a higher-level subset, this subset is a *routing domain*.

The fact that you can divide internetworks into logical groupings such as routing domains (or autonomous systems) gives rise to two kinds of routing protocols:

- Routing protocols that provide the routing of packets between routers in a routing domain
- Routing protocols that provide the routing of packets between routing domains

Exhibit 7   Routing Protocols

	Distance Vector	*Link State*	*Hybrid*
Examples	Interior Gateway Routing Protocol (IGRP), Routing Information Protocol (RIP)	Intermediate System to Intermediate System (IS-IS), NetWare Link Services Protocol (NLSP), Open Shortest Path First (OSPF)	Enhanced Interior Gateway Routing Protocol (EIGRP)
Convergence time	Slow	Fast	Fast
Bandwidth use	High	Low	Low
Resource use	Low	High	Low
Multi-path support	Yes	Yes	Yes
VLSM	No	Yes	Yes
Scales well	No; Yes for IGRP	Yes	Yes
Proprietary	No, Yes for IGRP	No	Yes
Routes non-IP Protocols	No	No	Yes

Interior gateway protocols (IGPs) route packets intradomain or among closely cooperating groups while Exterior gateway protocols (EGPs) route packets interdomain or between two independent administrative entities. One can classify dynamic routing protocols as either an EGP or an IGP. Examples of IGPs include Enhanced IGRP (EIGRP), Interior Gateway Routing Protocol (IGRP), Open Shortest Path First (OSPF), and Routing Information Protocol (RIP); and examples of EGPs include Border Gateway Protocol (BGP) and Exterior Gateway Protocol (EGP). The Internet is based on Border Gateway Protocol version 4.

IGPs do not scale well to extremely large networks. Designers developed EGPs to scale to the largest of networks, but their inherent complexity and overhead can quickly overwhelm a small or medium-sized network. On the other side, interior protocols are fairly simple and have less overhead but do not scale as well. IGPs operate within an autonomous system to exchange information with other routers in your organization.

Exhibit 7 groups some of the more popular protocols into the previous categories and lists some advantages and disadvantages of each. If you are an auditor or security professional, then it is unlikely that you will select the routing protocol; however, is important to know about the various protocols.

Practice Session

In this Practice Session, you will practice the following:

- Logging in
- Start and configure RIP

- Confirm our configuration
- Start and stop debugging
- Logging out

1. Log in to the SimRouter Web page.
2. Double-click on router 2501-1 to telnet to that router. This will open a console session.
3. Enter your **Username** and **Password** at the applicable prompt. These are the ones you set up in Chapter 2. You will need to hit the Enter key twice to get to the > prompt.
4. You need to enter the following to enable privileged EXEC mode:

   ```
   2501-1>enable
   ```

5. Then enter the following to configure the RIP protocol:

   ```
   2501-1#config t
   2501-1(config)#router rip
   2501-1(config-router)#network 10.0.0.0
   2501-1(config-router)#network 192.168.0.0
   ```

6. You need to enter the following commands to configure the router interfaces with IP addresses in the ranges that RIP will send updates:

   ```
   2501-1#config t
   2501-1(config)#interface s0
   2501-1(config-if)#ip address 10.10.10.1 255.0.0.0
   2501-1(config-if)#exit
   2501-1(config)#interface ethernet0
   2501-1(config-if)#ip address 192.168.0.1 255.255.255.0
   ```

7. Enter the **exit** command to get back to the 2501-1(config)# prompt. Enter the **exit** command again to get back to the 2501-1# prompt. (You can enter the end command to get right back to the # prompt.)
8. To turn on debugging, enter:

   ```
   2501-1#debug ip rip
   ```

Note: The debug command is CPU-intensive. You can use it on our network, but use it judiciously in the real world.

---

9. To turn off debugging, enter:

   ```
   2501-1#undebug ip rip
   ```

10. To return to user mode, type the **disable** command.
11. To see the effect of your change, enter the following command and review the results:

    ```
    2501-1>show ip protocol
    2501-1>show ip route
    ```

12. To see the contents of the ARP cache, enter the following command:

    router#**show arp**

13. To clear the contents of the ARP cache, enter the following command:

    router#**clear arp**

14. Exit your Telnet session by selecting the Disconnect option from the Connect menu in the Telnet window.
15. Click on Log Out on the SimRouter Web page.

Security and Audit Checklist

1. Does the router support static routing?
   - Yes
   - No
2. If yes, how was the static route determined?
3. Does the router support dynamic routing?
   - Yes
   - No
4. If dynamic routing is supported, what protocol for updating is used?
   - Distance vector
   - Link state
   - Hybrid
5. If dynamic routing is supported, what routing protocol is used?
   - BGP
   - EIGRP
   - IGRP
   - IS-IS
   - OSPF
   - RIP
   - Other
6. Do you have:
   - Access routers?
   - Core routers?
   - Distribution routers?
7. Are changes to routes:
   - Tested?
   - Approved?

Conclusion

In this chapter, you learned that you use routers to move packets from one network to another. Routers perform two basic activities: path determination and packet switching. You learned that there are different types of routing:

- Static and dynamic protocols
- Distance-vector, link-state, and hybrid routing protocols
- Interior gateway and exterior gateway protocols

You had an opportunity to configure some interfaces. Should you have time, enable other protocols and configure the interfaces.

Unless you are a network planner, this chapter is meant as a primer on routers and routing protocols. If you need to select protocols, then you should get yourself a book focusing on routing protocols.

In the next chapter, you will get a look at router management; that is, logging, troubleshooting, and debugging.

Chapter 4

Understanding
Router Basics

In this chapter, you will learn about:

- The user interface: user and privileged modes
- Context-sensitive help and the `history` command
- Router modes
- Router components: RAM, NVRAM, Flash, EPROM, ROM, and network interfaces

Router Overview

The Cisco IOS is the most important part of your router. Hardware is just metal without the software. The IOS is the program code that defines how the router functions. Without it, the router cannot route packets. The IOS is feature-rich and pretty much standard across the various Cisco platforms. So once you become familiar with IOS commands on one router, you do not have to learn new commands to work on a new router.

The IOS provides a labor-saving command line interface for configuring routers that is easy to navigate. This chapter introduces the various modes, the help function, and the router components.

User Interface

The Cisco IOS provides a robust user interface called EXEC for its routers. EXEC, short for executive, intercepts commands and executes them. For security purposes, EXEC supports two types of access:

- User mode
- Privileged mode

Exhibit 1   User EXEC Mode Commands

User Command	Function
access-enable	Create a temporary access-list entry
access-profile	Apply user profile to interface
clear	Reset functions
connect	Open a terminal connection
disable	Return to user mode and turn off privileged commands
disconnect	Disconnect an existing network connection
enable	Go to privileged mode and turn on privileged commands
exit	Leave the EXEC
help	View information from the interactive help system
lock	Lock the terminal
login	Log in as a particular user
logout	Log out from EXEC
mrinfo	Request neighbor and version information from a multicast router
mstat	Show statistics after multiple multicast traceroutes
mtrace	Trace reverse multicast path from destination to source
name-connection	Name an existing network connection
pad	Open an X.29 PAD connection
ping	Send ECHO messages
ppp	Start IETF Point-to-Point Protocol (PPP)
resume	Resume an active network connection
rlogin	Open an rlogin connection (trusted)
set	Set system parameter (not config)
show	Show system information
slip	Start serial-line IP (SLIP)
systat	Display information about terminal lines
telnet	Open a Telnet connection
terminal	Set terminal line parameters
traceroute	Trace route from source to destination
tunnel	Open a tunnel connection
where	List active connections
x28	Become an X.28 PAD
x3	Set X.3 parameters on PAD

User Mode

Upon logging in to the router, you are automatically put into *user mode*. EXEC commands in user mode allow you to display information but you cannot change router configuration settings. User mode commands are a subset of the larger privileged mode commands. Exhibit 1 lists the available commands in user EXEC mode. The actual commands depend on the router configuration and the Cisco IOS version.

Tip: You will know you are in user mode when you see the user EXEC mode prompt, which is the greater than symbol (>). If your router is named RouterA, then you will see the prompt of `RouterA>`.

Privileged Mode

Typically, you must enter a password before you can access privileged mode. Privileged mode allows execution of all of the user mode commands, as well as setting configuration parameters, performing extensive testing and debugging, and accessing the other router modes.

Exhibit 2 lists the available commands in privileged EXEC mode. The actual commands depend on the router configuration and the Cisco IOS version.

Tip: You will know you are in privileged mode when you see the privileged EXEC mode prompt, which is the pound symbol (#). If you named your router RouterA, then you will see the prompt of `RouterA#`.

Context-Sensitive Help

From Exhibits 1 and 2, you can see there are many commands. If you are not working day in and day out with these commands, then it is easy to forget the command or its syntax. Probably one of the most helpful features of the IOS is the context-sensitive help command. For example, entering "?" at the command prompt will generate a list of available commands for that particular EXEC mode.

Context-sensitive help provides assistance as you enter commands. Syntax checking, command prompting, and keyword completion are some of the context-sensitive help features available. Exhibit 3 highlights several features of context-sensitive help.

Suppose you enter the command sh c?. You would see the following:

```
2501-1>sh c?
clock compress configuration controllers
```

You will get different results, depending on where you place the question mark. If you entered sh cl?, then only information regarding the clock command would show.

Look at the following to gain an appreciation for the use of context-sensitive help:

```
2501-1>sh clock
*00:36:47.999 UTC Mon Mar 1 1993
2501-1>sh cloc
*00:36:53.671 UTC Mon Mar 1 1993
```

Exhibit 2   Privileged EXEC Mode Commands

User Command	Function
access-enable	Create a temporary access-list entry
access-profile	Apply user-profile to interface
access-template	Create a temporary access-list entry
bfe	For manual emergency modes setting
cd	Change current directory
clear	Reset functions
clock	Manage the clock system
configure	Enter configuration mode
connect	Open a terminal connection
copy	Copy configuration or image data
debug	Access debugging functions
delete	Delete a file
dir	List files on a file system
disable	Return to user mode and turn off privileged commands
disconnect	Disconnect an existing network connection
enable	Go to privileged mode and turn on privileged commands
erase	Erase Flash or configuration memory
exit	Leave the EXEC
help	View information from the interactive help system
lock	Lock the terminal
login	Log in as a particular user
logout	Log out from EXEC
more	Display the contents of a file
mrinfo	Request neighbor and version information from a multicast router
mstat	Show statistics after multiple multicast traceroutes
mtrace	Trace reverse multicast path from destination to source
name-connection	Name an existing network connection
no	Disable a function
pad	Open an X.29 PAD connection
ping	Send ECHO messages
ppp	Start IETF Point-to-Point Protocol (PPP)
pwd	Display current working directory
reload	Halt and perform a cold restart
resume	Resume an active network connection
rlogin	Open an rlogin connection (trusted)
rsh	Execute a remote command (trusted)
send	Send a message to other TTY lines
set	Set system parameter (not config)
setup	Run the SETUP command facility
show	Show system information
slip	Start serial-line IP (SLIP)
start-chat	Start a chat-script on a line
systat	Display information about terminal lines
telnet	Open a Telnet connection

Exhibit 2   Privileged EXEC Mode Commands (Continued)

User Command	Function
terminal	Set terminal line parameters
test	Test subsystems, memory, and interfaces
traceroute	Trace route from source to destination
tunnel	Open a tunnel connection
undebug	Disable debugging functions
verify	Verify the checksum of a Flash file
where	List active connections
write	Write running configuration to memory, network, or terminal
x28	Become an X.28 PAD
x3	Set X.3 parameters on PAD

Exhibit 3   Context-Sensitive Help

Command	Function
?	Displays a list of all available commands in the mode
help	Displays a brief description of the help system for any mode
<abbreviated command> ?	Displays a list of commands that begin with the character string specified in <abbreviated command>
<abbreviated command> <Tab>	Completes partial command
<command> ?	Displays the command's possible keywords
<command> <keyword> ?	Displays the keyword's possible arguments

```
2501-1>sh clo
*00:36:58.431 UTC Mon Mar 1 1993
2501-1>sh cl
*00:37:01.255 UTC Mon Mar 1 1993
2501-1>sh c
% Ambiguous command: "sh c"
```

You can see that when you get to sh c, there is ambiguity; that is, there are other show keywords starting with a "c" as you just saw. However, any of the other abbreviations is acceptable.

Looking at the clock's setting, you can see that it is incorrect. (No, I have not been working on this book since March 1, 1993.) You will set the clock in the Practice Session in this chapter.

Several common command abbreviations are provided in Exhibit 4.

Exhibit 4   Common Command Abbreviations

Abbreviation	Command
conf	configure
int	interface
sh	show
shut	shutdown
trace	traceroute

Tip: When you have completed enough of the command to make it unique and hit the Tab key, the IOS will complete the command. This is good for documentation purposes because it saves you time but shows the complete command. Try it with commands you do not use frequently.

Command History

EXEC also provides a record of recently executed commands. Command history is available to you in most of the router modes (see Router Modes section). The router stores the commands in a buffer with the oldest commands at the top. You can use the sh history command to display the previous ten commands (i.e., the default history size that the IOS enables by default). You also can use the history with editing commands to save yourself time and effort.

Tip: You can adjust the history buffer size using the terminal history size <number of lines> command.

Editing Commands

EXEC includes an enhanced editing mode that supports several editing functions. Used along with the command history, the editing commands prove quite useful. You can recall commands from the command history, edit them, and then re-execute them without re-entering the entire command line. Exhibit 5 provides some useful editing and history commands.

Tip: The IOS enables advanced editing by default. You can disable it using the terminal no editing command.

Exhibit 5   Editing Commands

Keystroke	Task
Ctrl-A	Moves to the beginning of the command line
Ctrl-B	Moves back one character
Ctrl-E	Moves to the end of the command line
Ctrl-F	Moves forward one character
Ctrl-N or down arrow	Recalls a newer or more recent command
Ctrl-P or up arrow	Recalls the last or previous command
Ctrl-R	Redisplays the current line when the screen gets overloaded with logging messages
Esc-B	Moves back one word
Esc-F	Moves forward one word

Finally, the IOS provides horizontal scrolling for long command lines. Should your cursor reach the end of the line while you are entering a command, the IOS shifts the command line ten characters to the left. A dollar sign ("$") at the beginning of the line indicates that the IOS shifted the line. Each time your cursor hits the end of the line, the IOS will shift the command line. You can then use the editing features in Exhibit 4 to edit the line.

Router Modes

Regardless of whether you use the console port, dial-up, or connect through a router interface, you can place it in several modes as follows:

- *User mode.* As stated, this mode provides a user display-only environment. It is a read-only mode. You can connect to some other devices, perform some tests, and look at some statistics.
- *Privileged mode.* As stated, this mode allows you to test, debug, and change the configuration. You have access to all commands on the router.
- *Setup mode.* This mode is triggered on start-up when there is no configuration file residing in Non-Volatile Random Access Memory (NVRAM). This mode executes an interactive prompted dialog to assist you in creating an initial router configuration.
- *ROM monitor mode.* This mode facilitates recovery functions when you lose the router password or something corrupts or erases the IOS file stored in Flash.
- *RXBOOT mode.* This mode is accessible by changing the config register settings and rebooting the router. RXBOOT mode loads a subset of the IOS to help you get the router running when it cannot find a valid version of the IOS.
- *Global configuration mode.* This mode allows you to perform simple configuration tasks such as naming the router, setting router passwords, and creating router banners.
- *Other configuration modes.* These modes allow you to perform complex router configuration tasks such as configuring interfaces, sub-interfaces, controllers, and routing protocols.

Exhibit 6 Router Modes

Type of User	Functions	How Accessed	Prompt
User	Limited display	Log in to the router	Router>
Privileged	Display, test, debug, and make configuration file changes	From user EXEC mode, enter the `enable` command	Router#
Setup	Create initial router configuration	During router start-up, when the configuration file is gone from NVRAM (console access only)	Interactive dialog prompts
ROM monitor	Bypass config file processing	Activated when the router cannot find a valid version of the IOS; from the privileged EXEC mode, use the `reload` command	> or rommon >
RXBOOT	Perform router recovery	Press Break key during router startup (console access only)	> or Router<boot>
Global	Perform a simple configuration	From privileged EXEC mode, enter the `configure` command	Router(config)#
Others	Perform complex and multi-line configurations	From within global configuration mode, the command entered varies	Router(config-<mode>)#

Note: There are more than 17 different config modes. Should you learn how one works, then you will understand how they all work.

Exhibit 6 summarizes the type of user, the commands they can execute, how to access the command, and the command prompt needed.

Router Components

Every router has the following components that make up its configuration: RAM, NVRAM, Flash, ROM, and interfaces. Exhibit 7 shows the various components of a router.

Random Access Memory (RAM)

RAM serves as a temporary working storage area for the router. RAM contains data such as routing tables, cache, buffers, and I/O queues. RAM also provides storage for temporary memory for the router's active IOS and configuration file (i.e., the *running-config*). You lose the entire contents of RAM when you power down or restart the router.

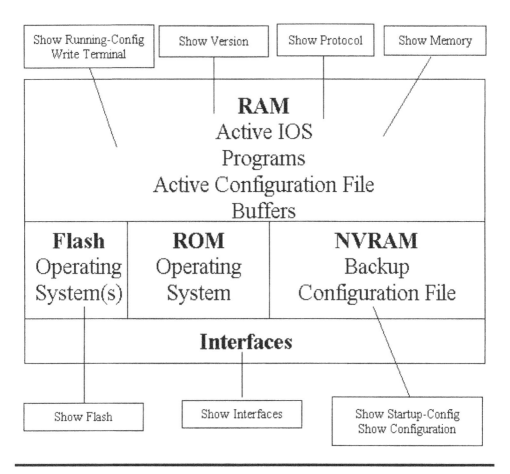

Exhibit 7   Router Components

Non-Volatile RAM (NVRAM)

Conversely, NVRAM is permanent and retains its contents when you power down or restart the router. NVRAM stores permanent information, such as the router's backup configuration file. The router retrieves the *startup-config* from NVRAM at start-up and loads into RAM.

Flash

Flash stores the Cisco IOS image and associated microcode. Flash is erasable, programmable, read-only memory (EPROM) that retains its contents when you power down or restart the router. You can store several versions of IOS images in Flash memory. Flash allows you to upgrade the router without adding, removing, or replacing microchips on the router.

Read-Only Memory (ROM)

ROM, like Flash, maintains a copy of the IOS but it is an older version of the IOS. ROM also stores the bootstrap program and power-on diagnostic programs. Unlike Flash, you can only upgrade ROM by replacing chips on the motherboard.

Interfaces

Interfaces provide the network connections where packets move in and out of the router. Depending on the router model, the interfaces might exist on the motherboard or on separate, modular interface cards.

Router Status

Routine administration of a router involves examining the status of the router and its components. Exhibit 7 provided some commands that you can use to do this. The show command allows you to view the status of the router's components. You can execute the show command from either user or privileged EXEC mode. You should know that the keywords are different in each mode.

You will have an opportunity to try the following commands in the Practice Session and see the results:

- The show version command displays the hardware configuration, software version, boot images, and names and sources of configuration files.
- The show memory command displays statistics about the router's memory.
- The show protocol command displays the network layer protocols and addresses currently configured on the router.
- The show running-config command displays the active configuration file.

Tip: Use the write terminal command instead of the show running-config command when your router is running IOS 10.3 or earlier.

- The show startup-config command displays the backup configuration file.

Tip: Use the show configuration command instead of the show startup-config command when your router is running IOS 10.3 or earlier. The show configuration command works for newer versions as well.

- The show interfaces command displays statistics for all of the router's interfaces or for a specific router interface.
- The show flash command displays information about the Flash memory.
- The show subsys command displays subsystem information.
- The show users command displays information about terminal lines.

Practice Session

In this Practice Session, you will practice the following:

- Logging in
- Saving log data
- Context-sensitive help
- show command

1. Log in to the SimRouter Web page.
2. Double-click on router 2501-1 to telnet to that router. This will open a console session.
3. Enter your **Username** and **Password** at the applicable prompt. These are the ones you set up in Chapter 2. You will need to hit the Enter key twice to get to the > prompt.
4. Let us save the log for your session today. To do this, select | Terminal | Start Logging | from the menu bar in the Telnet window. The Telnet client will ask you where you wish to store the log and with what name. Your choice.
5. Type **?**. As soon as you type ?, the IOS displays a list of commands. It stops at the end of the first page, where you should see −More−. If you press the Enter key, you will get the next line. Pressing the spacebar will display the next page. Review the commands available.
6. From the list in Step 5, you see that a valid command is show. Enter the following show commands and study the output:

```
2501-1>show version
```

You should see the following information:

```
2501-1>show version
Cisco Internetwork Operating System Software
IOS (tm) 2500 Software (C2500-D-L), Version 12.0(9),
   RELEASE SOFTWARE (fc1)
Copyright (c) 1986-2000 by Cisco Systems, Inc.
Compiled Mon 24-Jan-00 22:06 by bettyl
Image text-base: 0x030387D0, data-base: 0x00001000

ROM: System Bootstrap, Version 11.0(10c)XB2, PLATFORM
   SPECIFIC RELEASE SOFTWARE
(fc1)
BOOTFLASH: 3000 Bootstrap Software (IGS-BOOT-R),
   Version 11.0(10c)XB2, PLATFORM
SPECIFIC RELEASE SOFTWARE (fc1)

2501-1 uptime is 11 minutes
System restarted by reload
System image file is "flash:c2500-d-1.120-9.bin"

Cisco 2500 (68030) processor (revision D) with
   16384K/2048K bytes of memory.
```

```
Processor board ID 01881869, with hardware revision
   00000000
Bridging software.
X.25 software, Version 3.0.0.
1 Ethernet/IEEE 802.3 interface(s)
2 Serial network interface(s)
32K bytes of non-volatile configuration memory.
8192K bytes of processor board System flash (Read ONLY)

Configuration register is 0x2102
2501-1>sho memory
```

Tip: Hit the Esc key whenever you want to break out of a command.
Try it when the sh memory command is running.

```
2501-1>sh protocol
```

You should see the following information:

```
2501-1>sh protocol
Global values:
Internet Protocol routing is enabled
Ethernet0 is administratively down, line protocol is
   down
Serial0 is administratively down, line protocol is down
Serial1 is administratively down, line protocol is down
2501-1>show interfaces
```

You should see the following information:

```
2501-1>show interfaces
Ethernet0 is administratively down, line protocol is
   down
   Hardware is Lance, address is 0000.0c5d.433b (bia
      0000.0c5d.433b)
   MTU 1500 bytes, BW 10000 Kbit, DLY 1000 usec, rely
      255/255, load 1/255
   Encapsulation ARPA, loopback not set, keepalive set
      (10 sec)
   ARP type: ARPA, ARP Timeout 04:00:00
   Last input never, output never, output hang never
   Last clearing of "show interface" counters never
   Queueing strategy: fifo
   Output queue 0/40, 0 drops; input queue 0/75, 0 drops
   5 minute input rate 0 bits/sec, 0 packets/sec
   5 minute output rate 0 bits/sec, 0 packets/sec
```

```
            0 packets input, 0 bytes, 0 no buffer
            Received 0 broadcasts, 0 runts, 0 giants, 0
              throttles
            0 input errors, 0 CRC, 0 frame, 0 overrun, 0
              ignored, 0 abort
            0 input packets with dribble condition detected
            0 packets output, 0 bytes, 0 underruns
            0 output errors, 0 collisions, 9 interface resets
            0 babbles, 0 late collision, 0 deferred
            0 lost carrier, 0 no carrier
            0 output buffer failures, 0 output buffers swapped
              out
      Serial0 is administratively down, line protocol is down
        Hardware is HD64570
        MTU 1500 bytes, BW 1544 Kbit, DLY 20000 usec, rely
          255/255, load 1/255
        Encapsulation HDLC, loopback not set, keepalive set
          (10 sec)
        Last input never, output never, output hang never
        Last clearing of "show interface" counters never
        Input queue: 0/75/0 (size/max/drops); Total output
          drops: 0
        Queueing strategy: weighted fair
        Output queue: 0/1000/64/0 (size/max
          total/threshold/drops)
          Conversations 0/0/256 (active/max active/max total)
          Reserved Conversations 0/0 (allocated/max
            allocated)
        5 minute input rate 0 bits/sec, 0 packets/sec
        5 minute output rate 0 bits/sec, 0 packets/sec
            0 packets input, 0 bytes, 0 no buffer
            Received 0 broadcasts, 0 runts, 0 giants, 0
              throttles
            0 input errors, 0 CRC, 0 frame, 0 overrun, 0
              ignored, 0 abort
            0 packets output, 0 bytes, 0 underruns
            0 output errors, 0 collisions, 1 interface resets
            0 output buffer failures, 0 output buffers swapped
              out
            0 carrier transitions
            DCD=down DSR=down DTR=down RTS=down CTS=down
      Serial1 is administratively down, line protocol is down
        Hardware is HD64570
        MTU 1500 bytes, BW 1544 Kbit, DLY 20000 usec, rely
          255/255, load 1/255
```

```
      Encapsulation HDLC, loopback not set, keepalive set
         (10 sec)
      Last input never, output never, output hang never
      Last clearing of "show interface" counters never
      Input queue: 0/75/0 (size/max/drops); Total output
         drops: 0
      Queueing strategy: weighted fair
      Output queue: 0/1000/64/0 (size/max
         total/threshold/drops)
         Conversations 0/0/256 (active/max active/max
            total)
         Reserved Conversations 0/0 (allocated/max
            allocated)
      5 minute input rate 0 bits/sec, 0 packets/sec
      5 minute output rate 0 bits/sec, 0 packets/sec
         0 packets input, 0 bytes, 0 no buffer
         Received 0 broadcasts, 0 runts, 0 giants, 0
            throttles
         0 input errors, 0 CRC, 0 frame, 0 overrun, 0
            ignored, 0 abort
         0 packets output, 0 bytes, 0 underruns
         0 output errors, 0 collisions, 1 interface resets
         0 output buffer failures, 0 output buffers swapped
            out
         1 carrier transitions
         DCD=down DSR=down DTR=down RTS=down CTS=down
2501-1>sho flash
```

You should see the following information:

```
2501-1>sho flash

System flash directory:
File  Length     Name/status
   1  6888660    c2500-d-1.120-9.bin
[6888724 bytes used, 1499884 available, 8388608 total]
8192K bytes of processor board System flash (Read ONLY)
2501-1>sh users
```

You should see the following information:

```
2501-1>sh users
   Line     User     Host(s)          Idle Location
*  0        con 0    idle             00:00:00
2501-1>show buffers
```

You should see the following information:

```
2501-1#show buffers
```

```
Buffer elements:
  500 in free list (500 max allowed)
  16 hits, 0 misses, 0 created

Public buffer pools:
Small buffers, 104 bytes (total 50, permanent 50):
  49 in free list (20 min, 150 max allowed)
  17 hits, 0 misses, 0 trims, 0 created
  0 failures (0 no memory)
Middle buffers, 600 bytes (total 25, permanent 25):
  25 in free list (10 min, 150 max allowed)
  24 hits, 0 misses, 0 trims, 0 created
  0 failures (0 no memory)
Big buffers, 1524 bytes (total 50, permanent 50):
  50 in free list (5 min, 150 max allowed)
  4 hits, 0 misses, 0 trims, 0 created
  0 failures (0 no memory)
VeryBig buffers, 4520 bytes (total 10, permanent 10):
  10 in free list (0 min, 100 max allowed)
  0 hits, 0 misses, 0 trims, 0 created
  0 failures (0 no memory)
Large buffers, 5024 bytes (total 0, permanent 0):
  0 in free list (0 min, 10 max allowed)
  0 hits, 0 misses, 0 trims, 0 created
  0 failures (0 no memory)
Huge buffers, 18024 bytes (total 0, permanent 0):
  0 in free list (0 min, 4 max allowed)
  0 hits, 0 misses, 0 trims, 0 created
  0 failures (0 no memory)

Interface buffer pools:
Ethernet0 buffers, 1524 bytes (total 32, permanent 32):
  8 in free list (0 min, 32 max allowed)
  24 hits, 0 fallbacks
  8 max cache size, 8 in cache
Serial0 buffers, 1524 bytes (total 32, permanent 32):
  7 in free list (0 min, 32 max allowed)
  25 hits, 0 fallbacks
  8 max cache size, 8 in cache
Serial1 buffers, 1524 bytes (total 32, permanent 32):
  7 in free list (0 min, 32 max allowed)
  25 hits, 0 fallbacks
  8 max cache size, 8 in cache
```

7. Enter `enable` mode. Presently, the router is not set up with an enable password. You will set one in Chapter 6, "Implementing Non-AAA Authentication."

8. To see the current clock settings, type the following:

   ```
   2501-1#show cl
   ```

   To set the clock, type the following:

   ```
   2501-1#c?
   2501-1#clock ?
   ```

   From the keywords, select set and enter:

   ```
   2501-1#clock set ?
   ```

   Enter the time as specified in the format:

   ```
   2501-1#clock set 10:01:00 ?
   ```

   Enter the day of the month and month of the year:

   ```
   2501-1#clock set 10:01:00 22 August ?
   ```

   Enter the year:

   ```
   2501-1#clock set 10:01:00 22 August 2001
   ```

9. Enter the following commands and study the output:

   ```
   2501-1#show running-config
   ```

   You should see the following information:

   ```
   2501-1#show running-config
   Building configuration…

   Current configuration:
   !
   version 12.0
   service timestamps debug uptime
   service timestamps log uptime
   no service password-encryption
   !
   hostname 2501-1
   !
   !
   ip subnet-zero
   !
   !
   !
   interface Ethernet0
     no ip address
     no ip directed-broadcast
     shutdown
   !
   interface Serial0
     no ip address
   ```

```
    no ip directed-broadcast
    shutdown
!
interface Serial1
  no ip address
  no ip directed-broadcast
  shutdown
!
ip classless
!
!
line con 0
  transport input none
line aux 0
line vty 0 4
  login
!
end
2501-1#sho startup-config
```

You should see the following information:

```
2501-1#sho startup-config
Using 447 out of 32762 bytes
!
version 12.0
service timestamps debug uptime
service timestamps log uptime
no service password-encryption
!
hostname 2501-1
!
!
ip subnet-zero
!
!
!
interface Ethernet0
  no ip address
  no ip directed-broadcast
  shutdown
!
interface Serial0
  no ip address
  no ip directed-broadcast
  shutdown
```

```
!
interface Serial1
  no ip address
  no ip directed-broadcast
  shutdown
!
ip classless
!
!
line con 0
  transport input none
line aux 0
line vty 0 4
!

end
```

Because you have not made any changes, the startup-config and the running-config commands should give you the same information.

```
2501-1#sh subsya
```

10. As you can see, you got an error on the last command. It was spelled wrong; you should have entered **subsys**. Type **Ctrl-P** or use the up arrow. This returns you to the last command you entered. Press the Backspace key, enter an "s," and press the Enter key. Try some of the other editing commands.

11. To see a history of the commands you entered, type the following:

    ```
    2501-1#sh history
    ```

12. Exit your Telnet session by selecting the Disconnect option from the Connect menu in the Telnet window or by typing **quit** at the prompt.

13. Click on Log Out on the SimRouter Web page.

Security and Audit Checklist

1. What is the name of the router?
2. What is the current time and date for the router?
3. What is the IOS current version?
4. When was the IOS last compiled?
5. What is the system bootstrap version?
6. How long has the system been up?
7. What is the name of the Flash image file?
8. What is the router model?
9. How much memory does the router have?
10. Is there any bridging software installed?
    - Yes
    - No

11. If you answered Yes to Question 10, what version is it?
12. What version of X.25 software are you using?
13. Does the router have any of the following interfaces?
    - Ethernet
    - Token Ring
    - Serial
    - Other
14. The configuration register is set to:
    - 0x2100: will not boot unless you enter the boot command.
    - 0x2101: will boot from ROM.
    - 0x2102-0x210F: will look at the configuration file for boot command instructions.
15. What lines are up (i.e., active)?
16. What are the hardware addresses of the interfaces?
17. What are the IP addresses of the interfaces?
18. Are network addresses assigned to interfaces? If yes, what are they?
19. What is the value for the maximum transmission unit (MTU)?
20. What is the length of the Flash program?
21. Is the length of the Flash program ever checked for unauthorized changes?

Conclusion

In this chapter, you learned about router modes and components. You saw that you can obtain lots of information by just using the show commands in the user EXEC mode. To make changes to the existing configuration, you will need to enter privileged EXEC mode.

As a security or audit professional, you need to know the components of the router and what they do.

The point of this book is not to turn you into a CCNA, but you are well on your way. By the time you finish, you most likely will be able pass the examination. Take your time when you are on SimRouter and try different commands. You cannot really do any harm — and you always can reboot!

The next chapter proves to be the final one on routers and routing basics before you get into securing and controlling your router.

Chapter 5

Router Management

In this chapter, you will learn about:

- Router setup
- Upgrading the IOS
- Troubleshooting
- Logging
- Simple Network Management Protocol
- Cisco Discovery Protocol
- Router management techniques

Router Setup

Before you can use your router, you have to set it up by configuring it. There are several ways to configure your router, including using:

- The Setup script
- TFTP
- Config Maker
- The command line interface
- Boot system commands

The next several sections will will explore the various ways to configure your router.

Using the Setup Script

The most common way to configure a router is to use the Setup script. When you start a new router without a configuration, the router will ask whether you want to enter the system configuration dialog. Should you say yes, you will need to set information regarding:

- The router's name
- The enable secret, enable, and virtual terminal passwords
- The SNMP community string
- The various interfaces
- The various protocols

While undoubtedly useful, the script only allows you to set up some basic information. In this chapter's Practice Session, you will use Setup and preserve the running-config to use as the starting point in the next chapter.

Using TFTP

Network administrators like to store their router configuration in a text file, edit it with a text editor, and then upload it using the Trivial File Transfer Protocol (TFTP). (Keep in mind that TFTP is a cracker target.) Administrators can take a configuration from one router, modify it, and copy it to another.

You would use the following steps with TFTP:

```
2501-1#copy tftp running-config
Host or network configuration file [host]? host
Address of remote host [255.255.255.255]? 10.8.0.2
Name of configuration file [2501-1-config]? 2501-1-config
Configure using 2501-1-config from 10.8.0.2? [confirm]
Loading 2501-1-config
```

The above commands take the configuration 2501-1-config from the system 10.8.0.2 and load them into the running configuration. You could have entered the information with the original command and not walked through the various parameters. Your choice.

Note: This procedure does not overwrite the existing running configuration but appends to it. So this means anything not specifically mentioned in the new file is left unchanged.

Now, as a control specialist, this process should make you nervous. First, you might want to limit the use of TFTP to a particular host on a particular segment or subnet. You might also want to ensure there are no packet analyzers on the subnet that might grab a copy of the next running-config file. You will learn about the various passwords for the router in Chapter 6. The router does not automatically encrypt all passwords, so they might be available in cleartext in the file being uploaded. Thus, anyone who grabs a copy of the uploaded file might have cleartext passwords. Finally, you might want to make sure they have a rigorous process in place to ensure they protect the text file and provide backup and that they develop procedures for change control. Your network administrator will not be the first one to mistakenly load the wrong version of the text file.

Using Config Maker

Cisco offers Config Maker, which allows you to draw the network with a Visio-like program. Based on how you draw your network, Config Maker asks you for information; and based on the answers, configures the interfaces and protocols.

Using the Command Line Interface

Even with the various tools available, many administrators prefer to use the old-fashioned way — the command line interface (CLI). You can access the CLI through Telnet or the console port. The CLI is always available, whereas you might find a system without the other tools installed. So, using the CLI is a good way to go. Most Practice Sessions in this book use the CLI.

Using Boot System Commands

The boot system commands specify to the router where to load the IOS from and the fallback to use when the router cannot load the IOS. The router executes the boot system commands in the order it finds them. Following is an example of a boot system command sequence:

```
2501-1(config)#boot system flash c2500-d-1.120-9.bin
2501-1(config)#boot system tftp image.exe 10.8.0.2
2501-1(config)#boot system rom
2501-1(config)#exit
2501-1#copy run start
```

This command sequence tells the router to try to load the IOS file c2500-d-1.120-9.bin from Flash. If that fails, the router will try to load the file image.exe from the TFTP server. And if that fails, the router will load the IOS from ROM, which likely is a subset of the IOS and an older version, but a version of last resort. The last command takes the file used and copies it to the startup configuration file for the next time you boot the router.

The use of boot system commands is left to network administrators and operators and its discussion to scholarly tomes aimed at those professionals.

Caution: But, should you feel the urge to configure boot system commands, always establish a fallback boot image from ROM. Then, when something goes wrong and the Flash is empty or some other problem occurs, you can always boot from an older image. The prudent person plays not with boot system commands and might set the configuration register as follows:

```
2501-1(config)#config-register 0x2102
```

Updating the IOS

During the time your organization owns the router, there will be times when you need to upgrade the IOS. For example, the router might not have the latest version when you purchase it, so you will have to upgrade; or you might find a security exposure that requires an upgrade; or you might find that the version you are using does not give you all the features you want, so you will need to upgrade. You will obviously need to upgrade as Cisco phases out its support for your IOS. You can find out what version you are running using the `sh version` command. Also observe the amount of memory (`sh memory`) because you cannot upgrade when you do not have enough memory to support the current version.

There are two primary ways to upgrade the IOS:

- Using CPSWInst
- Using TFTP

Using CPSWInst

On every CD-ROM shipped, Cisco provides the CPSWInst tool for upgrading the IOS. This tools helps load the IOS from any workstation connecting to the console port.

Using TFTP

You also can upgrade the IOS using TFTP — as do most network administrators. You could use the commands shown in Exhibit 1.

After typing the original `copy` command, the router will prompt you for the source and destination files. Depending on the version, you may get the last confirmation message.

You can use any system as a TFTP server, including a workstation or another router. Thus, you can upgrade one router and then pull that version down to every other router. Pulling the configuration from another router is definitely a time-saver, but remember that the data is visible because it is in cleartext.

Troubleshooting

You (or your network administrator) have installed the router and configured it but it just does not seem to work. Of course, you can call support; but before you do, there are a number of applications you can run to try and isolate the problem. It is important to have tools to test the availability and connectivity of your network. Consequently, Cisco has included the following basic tools:

- Ping
- Traceroute
- Telnet
- Debug
- Cisco Discovery Protocol

Exhibit 1   Upgrading the IOS Using TFTP

```
2501-1#copy tftp flas
                    **** NOTICE ****
Flash load helper v1.0
This process will accept the copy options and then terminate
    the current system image to use the ROM based image for
    the copy.
Routing functionality will not bc available during that
    time.
If you are logged in via telnet, this connection will
    terminate.
Users with console access can see the results of the copy
    operation.
                ___ ******** ___
[There are active users logged into the system]
Proceed? [confirm]

System flash directory:
  File   Length    Name/status
    1    6888660   c2500-d-1.120-9.bin
[6888724 bytes used, 1499884 available, 8388608 total]
Address or name of remote host [10.8.0.3]: 10.8.0.2
Source file name? c2500-d-1.120-9.bin
Destination file name [c2500-d-1.120-9.bin]?
Accessing file 'c2500-d-1.120-9.bin' on 10.8.0.2. . .
Loading c2500-d-1.120-9.bin from 10.8.0.2 (via Ethernet): !
  [OK]

Erase flash device before writing? [confirm]
```

Using the Packet InterNetwork Groper (Ping)

Ping is the basic tool for testing IP connectivity because it checks end-to-end connectivity. Ping, as you can see in Appendix F, "ICMP Types and Codes," is an ICMP message type 8 with a response of message type 0. These message types are synonymous with Ping. The ping command lets you test the connection between two or more nodes on the network. You will get an opportunity to try Ping in the Practice Session at the end of this chapter.

Exhibit 2 provides information on several output characters for Echo reply for the ping command.

Tip: Ping taking too long. You can always break out using **Ctrl+Shift+6 X**, which will cancel it.

Exhibit 2   Echo Reply Characters

Character	Description
!	Successful receipt of a reply for each exclamation mark received
.	Network server timeout for each period (dot) displayed
?	Unknown packet type for each question mark received
&	Packet lifetime exceeded for each question mark received
U	PDU error or Destination Network Unreachable
C	An ICMP congestion experienced packet was received
I	User interrupted the test

Where you get 100 percent echo replies, your lower-layer protocols are working fine.

In the Practice Session, you only get to use the standard Ping. Cisco offers an extended ping command that lets you specify the protocol, among other things. With the extended Ping, you can change all the default information for the Ping. Supply the information requested at each step in the extended Ping format followed by **Enter**. Following is an example of the use of the extended Ping:

```
2501-1#ping
Protocol [ip]: ip
Target IP address: 10.16.0.1
Repeat count [5]: 10
Datagram size [100]:
Timeout in seconds [2]: 5
Extended commands [n]:
Sweep range of sizes [n]:
Type escape sequence to abort.
Sending 10, 100-byte ICMP Echos to 10.16.0.1, timeout is
   5 seconds:
!!!!!!!!!!
Success rate is 100 percent (10/10), round-trip min/avg/max =
   1/3/4 ms
```

With the extended Ping, you can test for more than connectivity. However, Ping provides limited information. For one thing, the echo request and echo reply may use different paths, as asymmetric routing is common in many large networks. So, a missing echo reply does not tell you what is broken, only that you could not reach the destination and get back. Also, the router may drop ICMP echo request packets due to congestion. In fact, your ICMP packets might be contributing to the congestion. However, the ping command remans a good starting point.

Using Traceroute

Traceroute fixes problems associated with Ping that were enumerated previously. Traceroute uses the ICMP to help determine what path the packets are taking to get to their final destination, and perchance the router that is failing to deliver the packet. The `traceroute` command takes advantage of the ICMP error messages generated by devices when a received datagram exceeds its time-to-live (TTL) value. When you initiate a `traceroute` or `trace` command, your router sends a datagram with a value of one (1). The first device will decrement the value to zero (0), discard the packet, and report back with time exceeded and destination unreachable messages. The Trace program displays the round-trip time and other information and then increases the TTL to two (2). The first packet decreases the TTL and passes it to the next hop. That device decreases the TTL to zero (0), discards the packet, and reports back. The Trace program continues in this fashion until it reaches the destination that you specified. When the timer goes off (ICMP is a connectionless protocol) before the router receives a response, Trace will report an asterisk ("*"). You will practice the `traceroute` command in this chapter's Practice Session.

A sample of the information you might see follows:

```
1 HSE-Toronto-ppp3481626.sympatico.ca (65.92.85.1)50 msec 60
  msec 50 msec
```

where

$$1 = \text{sequence number}$$
$$\text{HSE-Toronto-ppp3481626.sympatico.ca} = \text{DNS resolved name}$$
$$(65.92.85.1) = \text{IP address of the host}$$
$$50 \text{ msec } 60 \text{ msec } 50 \text{ msec} = \text{round-trip time from source to this host}$$

There is an extended `trace` command that works like the extended `ping` command.

The biggest problem with the `traceroute` command is that some administrators configure their firewall devices to block these datagrams.

Using Debug

A network administrator will find the `debug` command extremely useful because they show what is going on in the router and what traffic is passing through the interfaces. You should know that the `debug` command is very resource-intensive and you should only use it when absolutely needed. You will see a degradation of service when using `debug`. Do not use the `debug` command to monitor network traffic; there are better tools, such as Sniffer, for this. You can get a list of debug keywords using the command in Exhibit 3.

You will see that there are lots of categories with further keywords themselves. As you narrow in on the problem, you can get more specific information with the `debug` command, making the output more valuable for troubleshooting.

Using Telnet

Because Telnet works at the application layer, when you connect to another host, you know that all the other layers are working. If not, one of the lower levels is not working correctly. You can try Telnet to connect from one router to another in the Practice Session.

Exhibit 3   List of Debug Keywords

```
2501-1#debug ip ?
bgp                      BGP information
cache                    IP cache operations
cgmp                     CGMP protocol activity
drp                      Director response protocol
dvmrp                    DVMRP protocol activity
egp                      EGP information
eigrp                    IP-EIGRP information
error                    IP error debugging
ftp                      FTP dialogue
http                     HTTP connections
icmp                     ICMP transactions
igmp                     IGMP protocol activity
igrp                     IGRP information
interface                IP interface configuration changes
mcache                   IP multicast cache operations
mobile                   Mobility protocols
mpacket                  IP multicast packet debugging
mrouting                 IP multicast routing table activity
mtag                     IP multicast tagswitching activity
nat                      NAT events
ospf                     OSPF information
packet                   General IP debugging and IPSO
                            security transactions
peer                     IP peer address activity
pim                      PIM protocol activity
policy                   Policy routing
rip                      RIP protocol transactions
routing                  Routing table events
rsvp                     RSVP protocol activity
rtp                      RTP information
sd                       Session Directory (SD)
security                 IP security options
socket                   Socket event
tcp                      TCP information
tempacl                  IP temporary ACL
trigger-authentication   Trigger authentication
udp                      UDP based transactions
wccp                     WCCP information
```

You can use any IP address to gain access to a system provided you know the virtual terminal password (when one is required). Again, the firewall administrator may block access to port 23 and, thus, Telnet is not available.

Using Cisco Discovery Protocol (CDP)

The Cisco Discovery Protocol (CDP) provides a protocol-independent method for testing direct connectivity, that is, those routers who are your neighbors. This means it will collect information, regardless of whether the neighbor router supports IP, IPX, DECnet, etc. CDP is a layer two Cisco-proprietary protocol that provides information on directly connected neighbors. CDP uses data-link broadcasts to discover neighboring Cisco routers that also run CDP. The results will show you your neighbor's device ID, local port number, holdtime (in seconds), network device capability, hardware platform, and remote port type and number. The command `show cdp interface` displays CDP configuration and status information. You will use CDP in the Practice Session at the end of the chapter.

Note: CDP is on by default in IOS versions 10.3 and greater. But as you will see in the Practice Session, you can toggle it off and on using the `no cdp enable` and `cdp enable` commands.

Logging

Cisco routers can record information about a variety of events, many having security significance. Network administrators will find logs invaluable in characterizing and responding to security incidents. From a security point of view, the most important events usually recorded by system logging are interface status changes, changes to the system configuration, access list matches, and events detected by the optional firewall and intrusion detection features. The main types of logging used by Cisco routers include:

- *AAA logging,* which collects information about user dial-in connections, log ins, log outs, HTTP accesses, privilege-level changes, commands executed, and similar events. AAA log entries are sent to authentication servers using the TACACS+ and/or RADIUS protocols, and those servers record locally, typically in disk files. If you are using a TACACS+ or RADIUS server, you may wish to enable AAA logging of various sorts; this is done using AAA configuration commands such as `aaa accounting`. You will look at AAA logging in Chapter10, "AAA Accounting."
- *SNMP trap logging,* which sends notifications of significant changes in system status to SNMP management stations. You will probably want to use SNMP traps only when you have a preexisting SNMP management infrastructure; for example, you use H-P OpenView, Tivoli NetView, Novell NMS, or Cabletron Spectrum.
- *System logging,* which records a large variety of events, depending on the system configuration. You can configure your router to report system logging events to a variety of destinations, including the following:
  - The system console port (i.e., logging console)
  - A local logging buffer in router RAM (i.e., logging buffered)

Exhibit 4   System Logging Levels

Level #	Keyword	Syslog Definition	Description
0	Emergencies	SYS_EMERG	System is unusable
1	Alerts	SYS_ALERT	Immediate action needed
2	Critical	SYS_CRIT	Critical conditions
3	Errors	SYS_ERROR	Error conditions
4	Warnings	SYS_WARNING	Warning conditions
5	Notifications	SYS_NOTICE	Normal but significant conditions
6	Informational	SYS_INFO	Informational messages
7	Debugging	SYS_DEBUG	Debugging messages

- Remote sessions on VTYs and local sessions on TTYs (i.e., logging monitor, terminal monitor)
- Servers using the UNIX syslog protocol (i.e., logging ip-address, logging trap)

Because logging is not done by default, you must turn it on. That is simple. To control the logging of error messages, you use the logging on global configuration command as follows:

```
2501-1(config)#logging on
```

This command sends debug or error messages to a logging process, which logs messages to designated locations (e.g., console, buffer, monitor, or server) asynchronously to the processes generating the messages.

Let us look at system logging first, and then SNMP.

Console Port Logging

By default, the IOS only sends system logging information to the asynchronous console port. You can limit messages logged to the console based on severity as follows:

```
2501-1(config)#logging console <level>
```

This command limits the logging of messages displayed on the console terminal to a specified level. Exhibit 4 shows the logging levels.

Each system logging event is tagged with an urgency level. The levels range from debugging information (at the lowest urgency) to major system emergencies. You can configure each logging destination with a threshold urgency, and that destination will receive logging events only at or above that threshold.

When you select the logging level, the router will record all messages at that level or lower. For example, if you select warnings, the router will write warnings, errors, critical, alerts, and emergencies to the log.

You can use the no form of this command to disable logging to the console terminal.

Note: Actually, you might want to turn console logging off. When you turn on debugging, all those messages going to the console at 9600 baud might halt productive use of the router. Using the `logging buffered` command that follows will still make the information available via the `show logging` command, but in a more efficient, economical, and effective manner. It also provides local logging of messages in the event your log server is unreachable for whatever reason. You may find this particularly useful where you have out-of-band access to a remote router. Its logged error messages may shed light on why it became unreachable!

Saving Log Information

Because many administrators do not monitor the console ports, or they connect the ports to terminals without permanent memory and with relatively small displays, you may not have this information available when it is needed, especially when someone is trying to debug a problem over the network. Also, it is not always practical to attach a device to every console port on every router, switch, and hub. However, you will find the messages very valuable and you should save them.

Almost every router should save system logging information to a local RAM buffer. The logging buffer is of a fixed size and retains only the newest information. A big downside to buffered logging is that you lose the contents of the log whenever someone reloads the router. Even so, a moderately sized logging buffer is often of great value. On low-end routers, a reasonable buffer size might be 16,384 (i.e., 16K) or 32,768 bytes (i.e., 32K); on high-end routers with lots of memory (and many logged events), even 262,144 bytes (256K) might be appropriate. Sometimes you can take router memory and buffer to allow for logging. You can use the `show version` or `show flash` command to make sure that your router has enough free memory to support a logging buffer. To save messages to an internal buffer, use the following command.

```
2501-1(config)#logging buffered <buffer-size> <level>
```

You can use the no form of this command to cancel the use of the buffer. The optional buffer size is 4096 to 4,294,967,295 bytes. The default size varies by platform, but generally is 4K. The `default logging buffered` command returns the buffer size to the default size.

Caution: Remember that the more memory you allocate to logging, the less your router has to accomplish its primary tasks. You need to do some analysis to decide the optimum value — enough memory to troubleshoot the network but not so much that you do not route messages efficiently.

You can also specify the logging levels as shown in Exhibit 4.

Note: Pre-version 11.3, you could not set the logging level with the `logging buffered` command.

IOS appends the newest entries to the end of the log. When the log is full, the router will remove the older messages from the head of the log as it adds new ones to the end. How long it takes to fill the buffered log is a function of the length of the messages and the volume of messages.

Note: If you choose logging buffered, the error messages will not even show up on the console. This will keep the noise level down on the management console, especially when you are in debug mode and generating lots of error messages.

The IOS does not timestamp the log entries by default. This is not that useful when trying to troubleshoot a problem or for evidentiary purposes. But you do have two solutions. First, you can timestamp the record based on router uptime. That is, the IOS records a time that you would have to add to the time when you booted the router. To use this timestamp, use the following command:

```
2501-1(config)#service timestamps log uptime
```

If your router has a real-time clock or is running NTP, you will probably want to timestamp log entries using `service timestamps log datetime local-time msecs`.

To clear messages from the logging buffer, you will use the `clear logging` privileged EXEC command.

Syslog Servers

As mentioned, when you reboot your system, you lose buffered logging. This means you have to get to the console and do a `show logging` command to see the information before it is gone or overwritten. And no matter how large you make the logging buffer, it will fill up.

Consequently, larger installations will have syslog servers because they help solve these problems. Setting up a syslog server is fairly straightforward. You can export syslog data to any system supporting syslog. UNIX systems come with a system log daemon (syslogd); but whether the system administrator runs it is another question. The syslogd uses UDP and listens on port 514. If your organization favors Microsoft, there are even shareware syslog servers for Windows NT and 2000 Servers. You might have purchased Cisco Resource Manager, which comes with a syslog server and many good tools for analyzing the data. Your choices are bountiful. Saving to the syslog server provides another benefit: now you can use host-based tools for parsing, processing, and presenting the data.

Tip: If you do not currently have a syslog server and are wondering where to get one, you can rest assured that someone has made one available on the Internet. You will find at least the following software:

- CLS Syslogdaemon (http://www.cls.de)[2,3]
- EeSYSLOG (http://www.boson.com)[1,3]
- Kiwi Syslog Daemon (http://www.kiwi-enterprises.com/)[1,3]
- Mac NetLogger (http://www.laffeycomputer.com/)[1,4]
- SyslogX (http://download.cnet.com)[2,3]
- WinSyslog (http://www.adiscon.com/)[1,3]
- Sentinel (http://www.expnetworks.net/)[1,3]

where

[1] is freeware

[2] is shareware

[3] is Win32 software

[4] is MacOS software

To set up a log server is fairly straightforward; just use the following global configuration command:

```
2501-1(config)#logging ip-address <level>
```

This will direct messages to port 514 of the host specified by the IP address. You can get pretty sophisticated should you wish. First, you can have multiple log servers. Second, you can limit the types of messages you send to a syslog server. To limit messages logged to the syslog servers based on severity, use the `logging trap` global configuration command. You control the urgency threshold for logging to the server with `logging trap <level>`. This command limits the logging of error messages sent to syslog servers to only those messages at the specified level. The level is one shown in Exhibit 4. Selecting the debugging level is not going to hurt you, and might even help you in the future when you are trying to debug a particularly nasty problem. Surprisingly, it takes less CPU cycles to write to the syslog than to the console. If you are writing tons of messages, then you most likely have a problem and will need as much information as you can get. An obvious exception to this is the access list logging that you will cover in a later section. As usual, you can use the no form of this command to disable logging message levels to syslog servers.

The `logging facility` command tells the router how to interact with the syslog server. Local7 is the default and works with most servers, but you can use uucp, mail, news, line printer, or other logging facilities to interact with the syslog server. You have the choice of eight facilities (local0 to local7). To configure the syslog facility where you want the error messages sent, use the `logging facility` global configuration command as shown:

```
2501-1(config)#logging facility local7
```

To revert to the default of local7, use the no form of this command:

```
2501-1(config)#no logging facility
```

Even when you have a syslog server, you probably should still enable local logging. When you cannot get to the console, the syslog server provides backup and a complete record. When your router cannot get to the syslog server, you still have the data in the buffer and you do not want to lose it. A combination of syslog server and buffered logging provides your organization with the log data needed to perform troubleshooting.

Perhaps you are working on a problem and want the log messages sent to your terminal while you connect. If you want to see the messages when you telnet to the router, use the following command:

```
2501-1(config)#logging monitor <level>
```

This command limits the logging messages displayed on terminal lines other than the console line to messages with a level at or above the level. Use the no form of the command to disable logging to terminal lines other than the console line. You will need to type **terminal monitor** on the command line when you log in.

Note: All terminals monitoring will see the same message. There is no way to selectively send some error messages to one terminal and others to another terminal.

Recording Access List Violations

If you use access lists to filter traffic, you will want to log packets that violate your filtering criteria. Older Cisco IOS software versions support logging using the `log` keyword, which causes logging of the IP addresses and port numbers associated with packets matching an access list entry. Newer versions provide the `log-input` keyword, which adds information about the interface where the packet was received and the MAC address of the host that sent it.

Be selective in what you log. Do not configure logging for access list entries that will match a very large numbers of packets. Doing so will cause log files to grow excessively large and may cut into system performance. However, access list log messages are rate-limited, so the impact is not catastrophic.

You can also use access list logging to characterize traffic associated with network attacks by logging the suspect traffic. Examples of access list logging include:

```
2501-1(config)#access-list number action criteria log
2501-1(config)#access-list number action criteria log-input
```

In Chapter 15, "Basic Traffic Filtering, Part I," you will learn about access lists, so the discussion of the access list keywords is left until then. For now, it is sufficient to know that you can use `log` and `log-input` with the command.

Log Processing

Cisco routers can provide an immense quantity of real-time status information to support network management, simply by enabling the system logging facility. Your router can record the state transition of every line, along with call statistics, router configuration changes, software errors, environmental warnings, IOS reloads, and more. This level of detail can provide valuable insight into network operation that goes far beyond its normal use as a tool for resolving the cause of network failures. So, you turn on system logging and access list logging and you amass a mountain of data; now what?

Tremendous amounts of useful operations data and warnings of pending failures are available in the router logs. The challenge is that as the network gets larger, so do the number of entries in the logs, which can quickly grow to an unmanageable size. You need to process the data to provide some insight into the functioning of your router. Automating the analysis of router logs is essential should you wish to use the router logs as a proactive network management tool. Many organizations fail to take full advantage of the available information. But there are lots of solutions, so no excuses. Cisco provides CiscoWorks for Windows (CWW) and CiscoWorks 2000 Server. In addition to various other tasks, CiscoWorks provides Security Management, Server Process Status, and Useful Log Files.

The Cisco Resource Manager syslog analysis features provide a central error message logging system that you use to classify, sort, and integrate error messages and exceptions. All Resource Manager clients can generate message log reports, custom reports and summaries, and severity alert reports and summaries.

Of course, there are non-proprietary solutions as well. Freeware solutions include:

- *logsurfer* (ftp://ftp.cert.dfn.de/pub/tools/audit/logsurfer) was developed to address many of the underlying problems of swatch.
- *logcheck* (http://www.psionic.com/abacus/logcheck/) is not a real-time notification engine, but is run from `cron` and can read the new portions of the logs and process accordingly.
- *swatch* (ftp://ftp.Stanford.EDU/general/security-tools/swatch) tails the logs actively and performs its analysis and actions in real-time.
- *WOTS* (http://www.hpcc.uh.edu/~tonyc/tools/), a log file monitoring program, generates action reports based on patterns.
- UNIX `grep` and `awk` commands or C and Perl to parse the syslog.

Given the valuable information and operational insight available from the system logs, every network administrator should routinely perform a detailed analysis of syslog data. Unfortunately, this is a task frequently ignored, simply because of the difficulty of dealing with the huge quantity of raw data. So if there is any advice, it is: automate, automate, automate the process.

Simple Network Management Protocol (SNMP)

SNMP, another way to monitor a network, is commonly used for router monitoring and frequently for router configuration changes as well. SNMP uses a workstation as the point of entry and control for the Network Manager. In the Cisco environment, the router has an SNMP agent and a management information block (MIB). The MIB is a simple, hierarchical tree structure containing device information. The basic commands are the GET that retrieves information from an MIB and the SET that places data into an MIB variable. With SNMP, you also can gather statistics or configure the router. Gather statistics with get-request and get-next-request messages, and configure routers with set-request messages. You will need some software to communicate with your router. Typically, you would use a product such as the ones previously mentioned: NetView, OpenView, NMS, or Spectrum. But when you have a smaller budget or network, you can use Tobias Oetiker's freeware tool Multi Router Traffic Grapher or Ipswitch's modestly priced monitoring tool WhatsUp Gold. Should you wish to both monitor and configure your system, you would probably want to acquire CiscoWorks.

Before acquiring a product, your organization needs to develop a policy on the use of SNMP. First, decide whether you support it or not. Then, consider whether you will use software to poll the devices for useful information, enable traps on the device to automatically send back information, or both.

SNMP messages have a community string that is a cleartext password sent in every packet between a management station and the router, which has an SNMP agent. The SNMP community string is used to authenticate messages sent between the manager and agent. Briefly, a community string is a password that identifies a specific level of access for a device (either read-only or read-write). Only when the manager sends a message with the correct community string will the agent respond.

Unfortunately, version 1 of SNMP, which is the most widely used, uses a very weak authentication scheme based on only the community string, which amounts to a fixed password transmitted over the network unencrypted. SNMP version 1 is ill-suited for use across the public Internet for the following reasons:

- It uses cleartext authentication ASCII strings that anyone can capture on a network.
- Most SNMP implementations send the authentication strings as part of their periodic polling.
- It sends all data in cleartext.
- It uses UDP as a transport and is difficult to filter due to its connectionless state.
- It is an easily spoofable, datagram-based transaction protocol.

Grabbing the community string would allow unauthorized users to query or modify routers via SNMP. For this reason, using the `no snmp-server trap-authentication` command may prevent intruders from using trap messages (sent between SNMP managers and agents) to discover community strings.

The Internet community, recognizing the problems with SNMPv1, greatly enhanced the security of SNMP version 2 (SNMPv2) as described in RFC 1446. SNMPv2 uses an algorithm called MD5 (message digest 5) to authenticate communications between an SNMP server and agent. MD5 verifies the integrity of the communications, authenticates the origin, and checks for timeliness. Further, SNMPv2 can use the Data Encryption Standard (DES) for encrypting information should you desire. So, when available, your organization should use SNMPv2, which supports an MD5-based digest authentication scheme and allows for restricted access to various management data.

The SNMP agent on the router allows you to configure different community strings for non-privileged and privileged access. You configure community strings on the router via the global configuration command `snmp-server community` `<string>` `[RO | RW] [access-list]`. When you must use SNMPv1, carefully choose non-obvious community strings (not, for example, PUBLIC or PRIVATE). You should avoid using the same community strings for all your network devices; use a different string or strings for each device, or at least for each area of the network. Using different strings means that a breach of one router does not result in the compromise of the entire network, but compartmentalizes the problem to that device. You can even use multiple community strings on the same router for different network management groups. The following highlights this:

```
snmp-server community password1 RO
snmp-server community password2 RO 60
snmp-server community password3 RW 60
```

Avoid making the read-only (RO) string the same as the read-write (RW) string. When possible, you should do periodic SNMPv1 polling with a read-only community string; you should only use read-write strings for actual write operations.

In most networks, legitimate SNMP messages will come only from certain management stations. If this is true in your network, you can use the access list number option on the `snmp-server community` command to restrict SNMPv1 access to only the IP addresses of the management stations. Do not use the `snmp-server community` command for any purpose in a pure SNMPv2 environment; this command implicitly enables SNMPv1.

For SNMPv2, configure digest authentication with the authentication and MD5 keywords of the `snmp-server party` configuration command. When possible, use a different MD5 secret value for each router.

```
2501-1(config)#snmp-server party... authentication md5
   secret ...
```

SNMP management stations often have large databases of authentication information, such as community strings. This information may provide access to many routers and other network devices. This concentration of information makes the

SNMP management station a natural target for attack, and it should be secured accordingly.

Non-Privileged Mode

Use the RO keyword of the `snmp-server community` command to provide non-privileged access to your routers via SNMP. You also can specify a list of IP addresses that are allowed to send messages to the router using the access-list option with the `snmp-server community` command. In the following configuration example, you allow only hosts 10.8.0.4 and 10.16.0.4 non-privileged mode SNMP access to the router:

```
2501-1(config-if)#access-list 1 permit 10.8.0.4
2501-1(config-if)#access-list 1 permit 10.16.0.4
2501-1(config)#snmp-server community public RO 1
```

Privileged Mode

Give serious thought to the machines that can access your routers and others supporting SNMP. Use the RW keyword of the `snmp-server community` command to provide privileged access to your routers via SNMP. You also can specify a list of IP addresses that are allowed to send messages to the router by using the access-list option of the `snmp-server community` command. In the following configuration example, only hosts 10.8.0.4 and 10.16.0.4 are allowed privileged mode SNMP access to the router:

```
2501-1(config-if)#access-list 1 permit 10.8.0.4
2501-1(config-if)#access-list 1 permit 10.16.0.4
2501-1(config)#snmp-server community private RW 1
```

Again, these examples have easy-to-guess community strings. You should test your SNMP passwords using a tool such as SNMP Brute Force Attack available from SolarWinds.net. With such a tool, you can execute a dictionary attack on your SNMP-enabled routers. Use it on any SNMP-enabled devices such as servers, switches, hubs, or modems. A smart administrator will use this tool to test the strength of the community strings before someone else does.

If you suspect someone is trying to do a brute-force password attack or is just plain guessing passwords, you can use the trap capability of SNMP. Your router will then tell you when someone is sending SNMP commands with an incorrect community string. Following are the needed commands.

```
2501-1(config)#snmp-server enable traps
2501-1(config)#snmp-server trap-authentication
2501-1(config)#snmp-server host 10.8.0.4
```

The first command tells the router to enable SNMP traps. If this is not active, the router will not forward a trap. The second command tells the router to send a trap when authentication of the community string fails. The last command tells the router where to send the trap.

Tip: If you are counting on SNMP traps, it is wise to test them. There are several ways you can lose traps between your router and get an icon to blink in your network management software. It is wise to make sure you have not overlooked anything.

There are two SNMP variables that almost everyone seems to set. Use the following commands if you want to impress people with how well you manage your shop and to provide network documentation.

```
2501-1(config)#snmp-server contact ptdavis
2501-1(config)#snmp-server location Toronto
```

Finally, the dangerous aspects of SNMP mean that you should avoid the use of SNMP whenever possible. Unquestionably, SNMP aids with manageability in a large network, but the security exposures might not merit the benefit. You definitely should think twice about using it with a device that is part of your firewall configuration.

As a last comment on SNMP, use the `no snmp-server system-shutdown` command to prevent SNMP-triggered rebooting of the router. It is best to leave this feature turned off.

Cisco Discovery Protocol

Cisco Discovery Protocol (CDP) is used for some network management functions, but is dangerous in that it allows any system on a directly connected segment to learn that the router is a Cisco device, and to determine the model number and the Cisco IOS software version being run (see the following).

```
2524-1#show cdp neighbors
Capability Codes: R—Router, T—Trans Bridge, B—Source Route Bridge
                  S—Switch, H—Host, I—IGMP, r—Repeater

Device ID  Local Intrfce  Holdtme  Capability  Platform  Port ID
2501-1        Eth 0          138        R          2500     Eth 0
```

A cracker may in turn use this information to design attacks against the router. CDP information is accessible only to directly connected systems. You can disable CDP with the global configuration command `no cdp running`. CDP can be disabled on a particular interface with the `no cdp enable` command.

```
2501-1(config)#no cdp running
2501-1(config)#no cdp enable
```

Last Word on Management

Above, you learned some useful tools for managing the router. You must ensure that there are some management processes in place as well. For example, it is important to keep good records to handle and prevent network problems. Your organization should keep an accurate and complete record of all physical connections in your network. Ideally, your network administrator can take these records, and only these records, and physically trace a connection from any machine in your network to any other machine in your network without leaving her desk. The records should detail the media topology and the ports on all devices.

You must also keep detailed change records for all of your configurations. When looking at any line in the running-config, you have to attribute the change to a particular request and prove who authorized the changes. So, your records should show all lines or values added, changed, and deleted for every configuration change; the date and time of the change; the change agent and authority; and a description of the change itself. A good change management system can help in the gathering and reporting of the following information:

- Number of changes by type
- Number of changes by source
- Number of changes by risk category
- Number of changes planned in the next 30 days
- Number of incident-causing changes by source
- Number of emergency changes by source
- Percentage of incorrect categorization
- Percentage of problems due to change by type, source, risk, or category
- Average resolution time per problem
- Percentage of unrecorded changes causing problems
- Percentage of router availability
- Percentage of on-time changes
- Ratio of planned outage due to change versus actual duration

If you keep this level of documentation, then you can go back and look at the change when you are problem solving. You should also evaluate changes after-the-fact to determine whether your organization achieved the goal of the change. Finally, your organization should set a standard for how long you will keep these records.

Your organization should develop a framework for changes; that is, planning, testing, implementing, and evaluating all changes. An organization must closely monitor and control changes to systems and software so that they are completed on schedule while ensuring the stability of the environment. Best practices dictate that the process will include the following:

- Authorization for each requested change
- Performance by authorized personnel

- Identification and documentation of each feature being modified
- Ongoing tracking and communication of status

It is important that your network administrators think through all changes and the potential impact on security, efficiency, and economy. Furthermore, good practice dictates that someone reviews the plan to ensure that it is both viable and complete. The plan must identify the steps to take when someone needs to back-out the change for whatever reason. After thorough planning, try the change in a test environment. Better to have the SimRouter network crash than yours! Develop procedures for the implementation of all changes. Set standards on whether you allow network administrators to use TFTP, HTTP, or some other method of update. Decide on a procedure for accepting, reviewing, and implementing all IOS upgrades. Develop a procedure in the event the router does not initialize properly after a change. Finally, develop a process to do a post-implementation review or evaluation of all changes — good and bad.

In addition to change management, your organization needs to develop a standard for problem management. Problem management is an operational control in that it concerns itself with the day-to-day functioning of the business and contains a set of standards specifying exceptions. Best practices for problem management include:

- Establishment of a formal problem control mechanism that logs each problem and monitors its resolution
- Analysis of problem error statistics by component or problem type, recognizing trends or recurring problems, and taking corrective actions

You can address best practices by:

- Identifying, reporting, and logging the problem
- Determining the impact and extent of the problem
- Selecting predefined bypass and recovery procedures
- Initiating actions to resolve the problem and prevent reoccurrence
- Reporting and controlling all unresolved problems

The final management issue comes down to how your organization manages the devices themselves. Many administrators manage their routers remotely, and sometimes they do this over public networks such as the Internet. Any unencrypted remote access carries some risk, but access over a public network such as the Internet is especially dangerous. All remote management schemes, including interactive access, HTTP, and SNMP, are vulnerable. The best policy is to ensure that you have a secure channel when transmitting any data of a sensitive nature.

Well, you have seen enough for now. There are many good books on router management and you should look into this subject in more detail. Of course, there are many excellent texts on the subject of change and problem management as topics. Delve into these topics — they are important. Right now, try some practice exercises.

Practice Session

In this Practice Session, you will practice:

- Logging in
- Saving log data
- Switching modes
- Using router setup dialog
- Using `ping`, `traceroute`, and `telnet` to test connectivity
- Using CDP
- Enabling and saving syslog data

1. Log in to the SimRouter Web page.
2. Double-click on router 2501-1 to telnet to that router. This will open a console session.
3. Enter your **Username** and **Password** at the applicable prompt. These are the ones you set up in Chapter 2. You will need to hit the Enter key twice to get to the > prompt.
4. To save the log for this session, select | Terminal | Start Logging | from the menu bar in the Telnet window. The Telnet client will ask where you wish to store the log and with what name. Your choice. You are going to save the log so that when you build this configuration file, you can cut-and-paste it in Chapter 6 as a starting point, rather than having to enter the same information each Practice Session.
5. Enter the enable mode:

   `2501-1#`**`enable`**

6. Type **`terminal length 0`**. This command instructs the router to scroll through a long command output without pausing (the —More— message).
7. As you may have gathered from the Practice Session in Chapter 4, the routers do not have a valid configuration when you first log in. They boot up as a new router so you need to run setup. Type **`setup`** to launch setup mode.
8. When prompted to continue with the configuration dialog, enter **yes**.
9. Type **no** to Would you like to enter basic management setup.
10. When asked whether you want to see the current interface summary, enter **no**. You are more than welcome to look at it, but there is nothing of value. You are going to set these values.
11. At the Enter host name (2501-1) prompt, type **2501-1**.
12. When prompted to put in the enable secret password, enter **alpha**.
13. When prompted to enter the enable password, enter **bravo**.
14. When prompted to enter the virtual terminal password, enter **charlie**. You will learn about these different passwords in Chapter 6.
15. When asked whether you want to Configure SNMP Network Management, enter **yes**.
16. At the community string (public) prompt, enter a really strong passcode that you can remember. If you just hit the Enter key, the router will set the community string to `public`. Hopefully, none of the routers in your organization are using the default community string of public.

Caution: Your SNMPv1 community strings are sent unencrypted and someone with a packet analyzer could grab them. SNMPv2 offers encrypted passwords. Consider using different community strings for every router on your network to compartmentalize any password compromise.

---

17. Setup will ask you whether you want, in turn, to configure DECnet, AppleTalk, IPX, IP, IGRP, RIP, and bridging. Enter **yes** to configure IP and RIP, **no** to the others.

18. Now you must configure the interfaces. The router will ask whether you want to configure Ethernet0. The default is no, but enter **yes**. Type **yes** to configure the IP address for the interface. Enter **10.8.0.1** for the IP address for the interface and **255.0.0.0** for the subnet mask. Enter **no** to bypass configuring Serial0 and Serial1.

19. Once you complete Step 18, you should see the following:

```
The following configuration command script was created:

hostname 2501-1
enable secret 5 $1$FzEE$BdzxWGpwJv/TTKYAr/E300
enable password bravo
line vty 0 4
password charlie
snmp-server community public
!
no decnet routing
no appletalk routing
no ipx routing
ip routing
no bridge 1
!
interface Ethernet0
no shutdown
ip address 10.8.0.1 255.0.0.0
no mop enabled
!
interface Serial0
shutdown
no ip address
!
interface Serial1
shutdown
no ip address
dialer-list 1 protocol ip permit
dialer-list 1 protocol ipx permit
!
```

```
router rip
redistribute connected
network 10.0.0.0
!
end
```

```
[0] Go to the IOS command prompt without saving this
    config.
[1] Return back to the setup without saving this config.
[2] Save this configuration to nvram and exit.
```

```
Enter your selection [2]:
```

Review the configuration and type **2** to save the new configuration. The IOS will automatically save the configuration to NVRAM.

20. In the Telnet window for router 2501-1, select | Terminal | Stop Capture | from the menu bar to stop capturing the Telnet output.
21. Type **quit** to log out from router 2501-1. Close the Telnet window and return to the SimRouter Topology Map.
22. You can prepare this configuration for the Practice Session in Chapter 6. Open the log file with the text editor of your choice (e.g., use | Start | Programs | Accessories | Notepad |). Go to the end and look for the output of the command in Step 16 and copy from the first "!" to "end."
23. Double-click on router 2524-1 to telnet to that router. This will open a console session.
24. Repeat Steps 3 through 17. Of course, you must substitute **2524-1** wherever you see **2501-1**.
25. Bypass the ISDN configuration parameters by typing 0 to Choose ISDN BRI Switch Type. Type **no** to Do you want to configure BRI0 (BRI d-channel) interface.
26. Now you must configure the other interfaces. The router will ask you whether you want to configure Ethernet0. The default is no, but enter **yes**. Type **yes** to configure the IP address for the interface. Enter **10.16.0.1** for the IP address for the interface and **255.0.0.0** for the subnet mask. Enter **no** to bypass configuring Serial0 and Serial1.
27. Once you complete Step 26, you should see the following:

```
The following configuration command script was created:
```

```
hostname 2524-1
enable secret 5 $1$jO3i$y8Z8dHeV3XMCoKROKW1Ma1
enable password bravo
line vty 0 4
password charlie
snmp-server community public
!
no decnet routing
no appletalk routing
no ipx routing
ip routing
```

```
no bridge 1
isdn switch-type none
!
interface BRI0
shutdown
no ip address
!
interface Ethernet0
no shutdown
ip address 10.16.0.1 255.0.0.0
no mop enabled
!
interface Serial0
shutdown
no ip address
!
interface Serial1
shutdown
no ip address
dialer-list 1 protocol ip permit
dialer-list 1 protocol ipx permit
!
router rip
redistribute connected
network 10.0.0.0
!
end

[0] Go to the IOS command prompt without saving this
    config.
[1] Return back to the setup without saving this config.
[2] Save this configuration to nvram and exit.

Enter your selection [2]:
```

Review the configuration and type **2** to save the new configuration. The IOS will automatically save the configuration to NVRAM.

28. To verify your work, type **ping 10.8.0.1**. If you see the following, it worked:

```
2524-1#ping 10.8.0.1

Type escape sequence to abort.
Sending 5, 100-byte ICMP Echos to 10.8.0.1, timeout is
    2 seconds:
!!!!!

Success rate is 100 percent (5/5), round-trip
    min/avg/max = 4/4/4 ms
```

29. Also try **traceroute 10.8.0.1** or **trace 10.8.0.1**. You should see the following:

    2524-1#**traceroute 10.8.0.1**

    Type escape sequence to abort.
    Tracing the route to 10.8.0.1

    1 10.8.0.1 4 msec 0 msec *

    You can also test router connectivity using Telnet. Type **telnet 10.8.0.1**. You should see the following:

    2524-1#**telnet 10.8.0.1**
    Trying 10.8.0.1 … Open

    User Access Verification

    Password:
    2501-1>
    Type exit to disconnect from router 2501-1. You should see the 2524-1# prompt again.

30. To verify CDP is running, use the following command:

    2524-1#show cdp neighbors

    If CDP is not running, the output will be:

    "% CDP is not enabled"

    If CDP is running, the output will be:

    2524-1#show cdp neighbors
    Capability Codes: R—Router, T—Trans Bridge, B—Source Route Bridge
                       S—Switch, H—Host, I—IGMP, r—Repeater

Device ID	Local Intrfce	Holdtme	Capability	Platform	Port ID
2501-1	Eth 0	140		2500	Eth 0

31. Type **show cdp** to verify CDP has been enabled. The output should be:

    2524-1#**show cdp**
    Global CDP information:
      Sending CDP packets every 60 seconds
      Sending a holdtime value of 180 seconds

32. Now set up buffered logging. Enter the following commands:

    2524-1#logging buffered 4096 debugging

    Enter the following to prove logging is enabled.

    2524-1#sh logging

    Use the following command to timestamp the log records.

    2524-1#service timestamps log datetime

    Enter the following to look at the log.

    2524-1#sh logging

33. Should you have a problem and need to phone technical support, you can display general information about the router to use when reporting a problem. Use the following command:

    `2501-1#show tech-support ?`

    Select Page, which causes the output to display one page of information at a time. Use the Return key to display the next line of output or use the spacebar to display the next page of information. If not used, the output scrolls (i.e., does not stop for page breaks).

    `2501-1#show tech-support page ?`

    Select Password, as this causes IOS to leave passwords and other security information in the output. When not used, the IOS replaces passwords and other security-sensitive information in the output with the label "<removed>". If you were sending this off-site, you most likely would not want to print the passwords. Be extremely careful with any printout that has sensitive security information. You do not want to compromise the passwords.

    `2501-1#show tech-support page password`

34. Type **sh running-config**. The IOS displays the current running configuration as it is captured to the log file.
35. In the Telnet window for router 2524-1, select | Terminal | Stop Capture | from the menu bar to stop capturing the Telnet output.
36. You can prepare this configuration for the Practice Session in Chapter 6. Open the log file with any text editor of your choice (e.g., use | Start | Programs | Accessories | Notepad |). Go to the end and look for the output of the command in Step 32 and copy from the first "!" to "end".

Note: The procedure in Step 36 is important. In the real world, you can save printouts of your router's configuration. You can make changes to the saved material and copy it from one system to another. This is an especially good technique when you have a test lab. You can test changes in the lab and then pass them into the production router.

---

37. Type **quit** to log out from router 2524-1. Close the Telnet window and return to the SimRouter Topology Map.
38. Click on Log Out on the SimRouter Web page.

Security and Audit Checklist

1. Is logging turned on?
   - Yes
   - No

2. Are these logs part of the "Corporate History"?
   - Yes
   - No
3. What laws and organizational rules apply to the contents of the collected logs?
4. Logging is done to the:
   - Console?
   - Buffer?
   - Syslog server?
   - Terminal?
5. If logging is buffered, is the buffer size adequate?
   - Yes
   - No
6. Are you auditing the following:
   - State transition for every line?
   - Call statistics?
   - Router configuration changes?
   - Software errors?
   - Environmental warnings?
   - IOS reloads?
   - Other?
7. Are logs analyzed in real-time as part of an intrusion detection system (IDS)?
   - Yes
   - No
8. Do you use access list logging?
   - Yes
   - No
9. Does any one review all the log data?
   - Yes
   - No
10. Are the logs analyzed on a regular basis to detect abuse or find configuration errors?
    - Yes
    - No
11. Is this review timely?
    - Yes
    - No
12. What is the training and experience of the people who analyze the log files?
    - Excellent
    - Good
    - Fair
    - Poor
13. Do you have a standard for log retention?
    - Yes
    - No
14. Which log messages are archived?
    - Emergencies
    - Alerts

■ Critical
■ Errors
■ Warnings
■ Notifications
■ Informational
■ Debugging
■ None

15. Which log messages are archived in real-time?
■ Emergencies
■ Alerts
■ Critical
■ Errors
■ Warnings
■ Notifications
■ Informational
■ Debugging
■ None

16. Is there a requirement to archive every log message?
■ Yes
■ No

17. Are there any logs that must have the entire contents archived?
■ Yes
■ No

18. Does the central syslog server store all messages in a single file?
■ Yes
■ No

19. Are the logs and log data adequately protected?
■ Online
■ Offline

20. Does your router have the following ports open?
■ Echo (7)
■ Discard (9)
■ Telnet (23)
■ Finger (79)
■ HTTP (80)
■ Finger
■ SNMP over TCP (1993)
■ Auxiliary (AUX) port (2001)
■ Auxiliary (AUX) port (4001)
■ Auxiliary (AUX) port (6001)

21. Does the router support:
■ SNMP version 1?
■ SNMP version 2?

22. Is Cisco Discovery Protocol (CDP) enabled?
■ Yes
■ No

Conclusion

Router and network management is a complex subject. This chapter provides some simple tools you can use for testing connectivity and managing remote devices. When deciding to use any network management tool, someone in your organization must perform a risk analysis and determine the risks associated with using and not using the proposed tool.

Often, network administrators are loath to give up memory and disk space to logging, but logging is an essential application in any production environment. Decide what records your organization requires, and set up a procedure to review, analyze, and purge log data. You can gain a lot of information about logging by going to the CERT. The CERT has a Web page (http://www.cert.org/security-improvement/practices/p092.html) entitled "Manage logging and other data collection mechanisms." The CERT has listed things you should think about, such as log rotation and retention, and protection using encryption and access control. Visit this page when you start to set up your log server.

In Section II of this book, you will learn about preventing unauthorized access to the router itself. Specifically, Chapter 6 discusses authentication methods.

Take time to try the Practice Session in this chapter before moving on. Attempting various commands on the router is a good way to learn, as you will see as you progress through the remainder of the book.

PREVENTING UNAUTHORIZED ACCESS: NETWORKING DEVICE

II

Chapter 6

Implementing Non-AAA Authentication

In this chapter, you will learn about:

- Authentication
- Using router passwords
- Encrypting router passwords
- Configuring privilege
- Configuring line password protection
- Configuring username authentication
- Enabling CHAP or PAP authentication
- Using MS-CHAP
- Configuring TACACS and Extended TACACS password protection
- Controlling interactive access
- Configuring banners

Protecting who can access your router and make changes is an important topic. This chapter specifically tackles non-AAA authentication techniques. Cisco resolutely advocates the use of AAA security service, which this book covers in Chapters 7 through 10. The controls offered in this chapter cannot compare with the secure use of a protocol such as Kerberos. But any protection is better than no protection; so let us get started.

Authentication

A generally accepted technique for providing authentication is to exchange privileged information, or, in general terms, use a *password* or *passnumber*. Before granting any authority to anyone, your router must first identify, verify, and authenticate him or her. You implement identification through the use of a username, userID, usercode, or whatever you want to call it — an identifier that is public information. The user might identify himself as ptdavis, but you need to verify that it really is Peter Davis. A user provides a password or passnumber to verify that it truly is them and not someone else. A password is confidential and privileged information and, in general, the owners do not share passwords or passnumbers. The proper use of passwords and passnumbers is an essential first step in establishing effective access control. You can compose a password or passnumber of anything associated with an individual such that this association is a legally binding association (e.g., fingerprints, signature) or has an extremely low probability of discovery or duplication by an unauthorized individual. The system can authenticate the user by comparing the provided username and the associated password to the expected username/password pair.

Creating Strong Passcodes

For years, security practitioners have stressed the need for good password systems. The use of the term "password" is unfortunate because it focuses on the use of ordinary words. The use of ordinary words limits the passcode space. From now on, you should label these authentication keys as passcodes.

Note: There are approximately 100,000 entries in the *Unabridged Oxford Dictionary*, not including etymological (or the derivation of words) entries. One might consider this a standard for the English language. There are approximately 10,000 words in the *Abridged Webster* pocket edition you have on your desk. However, in prose (ordinary language), there are about 2000 words. Check the dictionary on your UNIX system or in Microsoft Word. Of course, Microsoft considers Microsoft and PowerPoint as valid words. If you watch television, you might think that most of them are four-letter words. Let us be generous and say that half of them are six to eight characters in length. Believe me; it does not take my Athlon 1-gigabyte processor long to cycle through those passwords!

A passcode is a sequence of characters selected or generated from a possible password space. The password space may have some passwords that are not acceptable. For example, all As is not a good passcode and you should avoid it. A good password system has a very large space of acceptable passcodes. The space should be large enough to make a brute-force attack undesirable because it is unprofitable. A brute-force attack occurs when the attacker breaks the system by trying all possible passcodes. Discovering the passcode through a search of all passcodes should cost more than the value of the information being protected.

The temptation for people to create weak passcodes is overpowering. They want to remember it so they make something that is memorable — the name of their dog, favorite city, or dream car. But making it memorable makes it predictable. There are some things you can do to create a strong passcode that you can remember. First, you should randomly generate passcodes to minimize the possibility of their determination by an unauthorized individual. There are some obvious passcodes to avoid. For example, avoid the use of:

- Words in the dictionary
- First and last names
- Street and city names
- Valid license plate numbers
- Room numbers, social security numbers, social insurance numbers, and telephone numbers
- Beer and liquor brands
- Athletic teams
- Days of the week and months of the year
- Repetitive characters
- Software default passwords

The passcode length impacts greatly on the potential security of your router. A passcode length of one reduces the potential passcode space to the number of characters in the composition set, for example, 0 to 9 for numeric characters and A to Z for alphabetic characters. Increasing the length of a random passcode can make it drastically more difficult to discover. With each additional character, both the number of possible combinations and the average time required to find the password increases exponentially. A passcode length of two characters squares the number, a length of three cubes this number, etc. Remember, a good passcode is one that is one that has an extremely low probability of discovery or duplication by an unauthorized individual. A passcode of aaa does not qualify. Using combinations of seven letters and numbers (exactly 78,364,164,096), there are enough for more than 314 passwords for every man, woman, and child in the United States. However, passcodes made up of truly random combinations are more difficult to remember the longer they get.

You should also consider the lifetime of the passcode (i.e., how long you can keep the passcode without changing it). The useful lifetime of a passcode depends on the following:

- Cost of passcode changes
- Risk associated with information disclosure
- Probability of guessing the passcode
- Number of times you use the passcode
- Susceptibility of passcode to a brute-force attack

Change passcodes regularly to reduce the risk of compromise. The period you select should fit both security and operational requirements. The maximum period for passcode usage should not exceed one year.

When needed, you must control the distribution of passcodes through a trusted means to ensure the non-disclosure of passcodes to unauthorized persons. Do not send them unencrypted over public networks.

Consecutive failed passcode submission trials permitted and the action taken by the system should be such that the system effectively prevents a person from guessing any passcode through trial and error.

Your system should maintain passcodes to protect them from disclosure or change. The passcode system should securely control passwords in the system. Specifically, the router must store and maintain the authentication list in such a manner to prevent unauthorized access. This may involve the encryption of the passcodes while residing on the system or during transmission.

Transmission is the communication of a passcode from its point of origin for comparison with a valid stored passcode. Passcodes typically authenticate the identity of a user accessing the network. To be authenticated, the passcode must be sent to the file server over the network. Unless the line is physically protected or the passcode is encrypted, the passcode is vulnerable to discovery during transmission.

As already shown, words from a dictionary are easily guessed and should be avoided. A comparison of your password file with a standard dictionary would probably result in the guessing of at least one in four passwords. This is the way most *crackers* and *sneakers* would obtain passwords.

It is amazing how many offices you can walk into and find passwords taped to the side of some device. You can write policies until you are blue in the face and you will not stop this practice. Bank campaigns have stressed to customers the need to avoid writing their personal identification number (PIN) on their card; yet bank investigators will tell you this practice accounts for most automated banking machine "fraud." Because you know that this is human nature, you must periodically look for passcodes.

One last comment on passcodes. Some security practitioners feel passcodes should not be pronounceable. The advantage to this approach is that a dictionary attack would not work. However, an unpronounceable passcode is likely to be written. This author personally does not agree with enforcing unpronounceable passcodes. Passcodes created by a transformation could be pronounceable but extremely difficult to guess.

Keep in mind that passcodes are not entirely effective — either because of user carelessness or the static nature of the codes themselves.

Enough of the theory and rhetoric for now. What does Cisco provide? Basically, the Cisco IOS software implementation of authentication is divided into two main categories:

- AAA authentication methods
- Non-AAA authentication methods

You implement authentication, for the most part, through the AAA security services. Whenever possible, use AAA to implement authentication. So, turn your attention to non-AAA authentication, starting with router passwords.

Using Router Passwords

Passwords (and similar secrets, such as SNMP community strings) are the primary defense against unauthorized access to your router. They stop snooping. Bear in mind that Cisco never designed IOS passwords to defend against a determined attack. The best way to handle most passwords is to maintain them on a TACACS+ or RADIUS authentication server. However, almost every router will still have a locally configured password for privileged access, and may also have other password information in its configuration file.

In the Practice Session in Chapter 5, the IOS prompted you for three passwords as follows:

```
The enable secret is a password used to protect access to
   privileged EXEC and configuration modes. This password,
   after entered, becomes encrypted in the configuration.
Enter enable secret: alpha
```

```
The enable password is used when you do not specify an enable
   secret password, with some older software versions, and
   some boot images.
Enter enable password: bravo
```

```
The virtual terminal password is used to protect access to
   the router over a network interface.
Enter virtual terminal password: charlie
```

The passwords shown in the example are static passwords; that is, they will not change until you change them. This means that if you do not change them for a year, they will remain alpha, bravo, and charlie for the year. Now, these are not particularly the strongest passcodes, so the chances are that someone — through either guessing, sniffing, shoulder-surfing (looking over your shoulder as you enter the code), or a brute-force attack — will figure them out.

In the following sections, you will learn about these passwords and other non-AAA authentication methods. First take a look at the five different password types: enable, enable secret, console, auxiliary, and virtual terminal.

Enable Password

The user EXEC mode is the first you encounter when you connect to a Cisco router. As you know, you can check connectivity and look at statistics and some configuration information. You cannot, however, make any changes to the configuration. To make changes, you need privileged EXEC mode. The enable password associated with privileged EXEC mode (sometimes called the enable mode) works with older versions of IOS that do not support encryption. When using the setup command, you must specify an enable password, although you will not use this password.

Caution: If you make the enable and enable secret passwords the same, then you are putting the enable secret at risk. First, unless you make a conscious effort, the router stores the enable password in cleartext and you can see it using the show running-config command. Second, if you encrypt the password (you will see the command to do this shortly), there are several Internet sites providing free password crackers. You will find Cisco password-cracking programs at:

http://www.boson.com/promo/utilities/getpass/getpass_utility.htm,
http://www.neotech.demon.co.uk/ciscopwd.htm, and
http://www.alcrypto.co.uk/cisco.

If you want to see how it works, you can find C code at:

http://www.alcrypto.co.uk/cisco/c/ciscocrack.c or PERL script at
http://www.alcrypto.co.uk/cisco/perl/ios7decrypt.pl and
http://www.alcrypto.co.uk/cisco/psion/cisco.opl.

You can even find programs that run on the PalmOS at
http://www.alcrypto.co.uk/cisco/pilot/ciscopw_1-0.zip or
http://www.l0pht.com/~kingpin/cisco.zip!

You can enter an enable password with the following command:

```
2501-1(config)#enable password alpha
```

You substitute whatever passcode you want for `alpha`.

If you want, you can specify privilege-level access with enable passwords. Thus, your real authority would depend on what password you enter. The command is:

```
2501-1(config)#enable password bravo [level level]
```

Replace the keyword `level` with a value between 0 and 15. Setting privileges are discussed later in this chapter. This command establishes a password for a privilege command mode.

Caution: Please do not use alpha or any other passcode shown in this book. They are far too easy to guess and are shown for illustrative purposes only.

Enable Secret Password

You can use the `enable secret` command to set the password that grants privileged administrative access to the IOS system. Your organization should always set an enable secret password. You should use enable secret, not the older enable password. The enable password uses a weak encryption algorithm (see the description of the service password-encryption command in the Encrypting Router Passwords section).

If no enable secret is set and a password is configured for the console TTY line, you can use the console password to get privileged access, even from a remote VTY session. This is almost certainly not what you want, and is another reason to ensure you configure an enable secret password. The command is:

```
2501-1(config)#enable secret password charlie
```

You substitute whatever passcode you want for `charlie`.

> **Note:** Cisco passwords are case sensitive, so the password `charlie` is not the same as the password `CHARLIE`. This greatly increases the password space.

If you want, you can specify privilege-level access with enable secret passwords. So your real authority would depend on what password you enter. The command is:

```
2501-1(config)#enable secret level level password delta
```

Replace the keyword `level` with a value between 0 and 15. When using this keyword, give the password to only those administrators who need access at the specified privilege level. You will use the `privilege level` configuration command to specify commands assigned to each level. The `privilege` command is discussed later in this chapter.

With the `enable secret` command, you can also specify encryption type. If you do, you must specify the encrypted password. You can copy the encrypted password from another router.

> **Note:** You cannot recover a lost encrypted password, but you can write it down, put it in a sealed, signed envelope, and give it to someone of authority to hold in trust for that day when you need it. Optionally, you can use the procedure in the Practice Session to recover a lost encrypted password. Should you forget an unencrypted password, just use the `show running-config` command and it will appear in the text.

Using Console and Auxiliary Passwords

Anyone who can log in to a Cisco router can display information that you probably do not want to make available to the general public. A user who can log in to the router can use it as a relay for further network attacks. Anyone who can get privileged access to the router can reconfigure it, with potentially disastrous results. To prevent inappropriate access and action, you need to control interactive logins to the router.

Although the IOS disables most interactive access by default, there are exceptions. The most obvious are interactive sessions from directly connected asynchronous terminals, such as the console terminal, and from integrated modem lines.

It is important to remember that the console port of an IOS device has special privileges. In particular, if a BREAK signal is sent to the console port during the first few seconds after a reboot, someone can easily perform the password recovery procedure to take control of the system. (You will practice the password recovery yourself in the Practice Session.) By interrupting power or inducing a system crash, attackers with access to the console port via a local terminal, modem, terminal server, or some other network device can take control of the system. This is true even when they do not have physical access to it or the ability to log in to it normally.

It follows that any modem or network device that gives access to the Cisco console port must itself be secured to a standard comparable to the security used for privileged access to the router. At a bare minimum, any console modem should be of a type that can require the dial-up user to supply a password for access, and the modem password should be carefully managed. The console and auxiliary passwords restrict user mode access via the console or auxiliary ports on the router. Use the following command sequence to create a password for the console.

```
2501-1(config)#line console 0
2501-1(config-line)#login
2501-1(config-line)#password echo
2501-1(config-line)#exit
2501-1(config)#exit
2501-1#
```

The first line specifies the one and only console device; there is only one console device. The `login` command specifies that users must enter a password each and every time they attempt to connect to the console. You substitute whatever passcode you want for `echo`. Passwords are visible using `sh running-config` because they are unencrypted. The two lines with **exit** are there to show you how to back out of a mode on the router.

Use the following command sequence to create a password for an auxiliary device.

```
2501-1(config)#line aux 0
2501-1(config-line)#login
2501-1(config-line)#password foxtrot
```

The first line specifies the actual device. The `login` command specifies that users must enter a password each and every time they attempt to connect to the console. You substitute whatever passcode you want for `foxtrot`. Passwords are visible using `sh running-config` because they are unencrypted.

Using Virtual Terminal Passwords

You use the virtual terminal or VTY password to restrict user mode access via a Telnet session. Anyone using a virtual terminal to telnet to the router will use the VTY password. You must set the VTY password or your clients cannot log in to the router using Telnet.

Your router supports multiple Telnet sessions at one time. The default is 5 (0-4). You can create more than five VTYs. For example, you can use the command line vty 0 8 and set up 9. You could have different passwords for each device, but this is really not pragmatic because you do not know which virtual terminal the router will assign.

Tip: You could use the feature that lets you use different passwords to support your network administrators. Assign the same password to the first three (8 or whatever number) devices and then assign a different pass to the last VTY. Keep the passcode for emergency use only. This way, if a network administrator needs to get in, but people are using all the available VTYs, she always can log in to the last device with the different passcode.

The commands are:

```
2501-1(config)#line vty 0 4
2501-1(config-line)#password golf
2501-1(config-line)#exit
2501-1(config)#line vty 5
2501-1(config)#config line
2501-1(config-line)#password hotel
```

This command specifies five virtual terminals with the password golf. It also shows an additional device with password hotel. These then are the passcodes you would use to telnet to the router.

Configuring Privilege Levels

Your default IOS configuration has two modes of password security: user mode and enable (or privileged) mode. Not the level of granularity you would want in a robust authentication system — either you have the keys to the farm or you do not! Realizing this shortcoming, Cisco allows you to set up to 16 hierarchical command levels for each mode. By configuring and controlling different passwords, you can allow different sets of administrators with different responsibilities to have different commands.

Perhaps you want to control the use of the configure command but you do not want to restrict the use of the clear line command. Assign level 2 to the latter and level 3 to the former. You would then guard more vigilantly the password associated with level 3 than the password for level 2.

To use this capability, you must first set the privilege and then set the password as shown in the following commands:

```
2501-1(config)#privilege mode level level command
2501-1(config)#enable password level level India
```

The first line sets the privilege level for a command and the second line sets the password for the level. Exhibit 1 shows the acceptable keywords for mode used with the privilege command.

Exhibit 1   Mode Keywords

Keyword	Mode
configuration	Global configuration
controller	Controller configuration
exec	EXEC
hub	Hub configuration
interface	Interface configuration
ipx-router	IPX router configuration
line	Line configuration
map-class	Map class configuration
map-list	Map list configuration
route-map	Route map configuration
router	Router configuration

For example, you could use the following to set the use of the `configure` command to level 14 and establish `juliet` as the password you must enter to use level 14 commands.

```
2501-1(config)#privilege exec level 14 config
2501-1(config)#enable password level 14 juliet
```

As stated, you can specify up to 16 levels (0 to 15). For example, you could set up level 0 to use only the `show  users` and `exit` commands. The system defaults are 15, which is the level of access permitted when using the enable password, and level 1, which is the normal user EXEC mode.

Note: Level 0 has the `disable,   enable,   exit,   help`, and `logout` commands associated with it by default.

When you set a command to a privilege level, it is reasonable that the IOS includes all subsets of the command.

Setting Line Privilege

You also can set a privilege level for a line. You could use this feature along with the special password for the last line previously mentioned to provide tighter security. While a useful feature, administrators can bypass this control by logging in to the line and then enabling a different privilege level. They also could lower the privilege using the `disable` command (not likely). Sensibly, use a high level to protect the console port to restrict usage. The following commands show you how to use this feature:

```
2501-1(config)#line aux 0
2501-1(config-line)#privilege level 7
```

Encrypting Router Passwords

Of the five different password types, the IOS only encrypts the enable secret password by default. For the remaining passwords, you must use the `service password-encryption` command. This command directs the IOS software to encrypt the passwords, CHAP secrets, and similar data that the IOS saves in its configuration file. This is useful for preventing casual observers from reading passwords, for example, when they happen to look at the screen over an administrator's shoulder. Furthermore, unencrypted passwords are at risk to disclosure because anyone with a protocol analyzer can examine the packet.

The following command encrypts the enable, console, auxiliary, virtual terminal, username, authentication key, and BGP neighbor passwords.

```
2501-1(config)#service password-encryption
```

Caution: The router only encrypts passwords entered after the `service password-encryption` command. Be aware that the encryption is really just a simple hash.

The service password-encryption algorithm is a simple Vigenere cipher, so any competent cryptographer could easily reverse it in, at most, a few hours. The algorithm was not designed to protect configuration files against serious analysis by even slightly sophisticated attackers, and should not be used for this purpose. Any Cisco configuration file that contains encrypted passwords should be treated with the same care used for a cleartext list of those same passwords.

Tip: Encrypted passwords are not a silver bullet. The encryption is weak. Use supplemental security measures to protect the router and its passwords. Do not leave configurations lying around. Allow only authorized individuals access to the user and privileged EXEC mode. Protect the console. Control Telnet access to the router. There are several excellent texts on general logical and physical security. Look in the bibliography in Appendix J for starters.

This weak encryption warning does not apply to passwords set with the `enable secret` command, but it does apply to passwords set with `enable password`. The `enable secret` command uses MD5 for password hashing. The algorithm has had considerable public review and is not reversible as far as anybody knows. It is, however, subject to dictionary attacks; a dictionary attack is having a computer try every word in a dictionary or other list of candidate passwords. It is therefore wise to keep your configuration file out of the hands of untrusted people, especially when you are not sure your passwords are robust. More information about password encryption is available on Cisco's Web site at http://www.cisco.com/warp/public/701/64.html.

Getting Around Lost Passwords

What happens if you forget the passwords you just created? Potentially, this is bad news. You cannot get into privileged mode to change your router's configuration. If you did not encrypt them, you can find them if you have a copy of the running-config in a file somewhere (you created just such a file in Chapter 5 to paste in the router) or a hardcopy listing. But if you are paying attention, you followed the advice in this chapter and encrypted all passwords. Do not despair; you can work around the forgotten password. Basically, you just fake out the router and start with an older version of the configuration.

Caution: If you are reading this section, then you must assume that either crackers know this or they are reading this at this very minute. Trust me; this is another reason to use AAA authentication.

In this chapter's Practice Session, you will follow steps to recover from a lost password.

Configuring Line Password Protection

You can provide access control on a terminal line by entering the password and establishing password checking. To do so, use the following commands in line configuration mode:

```
2501-1(config-line)#password kilo
2501-1(config-line)#login
```

You can disable line password verification by disabling password checking. To do so, use the no login command in line configuration mode.

If you configure line password protection and then configure TACACS or Extended TACACS, the TACACS username and password take precedence over line passwords. If you have not yet implemented a security policy, choose to use AAA Security Services. (See Chapter 7.)

Note: The login command only changes username and privilege level but does not execute a shell; therefore, the IOS will not execute autocommands (automatic commands). To execute autocommands in this circumstance, you need to establish a Telnet session back into the router (loop-back). Make sure that you configure the router configured for secure Telnet sessions if you choose to implement autocommands this way.

Setting TACACS Passwords for Privileged EXEC Mode

You can set the TACACS protocol to set whether an administrator can access privileged EXEC mode. Use the following global configuration command:

```
2501-1(config)#enable use-tacacs
```

When you use type **enable** and you have TACACS password protection, the IOS will prompt you for a username and password. The IOS will pass the username/password pair to the TACACS server for authentication.

Caution: Should you decide to use TACACS, you must also specify `tacacs-server authenticate enable` or you cannot access privileged EXEC mode.

Should you use XTACACS, the IOS also passes any existing UNIX user identification code to the TACACS server.

Caution: When you use the `enable use-tacacs` command without Extended TACACS, anyone with a valid username and password can access the privileged EXEC mode. This obviously is a serious security exposure. Why does this happen? Well, the TACACS query resulting from entering the `enable` command is indistinguishable from an attempt to log in without XTACACS.

Note: Throughout the text above, you will see the term "administrator" used when talking about logging in and using privilege. Logically, you could substitute the term "user" or "client." However, administrator was chosen purposely. When performing security reviews, you often find many people with high levels of authority, for example, root, supervisor, or administrator. A smart organization analyzes business needs to determine the correct number of people who need to know the enable password or have physical access to the router itself. There is no magical number. Every organization is different; so do the work and figure out who needs high privilege or the enable password. (I do not know the correct number in your organization, but intuitively I know it is not 50 out of 51 users as I have seen in some organizations.)

Establishing Username Authentication

You can create a username-based authentication system, which is useful in the following situations:

- To provide a TACACS-like username and encrypted password authentication system for networks that cannot support TACACS
- To provide special-case log-ins; for example, access list verification, no password verification, autocommand execution at log-in, and a "no escape" situation

To establish username authentication, use the following commands in global configuration mode as needed for your system configuration:

```
2501-1(config)#username name {nopassword | password password
[encryption-type encrypted-password]}
```

Caution: One more time: passwords appear unencrypted in your configuration unless you enable the `service password-encryption` command.

```
2501-1(config)#! Establish username authentication with
   encrypted passwords. Encryption types are 0 for not
   encrypted or 7 for encrypted with a Cisco-defined
   encryption algorithm
```

Note: The lines starting with a bang or exclamation mark (!) are there to explain the previous line.

```
2501-1(config)#username name password secret
2501-1(config)#! Use for CHAP to specify secret for the
   local/remote device
2501-1(config)#username name [access-class number]
2501-1(config)#! Establish username authentication by access
   list
2501-1(config)#username name [autocommand command]
2501-1(config)#! Specify a command to automatically execute.
   Since commands are any length and contain embedded spaces,
   must use as last option on line
2501-1(config)#username name [callback-dialstring telephone-
   number]
2501-1(config)#! Specify an asynchronous callback number to
   pass to the DCE
```

```
2501-1(config)#username name [callback-rotary rotary-group-
  number]
2501-1(config)#! Specify a rotary group number so that the
  next available line will do asynchronous callback. Its
  number is 1-100
2501-1(config)#username name [callback-line [tty] line-
  number [ending line-number]]
2501-1(config)#! Specify line where you want username to
  callback. TTY is a standard asynchronous line. Numbering
  begins with 0. If you omit keyword tty, then numbers are
  absolute rather than relative
2501-1(config)#username name [nocallback-verify]
2501-1(config)#! Specify authentication not required for
  EXEC callback on the specified line
2501-1(config)#username name [noescape] [nohangup]
2501-1(config)#! Set a "no escape" login environment. The
  keyword noescape prevents users from using escape
  characters on the hosts to which they are connected. The
  nohangup feature does not disconnect after using the
  autocommand
2501-1(config)#username name [privilege level]
2501-1(config)#! Set the privilege level for the user
```

Multiple username commands for a single user are alright. You must create a username/password entry for every authenticating router in every router. That is, configure an entry referring to each communicating router. For CHAP, you must place username statements in each router doing the authentication.

Tip: You can use the username command to define users getting special treatment of one kind or another. For example, you could define an audit account that allows an auditor to execute automatically some show commands. In addition, you could set up an info username without a password that allows individuals on your local subnet to use a general-purpose information service (e.g., username info nopassword noescape autocommand show users).

Enabling CHAP or PAP Authentication

Most Internet service providers (ISPs) support the Point-to-Point Protocol (PPP) for dial-up. RFCs 1661, 1331, and 2153 describe PPP. Traditionally, remote users dial in to an access server to initiate a PPP session. After PPP has been negotiated, remote users are connected to the ISP network and to the Internet. PPP encapsulates network layer information for transmission over point-to-point links.

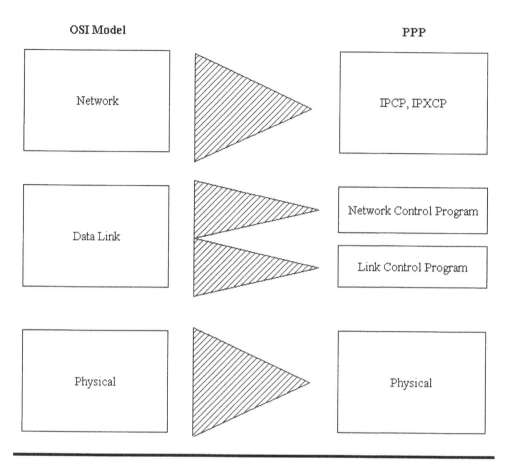

Exhibit 2   OSI and PPP Compared

Because ISPs want only customers to connect to their access servers, the access server usually authenticates remote users before allowing them to start a PPP session. Normally, a remote user authenticates by typing in a username and password when prompted by the access server. Although this is a workable solution, it is difficult to administer and awkward for the remote user.

A better solution is to use the authentication protocols built into PPP. In this case, the remote user dials in to the access server and starts up a minimal subset of PPP with the access server. This does not give the remote user access to the ISP's network — it merely allows the access server to talk to the remote device.

Like TCP/IP, PPP is a layered architecture. Exhibit 2 compares the PPP stack to the OSI model. The Link Control Program establishes, configures, and tests the connection, while the Network Control Program configures the network layer protocols.

PPP supports authentication, compression, error detection, and multilink. The first three are self-explanatory, but the fourth needs one. Multilink allows the aggregation of multiple channels of communication. It is useful when using ISDN. PPP authentication occurs during the link quality determination phase of the Link Control Protocol. Authentication is optional. The calling side of the link must transmit authentication information to ensure that the caller is authorized to establish the connection. PPP currently supports two authentication protocols:

Password Authentication Protocol (PAP) and Challenge Handshake Authentication Protocol (CHAP). Both are specified in RFC 1334 and are supported on synchronous and asynchronous interfaces. Authentication via PAP or CHAP is equivalent to typing in a username and password when prompted by the server. Because the remote user's password is never sent across the connection, CHAP is more secure.

Cisco supports PPP (with or without PAP or CHAP authentication) for dial-out as well. An access server utilizes a dial-out feature when it initiates a call to a remote device and attempts to start up a transport protocol such as PPP.

Note: To use CHAP or PAP, you must run PPP encapsulation.

Password Authentication Protocol

PAP uses a two-way handshake for identification. After link establishment, PAP performs the following steps:

1. The remote router attempting to connect to the access server must send an authentication request. The request consists of a username and password. The remote host will send the information until the local host either accepts or rejects the request.
2. The local host receives the call and either accepts or rejects the username and password specified in the authentication request. If the receiving device accepts the request, the Cisco IOS software sends an authentication acknowledgment. If the local host rejects the information, it terminates the connection.

Challenge Handshake Authentication Protocol

CHAP uses a three-way handshake for identification. After link establishment, CHAP performs the following steps:

1. When you enable CHAP on an interface and a remote device attempts to connect to it, the access server sends a CHAP packet to the remote device.
2. The CHAP packet requests or "challenges" the remote device to respond. The challenge packet consists of an ID, a random number, and the host name of the local router or the name of a username on the remote host.
3. When the remote device receives the challenge packet, it concatenates the ID, the remote device's password, and the random number, and then encrypts all of it using the remote device's password. The remote device sends the results back to the local host, along with the name associated with the password used in the encryption process. This step prevents the password from actually being sent, as the remote device uses it only as an encryption key.

4. When the local host receives the response, it uses the name it received to retrieve a password stored in its user database. Assuming everything is correct, the retrieved password is the same password the remote device used in its encryption process. The local host then encrypts the concatenated information with the newly retrieved password — when the result matches the result sent in the response packet, authentication succeeds.

The benefit of using CHAP authentication is that the remote device's password is never transmitted in cleartext. This prevents other devices from stealing it and gaining illegal access to the ISP's network.

CHAP transactions occur only at the time a link is established. The access server does not request a password during the remainder of the call. (The local device can, however, respond to such requests from other devices during a call.)

Microsoft Challenge Handshake Authentication Protocol (MS-CHAP) is the Microsoft version of CHAP and is an extension to RFC 1994. Like CHAP, you will use MS-CHAP for PPP authentication. However, authentication occurs between a computer with Microsoft Windows 95, 98, Me, NT, or 2000 and a Cisco router or access server acting as a network access server. Among other differences, MS-CHAP provides authenticator-controlled authentication retry and change password mechanisms.

After you have enabled CHAP, MS-CHAP, or PAP, the access server will require authentication from remote devices dialing in to the access server. If the remote device does not support the enabled protocol, the local host will drop the call.

To use CHAP, MS-CHAP, or PAP, you must perform the following tasks:

1. Enable PPP encapsulation. To enable PPP encapsulation, use the following command in interface configuration mode:

    ```
    2501-1(config-if)#encapsulation ppp
    ```

Note: You can monitor PPP activity with the `show interface` and `debug ppp {chap | ms-chap | pap}` commands. The show interface command lets you view PPP LCP and NCP information. The `debug ppp {chap | ms-chap | pap}` command lets you display CHAP or PAP packet exchanges.

---

2. Enable CHAP, MS-CHAP, or PAP on the interface. To enable pap or chap, use the following command in interface configuration mode:

    ```
    2501-1(config-if)#ppp authentication {chap | chap pap |
        pap | pap chap | ms-chap} [if-needed] [callin] [one-
        time]
    ```

    The following section provides information on the command itself.

3. For CHAP and MS-CHAP, configure host name authentication and the secret or password for each remote system where you require authentication:

    ```
    2501-1(config)#username admin1 password lima level 14
    ```

Enabling PAP or CHAP

Should you `configure ppp authentication chap` on an interface, the local host will authenticate all incoming calls on that interface that start a PPP connection with the CHAP. Similarly, should you `configure ppp authentication pap`, the access server will authenticate all incoming calls that start a PPP connection with the PAP.

Should you `configure ppp authentication chap pap`, the access server will attempt to authenticate all incoming calls that start a PPP session with CHAP. Where the remote device does not support CHAP, the access server will try to authenticate the call with PAP. When the remote device does not support either CHAP or PAP, authentication fails and the local host will drop the call.

Should you `configure ppp authentication pap chap`, the access server will attempt to authenticate all incoming calls that start a PPP session with PAP. Where the remote device does not support PAP, the access server will try to authenticate the call with CHAP. When the remote device does not support either protocol, authentication fails and the local host will drop the call.

Should you `configure ppp authentication ms-chap`, the access server will attempt to authenticate all incoming calls that start a PPP session with MS-CHAP.

The `if-needed` keyword is only available when using TACACS or Extended TACACS (see Chapter 11). The `ppp authentication` command with the `if-needed` keyword means that PPP will only authenticate the remote device with CHAP, MS-CHAP, or PAP when they have not yet authenticated during the life of the current call. If the remote device authenticated via a standard log-in procedure and initiated PPP from the EXEC prompt, then PPP will not authenticate via CHAP or MS-CHAP when you `configure ppp authentication chap if-needed` or `ppp authentication ms-chap if-needed` on an interface.

When you configure the `ppp authentication` command with the `callin` keyword, the access server will only authenticate the remote device when the remote device initiated the call.

The `ppp authentication` command with the `one-time` keyword enables support for one-time passwords during authentication.

For information about adding a username entry for each remote system from which the local router or access server requires authentication, see the section "Establishing Username Authentication."

Inbound and Outbound Authentication

PPP supports two-way authentication. Normally, when a remote device dials in to an access server, the access server requests that the remote device prove that it is allowed access. This is known as inbound authentication.

At the same time, the remote device can also request that the access server prove that it is who it says it is. This is known as outbound authentication. An access server also performs outbound authentication when it initiates a call to a remote device.

Enabling Outbound PAP Authentication

To enable outbound PAP authentication, use the following command in interface configuration mode:

```
2501-1(config-if)#ppp pap sent-username <username> password
  <password>
```

The access server uses the username and password specified by the ppp pap sent-username command to authenticate itself whenever it initiates a call to a remote device or when it has to respond to a remote device's request for outbound authentication.

Creating a Common CHAP Password

For remote CHAP authentication only, you can configure your router to create a common CHAP secret password to use in response to challenges from an unknown peer. The ppp chap password command allows you to replace several username and password configuration commands with a single copy of this command on any dialer interface or asynchronous group interface. To enable a router calling a collection of routers to configure a common CHAP secret password, use the following command in interface configuration mode:

```
2501-1(config-if)#ppp chap password mike
```

Refusing CHAP Authentication Requests

To disable CHAP authentication from peers requesting it, use the following command in interface configuration mode:

```
2501-1(config-if)#ppp chap refuse [callin]
```

If you use the callin keyword, the router will refuse to answer CHAP authentication challenges received from the peer, but will still require the peer to answer any CHAP challenges the router sends.

If you enable outbound PAP (using the ppp pap sent-username command), the router will suggest PAP as the authentication method in the refusal packet.

Delaying CHAP Authentication until Peer Authenticates

To specify that the router will not authenticate to a peer requesting CHAP authentication until after the peer has authenticated itself to the router, use the following command in interface configuration mode:

```
2501-1(config-if)#ppp chap wait secret
```

This command (which is the default) specifies that the router will not authenticate to a peer requesting CHAP authentication until the peer has authenticated itself to the router. The no ppp chap wait command specifies that the router will respond immediately to an authentication challenge.

Configuring TACACS and Extended TACACS Password Protection

CHAP, MS-CHAP, and PAP provide some additional security but you can also use TACACS or Extended TACACS to control log-in access to the router. To do this, you need to perform the following tasks:

1. Set TACACS password protection at the user level. You enable TACACS password checking at log-in with the following configuration command:

   ```
   2501-1(config)#login tacacs
   ```

2. Disabling password checking at the user level. By default, IOS denies the request when a TACACS server does not respond to a log-in request. However, you can prevent log-in failure by allowing a user to access privileged EXEC mode:

   a. When that user enters the correct enable password
   b. Whenever without further challenge

   To specify one of these features, use either of the following global configuration commands:

   ```
   2501-1(config)#tacacs-server last-resort password
   2501-1(config)#tacacs-server last-resort succeed
   ```

   The first command disables password checking at the user level, while the latter command allows a user to access privileged EXEC mode.

General Interactive Access

There are more ways of getting interactive connections to routers than users may realize. Cisco IOS software, depending on the configuration and software version, may support connections via Telnet; rlogin; SSH; non-IP-based network protocols like LAT, MOP, X.29, and V.120; and possibly other protocols; as well as via local asynchronous connections and modem dial-ins. Cisco is always adding additional protocols for interactive access. Interactive Telnet access is available not only on the standard Telnet TCP port (port 23), but on a variety of higher-numbered ports as well (e.g., port 80 or http).

All interactive access mechanisms use the IOS TTY abstraction (that is, they all involve sessions on lines of one sort or another). Local asynchronous terminals and dial-up modems use standard lines, known as TTYs. Remote network connections, regardless of the protocol, use virtual TTYs, or VTYs. The best way to protect a system is to make certain that appropriate controls are applied on all lines, including both VTY lines and TTY lines. Above, you saw how to assign passwords and privileges to TTYs and VTYs.

It is certainly difficult for administrators to ensure that they have blocked all possible modes of access. So administrators should make sure that they control log-ins to all lines using some sort of authentication mechanism, even on supposedly inaccessible routers. This is especially important for VTY lines and for lines connected to modems or other remote access devices.

Prevent interactive log-ins completely on any line by configuring it with the `login` and `no password` commands. Fortunately, this is the default configuration for VTYs; but unfortunately, it is not for TTYs. You have already seen various ways to configure passwords and other forms of user authentication for TTY and VTY lines.

Controlling TTYs

Local asynchronous terminals are less common than they once were, but they still exist in some installations. Unless you can physically secure the terminals, and usually even when they are, you should configure the router to require users on local asynchronous terminals to log in before using the system. Most TTY ports in modern routers connect either to external modems or integrated modems; so securing these ports is obviously even more important than securing local terminal ports.

By default, a remote user can establish a connection to a TTY line over the network; this is known as *reverse Telnet*, and allows the remote user to interact with the terminal or modem connected to the TTY line. It is possible to apply password protection for such connections. It is often desirable to allow users to make connections to modem lines so that they can make outgoing calls. However, this feature may allow a remote user to connect to a local asynchronous terminal port, or even to a dial-in modem port, and simulate the router's `login` prompt (through the use of a Trojan horse) to steal passwords, or to do other things that may trick local users or interfere with their work.

To disable the reverse Telnet feature, apply the `transport input none` configuration command to any asynchronous or modem line that you do not want receiving connections from network users. If at all possible, do not use the same modems for both dial-in and dial-out, and do not allow reverse Telnet connections to the lines you use for dial-in.

Caution: One reason not to use the same line in and out is because of a phenomenon called glare. Glare occurs when two users seize both ends of a telephone line or trunk at the same time for different purposes. Perhaps you have experienced this firsthand. Have you ever tried to dial out at the same time someone called you, and you both say "hello"? Well, imagine your system calling back and someone else calls in. Because of glare, your system might think it connected to the person being called back and potentially give the authority to the new caller. It is a low probability, but not an impossibility.

Controlling VTYs and Ensuring VTY Availability

Configure any VTY to accept connections to only supported protocols using the `transport input` command. For example, configure a VTY expecting only

Telnet sessions with `transport input telnet`, and a VTY permitting both Telnet and SSH sessions with `transport input telnet ssh`. When your software supports an encrypted access protocol such as SSH, enable only that protocol, and disable, for example, cleartext Telnet. Furthermore, use the `ip access-class` command to restrict acceptable IP addresses for VTY connections.

In a preceding section, you learned that a Cisco IOS device has a limited number of VTY lines (usually five). When all of the VTYs are in use, your administrators cannot establish another remote interactive connection, thereby creating an opportunity for a denial-of-service attack. Should an attacker open remote sessions to all the VTYs on the system, the legitimate administrator cannot log in. The attacker does not have to log in to accomplish this dastardly deed (so he or she does not need an account or password); the pest can simply leave the sessions at the `login` prompt. Reduce your exposure by configuring a more restrictive `ip access-class` command on the last VTY in the system than on the other VTYs. You already saw how to configure a different password on the last VTY, but you can further restrict it to accept connections only from a single, specific administrative workstation, whereas the other VTYs might accept connections from any address in your network.

Along with restricting it to a specific IP address, configure VTY timeouts using the `exec-timeout` command to prevent an idle session from indefinitely consuming a VTY. Then, when it reaches the timeout limit without any action, it will drop the connection and free it up for an administrator. Although the effectiveness of timeouts is relatively limited against deliberate attacks, it also provides some help for sessions accidentally left idle. Your administrator had to unexpectedly leave, forgot to log out, and left the workstation unattended, thus exposing his authority. Time him out. Similarly, enabling TCP keepalives on incoming connections (with `service tcp-keepalives-in`) can help to guard against both malicious attacks and orphan sessions caused by remote system crashes.

Complete VTY protection by disabling all non-IP-based remote access protocols and using IPSec encryption for all remote interactive connections to the router. IPSec is discussed in Chapter 21, "Configuring IPSec."

Warning Banners and Router Identification

Before setting banner messages, focus first on identifying the router itself. A router's name is referred to as its *host name*. The default host name for all routers is "Router." You can change the host name of a router using the `hostname` global configuration command as follows:

```
2501-1(config)#hostname PDAConsulting
PDAConsulting(config)#
```

You also can add a description to any interface. The IOS limits the description to 80 characters, but this is more than enough to describe the purpose of the link. As a control specialist, you should strive for good documentation. Use the `description` interface configuration command as follows to document your interfaces.

```
PDAConsulting(config)#int s0
PDAConsulting(config-line)#description 56k link between
  Toronto and New York for the wireroom
```

The first command identifies the interface you want to describe, and the second command provides the description of the serial interface labeled as 0.

In some jurisdictions, civil and criminal prosecution of crackers who break into your systems is made much easier if you provide a banner informing unauthorized users that their use is, in fact, unauthorized. In other jurisdictions, you may not monitor the activities of even unauthorized users unless you have taken steps to notify them of your intent to do so. One way of providing this notification is to put it into a banner message configured with the Cisco IOS banner login command.

Note: An urban myth making the rounds several years ago had the accused getting acquitted at trial because the defense argued that the system offered the message "Welcome to XYZ Company" when the accused logged in. The Internet LACC mailing list participants could find no such citation. They did, however, find someone threatening to use this defense, but the accused settled out of court. We will never know. Almost every jurisdiction has some sort of electronic trespassing law, but it is not strictly required that you have a warning banner. But when you have a sign that says "Beware of Dog" and someone comes on your property uninvited and the dog bites them, well *c'est la vie*. Now, some societies are more litigious than others (you know who you are), so you know what free advice is worth — although, it should make it easier to convince a jury of peers that you intended to protect your system when you present a warning saying "Private Property: Keep Out."

Legal notification requirements are complex and vary in each jurisdiction and situation. Even within jurisdictions, legal opinions vary, so your legal counsel needs to step up to the plate and get involved in this issue. In cooperation with counsel, you should consider putting the following information into your banner:

- A notice that you must log in to or use the system only where specifically authorized, and perhaps information about who may authorize use
- A notice that any unauthorized use of the system is unlawful, and subject to civil or criminal penalties
- A notice that you may log or monitor any use of the system without further notice and that you may use the resulting logs as evidence in court
- Specific notices required by specific local laws

From a security, rather than a legal, point of view, your log-in banner should usually not contain any specific information about your router, its name, its model, what version it is running, or who owns it because crackers can use such information to abuse you. Change the router's prompt back to 2501-1 and check out the banner global configuration command:

```
PDAConsulting(config)#hostname 2501-1
2501-1(config)#banner ?
LINE      c banner-text c, where 'c' is a delimiting character
exec      Set EXEC process creation banner
incoming  Set incoming terminal line banner
login     Set login banner
motd      Set Message of the Day banner
```

There are five potential keywords. Use them as follows:

```
2501-1(config)#banner 'Private system. Authorized use only.'
2501-1(config)#banner exec 'Welcome to router 2501-1'
2501-1(config)#banner incoming 'Welcome to router 2501-1'
2501-1(config)#banner motd * Authorized use only, violators
   face prosecution. Your activity on this system is logged
   and potentially monitored. *
```

In the examples above, you see two different message delimiters: ' and *. You can use any special character as a delimiter (ASCII-delimiting character). The delimiter tells the IOS where the message starts and stops. Choose the delimiter wisely because you cannot also use it as part of the message.

Originally, the developers designed motd or Message of the Day to display daily messages; but now, organizations use it to display security information to individuals when they connect. The other messages are not universal and will only display upon an event, such as log-in message displaying when you must log in.

You saw many commands in this chapter; now it is appropriate and timely that you practice some.

Practice Session

In this Practice Session, you will practice the following:

- Logging in
- Saving log data
- Switching modes
- Pasting configuration files
- Recovering from a lost enable secret password
- Renaming the router
- Setting a console password
- Encrypting passwords
- Determining your privilege level
- Creating a new privilege level
- Testing privilege levels

- Creating a local user
- Enabling and saving syslog data
- Logging out

1. Log in to the SimRouter Web page.
2. Double-click on router 2501-1 to telnet to that router. This will open a console session.
3. Enter your **Username** and **Password** at the applicable prompt. These are the ones that you set up in Chapter 2. You will need to hit the Enter key twice to get to the > prompt.
4. Save the log for this session. To do this, select | Terminal | Start Logging | from the menu bar in the Telnet window. The Telnet client will ask you where you wish to store the log and with what name. Your choice. You are going to save the log so that when you build this configuration file, you can cut-and-paste it into the Chapter 7 Practice Session as a starting point, rather than having to enter the same information for each Practice Session.
5. Enter the enable mode:

   `2501-1#`**`enable`**

6. When prompted for the enable secret password, enter **alpha**.
7. Type **terminal length 0**. This command instructs the router to scroll through a long command output without pausing (the —More— message).
8. As you may have gathered from the Practice Session in Chapter 5, the routers do not have a valid configuration when you first log in. You will paste the `running-config` that you saved from the Chapter 5 Practice Session log. At the 2501-1# prompt, type `config t`.
9. If you did not do this, open your log file with any text editor of your choice (e.g., use | Start | Programs | Accessories | Notepad |). Do a find on `sh running-config` and copy from the first "!" to "end." At the `2501-1(config)#` prompt, paste this configuration. You should use this same technique to review and edit your router configuration offline and then use it to update any router, be it the SimRouter or any other network.
10. Turn off your router, wait at least five seconds, and then turn it back on. As the router reboots, press `^Break` (i.e., **Ctrl-Break**). You must break in the first 60 seconds after turning the router back on. This will put you in ROM Monitor mode. (Remember the various modes discussed in Chapter 4, "Understanding Router Basics.") You should see a > prompt.
11. Type **e/s 2000002**, and then press Enter. Write down the virtual configuration number that you see; you will need it later.
12. At the prompt, type **o/r 0x2142** and press Enter. This command makes your router ignore whatever is in NVRAM.
13. At the prompt, type **i**, and then press Enter. This will cause the router to reboot and enter the configuration dialog.
14. At the prompt, type **no** and press Enter.
15. Type **enable** and press Enter to enter the enable mode.
16. Type **copy startup-config running-config** and then press Enter. This will copy your original configuration into the router's RAM.

17. At the privileged prompt, type **config** and then press Enter. You are now in configuration mode.
18. Type **enable secret <new password>** and then press Enter. Select a strong passcode that you can remember. For our purposes, enter **november** as the new password.
19. Now you must set the contents of the register back to its original contents. Type **config t** and then press Enter.
20. At the config prompt, type **config-register 0x** and the virtual configuration number you wrote down; then press Enter.
21. Type **end** and press Enter to get out of configuration mode. Reboot the router. Your router should have a new password and its normal configuration.
22. Double-click on router 2501-1 to telnet to that router. This will open a console session.
23. Enter your **Username** and **Password** at the applicable prompt. These are the ones you set up in Chapter 2. You will need to hit the Enter key twice to get to the > prompt.
24. Save the log for the remainder of this session. To do this, select | Terminal | Start Logging | from the menu bar in the Telnet window. The Telnet client will ask you where you wish to store the log and with what name. Your choice.
25. Enter the enable mode:

    2501-1#**enable**

26. When prompted to put in the enable secret password, enter **november**.
27. Type **terminal length 0**. This command instructs the route to scroll through the long command output without pausing (the —More— message).
28. At the 2501-1# prompt, type **config t**.
29. Type **hostname SimRouter** and press Enter. You should see the new prompt as shown:
    SimRouter(config)#
30. Type **line console 0** and press Enter. Now, type **login** and press Enter. Finally, type **password oscar** and press Enter. You set a password for the console. Because it is unencrypted, let us encrypt it.
31. Type **service password-encryption** and press Enter.
32. Type **sh running-config** and press Enter. You will use this new configuration to start the next Practice Session (Chapter 7).
33. Type **quit** to log out from router 2501-1. Close your Telnet window and return to the SimRouter Topology Map.
34. Repeat Steps 2 through 9 for router 2524-1, substituting **2524-1** for 2501-1.
35. Type **sh privilege** and press Enter. Note your privilege level.
36. Type **config t** and press Enter.
37. Type **privilege exec level 2 show users** and press Enter.
38. Type **privilege exec level 2 exit**, press Enter, and then exit.
39. Type **enable 2**, and press Enter. Type **sh running-config**, press Enter, and note the results. Type **sh users**, press Enter, and note the results.
40. Now create a local user. Type **username peter password papa autocommand sh users** and press Enter.

41. Type **quit** to log out from router 2524-1. Close your Telnet window and return to the SimRouter Topology Map.
42. Click on Log Out on the SimRouter Web page.
43. Study the `running-configs` from SimRouter (2501-1) and 2524-1. Try to find the effects of the Practice Session in the configuration file; for example, look for encrypted passwords or user `peter`.

Security and Audit Checklist

1. Do you have passcode standards?
   - Yes
   - No
2. If you answered Yes to Question 1, does it cover:
   - Syntax?
   - Passcode length?
   - Passcode interval?
   - Passcode change?
   - Ownership?
3. Are all passwords protected?
   - Yes
   - No
4. Do you periodically test password strength?
   - Yes
   - No
5. Do you automatically change weak passwords?
   - Yes
   - No
6. Do you change router passwords when someone who knows it leaves the organization?
   - Yes
   - No
7. Does your organization use:
   - Enable passwords?
   - Enable secret passwords?
   - Console passwords?
   - Auxiliary line passwords?
   - Virtual terminal (VTY) passwords?
8. Do you encrypt all passwords?
   - Yes
   - No
9. If No, do you protect any listings that might have cleartext passwords?
   - Yes
   - No
10. Did you create a different password for the last VTY?
    - Yes
    - No

11. Do you use privilege levels for the following?
    - User mode
    - Enable mode
    - User and enable mode
    - Neither user nor enable mode
12. Do you have a record of the privilege level and the commands associated with the level?
    - Yes
    - No
13. Are the levels appropriate?
    - Yes
    - No
14. Are the passwords to the various levels provided on a need-to-access basis?
    - Yes
    - No
15. Do you use line privilege?
    - Yes
    - No
16. Is the use of line privilege appropriate?
    - Yes
    - No
17. Do you use line passwords?
    - Yes
    - No
18. Are the line passwords given out on a need-to-know basis?
    - Yes
    - No
19. Do you use:
    - TACACS?
    - Extended TACACS?
20. Do you support a local username database?
    - Yes
    - No
21. Is the local username database used:
    - Instead of TACACS?
    - To provide special-case logins?
22. If the local username database is used to provide special-case log-ins, is the use appropriate?
    - Yes
    - No
23. Does your organization support:
    - Leased lines: T1/E1?
                                 T3/E3?
    - Circuit-switched circuits: ISDN?
    - Packet-switched circuits: Asynchronous transfer mode (ATM)?
                                 Frame Relay?
                                 Switched multimegabit data services (SMDS)?
                                 X.25?

24. Does your organization support High-Level Data Link Control (HDLC) for leased lines and ISDN?
    - Yes
    - No
25. Does your organization support PPP?
    - Yes
    - No
26. If you answered Yes to the previous question, do you use?
    - PAP
    - CHAP
    - MS-CHAP
    - TACACS
    - XTACACS
27. Do you support the following for PPP?
    - Asynchronous Serial
    - Synchronous Serial
    - High-Speed Serial Interface (HSSI)
    - Integrated Services Digital Network (ISDN)
28. If you support ISDN, do you support dial-on-demand routing (DDR)?
    - Yes
    - No
29. Do your network management procedures involve monitoring your WAN connections?
    - Yes
    - No
30. Do you control the activity of VTYs?
    - Yes
    - No
31. Do you review the activity of VTYs?
    - Yes
    - No
32. Have you disabled the reverse Telnet feature?
    - Yes
    - No
33. Have you restricted services to specific IP addresses?
    - Yes
    - No
34. Do you use timeout on VTY sessions?
    - Yes
    - No
35. Do you use the keepalives feature for VTYs?
    - Yes
    - No
36. Do you use the following banners?
    - Line
    - Exec
    - Incoming
    - Login

■ Motd

■ None

37. Has someone reviewed the messages to ensure that they are:

■ Legal?

■ Appropriate?

38. Do you inform people that:

■ The system is proprietary?

■ To use only when authorized?

■ Their activity is logged?

■ They might be monitored?

■ You may take the appropriate legal action for infractions or violations?

Conclusion

These are a lot of controls to ponder. Authentication is a primary method for preventing unauthorized access to the network device. There are five types of router passwords: enable secret, enable, console, auxiliary, and virtual terminal. Only the first password listed is encrypted by default, so there is a need to encrypt the others. You saw that you could add privilege to user and privileged EXEC mode. If you support PPP, set up encapsulation; enable CHAP, MS-CHAP, or PAP; and configure username authentication. You saw additional thoughts on controlling interactive access and the banners these users will see.

Protecting who can access your router and make changes is an important topic. This chapter specifically tackles non-AAA authentication techniques. Cisco resolutely advocates the use of AAA security service, which this book covers in Chapters 7 through 10. The controls offered in this chapter cannot compare with the secure use of a protocol such as Kerberos. However, any protection is better than no protection; so get started.

Chapter 7

Implementing AAA Security Services

In this chapter, you will learn about:

- Authentication, authorization, and accounting security services
- Selecting a security server
- TACACS+
- RADIUS
- Kerberos

Chapter 6 began the issue of authentication. This chapter delves further into this topic.

Accessing the Network

When thinking about securing your network, keep in mind the three primary ways someone can gain access to your network:

1. Through public networks, such as the Internet
2. Through virtual private networks (VPNs)
3. Through dial-in

The first two access points are relatively easy to cover and their security is addressed in Chapter 8. However, the requirement to support dial-in users might prove to be the security administrator's biggest challenge. This is especially true if you allow users to dial in directly to their workstations or servers, bypassing all other security methods in place.

Either the plain old telephone system (POTS) or an ISDN connection can provide dial-in access. Because ISDN connections are relatively expensive, there are usually fewer individuals who have an ISDN connection to the desktop. However, the cost of telephone connections is so low that it is reasonable for individuals to have dedicated lines at the desktop.

Within some organizations, there are individuals or groups who insist that they must skirt ordinary security controls because it interferes with their business objectives. They cite the perceived needless expense as compromising the business case of an otherwise profitable venture. They lobby hard to senior management to accept the risk. They often claim that they will put in mitigating manual procedures or that the risk is so low that it is not worth the worry.

Other times, you will find application developers who state that they cannot support the application in a timely manner when they cannot have dial-in. Likewise, administrators cannot guarantee timely support for the network or the system without dial-up. Senior and Executive Management are also the culprits. They want to access e-mail or their systems with limited hassles and delay; and they cannot bother with access tokens or one-time passwords. After all, they say it is only e-mail and not anything sensitive or confidential. This poses a dilemma for the person tasked with maintaining the perimeter and network security. Superficially, the arguments are compelling. It usually involves something quite rational: someone wants dial-up to test an application; another person wants to debug software or hardware; a salesperson wants to demo a product or get the latest production schedule.

These requirements often lead to multiple entry points into the organization. A system administrator gets Windows 2000 Server, implements Routing and Remote Access Services (RRAS), and allows dial-in. Someone else implements dial-up on the new UNIX system. Once the network starts to become open to unfettered remote access, it is very difficult for the security or network administrator to regain control. For one thing, backing out anything in place is next to impossible. God created the Earth in six days only because there was no installed base! Taking away their dial-up is close to impossible once they taste freedom.

Looking at Dial-In Issues

The use of dial-in raises some serious issues in an organization, including:

- *Loss of network management effectiveness*. Individuals can add new nodes, connect to public networks, and offer users an entry point into your network. How can you manage a network when you do not know what it really looks like? Where are all the entry points?
- *Decentralization of security*. Allowing users to directly access other networks or their system decentralizes security. You have now placed the control in their hands. These individuals might have a different view of security and might not set up access at all, or might use an easily guessed passcode. How do you manage this?
- *Cost of additional analog lines*. When you can eliminate phone lines through consolidation, you will see real savings. Not everyone can use a modem all the time and at the same time; so, intuitively, your organization is paying for more lines than it really needs. (If someone is using his or her modem all the time, then perhaps you should look at a dedicated line,

ISDN, cable, or DSL — something a little more cost-effective and efficient than direct demand dial.) How much do all the phone lines cost your organization in hard money?

- *Lack of global authentication.* Windows NT and 2000 Servers have challenge/response, which is different from PCAnywhere authentication, which is different from OS/390 Security Server, etc. You start to rely on the built-in security of the various operating systems and all the vagaries of this. How do you ensure every operating system is up-to-date on all fixes, patches, put tapes, releases, and versions? How do you ensure they are secure?

- *Backdoor circumvention of the firewall system.* You can put very good rules in your firewall devices; but when someone can dial in to some device behind the firewall, then they can bypass your rules and, hence your policy. How do you enforce your policy at the front door when everybody is running in and out the backdoor?

- *Bypass censorship.* Your policy prohibits staff from accessing a neo-Nazi or other pornographic site, but now they can dial direct. Further, a user has the ability to transfer data of a sensitive nature outside the organization — explicitly against your policy. Under normal conditions, the proxy server or some other device would have blocked such transfers. How do you prevent users from accessing sites that might lead to sexual harassment or other litigation?

- *Heightened risk to host systems.* Without the benefits of rigorous and robust security controls, your hosts are at more risk to viruses, Trojan horses, worms, and other malware. How do you scan for malware at the perimeter when you are not sure where the perimeter is?

- *Lack of attention.* Unless the administrator is totally aware of the dial-in connections and has control over them, it is unlikely that he or she will attempt to control the connections, preferring instead to wait for a problem. At this point, the administrator will leap right in and say that they should not have dial-up and should have used the corporate authorized method. That is, they will assist in shooting the wounded. This also might result in the lack of differentiation between the dial-up user and a local user — with potentially disastrous results. Who is responsible for securing the access point? How do you ensure that the individual upholds the responsibility? How do you hold that person accountable?

Developing Your Policy

Thus, there are issues that need resolution. Accordingly, your organization needs to develop a well-defined policy on dial-up and the requisite controls. Base your policy on a formal risk analysis. A good policy will answer the following questions:

1. Who will have authority to use dial-in?
2. What can they access?
3. Where can they access the network?
4. When can they access the network?
5. How can they access the network?

The policy, at a minimum, should cover the following:

1. Authorization required to use dial-up
2. Use of a separate security layer
3. Controlled access path
4. User destination filtering
5. Controls over the use of lines (especially analog lines)
6. Policy on the use of remote node (i.e., access servers)
7. Policy on remote control and desktop modems
8. Session integrity (e.g., how the system deals with drop-off or add-on sessions)
9. Authentication (based on risk analysis)

It is much easier to maintain than to regain control. But having said that, it still is possible to move from a less secure environment to a more secure environment. So, as much as practical, centralize dial-in and implement strong access control. Put your eggs in one basket and watch the basket very carefully. Having users enter your network at a single point simplifies administration.

Authenticating Dial-In Users

The most commonly used protocols for dial-in are the Point-to-Point Protocol (PPP) and Serial Line Internet Protocol (SLIP). Access control is the way one controls who is allowed access to the network server and what services they are allowed to use once they have access. Cisco routers employ user-based authentication and authorization for access to network resources, including access to the router itself. Authentication is the process that verifies the identity of the user. Authorization generally follows immediately after authentication and ensures that a user actually has the permissions necessary to access a resource. Chapter 6 revealed that you could accomplish some of your security goals using the Password Authentication Protocol (PAP) and Challenge Handshake Authentication Protocol (CHAP) for dial-in. Chapter 6 also discussed TACACS and XTACACS for authentication; both allow you to build a database of users and passwords. Imagine the overhead required to implement a policy that requires 500 users to have access and requires them to change their passcode on a monthly basis. These solutions are viable for small environments, but the overhead might become unmanageable in a larger environment. Consequently, separate security services are commonly used (e.g., RADIUS and TACACS+). To authenticate large numbers of users, you need to have a database that stores usernames and passwords. This is where TACACS+ and RADIUS servers come into play. Refer to the section "Selecting Security Servers" later in this chapter when you are in the position where you must make a choice between security servers. These solutions provide the added benefit of including authorization and accounting as well. Authentication, authorization, and accounting (AAA) network security services provide the primary framework for setting up access control on your router or access server.

Defining AAA

AAA is an architectural framework for configuring a set of three independent security functions in a consistent manner. AAA provides a modular way of performing the following services: authentication, authorization, and accounting.

Authentication

Authentication provides the method for identifying users, including log-in and password dialog; challenge and response; messaging support; and, depending on the security protocol selected, encryption. An example is the system authenticates user Peter through the use of a passcode known only to Peter.

Authentication is the way your system identifies a user prior to allowing access to the network and network services. You configure AAA authentication by defining a named list of authentication methods and then applying that list to various interfaces. The method list defines the types of authentication and the sequence for querying; you must apply a method list to a specific interface before the router will perform any of the defined authentication methods.

The only exception is the default method list (which, coincidentally, is named "default"). The router automatically applies the default method list to all interfaces when you do not define another method list. A defined method list overrides the default method list.

There are various options for authentication. For example, TACACS+ and RADIUS allow for multiple forms of authentication, including:

- Digital certificates
- One-time passwords
- Changeable passwords
- Static passwords
- UNIX authentication using the /etc/passwd file
- NT and 2000 challenge and response

You must define all authentication methods, except for local, line password, and enable authentication, using AAA. For information about configuring authentication methods, refer to Chapter 8, "AAA Authentication." For local, line, and enable passwords, refer to Chapter 6.

Authorization

Authorization provides the method for remote access control, including one-time authorization or authorization for each service; per-user account list and profile; user group support; and support of IP, IPX, ARA, and Telnet. For example, Peter works in the payroll department; thus, his manager authorizes him to access payroll data in the fulfillment of his job.

AAA authorization works by assembling a set of attributes describing the user's authorities; for example, programs, databases, rows, columns, and data. The system compares these attributes to the information contained in a database for a given user and AAA receives the result to determine the user's actual capabilities and restrictions. You can maintain a local database on the access server or router, or you can host it remotely on a RADIUS or TACACS+ security server. Remote security servers such as RADIUS and TACACS+ authorize users for specific rights by associating attribute-value (AV) pairs, which define those rights, with the appropriate user.

You use AAA to define all authorization methods. As with authentication, you configure AAA authorization by defining a named list of authorization methods and then applying that list to various interfaces. For information about configuring authorization using AAA, refer to Chapter 9, "AAA Authorization."

Accounting

Accounting provides the method for collecting and sending security server information used for billing, auditing, and reporting, such as user identities, start and stop times, executed commands (such as PPP), number of packets, and number of bytes. When Peter passes authentication and authorization, you can record data about the user and the time and date of the access.

With accounting, you can track the services users access as well as the amount of network resources they consume. When you activate AAA accounting, the network access server reports user activity to the TACACS+ or RADIUS security server (depending on the security method you have implemented) in the form of accounting records. Each accounting record is comprised of accounting AV pairs and is stored on the access control server. The administrator can analyze this data for network management, client billing, or auditing purposes. All accounting methods must be defined through AAA. As with authentication and authorization, you configure AAA accounting by defining a named list of accounting methods and then applying that list to various interfaces. For information about configuring accounting using AAA, refer to Chapter 10, "AAA Accounting."

In many circumstances, AAA uses protocols such as RADIUS, TACACS+, and Kerberos to administer its security functions. If your router or access server is acting as a network access server, AAA is the way you establish communication between your network access server and your RADIUS, TACACS+, or Kerberos security server. For information about TACACS+, RADIUS, and Kerberos refer to Chapters 12 through 14.

Although AAA is the primary (and recommended) method for access control, Cisco IOS software provides additional features for simple access control (refer back to Chapter 6, "Non-AAA Authentication") that are outside the scope of AAA, such as local username authentication, line password authentication, and enable password authentication. However, these features do not provide the same degree of access control possible using AAA.

In some cases, you might implement one, two, or all three AAA functions. For example, your company only wishes to authenticate users when they attempt to access a certain resource, so you only need to configure authentication. But when you want to create an audit trail to record what accessed the resource, you would need to configure authentication and accounting.

Exhibit 1 shows how an Internet service provider (ISP) might implement AAA. A dial-in client wants to browse the site www.pdaconsulting.com. So the client

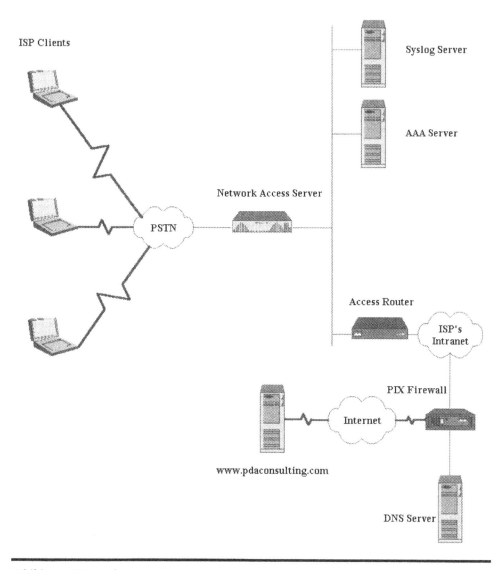

Exhibit 1   ISP Implementation

dials out through the public switched telephone network (PSTN) to connect to the ISP. The client must log on when prompted by the network access server (NAS) or they cannot access the Internet. The NAS queries the AAA server with the credentials provided by the client. The AAA server validates the credentials and returns the response to the NAS, which lets them connect and request www.pdaconsulting.com. Most likely, the ISP is logging all customer connections to the syslog server. This is an example of authentication and accounting.

Benefits of Using AAA

AAA provides a security mechanism to implement an organization's policy and protect assets by permitting only certain authorized entities to access those assets. AAA governs what those entities can do once they are authenticated and can log what actions those entities perform.

AAA provides the following benefits when implemented correctly:

- Increased flexibility and control
- Scalability
- Centralized administration
- Standardized authentication methods, such as TACACS+ and RADIUS
- Multiple backup systems

For example, you have 100 Cisco routers, PIX firewalls, or switches. By default, each and every device will need one password for user mode (where configured on the console or VTY lines) and one password for privileged mode. If you practice safe-hex, then you will need to change those passwords within a reasonable time period (e.g., a month). You would need to communicate these passwords to every administrator. This is an administrative nightmare. So instead, you can use a centralized database for defining user accounts. You could also define the authorities for each user so that you can define users and their privileges.

AAA provides a template that allows dynamic configuration of the type of authentication, authorization, and accounting on a per-entity basis (i.e., user, group, system, or system process). You can create lists that specify the method for authentication and then apply the lists to interfaces or services.

Using a centralized security server for AAA implies a centralized database containing the following information:

- User accounts for PPP, router access, firewall access, etc.
- User authorization information
- User activities

Having a centralized security server allows the network administrator to manage all the user accounts and accounting information from a single database. This makes user account management scalable.

You can specify backup systems in the event that your system cannot reach your primary authentication mechanism or it is down. If the authentication server fails to respond to a request, AAA will automatically redirect the request to the next server in sequence.

Implementing AAA

AAA is designed to enable you to dynamically configure the type of authentication and authorization you want on a per-line (per-user) or per-service (e.g., IP, IPX, or VPN) basis. You define the type of authentication and authorization you want by creating method lists and then applying those method lists to specific services or interfaces.

Note: The older, not recommended protocols, TACACS and Extended TACACS, are not compatible with AAA. Thus, if you select these security protocols, you cannot take advantage of the AAA security services.

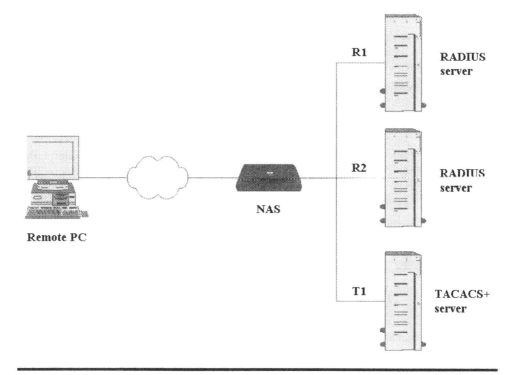

Exhibit 2   Typical AAA Network Configuration

Method Lists

A method list is simply a list defining the authentication methods to be used, in sequence, to authenticate a user. Method lists enable you to designate one or more security protocols to be used for authentication, thus ensuring a backup system for authentication in case the initial method fails. Cisco IOS software uses the first listed method to authenticate users; should that method not respond, the Cisco IOS software selects the next authentication method listed in the method list. This process continues until there is successful communication with a listed authentication method or the authentication method list is exhausted, in which case authentication fails.

Note: Cisco IOS software attempts authentication with the next listed authentication method only when there is no response from the previous method. If authentication fails at any point in this process — meaning that the security server or local username database responds by denying the user access — the authentication process stops and the router will not attempt other authentication methods.

Using AAA

Exhibit 2 shows a typical AAA network configuration that includes three security servers: R1and R2 are RADIUS servers and T1 is a TACACS+ server.

Suppose your network administrator has defined a method list where the router will contact R1 first for authentication information, then R2, T1, and then finally the local username database on the access server itself. When a remote user attempts to dial in to the network, the network access server first queries R1 for authentication information. If R1 authenticates the user, it issues a PASS response to the network access server and the router allows the user to access the network. If R1 returns a FAIL response, the router denies access to the user and terminates the session. When R1 does not respond, then the network access server processes that as an ERROR and queries R2 for authentication information. This pattern would continue through the remaining designated methods until the router either authenticates or rejects the user or terminates the session. If all the authentication methods return ERRORS, which the network access server would process as a failure, the router would terminate the session.

Note: A FAIL response is significantly different from an ERROR. FAIL means that the user has not met the criteria contained in the applicable authentication database for successful authentication. Authentication ends with a FAIL response. ERROR means that there is no response to an authentication query from the security server. Because of this, no device has attempted authentication. Only when the IOS detects an ERROR will AAA select the next authentication method defined in the authentication method list. Again, it terminates on a FAIL.

Setting up AAA

You must first decide what kind of security solution you want to implement. You need to assess the security risks in your particular network and decide on the appropriate means to prevent unauthorized entry and attack. For more information about assessing your security risks and possible security solutions, refer to Chapter 1, "The Need for Security." Cisco recommends the use of AAA, no matter how minor your security needs. (And so does this author.)

Configuring AAA is relatively simple once you understand the basic process involved. To configure security on a Cisco router or access server using AAA, follow this process:

1. Enable AAA using the `aaa new-model` global configuration command. See the section "Enabling AAA" that follows.
2. If you decide to use a separate security server, configure the security server protocol parameters. You need to set up RADIUS, TACACS+, or Kerberos, whichever you choose. See Chapters 12 through 14 for help on setting up your server. For TACACS+, the commands look like this:

```
2501-1(config)#tacacs-server host <ip-address>
2501-1(config)#tacacs-server key <serverkey>
```

The first command tells the router the IP address of the TACACS+ server. The second line tells the router the shared password key with the security server. The password key always appears unencrypted in the configuration file. See the section "Using Security Servers" for help with this step.

3. Define the method lists for authentication using the `aaa authentication` command. You will learn about this subject in its entirety in Chapter 8 and do it yourself in the Practice Session.

4. Apply the method lists to a particular interface or line, where required. See the section "Applying a Method List" that follows.

5. Optionally, configure authorization using the `aaa authorization` command. Refer to Chapter 9, "AAA Authorization," for a complete discussion of this topic.

6. Optionally, configure accounting using the `aaa accounting` command. Refer to Chapter 10, "AAA Accounting," for a complete discussion of this topic.

Enabling AAA

Before you can use any of the services that AAA network security services provide, you need to enable AAA. When you enable AAA, you add a lot more auditing, authentication, and accounting functionality. You can require authentication to run a command at a specific level, enter enable mode, start an outbound Telnet or rlogin session, or any type of network-related service request. Enabling AAA is simple. To enable AAA, use the following command in global configuration mode:

```
2501-1(config)#aaa new-model
```

> **Note:** When you enable AAA, you can no longer access the commands to configure the older disparaged protocols: TACACS or XTACACS. Should you decide to use TACACS or Extended TACACS in your security solution, do not enable AAA.

You can disable AAA functionality with a single command when, for some reason, you decide that AAA cannot meet your security needs but can be met by using TACACS, Extended TACACS, or a line security method that you can implement without AAA. To disable AAA, use the following command in global configuration mode:

```
2501-1(config)#no aaa new-model
```

Using Security Servers

Once you enable AAA, you are ready to configure the other elements relating to your selected security solution. Exhibit 3 describes AAA configuration tasks and where to find more information.

Exhibit 3   AAA Access Control Security Solutions Methods

Task	Book Chapter
Configuring local log-in authentication	Chapter 6, "Non-AAA Authentication"
Controlling log-in using security server authentication	Chapter 6, "Non-AAA Authentication"
Defining method lists for authentication	Chapter 8, "AAA Authentication"
Applying method lists to a particular interface or line	Chapter 7, "AAA Security Service," section: Applying a Method List
Configuring TACACS+ security protocol parameters	Chapter 12, "Configuring TACACS+"
Configuring RADIUS security protocol parameters	Chapter 13, "Configuring RADIUS"
Configuring Kerberos security protocol parameters	Chapter 14, "Configuring Kerberos"
Enabling TACACS+ authorization	Chapter 9, "AAA Authorization"
Enabling RADIUS authorization	Chapter 9, "AAA Authorization"
Enabling accounting	Chapter 10, "AAA Accounting"

Applying a Method List

Once you configure the model and method list statements, you simply apply them to individual interfaces. Take a look at an example in which you have a wide area network connection to your remote office (serial interface 0 or S0) and you have configured AAA as follows.

```
aaa new-model
! You will use AAA
tacacs-server 10.0.1.6
! Tell the system the TACACS+ server has this address
tacacs-server key mysecretkey
! The router and the server will use this key for encryption
   when the router sends the key to the server
aaa authentication ppp remote-users tacacs+ login
! Set ppp authentication to use TACACS+ and local database
   respectively. The list is named remote-users
```

You will now apply this to an interface. In Chapter 6, you saw that you could use the following:

```
interface serial 0
! Connected to the remote office
ppp authentication chap pap
```

This is similar to what you did in Chapter 6, and does not accomplish our goal of using AAA security services. To use TACAS+, you need to tweak the last statement a little. Change it to:

```
ppp authentication chap pap if needed remote-users callin
```

You will learn more about this command in Chapter 8. For now, this statement tells the router to use CHAP for incoming PPP authentication when the router has not previously authenticated the user with TACACS+. If CHAP is not available, use PAP. You have defined the method list for TACACS and then used it with the `ppp authentication` command that you applied to the interface.

There is one other thing you should probably do that you learned in Chapter 6. You define how remote users using PPP will authenticate, but you must configure how you log into the router for administrative purposes. If you rely on the TACACS+ server, you might find yourself locked out when that server is down or there is no communication between the router and the server for some unknown reason. Therefore, you need to configure another method to access the console. You saw how to do this in Chapter 6.

Selecting Security Servers

Cisco supports TACACS+, RADIUS, and Kerberos for authentication. The first two provide the added benefit of supporting authorization and accounting as well. They are also the most widely used. When considering your security server, consider:

- Vendor support
- Open standard support
- Product interoperability
- Application compatibility
- Security features
- Protocol support
- Password database protection

Also consider the following questions for your organization:

- Do you already support a security server?
- Is this only for your Cisco routers?
- Should you have only one dedicated security server? Or more than one?
- For which services should you configure AAA?
- Is one security server easier to configure than another?

Looking at TACACS+

Terminal Access Controller Access Control System Plus (TACACS+) is an enhancement to the TACACS protocol developed by Cisco. The enhancements include the separation of authentication, authorization, and accounting. You can use the services independently or together. For example, you could use Kerberos to provide robust user authentication services and TACACS+ to provide authorization and accounting services. The TACACS+ server:

- Uses TCP port 49 to provide reliable and acknowledged transport
- Can encrypt the entire payload of the packet
- Supports multiple protocols, such as AppleTalk Remote Access, IP, NetWare Asynchronous Services Interface, X.25, and NetBIOS
- Supports AAA
- Can provide greater control over router commands in user and privileged EXEC mode

TACACS Authentication Examples

There is nothing like an example, so the following is an example showing TACACS enabled for PPP authentication:

```
int async 1
ppp authentication chap
ppp use-tacacs
```

The next example shows TACACS enabled for ARAP authentication:

```
line 3
arap use-tacacs
```

You will learn more about TACACS+ in Chapter 12.

Looking at RADIUS

RADIUS is a client/server protocol. The client is typically an NAS, router, or switch that requests a service such as authentication or authorization from the RADIUS server. A RADIUS server is usually a daemon running on a UNIX machine or service running on a Windows NT or 2000 Server. The RADIUS server:

- Uses UDP port so delivery is on a best-effort basis
- Can encrypt only the password sent from the client to the server
- Supports only IP
- Combines authentication and authorization
- Does not provide control over router commands in user and privileged EXEC mode

You will learn more about RADIUS in Chapter 13.

Looking at Kerberos

Kerberos is an authentication mechanism only. You must adapt your host applications, in most instances, to support Kerberos. Project Athena at some Boston-based universities (primarily MIT) developed Kerberos as a secure single sign-on and ticket granting service. Because it only supports authentication, you would either need to not use it or use it in conjunction with RADIUS or TACACS+ when

Exhibit 4   Security Server Protocol Comparison

Protocol	Authentication	Authorization	Accounting
TACACS+	Yes	Yes	Yes
RADIUS	Yes	Yes	Yes
Kerberos	Yes	No	No

you want both authorization and accounting services. You will learn more about Kerberos in Chapter 14.

Exhibit 4 summarizes the three server security protocols and the functions they serve.

Practice Session

In this Practice Session, you will practice the following:

- Logging in
- Saving log data
- Switching modes
- Pasting configuration files
- Enabling AAA security services
- Enabling and saving syslog data
- Logging out

1. Log in to the SimRouter Web page.

Tip: This Practice Session should not take even one hour. So, if you are using SimRouter, wait until Chapter 8 and then schedule your session. Of course, you can always schedule a session and catch up on the material to this point. Practice only enhances your learning experience. And, in addition, it is fun!

---

2. Double-click on router 2501-1 to telnet to that router. This will open a console session.
3. Enter your **Username** and **Password** at the applicable prompt. These are the ones you set up in Chapter 2. You will need to hit the Enter key twice to get to the > prompt.
4. Again, save the log for your session. To do this, select | Terminal | Start Logging | from the menu bar in the Telnet window. The Telnet client will ask you where you wish to store the log and with what name. Your choice. You are going to save the log so when you build this configuration file, you can cut-and-paste this as a starting point in Chapter 8, rather than having to enter the same information for every Practice Session.

5. Enter the enable mode:

   `2501-1#`**`enable`**

6. When prompted to put in the enable secret password, enter **november**.
7. Type **terminal length 0**. This command instructs the router to scroll through long command output without pausing (the —More— message).
8. You will paste the `running-config` that you saved from the Chapter 6 log. At the `2501-1#` prompt, type **config t**.
9. If you did not do this in Chapter 6, open your log file with the text editor of your choice (e.g., use | Start | Programs | Accessories | Notepad |). Do a find on `sh running-config` and copy from the first "!" to "end." At the `2501-1(config)#` prompt, paste this configuration.
10. Type **aaa new-model** and press Enter.
11. Type **aaa authentication ?** and press Enter. Note the various options for the `aaa authentication` command.
12. Type **aaa authorization ?** and press Enter. Note the various options for the `aaa authorization` command.
13. Type **aaa accounting ?** and press Enter. Note the various options for the `aaa accounting` command.
14. Type **tacacs-server ?** and press Enter. Note the various options for the `tacacs-server` command.
15. Type **sh running-config** and press Enter. You will use this new configuration to start the next Practice Session.
16. Type **quit** to log out from router 2501-1. Close the Telnet window and return to the SimRouter Topology Map.
17. Repeat Steps 2 through 9 for router 2524-1, substituting **2524-1** for `2501-1`.
18. Type **aaa new-model** and press Enter.
19. Type **sh running-config** and press Enter. You will use this new configuration to start the next Practice Session.
20. Type **quit** to log out from router 2524-1. Close the Telnet window and return to the SimRouter Topology Map.
21. Click on Log Out on the SimRouter Web page.
22. Study the `running-configs` from SimRouter (2501-1) and 2524-1. Try to find the effects of the Practice Session in the configuration file. For example, look for encrypted passwords or user peter.

Security and Audit Checklist

1. Is there a policy about the use of authentication services in your organization?
   - Yes
   - No
2. Does your organization support AAA security services?
   - Yes
   - No

3. Does your organization support:
   - Authentication?
   - Authorization?
   - Accounting?
   - All of the above?
   - None of the above?
4. Does your organization support:
   - TACACS?
   - XTACACS?
   - TACACS+?
   - RADIUS?
   - Kerberos?

Conclusion

This chapter introduces you to the concept of AAA security services. Cisco recommends that you use AAA instead of TACACS, XTACACS, or local passwords. AAA provides a practical mechanism to implement your security policy. Use TACACS+, RADIUS, or Kerberos to create a centralized database for user accounts and their privileges. This makes user account management flexible and scalable.

Deciding between TACACS+, RADIUS, and Kerberos is a big decision. They receive further coverage in Chapters 12 through 14. Consider your existing security services, vendor support, protocol support, overhead, and cost. Make this decision after thorough analysis because it is key to the success of your authentication scheme for dial-in public and private networks.

In the next chapter, you will configure the authentication methods you want for your organization.

Chapter 8

Implementing AAA Authentication

In this chapter, you will learn about:

- Creating method lists
- Configuring ARA authentication
- Configuring enable authentication
- Configuring log-in authentication
- Configuring NASI authentication
- Configuring PPP authentication
- Specifying the log-in input amount of time
- Enabling password protection
- Configuring message banners

As you saw in Chapter 7, you use the `aaa new-model` command to enable AAA security services. Enabling it is not enough; you must also configure authentication, which is the purpose of this chapter. To recap, you must complete the following steps to use AAA authentication.

1. Enable AAA with the `aaa new-model` command.
2. If using a separate security server, configure RADIUS, TACACS+, or Kerberos.
3. Define the method lists for authentication with the `aaa authentication` command. The default method list applies to all interfaces.
4. Apply the method lists to a particular interface or line, where required.

In Chapter 7 you also learned that:

- The router queries the methods in sequence to authenticate a user.
- You can designate one or more protocols for authentication.

- The software uses the first method listed to authenticate, etc.
- If authentication fails at any point, the process stops.

Creating method lists is key to unlocking the mysteries of AAA authentication. Now, turn your attention to creating method lists.

Using Method Lists

In Chapter 7 you saw that it was fairly easy to use AAA authentication. To configure AAA authentication, first define a named list of authentication methods and then apply that list to various interfaces. The method list defines the types of authentication the router will perform and their sequence. As a rule, you must apply the method list to a specific interface before the router will perform any of the defined authentication methods. The only exception is the default method list (which Cisco, coincidentally, named "default"). The router automatically applies the default method list to all interfaces except those that have a named method list explicitly defined. A defined method list overrides the default method list.

A method list is simply a list describing the authentication methods to query, in sequence, for user authentication. Method lists enable you to designate one or more security protocols for use in authentication, thus ensuring a backup system for authentication in the event the initial method fails or is unavailable. Cisco IOS software uses the first method listed to authenticate users; when that method fails to respond, Cisco IOS software selects the next authentication method listed in the method list. This process continues until there is successful communication with a listed authentication method, or the router exhausts all defined methods.

As stated in Chapter 7, Cisco IOS software attempts authentication with the next listed authentication method only when there is no response from the previous method. If authentication fails at any point in this cycle — meaning that the security server or local username database responds by denying the user access — the authentication process stops and the IOS software attempts no other authentication methods. Thus, the order of authentication methods is important.

Creating a Method List

The syntax for specifying an authentication method list is:

```
aaa authentication service {default | list-name} method1
    [method2] [method3] [method4]
```

For authentication, there are five valid arguments for service, as shown in Exhibit 1: `arap`, `enable`, `login`, `nasi`, and `ppp`. Exhibit 1 provides a brief description of these services.

You can have up to four authentication methods per method list. Method2 through method4 are optional and the router will use them when looking for another authentication mechanism. The access server or router uses the first method and only uses the second when the first does not respond. There are 11 authentication methods in total, as shown in Exhibit 2.

Exhibit 1   AAA Authentication Service Types

Service	Description
arap	Uses AppleTalk Remote Access Protocol list
enable	Uses the enable mode list
login	Uses the character mode connections
nasi	Uses the NetWare Asynchronous Services Interface
ppp	Uses the Point-to-Point Protocol

Exhibit 2   AAA Authentication Methods

Method	Description
auth-guest	Allows a guest log-on only after the user has already logged in to the EXEC mode
enable	Uses the enable password for authentication
guest	Allows a guest log-on
if-needed	Authenticates only when the user has not already been authenticated
krb5	Uses Kerberos v5 for authentication
krb5-telnet	Uses Kerberos v5 for authentication of Telnet sessions; this method, if used, must lead the list
line	Uses the line password for authentication
local	Uses the local database for authentication
none	No authentication takes place
radius	Uses RADIUS for authentication
tacacs+	Uses TACACS+ for authentication

So, you have five services and eleven authentication methods. This provides for several options, but not all authentication methods are available for every service. Exhibit 3 shows a compatibility matrix of the available services (first row) and authentication methods (first column).

You can select any string value except default for list-name you desire. As just stated, AAA reserves the list name of default, which you can use to apply an authentication method to all your router's interfaces for all valid connections without further configuration. This is a fairly useful feature but you might also find that you want to use AAA for VTY authentication and not PPP. So be careful how you apply authentication to interfaces. The following global configuration command demonstrates the use of the default.

```
2501-1(config)#aaa authentication login default tacacs+ local
```

This command sets up log-in authentication for all interfaces using TACACS+ as the primary authentication method and, when TACACS+ does not respond, the local database of the router. If you want to label the method list, you must apply it to an interface. For example, the following creates a method list called admin1.

```
2501-1(config)#aaa authentication login admin1 tacacs+ local
```

Exhibit 3 Authentication Services and Methods Compatibility

Method	*Service*				
	arap	**enable**	**login**	**nasi**	**ppp**
auth-guest	Yes	No	No	No	No
enable	No	Yes	Yes	Yes	No
guest	Yes	No	No	No	No
if-needed	No	No	No	No	Yes
krb5	No	No	Yes	No	Yes
krb5-telnet	No	No	Yes	No	No
line	Yes	Yes	Yes	Yes	No
local	Yes	No	Yes	Yes	Yes
none	Yes	Yes	Yes	Yes	Yes
radius	Yes	Yes	Yes	No	Yes
tacacs+	Yes	Yes	Yes	Yes	Yes

Again, this list authenticates with TACACS+ and, failing a response, the local database. You would then need to apply it to an interface, as follows:

```
2501-1(config)#line vty 0 4
2501-1(config-line)#log-in authentication admin1
```

These commands apply the list admin1 to the VTY lines.

AAA Authentication Methods

The remainder of this chapter shows you how to configure AAA authentication to implement Exhibit 3. You can see that you do have great flexibility in setting up AAA authentication. Again, remember that you cannot use AAA features until you enable AAA globally by issuing the aaa new-model command. For more information on enabling AAA, refer to Chapter 7.

Configuring Log-In Authentication

The AAA security services facilitate a variety of log-in authentication methods. Use the aaa authentication login command to enable AAA authentication no matter what supported log-in authentication methods you decide to use. With the aaa authentication login command, you create one or more lists of authentication methods that the software tries at log-in.

To configure AAA log-in authentication, use the following commands, beginning in global configuration mode.

```
2501-1(config)#aaa new-model
2501-1(config)#! Enable AAA globally
2501-1(config)#aaa authentication login {default |
  list-name} method1 [method2...]
```

```
2501-1(config)#! Create a local authentication list
2501-1(config)#line [aux | console | tty | vty] line-number
    [ending-line-number]
2501-1(config)#! Enter line configuration mode
2501-1(config-line)#login authentication {default |
    list-name}
2501-1(config-line)#! Apply the authentication list
```

The keyword list-name is a character string used to name the list you are creating. The keyword method1 refers to the actual method the authentication algorithm tries first. The router uses the additional methods of authentication (method2 to method4) only when the previous method returns an error, not when it fails. To specify that the authentication should succeed even when all methods return an error, specify **none** as the final method in the command line.

For example, to specify that authentication should succeed even when (in this example) the TACACS+ server returns an error, enter the following:

```
2501-1(config)#aaa authentication login default tacacs+ none
```

Note: Because the none keyword enables any user logging in to successfully authenticate, use it only as a backup method of authentication. And use it with discretion. Most likely, you would not make the default none because this allows anyone in. But you might apply it to a particular interface after performing a threat/risk assessment.

To create a default list that the router uses for log-in authentication, use the default argument followed by the methods you want used in default situations. The IOS software automatically applies the default method list to all interfaces. For example, to specify RADIUS as the default method for user authentication during log-in, enter the following:

```
2501-1(config)#aaa authentication login default radius
```

Refer to Exhibit 3, which lists the supported log-in authentication methods. From the list, you have the following options: enable, Kerberos, line, local, RADIUS, and TACACS+.

Note: The login command only changes username and privilege level but it does not execute a shell. Therefore, the client cannot execute autocommands. Should you want the user to execute autocommands, you need to establish a Telnet session back into the router (loop-back). Make sure that you configure the router for secure Telnet sessions when you choose to implement autocommands this way.

Log-In Authentication Using Enable Password

Use the aaa authentication login command with the enable method keyword when you want to specify the enable password as the log-in authentication method. For example, to specify the enable password as the method of user authentication at log-in when you have not defined any other method list, enter:

```
2501-1(config)#aaa authentication login default enable
```

Before you can use the enable password as the log-in authentication method, you need to define the enable password. Refresh your memory on this topic by looking at Chapter 6, "Implementing Non-AAA Authentication."

Log-In Authentication Using Kerberos

Authentication via Kerberos is different from most other authentication methods: the user never sends the password to the remote access server. Before you can use Kerberos as the log-in authentication method, you need to enable communication with the Kerberos security server. For more information about establishing communication with a Kerberos server, refer to Chapter 14, "Configuring Kerberos."

Use the aaa authentication login command with the krb5 method keyword to specify Kerberos as the log-in authentication method. For example, to specify Kerberos as the method of user authentication at log-in when you have not defined any other method list, enter the following:

```
2501-1(config)#aaa authentication login default krb5
```

Log-In Authentication Using Line Password

Use the aaa authentication login command with the line method keyword to specify the line password as the log-in authentication method. For example, to specify the line password as the method of user authentication at log-in when you have not defined any other method list, enter the following:

```
2501-1(config)#aaa authentication login default line
```

Before you can use a line password as the log-in authentication method, you need to define a line password.

Log-In Authentication Using Local Password

Use the aaa authentication login command with the local method keyword to specify that the Cisco router or access server will use the local username database for authentication. For example, to specify the local username database as the method of user authentication at log-in when you have not defined any other method list, enter the following:

```
2501-1(config)#aaa authentication login default local
```

Log-In Authentication Using RADIUS

Use the `aaa authentication login` command with the `radius` method keyword to specify RADIUS as the log-in authentication method. For example, to specify RADIUS as the method of user authentication at log-in when you have not defined any other method list, enter the following:

```
2501-1(config)#aaa authentication login default radius
```

Before you can use RADIUS as the log-in authentication method, you need to enable communication with the RADIUS security server. For more information about establishing communication with a RADIUS server, refer to Chapter 13, "Configuring RADIUS."

Log-In Authentication Using TACACS+

Use the `aaa authentication login` command with the `tacacs+` method keyword to specify TACACS+ as the log-in authentication method. For example, to specify TACACS+ as the method of user authentication at log-in when you have not defined any other method list, enter the following:

```
2501-1(config)#aaa authentication login default tacacs+
```

Before you can use TACACS+ as the log-in authentication method, you need to enable communication with the TACACS+ security server. For more information about establishing communication with a TACACS+ server, refer to Chapter 12, "Configuring TACACS+."

Configuring PPP Authentication

Many users access network access servers through dial-up using the POTS or ISDN. Dial-up via POTS or ISDN bypasses the CLI completely because the router starts a network protocol, such as PPP or ARA, as soon as it establishes the connection.

The AAA security services facilitate a variety of authentication methods for use on serial interfaces running PPP. Use the `aaa authentication ppp` command to enable AAA authentication no matter what supported PPP authentication methods you decide to use.

To configure AAA authentication methods for serial lines using PPP, use the following commands in global configuration mode:

```
2501-1(config)#aaa new-model
2501-1(config)#! Enable AAA globally
2501-1(config)#aaa authentication ppp {default | list-name}
  method1 [method2...]
```

```
2501-1(config)#! Create a local authentication list
2501-1(config)#interface interface-type interface-number
2501-1(config)#! Enter interface configuration mode
2501-1(config)#ppp authentication {chap | pap | chap pap |
  pap chap} [if-needed] {default | list-name} [callin]
2501-1(config)#! Apply the authentication list
```

The keyword list-name is any character string used to name the list you are creating. The keyword method1 refers to the actual method the authentication algorithm tries. The IOS only uses the additional methods of authentication (method2 through method4) when the previous method returns an error, not when it fails. To specify that the authentication should succeed even when all methods return an error, specify none as the final method in the command line.

With the aaa authentication ppp command, you can create one or more lists of authentication methods that the IOS tries when a user attempts to authenticate using PPP. You apply these lists using the ppp authentication line configuration command.

To create a default list to use when you do not specify a named list in the ppp authentication command, use the default argument followed by the methods you want used in default situations. For example, to specify the local username database as the default method for user authentication, enter the following:

```
2501-1(config)#aaa authentication ppp default local
```

For example, to specify that authentication should succeed even when the TACACS+ server returns an error, enter the following:

```
2501-1(config)#aaa authentication ppp default tacacs+ none
```

Exhibit 3 lists the supported log-in authentication methods. From the list, you can see that you have the following options: Kerberos, local, RADIUS, and TACACS+.

PPP Authentication Using Kerberos

Use the aaa authentication ppp command with the krb5 method keyword to specify Kerberos as the authentication method for use on interfaces running PPP. For example, to specify Kerberos as the method of user authentication when you have not defined any other method list, enter the following:

```
2501-1(config)#aaa authentication ppp default krb5
```

Before you can use Kerberos as the log-in authentication method, you need to enable communication with the Kerberos security server. For more information about establishing communication with a Kerberos server, refer to Chapter 14, "Configuring Kerberos."

Note: Kerberos log-in authentication works only with PPP PAP authentication.

PPP Authentication Using Local Password

Use the aaa authentication ppp command with the local method keyword to specify that the Cisco router or access server will use the local username database for authentication. For example, to specify the local username database as the method of authentication for use on lines running PPP when you have not defined any other method, enter the following:

```
2501-1(config)#aaa authentication ppp default local
```

PPP Authentication Using RADIUS

Use the aaa authentication ppp command with the radius method keyword to specify RADIUS as the authentication method for use on interfaces running PPP. For example, to specify RADIUS as the method of user authentication when you have not defined any other method list, enter the following:

```
2501-1(config)#aaa authentication ppp default radius
```

Before you can use RADIUS as the authentication method, you need to enable communication with the RADIUS security server. For more information about establishing communication with a RADIUS server, refer to Chapter 13, "Configuring RADIUS."

PPP Authentication Using TACACS+

Use the aaa authentication ppp command with the tacacs+ method keyword to specify TACACS+ as the authentication method for use on interfaces running PPP. For example, to specify TACACS+ as the method of user authentication when you have not defined any other method list, enter the following:

```
2501-1(config)#aaa authentication ppp default tacacs+
```

Before you can use TACACS+ as the authentication method, you need to enable communication with the TACACS+ security server. For more information about establishing communication with a TACACS+ server, refer to Chapter 12, "Configuring TACACS+."

Configuring AAA Scalability for PPP Requests

You can configure and monitor the number of background processes allocated by the PPP manager to deal with AAA authentication and authorization requests.

In previous Cisco IOS releases, the IOS only allocated one background process to handle all AAA requests for PPP. This meant that you could not fully exploit parallelism in AAA servers, and it created a bottleneck. The new AAA scalability feature enables you to configure the number of processes you want to handle AAA requests for PPP, thus increasing the number of users that your system can simultaneously authenticate or authorize.

To allocate a specific number of background processes to handle AAA requests for PPP, use the following command in global configuration mode:

```
2501-1(config)#aaa processes number
2501-1(config)#! Allocate a specific number of background
    processes for PPP authentication and authorization
    requests
```

The argument number defines the number of background processes earmarked to process AAA authentication and authorization requests for PPP and you can configure the number from 1 to 2,147,483,647. Because of the way the PPP manager handles requests for PPP, this argument also defines the number of new users that your router can simultaneously authenticate. Of course, you can increase or decrease this argument at any time.

Note: Allocating additional background processes is not without cost and may be expensive. You should configure the minimum number of background processes capable of handling the AAA requests for PPP. There is no set formula for calculating this value, other than trial and error.

Enabling Double Authentication

Double authentication provides additional authentication for Point-to-Point Protocol (PPP) sessions. Previously, you could only authenticate PPP sessions using a single authentication method: either PAP or CHAP. Double authentication requires remote users to pass a second stage of authentication — after CHAP or PAP authentication — before gaining network access.

This second (or double) authentication requires a password known to the user but not stored on the user's remote host. Therefore, the second authentication is specific to a user, not to a host. This provides an additional level of security that will be effective even when someone steals information from the remote host. In addition, this provides greater flexibility by allowing customized network privileges for each and every user.

The second-stage authentication can use one-time passwords such as token card passwords, which are not supported by CHAP. If you use one-time passwords, a stolen user password is of little use to the perpetrator.

Understanding Double Authentication

With double authentication there are two authentication/authorization stages. These two stages occur after a remote user dials in and initiates a PPP session.

In the first stage, the user logs in using the remote host name. CHAP (or PAP) authenticates the remote host and then PPP negotiates with AAA to authorize the remote host. In this process, the router assigns the network access privileges associated with the remote host to the user.

Tip: The network administrator should restrict authorization at this first stage to allow only Telnet connections to the local host.

In the second stage, the remote user must telnet to the network access server for authentication. When the remote user logs in, AAA log-in authentication must authenticate the user. The user must then enter the `access-profile` command for AAA reauthorization. When this authorization is complete, the router has double authenticated the user and the user can access the network according to per-user network privileges.

The system administrator determines what network privileges remote users will have after each stage of authentication by configuring appropriate parameters on a security server. To use double authentication, the user must activate it by issuing the `access-profile` command.

Caution: Double authentication can cause certain undesirable events if multiple hosts share a PPP connection to a network access server.

Configuring Double Authentication

To configure double authentication, you must complete the following steps:

1. Enable AAA using the `aaa-new model` global configuration command. For more information on enabling AAA, refer to Chapter 7, "Implementing AAA Security Services."
2. Use the `aaa authentication` command to configure your network access server to use log-in and PPP authentication method lists; then apply those method lists to the appropriate lines or interfaces.
3. Use the `aaa authorization` command to configure AAA network authorization at log-in. For more information on configuring network authorization, refer to Chapter 9, "Implementing AAA Authorization."
4. Configure security protocol parameters (e.g., RADIUS or TACACS+). For more information on TACACS+ and RADIUS, refer to Chapters 12 and 13, respectively.

5. Use access control list AV pairs on the security server that the user can connect to the local host only by establishing a Telnet connection.

6. Optionally, configure the `access-profile` command as an autocommand. If you configure the autocommand, remote users will not have to manually enter the `access-profile` command to access authorized rights associated with their personal user profile.

Note: If the `access-profile` command is configured as an autocommand, users will still need to telnet to the local host and log in to complete double authentication.

Access User Profile after Double Authentication

In double authentication, when a remote user establishes a PPP link to the local host using the local host name, the router authenticates the remote host with CHAP (or PAP). After CHAP (or PAP) authentication, PPP negotiates with AAA to assign network access privileges associated with the remote host to the user. Restrict privileges at this point to allow the user to connect to the local host only by establishing a Telnet connection.

When the user needs to initiate the second phase of double authentication — establishing a Telnet connection to the local host — the user enters a personal username and password (different from the CHAP or PAP username and password). AAA performs re-authentication according to the personal username/password. The initial rights associated with the local host, however, are still in place. By using the `access-profile` command, the rights associated with the local host are replaced by or merged with those defined for the user in the user's profile.

Use the following command in EXEC configuration mode:

```
2501-1(config)#access profile [merge | replace | ignore-
    sanity-checks]
```

If you configured the `access-profile` command to be executed as an autocommand, it will be executed automatically after the remote user logs in.

Enabling Automated Double Authentication

You can make the double authentication process easier for users by implementing automated double authentication. Automated double authentication provides all of the security benefits of double authentication but offers a simpler, user-friendlier interface for remote users. With double authentication, a second level of user authentication is achieved when the user telnets to the network access server or router and enters a username and password. With automated double authentication, the user does not have to telnet to the network access server; instead, the user responds to a dialog box request for a username and password or personal identification number (PIN). To use the automated double authentication feature, the remote user hosts must run a companion client application. This presently is the kicker because there is currently only one such program.

> **Note:** Automated double authentication, like the existing double authentication feature, works with Multilink PPP ISDN connections only. You cannot use automated double authentication with other protocols such as X.25 or SLIP.

To configure automated double authentication, use the following commands starting in global configuration mode:

```
2501-1(config)#ip trigger-authentication [timeout seconds]
  [port number]
2501-1(config)#interface bri number
```

or

```
2501-1(config)#interface serial number:23
2501-1(config)#ip trigger-authentication
```

Troubleshooting Double Authentication

To troubleshoot automated double authentication, use the following privileged commands:

```
2501-1#show ip trigger-authentication
2501-1#! Views the list of remote hosts where automated
  double authentication has been attempted
2501-1#clear ip trigger-authentication
2501-1#! Clear the list of remote trigger-authentication
  hosts where automated double authentication has been
  attempted
2501-1#! This clears the table displayed by the show ip
  trigger-authentication command
2501-1#debug ip trigger-authentication
2501-1#! View debug output related to trigger-authentication
  automated double authentication.
```

Configuring ARA Authentication

With the `aaa authentication arap` command, you create one or more lists of authentication methods that the IOS tries when AppleTalk Remote Access (ARA) users attempt to log in to the router. You use these lists with the `arap authentication` line configuration command.

> **Note:** ARA authentication is shown here for completeness. The emphasis, however, of this book has been and is on IP.

Use at least the first of the following commands starting in global configuration mode:

```
2501-1(config)#aaa new-model
2501-1(config)#! Enable AAA globally
2501-1(config)#aaa authentication arap {default | list-name}
    method1 [method2...]
2501-1(config)#! Enable authentication for ARA users
2501-1(config)#line number
2501-1(config)#! Change to line configuration mode
2501-1(config-line)#autoselect arap
2501-1(config-line)#! Enable autoselection of ARA
2501-1(config-line)#autoselect during-login
2501-1(config-line)#! Start the ARA session automatically at
    login
2501-1(config-line)#arap authentication list-name
2501-1(config-line)#! Enable TACACS+ authentication for ARA
```

The list-name is any character string used to name the list you are creating. The method refers to the actual list of methods the authentication algorithm tries, in the sequence entered. The IOS only uses the additional methods of authentication (method2 through method4) when the previous method returns an error, not when it fails. To specify that the authentication should succeed even when all methods return an error, specify none as the final method in the command line.

To create a default list to use when you do not specify a named list in the arap authentication command, use the default argument followed by the methods you want used in default situations. For example, to create a default AAA authentication method list used with the ARA protocol, enter the following:

```
2501-1(config)#aaa authentication arap default if-needed
    none
```

To create the same authentication method list for the ARA protocol but name the list MIS-access, enter the following:

```
2501-1(config)#aaa authentication arap MIS-access if-needed
    none
```

Exhibit 3 lists the supported log-in authentication methods. From the list, you can see that you have the following options: auth-guest, guest, line, local, and TACACS+.

ARA Authentication Allowing Authorized Guest Log-Ins

Use the aaa authentication arap command with the auth-guest method keyword to allow guest log-ins only when the user has already successfully logged in to the EXEC. You must list this method first in the ARA authentication method list but you can follow it with other methods where it does not succeed.

For example, to allow all authorized guest log-ins — meaning log-ins by users who have already successfully logged in to the EXEC — as the default method of authentication, using RADIUS only when that method fails, enter the following:

```
2501-1(config)#aaa authentication arap default auth-guest
   radius
```

> **Note:** By default, IOS disables guest log-ins through ARAP when you initialize AAA. To allow guest log-ins, you must use the aaa authentication arap command with either the guest or auth-guest keyword.

ARA Authentication Allowing Guest Log-Ins

Use the aaa authentication arap command with the guest method keyword to allow guest log-ins. You must list this method first in the ARA authentication method list but you can follow it with other methods where it does not succeed.

For example, to allow all guest log-ins as the default method of authentication, using RADIUS only when that method fails, enter the following:

```
2501-1(config)#aaa authentication arap default guest radius
```

> **Note:** By default, IOS disables guest log-ins through ARAP when you initialize AAA. To allow guest log-ins, you must use the aaa authentication arap command with either the guest or auth-guest keyword.

ARA Authentication Using Line Password

Use the aaa authentication arap command with the line method keyword to specify the line password as the authentication method. For example, to specify the line password as the method of ARA user authentication when you have not defined any other method list, enter the following:

```
2501-1(config)#aaa authentication arap default line
```

Before you can use a line password as the ARA authentication method, you need to define a line password.

ARA Authentication Using Local Password

Use the aaa authentication arap command with the local method keyword to specify that the Cisco router or access server will use the local username database for authentication. For example, to specify the local username database as the method of ARA user authentication when you have not defined any other method list, enter the following:

```
2501-1(config)#aaa authentication arap default local
```

For information about adding users to the local username database, see Chapter 6, "Implementing Non-AAA Authentication."

ARA Authentication Using TACACS+

Use the aaa authentication arap command with the tacacs+ method keyword to specify TACACS+ as the ARA authentication method. For example, to specify TACACS+ as the method of ARA user authentication when you have not defined any other method list, enter the following:

```
2501-1(config)#aaa authentication arap default tacacs+
```

Before you can use TACACS+ as the ARA authentication method, you need to enable communication with the TACACS+ security server. For more information about establishing communication with a TACACS+ server, refer to Chapter 12, "Configuring TACACS+."

Configuring NASI Authentication

With the aaa authentication nasi command, you can create one or more lists of authentication methods that the router or network access server tries when NetWare Asynchronous Services Interface (NASI) users attempt to log in to the router. You use these lists with the nasi authentication line configuration command.

Note: NASI authentication is shown here for completeness. The emphasis, however, of this book has been and is on IP.

Use at least the first of the following commands starting in global configuration mode:

```
2501-1(config)#aaa new-model
2501-1(config)#! Enable AAA globally
2501-1(config)#aaa authentication nasi {default | list-name}
  method1 [method2...]
2501-1(config)#! Enable authentication for NASI users
2501-1(config)#line number
2501-1(config-line)#! Change to line configuration mode
2501-1(config-line)#nasi authentication list-name
2501-1(config-line)#! Enable authentication for NASI
```

The list-name is any character string used to name the list you are creating. The method refers to the actual list of methods the authentication algorithm tries, in the sequence entered.

The IOS uses the additional authentication methods only when the previous method returns an error, not when it fails. To specify that the authentication should succeed even when all methods return an error, specify none as the final method in the command line.

To create a default list that is used when a named list is not specified in the aaa authentication nasi command, use the default argument followed by the methods you want to be used in default situations. For example, you might use:

```
2501-1(config)#aaa authentication nasi default enable
```

Exhibit 3 lists the supported log-in authentication methods. From the list, you can see you have the following options: enable, line, local, and TACACS+.

NASI Authentication Using Enable Password

Use the aaa authentication nasi command with the enable argument to specify the enable password as the authentication method. For example, to specify the enable password as the method of NASI user authentication when you have not defined any other method list, enter the following:

```
2501-1(config)#aaa authentication nasi default enable
```

Before you can use the enable password as the authentication method, you need to define the enable password.

NASI Authentication Using Line Password

Use the aaa authentication nasi command with the line method keyword to specify the line password as the authentication method. For example, to specify the line password as the method of NASI user authentication when you have not defined another method list, enter the following:

```
2501-1(config)#aaa authentication nasi default line
```

Before you can use a line password as the NASI authentication method, you need to define a line password.

NASI Authentication Using Local Password

Use the aaa authentication nasi command with the local method keyword to specify that the Cisco router or access server will use the local username database for authentication information. For example, to specify the local username database as the method of NASI user authentication when you have not defined another method list, enter the following:

```
2501-1(config)#aaa authentication nasi default local
```

NASI Authentication Using TACACS+

Use the aaa authentication nasi command with the tacacs+ method keyword to specify TACACS+ as the NASI authentication method. For example, to specify TACACS+ as the method of NASI user authentication when you have not defined any other method list, enter the following:

```
2501-1(config)#aaa authentication nasi default tacacs+
```

Before you can use TACACS+ as the authentication method, you need to enable communication with the TACACS+ security server. For more information about establishing communication with a TACACS+ server, refer to Chapter 12, "Configuring TACACS+."

Specifying the Amount of Time for Log-In Input

The timeout login response command allows you to specify how long the system will wait for log-in input (such as username and password) before timing out. The default log-in value is 30 seconds; with the timeout login response command, you can specify a timeout value from 1 to 300 seconds.

Use the following command in interface configuration mode to change the log-in timeout value from the default of 30 seconds for an interface:

```
2501-1(config-if)#timeout login response seconds
```

To change for a line, use the following command:

```
2501-1(config-line)#timeout login response seconds
```

Enabling Password Protection at the Privileged Level

Use the aaa authentication enable default command to create a series of authentication methods that the router uses to determine whether a user can access the privileged EXEC command level. You can specify up to four authentication methods. The IOS uses the additional authentication methods only when the previous method returns an error, not when it fails. To specify that the authentication should succeed even when all methods return an error, specify none as the final method in the command line.

Use the following command in global configuration mode:

```
2501-1(config)#aaa authentication enable default method1
    [method2...]
```

The method refers to the actual list of methods the authentication algorithm tries, in the sequence entered. Exhibit 3 lists the supported log-in authentication methods.

Changing the Text Displayed at the Password Prompt

Use the aaa authentication password-prompt command to change the default text that the Cisco IOS software displays when prompting a user to enter a password. This command changes the password prompt for the enable password as well as for log-in passwords that remote security servers do not supply. The no form of this command returns the password prompt to the following default value:

```
Password:
```

The aaa authentication password-prompt command works when using RADIUS as the log-in method. You can see the password prompt defined in the command shown even when the RADIUS server is unreachable.

The aaa authentication password-prompt command does not change any dialog supplied by a remote TACACS+ server. The aaa authentication password-prompt command does not work with TACACS+. TACACS+ supplies the NAS the password prompt to display to the users. When the TACACS+ server is reachable, the NAS gets the password prompt from the server and uses that prompt instead of the one defined in the aaa authentication password-prompt command. When the TACACS+ server is not reachable, the router will use the password prompt defined in the aaa authentication password-prompt command.

Use the following command in global configuration mode:

```
2501-1(config)#aaa authentication password-prompt text-
    string
```

Configuring Message Banners for AAA Authentication

AAA supports the use of configurable, personalized log-in and failed log-in banners. You can configure message banners that the router will display when a user logs in to the system to be authenticated using AAA and when authentication, for whatever reason, fails.

Configuring a Log-In Banner

To create a log-in banner, you need to configure a delimiting character that notifies the system that the following text string is to be displayed as the banner, and then the text string itself. You repeat the delimiting character at the end of the text string to signify the end of the banner. Use any single character in the extended ASCII character set as the delimiting character; but once defined as the delimiter, you cannot use that character in the text string making up the banner.

To configure a banner that the router will display whenever a user logs in (replacing the default message for log-in), use the following commands in global configuration mode:

```
2501-1(config)#aaa new-model
2501-1(config)#aaa authentication banner delimiter string
    delimiter
```

The maximum number of characters that you can display in the log-in banner is 2996.

Configuring a Failed Log-In Banner

To create a failed log-in banner, you need to configure a delimiting character that notifies the system that the following text string is to be displayed as the banner, and then the text string itself. You repeat the delimiting character at the end of the text string to signify the end of the banner. Use any single character in the extended ASCII character set as the delimiting character; but once defined as the delimiter, you cannot use that character in the text string making up the banner.

To configure a message that the router will display whenever a user fails log-in (replacing the default message for failed log-in), use the following commands in global configuration mode:

```
2501-1(config)#aaa new-model
2501-1(config)#aaa authentication fail-message delimiter
    string delimiter
```

The maximum number of characters that you can display in the failed log-in banner is 2996.

Log-In and Failed Log-In Banner Configuration Examples

The following example configures a log-in banner (in this case, the phrase "Authorized Access Only") to display when a user logs in to the system. An asterisk (*) is the delimiting character. RADIUS is specified as the default log-in authentication method.

```
aaa new-model
aaa authentication banner *Authorized Access Only*
aaa authentication login default radius
```

This configuration produces the following log-in banner:

```
Authorized Access Only
Username:
```

The following example additionally configures a failed log-in banner (in this case, the phrase "Failed login. Please try again.") to display when a user tries to log in to the system and fails. An asterisk (*) is the delimiting character. Again, RADIUS is specified as the default log-in authentication method.

```
aaa new-model
aaa authentication banner *Authorized Access Only*
aaa authentication fail-message *Failed login. Please try
   again.*
aaa authentication login default radius
```

This configuration produces the following log-in and failed log-in banner:

```
Authorized Access Only
Username:
Password:
Failed login. Please try again.
```

At this point you should have a good grounding in AAA authentication. It is now time to practice some of the commands from the chapter.

Practice Session

In this Practice Session, you will practice the following:

- Logging in
- Saving log data
- Switching modes
- Pasting configuration files
- Enabling AAA security services
- Enabling and saving syslog data
- Logging out

1. Log in to the SimRouter Web page.
2. Double-click on router 2501-1 to telnet to that router. This will open a console session.
3. Enter your Username and Password at the applicable prompt. These are the ones you set up in Chapter 2. You will need to hit the Enter key twice to get to the > prompt.
4. Again, save the log for your session. To do this, select | Terminal | Start Logging | from the menu bar in the Telnet window. The Telnet client will ask you where you wish to store the log and with what name. Your choice.

You are going to save the log so that when you build the configuration file in this session, you can cut-and-paste it as a starting point in Chapter 9, rather than having to enter the same information each session.

5. Enter the enable mode:

   `2501-1#`**`enable`**

6. When prompted to put in the enable secret password, enter **november**.
7. Type **`terminal length 0`**. This command instructs the route to scroll through long command output without pausing (the —More— message).
8. You will paste the `running-config` that you saved from the Chapter 7 log. At the `2501-1#` prompt, type **`config t.`**
9. If you did not do it in Chapter 7, open your log file with the text editor of your choice (e.g., use | Start | Programs | Accessories | Notepad |). Do a find on `sh running-config` and copy from the first "!" to "end." At the `2501-1(config)#` prompt, paste this configuration.
10. Type **`aaa new-model`** and press Enter.
11. Type **`aaa authentication login radius-login RADIUS local`** and press Enter. This command configures the router to use RADIUS for authentication at the log-in prompt. If RADIUS returns an error, the user is authenticated using the local database.
12. Type **`aaa authentication ppp radius-ppp if-needed radius`** and press Enter. This command configures the Cisco IOS software to use PPP authentication using CHAP or PAP if the user has not already logged in. If the EXEC facility has authenticated the user, PPP authentication is not performed.
13. Type **`line 3`** and press Enter.
14. Type **`log-in authentication radius-login`** and press Enter. This command enables the use-radius method list for line 3.
15. Type **`interface serial 0`** and press Enter.
16. Type **`ppp authentication radius-ppp`** and press Enter. This command enables the user-radius method list for serial interface 0.
17. Type **`sh running-config`** and press Enter. You will use this new configuration to start the next Practice Session.
18. Type **`quit`** to log out from router 2501-1. Close the Telnet window and return to the SimRouter Topology Map.
19. Repeat Steps 2 through 9 for router 2524-1, substituting **2524-1** for 2501-1.
20. Type **`aaa new-model`** and press Enter.
21. Type **`aaa authentication ppp test tacacs+ local`** and press Enter. This `aaa authentication` command defines a method list, "test," to be used on serial interfaces running PPP. The keyword `tacacs+` means that authentication will be done through TACACS+. If TACACS+ returns an ERROR of some sort during authentication, the keyword `local` indicates that authentication will be attempted using the local database on the network access server.
22. Type **`interface serial 0`** and press Enter.
23. Type **`ppp authentication chap pap test`** and press Enter. This `ppp authentication` command applies the test method list to this line.

24. Type **tacacs-server host 10.1.2.3** and press Enter. This tacacs-server host command identifies the TACACS+ daemon as having an IP address of 10.1.2.3.

25. Type **tacacs-server key secret** and press Enter. This tacacs-server key command defines the shared encryption key to be "secret."

26. Type **aaa authentication ppp default if-needed tacacs+ local** and press Enter. The keyword default applies PPP authentication to all interfaces. The if-needed keyword means that when the user has already authenticated by going through the ASCII log-in procedure, then PPP is not necessary and is skipped. If authentication is needed, the keyword tacacs+ means that authentication will be done through TACACS+. If TACACS+ returns an ERROR of some sort during authentication, the keyword local indicates that authentication will be attempted using the local database on the network access server.

27. Type **sh running-config** and press Enter. You will use this new configuration to start the next Practice Session.

28. Type **quit** to log out from router 2524-1. Close the Telnet window and return to the SimRouter Topology Map.

29. Click on Log Out on the SimRouter Web page.

30. Study the running-configs from SimRouter (2501-1) and 2524-1. Try to find the effects of the Practice Session in the configuration file. For example, look for encrypted passwords or user peter.

Security and Audit Checklist

1. Do you use AAA authentication in your organization?
   - Yes
   - No

2. Do you have a default method for:
   - ARAP?
   - Enable?
   - Login?
   - NASI?
   - PPP?

3. Are the default methods reasonable?
   - Yes
   - No

4. Which of the following enable authentication methods do you use?
   - Enable
   - Line
   - RADIUS
   - TACACS+
   - None

5. Which of the following log-in authentication methods do you use?
   - Enable
   - Krb5
   - Krb5-Telnet

- Line
- Local
- RADIUS
- TACACS+
- None

6. Which of the following PPP authentication methods do you use?
   - If-needed
   - Krb5
   - Local
   - RADIUS
   - TACACS+
   - None

7. Which of the following ARAP authentication methods do you use?
   - Auth-guest
   - Guest
   - Line
   - Local
   - RADIUS
   - TACACS+

8. Which of the following NASI authentication methods do you use?
   - Enable
   - Line
   - Local
   - TACACS+
   - None

9. Are all the authentication methods appropriate?
   - Yes
   - No

10. Which of the following authentication enable default methods do you use?
    - Enable
    - Line
    - RADIUS
    - TACACS+
    - None

11. Does you organization configure the number of processes allocated to PPP?
    - Yes
    - No

12. Do you use:
    - Log-in banner?
    - Failed log-in banner?

13. Did legal counsel review the legality of any banners?
    - Yes
    - No

14. Do you use double authentication?
    - Yes
    - No

15. Do you use automated double authentication?
    - Yes
    - No

Conclusion

There is lots to reflect on. You started with the syntax for the aaa authentication command. You learned that there are five services you can configure authentication: arap, enable, login, nasi, and ppp. In addition, there are eleven authentication methods. The remainder of the chapter focused on providing examples of the various service/method combinations. Finally, you learned how to configure banners for log-in and failed log-in.

Chapter 9 continues with AAA security services by configuring `aaa authorization` commands.

Chapter 9

Implementing AAA Authorization

In this chapter, you will learn about:

- Configuring authorization
- AAA authorization types
- AAA authorization methods
- Disabling authorization for global configuration commands
- Authorization for reverse Telnet
- Authorization attribute-value (AV) pairs

AAA authorization enables you to limit the services available to a user. When you enable AAA authorization, the network access server uses information retrieved from the user's profile, which is located either in the local user database or on the security server, to configure the user's session. Once this is done, the router will grant the user access to a requested service only when the information in the user profile allows it.

The second part of AAA security services is authorization. Authorization is the act of granting permission to a user, group of users, system, or system process. For example, when users log in to a server, the administrator will preauthorize them to use certain services such as file access or printing. On a router or network access server, authorization may include the capability to access the network when logging in using PPP or the capability to use a certain protocol such as FTP.

Note: Authorization method lists for SLIP follow whatever is configured for PPP on the relevant interface. If you do not define lists and apply them to a particular interface (or no PPP settings are configured), the default setting for authorization applies.

You can use a Cisco router to restrict user access to the network so that the user can only perform certain functions after successful authentication. As with authentication, you can use a local database or a security server to define the capability of a user once authenticated.

Caution: Authenticated users who log in to the console line bypass authorization, even when you configure authorization.

The capability to enter privileged EXEC mode is an example of authorization enabled by default. Once you enter **enable** at the EXEC prompt, the IOS prompts you for the enable router (assuming there is one). Should you enter the correct password, the router authorizes you to use privilege EXEC mode. Instead of having an enable password on every device, you can create a database of users who may or may not access privileged EXEC mode. If your organization previously configured a RADIUS or TACACS+ server (see Chapters 12 and 13), then you can also specify who can access privileged mode, and the router will not rely on the configured enable password or rely on it only in a fail-safe configuration on the router.

Caution: There are five commands associated with privilege level 0: `disable, enable, exit, help,` and `logout.` Should you configure AAA authorization for a privilege level greater than 0, the IOS will not include those five commands in the privilege level command set. This obviously might cause you some grief.

Starting with AAA Authorization

Before configuring authorization using named method lists, you must first perform the following tasks:

1. Enable AAA on your network access server. For more information about enabling AAA on your Cisco router or access server, refer to Chapter 7, "Implementing AAA Security Services."
2. Configure AAA authentication. Authorization generally takes place after authentication and relies on authentication to work properly. For more information on AAA authentication, refer to the Chapter 8, "Implementing AAA Authentication."
3. Define the characteristics of your RADIUS or TACACS+ security server if you are issuing RADIUS or TACACS+ authorization. For more information about configuring your Cisco network access server to communicate with your RADIUS and TACACS+ security servers, refer to Chapters 12 and 13, "Configuring TACACS+" and "Configuring RADIUS," respectively.
4. Define the rights associated with specific users by using the `username` command when you are issuing local authorization.

5. Create the administrative instances of users in the Kerberos key distribution center by issuing the `kerberos instance map` command when using Kerberos. For more information about Kerberos, refer to Chapter 14, "Configuring Kerberos."

Understanding AAA Authorization

Once the router authenticates the user, you can apply authorization to that user. As with authentication, the first step is to create a method list. Both the syntax and the reasoning behind the method list are similar to that for authentication. One major difference is that you do not have to name the method list. The `aaa authorization` command allows you to set parameters that restrict a user's network access. To enable AAA authorization, use the following commands starting in global configuration mode:

```
2501-1(config)#aaa authorization {network | exec | commands
   level | reverse-access} {default | list-name} {tacacs+ |
   if-authenticated | none | local | radius | krb5-instance}
2501-1(config)#line [aux | console | tty | vty] line-number
   [ending-line-number}
2501-1(config-line)#authorization {arap | commands level |
   exec | reverse-access}{default | list-name}
2501-1(config)#ppp authorization {default | list-name}
```

Note: You cannot use this command with TACACS and Extended TACACS.

In the command (first set of braces), you can see that the Cisco IOS software supports four different types of authorization:

■ exec applies to the attributes associated with a user EXEC terminal session. This determines whether the user has the authorization to run an EXEC shell.

■ commands applies to the EXEC mode commands a user can issue. Command authorization attempts authorization for all EXEC mode commands, including global configuration commands, associated with a specific privilege level.

■ network applies to a network connection, including a PPP, SLIP, or ARAP connection. This means that authorization is in effect for all network-related service requests.

■ reverse-access applies to reverse Telnet sessions.

Method lists for authorization define the ways the router will perform authorization and the method sequence. This concept is identical to the way it works with the authentication methods. A method list is simply a named list describing the authorization methods to query (e.g., RADIUS or TACACS+), in sequence. Method lists enable you to designate one or more security protocols to use for authorization, thus ensuring a backup system in case the initial method fails. Cisco IOS software uses the first method listed to authorize users for specific network services. If that method fails to respond, the Cisco IOS software selects the next method listed in the method list. This process continues until there is successful communication with a listed authorization method, or the router exhausts all defined methods.

Note: The Cisco IOS software attempts authorization with the next listed method only when there is no response from the previous method. If authorization fails at any point in this cycle — meaning that the security server or local username database responds by denying the user services — the authorization process stops and the router or NAS will attempt no other authorization methods.

Cisco IOS software supports the following methods for authorization:

- *if-authenticated*. The user can access the requested function provided the router has successfully authenticated the user.
- *krb5-instance*. The network access server uses the instance defined by the `Kerberos Instance Map` command for authorization.
- *local*. The router or access server consults its local database, as defined by the `username` command, to authorize specific rights for users. You can only control a limited set of functions using the local database.
- *none*. The network access server does not request authorization information; the router does not perform authorization over this line/interface.

Note: By default, the router disables authorization for all actions (which is equivalent to the keyword `none`).

- *RADIUS*. The network access server requests authorization information from the RADIUS security server. RADIUS authorization defines specific user rights by associating attributes, which are stored in a database on the RADIUS server, with the appropriate user.
- *TACACS+*. The network access server exchanges authorization information with the TACACS+ security daemon. TACACS+ authorization defines specific user rights by associating attribute-value (AV) pairs, which are stored in a database on the TACACS+ security server, with the appropriate user.

When you create a named method list, you are defining a particular list of authorization methods for the indicated authorization type.

Once defined, you must apply method lists to specific lines or interfaces before the IOS will perform any of the defined methods. The only exception is the default method list (which Cisco, coincidentally, named "default"). If you issue the `aaa authorization` command for a particular authorization type without a named method list specified, the router automatically applies the default method list to all interfaces or lines except those with an explicitly defined named method list. Thus, a defined method list overrides the default method list. When you do not define a default method list, then no authorization takes place.

Let us recap the rules for authorization. To enable authorization for all network-related service requests (including SLIP, PPP, PPP NCPs, and ARA protocols), use the `network` keyword. To enable authorization to determine whether a user can run an EXEC shell, use the `exec` keyword. To enable authorization for specific, individual EXEC commands associated with a specific privilege level, use the `command` keyword. This allows you to authorize all commands associated with a specified command level from 0 to 15. To create a method list to enable authorization for reverse Telnet functions, use the `reverse-access` keyword.

Using the above command syntax to apply authorization against RADIUS for all commands at exec level 5, the command is:

```
2501-1(config)#aaa authorization commands 5 default radius
```

TACACS+ Authorization

To have the network access server request authorization information via a TACACS+ security server, use the `aaa authorization` command with the `tacacs+` method keyword. The following example uses a TACACS+ server to authorize the use of network services, including PPP and ARA. When the TACACS+ server is not available or an error occurs during the authorization process, the fallback method (none) is to grant all authorization requests:

```
2501-1(config)#aaa authorization network tacacs+ none
```

The following example allows network authorization using TACACS+:

```
2501-1(config)#aaa authorization network tacacs+
```

The following example provides the same authorization, but also creates address pools called mci and att:

```
2501-1(config)#aaa authorization network tacacs+
2501-1(config)#ip address-pool local
2501-1(config)#ip local-pool mci 10.1.0.1 10.1.0.255
2501-1(config)#ip local-pool att 10.2.0.1 10.2.0.255
```

For more specific information about configuring authorization using a TACACS+ security server, refer to Chapter 12, "Configuring TACACS+."

If-Authenticated Authorization

To allow users to have access to the functions they request as long as they have been authenticated, use the aaa authorization command with the if-authenticated method keyword. If you select this method, the router automatically grants all requested functions to authenticated users. To apply authorization to network connections when already authenticated, use the following command:

```
2501-1(config)#aaa authorization network default
   if-authenticated
```

None Authorization

There may be times when you do not want to run authorization from a particular interface or line. To perform no authorization for the actions associated with a particular type of authentication, use the aaa authorization command with the none method keyword. If you select this method, the router disables authorization for all actions. To apply no authorization to network connections, use the following command:

```
2501-1(config)#aaa authorization network default none
```

Local Authorization

To select local authorization, which means that the router or access server consults its local user database to determine the functions a user is permitted, use the aaa authorization command with the local method keyword. To specify that authorization is the local user database for EXEC commands, use the following command:

```
2501-1(config)#aaa authorization exec default local
```

The functions associated with local authorization are defined using the username global configuration command.

RADIUS Authorization

To have the network access server request authorization via a RADIUS security server, use the aaa authorization command with the radius method keyword. The following example shows how to configure the router to authorize using RADIUS:

```
2501-1(config)#aaa authorization exec radius if-
   authenticated
2501-1(config)#! Configures the NAS to contact the RADIUS
   server to determine whether users are permitted to start
```

an EXEC shell when they log in. If an error occurs when the
network access server contacts the RADIUS server, the
fallback method is to permit the CLI to start, provided
the user has been properly authenticated
```
2501-1(config)#aaa authorization network radius
2501-1(config)#! Configures network authorization via
   RADIUS: use to govern address assignment, the application
   of access lists, and various other per-user quantities
```

The RADIUS information returned can be used to specify that an autocommand
or a connection access list be applied to this connection.

Note: Because no fallback method is specified in this example,
authorization will fail when, for any reason, there is no response
from the RADIUS server.

For more specific information about configuring authorization using a RADIUS
security server, refer to Chapter 13, "Configuring RADIUS."

Kerberos Authorization

To run authorization to determine whether a user can run an EXEC shell at a
specific privilege level based on a mapped Kerberos instance, use the krb5-
instance method keyword. The following global configuration example maps
the Kerberos instance, admin, to enable mode:

```
2501-1(config)#kerberos instance map admin 15
```

The following example configures the router to check the user's Kerberos
instance and set appropriate privilege levels:

```
2501-1(config)#aaa authorization exec krb5-instance
```

For more information, refer to Chapter 14, "Configuring Kerberos."

Disabling Authorization for Global Configuration Commands

The aaa authorization command with the keyword command attempts
authorization for all EXEC mode commands, including global configuration commands, associated with a specific privilege level. Because there are configuration
commands that are identical to some EXEC-level commands, there can be some
confusion in the authorization process. Using the no aaa authorization
config-command command stops the network access server from attempting
configuration command authorization. To disable AAA authorization for all global

configuration commands, use the following command in global configuration mode:

```
2501-1(config)#no aaa authorization config-command
```

After you issue the `aaa authorization` command `level method` command, the router enables the `no aaa authorization config-command` command by default. This means that all configuration commands in the EXEC mode are authorized.

Be careful when using the no form of this command because it potentially reduces the amount of administrative control over configuration commands.

Authorization for Reverse Telnet

In Chapter 5, "Managing Your Router," you used Telnet to test connectivity between one router and another. Telnet is a standard terminal emulation protocol used for remote terminal connection. Normally, you log in to a network access server (typically through a dial-up connection) and then use Telnet to access other network devices from that network access server. There are times, however, when it is necessary to establish a reverse Telnet session. In reverse Telnet sessions, you establish the Telnet connection in the opposite direction — from inside a network to a network access server on the network periphery to gain access to modems or other devices connected to that network access server. Reverse Telnet can provide users with dial-out capability by allowing them to Telnet to modem ports attached to a network access server.

You must control access to ports accessible through reverse Telnet. Failure to do so could, for example, allow unauthorized users free access to modems where they can trap and divert incoming calls or make outgoing calls to unauthorized destinations. The phreakers and crackers out there will run up your phone bills and use your site to launch attacks on other people.

The router authenticates the user during reverse Telnet through the standard AAA log-in procedure for Telnet. Typically, the user must provide a username and password to establish either a Telnet or reverse Telnet session.

Reverse Telnet authorization provides an additional, but optional, level of security by requiring authorization in addition to authentication. When enabled, reverse Telnet authorization can use RADIUS or TACACS+ to authorize, whether or not this user is allowed reverse Telnet access to specific asynchronous ports, after the user successfully authenticates through the standard Telnet log-in procedure.

Reverse Telnet authorization offers the following benefits:

- An additional level of protection by ensuring that users engaged in reverse Telnet activities are indeed authorized to access a specific asynchronous port using reverse Telnet.
- An alternative method (other than access lists) to manage reverse Telnet authorization.

To configure a network access server to request authorization information from a TACACS+ or RADIUS server before allowing a user to establish a reverse Telnet session, use the following command in global configuration mode:

```
2501-1(config)#aaa authorization reverse-access {radius |
  tacacs+}
```

This feature enables the network access server to request reverse Telnet authorization information from the security server, whether RADIUS or TACACS+. You must configure the specific reverse Telnet privileges for the user on the security server itself.

The following example causes the network access server to request authorization information from a TACACS+ security server before allowing a user to establish a reverse Telnet session:

```
2501-1(config)#aaa new-model
2501-1(config)#! Enables AAA
2501-1(config)#aaa authentication login default tacacs+
2501-1(config)#! Specifies TACACS+ as the default method for
  user authentication during login
2501-1(config)#aaa authorization reverse-access tacacs+
2501-1(config)#! Specifies TACACS+ as the method for user
  authorization when trying to establish a reverse Telnet
  session
2501-1(config)#tacacs-server host 10.1.0.8
2501-1(config)#! Identifies the TACACS+ server
2501-1(config)#tacacs-server timeout 90
2501-1(config)#! Sets the interval that the network access
  server waits for the TACACS+ server to reply
2501-1(config)#tacacs-server key secret1
2501-1(config)#! Defines the encryption key used for all
  communication between the NAS and the TACACS+ server
```

You also need to configure the TACACS+ server to grant a user, say Peter, reverse Telnet access to a port, say TTY2, on the network access server named NAS1. You do that with the following configuration in TACACS+:

```
user = peter
login = cleartext SimRouter
service = raccess {
port#1 = nas1/tty2
```

For information on configuring TACACS+, refer to Chapter 12.

The following example causes the network access server to request authorization from a RADIUS security server before allowing a user to establish a reverse Telnet session:

```
2501-1(config)#aaa new-model
2501-1(config)#! Enables AAA
2501-1(config)#aaa authentication login default radius
2501-1(config)#! Specifies RADIUS as the default method for
  user authentication during login
2501-1(config)#aaa authorization reverse-access radius
2501-1(config)#! Specifies RADIUS as the method for user
  authorization when trying to establish a reverse Telnet
  session
2501-1(config)#radius-server host 10.1.0.9
2501-1(config)#! Identifies the RADIUS server
2501-1(config)#radius-server key secret2
2501-1(config)#! Defines the encryption key used for all
  communication between the NAS and the RaDIUS server
```

You also need to configure the RAIDUS server to grant a user, say Peter, reverse Telnet access to a port, say TTY2, on the network access server named NAS1. You do that with the following configuration in RADIUS:

```
Password = "secret2"
User-Service-Type = Shell-User
cisco-avpair = "raccess:port#1=nas1/tty2"
```

For information on configuring RADIUS, refer to Chapter 13.

Authorization Attribute-Value Pairs

RADIUS and TACACS+ authorization both define specific rights for users by processing attributes, which you store in a database on the security server. For both RADIUS and TACACS+, you define the attributes associated with the user on the security server, and the security server sends them to the network access server where they are applied to the user's connection.

Practice Session

In this Practice Session, you will practice the following:

- Logging in
- Saving log data
- Switching modes
- Pasting configuration files
- Enabling AAA security services
- Enabling and saving syslog data
- Logging out

1. Log in to the SimRouter Web page.
2. Double-click on router 2501-1 to telnet to that router. This will open a console session.
3. Enter your **Username** and **Password** at the applicable prompt. These are the ones you set up in Chapter 2. You will need to hit the Enter key twice to get to the > prompt.
4. Again, save the log for your session. To do this, select | Terminal | Start Logging | from the menu bar in the Telnet window. The Telnet client will ask you where you wish to store the log and with what name. Your choice. You are going to save the log so that when you build a configuration file in this Practice Session, you can cut-and-paste this in Chapter 10 as a starting point, rather than having to enter the same information for each Practice Session.
5. Enter the enable mode:

   2501-1#**enable**

6. When prompted to put in the enable secret password, enter **november**.
7. Type **terminal length 0**. This command instructs the route to scroll through long command output without pausing (the —More— message).
8. You will paste the running-config that you saved from the Chapter 8 log. At the 2501-1# prompt, type **config t**.
9. If you did not do this in Chapter 8, open your log file with any text editor of your choice (e.g., use | Start | Programs | Accessories | Notepad |). Do a find on sh running-config and copy from the first "!" to "end." At the 2501-1(config)# prompt, paste this configuration.
10. Type **aaa authorization exec radius if-authenticated** and press Enter. The aaa authorization exec radius if-authenticated command queries the RADIUS database for information that is used during EXEC authorization, such as autocommands and privilege levels, but only provides authorization if the user has successfully authenticated.
11. Type **aaa authorization network radius** and press Enter. The aaa authorization network radius command queries RADIUS for network authorization, address assignment, and other access lists.
12. Type **sh running-config** and press Enter. You will use this new configuration to start the next Practice Session.
13. Type **quit** to log out from router 2501-1. Close the Telnet window and return to the SimRouter Topology Map.
14. Repeat Steps 2 through 5 for router 2501-2, substituting **2501-2** for 2501-1.
15. Type **aaa new-model** and press Enter.
16. Type **setup** to launch setup mode.
17. When prompted to continue with the configuration dialog, enter **yes**.
18. Type **no** to Would you like to enter basic management setup.
19. When asked whether you want to see the current interface summary, enter **no**. You are more than welcome to look at it, but there is nothing of value. You are going to set these values.
20. At the Enter host name (2501-1) prompt, type **2501-2**.
21. When prompted to put in the enable secret password, enter **oscar**.

22. When prompted to enter the enable password, enter **papa**.
23. When prompted to enter the virtual terminal password, enter **quebec**.
24. When asked whether you want to Configure SNMP Network Management, enter **yes**.
25. At the community string (public) prompt, enter a really strong passcode that you can remember. If you just hit the Enter key, the router will set the community string to public. Hopefully, none of the routers in your organization are using the default community string of public.

Caution: Your SNMPv1 community strings are sent unencrypted and someone with a packet analyzer could grab them. SNMPv2 offers encrypted passwords. Consider using different community strings for every router on your network to compartmentalize any password compromise.

---

26. Setup will ask you whether you want, in turn, to configure DECnet, AppleTalk, IPX, IP, IGRP, RIP, and bridging. Enter **yes** to configure IP and RIP; **no** to the others.
27. Now you must configure the interfaces. The router will ask you whether you want to configure Ethernet0. The default is no, but enter **yes**. Type **yes** to configure the IP address for the interface. Enter **10.9.0.1** for the IP address for the interface and **255.0.0.0** for the subnet mask. Enter **no** to bypass configuring Serial0 and Serial1.
28. Once you complete step 27, you should see the following:

```
The following configuration command script was created:
hostname 2501-2
enable secret 5 $1$FzEE$BdzxWGpwJv/TTKYAr/E300
enable password papa
line vty 0 4
password quebec
snmp-server community public
!
no decnet routing
no appletalk routing
no ipx routing
ip routing
no bridge 1
!
interface Ethernet0
no shutdown
ip address 10.9.0.1 255.0.0.0
no mop enabled
!
interface Serial0
```

```
shutdown
no ip address
!
interface Serial1
shutdown
no ip address
dialer-list 1 protocol ip permit
dialer-list 1 protocol ipx permit
!
router rip
redistribute connected
network 10.0.0.0
!
end
```

```
[0] Go to the IOS command prompt without saving this
    config.
[1] Return back to the setup without saving this config.
[2] Save this configuration to nvram and exit.
Enter your selection [2]:
```

29. Review the configuration and type **2** to save the new configuration. The IOS will automatically save the configuration to NVRAM.

30. Type **aaa new-model** and press Enter. The aaa new-model command enables AAA network security services.

31. Type **aaa authentication login admins local** and press Enter. This command names a method list, admins, for log-in authentication.

32. Type **aaa authentication ppp dialins radius local** and press Enter. This command names the authentication method list dialins, which specifies that RADIUS authentication then local authentication for serial lines using PPP.

33. Type **aaa authorization network mylan radius local** and press Enter. This command defines the network authorization method list named mylan, which specifies to use RADIUS authorization on serial lines using PPP. If the RADIUS server fails to respond, then the router will perform local network authorization.

34. Type **username root password romeo** and press Enter. This command defines the username root and password for the PPP Password Authentication Protocol (PAP) caller identification.

35. Type **radius-server host radius1** and press Enter. This command defines the name of the RADIUS server host — radius1.

36. Type **radius-server key sierra** and press Enter. This command defines the shared secret text string (sierra) between the network access server and the RADIUS server host.

37. Type **interface group-async 1** and press Enter. This command selects and defines an asynchronous interface group.

38. Type **group-range 1 16** and press Enter. This command defines the member asynchronous interfaces in the interface group.

39. Type **encapsulation ppp** and press Enter. This command sets PPP as the encapsulation method used on the specified interfaces.

40. Type **ppp authentication chap dialins** and press Enter. This command selects Challenge Handshake Authentication Protocol (CHAP) as the method of PPP authentication and applies the named dialins method list to the specified interfaces.

41. Type **ppp authorization mylan** and press Enter. This command applies the mylan network authorization method list to the specified interfaces.

42. Type **line 1 16** and press Enter. This command switches the configuration mode from global configuration to line configuration and identifies the specific lines being configured.

43. Type **autoselect ppp** and press Enter. This command allows a PPP session to start up automatically on these selected lines.

44. Type **autoselect during-login** and press Enter. Use this command to display the username and password prompt without pressing the Return key. After the user logs in, the autoselect function (in this case, PPP) begins.

45. Type **login authentication admins** and press Enter. This command applies the admins method list for log-in authentication.

46. Type **modem dialin** and press Enter. This command configures attached modems to accept incoming calls only.

47. Type **sh running-config** and press Enter. You will use this new configuration to start the next Practice Session.

48. Type **quit** to log out from router 2524-1. Close the Telnet window and return to the SimRouter Topology Map.

49. Click on Log Out on the SimRouter Web page.

50. Study the **running-configs** from SimRouter (2501-1) and 2524-1. Try to find the effects of the Practice Session in the configuration file. For example, look for encrypted passwords or user peter.

Security and Audit Checklist

1. Do you use AAA authorization in your organization?
   - Yes
   - No
2. Does your organization have a policy for AAA authorization?
   - Yes
   - No
3. Do you use authorization for the following:
   - Commands?
   - Exec?
   - Network?
   - Reverse-access?

4. Which of the following enable authorization methods do you use?
   - If-authenticated
   - Krb5-instance
   - Local
   - None
   - RADIUS
   - TACACS+
5. Are all the authorization methods appropriate?
   - Yes
   - No
6. Have you disabled authorization for global configuration commands?
   - Yes
   - No
7. Do you use authorization for reverse Telnet?
   - Yes
   - No

Conclusion

In this chapter, you saw how to configure authorization. AAA authorization enables you to limit the services available to a user. You have to decide what authorization (network, exec, commands, or reverse Telnet) a user gets, and then decide on the authorization method (if-authenticated, krb5-instance, local, none, RADIUS, or TACACS+) itself. When you AAA enable authorization, the network access server uses information it retrieves from the user's profile, located either in the local user database or on the security server, to configure the user's session. Once done, the user gains access to a requested service only when someone provides prior permission.

So there you have the second part of AAA security services. The last piece of our AAA puzzle is accounting, which you will look at in Chapter 10.

Before moving on, make sure you have a good handle on both authentication and authorization. Understand when and why you would use these functions.

Chapter 10

Implementing
AAA Accounting

In this chapter, you will learn about:

- Configuring AAA accounting
- AAA accounting event types
- AAA accounting triggers
- AAA accounting methods
- Monitoring accounting
- Accounting attribute-value (AV) pairs

The previous two chapters covered AAA authentication and authorization. These subjects are pretty intense. AAA accounting, the subject of this chapter, is not quite as intense.

The concept of AAA accounting is pretty straightforward. Your organization wishes to track which resources individuals or groups use. You might want to track this information because you charge back for network use. That is, the IS department charges other departments for access and resources consumed. You also might provide support to other departments and need the information on usage, dial-in access, and other data to do your job; or perhaps you are an ISP and you want to track dial-in access for billing. There are myriad reasons for accounting data. AAA accounting provides the capability to collect this data.

Although accounting is generally considered a management control, whether it is network or financial, it also is a key security control. For example, using accounting data, you can create a list of users and the time of day that they dialed in to the network. You can record start and stop times, commands executed, number of packets sent and received, and the number of bytes sent and received. Obviously, this is useful information when trying to trace a particular problem on your system.

Another important use of accounting data is for change management purposes. Assuming you set up accounting to collect the data, you can gather information on who made a change and the nature of that change. Again, this information is extremely useful in troubleshooting. You can now determine whether or not the change is legitimate, that is, an authorized or unauthorized change.

When you enable `aaa accounting`, the network access server (NAS) reports user activity to the TACACS+ or RADIUS security server in the form of accounting records. Where the NAS sends the data obviously depends on which security server you configure in your organization. You might support both and the NAS can write to both should you choose. Each accounting record contains accounting attribute-value (AV) pairs. For example, the pair might be "address=10.8.0.6," where 10.8.0.6 is the value of the attribute address. The security server will store all AV pairs it receives. You can then analyze the data for network management, change management, client billing, and auditing purposes.

Starting with AAA Accounting

You must define all accounting methods through AAA security services. When you activate accounting, the IOS globally applies it to all interfaces or lines on the router or NAS, so you need not specify whether you want to apply accounting enabled on an interface-by-interface or line-by-line basis. But you can! Before configuring accounting using named method lists, you must first perform the following tasks:

1. Enable AAA on your network access server. For more information about enabling AAA on your Cisco router or access server, refer to Chapter 7, "Implementing AAA Security Services."
2. Configure AAA authentication. For more information on AAA authentication, refer to Chapter 8, "Implementing AAA Authentication."
3. Configure AAA authorization. For more information on AAA authorization, refer to Chapter 9, "Implementing AAA Authorization."
4. Define the characteristics of your RADIUS or TACACS+ security server when you are issuing RADIUS or TACACS+ authorization. For more information on configuring your Cisco network access server to communicate with your RADIUS and TACACS+ security servers, refer to Chapters 12 and 13, "Configuring TACACS+" and "Configuring RADIUS," respectively.
5. Apply accounting to an interface or line.
6. Monitor accounting.

Configuring AAA Accounting

The AAA accounting feature enables you to track the services users are accessing as well as the amount of network resources they are consuming. When you enable `aaa accounting`, the network access server reports user activity to the TACACS+ or RADIUS security server (depending on the security method you implemented) in the form of accounting records. Each accounting record contains accounting attribute-value (AV) pairs and the IOS stores them on the security server. The network access server monitors the accounting functions defined in either TACACS+ attribute/value (AV) pairs or RADIUS attributes, depending on which

Exhibit 1   AAA Accounting Event Types

Event Type	Description
commands *level*	Implements accounting for all commands at the specified privilege level (0 to 15). Applies to the EXEC mode commands a user issues. Command authorization attempts for all EXEC mode commands, including global configuration commands, associated with a specific privilege level. Data includes username, executed commands, date, and time.
connection	Implements accounting for outbound connections made from the network access server, such as Telnet, local area transport (LAT), packet assembler/disassembler (PAD), and rlogin.
exec	Implements accounting for all user shell EXEC commands. Provides information about user EXEC terminal sessions to the network access server. Data includes username, date, start and stop times, NAS or router IP address, and calling telephone number (for dial-in clients) when you have CallerID enabled.
network	Implements accounting for all network-related events, such as SLIP, PPP, PPP NCPs, and ARA. Data includes packet and byte counts.
system	Implements accounting for system-level events not associated with users; for example, a reboot command.

security method you have implemented. Your system, network, or security administrator can analyze this data for network management, client billing, and auditing.

Following is the syntax for the aaa accounting global configuration command.

```
2501-1(config)#aaa accounting event-type {default | list-
  name} {start-stop | wait-start | stop-only | none} method1
  [method2]
```

Accounting method lists are specific to the requested type of accounting. AAA supports five different event types for accounting, as shown in Exhibit 1.

The command syntax shows a trigger following the event type. The trigger tells the security server when to start recording. In Exhibit 2, you have four options for the trigger.

Tip: For minimal accounting, use the stop-only keyword, which instructs the specified authentication system (RADIUS or TACACS+) to send a stop record accounting notice, at the end of the requested user process. For more accounting information, use the start-stop keyword to send a start accounting notice at the beginning of the requested event and a stop accounting notice at the end of the event. You can further control access and accounting by using the wait-start keyword, which ensures that the RADIUS or TACACS+ security server acknowledges the start notice before granting the user's process request.

Exhibit 2   AAA Accounting Trigger

Trigger	Description
start-stop	Starts accounting at beginning and stops at end, which means the IOS sends an accounting record as soon as a session begins. The IOS also sends another record as soon as the session ends. The process will start regardless of whether or not the security server received the start command.
wait-start	Start accounting at beginning and stop at end when acknowledged, which means the IOS sends an accounting record after receiving an acknowledgment from the security server that it started a session. The IOS also sends another record as soon as the session ends.
stop-only	Sends stop accounting notice at end of requested user process, which means the IOS only sends a record when the session ends. The record includes session statistics.
none	Disables accounting services on the line or interface.

The parameters `method1` and `method2` only have two possible values. Cisco IOS software supports only two methods for accounting:

- *TACACS+.* The network access server reports user activity to the TACACS+ security server in the form of accounting records. Each accounting record contains accounting attribute-value (AV) pairs and is stored on the security server.
- *RADIUS.* The network access server reports user activity to the RADIUS security server in the form of accounting records. Each accounting record contains accounting attribute-value (AV) pairs and is stored on the security server.

To have the network access server send accounting information from a TACACS+ security server, use the `tacacs+` method keyword. For more specific information about configuring TACACS+ for accounting services, refer to Chapter 12, "Configuring TACACS+."

To have the network access server send accounting information from a RADIUS security server, use the `radius` method keyword. For more specific information about configuring RADIUS for accounting services, refer to Chapter 13, "Configuring RADIUS."

In the following sample configuration, you use RADIUS-style accounting to track all usage of EXEC commands and network services, such as SLIP, PPP, and ARAP:

```
2501-1(config)#aaa accounting exec start-stop radius
2501-1(config)#aaa accounting network start-stop radius
```

Named Method Lists for Accounting

Similar to authentication and authorization method lists, method lists for accounting define the way the router will perform accounting. Named accounting method lists enable you to designate accounting services for a particular security protocol to specific lines or interfaces.

Note: System accounting does not use named accounting lists; you can only define the default list for system accounting.

Once again, when you create a named method list, you are defining a particular list of accounting methods for the indicated accounting type.

You must apply accounting method lists to specific lines or interfaces before the router or NAS will perform any of the defined methods. The only exception is the default method list (which Cisco coincidentally named "default"). If you configure the aaa accounting command for a particular accounting type without specifying a named method list, the router or NAS automatically applies the default method list to all interfaces or lines except those where you have explicitly defined a named method list. A defined method list always trumps the default method list. If you do not define a default method list, then no accounting takes place.

Understanding AAA Accounting Types

As you just saw, Cisco IOS software supports five different kinds of accounting:

- Command accounting
- Connection accounting
- EXEC accounting
- Network accounting
- System accounting

Command Accounting

Command accounting provides information about the EXEC shell commands for a specified privilege level that is being executed on a network access server. Each command accounting record includes a list of the commands executed for that privilege level, as well as the date and time each command was executed and the user who executed it.

The following example shows the information contained in a TACACS+ command accounting record for privilege level 1:

```
Mon Sep 11 09:39:11 2001 10.8.0.10 ptdavis tty5
  5622329430/4327528 stop task_id=3 service=shell priv-
  lvl=1 cmd=sh version <cr>
Mon Sep 11 09:39:23 2001 10.8.0.10 ptdavis tty5
  5622329430/4327528 stop task_id=4 service=shell priv-
  lvl=1 cmd=sh interface e0 <cr>
```

```
Mon Sep 11 09:39:37 2001 10.8.0.10 ptdavis tty5
   5622329430/4327528 stop task_id=5 service=shell priv-
   lvl=1 cmd=sh ip route <cr>
```

In this example, you see an attribute pair in the first record of cmd=sh version <cr>. The attribute is the command (cmd) and the value is the command the user executed, that is, show version.

The following example shows the information contained in a TACACS+ command accounting record for privilege level 15:

```
Mon Sep 11 09:44:22 2001 10.8.0.10 ptdavis tty5
   5622329430/4327528 stop task_id=6 service=shell priv-
   lvl=15 cmd=config t <cr>
Mon Sep 11 09:44:38 2001 10.8.0.10 ptdavis tty5
   5622329430/4327528 stop task_id=7 service=shell priv-
   lvl=15 cmd=interface s0 <cr>
Mon Sep 11 09:44:51 2001 10.8.0.10 ptdavis tty5
   5622329430/4327528 stop task_id=8 service=shell priv-
   lvl=15 cmd=ip address 10.8.0.1 255.255.255.0 <cr>
```

Note: Cisco's implementation of RADIUS does not support command accounting.

In this example, you see an attribute pair in the first record of priv-lvl=15. The attribute is the privilege level (priv-lvl) and the value is 15, the highest privilege level.

Connection Accounting

Connection accounting provides information about all outbound connections made from the network access server, such as Telnet, local area transport (LAT), TN3270, packet assembler/disassembler (PAD), and rlogin.

The example in Exhibit 3 shows the information contained in a RADIUS connection accounting record for an outbound Telnet connection.

In Exhibit 3, you see an attribute pair of User-Id = "ptdavis." The attribute is the user identifier (User-Id) and the value is the userid or username of the user, that is, ptdavis. While looking at the examples, review the AV pairs.

The example in Exhibit 4 shows the information contained in a TACACS+ connection accounting record for an outbound Telnet connection.

The example in Exhibit 5 shows the information contained in a RADIUS connection accounting record for an outbound rlogin connection, and the following example shows the information contained in a TACACS+ connection accounting record for an outbound rlogin connection:

**Exhibit 3   RADIUS Connection Accounting
Record for an Outbound Telnet Connection**

```
Mon Sep 11 09:47:07 2001
   NAS-IP-Address = "10.8.0.10"
   NAS-Port = 2
   User-Name = "ptdavis"
   Client-Port-DNIS = "4327528"
   Caller-ID = "5554101234"
   Acct-Status-Type = Start
   Acct-Authentic = RADIUS
   Service-Type = Login
   Acct-Session-ID = "00000009"
   Login-Service = Telnet
   Login-IP-Host = "10.8.0.7"
   Acct-Delay-Time = 0
   User-Id = "ptdavis"
   NAS-Identifier = "10.8.0.10"
Mon Sep 11 09:47:51 2001
   NAS-IP-Address = "10.8.0.10"
   NAS-Port = 2
   User-Name = "ptdavis"
   Client-Port-DNIS = "4327528"
   Caller-ID = "5554101234"
   Acct-Status-Type = Stop
   Acct-Authentic = RADIUS
   Service-Type = Login
   Acct-Session-ID = "00000009"
   Login-Service = Telnet
   Login-IP-Host = "10.8.0.7"
   Acct-Input-Octets = 16590
   Acct-Output-Octets = 123
   Acct-Input-Packets = 89
   Acct-Output-Packets = 147
   Acct-Session-Time = 44
   Acct-Delay-Time = 0
   User-Id = "ptdavis"
   NAS-Identifier = "10.8.0.10"
```

```
Mon Sep 11 10:13:05 2001 10.8.0.10 ptdavis tty5
  5622329430/4327528 start task_id=10 service=connection
  protocol=rlogin addr=10.8.0.7 cmd=rlogin 10.8.0.7 /user
  ptdavis
```

Exhibit 4   TACACS+ Connection Accounting Record for an Outbound Telnet Connection

---

```
Mon Sep 11 10:05:44 2001 10.8.0.10 ptdavis tty5
   5622329430/4327528 start task_id=9 service=connection
   protocol=telnet addr=10.8.0.7 cmd=telnet 10.8.0.7
Mon Sep 11 10:05:44 2001 10.8.0.10 ptdavis tty5
   5622329430/4327528 stop task_id=9 service=connection
   protocol=telnet addr=10.8.0.7 cmd=telnet 10.8.0.7
   bytes_in=16590 bytes_out=123 paks_in=89 paks_out=147
   elapsed_time=44
```

```
Mon Sep 11 10:13:27 2001 10.8.0.10 ptdavis tty5
   5622329430/4327528 stop task_id=10 service=connection
   protocol=rlogin addr=10.8.0.7 cmd=rlogin 10.8.0.7 /user
   ptdavis bytes_in=18867 bytes_out=88 paks_in=90
   paks_out=137 elapsed_time=22
```

The following example shows the information contained in a TACACS+ connection accounting record for an outbound LAT connection:

```
Mon Sep 11 10:18:13 2001 10.8.0.10 ptdavis tty5
   5622329430/4327528 start task_id=11 service=connection
   protocol=lat addr=VAX cmd=lat VAX
Mon Sep 11 10:18:19 2001 10.8.0.10 ptdavis tty5
   5622329430/4327528 stop task_id=11 service=connection
   protocol=lat addr=VAX cmd=lat VAX bytes_in=0 bytes_out=0
   paks_in=0 paks_out=0 elapsed_time=6
```

EXEC Accounting

EXEC accounting provides information about user EXEC terminal sessions (user shells) on the network access server, including username, date, start and stop times, the access server IP address, and (for dial-in users) the originating telephone number.

The example in Exhibit 6 shows the information contained in a RADIUS EXEC accounting record for a dial-in user, and the following example shows the information contained in a TACACS+ EXEC accounting record for a dial-in user:

```
Mon Sep 11 10:23:18 2001 10.8.0.10 ptdavis tty5
   5622329430/4327528 start task_id=12 service=shell
Mon Sep 11 10:24:19 2001 10.8.0.10 ptdavis tty5
   5622329430/4327528 stop task_id=12 service=shell
   elapsed_time=61
```

**Exhibit 5   RADIUS Connection Accounting
Record for an Outbound rlogin Connection**

```
Mon Sep 11 10:10:47 2001
  NAS-IP-Address = "10.8.0.10"
  NAS-Port = 2
  User-Name = "ptdavis"
  Client-Port-DNIS = "4327528"
  Caller-ID = "5554101234"
  Acct-Status-Type = Start
  Acct-Authentic = RADIUS
  Service-Type = Login
  Acct-Session-ID = "0000000A"
  Login-Service = Rlogin
  Login-IP-Host = "10.8.0.7"
  Acct-Delay-Time = 0
  User-Id = "ptdavis"
  NAS-Identifier = "10.8.0.10"
Mon Sep 11 10:11:11 2001
  NAS-IP-Address = "10.8.0.10"
  NAS-Port = 2
  User-Name = "ptdavis"
  Client-Port-DNIS = "4327528"
  Caller-ID = "5554101234"
  Acct-Status-Type = Stop
  Acct-Authentic = RADIUS
  Service-Type = Login
  Acct-Session-ID = "0000000A"
  Login-Service = Rlogin
  Login-IP-Host = "10.8.0.7"
  Acct-Input-Octets = 18867
  Acct-Output-Octets = 88
  Acct-Input-Packets = 90
  Acct-Output-Packets = 137
  Acct-Session-Time = 44
  Acct-Delay-Time = 0
  User-Id = "ptdavis"
  NAS-Identifier = "10.8.0.10"
```

The example in Exhibit 7 shows the information contained in a RADIUS EXEC accounting record for a Telnet user, and the following example shows the information contained in a TACACS+ EXEC accounting record for a Telnet user:

Exhibit 6   RADIUS EXEC Accounting Record for a Dial-In User

```
Mon Sep 11 10:20:10 2001
  NAS-IP-Address = "10.8.0.10"
  NAS-Port = 2
  User-Name = "ptdavis"
  Client-Port-DNIS = "4327528"
  Caller-ID = "5554101234"
  Acct-Status-Type = Start
  Acct-Authentic = RADIUS
  Service-Type = Exec-User
  Acct-Session-ID = "00000007"
  Acct-Delay-Time = 0
  User-Id = "ptdavis"
  NAS-Identifier = "10.8.0.10"
Mon Sep 11 10:21:11 2001
  NAS-IP-Address = "10.8.0.10"
  NAS-Port = 2
  User-Name = "ptdavis"
  Client-Port-DNIS = "4327528"
  Caller-ID = "5554101234"
  Acct-Status-Type = Stop
  Acct-Authentic = RADIUS
  Service-Type = Exec-User
  Acct-Session-ID = "00000007"
  Acct-Session-Time = 61
  Acct-Delay-Time = 0
  User-Id = "ptdavis"
  NAS-Identifier = "10.8.0.10"
```

```
Mon Sep 11 10:29:23 2001 10.8.0.10 ptdavis tty5 10.8.0.115
  start task_id=13 service=shell
Mon Sep 11 10:30:19 2001 10.8.0.10 ptdavis tty5 10.8.0.115
  stop task_id=13 service=shell elapsed_time=56
```

Network Accounting

Network accounting provides information for all PPP, SLIP, or ARAP sessions, including packet and byte counts. The example in Exhibit 8 shows the information contained in a RADIUS network accounting record for a PPP user who comes in through an EXEC session, and the following example shows the information contained in a TACACS+ network accounting record for a PPP user who first started an EXEC session:

**Exhibit 7 RADIUS EXEC Accounting
Record for a Telnet User**

```
Mon Sep 11 10:25:20 2001
  NAS-IP-Address = "10.8.0.10"
  NAS-Port = 2
  User-Name = "ptdavis"
  Caller-ID = 10.8.0.115
  Acct-Status-Type = Start
  Acct-Authentic = RADIUS
  Service-Type = Exec-User
  Acct-Session-ID = "00000010"
  Acct-Delay-Time = 0
  User-Id = "ptdavis"
  NAS-Identifier = "10.8.0.10"
Mon Sep 11 10:26:11 2001
  NAS-IP-Address = "10.8.0.10"
  NAS-Port = 2
  User-Name = "ptdavis"
  Caller-ID = 10.8.0.115
  Acct-Status-Type = Stop
  Acct-Authentic = RADIUS
  Service-Type = Exec-User
  Acct-Session-ID = "00000010"
  Acct-Session-Time = 51
  Acct-Delay-Time = 0
  User-Id = "ptdavis"
  NAS-Identifier = "10.8.0.10"
```

```
Mon Sep 11 10:47:29 2001 10.8.0.10 ptdavis tty5 562/4327528
  start task_id=19 service=shell
Mon Sep 11 10:48:19 2001 10.8.0.10 ptdavis tty5 562/4327528
  start task_id=21 addr=10.8.0.205 service=ppp
Mon Sep 11 10:48:19 2001 10.8.0.10 ptdavis tty5 562/4327528
  update task_id=21 addr=10.8.0.205 service=ppp protocol=ip
  addr=10.8.0.205
Mon Sep 11 10:47:29 2001 10.8.0.10 ptdavis tty5 562/4327528
  stop task_id=21 addr=10.8.0.205 service=ppp protocol=ip
  addr=10.8.0.205 bytes_in=4025 bytes_out=123 pks_in=89
  paks_out=147 elapsed_time=170
Mon Sep 11 10:53:19 2001 10.8.0.10 ptdavis tty5 562/4327528
  stop task_id=19 service=shell elapsed_time=230
```

**Exhibit 8   RADIUS Network Accounting Record for a PPP
User Who Comes in through an EXEC Session**

```
Mon Sep 11 10:39:25 2001
  NAS-IP-Address = "10.8.0.10"
  NAS-Port = 2
  User-Name = "ptdavis"
  Client-Port-DNIS = "4327528"
  Caller-ID = "562"
  Acct-Status-Type = Start
  Acct-Authentic = RADIUS
  Service-Type = Exec-User
  Acct-Session-ID = "00000011"
  Acct-Delay-Time = 0
  User-Id = "ptdavis"
  NAS-Identifier = "10.8.0.10"
Mon Sep 11 10:40:11 2001
  NAS-IP-Address = "10.8.0.10"
  NAS-Port = 2
  User-Name = "ptdavis"
  Client-Port-DNIS = "4327528"
  Caller-ID = "562"
  Acct-Status-Type = Start
  Acct-Authentic = RADIUS
  Service-Type = Framed
  Acct-Session-ID = "00000012"
  Framed-Protocol = PPP
  Framed-IP-Address = "10.8.0.205"
  Acct-Delay-Time = 0
  User-Id = "ptdavis"
  NAS-Identifier = "10.8.0.10"
Mon Sep 11 10:42:15 2001
  NAS-IP-Address = "10.8.0.10"
  NAS-Port = 2
  User-Name = "ptdavis"
  Client-Port-DNIS = "4327528"
  Caller-ID = "562"
  Acct-Status-Type = Stop
  Acct-Authentic = RADIUS
  Service-Type = Framed
  Acct-Session-ID = "00000012"
  Framed-Protocol = PPP
  Framed-IP-Address = "10.8.0.205"
  Acct-Input-Octets = 4025
  Acct-Output-Octets = 123
```

Exhibit 8 RADIUS Network Accounting Record for a PPP User Who Comes in through an EXEC Session (Continued)

```
Acct-Input-Packets = 89
Acct-Output-Packets = 147
Acct-Session-Time = 170
Acct-Delay-Time = 0
User-Id = "ptdavis"
NAS-Identifier = "10.8.0.10"
Mon Sep 11 10:46:15 2001
NAS-IP-Address = "10.8.0.10"
NAS-Port = 2
User-Name = "ptdavis"
Client-Port-DNIS = "4327528"
Caller-ID = "562"
Acct-Status-Type = Stop
Acct-Authentic = RADIUS
Service-Type = Exec-User
Acct-Session-ID = "00000011"
Framed-Protocol = PPP
Framed-IP-Address = "10.8.0.205"
Acct-Delay-Time = 0
User-Id = "ptdavis"
NAS-Identifier = "10.8.0.10"
```

Note: As they say in advertising circles, results may vary. The precise format of accounting packets records may vary, depending on your particular security server daemon.

The example in Exhibit 9 shows the information contained in a RADIUS network accounting record for a PPP user who comes in through autoselect, and the following example shows the information contained in a TACACS+ network accounting record for a PPP user who comes in through autoselect:

```
Mon Sep 11 11:00:47 2001 10.8.0.10 ptdavis Async 562/4327528
   start task_id=23 service=ppp
Mon Sep 11 11:01:19 2001 10.8.0.10 ptdavis Async 562/4327528
   update task_id=23 service=ppp protocol=ip addr=10.8.0.205
Mon Sep 11 11:02:29 2001 10.8.0.10 ptdavis Async 562/4327528
   stop task_id=23 service=ppp protocol=ip addr=10.8.0.205
   bytes_in=4025 bytes_out=123 pks_in=89 paks_out=147
   elapsed_time=102
```

Exhibit 9   RADIUS Network Accounting Record for a PPP User Who Comes in through Autoselect

```
Mon Sep 11 10:55:40 2001
  NAS-IP-Address = "10.8.0.10"
  NAS-Port = 2
  User-Name = "ptdavis"
  Client-Port-DNIS = "4327528"
  Caller-ID = "562"
  Acct-Status-Type = Start
  Acct-Authentic = RADIUS
  Service-Type = Framed
  Acct-Session-ID = "00000013"
  Framed-Protocol = PPP
  Framed-IP-Address = "10.8.0.205"
  Acct-Delay-Time = 0
  User-Id = "ptdavis"
  NAS-Identifier = "10.8.0.10"
Mon Sep 11 10:59:15 2001
  NAS-IP-Address = "10.8.0.10"
  NAS-Port = 2
  User-Name = "ptdavis"
  Client-Port-DNIS = "4327528"
  Caller-ID = "562"
  Acct-Status-Type = Stop
  Acct-Authentic = RADIUS
  Service-Type = Framed
  Acct-Session-ID = "00000013"
  Framed-Protocol = PPP
  Framed-IP-Address = "10.8.0.205"
  Acct-Input-Octets = 4025
  Acct-Output-Octets = 123
  Acct-Input-Packets = 89
  Acct-Output-Packets = 147
  Acct-Session-Time = 215
  Acct-Delay-Time = 0
  User-Id = "ptdavis"
  NAS-Identifier = "10.8.0.10"
```

System Accounting

System accounting provides information about all system-level events; for example, when the system reboots or when someone turns accounting on or off. The following accounting record is an example of a typical TACACS+ system accounting record server indicating that an unknown person turned AAA accounting off:

```
Mon Sep 11 10:31:23 2001 10.8.0.10 unknown unknown unknown
   start task_id=14 service=system event=sys_acct
   reason=reconfigure
```

Note: The precise format of accounting packets records may vary, depending on your particular TACACS+ daemon.

The following accounting record is an example of a TACACS+ system accounting record indicating that that unknown person turned AAA accounting on:

```
Mon Sep 11 10:33:31 2001 10.8.0.10 unknown unknown unknown
   stop task_id=15 service=system event=sys_acct
   reason=reconfigure
```

Note: Where is the RADIUS example? Cisco's implementation of RADIUS does not support system accounting.

Applying a Named List

Earlier you learned how to configure AAA accounting using named method lists. Now you need to learn how to apply the named lists to lines or interfaces. To enable AAA accounting services on a specific line or a group of lines, you use the accounting line configuration command. First, enter the line configuration mode for the lines where you want to apply the accounting method list. Use the all too familiar command following:

```
2501-1(config)#line [aux | console | tty | vty] line-number
   [ending-line-number]
```

Next, you apply the accounting method list to a line or set of lines as follows.

```
2501-1(config-line)#accounting {arap | exec | connection |
   commands level}{default | list-name}
```

Named accounting method lists are specific to the indicated type of accounting. To create a method list to provide accounting information for ARAP (network) sessions, use the arap keyword. To create a method list to provide accounting records about user EXEC terminal sessions on the network access server, including username, date, and start and stop times, use the exec keyword. To create a method list to provide accounting information about specific, individual EXEC commands associated with a specific privilege level, use the commands keyword. To create a method list to provide accounting information about all outbound connections made from the network access server, use the `connection` keyword. System accounting does not support named method lists.

Note: System accounting does not use named method lists. For system accounting, you can only define the default method list.

Following is a simple example of the use of the commands that enables command accounting for level 15 using the named method list tech-support:

```
2501-1(config)#line 9
2501-1(config-line)#accounting commands 15 tech-support
```

If you want to enable AAA accounting services on an interface, use the `ppp accounting interface configuration` command. First, enter the interface configuration mode for the interfaces where you want to apply the accounting method list:

```
2501-1(config)#interface interface-type interface-number
```

Next, apply the accounting method list to that interface or set of interfaces:

```
2501-1(config-if)#encapsulation ppp
2501-1(config-if)#ppp accounting {default | list-name}
```

Note: Accounting method lists for SLIP follow whatever you configure for PPP on the relevant interface. If you do not define lists and apply them to a particular interface (or you do not configure any PPP settings), the default setting for accounting applies.

If you do not specify a list-name, the IOS assumes it is the default.

Following is a simple example of the use of the commands that enables an asynchronous interface 1 using the named method list tech-support:

```
2501-1(config)#interface async 1
2501-1(config-if)#encapsulation ppp
2501-1(config-if)#ppp accounting tech-support
```

Suppress Generation of Accounting Records for Null Username Sessions

When you activate aaa accounting, the Cisco IOS software issues accounting records for all users on the system, including users whose username string, because of protocol translation, is NULL. This can happen to users who come in on lines where you have applied the aaa authentication login *method-list* none command. To prevent the IOS from generating accounting records for sessions that do not have usernames associated with them, use the following command in global configuration mode:

```
2501-1(config)#aaa accounting suppress null-username
```

This command prevents the router or NAS from generating accounting records for users whose username string is NULL.

Generating Interim Accounting Records

To enable the sending of periodic interim accounting records to the accounting server, use the following command in global configuration mode:

```
2501-1(config)#aaa accounting update {newinfo | periodic
   number}
```

When you use the aaa accounting update command, the Cisco IOS software issues interim accounting records for all users on the system. If you use the keyword newinfo, the IOS will send interim accounting records to the accounting server every time there is new accounting information to report. An example of this would be when IPCP completes IP address negotiation with the remote peer. The interim accounting record will include the negotiated IP address used by the remote peer.

When used with the keyword periodic, the IOS sends interim accounting records periodically as defined by the argument number. The keyword number is some value from 1 to 2,147,483,647 minutes. That is a lot of minutes! The interim accounting record contains all of the accounting information recorded for that user up to the time the interim accounting record is sent.

Both of these keywords are mutually exclusive, meaning that whichever keyword you configured last takes precedence over the previous configuration. For example, if you configure aaa accounting update periodic and then configure aaa accounting update newinfo, all users currently logged in will continue to generate periodic interim accounting records. All new users will generate accounting records based on the newinfo algorithm.

Caution: Using the aaa accounting update periodic command can cause heavy congestion when many users are logged in to the network. So use this command judiciously and when risks justify.

Monitoring Accounting

No specific show command exists for either RADIUS or TACACS+ accounting. To obtain accounting records displaying information about users currently logged in, use the following command in privileged EXEC mode:

Exhibit 10   Show Accounting Field Descriptions

Field	Description
Active Accounted actions on	Name of terminal line or interface where the user logged in
User	Username
Priv	User's privilege level
Task ID	Unique identifier for each accounting session
Accounting record	Type of accounting session; that is, command, connection, exec, network, or system
Elapsed	Length of time (hh:mm:ss) for this session type
attribute=value	AV pairs associated with this accounting session

2501-1#**show accounting**

You can use this command to step through all active sessions and print all the accounting records for the actively accounted functions.

You previously saw the following commands:

2501-1(config)#**aaa accounting exec start-stop radius**
2501-1(config)#**aaa accounting network start-stop radius**

The show accounting command yields the following output for the above configuration and Exhibit 10 describes the displayed fields:

```
Active Accounted actions on tty1, User ptdavis Priv 15
Task ID 17, EXEC Accounting record, 00:00:22 Elapsed
task_id=17 service=shell
```

You can also use related commands, show users and show line, to find out about the users and line status. To refresh your memory, here is sample output from these commands:

2501-1#**sh users**

```
    Line          User        Host(s)       Idle Location
*   0 con 0                    idle          00:00:00
```

2501-1#**sh line**

Tty	Typ	Tx/Rx	A	Modem	Roty	AccO	AccI	Uses	Noise	Overruns	Int
* 0	CTY		−	−	−	−	−	0	0	0/0	−
1	AUX	9600/9600	−	−	−	−	−	0	0	0/0	−
2	VTY		−	−	−	−	−	0	0	0/0	−
3	VTY		−	−	−	−	−	0	0	0/0	−
4	VTY		−	−	−	−	−	0	0	0/0	−
5	VTY		−	−	−	−	−	0	0	0/0	−
6	VTY		−	−	−	−	−	0	0	0/0	−

Finally you have a general idea of the format of the various accounting records. Review the record formats for your particular vendor. Once you understand the format, it is relatively easy to dump the records into an Access, MySQL, SQLServer, DB2, Paradox, or Oracle database and interrogate the records. You should develop some standard routines, such as looking for reconfigurations, and set up a schedule to run the routines. Of course, you will need to schedule some time to review the output.

Practice Session

In this Practice Session, you will practice the following:

- Logging in
- Saving log data
- Switching modes
- Pasting configuration files
- Enabling AAA security services
- Enabling aaa accounting
- Applying a named list
- Enabling and saving syslog data
- Logging out

1. Log in to the SimRouter Web page.
2. Double-click on router 2501-2 to telnet to that router. This will open a console session.
3. Enter your **Username** and **Password** at the applicable prompt. These are the ones you set up in Chapter 2. You will need to hit the Enter key twice to get to the > prompt.
4. Again, save the log for your session. To do this, select | Terminal | Start Logging | from the menu bar in the Telnet window. The Telnet client will ask you where you wish to store the log and with what name. Your choice. You are going to save the log so that when you build a configuration file in this session, you can cut-and-paste this in Chapter 11 as a starting point, rather than having to enter the same information each Practice Session.
5. Enter the enable mode:

   `2501-1#`**`enable`**

6. When prompted to put in the enable secret password, enter **oscar**.
7. Type **terminal length 0**. This command instructs the router to scroll through long command output without pausing (the —More— message).
8. You will paste the running-config that you saved from the Chapter 9 log. At the 2501-2# prompt, type **config t**.
9. If you did not do it in Chapter 9, open your log file with any text editor of your choice (e.g., use | Start | Programs | Accessories | Notepad |). Do a find on sh running-config and copy from the first "!" to "end." At the 2501-2(config)# prompt, paste this configuration.
10. Type **aaa accounting network mylan start-stop radius** and press Enter. This command defines the network accounting method list named charley, which specifies that RADIUS accounting services (in this

case, start and stop records for specific events) will be used on serial lines using PPP.

11. Type **aaa accounting commands 15 default start-stop tacacs+** and press Enter. This command sends accounting records to the TACACS+ server for any commands entered.

12. Type **interface group-async 1** and press Enter. This command selects and defines an asynchronous interface group.

13. Type **group-range 1 16** and press Enter. This command defines the member asynchronous interfaces in the interface group.

14. Type **ppp accounting mylan** and press Enter. This command applies the `charley` network accounting method list to the specified interfaces.

15. Type **sh running-config** and press Enter. You will use this new configuration to start the next Practice Session.

16. Type **quit** to log out from router 2501-2. Close the Telnet window and return to the SimRouter Topology Map.

17. Click on Log Out on the SimRouter Web page.

Security and Audit Checklist

1. Do you use AAA accounting in your organization?
   - Yes
   - No
2. Do you use have a policy for the review of accounting data?
   - Yes
   - No
3. Does someone have responsibility for reviewing accounting data?
   - Yes
   - No
4. Does this person review the accounting data in a timely manner?
   - Yes
   - No
5. Is there a schedule for the retention of the accounting data?
   - Yes
   - No
6. Is the schedule appropriate?
   - Yes
   - No
7. Is the accounting data adequately protected?
   - Yes
   - No
8. Do you have accounting on for:
   - Commands?
   - Connection?
   - Exec?
   - Network?
   - System?

9. Do you use named lists?
    ■ Yes
    ■ No
10. Do you use the named lists for:
    ■ Commands?
    ■ Connection?
    ■ Exec?
    ■ Network?
11. Are the named lists applied to:
    ■ Interfaces?
    ■ Lines?
12. Do you have a default list for:
    ■ Commands?
    ■ Connection?
    ■ Exec?
    ■ Network?
    ■ System?
13. Is the default list appropriate for commands?
    ■ Yes
    ■ No
14. Is the default list appropriate for connection?
    ■ Yes
    ■ No
15. Is the default list appropriate for exec?
    ■ Yes
    ■ No
16. Is the default list appropriate for network?
    ■ Yes
    ■ No
17. Is the default list appropriate for system?
    ■ Yes
    ■ No
18. Do you use the default list on:
    ■ Interfaces?
    ■ Lines?
19. Which security server does your organization use for AAA accounting?
    ■ TACACS+
    ■ RADIUS

Conclusion

Having the capability to track what people are doing on your routers is a good idea, and AAA accounting provides some great functionality. It is always nice to tell who did what and when, especially when you are troubleshooting a problem. The first step is to gather the data by turning on AAA security and accounting. You can then analyze the data for network management, change management, client billing, and auditing purposes.

That concludes Section II on authentication, authorization, and accounting, which was preventing unauthorized access to the networking device. If you have a small network and you want to keep it simple, you saw in Chapter 6 that you could create a local username database and use that to authenticate users trying to telnet or log in locally. For larger, more sophisticated networks, this is not a viable solution — too many devices, too many administrators, no real control of functionality, and limited recording of router events. Chapters 7 through this one covered Cisco's AAA security services. You can implement authentication, authorization, and accounting for various access lines or interfaces, types, services, and methods.

As always, when you are unsure of the command, use Cisco's context-sensitive help. Start with, for example, **aaa authentication ?** and follow along. Speaking of following along, let us complete this subject by configuring our security server. If you have decided to use non-AAA authentication, you will want to go to Chapter 11; however, if you have decided to use AAA, then Chapters 12, 13, and 14 cover TACACS+, RADIUS, and Kerberos, respectively.

Chapter 11

Configuring TACACS and Extended TACACS

In this chapter, you will learn about:

- Distinguishing the various security servers
- Establishing the server host
- Setting limits on log-in attempts
- Enabling standard TACACS
- Enabling Extended TACACS
- Specifying a TACACS server at log-in

Breaking Down the Protocols

Network managers tasked with securing organizational resources need to control who can access network devices and what they can do. In Chapter 6, "Implementing Non-AAA Authentication," you learned about enable, console, line, and local passwords. Using these passwords is not without problems. Briefly, the problems are:

- You must maintain local passwords on all your routers and update them all when you change passwords. Now, in a small network, this might not seem like such a big deal; but when you have hundreds of routers, this is a mammoth task guaranteed to go wrong. You could forget one device or you might not change the password in a timely manner, not to mention the labor associated with the task itself.
- You must communicate the change to people who have a need-to-know; and you must do this in a secure manner. Unfortunately, share-level passwords have a way of getting around. Perhaps you remember the vintage Clairol commercial: you tell two people, they tell two people and

before you know it, everybody is using Clairol. Well, it is the same with share-level passwords. These passwords are supposedly secret. The problem is that a secret is only secret when one person knows it.

■ You are stymied in trying to implement your security policy to give different access levels to different individuals. Once a user gains access, it becomes difficult to control his actions. You will not get the type of granularity you need to implement robust security.

■ You log in over the network with cleartext passwords. Any individual with a packet analyzer could intercept the packets and extract the password. If you have static passwords, and the password is valid for another 89 days, then an unauthorized individual could use the password undetected for that long.

To deal with these problems and more, Cisco IOS gives you alternative methods for validating access to a router or NAS and to privileged commands on the router. One such method is Terminal Access Controller Access Control System (TACACS) — now that is a mouthful. Not only TACACS, but Cisco also gave us XTACACS and TACACS+. Cisco must like the acronym TACACS. This chapter explores TACACS and XTACACS, and compares them to TACACS+, which you will cover in Chapter 12. In addition, Cisco adopted the RADIUS and Kerberos open standards, which you will cover in Chapters 13 and 14, respectively.

Whatever system you elect to use, you will need an appropriate server. Generally, the TACACS server is a daemon running on a UNIX host. You can acquire a commercial off-the-shelf (COTS) server or you can develop it yourself. The following links provide information on TACACS/XTACACS servers:

■ Shiva LanRover Access Switch, Remote Access Server (http://www.intel.com)
■ SIPRNET XTACACS server (http://www.nic.mil/ftp/)
■ TACACS and XTACACS (http://www.linux.org.ve/pub/Linux/network/daemons/readme.XTACACS)
■ xtacacsd (http://www.netplex-tech.com)

Configuring these servers is highly dependent on the server you choose and your specific needs. These servers are more complex than simple passwords, with little control over authorization granularity. What server your organization selects is a function of your risk and your comfort level. Again, your organization needs to do the tough stuff — risk assessment and analysis. Notwithstanding these issues, you will learn some of the configuration commands and a little of the capability of the various protocols in this chapter as well as Chapters 12, 13, and 14. You will start with the simplest and least secure method of authentication.

TACACS provides a way to centrally validate users attempting to gain access to a router or access server. Cisco modeled basic TACACS support after the original Defense Data Network (DDN) application. TACACS and its mutations have some similarity to RADIUS and Kerberos because they all provide a centralized server that responds to client requests to authenticate. You maintain authentication information in a database on a TACACS server running, typically, on a UNIX workstation. You must configure your TACACS server before configuring the TACACS features on your Cisco router.

Cisco implemented TACACS to allow centralized control over access to routers and access servers. TACACS also provides authentication features for Cisco IOS administration tasks on the router and access server user interfaces. Should you enable TACACS, the router or access server prompts for a username and password, and then verifies the username/password pair with the TACACS server. That in a nutshell is TACACS. The remainder of this chapter describes the TACACS and Extended TACACS protocols and the various ways you can use them to secure access to your network.

Note: Cisco says TACACS and Extended TACACS are now deprecated. This author thinks that this is a fancy way for Cisco to say that they no longer support TACACS and XTACACS. But having said that, they are available for use on your router.

Understanding the TACACS Protocols

There are three variants of TACACS protocols — TACACS, XTACACS, and TACACS+ — that the Cisco IOS software currently supports. Each is a separate and unique protocol. Briefly, they are:

- TACACS. Cisco's oldest access protocol is not compatible with the TACACS+ protocol. Cisco has "deprecated" the protocol. TACACS provides for centralized user password administration. As well, it provides password checking and authentication, and notification of user actions for security and accounting purposes. Whenever a user requests some action, the router sends the username and password to a central TACACS server. The centralized server can either be a TACACS database or a database like the UNIX password file with TACACS protocol support. The server consults its access control database and either permits or denies the requested action. If you use TACACS to control access to the router and to control access to the router's privileged commands, any user with access to the router has access to the privileged commands because TACACS cannot distinguish a log-in attempt from a request to escalate one's privilege. TACACS provides authentication only. TACACS provides the advantage of being a standards-based solution that simplifies administration of security systems in multi-vendor environments. On the negative side, this protocol only works with basic password exchanges used in PAP authentication servers and does not permit configuration options. RFC 1492 provides more information on the open TACACS.
- Extended TACACS (XTACACS). An extension to the older TACACS protocol, XTACACS adds functionality to TACACS and attempts to resolve some of the limitations of the older protocol. For example, where TACACS cannot tell the difference between a log-in attempt and a request for increased privileges, XTACACS can. Extended TACACS provides information about protocol translator and router use for use in UNIX auditing trails and

accounting files. It also provides greater detail in its logging. XTACACS provides authentication as well as accounting services. Specifically, XTA-CACS supports:

- Multiple TACACS servers
- syslog: sends accounting information to a UNIX host
- connect: where the user is authenticated into the access server "shell" and can telnet or initiate SLIP, PPP, or ARA after initial authentication
- Multiple protocols and can authorize connections with SLIP, enable, PPP, ARA, EXEC, Telnet.

XTACACS has built-in support for SecurID, but it will not support any challenge-response systems. It can only take the user-supplied password and call an administrator-defined program to verify it. You will find a module that does SecurID verification supplied with it. XTACACS provides the advantage of being a standards-based solution that simplifies administration of security systems in multi-vendor environments. XTACACS is not compatible with TACACS+ and Cisco has also "deprecated" it.

- TACACS+: Cisco's newest TACACS protocol, which Cisco introduced in IOS 10.3 in the first half of 1995, is part of the AAA model. It was a total rewrite of the XTACACS protocol. TACACS+ and XTACACS are not compatible. TACACS+ was the first protocol built into AAA security services and is a logical extension of the older TACACS protocol. It provides detailed accounting information and flexible administrative control over authentication and authorization processes. Unlike TACACS, TACACS+ encrypts sensitive information (but not the header) as it crosses the network. Of the three TACACS variants, TACACS+ provides the most flexibility and control but is more complex. With TACACS+, you can separate authentication, authorization, and accounting mechanisms. Consequently, you can implement each service independently. The three services can each have a separate database. TACACS+ has built-in support for S/key. The basic protocol supports challenge/response and allows you to easily add authentication modules. The strength of TACACS+ is its flexibility. Because it is a Cisco proprietary protocol, it is not an industry standard and, consequently, not interoperable or compatible in a multi-vendor environment. You enable the use of TACACS+ through the AAA commands discussed in Chapters 8 through 10.

In Chapters 6 through 10, you learned some useful authentication, authorization, and accounting commands. Exhibit 1 identifies these alphabetically sorted Cisco IOS commands and others and their application in the various versions of TACACS. The exhibit proves something: TACACS and XTACACS are not compatible with AAA security services, only TACACS+.

Configuring TACACS and Extended TACACS

This section discusses how to enable and configure TACACS and XTACACS. You can establish TACACS-style password protection on both user and privileged levels of the system EXEC.

Exhibit 1 TACACS Command Comparison

Cisco IOS Command	TACACS	XTACACS	TACACS+
aaa accounting	No	No	Yes
aaa authentication arap	No	No	Yes
aaa authentication enable default	No	No	Yes
aaa authentication login	No	No	Yes
aaa authentication local override	No	No	Yes
aaa authentication ppp	No	No	Yes
aaa authorization	No	No	Yes
aaa new-model	No	No	Yes
arap authentication	No	No	Yes
arap use-tacacs	Yes	Yes	No
enable last-resort	Yes	Yes	No
enable use-tacacs	Yes	Yes	No
ip tacacs source-interface	Yes	Yes	Yes
login authentication	No	No	Yes
login tacacs	Yes	Yes	No
ppp authentication	Yes	Yes	Yes
ppp use-tacacs	Yes	Yes	Yes
tacacs-server attempts	Yes	No	No
tacacs-server authenticate	Yes	Yes	No
tacacs-server directed-request	Yes	Yes	Yes
tacacs-server extended	No	Yes	No
tacacs-server host	Yes	Yes	Yes
tacacs-server key	No	No	Yes
tacacs-server last-resort	Yes	Yes	No
tacacs-server notify	Yes	Yes	No
tacacs-server optional-passwords	Yes	Yes	No
tacacs-server retransmit	Yes	Yes	No
tacacs-server timeout	Yes	Yes	Yes

To use TACACS or XTACACS for router authentication, you must first set up and administer a server. This host gives you the facility to centrally manage the authentication mechanism for the routers in your organization. This way, you do not have to manage the passwords on all the routers, only the one on the server.

Should you decide to use Extended TACACS, you can download the software from Cisco's Using File Transfer Protocol (FTP) site.

Note: You cannot use TACACS and Extended TACACS commands after you have initialized AAA. To identify the commands you can use with the three versions, refer to Exhibit 1.

The first thing you need to do is declare the TACACS server or host.

Establishing the TACACS Server Host

The `tacacs-server host` command allows you to specify the names of the IP host or hosts maintaining a TACACS server. Because the TACACS software searches for the hosts in the order specified, this feature can be useful for setting up a list of preferred servers.

With TACACS and XTACACS, the `tacacs-server retransmit` command allows you to modify the number of times the system software searches the list of TACACS servers (from the default of two times) and the interval it waits for a reply (from the default of five seconds).

To define the number of times the Cisco IOS software searches the list of servers, and how long the server waits for a reply, use the following commands in global configuration mode as needed for your system configuration:

```
2501-1(config)#tacacs-server host hostname [port integer]
    [timeout integer]
```

For the keyword `hostname`, you specify either a TACACS hostname or the IP address of the host. To explain by example:

```
2501-1(config)#tacacs-server host 10.1.0.6
```

This tells the router that it can find the TACACS server at the IP address 10.1.0.6. This in itself is dangerous because the router will not allow anyone in when it cannot communicate with the host at address 10.1.0.6.

Use the `port` keyword to specify you want to enumerate the port with the `integer` keyword. The default port is 49. You can specify any value from 1 to 65,535.

Another optional keyword is `timeout`. This selection, when chosen, overrides the global timeout value set with the `tacacs-server timeout` global configuration command for the server. You can specify timeout with the keyword `integer`, which is the value in seconds of the timeout interval. The value of `integer` is any number from 1 to 1000.

Enabling the Extended TACACS Mode

While standard TACACS provides only username and password information, XTACACS mode provides information about the terminal requests to help set up UNIX auditing trails and accounting files for tracking the use of protocol translators, access servers, and routers. The information includes responses from these network devices and validation of user requests.

An unsupported XTACACS server is available via FTP from the Cisco site for UNIX users who want to create the auditing programs.

Once you configure TACACS, moving to XTACACS is child's play. Just issue the following global configuration command:

```
2501-1(config)#tacacs-server extended
```

To disable XTACACS, use the **no tacacs-server extended** command.

> **Note:** When configuring XTACACS, any usernames that you define locally the router will use. The router will not go to the TACACS server for authentication.

Disabling Password Checking at the User Level

When the TACACS server does not respond to a log-in request, the Cisco IOS software denies the request by default. Naturally, this may cause problems. However, you can prevent that log-in failure in one of the following two ways:

- Allow a user to access privileged EXEC mode when that user enters the password set by the enable command.
- Allow the user to access the privileged EXEC mode without further question.

To specify one of these features, use either of the following commands in global configuration mode:

```
2501-1(config)#tacacs-server last-resort password
2501-1(config)#tacacs-server last-resort succeed
```

The first command allows the router to use the enable secret EXEC password to authenticate a user when it cannot talk to the TACACS server. The second command allows the user to enable without further question. The tacacs-server last-resort {password | succeed} command is not available with TACACS+.

> **Caution:** Although Cisco provides it, never use the tacacs-server last-resort succeed command. Configuring this allows any user to authenticate automatically when the server is unreachable. So, your friendly neighborhood cracker perpetrates a denial-of-service attack on your TACACS server and then logs into the router. Bingo, bango, bongo; the cracker got control. It is even more insidious. The cracker does not even have to crash your server; he just needs to prevent your router from talking to the TACACS server for a period sufficiently long enough to get authenticated.

Setting Optional Password Verification

You can specify that the router makes the first TACACS request to a TACACS server without password verification. To do so, use the following command in global configuration mode:

```
2501-1(config)#tacacs-server optional-passwords
```

When the user enters the log-in name, the router transmits the log-in request with the name and a zero-length password. If the TACACS server accepts, the router completes the log-in procedure. Should the TACACS server refuse this request, the terminal server prompts for a password and tries again when the user supplies a password.

The TACACS server must support authentication for users without passwords to make use of this feature. This feature supports all TACACS requests, including login, SLIP, and enable.

Setting Notification of User Actions

The `tacacs-server notify` command allows you to configure the XTACACS server to send a message when a user does the following:

- Makes a TCP connection
- Enters the `enable` command
- Logs out

To specify that the TACACS server sends notification, use the following command in global configuration mode:

```
2501-1(config)#tacacs-server notify {connections [always] |
   enable | logout [always] | slip [always]}
```

In the above command, the keyword `connections` specifies that the router transmits a message when a user makes a TCP connection. Optionally, for SLIP and PPP connections, you can specify that the router sends this message even when a user is not logged in with the keyword `always`. You can only use this keyword with the `logout` and `slip` keywords. The `enable` keyword specifies that the router transmits a message when a user enters the `enable` command. Use the `logout` keyword to specify that the router transmits a message when a user logs out. And finally, the `slip` keyword specifies that the router transmits a message when a user starts a SLIP or PPP session.

A router background process tries the retransmission of the message for up to five minutes. The terminal user, however, receives an immediate response, allowing access to the terminal.

Note: The `tacacs-server notify` command is available only when you have set up an XTACACS server using the latest Cisco XTACACS server software, available via FTP. It is not available in TACACS+ because Cisco replaced it with `aaa accounting` commands.

Setting Authentication of User Actions

For a SLIP or PPP session, you can specify that if a user tries to start a session, the TACACS software requires a response (either from the TACACS server host or the router) indicating whether the user can start the session. You can specify that the TACACS software perform authentication even when a user is not logged in; you can also request that the TACACS software install access lists.

If a user issues the `enable` command, the TACACS software must respond, indicating whether the user can give the command. You can also specify authentication when a user enters the `enable` command.

To configure any of these scenarios, use the following command in global configuration mode:

```
2501-1(config)#tacacs-server authenticate {connections
  [always] enable | slip [always] [access-lists]}
```

In the above command, the keyword `connections` specifies that the router transmits a message when a user makes a TCP connection. Optionally, for SLIP and PPP connections, you can specify that the router sends this message even when a user is not logged in with the keyword `always`. You can only use this keyword with the `logout` and `slip` keywords. The `enable` keyword specifies that the router transmits a message when a user enters the `enable` command. Use the `logout` keyword to specify that the router transmits a message when a user logs out. And finally, the `slip` keyword specifies that the router transmits a message when a user starts a SLIP or PPP session.

Note: The `tacacs-server authenticate` command is available only when you have set up an XTACACS server using the latest Cisco XTACACS server software, which is available via FTP.

You can configure the router or NAS to send only the username to the TACACS server when a direct request is issued. That is, the IOS sends only the username before the @ sign to the server. This allows you to redirect a request to any server, and the router or NAS will send only the username. When you use the no form of the command, the router queries the list of servers, starts with the first one in the list, sends the whole string, and accepts the first response that it gets from the server. Use the following global configuration command:

```
2501-1(config)#tacacs-server directed-request
```

This command is useful for sites that developed a TACACS server that parses the whole string and makes decisions based on it. When you enable this command, your users can only log in with configured servers. When the host name specified by the user does not match the IP address of a TACACS server, then the router rejects user input.

Setting Limits on Log-In Attempts

The `tacacs-server attempts` command allows you to specify the number of log-in attempts that a user can make on a line set up for TACACS. Use the following command in global configuration mode to limit log-in attempts:

```
2501-1(config)#tacacs-server attempts count
```

Any number from 1 to 1000 is acceptable for the keyword `count`. Select a number that is reasonable for the keyword `count` (e.g., 3). Otherwise, attackers will attempt dictionary or brute-force password attacks.

Specify the number of times the server will search the list of TACACS and XTACACS server hosts before giving up with the following command:

```
2501-1(config)#tacacs-server retransmit retries
```

Keyword `retries` is an integer specifying the retransmit count. You can specify any number from 0 to 100 for this keyword.

Use the following global configuration command to set the interval the server waits for a TACACS or XTACACS server host to reply:

```
2501-1(config)#tacacs-server timeout seconds
```

Use a value for the keyword `seconds` from 1 to 1000 to specify the interval in seconds. The default is 5 seconds.

Setting TACACS Password Protection at the User Level

You need to configure the lines and the console that will use TACACS. To enable the TACACS-style user ID and password-checking, use the following commands starting first in global configuration mode:

```
2501-1(config)#line vty 0 4
2501-1(config-line)#login tacacs
2501-1(config-line)#exit
2501-1(config)#line console 0
2501-1(config-line)#login tacacs
```

Note: When configuring TACACS, the router will use any usernames locally defined. The router will not go to the TACACS server for authentication.

Setting TACACS Password Protection at the Privileged Level

You can set the TACACS protocol to determine whether a user can access the privileged EXEC level. To do so, use the following command in global configuration mode:

```
2501-1(config)#enable use-tacacs
```

This will set the TACACS-style user ID and password-checking mechanism at the privileged EXEC level. When you set TACACS password protection at the privileged EXEC level, the EXEC enable command will ask for both a new username and a password. Then the router passes this information to the TACACS server for authentication. If you are using the XTACACS, it also passes any existing UNIX user identification code to the server.

Caution: If you use the enable use-tacacs command, you must also specify tacacs-server authenticate enable; otherwise, you will lock yourself out.

For example, to set TACACS verification on the privileged EXEC-level log-in sequence, use the following global configuration commands:

```
2501-1(config)#enable use-tacacs
2501-1(config)#tacacs-server authenticate enable
```

Note: When used without XTACACS, this task allows anyone with a valid username and password to access the privileged command level, creating a potential security problem. This is because the TACACS query resulting from entering the enable command is indistinguishable from an attempt to log in without XTACACS.

Enabling TACACS and XTACACS for Use

This section provides examples of how to apply TACACS and XTACACS to PPP and ARA.

Enabling Extended TACACS for PPP Authentication

You can use XTACACS for authentication within PPP sessions. To do so, use the following commands in interface configuration mode:

```
2501-1(config-if)#ppp authentication {chap | chap pap | pap
   chap | pap} [if-needed] [list-name | default] [callin]
2501-1(config-if)#ppp use-tacacs [single-line]
```

Enabling Standard TACACS for ARA Authentication

You can use the standard TACACS protocol for authentication within AppleTalk
Remote Access (ARA) protocol sessions. To do so, use the following commands
starting in line configuration mode:

```
2501-1(config-line)#arap use-tacacs
2501-1(config-line)#autoselect arap
2501-1(config-line)#autoselect during-login
2501-1(config-line)#! Optionally, have the ARA session start
   automatically at user login
```

The arap use-tacacs single-line command is useful when integrating
TACACS with other authentication systems that require a cleartext version of the
user's password. Such systems include one-time passwords, token card systems,
and others.

By using the optional during-login argument with the autoselect command, you can display the username or password prompt without pressing the
Return key. While the router displays username or password name, you can
choose to answer these prompts or start sending packets from an autoselected
protocol.

The remote user logs in through ARA as follows:

Step 1. When prompted for a username by the ARA application, the remote user
enters **username*password** and presses Enter.
Step 2. When prompted for password by the ARA application, the remote user
enters **arap** and presses Enter.

Enabling Extended TACACS for ARA Authentication

You can use XTACACS for authentication for AppleTalk Remote Access (ARA)
protocol sessions. The XTACACS server software is available via FTP (see the
README file in the ftp.cisco.com directory).

After installing an XTACACS server with ARA support, use the following
commands in line configuration mode on each line:

```
2501-1(config-line)#arap use-tacacs
2501-1(config-line)#autoselect arap
2501-1(config-line)#! Optionally, enable autoselection of
   ARA
2501-1(config-line)#autoselect
2501-1(config-line)#! Optionally, have the ARA session start
   during-login automatically at user login
```

By using the optional during-login argument with the `autoselect` command, you can display the username or password prompt without pressing the Return key. While the router presents the Username or Password, you can choose to answer these prompts, or to start sending packets from an autoselected protocol.

Enabling TACACS to Use a Specific IP Address

You can designate a fixed source IP address for all outgoing TACACS packets. The feature enables TACACS to use the IP address of a specified interface for all outgoing TACACS packets. This is especially useful when your router has many interfaces and you want to make sure that all TACACS packets from a particular router have the same IP address.

To enable TACACS to use the address of a specified interface for all outgoing TACACS packets, use the following global configuration command:

```
2501-1(config)#ip tacacs source-interface subinterface-name
```

You must substitute the interface name to for the keyword `subinterface-name` to enable TACACS to use the IP address of a specified interface for all outgoing TACACS packets.

Specifying a TACACS Host at Log-In

You can specify a TACACS host when you dial in or use the `login` command. The router will only search the specified host for user authentication information. For example, user ptdavis specifies the TACACS host `host1` to authenticate the password.

```
2501-1>login
Username: ptdavis@host1
Translating "HOST1"...domain server (10.1.0.111) [OK]
```

Practice Session

In this Practice Session, you will practice the following:

- Logging in
- Saving log data
- Switching modes
- Pasting configuration files
- Enabling TACACS
- Enabling XTACACS
- Enabling and saving syslog data
- Logging out

1. Log in to the SimRouter Web page.
2. Double-click on router 2501-1 to telnet to that router. This will open a console session.

3. Enter your **Username** and **Password** at the applicable prompt. These are the ones you set up in Chapter 2. You will need to hit the Enter key twice to get to the > prompt.
4. Again, save the log for your session. To do this, select | Terminal | Start Logging | from the menu bar in the Telnet window. The Telnet client will ask you where you wish to store the log and with what name. Your choice. You are going to save the log so that when you build a configuration file in this Practice Session, you can cut-and-paste this in Chapter 12 as a starting point, rather than having to enter the same information each Practice Session.
5. Enter the enable mode:

```
2501-1#enable
```

6. When prompted to put in the enable secret password, enter **oscar**.
7. Type **terminal length 0**. This command instructs the router to scroll through long command output without pausing (the —More— message).
8. You will paste the running-config that you saved from the Chapter 10 log. At the 2501-2# prompt, type **config t**.
9. If you did not do it in Chapter 10, open your log file with the text editor of your choice (e.g., use | Start | Programs | Accessories | Notepad |). Do a find on sh running-config and copy from the first "!" to "end." At the 2501-2(config)# prompt, paste this configuration.
10. Start by turning on extended TACACS mode. Type **tacacs-server extended** and press Enter.
11. Next, tell the router the address of the TACACS servers. Type **tacacs-server host 10.8.0.5** and press Enter.
12. Tell the router to use TACACS to authenticate enabled mode access, with the configured enable password as fallback should the TACACS server become inaccessible. Type **enable use-tacacs** and press Enter.
13. Type **tacacs-server authenticate enable** and press Enter.
14. Type **enable last-resort password** and press Enter.
15. Similarly, should the TACACS server fail to respond, configure the router to allow users to use a local password or the enable password to log in to the router. Type **tacacs-server last-resort password** and press Enter.
16. Configure the router to authenticate users before they can use certain commands at the router EXEC prompt. Type **tacacs-server authenticate connections** and press Enter.
17. Type **tacacs-server authenticate enable** and press Enter.
18. Authenticate SLIP as well. Type **tacacs-server authenticate slip** and press Enter.
19. Now use TACACS instead of CHAP or PAP. Type **ppp use-tacacs** and press Enter.
20. Of course, you will want to log action on the router. Type the following and press Enter after each command:

```
2501-1(config)#tacacs-server notify connections
2501-1(config)#tacacs-server notify enable
2501-1(config)#tacacs-server notify slip
2501-1(config)#tacacs-server notify logout
```

21. Now you must apply TACACS authentication to an interface or line. Type the following and press Enter after each command:

```
2501-1(config)#line console 0
2501-1(config-line)#login tacacs
2501-1(config-line)#exit
2501-1(config)#line aux 0
2501-1(config-line)#no exec
2501-1(config-line)#login tacacs
```

22. Type **sh running-config** and press Enter. You will use this new configuration to start the next Practice Session.
23. Type **quit** to log out from router 2501-1. Close the Telnet window and return to the SimRouter Topology Map.
24. Click on Log Out on the SimRouter Web page.

Security and Audit Checklist

1. Do you use TACACS service in your organization?
   - Yes
   - No
2. Do you use the features of XTACACS in your organization?
   - Yes
   - No
3. Do you know the vendor of your TACACS/XTACACS server?
   - Yes
   - No
4. Is there support for your software?
   - Vendor
   - Open source
   - Third-party
   - In-house
   - Other
   - None
5. Do you support multiple XTACACS servers?
   - Yes
   - No
6. Are you using syslog for accounting information?
   - Yes
   - No
7. Are you using any form of extended user authentication?
   - Yes
   - No
8. Do you use the last-resort function of TACACS?
   - Yes
   - No
9. Do you use the tacacs-server last-resort succeed command?
   - Yes
   - No

10. Do you use the `tacacs-server optional-passwords` command?
    - Yes
    - No
11. Do you use the `tacacs-server notify` command?
    - Yes
    - No
12. Do you use the `notify` keyword for:
    - Connections?
    - Enable?
    - Log-out?
    - SLIP?
13. Do you use the `tacacs-server authenticate` command?
    - Yes
    - No
14. Do you use the `authenticate` keyword for:
    - Connections?
    - Enable?
    - Log-out?
    - SLIP?
15. Do you use the `tacacs-server directed-response` command?
    - Yes
    - No
16. Is the use of this command appropriate?
    - Yes
    - No
17. Do you use the `tacacs-server attempts` command?
    - Yes
    - No
18. Is the number of attempts appropriate?
    - Yes
    - No
19. Does it adhere to the organization's password policy and standard?
    - Yes
    - No
20. Do you use the `tacacs-server retransmit` command?
    - Yes
    - No
21. Is the number of retries appropriate?
    - Yes
    - No
22. Do you use the `tacacs-server timeout` command?
    - Yes
    - No
23. Is the timeout interval appropriate?
    - Yes
    - No
24. Does it adhere to the organization's password policy and standard?
    - Yes
    - No

25. Does TACACS apply to:
    - Lines?
    - Console?
    - Enable?
    - PPP?
    - ARAP?

Conclusion

So there you have TACACS and XTACACS (extended TACACS). Cisco has deprecated these protocols and suggest that you do not use them. However, there is service software available and their use does beat just line, console, and enable passwords — especially if you have many routers. Maintaining all the passwords on all the devices starts to become a nightmare. TACACS/XTACACS helps a little. The chapter began with a short discussion of the various TACACS flavors: TACACS, XTACACS, and TACACS+. In this chapter, you learned how to establish the server host and how to enable standard and XTACACS. You also saw how to set limits on log-in attempts.

In Chapter 12, you continue your exploration of security servers. Chapter 12 covers TACACS+, a protocol that Cisco definitely supports.

Chapter 12

Configuring TACACS+

In this chapter, you will learn about:

- Understanding TACACS+
- Comparing TACACS+ to RADIUS
- Establishing the server host
- Enabling TACACS+

Understanding the TACACS+ Protocol

TACACS+ is a security application that provides centralized validation of users attempting to gain access to a router or network access server. TACACS+ services are maintained in a database on a TACACS+ daemon running, typically, on a UNIX or Windows NT workstation. You must have access to and configure a TACACS+ server before the configured TACACS+ features on your network access server are available.

Note: TACACS+, in conjunction with AAA, is a separate and distinct protocol from the earlier TACACS or XTACACS, which are now deprecated. After you enable AAA, you can no longer configure many of the original TACACS and XTACACS commands.

TACACS+ provides for separate and modular authentication, authorization, and accounting facilities. TACACS+ allows for a single access control server (the TACACS+ daemon) to provide each service — authentication, authorization, and accounting — independently. Each service can be tied into a database of its own to take advantage of other services available on that server or on the network, depending on the capabilities of the daemon.

The goal of TACACS+ is to provide a methodology for managing multiple network access points from a single management service. The Cisco family of access servers and routers and the Cisco IOS user interface (for both routers and access servers) can be network access servers.

Network access points enable traditional "dumb" terminals, terminal emulators, workstations, personal computers (PCs), and routers in conjunction with suitable adapters (e.g., modems or ISDN adapters) to communicate using protocols such as the Point-to-Point Protocol (PPP), Serial Line Internet Protocol (SLIP), Compressed SLIP (CSLIP), or AppleTalk Remote Access (ARA) Protocol. That is, a network access server provides connections to a single user, to a network or subnetwork, and to interconnected networks. The entities connected to the network through a network access server are called network access clients; for example, a PC running PPP over a voice-grade circuit is a network access client. TACACS+, administered through the AAA security services, can provide the following services:

- *Authentication:* Provides complete control of authentication through log-in and password dialog, challenge and response, and messaging support. The authentication facility provides the ability to conduct an arbitrary dialog with the user (e.g., after the client provides a log-in and password, to challenge the user with a number of questions, such as home address, mother's maiden name, service type, and social insurance or security number). In addition, the TACACS+ authentication service supports sending messages to user screens. For example, a message could notify users that they must change their existing password to comply with the company's password aging standard.
- *Authorization:* Provides fine-grained control over user capabilities for the duration of the user's session, including but not limited to setting auto-commands, access control, session duration, and protocol support. You can also enforce restrictions on what commands a user can execute with the TACACS+ authorization feature.
- *Accounting:* Collects and sends information used for billing, auditing, and reporting to the TACACS+ daemon. Network managers can use the accounting facility to track user activity for a security audit or to provide information for user billing. Accounting records include user identities, start and stop times, executed commands (such as PPP), number of packets, and number of bytes.

The TACACS+ protocol provides authentication between the network access server and the TACACS+ daemon, and it ensures confidentiality because all protocol exchanges between a network access server and a TACACS+ daemon are encrypted.

You need a system running TACACS+ daemon software to use the TACACS+ functionality on your network access server. Cisco makes the TACACS+ protocol specification available as a draft RFC for those customers interested in developing their own TACACS+ software.

You have choices for your TACACS+ server. Of course, Cisco provides one solution but there are others. For example, you can get the following TACACS+ servers:

- 802.1X/TACACS+ (http://www.mtghouse.com/products_priv.html)
- ActivPack for Windows NT (http://www.safedata.com/)
- Ascend TACACS+ (ftp://ftp.ascend.com)
- Defender TACACS+ Servers (http://www.symantec.com)
- Free TACACS+ daemon (http://www.lirex.com/~delian/tacacs/)
- SafeWord TACACS+ servers (http://www.securecomputing.com)
- tac_plusv2.1.tar (ftp://cio.cisco.com)

The underlying architecture of the TACACS+ protocol complements the independent AAA architecture. The protocol designers intended that TACACS+ scale as networks grow and adapt to new security technology as the market matures.

Comparing TACACS+ and RADIUS

Should you wish to use a security server and Cisco's AAA security, then you have two primary choices for the security protocols to control dial-up access into networks: Cisco's TACACS+ and Livingston Enterprise's RADIUS. Cisco commits to supporting both protocols. With the release of Cisco IOS Release 11.1 in February 1996, Cisco offered support for the RADIUS protocol. Cisco does not intend to compete with RADIUS or influence their clients to use TACACS+. So, choose the solution that best meets your needs. Chapter 13 covers RADIUS in more detail; the intent of this section is to compare and contrast TACACS+ and RADIUS so that you can make an educated choice between the two at some point.

Cisco seriously evaluated RADIUS as a security protocol before developing TACACS+. Consequently, Cisco included many RADIUS features in the TACACS+ protocol to meet the needs of the growing dial-up access control and security market.

In Chapter 7, "Implementing AAA Security Services," you saw a high-level comparison of TACACS+ and RADIUS. Before continuing with TACACS+ in this chapter and RADIUS in the next, take a deeper look into these two protocols. A good place to start is communicating with the server.

Transport Protocol

RADIUS uses UDP while TACACS+ uses TCP. TCP offers several advantages over UDP. As you learned in Chapter 2, TCP offers a connection-oriented transport while UDP offers best-effort delivery. RADIUS requires additional programmable variables such as retransmit attempts and timeouts to compensate for best-effort transport, but it lacks the level of built-in support that a TCP transport offers; for example:

- Using TCP, the back-end authentication mechanism provides a separate acknowledgment (TCP ACK) that it has received a request, regardless of its load or capacity.
- TCP provides an immediate indication of a crashed (or not running) server (RST packets). You can determine when a server has crashed and recovered when you use long-lived TCP connections. UDP cannot tell the difference between a downed server, a slow server, and a nonexistent server.

- Using TCP keepalives, you can detect server crashes out-of-band with actual requests. Your router can maintain simultaneous connections to multiple servers and you only need to send messages to the ones that are known to be up and running.
- TCP is more scalable and adapts to growing as well as congested networks.

Packet Encryption

RADIUS encrypts only the password in the access-request packet from the client to the server. The remainder of the packet remains in the clear. An unauthorized third party could capture other information, such as username, authorized services, and accounting data.

TACACS+ encrypts the entire body of the packet but leaves a standard TACACS+ header. Within the header is a field that indicates whether or not the body is encrypted. For debugging network problems, it is useful to have the body of the packets in the clear. However, normal operation will fully encrypt the body of the packet for more secure communications.

Authentication and Authorization

RADIUS combines authentication and authorization. The access-accept packets sent by the RADIUS server to the client contain authorization information. This makes it difficult to decouple authentication and authorization.

TACACS+ uses the AAA architecture, thereby separating authentication, authorization, and accounting. This allows separate authentication solutions that can still use TACACS+ for authorization and accounting. To illustrate, you may want to use Kerberos authentication and TACACS+ authorization and accounting. This is entirely possible with TACACS+, but not with RADIUS. After a NAS authenticates on a Kerberos server, it requests authorization information from a TACACS+ server without having to re-authenticate. The NAS (network access server) informs the TACACS+ server that it has successfully authenticated on a Kerberos server, and the server then provides the authorization information.

During a session, when you require additional authorization checking, the access server checks with a TACACS+ server to determine whether the user is granted permission to use a particular command. This provides greater control over executable commands on the access server while decoupling from the authentication mechanism.

Multi-Protocol Support

TACACS+ supports the following protocols:

- AppleTalk Remote Access (ARA) protocol
- NetBIOS Frame Protocol Control protocol
- Novell Asynchronous Services Interface (NASI)
- X.25 PAD connection

RADIUS does not offer multi-protocol support.

Router Management

RADIUS does not allow users to control executable commands on a router; therefore, it is not as useful for router management or as flexible for terminal services.

TACACS+ provides two ways to control the authorization of router commands on a per-user or per-group basis. First, you can assign privilege levels to commands and have the router verify with the TACACS+ server whether or not the user is authorized at the specified privilege level. Second, you can explicitly specify in the TACACS+ server, on a per-user or per-group basis, the allowable commands.

Interoperability

The RADIUS standard does not guarantee interoperability. Although several vendors implement RADIUS clients, this does not mean they are interoperable. There are approximately 45 standard RADIUS ATTRIBUTES. Cisco currently implements most of them and is adding more. If you use only the standard ATTRIBUTES in your servers, you can probably interoperate between several vendors, providing those vendors implement the same ATTRIBUTES. However, many vendors implement extensions that are proprietary ATTRIBUTES. When a customer uses one of those vendor-specific extended ATTRIBUTES, interoperability is not possible.

Overhead

Owing to the previous differences between TACACS+ and RADIUS, the amount of traffic generated between the client and server will differ. In general, traffic for RADIUS is less because it uses UDP, a connectionless protocol.

In addition, RADIUS uses less CPU overhead and consumes less memory than TACACS+.

Understanding TACACS+ Operation

Exhibit 1 illustrates the log-in process. When a user attempts a simple ASCII log-in by authenticating to a network access server using TACACS+, the following process typically occurs:

1. After connection establishment, the network access server will contact the TACACS+ server to obtain a username prompt, which the router then displays to the user. The user enters a username and the NAS then contacts the TACACS+ daemon to obtain a password prompt. The NAS displays the password prompt to the user, and the user enters a password.
2. The router then sends the username and password credentials to the TACACS+ daemon.

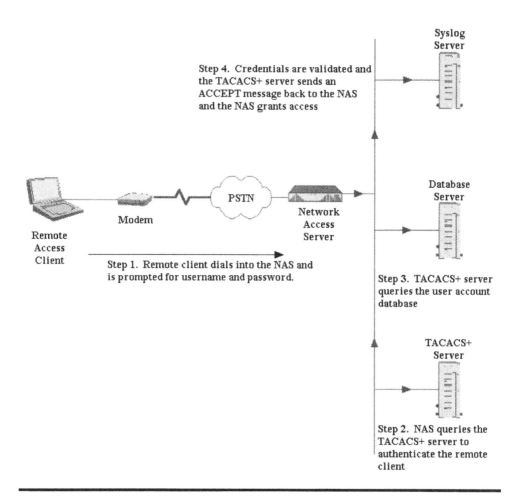

Step 4. Credentials are validated and the TACACS+ server sends an ACCEPT message back to the NAS and the NAS grants access

Step 1. Remote client dials into the NAS and is prompted for username and password.

Step 3. TACACS+ server queries the user account database

Step 2. NAS queries the TACACS+ server to authenticate the remote client

Exhibit 1   TACACS+ Log-On Process

> **Note:** TACACS+ allows an arbitrary conversation to be held between the daemon and the user until the daemon receives enough information to authenticate the user. This is usually done by prompting for a username and password combination, but may include other items (e.g., mother's maiden name), all under the control of the TACACS+ daemon.

3. The TACACS+ server will query a user database and compare the credentials with the information stored for the user.
4. The NAS will eventually receive one of the following responses from the TACACS+ daemon:
    a. *ACCEPT.* TACACS+ authenticates the user and service can begin. If you configure the NAS to require authorization, authorization will begin at this time.

    b. *REJECT.* The user fails to authenticate. Depending on the TACACS+ version, the daemon will deny the user further access or prompt the user to retry the log-in sequence.

    c. *ERROR.* An error occurred at some time during authentication. The error is either with the daemon or with the network connection between the daemon and the NAS. When the NAS receives an ERROR response, it typically tries to use an alternative method for authenticating the user.

    d. *CONTINUE.* The NAS prompts the user for additional authentication information.

A further explanation of the log-in process is needed. A PAP log-in is similar to an ASCII log-in, except that the username and password arrive at the NAS in a PAP protocol packet instead of the user typing, so the server does not prompt the user. PPP CHAP log-ins are also similar in principle. Both PAP and CHAP, used as authentication methods for the Point-to-Point Protocol, send credentials through the PPP link rather than prompting the user after the establishment of a connection. For example, when a client dials the ISP, client software uses PPP to encapsulate traffic between the remote user and the router or NAS. PPP can send authentication information in the form of PAP and CHAP packets to the NAS for authentication and authorization purposes. Remember that PAP sends passwords in cleartext, whereas CHAP uses a three-way handshake to validate each side of the PPP link. As you learned earlier, CHAP encrypts the username and password exchanged during the handshake.

Following authentication, the router will also require the user to undergo an additional authorization phase when you have enabled authorization on the NAS. Users must first successfully complete TACACS+ authentication before proceeding to TACACS+ authorization.

When you require TACACS+ authorization, the router again contacts the TACACS+ daemon and it returns an ACCEPT or REJECT authorization response. If TACACS+ returns an ACCEPT response, the response will contain data in the form of attributes that the IOS uses to direct the EXEC or NETWORK session for that user, determining the services that the user can access. Services the user may have authority for include the following:

- Telnet, rlogin, Point-to-Point Protocol (PPP), Serial Line Internet Protocol (SLIP), or EXEC services
- Connection parameters, including the host or client IP address, access list, and user timeouts

TACACS+ Configuration Task List

To configure your router to support TACACS+, you must perform the following tasks:

1. Use the `aaa new-model` global configuration command to enable AAA. You must configure AAA when you plan to use TACACS+. For more information about using the `aaa new-model` command, refer to Chapter 7, "Implementing AAA Security Services."

2. Use the `tacacs-server host` command to specify the IP address of one or more TACACS+ daemons. Use the `tacacs-server key` command to specify an encryption key that the network access server and the TACACS+ daemon will use to encrypt all exchanges. Configure this same key on the TACACS+ daemon.

3. Use the `aaa authentication` global configuration command to define method lists that use TACACS+ for authentication. For more information on using the `aaa authentication` command, refer to Chapter 8, "Implementing AAA Authentication."

4. Use `line` and `interface` commands to apply the defined method lists to various interfaces.

5. Where needed, use the `aaa authorization` global command to configure authorization for the network access server. Unlike authentication, which you can configure per line or per interface, you configure authorization globally for the entire network access server. For more information on using the `aaa authorization` command, refer to Chapter 9, "Implementing AAA Authorization."

6. Where needed, use the `aaa accounting` command to enable accounting for TACACS+ connections. For more information on using the `aaa accounting` command, refer to Chapter 10, "Implementing AAA Accounting."

Configuring TACACS+

Configuring TACACS+ is fairly straightforward. You just perform the following tasks:

1. Identify the TACACS+ server host
2. Set the TACACS+ authentication key
3. Specify TACACS+ authentication
4. Specify TACACS+ authorization
5. Specify TACACS+ accounting

Identifying the TACACS+ Server Host

The `tacacs-server host` command enables you to specify the names of the IP host or hosts hosting a TACACS+ server. Because the TACACS+ software searches for the hosts in the order specified, this feature can be useful for setting up a list of preferred daemons.

To specify a TACACS+ host, use the following command in global configuration mode:

```
2501-1(config)#tacacs-server host name [single-connection]
   [port integer] [timeout integer] [key string]
```

Substitute the IP address or host name of the remote TACACS+ server for the keyword host. Use the `single-connection` keyword to specify single-connection (only valid with CiscoSecure Release 1.0.1 or later). Rather than have the router open and close a TCP connection to the daemon each time it must communicate, the single-connection option maintains a single open connection between the router and the daemon. That is, the client will maintain a single open connection when exchanging information with the TACACS+ server. This is more efficient because it allows the daemon to handle a higher number of TACACS operations.

Note: The daemon must support single-connection mode for this to be effective; otherwise, the connection between the network access server and the daemon will lock up or you will receive spurious errors.

Use the port `integer` argument to specify the TCP port number to use when making connections to the TACACS+ daemon. This is the port where the client will send requests. Obviously, this value should match what you set up as the port on the TACACS+ server. The default port number is 49. You can, however, select any port from 1 to 65,535.

Use the timeout `integer` argument to specify the period of time (in seconds) the router will wait for a response from the daemon before it times out and declares an error. The *integer* can be any number from 1 to 1000.

Note: Specifying the timeout value with the `tacacs-server host` command overrides the default timeout value set with the `tacacs-server timeout` command for this server only.

Use the key `string` argument to specify an encryption key for encrypting and decrypting all traffic between the network access server and the TACACS+ daemon.

Note: Specifying the encryption key with the `tacacs-server host` command overrides the default key set by the global configuration `tacacs-server key` command for this server only.

Because some of the parameters of the `tacacs-server host` command override global settings made by the `tacacs-server timeout` and `tacacs-server key` commands, you can use this command to enhance security on your network by uniquely configuring individual TACACS+ connections.

Thus, a simple example of the commands you need is:

```
2501-1(config)#aaa new-model
2501-1(config)#tacacs-server host 10.8.0.8
```

The first command sets up the AAA features on the router. The second command specifies the IP address of the TACACS+ server.

Setting the TACACS+ Authentication Key

To set the TACACS+ authentication key and encryption key, use the following command in global configuration mode:

```
2501-1(config)#tacacs-server key key
```

Set the keyword key to match the one that you used on the TACACS+ daemon.

Note: You must configure the same key on the TACACS+ daemon for encryption to be successful.

To continue the simple example started above:

```
2501-1(config)#aaa new-model
2501-1(config)#tacacs-server host 10.8.0.8
2501-1(config)#tacacs-server key secret
```

The last command sets the encryption key to secret, which coincidentally is the most popular six-character password. So, perhaps you should not use it yourself.

Specifying TACACS+ Authentication

After you have identified the TACACS+ daemon and defined an associated TACACS+ encryption key, you need to define method lists for TACACS+ authentication. Because AAA facilitates TACACS+ authentication, you need to issue the aaa authentication command, specifying TACACS+ as the authentication method.

To use the TACACS+ server for authentication, you would use a command such as:

```
2501-1(config)#aaa authentication commands 15 default
    tacacs+ none
```

This command forces authentication for all commands a user enters in the router for privilege levels 1 to 15. This command also specifies (keyword none) that no authentication takes place when TACACS+ authentication returns an error to the router.

Take a look at some more detailed examples. The following commands configure TACACS+ as the security protocol for PPP authentication.

```
2501-1(config)#aaa new-model
2501-1(config)#! Enables the AAA security services
2501-1(config)#aaa authentication ppp test tacacs+ local
```

```
2501-1(config)#! Defines the test method list for serial
   interfaces running PPP. Keyword tacacs+ specifies
   authenticate using TACACS+. When TACACS+ returns an ERROR,
   the keyword local specifies the local database as backup
2501-1(config)#tacacs-server host 10.8.0.8
2501-1(config)#! Identifies the IP address of 10.8.0.8 as the
   address of the TACACS+ server
2501-1(config)#tacacs-server key keepout
2501-1(config)#! Defines the shared encryption key as keepout
2501-1(config)#interface serial 0
2501-1(config)#! Selects the line
2501-1(config-if)#ppp authentication chap pap test
2501-1(config-if)#! Applies the test method list to s0
```

The following example configures TACACS+ as the security protocol to be used for PPP authentication, but instead of the method list "test," it uses the default method list.

```
2501-1(config)#aaa new-model
2501-1(config)#! Enables AAA security services
2501-1(config)#aaa authentication ppp default if-needed
   tacacs+ local
2501-1(config)#! Defines the default method list for serial
   interfaces running PPP. If-needed keyword means that where
   user already authenticated via ASCII login, then PPP
   authentication not. If authentication needed, the keyword
   tacacs+ specifies to use TACACS+. When TACACS+ returns an
   ERROR, the keyword local specifies the local database as
   backup
2501-1(config)#tacacs-server host 10.8.0.8
2501-1(config)#! Identifies the IP address of 10.8.0.8 as the
   address of the TACACS+ server
2501-1(config)#tacacs-server key security
2501-1(config)#! Defines the shared encryption key as
   security
2501-1(config)#interface serial 0
2501-1(config)#! Selects the line
2501-1(config)#ppp authentication default
2501-1(config-if)#! Applies the default method list to s0
```

For more information or to refresh your memory, refer to Chapter 8, "Implementing AAA Authentication."

Specifying TACACS+ Authorization

AAA authorization enables you to set parameters restricting a user's network access. You can apply authorization via TACACS+ to commands, network connections, and

EXEC sessions. Because AAA facilitates TACACS+ authorization, you need to issue the aaa authorization command, specifying TACACS+ as the authorization method.

To use the TACACS+ server for authorization, you would use a command such as:

```
2501-1(config)#aaa authorization commands 15 tacacs+ none
```

This command applies authorization against TACACS+ for all commands at exec level 15 or lower. Again, the none keyword specifies that no authorization occurs when the TACACS+ server returns an error, but not a reject or accept message.

The following example configures TACACS+ as the security protocol to be used for PPP authentication using the default method list, and configures network authorization via TACACS+.

```
2501-1(config)#aaa new-model
2501-1(config)#! Enables AAA security services
2501-1(config)#aaa authentication ppp default if-needed
    tacacs+ local
2501-1(config)#! Defines the default method list for serial
    interfaces running PPP. If-needed keyword means that where
    user already authenticated via ASCII login, then PPP
    authentication not. If authentication needed, the keyword
    tacacs+ specifies to use TACACS+. When TACACS+ returns an
    ERROR, the keyword local specifies the local database as
    backup
2501-1(config)#aaa authorization network tacacs+
2501-1(config)#! Configures TACACS+ authorization for all
    incoming network connections
2501-1(config)#tacacs-server host 10.8.0.8
2501-1(config)#! Identifies the IP address of 10.8.0.8 as the
    address of the TACACS+ server
2501-1(config)#tacacs-server key security
2501-1(config)#! Defines the shared encryption key as
    security
2501-1(config)#interface serial 0
2501-1(config)#! Selects the line
2501-1(config)#ppp authentication default
2501-1(config-if)#! Applies the default method list to s0
```

For more information, refer to Chapter 9, "Implementing AAA Authorization."

Specifying TACACS+ Accounting

AAA accounting allows you to track the services that users are accessing as well as the amount of network resources they are consuming. Because TACACS+

accounting is facilitated through AAA, you need to issue the `aaa accounting` command, specifying TACACS+ as the accounting method.

To use the TACACS+ server for accounting, you would use a command such as:

```
2501-1(config)#aaa accounting commands 15 default start-stop
    tacacs+
```

This command sets up logging for any command a user enters.

The following example configures TACACS+ as the security protocol to be used for PPP authentication using the default method list and configures accounting via TACACS+.

```
2501-1(config)#aaa new-model
2501-1(config)#! Enables AAA security services
2501-1(config)#aaa authentication ppp default if-needed
    tacacs+ local
2501-1(config)#! Defines the default method list for serial
    interfaces running PPP. If-needed keyword means that where
    user already authenticated via ASCII login, then PPP
    authentication not. If authentication needed, the keyword
    tacacs+ specifies to use TACACS+. When TACACS+ returns an
    ERROR, the keyword local specifies the local database as
    backup
2501-1(config)#aaa accounting network stop-only tacacs+
2501-1(config)#! Specifies that accounting records for the
    session are sent to the TACACS+ daemon at termination of
    a network connection
2501-1(config)#tacacs-server host 10.8.0.8
2501-1(config)#! Identifies the IP address of 10.8.0.8 as the
    address of the TACACS+ server
2501-1(config)#tacacs-server key security
2501-1(config)#! Defines the shared encryption key as
    security
2501-1(config)#interface serial 0
2501-1(config)#! Selects the line
2501-1(config)#ppp authentication default
2501-1(config-if)#! Applies the default method list to s0
```

For more information, refer to Chapter 10, "Implementing AAA Accounting."

TACACS+ AV Pairs

The network access server implements TACACS+ authorization and accounting functions by transmitting and receiving TACACS+ attribute-value (AV) pairs for each user session. Exhibit 2 lists supported TACACS+ AV pairs.

Exhibit 2   IOS V12.0 Supported TACACS+ AV Pairs

Attribute

acl=x
addr-pool=x
addr=x
autocmd=x
callback-dialsting
callback-line
callback-rotary
cmd-arg=x
cmd=x
dns-servers=
gw-password
idletime=x
inacl#<n>
inacl=x
interface-config=
ip-addresses
link-compressions
load-threshold=<n>
max-links=<n>
nas-password
nocallback-verify
noescape=x
nohangup=x
old-prompts
outacl#<n>
outacl=x
pool-def#<n>
pool-timeout=
ppp-vj-slot-compression
priv-lvl=x
protocol=x
route
route#<n>
routing=x
rte-ftr-in#<n>
rte-ftr-out#<n>
sap#<n>
sap-ftr-in#<n>
sap-ftr-out#<n>
service=x
source-ip=x
timeout=x
tunnel-id
wins-servers=
zonelist=x

Practice Session

In this Practice Session, you will practice the following:

- Logging in
- Saving log data
- Switching modes
- Pasting configuration files
- Enabling TACACS+
- Enabling and saving syslog data
- Logging out

1. Log in to the SimRouter Web page.
2. Double-click on router 2501-1 to telnet to that router. This will open a console session.
3. Enter your **Username** and **Password** at the applicable prompt. These are the ones you set up in Chapter 2. You will need to hit the Enter key twice to get to the > prompt.
4. Again, save the log for your session. To do this, select | Terminal | Start Logging | from the menu bar in the Telnet window. The Telnet client will ask you where you wish to store the log and with what name. Your choice. You are going to save the log so that when you build this configuration file, you can cut-and-paste it in Chapter 13 as a starting point, rather than having to enter the same information each Practice Session.
5. Enter the enable mode:

   `2501-1#`**`enable`**

6. When prompted to put in the enable secret password, enter **oscar**.
7. Type **terminal length 0**. This command instructs the router to scroll through long command output without pausing (the —More— message).
8. You will paste the running-config that you saved from the Chapter 11 log. At the 2501-2# prompt, type **config t**.
9. If you did not do it in Chapter 11, open your log file with the text editor of your choice (e.g., use | Start | Programs | Accessories | Notepad |). Do a find on sh running-config and copy from the first "!" to "end." At the 2501-2(config)# prompt, paste this configuration.
10. Type aaa new-model and press Enter. This command enables the AAA security services.
11. Type **aaa authentication ppp support if-needed tacacs+ local** and press Enter. This command defines the support method list for serial interfaces running PPP. The use of the if-needed keyword means when the user has already authenticated by going through the ASCII log-in procedure, then the router will skip PPP authentication. If authentication is needed, the keyword tacacs+ specifies that the router will use TACACS+ for authentication. When TACACS+ returns an ERROR, the keyword local indicates that the router attempt authentication with the local database.
12. Type **tacacs-server host 10.8.0.8** and press Enter. This command identifies the TACACS+ daemon as having an IP address of 10.8.0.8.

13. Type **tacacs-server key keepout** and press Enter. This command defines the shared encryption key as keepout.

14. Type **interface s0** and press Enter. The `interface` command selects the line.

15. Type **ppp authentication ppp support** and press Enter. This command applies the default method list to the serial line 0.

16. Type **sh running-config** and press Enter. You will use this new configuration to start the next Practice Session.

17. Type **quit** to log out from router 2501-1. Close the Telnet window and return to the SimRouter Topology Map.

18. Click on Log Out on the SimRouter Web page.

Security and Audit Checklist

1. Do you use TACACS+ service in your organization?
   - Yes
   - No

2. Do you know the vendor of your TACACS+ server?
   - Yes
   - No

3. Is there support for your software?
   - Vendor
   - Open source
   - Third-party
   - In-house
   - Other
   - None

4. Do you support multiple TACACS+ servers?
   - Yes
   - No

5. Do you use TACACS+ for:
   - Authentication?
   - Authorization?
   - Accounting?

6. Are you using syslog for accounting information?
   - Yes
   - No

7. Are you using any form of extended user authentication?
   - Yes
   - No

8. Does TACACS+ apply to:
   - Lines?
   - Console?
   - Enable?
   - PPP?
   - ARAP?

9. What protocols does TACACS+ apply to:
   - ARAP?
   - NetBIOS frame protocol?
   - NASI?
   - X.25?

10. Do you use TCP port 49 for the TACACS+ server?
    - Yes
    - No

11. Do you use TACACS+ encryption?
    - Yes
    - No

12. Have you specified a backup authentication service for when TACACS+ is unavailable?
    - Yes
    - No

Conclusion

This chapter concludes the discussion of the various TACACS flavors: TACACS, XTACACS, and TACACS+. In the previous chapter, you covered TACACS and XTACACS (Extended TACACS). Cisco strongly suggests that you use TACACS+, especially when compared to TACACS and XTACACS. Several companies provide TACACS+ service software, including, of course, Cisco itself. The chapter started with a short comparison of the competing TACACS+ and RADIUS protocols. You will learn more about the RADIUS protocol in Chapter 13. In this chapter, you learned how to establish the server host and how to enable TACACS+.

Chapter 13 continues the exploration of security servers with a discussion of RADIUS.

Chapter 13

Configuring RADIUS

In this chapter, you will learn about:

- Understanding RADIUS
- Establishing the server host
- Enabling RADIUS

RADIUS Overview

While the original TACACS protocol was an open IETF standard, later enhancements by Cisco made it more of a proprietary one. RADIUS, on the other hand, is an open standard designed to provide remote access and accounting information for all kinds of network requests. RADIUS (Remote Authentication Dial-In User Service) is an access server authentication, authorization, and accounting protocol originally developed by Livingston Enterprises, Inc. Livingston, acquired by Lucent Technologies, was a direct competitor of Cisco, making routers and remote access products. The RADIUS specification (originally RFC 2138, but made obsolete by RFC 2865 and updated by RFC 2868) is a proposed security standard and the RADIUS accounting standard (originally RFC 2139, but made obsolete by RFC 2866 and updated by RFC 2867) is informational for accounting purposes.

RADIUS is a robust protocol that simplifies security administration by providing central management services to the authentication servers. Not only is it robust, but it is an inexpensive solution for simplifying security administration while maintaining multi-vendor interoperability. Whether large or small, RADIUS suits organizations looking for a remote access solution. RADIUS functions as an information clearinghouse that stores authentication information, such as access restrictions, destination-specific routing, packet filtering, and billing, about all network users in individual profiles. Used with CHAP or third-party authentication servers, a single RADIUS database server can administer multiple security systems across complex networks, maintaining security profiles for thousands of users.

RADIUS is a distributed client/server system that secures networks against unauthorized access. It has three basic components:

- Protocol with a frame format that uses the User Datagram Protocol
- Server
- Client

The server runs on a central computer typically at the customer's site, while the client resides in the dial-up access servers or is distributed throughout the network. The RADIUS client typically is a terminal access server (NAS) router or switch that requests a service such as authentication or authorization from the RADIUS server. Cisco incorporated the RADIUS client into the IOS starting with version 11.1. The server is typically a daemon on a UNIX box or a service on a Windows NT or 2000 server.

In the Cisco implementation, RADIUS clients run on Cisco routers and send authentication requests to a central RADIUS server that contains all user authentication and network service access information. The client is responsible for passing user information to designated RADIUS servers, and then acting on the response it receives in turn. RADIUS servers are responsible for receiving user connection requests, authenticating the user, and then returning all configuration information necessary for the client to deliver service to the user. The RADIUS servers can act as proxy clients to other kinds of authentication servers.

The client and RADIUS server authenticate transactions using a shared secret that is never sent over the network. In addition, the IOS sends any user passwords encrypted between the client and RADIUS server, to reduce the possibility that someone snooping on an unsecured network could determine a user's password.

Cisco and Other Vendor Support

Cisco supports RADIUS under its AAA security paradigm. You can use RADIUS with other AAA security protocols, including TACACS+, Kerberos, or local username lookup. RADIUS is supported on all Cisco platforms.

As stated, RADIUS is an IETF standard and a fully open protocol, distributed in source code format so you can modify it to work with any security system currently available on the market. Over the years, well-known vendors such as 3COM and Ascend have supported RADIUS. Following are just some of the companies now offering RADIUS servers:

- 802.1X/RADIUS (http://www.mtghouse.com/products_priv.html)
- ActivPack for Windows NT (http://www.safedata.com/)
- Ascend RADIUS (ftp://ftp.ascend.com)
- BorderManager Authentication Services 3.6 (http://www.novell.com)
- Cisco Secure Access Control Server (ACS)/Cisco Access Registrar (http://www.cisco.com/)
- Cistron RADIUS (http://www.miquels.cistron.nl)
- Defender RADIUS Servers (http://www.symantec.com)
- DialWays (http://www.mastersoft-group.com/)
- Esva RADIUS (ftp://ftp.esva.net)

- GNU-radius (http://www.gnu.org/software/radius/)
- IC-RADIUS (http://radius.innercite.com)
- Interlink Networks AAA Radius Server (http://www.interlinknetworks.com/)
- Internet Authentication Service/RadiusNT (http://www.microsoft.com)
- MacRadius (http://www.mcfsoftware.com/)
- Merit Radius (ftp://ftp.merit.edu/radius/releases)
- NavisRadius Authentication Server (http://www.lucent.com/)
- Nokia IP Authenticator (http://www.nokia.com/)
- PerlRADIUS (http://members.iinet.net.au/~michael/radius.html)
- Radiator (http://www.open.com.au/radiator/)
- Radius NT Server/RadiusX (http://www.iea-software.com/)
- RBS RADIUS (http://www.extent.com/)
- SafeWord RADIUS servers (http://www.securecomputing.com)
- Shiva's Access Manager RADIUS (http://www.intel.com)
- Steel-Belted Radius Service (http://www.funk.com)
- SuperStack Remote Access System (http://www.3com.com)
- VOP Radius (http://www.vircom.com)
- XTRADIUS (http://www.xtradius.com)
- YARD RADIUS (http://sourceforge.net/projects/yardradius)

Lately, firewall vendors, such as CheckPoint FireWall-1 and Cisco PIX, have supported RADIUS as well.

Using RADIUS

Organizations have implemented RADIUS in a variety of network environments requiring high levels of security while maintaining network access for remote users. You can use RADIUS in the following network environments requiring access security:

- *Networks with multiple-vendor access servers, each supporting RADIUS.* For example, access servers from several vendors use a single RADIUS server-based security database. In an IP-based network with multiple vendors' access servers, you can authenticate dial-in users through a customized RADIUS server that works with, for example, a Kerberos security system.
- *Turnkey network security environments in which applications support the RADIUS protocol, such as in an access environment that uses a smart card access control system.* For example, RADIUS and Enigma's security cards work together to validate users and grant access to network resources.
- *Networks already using RADIUS.* You can add a Cisco router with RADIUS to the network. This might be the first step when you make a transition to a Terminal Access Controller Access Control System Plus (TACACS+) server.
- *Networks in which a user must only access a single service.* Using RADIUS, you can control user access to a single host, to a single utility such as Telnet, or to a single protocol such as Point-to-Point Protocol (PPP). For example, when a user logs in, RADIUS identifies this user as having authorization to run PPP using IP address 10.2.3.4 and the IOS starts the defined access list.

- *Networks that require resource accounting.* You can use RADIUS accounting independent of RADIUS authentication or authorization. The RADIUS
  accounting functions allow data to be sent at the start and stop of services,
  indicating the amount of resources (e.g., time, packets, bytes, etc.) consumed during the session. An Internet service provider (ISP) might use
  customized RADIUS access control and accounting software to meet special
  customer security and billing needs.

RADIUS is not suitable in the following network security situations:

- *Multi-protocol access environments.* RADIUS does not support the following
  protocols:
  - AppleTalk Remote Access (ARA) Protocol
  - NetBIOS Frame Control Protocol (NBFCP)
  - NetWare Asynchronous Services Interface (NASI)
  - X.25 PAD connections
- *Router-to-router situations.* RADIUS does not provide two-way authentica-
  tion. You can use RADIUS to authenticate from one router to a non-Cisco
  router when the non-Cisco router requires RADIUS authentication.
- *Networks using a variety of services.* RADIUS generally binds a user to one
  service model.

Understanding RADIUS Operation

When the client requires authorization information, it queries the RADIUS server
and passes the user credentials to the designated RADIUS server. The server then
acts on the configuration information necessary for the client to deliver services
to the user. A RADIUS server can also act as a proxy client to other RADIUS
servers or to other authentication servers, such as NetWare Directory Service
(NDS), Active Directory Service (ADS), or Kerberos. Exhibit 1 illustrates the log-
in process for RADIUS. When a user attempts to access a RADIUS-managed
network, the following steps occur:

1. The remote user dials into the NAS (network access server) or router and
    the device prompts the user for credentials, such as a username and
    password. The remote access server answering the call requests the user's
    profile from the RADIUS server.
2. The username and encrypted password are sent over the network to the
    RADIUS server.
3. The RADIUS server looks up the user using the username and passes the
    request to the authentication server for that user. The RADIUS server may
    store the authentication information itself.
4. The RADIUS server receives the authentication response and passes the
    information, along with user profile information contained in its database,
    back to the remote access server. The remote access server then uses this
    information to either grant or deny access to the network according to the
    parameters contained in the RADIUS profile. The access server receives
    one of the following responses from the RADIUS server:

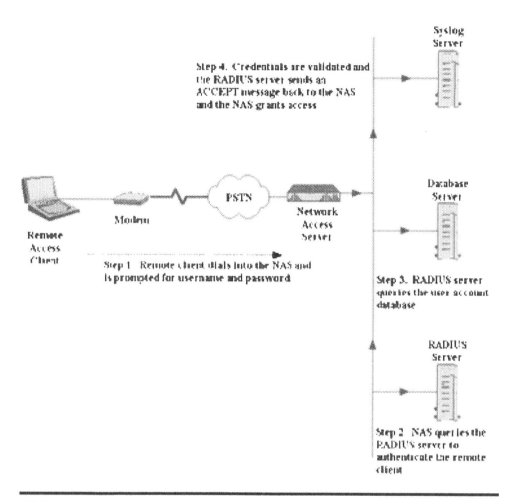

Exhibit 1   RADIUS Log-On Process

- *ACCEPT.* The user is authenticated.
- *REJECT.* The user is not authenticated and is prompted to reenter the username and password, or access is denied.
- *CHALLENGE.* The RADIUS server issues a challenge. The challenge collects additional data from the user.
- *CHANGE PASSWORD.* The RADIUS server issues a request asking the user to select a new password.

The RADIUS server supports a variety of methods for authenticating users. When the access server provides it with the username and original password given by the user, the RADIUS server can support PPP PAP or CHAP, UNIX log-in, and other authentication mechanisms.

The ACCEPT or REJECT response is bundled with additional data that the IOS uses for EXEC or network authorization. You must first complete RADIUS authentication before using RADIUS authorization. The additional data included with the ACCEPT or REJECT packets consists of the following:

- Services the user can access, including Telnet, rlogin, or local area transport (LAT) connections, and PPP, Serial Line Internet Protocol (SLIP), or EXEC services.
- Connection parameters, including the host or client IP address, access list, and user timeouts.

RADIUS Configuration Task List

To configure RADIUS on your Cisco router or access server, you must perform the following tasks:

1. Use the `aaa new-model` global configuration command to enable AAA. You must configure AAA if you plan to use RADIUS. For more information on using the `aaa new-model` command, refer to Chapter 7, "Implementing AAA Security Services."
2. Use the `aaa authentication` global configuration command to define method lists for RADIUS authentication. For more information on using the `aaa authentication` command, refer to Chapter 8, "Implementing AAA Authentication."
3. Use `line` and `interface` commands to apply the defined method lists to various interfaces.
4. Where needed, use the `aaa authorization` global command to authorize specific user functions. For more information on using the `aaa authorization` command, refer to Chapter 9, "Implementing AAA Authorization."
5. Where needed, use the `aaa accounting` command to enable accounting for RADIUS connections. For more information on using the `aaa accounting` command, refer to Chapter 10, "Implementing AAA Accounting."

Configuring RADIUS

Configuring RADIUS for authentication, authorization, and accounting on your network is fairly straightforward. You just perform the following tasks:

1. Configure the router to communicate with the RADIUS server
2. Specify RADIUS authentication
3. Specify RADIUS authorization
4. Specify RADIUS accounting

Configuring Router-to-RADIUS Server Communication

The RADIUS host is normally a multi-user system running RADIUS server software from Livingston, Merit, Microsoft, or another software provider. A RADIUS server and a Cisco router acting as a client use a shared-secret text string to encrypt passwords and exchange responses.

To configure RADIUS to use the AAA security commands, you must specify the host running the RADIUS server daemon and a secret text string that it shares with the router. Use the `radius-server` commands to specify the RADIUS server host and a secret text string. The available `radius-server` commands include:

```
2501-1(config)#radius-server ?
attribute           Customize selected radius attributes
challenge-noecho    Data echoing to screen is disabled
                      during Access-Challenge
configure-nas       Attempt to upload static routes and IP
                      pools at startup
deadtime            Time to stop using a server that does not
                      respond
host                Specify a RADIUS server
key                 encryption key shared with the radius
                      servers
optional-passwords  The first RADIUS request can be made
                      without requesting a password
retransmit          Specify the number of retries to active
                      server
timeout             Time to wait for a RADIUS server to reply
vsa                 Vendor specific attribute configuration
```

To specify a RADIUS server host and shared-secret text string, use the following commands in global configuration mode.

```
2501-1(config)#radius-server host {hostname | ip-address}
  [auth-port port-number] [acct-port port-number]
```

Use this command to specify the IP address or host name of the remote RADIUS server host and assign authentication and accounting destination port numbers. `hostname` is the DNS name and `ip-address` is the IP address of the RADIUS server host. As shown, `auth-port` is an optional keyword used to specify the UDP destination port for authentication requests and `port-number` is the actual port itself. The default `auth-port` is 1645. Should you set the `port-number` to 0, then the router will not use this host for authentication. In addition, `acct-port` is an optional keyword used to specify the UDP destination port for accounting requests and this `port-number` is the actual port itself for accounting. The default `acct-port` is 1646. Similar to authentication, if you set the `port-number` to 0, then the router will not use this host for authentication. The keyword `port-number` for auth-port and acct-port is any value from 0 to 65,535.

To illustrate, the following example specifies host1 as the RADIUS server and uses default ports for both accounting and authentication.

```
2501-1(config)#radius-server host host1.pdaconsulting.com
```

To specify different servers for authentication and accounting, use the port 0 as appropriate. In the following example, RADIUS server host1 is used for accounting but not for authentication, and server host2 is used for authentication but not for accounting.

```
2501-1(config)#radius-server host host1.pdaconsulting.com
  auth-port 0
2501-1(config)#radius-server host host2.pdaconsulting.com
  acct-port 0
```

This sets up two different servers: host1 for accounting and host2 for authentication.

From the syntax, you see that you can use the ports in another fashion. If you have a server host1 and you want to set up different ports for accounting and authentication, you would use something similar to:

```
2501-1(config)#radius-server host host1.pdaconsulting.com
  auth-port 12 acct-port 16
```

This command sets up port 12 as the destination for authentication and port 16 as the destination for accounting.

To set the authentication and encryption key for all RADIUS communications between the router and the RADIUS daemon, use the radius-server key command in global configuration mode. After enabling AAA authentication with the aaa new-model command, you must set the authentication and encryption key. The following is the syntax of the command to specify the shared-secret text string used between the router and the RADIUS server.

```
2501-1(config)#radius-server key string
```

The key you use on the router must match the key set up in the RADIUS server. When selecting your string, you should know that the IOS ignores all leading spaces but uses spaces within or at the end of the key.

Caution: When you use spaces in your key, do not enclose the key with quotation marks. The IOS would consider the quotation marks as part of the key.

To illustrate the use of the command to set a RADIUS authentication and encryption key with spaces:

```
2501-1(config)#radius-server key my secret key
```

This command sets the key that the router and the RADIUS server will use for authentication and encryption to "my secret key."

Another optional radius-server global configuration command that you can utilize to customize communication between the router and the RADIUS server is the radius-server retransmit command. Use this command to specify the number of times the IOS will search the list of RADIUS server hosts before giving up.

```
2501-1(config)#radius-server retransmit retries
```

Specify the number of times the router transmits each RADIUS request to the server before giving up by setting a value for `retries`. The default value is 3, but you can use any number from 0 to 100. To set the value to 5, use the following global configuration command.

```
2501-1(config)#radius-server retransmit 5
```

You might want to set the interval the router will wait for a response from the server host. The default is 5 seconds, but you can configure any value from 0 to 1000. Use the following command to change the interval.

```
2501-1(config)#radius-server timeout seconds
```

So to change it to 10 seconds, specify 10 for the keyword `seconds`.

To improve RADIUS response times when servers are unavailable, use the `radius-server deadtime` command. You can specify the number of minutes a RADIUS server that is not responding to authentication requests is passed over by requests for RADIUS authentication.

```
2501-1(config)#radius-server deadtime minutes
```

Tip: Remember that you can turn off any parameters you set using the `no` version of the command. For example, to revert the dead time to 0, use the `no radius-server deadtime` command.

You can set any value for deadtime from 1 to 1440 minutes (or 24 hours). Again, this command will cause the IOS to mark any RADIUS server as "dead" that fails to respond to authentication requests, thus avoiding the wait for request to timeout before trying the next configured server. The IOS will skip any RADIUS server marked as dead for the duration that you specify with the `seconds` keyword or there are no servers left that are not marked dead.

Configuring Router to Use Vendor-Specific RADIUS Attributes

The Internet Engineering Task Force (IETF) draft standard specifies a method for communicating vendor-specific information between the network access server or router and the RADIUS server by using the vendor-specific attribute (Attribute 26). (For a list of supported attributes, see Exhibit 2.) Vendor-specific attributes (VSAs) allow vendors to support extended attributes not suitable for general use. The Cisco RADIUS implementation supports one vendor-specific option using the format recommended in the specification. Cisco's vendor-ID is 9, and the supported option has vendor-type 1, which is named "cisco-avpair." The value is a string of the format:

```
protocol: attribute sep value *
```

Exhibit 2   Supported RADIUS Attributes

Number	Attribute	V12.0 Supported
1	User-Name	Yes
2	User-Passwrod	Yes
3	CHAP-Password	Yes
4	NAS-IP-Address	Yes
5	NAS-Port	Yes
6	Service-Type	Yes
7	Framed-Protocol	Yes
8	Framed-IP-Address	Yes
9	Framed-IP-Netmask	Yes
10	Framed-Routing	Yes
11	Filter-ID	Yes
12	Framed-MTU	Yes
13	Framed-Compression	Yes
14	Login-IP-Host	Yes
15	Login-Service	Yes
16	Login-TCP-Port	Yes
18	Reply-Message	Yes
19	Callback-Number	No
20	Callback-ID	No
22	Framed-Route	Yes
23	Framed-IPX-Network	No
24	State	Yes
25	Class	Yes
26	Vendor-Specific	Yes
27	Session-Timeout	Yes
28	Idle-Timeout	Yes
29	Termination-Action	No
30	Called-Station-ID	Yes
31	Calling-Station-ID	Yes
32	NAS-Identifier	No
33	Proxy-State	No
34	Login-LAT-Service	Yes
35	Login-LAT-Node	No
36	Login-LAT-Group	No
37	Framed-AppleTalk-Link	No
38	Framed-AppleTalk-Network	No
39	Framed-AppleTalk-Zone	No
40	Acct-Status-Type	Yes
41	Acct-Delay-Time	Yes
42	Acct-Input-Octets	Yes
43	Acct-Output-Octets	Yes
44	Acct-Session-ID	Yes
45	Acct-Authentic	Yes
46	Acct-Session-Time	Yes
47	Acct-Input-Packets	Yes

Exhibit 2   Supported RADIUS Attributes (Continued)

Number	Attribute	V12.0 Supported
48	Acct-Output-Packets	Yes
49	Acct-Terminate-Cause	Yes
50	Acct-Multi-Session-ID[a]	No
51	Acct-Link-Count[b]	No
60	CHAP-Challenge	No
61	NAS-Port-Type	Yes
62	Port-Limit	Yes
63	Login-LAT-Port	No
200	IETF-Token-Immediate	No

[a] Only stop records containing multi-session IDS because the IOS issues start records before any multi-link processing takes place.

[b] Only stop records containing link counts because the IOS issues start records before any multi-link processing takes place.

where protocol is a value of the Cisco "protocol" attribute for a particular type of authorization; `attribute` and `value` are an appropriate attribute/value (AV) pair defined in the Cisco TACACS+ specification; and `sep` is "=" for mandatory attributes and "*" for optional attributes. This allows the full set of features available for TACACS+ authorization to also be used for RADIUS.

For example, the following AV pair causes the IOS to activate during IP authorization (during PPP's IPCP address assignment) Cisco's "multiple named ip address pools" feature:

```
cisco-avpair= "ip:addr-pool=first"
```

The following example causes a user logging in from a network access server to have immediate access to EXEC commands.

```
cisco-avpair= "shell:priv-lvl=15"
```

Other vendors have their own unique vendor-IDs, options, and associated VSAs. For more information about vendor-IDs and VSAs, refer to RFC 2138, "Remote Authentication Dial-In User Service (RADIUS)." Exhibit 3 provides a list of vendor-specific attributes.

To configure the network access server to recognize and use VSAs, use the following command in global configuration mode:

```
2501-1(config)#radius-server vsa send [accounting |
  authentication]
```

This command enables the network access server to recognize and use VSAs as defined by RADIUS IETF attribute 26. The use of the `accounting` keyword limits the set of recognized vendor-specific attributes to only accounting attributes, and

Exhibit 3   Supported Vendor-Proprietary RADIUS Attributes

Number	Attribute	V12.0 Supported
17	Change-Password	Yes
21	Password-Expiration	Yes
64	Tunnel-Type	No
65	Tunnel-Medium-Type	No
66	Tunnel-Client-Endpoint	No
67	Tunnel-Server-Endpoint	No
68	Tunnel-ID	No
108	My-Endpoint-Disc-Alias	No
109	My-Name-Alias	No
110	Remote-FW	No
111	Multicast-Gleave-Delay	No
112	CBCP-Enable	No
113	CBCP-Mode	No
114	CBCP-Delay	No
115	CBCP-Trunk-Group	No
116	AppleTalk-Route	No
117	AppleTalk-Peer-Mode	No
118	Route-AppleTalk	No
119	FCP-Parameter	No
120	Modem-PortNo	No
121	Modem-SlotNo	No
122	Modem-ShelfNo	No
123	Call-Attempt-Limit	No
124	Call-Block-Duration	No
125	Maximum-Call-Duration	No
126	Router-Preference	No
127	Tunneling-Protocol	No
128	Shared-Profile-Enable	No
129	Primary-Home-Agent	No
130	Secondary-Home-Agent	No
131	Dialout-Allowed	No
133	BACP-Enable	No
134	DHCP-Maximum-Leases	No
135	Primary-DNS-Server	Yes
136	Secondary-DNS-Server	Yes
137	Client-Assign-DNS	No
138	User-Acct-Type	No
139	User-Acct-Host	No
140	User-Acct-Port	No
141	User-Acct-Key	No
142	User-Acct-Base	No
143	User-Acct-Time	No
144	Assign-IP-Client	No
145	Assign-IP-Server	No

**Exhibit 3   Supported Vendor-Proprietary
RADIUS Attributes (Continued)**

Number	Attribute	V12.0 Supported
146	Assign-IP-Global-Pool	No
147	DHCP-Reply	No
148	DHCP-Pool-Number	No
149	Expect-Callback	No
150	Event-Type	No
151	Session-Svr-Key	No
152	Multicast-Rate-Limit	No
153	IF-Netmask	No
154	Remote-Addr	No
155	Multicast-Client	No
156	FR-Circuit-Name	No
157	FR-LinkUp	No
158	FR-Nailed-Grp	No
159	FR-Type	No
160	FR-Link-Mgt	No
161	FR-N391	No
162	FR-DCE-N392	No
163	FR-DTE-N392	No
164	FR-DCE-N393	No
165	FR-DTE-N393	No
166	FR-T391	No
167	FR-T392	No
168	Bridge-Address	No
169	TS-Idle-Limit	No
170	TS-Idle-Mode	No
171	DBA-Monitor	No
172	Base-Channel-Count	No
173	Maximum-Channels	No
174	IPX-Route	No
175	FT1-Caller	No
176	Backup	No
177	Call-Type	No
178	Group	No
179	FR-DLCI	No
180	FR-Profile-Name	No
181	ARA-PW	No
182	IPX-Node-Addr	No
183	Home-Agent-IP-Addr	No
184	Home-Agent-Password	No
185	Home-Network-Name	No
186	Home-Agent-UDP-Port	No
187	Multilink-ID	Yes
188	Num-In-Multilink	Yes
189	Firs-Dest	No

Exhibit 3   Supported Vendor-Proprietary RADIUS Attributes (Continued)

Number	Attribute	V12.0 Supported
190	Pre-Input-Octets	Yes
191	Pre-Output-Octets	Yes
192	Pre-Input-Packets	Yes
193	Pre-Output-Packets	Yes
194	Maximum-Time	Yes
195	Disconnect-Cause	Yes
196	Connect-Progress	No
197	Data-Rate	Yes
198	PreSession-Time	Yes
199	Token-Idle	No
201	Require-Auth	No
202	Number-Sessions	No
203	Authen-Alias	No
204	Token-Expiry	No
205	Menu-Selector	No
206	Menu-Item	No
207	PW-Warntime	No
208	PW-Lifetime	Yes
209	IP-Direct	Yes
210	PPP-VJ-Slot-Comp	Yes
211	PPP-VJ-1172	No
212	PPP-Async-Map	No
213	Third-Prompt	No
214	Send-Secret	No
215	Receive-Secret	No
216	IPX-Peer-Mode	No
217	IP-Pool-Definition	Yes
218	Assign-IP-Pool	Yes
219	FR-Direct	No
220	FR-Direct-Profile	No
221	FR-Direct-DLCI	No
222	Handle-IPX	No
223	Netware-Timeout	No
224	IPX-Alias	No
225	Metric	No
226	PRI-Number-Type	No
227	Dial-Number	No
228	Route-IP	Yes
229	Route-IPX	No
230	Bridge	No
231	Send-Auth	No
232	Send-Passwd	No
233	Link-Compression	Yes
234	Target-Util	Yes

**Exhibit 3   Supported Vendor-Proprietary
RADIUS Attributes (Continued)**

Number	Attribute	V12.0 Supported
235	Maximum-Channels	Yes
236	Inc-Channel-Count	No
237	Dec-Channel-Count	No
238	Seconds-of-History	No
239	History-Weigh-Type	No
240	Add-Seconds	No
241	Remove-Seconds	No
242	Data-Filter	Yes
243	Call-Filter	Yes
244	Idle-Limit	Yes
245	Preempt-Limit	No
246	Callback	No
247	Data-Svc	No
248	Force-56	No
249	Billing-Number	No
250	Call-By-Call	No
251	Transit-Number	No
252	Host-Info	No
253	PPP-Address	No
254	MPP-Idle-Percent	No
255	Xmit-Rate	No

the use of the `authentication` keyword limits the set of recognized vendor-specific attributes to the authentication attributes.

Configuring Router for Vendor-Proprietary RADIUS Server Communication

Although an Internet Engineering Task Force (IETF) draft standard for RADIUS specifics a method for communicating vendor-proprietary information between the network access server and the RADIUS server, some vendors have extended the RADIUS attribute set in a unique way. Cisco IOS software supports a subset of vendor-proprietary RADIUS attributes.

As mentioned, to configure RADIUS (whether vendor-proprietary or IETF draft-compliant), you must specify the host running the RADIUS server daemon and the secret text string it shares with the Cisco device. You specify the RADIUS host and secret text string using the `radius-server` commands. To identify that the RADIUS server is using a vendor-proprietary implementation of RADIUS, use the `radius-server host non-standard` command.

The router will not support vendor-specific attributes unless you use the `radius-server host non-standard` command. To specify a vendor-proprietary RADIUS server host and a shared-secret text string, use the following commands in global configuration mode:

```
2501-1(config)#radius-server host {hostname | ip-address}
   non-standard
2501-1(config)#radius-server key string
```

Specify the IP address or host name of the remote RADIUS server host and identify that it is using a vendor-proprietary implementation of RADIUS. Specify the shared-secret text string used between the router and the vendor-proprietary RADIUS server. The router and the RADIUS server use this text string to encrypt passwords and exchange responses.

Configuring Router to Query RADIUS Server for Static Routes and IP Addresses

Some vendor-proprietary implementations of RADIUS allow the user to define static routes and IP pool definitions on the RADIUS server instead of on each individual network access server in the network. Each network access server then queries the RADIUS server for static route and IP pool information.

To have the Cisco router or access server query the RADIUS server for static routes and IP pool definitions when the device first starts up, use the following command in global configuration mode:

```
2501-1(config)#radius-server configure-nas
```

Use this command to tell the Cisco router or access server to query the RADIUS server for the static routes and IP pool definitions used throughout its domain when the router first starts up.

Note: Because the IOS performs the `radius-server config-ure-nas` command upon start-up, it will not take effect until you issue a `copy system:running config nvram:startup-config` command.

Configuring Router to Expand Network Access Server Port Information

There are some situations when PPP or log-in authentication occurs on an interface different from the interface where the call itself comes in. For example, in a V.120 ISDN call, log-in or PPP authentication occurs on a virtual asynchronous interface "ttt" but the call itself occurs on one of the channels of the ISDN interface.

The `radius-server attribute nas-port` extended command configures RADIUS to expand the size of the NAS-Port attribute (RADIUS IETF Attribute 5) field to 32 bits. The upper 16 bits of the NAS-Port attribute display the type and number of the controlling interface; the lower 16 bits indicate the interface undergoing authentication.

To display expanded interface information in the NAS-Port attribute field, use the following command in global configuration mode:

```
2501-1(config)#radius-server attribute nas-port extended
```

This command expands the size of the NAS-Port attribute from 16 to 32 bits to display extended interface information.

Note: This command replaces the deprecated `radius-server extended-portnames` command.

On platforms with multiple interfaces (ports) per slot, the Cisco RADIUS implementation will not provide a unique NAS-Port attribute that allows you to distinguish between the interfaces. For example, when a dual PRI interface is in slot 1, calls on both Serial1/0:1 and Serial1/1:1 will appear as NAS-Port = 20101. Once again, this is because of the 16-bit field size limitation associated with RADIUS IETF NAS-Port attribute. In this case, you can replace the NAS-Port attribute with a vendor-specific attribute (RADIUS IETF Attribute 26). Cisco's vendor-ID is 9, and the Cisco-NAS-Port attribute is subtype 2. Entering the `radius-server vsa send` command can turn on vendor-specific attributes (VSAs). The port information in this attribute is provided and configured using the `aaa nas port extended` command.

To replace the NAS-Port attribute with RADIUS IETF Attribute 26 and to display extended field information, use the following commands in global configuration mode:

```
2501-1(config)#radius-server vsa send [accounting |
   authentication]
```

This command enables the network access server to recognize and use vendor-specific attributes as defined by RADIUS IETF Attribute 26.

```
2501-1(config)#aaa nas port extended
```

This command expands the size of the VSA NAS-Port field from 16 to 32 bits to display extended interface information.

The router will continue to send the standard NAS-Port attribute (RADIUS IETF Attribute 5). Should you not want this information sent, you can suppress it by using the `no radius-server attribute nas-port` command. When you configure this command, the router will no longer send the standard NAS-Port attribute.

Specifying RADIUS Authentication

After you have identified the RADIUS server and defined the RADIUS authentication key, you need to define method lists for RADIUS authentication. Because you facilitate RADIUS authentication through AAA, you need to enter the `aaa authentication` command, specifying RADIUS as the authentication method.

Look at the following command that defines the `dialins` named method list and specifies RADIUS authentication, with `local` authentication in the event the RADIUS server does not respond.

```
2501-1(config)#aaa authentication ppp dialins radius local
```

As you know by now, you must apply the method list to an interface or line. The following applies the `dialins` method list just created to the asynchronous line. CHAP is used when both devices support it; otherwise, PAP is used.

```
2501-1(config)#interface async 1
2501-1(config-if)#encapsulation ppp
2501-1(config-if)#ppp authentication chap pap dialins
```

The next example shows how to configure the router to authenticate using RADIUS:

```
2501-1(config)#aaa authentication login use-radius radius
   local
2501-1(config)#! This command configures the use-radius
   method list to use RADIUS for authentication at the login
   prompt. If RADIUS returns an error, the user is
   authenticated using the local database
2501-1(config)#aaa authentication ppp user-radius if-needed
   radius
2501-1(config)#! This command configures user-radius method
   list to use RADIUS authentication for lines using Point-
   to-Point Protocol (PPP) with CHAP or PAP when the user has
   not already been authorized
```

Finally, you might want to be careful when configuring authentication for users to the console. If you rely solely on RADIUS (or TACACS+ for that matter), then you might set up a situation where no one can access the router when the RADIUS server is down. Therefore, you should set up another method for accessing the console as a last resort. First set up RADIUS as the default authentication method for log-in via the console and TTY, and then create a list requiring no authentication. At that point, associate this last list with the console. The following commands demonstrate these steps:

```
2501-1(config)#aaa authentication login default radius
2501-1(config)#aaa authentication login administrative none
2501-1(config)#line con 0
2501-1(config-line)#log-in authentication administrative
```

You have created a minor problem for yourself with this sequence of commands. Anyone who can physically access the router can log in and bypass RADIUS authentication. Nonetheless, anyone who can physically access the router can also reset the router and bypass the current configuration. So, lesson 1: ensure that you physically protect *all* network devices.

For more information on authentication, refer to Chapter 8, "Implementing AAA Authentication."

Specifying RADIUS Authorization

AAA authorization lets you set parameters that restrict a user's network access. Authorization using RADIUS provides one method for remote access control, including one-time authorization or authorization for each service, per-user account list and profile, user group support, and support of IP, IPX, and Telnet. Because RADIUS authorization is facilitated through AAA, you need to issue the aaa authorization command, specifying RADIUS as the authorization method.

The following example shows how to configure the router to authenticate and authorize using RADIUS:

```
2501-1(config)#aaa authorization exec radius
2501-1(config)#! This command sets the RADIUS information
   that is used for EXEC authorization, autocommands, and
   access lists
2501-1(config)#aaa authorization network radius
2501-1(config)#! This command sets RADIUS for network
   authorization, address assignment, and access lists
```

For more information on authorization, refer to Chapter 9, "Implementing AAA Authorization."

Specifying RADIUS Accounting

The AAA accounting feature enables you to track the services users are accessing as well as the amount of network resources they are consuming.

Because you facilitate RADIUS accounting through AAA, you need to issue the aaa accounting command, specifying RADIUS as the accounting method. The following example is a general configuration using RADIUS with the AAA command set:

```
2501-1(config)#radius-server host 10.8.0.25
2501-1(config)#radius-server key my secret key
2501-1(config)#username root password AStrongPassword
2501-1(config)#aaa authentication ppp dialins radius local
2501-1(config)#aaa authorization network radius local
2501-1(config)#aaa accounting network start-stop radius
2501-1(config)#aaa authentication login admins local
2501-1(config)#aaa authorization exec local
2501-1(config)#line 1 6
```

```
2501-1(config-line)#autoselect ppp
2501-1(config-line)#autoselect during-login
2501-1(config-line)#log-in authentication admins
2501-1(config-line)#modem ri-is-cd
2501-1(config-line)#exit
2501-1(config)#interface group-async 1
2501-1(config-if)#encaps ppp
2501-1(config-if)#ppp authentication pap dialins
```

The lines in this example RADIUS authentication, authorization, and accounting configuration are defined as follows:

- The `radius-server` host command defines the IP address of the RADIUS server host.
- The `radius-server` key command defines the shared-secret text string between the network access server and the RADIUS server host.
- The `aaa authentication ppp dialins radius local` command defines the authentication method list `dialins`, which specifies that the router use RADIUS authentication; then, should the RADIUS server does not respond, the router will use local authentication on serial lines using PPP.
- The `ppp authentication pap dialins` command applies the dialins method list to the specified lines.
- The `aaa authorization network radius local` command assigns an address and other network parameters to the RADIUS user.
- The `aaa accounting network start-stop radius` command turns on accounting and tracks PPP usage.
- The `aaa authentication login admins local` command defines another method list, `admins`, for log-in authentication.
- The `login authentication admins` command applies the `admins` method list for log-in authentication.

For more specific accounting information, refer to Chapter 10, "Implementing AAA Accounting."

RADIUS Attributes

The network access server monitors the RADIUS authorization and accounting functions defined by RADIUS attributes in each user profile. Exhibit 2 shows Cisco support in version IOS 12.0 for IETF attributes.

Vendor-Proprietary RADIUS Attributes

An Internet Engineering Task Force (IETF) draft standard for RADIUS specifies a method for communicating vendor-proprietary information between the network access server and the RADIUS server. Some vendors, nevertheless, have extended the RADIUS attribute set in a unique way. Cisco IOS software supports a subset of vendor-proprietary RADIUS attributes. Exhibit 3 provides a list of Cisco-supported vendor-proprietary RADIUS attributes.

The following example is a general configuration using vendor-proprietary RADIUS with the AAA command set:

```
2501-1(config)#radius-server host host non-standard
2501-1(config)#radius-server key my secret key
2501-1(config)#radius-server configure-nas
2501-1(config)#username root password AStrongPassword
2501-1(config)#aaa authentication ppp dialins radius local
2501-1(config)#aaa authorization network radius local
2501-1(config)#aaa accounting network start-stop radius
2501-1(config)#aaa authentication login admins local
2501-1(config)#aaa authorization exec local
2501-1(config)#line 1 6
2501-1(config-line)#autoselect ppp
2501-1(config-line)#autoselect during-login
2501-1(config-line)#log-in authentication admins
2501-1(config-line)#modem ri-is-cd
2501-1(config)#exit
2501-1(config)#interface group-async 1
2501-1(config-if)#encaps ppp
2501-1(config-if)#ppp authentication pap dialins
```

The lines in this example RADIUS authentication, authorization, and accounting configuration are defined as follows:

- The `radius-server host non-standard` command defines the name of the RADIUS server host and identifies that this RADIUS host uses a vendor-proprietary version of RADIUS.
- The `radius-server key` command defines the shared-secret text string between the network access server and the RADIUS server host.
- The `radius server configure-nas` command defines that the Cisco router or access server will query the RADIUS server for static routes and IP pool definitions when the device first starts up.
- The `aaa authentication ppp dialins radius local` command defines the authentication method list `dialins`, which specifies that the router use RADIUS authentication; then, when the RADIUS server does not respond, the router will use local authentication on serial lines using PPP.
- The `ppp authentication pap dialins` command applies the `dialins` method list to the specified lines.
- The `aaa authorization network radius local` command assigns an address and other network parameters to the RADIUS user.
- The `aaa accounting network start-stop radius` command turns on accounting and tracks PPP usage.

- The aaa authentication login admins local command defines another method list, admins, for log-in authentication.
- The log-in authentication admins command applies the admins method list for log-in authentication.

Practice Session

In this Practice Session, you will practice the following:

- Logging in
- Saving log data
- Switching modes
- Pasting configuration files
- Enabling RADIUS
- Enabling and saving syslog data
- Logging out

1. Log in to the SimRouter Web page.
2. Double-click on router 2501-1 to telnet to that router. This will open a console session.
3. Enter your **Username** and **Password** at the applicable prompt. These are the ones you set up in Chapter 2. You will need to hit the Enter key twice to get to the > prompt.
4. Again, save the log for your session. To do this, select | Terminal | Start Logging | from the menu bar in the Telnet window. The Telnet client will ask you where you wish to store the log and with what name. Your choice. You are going to save the log so that when you build this configuration file, you can cut-and-paste this in Chapter 14 as a starting point, rather than having to enter the same information each Practice Session.
5. Enter the enable mode:

   2501-1#**enable**

6. When prompted to put in the enable secret password, enter **oscar**.
7. Type **terminal length 0**. This command instructs the router to scroll through long command output without pausing (the —More— message).
8. You will paste the running-config that you saved from the Chapter 12 log. At the 2501-2# prompt, type **config t**.
9. If you did not do this, open your log file with the text editor of your choice (e.g., use | Start | Programs | Accessories | Notepad |). Do a find on sh running-config and copy from the first "!" to "end." At the 2501-2(config)# prompt, paste this configuration.
10. Type aaa new-model and press Enter. This command enables the AAA security services.
11. Type aaa authentication ppp support if-needed radius local and press Enter. This command defines the support method list for serial interfaces running PPP. The if-needed keyword means when

the user has already authenticated by going through the ASCII log-in procedure, then the router will skip PPP authentication. If authentication is needed, the keyword `radius` specifies that the router will use RADIUS for authentication. When RADIUS returns an ERROR, the keyword `local` indicates that the router attempt authentication with the local database.

12. Type **radius-server host 10.8.0.8** and press Enter. This command identifies the TACACS+ daemon as having an IP address of 10.8.0.8.

13. Type **radius-server key keepout** and press Enter. This command defines the shared encryption key as keepout.

14. Type **interface s0** and press Enter. The `interface` command selects the line.

15. Type **ppp authentication ppp support** and press Enter. This command applies the default method list to the serial line 0.

16. Type **sh running-config** and press Enter. You will use this new configuration to start the next Practice Session.

17. Type **quit** to log out from router 2501-1. Close the Telnet window and return to the SimRouter Topology Map.

18. Click on Log Out on the SimRouter Web page.

Security and Audit Checklist

1. Do you use RADIUS service in your organization?
   - Yes
   - No
2. Do you know the vendor of your RADIUS server?
   - Yes
   - No
3. Is there support for your software?
   - Vendor
   - Open source
   - Third-party
   - In-house
   - Other
   - None
4. Do you support multiple RADIUS servers?
   - Yes
   - No
5. Do you use RADIUS for:
   - Authentication?
   - Authorization?
   - Accounting?
6. Are you using syslog for accounting information?
   - Yes
   - No
7. Are you using any form of extended user authentication?
   - Yes
   - No

8. Does RADIUS apply to:
    - Lines?
    - Console?
    - Enable?
    - PPP?
9. Have you specified a backup authentication service for when RADIUS is unavailable?
    - Yes
    - No

Conclusion

In this chapter, you learned how to establish the server host and how to enable RADIUS. The open RADIUS protocol offers an extensible and independent platform for authentication and authorization. Not only does this allow for customizable authentication schemes, such as smart cards or biometric devices, but the RADIUS server helps offload the actual authentication work from either your terminal access server, network access server, router, switch, firewall, or any other LDAP-compliant directory server. By providing an infrastructure dedicated to authentication and authorization, RADIUS simplifies and strengthens the authentication and authorization process.

The biggest impediment to widespread use of RADIUS is its lack of support for encryption. While RADIUS may provide strong authentication, it cannot protect the confidentiality or integrity of the data once your client establishes a connection. Should you decide to use RADIUS to provide strong authentication for your router, you must use another solution to protect the data between your administrator and the router.

Chapter 14 continues the exploration with a discussion of another strong authentication solution — Kerberos.

Chapter 14

Configuring Kerberos

In this chapter, you will learn about:

- ■ Understanding Kerberos
- ■ Establishing the server host
- ■ Enabling Kerberos

Kerberos Overview

You previously learned that Cisco supports RADIUS, TACACS+, and Kerberos for authentication. You covered RADIUS and TACACS+, so it is time for Kerberos. Kerberos is a secret-key network authentication protocol, developed in the mid-1980s at the Massachusetts Institute of Technology (MIT) and other Boston-based educational institutions as part of Project Athena, that uses the Data Encryption Standard (DES) cryptographic algorithm for encryption and authentication. If you remember your Greek mythology, Kerberos (or Cerberus) is the three-headed dog guarding the gates to Hades. The three-headed part works in that the dog is a fierce animal looking all around to protect Hades. Let us hope, however, that your network is not like Hades! The designers intended Kerberos as a network authentication solution that provides secure single sign-on and a ticket granting service.

Kerberos provides mutual authentication and encrypted communication between clients and services. Unlike security tokens, Kerberos relies on each user to remember and maintain a unique password. Unlike other access control mechanisms, Kerberos does not require you to send your password either encrypted or unencrypted across a network.

When a user authenticates to the local operating system, a local agent sends an authentication request to the Kerberos server. The server responds by sending the encrypted credentials for the user attempting to authenticate to the system. The local agent then tries to decrypt the credentials using the user-supplied password. If the user supplies the correct password, the router validates the user and gives authentication tickets, which allow the user to access other Kerberos-authenticated services. The authentication server also gives the user a set of cipher keys for encrypting all data sessions.

The primary use of Kerberos is to verify that users and the network services they use are really who and what they claim to be. To accomplish this, a trusted Kerberos server issues tickets to users. These tickets, which have a limited lifetime, are stored in a user's credential cache and can be used in place of the standard username-and-password authentication mechanism.

Once validated, the user need not authenticate with any Kerberos-aware servers or applications. The tickets issued by the Kerberos server provide the credentials required to access additional network resources. The Kerberos credential scheme embodies a concept called "single log-on." This process requires authenticating a user once, and then allows secure authentication (without encrypting another password) wherever that user's credential is accepted. Although the user must still remember a password, the user benefits by only needing one password to access all systems on the network where the administrator has granted access.

Another big benefit of Kerberos is that it is freely available. You can download and use the source code without cost.

A major concern for networks is the usage of network monitoring tools to capture packets on the network. Sensitive information such as user's log-in ID and password is contained in these packets. Protocols such as Telnet, FTP, and POP3 send the information in cleartext. This means that anyone with a packet analyzer can look at the contents of the packet (the data portion) and see everything. Many organizations have implemented firewall systems to protect against intrusions originating from outside the network. However, these devices do little to prevent attacks that originate from the inside. Kerberos helps because you can use the exchanged keys to encrypt sessions and protect data.

Starting with Cisco IOS Release 11.2, Cisco IOS software includes Kerberos 5 support, which allows organizations already deploying Kerberos 5 to use the same Kerberos authentication database on their routers that they are already using on their other network hosts (such as UNIX servers and PCs).

The following network services are supported by the Kerberos authentication capabilities in Cisco IOS software:

- Telnet
- rlogin
- rsh
- rcp

Note: Cisco has based its implementation of Kerberos client support on code developed by CyberSafe, which was derived from the MIT code. As a result, the Cisco Kerberos implementation has successfully undergone full compatibility testing with the CyberSafe Challenger commercial Kerberos server and MIT's server code, which is freely distributed.

Supporting Kerberos Client

This section describes how the Kerberos security system works with a Cisco router functioning as the security server. Although (for convenience or technical reasons) you can customize Kerberos in a number of ways, remote users attempting to access network services must pass through the following three layers of security before they can access network services:

1. Authenticate to the boundary router
2. Obtain a TGT from the KDC
3. Authenticate to network services

Authenticating to the Boundary Router

The developers based Kerberos, like other secret-key systems, on the concept of a trusted third party that performs secure verification of users and services. In the Kerberos protocol, this trusted third party is called the key distribution center (KDC). The KDC is a key player (pardon the pun) in the Kerberos architecture.

The first step in the Kerberos authentication process is for users to authenticate themselves to the boundary router. The following process describes the first layer of security that remote users must pass through when they attempt to access a network and authenticate to a boundary router:

1. The remote user opens a PPP connection to the corporate site router.
2. The router prompts the user for a `username` and `password`.
3. The router requests a TGT from the KDC for this particular user.
4. The KDC sends an encrypted TGT to the router that includes (among other things) the user's identity.
5. The router attempts to decrypt the TGT using the password the user entered. If the decryption is successful, the remote user has a ticket for the user.

A remote user who successfully initiates a PPP session and authenticates to the boundary router is inside the firewall but still must authenticate to the KDC directly before being allowed to access network services. This is because the router stores the TGT issued by the KDC in memory, so the TGT is not useful for additional authentication unless the user physically logs on to the router.

Obtaining a TGT from the KDC

When a remote user authenticates to a boundary router, that user technically becomes part of the network; that is, the network is extended to include the remote user and the user's machine or network. To gain access to network services, however, the remote user must obtain a TGT from the KDC. The following process describes how remote users authenticate to the KDC:

1. The remote user, at a workstation on a remote site, launches the KINIT program (part of the client software provided with the Kerberos protocol).
2. The KINIT program finds the user's identity and requests a TGT from the KDC.

3. The KDC creates a TGT, which contains the identity of the user, the identity of the KDC, and the TGT's expiration time.
4. Using the user's password as a key, the KDC encrypts the TGT and sends the TGT to the workstation.
5. When the KINIT program receives the encrypted TGT, it prompts the user for a password (this is the password that the KDC has defined for the user).
6. If the KINIT program can decrypt the TGT with the password the user enters, the user is authenticated to the KDC and the KINIT program stores the TGT in the user's credential cache.

At this point, the user has a TGT and can communicate securely with the KDC. In turn, the TGT allows the user to authenticate to other network services.

Authenticating to Network Services

The following process describes how a remote user with a TGT authenticates to network services within a given Kerberos realm. Assume the user is on a remote workstation and wants to log in to a server.

1. The remote user initiates a Kerberized application (such as Telnet) to the desired server. The Kerberized application builds a service credential request and sends it to the KDC. The service credential request includes (among other things) the user's identity and the identity of the desired network service. The user's client uses the TGT to encrypt the service credential request.
2. The KDC tries to decrypt the service credential request with the TGT that it issued to the remote user. If the KDC can decrypt the packet, it is assured that the authenticated user sent the request.
3. The KDC notes the network service identity in the service credential request.
4. The KDC builds a service credential for the appropriate network service on the server on behalf of the user. The service credential contains the client's identity and the desired network service's identity.
5. The KDC then encrypts the service credential twice. It first encrypts the credential with the SRVTAB that it shares with the network service identified in the credential, and then encrypts the resulting packet with the TGT of the user.
6. The KDC sends the twice-encrypted credential to the user.
7. The user's client software attempts to decrypt the service credential with the user's TGT. If the user can decrypt the service credential, it is assured the credential came from the real KDC.
8. The user sends the service credential to the desired network service. Note that the credential is still encrypted with the SRVTAB shared by the KDC and the network service.
9. The network service attempts to decrypt the service credential using its SRVTAB.
10. If the network service can decrypt the credential, it is assured the credential was in fact issued by the KDC. Note that the network service trusts anything it can decrypt from the KDC, even when it receives it indirectly from a user. This is because the user first authenticated with the KDC.

At this point, the user is authenticated to the network service on the server. This process is repeated each time a user wants to access a network service in the Kerberos realm.

Configuring the Router to Use the Kerberos Protocol

To configure a Cisco router to function as a network security server and authenticate users using the Kerberos v5 protocol, you must complete the following tasks:

1. Define a Kerberos realm where the router or NAS resides.
2. Copy SRVTAB files from the KDC to the router or NAS.
3. Retrieve STVTAB files from the KDC.
4. Specify Kerberos authentication on the router or NAS.
5. Enable credentials forwarding on the router or NAS.

These steps assume that you have a Kerberos server configured and operational. Configuring your Kerberos server is well beyond the scope of this book. This task is not trivial, so either get yourself some help or RTFM.

Defining a Kerberos Realm

To authenticate a user defined in the Kerberos database, the router must know the host name or IP address of the KDC, the name of the Kerberos realm, and, optionally, know how to map the host name or Domain Name System (DNS) domain to the Kerberos realm.

To configure the router to authenticate to a specified KDC in a specified Kerberos realm, use the following commands in global configuration mode.

```
4500(config)#kerberos local-realm kerberos-realm
```

Note: The Kerberos realm is a domain name and, by convention, DNS domain names must begin with a leading dot (.).

```
4500(config)#kerberos server kerberos-realm {hostname | ip-
  address} [port-number]
4500(config)#kerberos realm {dns-domain | host} kerberos-
  realm
```

Note: Because the machine running the KDC and all Kerberized hosts must interact within a five-minute window or authentication fails, all Kerberized machines, and especially the KDC, should use the Network Time Protocol (NTP).

The first command defines the default realm for the router. A Kerberos realm consists of users, hosts, and network services registered to the server. You must use uppercase (capital letters) to specify the `kerberos-realm` keyword. The Kerberos `local realm`, `Kerberos realm`, and `Kerberos server` commands are equivalent to the UNIX `krb.conf` file. Your router can exist in more than one realm at anytime. However, you can only have one instance of `Kerberos local-realm`. The realm you specify with this command is the default realm.

The second command tells the router what KDC to use in a given Kerberos realm and, optionally, the port number the KDC is monitoring. (The default is 88.) The third optional command maps a host name or DNS domain to a Kerberos realm.

For example, the following global configuration command defines PDACON-SULTING.COM as the default Kerberos realm:

`4500(config)#`**`kerberos local-realm PDACONSULTING.COM`**

To tell the router that the PDACONSULTING.COM KDC is running on host 10.8.0.15 at port number 170, use the following Kerberos command:

`4500(config)#`**`kerberos server PDACONSULTING.COM 10.8.0.15 170`**

The following global configuration command maps the DNS domain pdacon-sulting.com to the Kerberos realm PDACONSULTING.COM.

`4500(config)#`**`kerberos realm .pdaconsulting.com`**
   `PDACONSULTING.COM`

Copying SRVTAB Files

When you want remote users to authenticate to the router using Kerberos credentials, the router or NAS must share a secret key with the KDC. To share keys, you must give the router a copy of the SRVTAB you extracted on the KDC.

The most secure method for copying SRVTAB files to the hosts in your Kerberos realm is to copy them onto physical media and go to each host in turn and manually copy the files onto the system. To copy SRVTAB files to the router, which does not have a physical media drive, you must transfer them via the network using the Trivial File Transfer Protocol (TFTP). If you do not have a copy of TFTP, you can download one from http://www.cisco.com.

Note: The SRVTAB is at the core of Kerberos security, so think twice about using TFTP to copy this important file from one system to the router over your network. You can minimize the risk by using a crossover cable to connect a workstation to the router's interface. Configure both interfaces with IP addresses in the same subnet. Doing your copy this way makes it physically impossible for someone to grab the packets.

To remotely copy SRVTAB files to the router from the KDC, use the following command in global configuration mode:

```
4500(config)#kerberos srvtab remote {hostname | ip-address}
  {file name}
```

Substitute the host name of the KDC where the SRVTAB file exits for the keyword hostname. Alternatively, you can substitute the IP address of the KDC for the ip-address keyword. Finally, use the file name keywords to specify the name of the SRVTAB file on the KDC. The command shows the following as acceptable for hostname and ip-address keywords:

```
bootflash:URL of srvtab file
flash:URL of srvtab file
ftp:URL of srvtab file
null:URL of srvtab file
nvram:URL of srvtab file
rcp:URL of srvtab file
system:URL of srvtab file
tftp:URL of srvtab file
```

To copy over the SRVTAB file on a host named host123.pdaconsulting.com for a router named router1.pdaconsulting.com, the command would look like this:

```
4500(config)#kerberos srvtab remote
  host123.pdaconsulting.com new-srvtab
```

Retrieving a SRVTAB File from the KDC

When you copy the SRVTAB file from the router to the KDC, the kerberos srvtab remote command parses the information in this file and stores it in the router's running-configuration in the kerberos srvtab entry format. To retrieve a SRVTAB file from a remote host and automatically generate a SRVTAB entry configuration, use the following global configuration command.

```
4500(config)#kerberos srvtab entry kerberos-principal
  principal-type timestamp key-version number key-type key-
  length encrypted-keytab
```

The kerberos-principal keyword specifies a service on the router. The keyword principal-type represents the version of the Kerberos SRVTAB. The keyword timestamp is a number representing the date and time of creation of the SRVTAB. Use the key-type keyword to specify the type of encryption used and the key-length keyword to specify the length of the encryption key in bytes. Finally, the encrypted-keytab keyword is the encrypted secret key shared with the KDC. By way of illustration:

```
4500(config)#kerberos srvtab entry host/new-
    router.pdaconsulting.com@PDACONSULTING.COM 0 8176980774 1
    1 8 .eNcryPt.KeY
```

In this example, host/new-router.pdaconsulting.com@PDACONSULTING.COM is the host, 0 is the type, 8176980774 is the timestamp, 1 is the version key, 1 is DES encryption, 8 is the number of bytes, and .eNcryPt.KeY is the encrypted key.

To ensure that the SRVTAB is available (that is, it does not need to be acquired from the KDC) when you reboot the router, use the write memory configuration command to write your running-configuration (which contains the parsed SRVTAB file) to NVRAM.

Specifying Kerberos Authentication

You have now configured Kerberos on your router. This makes it possible for the router to authenticate using Kerberos. The next step is to set up the router to do so. Because AAA facilitates Kerberos authentication, you need to enter the aaa authentication command, specifying Kerberos as the authentication method.

The following example sets authentication at log-in to use the Kerberos 5 Telnet authentication protocol for clients using Telnet to connect to the router.

```
4500(config)#aaa authentication login default krb5-telnet
    krb5
```

For more information, refer to Chapter 8, "Implementing AAA Authentication."

Enabling Credentials Forwarding

With Kerberos configured thus far, a user authenticated to a Kerberized router has a TGT and can use it to authenticate to a host on the network. However, should the user try to list credentials after authenticating to a host, the output will show no Kerberos credentials present.

You have the option to configure the router or NAS to forward users' TGTs with them as they authenticate from the router to Kerberized remote hosts on the network when using Kerberized Telnet, rcp, rsh, and rlogin (with the appropriate flags). For example, when a user telnets to a router that uses Kerberos for authentication, the router can forward the credentials to any host where the user attempts access. Of course, this host must also support Kerberos as an authentication protocol. To have all clients forward users' credentials as they connect to other hosts in the Kerberos realm, use the following command in global configuration mode:

```
4500(config)#kerberos credential forward
```

There are no optional keywords for this command. Again, this command forces all clients to forward user credentials upon successful Kerberos authentication.

With credentials forwarding enabled, the router automatically forwards the users' TGTs to the next host where they try to authenticate. In this case, users can connect to multiple hosts in the Kerberos realm without running the KINIT program each time to get a new TGT.

Telneting to the Router

To use Kerberos to authenticate users opening a Telnet session to the router from within the network, use the following command in global configuration mode:

```
4500(config)#aaa authentication login {default | list-name}
  krb5_telnet
```

This command sets log-in authentication to use the Kerberos 5 Telnet authentication protocol when using Telnet to connect to the router.

Although the router authenticates the Telnet sessions, users still must enter a cleartext password when they want to enter enable mode. You can, however, use the `kerberos instance map` command to allow them to authenticate to the router at a predefined privilege level. A better way to control Telnet sessions to other hosts from the router or the NAS is to encrypt the session.

Establishing an Encrypted Kerberized Telnet Session

To open a secure Telnet session, Cisco supports Encrypted Kerberized Telnet for users. With Encrypted Kerberized Telnet, the router authenticates users by their Kerberos credentials before establishing a Telnet session. You can use Kerberos to encrypt the Telnet session using 56-bit Data Encryption Standard (DES) encryption with 64-bit Cipher Feedback (CFB). Because Kerberos encrypts data sent or received, an attacker cannot alter or view session data between the dialed router (or access server) and the user.

Note: This feature is available only when you have the 56-bit encryption image. Strong encryption is subject to control in the United States. The 56-bit DES encryption algorithm is subject to U.S. Government export control regulations and requires approval from the U.S. Department of Commerce for export.

To establish an encrypted Kerberized Telnet session from a router to a remote host, use either of the following commands in EXEC command mode:

```
4500#connect host [port] /encrypt kerberos
```

or

```
4500#telnet host [port] /encrypt kerberos
```

The first command allows you to log in to a host that supports Telnet, rlogin, or LAT. Substitute a host name or IP address for the keyword *host*. You can optionally specify the TCP port of your choice. The default is Telnet or port 23 on the host. In this example, you see the keywords /encrypt kerberos. This is actually a Telnet connection option. Exhibit 1 provides other available options.

From Exhibit 1, you can see that the following are valid commands that accomplish the same thing:

```
4500#telnet host1 /encrypt kerberos
4500#telnet host1 23 /encrypt kerberos
4500#telnet host1 telnet /encrypt kerberos
```

The last two commands are somewhat redundant, but valid anyhow.

The keywords and options with the telnet command are the same as that for the connect command. If you are unsure of the host name, you can use the show hosts command, which will provide a list of all available hosts.

When a user opens a Telnet session from a Cisco router to a remote host, the router and remote host negotiate to authenticate the user using Kerberos credentials. If this authentication is successful, the router and remote host then negotiate whether or not to use encryption. If this negotiation is successful, both inbound and outbound traffic is encrypted using 56-bit DES encryption with 64-bit CFB.

When a user dials in from a remote host to a Cisco router configured for Kerberos authentication, the host and router will attempt to negotiate whether or not to use encryption for the Telnet session. If this negotiation is successful, the router will encrypt all outbound data during the Telnet session.

If the router and remote host do not successfully negotiate encryption, the router will terminate the session and the user will receive a message stating that the encrypted Telnet session was not successfully established.

For information about enabling bi-directional encryption from a remote host, refer to the documentation specific to the remote host device.

The following example establishes an encrypted Telnet session from a router to a remote host named "host1":

```
4500#telnet host1 /encrypt kerberos
```

Enabling Mandatory Kerberos Authentication

As an added layer of security, you can optionally configure the router so that after remote users authenticate to it, these users can authenticate to other services on the network only with Kerberized Telnet, rlogin, rsh, and rcp. If you do not make Kerberos authentication mandatory and Kerberos authentication fails, the application attempts to authenticate users using the default method of authentication for that network service. For example, Telnet and rlogin prompt for a password, and rsh attempts to authenticate using the local .rhost file.

To make Kerberos authentication mandatory, use the following command in global configuration mode:

```
4500(config)#kerberos clients mandatory
```

Exhibit 1   Telnet Connection Options

Option	Description
/debug	Enables debugging mode
/encrypt kerberos	Enables an encrypted session
/line	Enables line mode
/noecho	Disables local echo
/route path	Enables loose source routing
/source-interface	Specifies the source interface
/stream	Enables stream processing
port-number	Specify port number
bgp	Border Gateway Protocol
chargen	Character Generator
cmd rcmd	Remote commands
daytime	Daytime
domain	Domain Name System
echo	Echo
exec	EXEC
finger	Finger
ftp	File Transfer Protocol
ftp-data	FTP data connections (not often used)
gopher	Gopher
hostname	Network Information Center (NIC) host name server
ident	Indent Protocol
irc	Internet Relay Chat
klogin	Kerberos log-in
kshell	Kerberos shell
login	Log-in (rlogin)
lpd	Line printer daemon; print service
nntp	Network News Transport Protocol
node	Connect to a specific LAT node
pop2	Post Office Protocol version 2
pop3	Post Office Protocol version 3
port	Destination LAT port name
smtp	Simple Mail Transfer Protocol
sunrpc	Sun Remote Procedure Call
syslog	Syslog daemon
tacacs	Specify TACACS security
talk	Talk
telnet	Telnet
time	Time
uucp	UNIX-to-UNIX Copy Program
whois	Nickname
www	World Wide Web (HTTP)

This command sets Telnet, rlogin, rsh, and rcp to fail when they cannot negotiate the Kerberos protocol with the remote server.

Should you not configure this command and the user has locally stored Kerberos credentials, the rsh, rcp, rlogin, and Telnet commands will attempt to negotiate the Kerberos protocol with the remote server and will use the non-Kerberized protocols when successful. When the user does not have credentials, the standard protocols for rcp and rsh are used to negotiate the Kerberos protocol.

Enabling Kerberos Instance Mapping

You can create administrative instances of users in the KDC database. The kerberos instance map command allows you to map those instances to Cisco IOS privilege levels so that users can open secure Telnet sessions to the router at a predefined privilege level, obviating the need to enter a cleartext password to enter enable mode.

To map a Kerberos instance to a Cisco IOS privilege level, use the following command in global configuration mode:

```
4500(config)#kerberos instance map instance privilege-level
```

You substitute the name of a Kerberos instance for the keyword instance. An instance is an authorization level label for Kerberos principals. A Kerberos principal with a Kerberos instance has the form user/instance@REALM; for example, ptdavis/admin@PDACONSULTING.COM. Substitute the privilege level you want the user to have for the keyword privilege-level. You can specify 16 privilege levels, using numbers 0 through 15. Level 1 is EXEC-mode user privileges, which is the default.

As an example, if you want to set the privilege level to 15 for all authenticated Kerberos users with the admin instance in the Kerberos realm, use the following global configuration command:

```
4500(config)#kerberos instance map admin 15
```

Mapping a Kerberos Instance to a Cisco IOS Privilege Level

If there is a Kerberos instance for user ptdavis in the KDC database (e.g., ptdavis/admin), user ptdavis can now open a Telnet session to the router as ptdavis/admin and authenticate automatically at privilege level 15, assuming you mapped instance admin to privilege level 15. You can set Cisco IOS commands to various privilege levels using the privilege level command.

After you map a Kerberos instance to a Cisco IOS privilege level, you must configure the router to check for Kerberos instances each time a user logs in. To run authorization to determine whether a user can run an EXEC shell based on a mapped Kerberos instance, use the aaa authorization command with the krb5-instance keyword. To illustrate, look at the following command:

```
4500(config)#aaa authorization exec default krb5-instance
```

When you use the preceding command, the router or NAS will use the instance defined by the `kerberos instance map` command for authorization.

For more information, refer to Chapter 9, "Implementing AAA Authorization."

Using Kerberos Preauthentication

You can specify a preauthentication method to use for communicating with the KDC. To do so, use the following global configuration command.

```
4500(config)#kerberos preauth [encrypted-kerberos-timestamp
  | encrypted-unix-timestamp | none]
```

The `encrypted-kerberos-timestamp` keyword specifies the use of the RFC1510 timestamp. The optional `encrypted-unix-timestamp` keyword specifies an encrypted UNIX timestamp as a quick authentication method when communicating with the KDC. It is more secure to use a preauthentication for communications with the KDC. However, communication with the KDC will fail when the KDC does not support the `kerberos preauth` command. When that happens, turn off preauthentication with the `kerberos preauth none` command. The no form of this command is functionally equivalent to using the none keyword.

By way of illustration, look at the following examples that disable Kerberos preauthentication.

```
4500(config)#kerberos preauth none
4500(config)#no kerberos preauth
```

Monitoring and Maintaining Kerberos

When users authenticate themselves, Kerberos issues an authentication ticket called a credential. The router stores the credential in a credential cache. To display or remove a current user's credentials, use the following commands in EXEC mode:

```
4500#show kerberos creds
4500#clear kerberos creds
```

The first command lists the credentials in a current user's credentials cache, while the second command destroys all credentials in a current user's credential cache. If credentials do not exist in the credential cache, you will see the following:

```
No Kerberos credentials to free!
```

Practice Session

In this Practice Session, you will practice the following:

- Logging in
- Saving log data
- Switching modes
- Entering configuration mode
- Mapping the Kerberos instance `admin` to privilege level 15
- Mapping the Kerberos instance `restricted` to privilege level 3
- Specifying the instance defined by the `Kerberos instance map` command for AAA authorization
- Writing the configuration to the terminal
- Enabling and saving syslog data
- Logging out

1. Log in to the SimRouter Web page.
2. Double-click on router 4500 to telnet to that router. This will open a console session.
3. Enter your **Username** and **Password** at the applicable prompt. These are the ones you set up in Chapter 2. You will need to hit the Enter key twice to get to the > prompt.
4. Again, save the log for your session. To do this, select | Terminal | Start Logging | from the menu bar in the Telnet window. The Telnet client will ask you where you wish to store the log and with what name. Your choice. You are going to save the log so that when you build this configuration file, you can cut-and-paste this in Chapter 15 as a starting point, rather than having to enter the same information each Practice Session.
5. Enter the enable mode:

    `4500#`**`enable`**

6. When prompted to put in the enable secret password, enter **oscar**.
7. Type **terminal length 0**. This command instructs the router to scroll through long command output without pausing (the —More— message).
8. You will paste the `running-config` that you saved from the Chapter 13 log. At the `2501-2#` prompt, type **config t**.
9. If you did not do it, open your log file with the text editor of your choice (e.g., use | Start | Programs | Accessories | Notepad |). Do a find on sh running-config and copy from the first "!" to "end." At the `2501-2(config)#` prompt, paste this configuration.
10. Type **aaa new-model** and press Enter. This command enables the AAA security services.
11. Type **kerberos local-realm pdaconsulting.com** and press Enter. This sets the Kerberos local realm to pdaconsulting.com.
12. Type **kerberos server pdaconsulting.com krbsvr** and press Enter. This specifies the KDC for the pdaconsulting.com realm.
13. Type **kerberos credentials forward** and press Enter. This enables the forwarding of credentials when initiating sessions from the router or NAS to another device supporting Kerberos.
14. Type **kerberos srvtab remote krbsvr srvtab** and press Enter. This specifies where the SRVTAB will come from.
15. Type **aaa authentication login default krb5** and press Enter. This specifies that the default authentication method is Kerberos.

16. Type **aaa authorization exec krb5-instance** and press Enter. This specifies that the default authorization method for exec is Kerberos.
17. Type **write term** and press Enter.
18. Type **sh running-config** and press Enter. You will use this new configuration to start the next Practice Session.
19. Type **quit** to log out from router 4500. Close the Telnet window and return to the SimRouter Topology Map.
20. Click on Log Out on the SimRouter Web page.

Security and Audit Checklist

1. Do you use Kerberos service in your organization?
   - Yes
   - No
2. Do you know the vendor of your Kerberos server?
   - Yes
   - No
3. Is there support for your software?
   - Vendor
   - Open source
   - Third-party
   - In-house
   - Other
   - None
4. Do you support the following network services:
   - Telnet?
   - rlogin?
   - rsh?
   - rcp?
5. Are you using the standard port of 88 for Kerberos?
   - Yes
   - No
6. Do you use Network Time Protocol (NTP)?
   - Yes
   - No
7. Do you have a procedure for copying and retrieving SRVTAB files?
   - Yes
   - No
8. Is the method of copying and retrieving SRVTAB files secure?
   - Yes
   - No
9. Do you use credentials forwarding?
   - Yes
   - No
10. Does your router support 56-bit DES encryption in the 64-bit Cipher Feedback mode?
    - Yes
    - No

11. Did your organization enable mandatory Kerberos authentication?
    - Yes
    - No
12. Do you map instances to privilege levels?
    - Yes
    - No
13. Is this instance mapping appropriate?
    - Yes
    - No
14. Do you use Kerberos preauthentication?
    - Yes
    - No

Conclusion

In this chapter, you learned how to enable your router to use Kerberos authentication. Kerberos provides a secure sign-on and ticket granting solution. The protocol is not trivial and, to date, organizations have not widely deployed it. That may change now that Windows 2000 Server and Cisco provide native support.

The downside to Kerberos is that the developers hard-coded the DES algorithm into it. Kerberos is highly dependent on DES. It only supports 56-bit keys. This implementation of DES is no longer supported by the U.S. Department of Finance, who has thrown its weight behind the Rijndael algorithm as the DES replacement. ICL in Europe developed SESAME, a Kerberos competitor. However, SESAME is not algorithm dependent.

Notwithstanding these concerns, Kerberos is a good start at the elusive "Holy Grail" of an easy-to-manage, multi-platform, economical, effective, and secure single sign-on product.

This concludes the chapters on authentication, authorization, and accounting solutions for your router. In Chapter 15, you wade in on access lists. You start slow with standard access lists.

PREVENTING UNAUTHORIZED ACCESS: NETWORKING

III

Chapter 15

Basic Traffic Filtering, Part 1

In this chapter, you will learn about:

- Defining criteria for forwarding or blocking packets
- Creating standard and extended IP access lists
- Assigning a unique number to each access list
- Applying access lists to interfaces
- Creating and editing access list statements on a TFTP server

Cisco provides basic traffic filtering capabilities with access control lists (also referred to as access lists). You can configure access lists for all routed network protocols (IP, AppleTalk, etc.) to filter those protocols' packets as the packets pass through a router.

You can configure access lists at your router to control access to a network; access lists can prevent certain traffic from entering or exiting a network. This chapter explores access lists and their application to interfaces.

Access List Overview

Before you can begin to write access lists, you need a security policy. Hopefully, your organization has a security architecture document that you can review. The documentation should provide the data to create your organization's security policy. Your review should concentrate on your security policy. The access lists your organization creates are the extension and the execution of the security policy. Good policy should provide the "What" and "How" of your security. The "What" are the objects included in the policy. The "How" describes how the policy affects these objects. When you enforce your policy, you evaluate whether a set of objects is effective by a particular action. This is how the policy in the router works as well. A remote site tries to use FTP to download a file from the system.

So you have the objects — the remote and local system — and the action — FTP download. Your policy will state whether you accept or reject this action and others like it.

Once you create your policy, Cisco provides you with a policy toolkit on your router. So define your "Whats" of the policy and use the tools to control the "How." The toolkit consists of tools to control the following:

- Router resources
- Packets passing through the router
- Routes accepted and distributed
- Routes based on the characteristics of those routes

To provide the security benefits of access lists, you should, at a minimum, configure access lists on border routers — routers situated at the edges of your networks. This provides a basic buffer from the outside network, or from a less-controlled area of your network, to a more sensitive area of your network. You can use a packet-filtering router with access lists as part of your firewall configuration, which is often positioned between your internal network and an external network such as the Internet. You can also use access lists on a router positioned between two parts of your network to control traffic entering or exiting a specific part of your internal network.

Caution: Do not use packet filtering as the only component of your firewall configuration unless you have a simple environment. You can get by with packet filtering when you have only DNS, HTTP, and SMTP traffic.

On these routers, you should configure access lists for each network protocol configured on the router's interfaces. You can configure access lists so that the router filters inbound traffic, or outbound traffic, or both, on an interface.

You must define access lists on a per-protocol basis. That is, you should define access lists for every protocol enabled on an interface where you want to control traffic flow for that protocol.

Note: Some protocols refer to access lists as filters and refer to the act of applying the access lists to interfaces as filtering. Clearly, blocking is the most extreme form of filtering, but it is filtering nonetheless.

Access lists filter network traffic by controlling whether the router will forward routed packets or block them at the router's interfaces. Your router examines each packet to determine whether to forward or drop the packet, based on the criteria you specify with access lists. When a packet enters the router, it looks up a route for the packet's destination and determines an interface for the packet to exit the router. When using access lists, before the packet enters or exits the router, the router applies a stack of filters to the interface where the packet must pass. The stack the router applies is the commands you enter in an access list, then group together and apply to an interface.

Access list criteria could be the source address of the traffic, the destination address of the traffic, the upper-layer protocol, or other information. Note that sophisticated users can sometimes successfully evade or fool basic access lists because most organizations do not require authentication.

An access list consists of rules or statements that the router sequentially tests against incoming or outgoing packets. Access lists define the actual traffic that the router will permit or deny, whereas an access group applies an access list definition to an interface. You can use access lists to deny connections known to be a security risk and then permit all other connections, or to permit those connections your security policy considers acceptable and deny all the rest. The router invokes an access list after it makes a routing decision but before it sends the packet out on an interface. The best place to apply an access list is as close as possible to the source when you are denying, and to the destination when you are permitting. The best place to define an access list is on a preferred host using your favorite text editor. You can create a file that contains the `access list` commands, place the file (marked readable) in the default TFTP directory, and then network load the file onto the router.

Understanding Access List Configuration

Although each protocol has its own set of specific tasks and rules required for you to provide traffic filtering, in general most protocols require at least two basic steps:

1. Creating access lists
2. Applying access lists to interfaces

Creating Access Lists

Create access lists for each protocol you wish to filter, per router interface. For some protocols, you create one access list to filter inbound traffic and another access list to filter outbound traffic.

To create an access list, you specify the protocol to filter, you assign a unique name or number to the access list, and you define packet filtering criteria. A single access list can have multiple filtering criteria statements.

Cisco recommends that you create your access lists on a TFTP server and then download the access lists to your router. This can considerably simplify maintenance of your access lists. For details, see the section on creating and editing access list statements later in this chapter.

The protocols for which you can configure access lists are identified in Exhibits 1 and 2.

**Exhibit 1   Protocol with
Access Lists Specified by Names**

Protocol

Apollo Domain
IP
IPX
ISO CLNS
NetBIOS IPX
Source-route bridging NetBIOS

Exhibit 2   Protocols with Access Lists Specified by Numbers

Protocol	List Number
Standard IP	1–99
Standard VINES	1–100
Extended IP	100–199
Extended VINES	101–200
Ethernet type code	200–299
Transparent bridging (protocol type)	200–299
Source-route bridging (protocol type)	200–299
Simple VINES	201–300
DECnet and extended DECnet	300–399
XNS	400–499
Extended XNS	500–599
AppleTalk	600–699
Ethernet address	700–799
Transparent bridging (vendor code)	700–799
Source-route bridging (vendor code)	700–799
Standard IPX	800–899
Extended IPX	900–999
IPX SAP	1000–1099
IPX SAP SPX	1000–1099
Extended transparent bridging	1100–1199
IPX summary address	1200–1299
Standard IP	1300–1999
Extended IP	2000–2699

Assigning a Unique Name or Number to Each Access List

When configuring access lists on a router, you must identify each access list uniquely within a protocol by assigning either a name or a number to the protocol's access list.

> **Note:** Cisco requires that you name some access lists of some pro-
> tocols, while you can identify access lists of other protocols by a
> number. Cisco also allows you to identify some protocols by either
> a name or a number. When you use a number to identify an access
> list, you must use a number within the specific range of numbers
> that is valid for the protocol. Refer to Exhibit 2 for the proper number
> ranges.

You can specify access lists by name for the protocols listed in Exhibit 1, and by number for the protocols listed in Exhibit 2. Exhibit 2 also lists the range of access list numbers that is valid for each protocol.

Looking at Exhibit 2, you can see that some access lists have the same access list number; for example, Ethernet type code and source route bridging. The IOS will distinguish between them based on the syntax of the rule rather than relying strictly on the access list number to parse the rule. You generally use a different command to create the access list. For example, the command to create a Vines access list is `vines access-list 101`, as opposed to `ip access-list 101`.

IP, which is the focus of this book, allows numbers or names to identify access lists. You can pick any access list number within the range; you do not need to start with the first number in the range, although it is probably wise to do so. You can pick any name within some simple constraints you will learn about in Chapter 16.

Defining Criteria for Forwarding or Blocking Packets

When creating an access list, you define criteria and apply that criteria to each packet that the router processes. The router decides whether to forward or block each packet, based on whether or not the packet matches the criteria.

Typical criteria defined in access lists include packet source addresses, packet destination addresses, or the upper-layer protocol of the packet. To define an access list, you generally need the following information:

- Interface: router physical port
- Direction: in or out
- IP source address range: dotted decimal format
- IP destination address range: dotted decimal format
- IP type: ICMP/TCP/UDP
- TCP/UDP source port: remote host port
- TCP/UDP destination port: application
- Action: permit or deny

However, each protocol has its own specific set of criteria that you can define.

For a single access list, you can define multiple criteria in multiple, separate access list statements. Each of these statements should reference the same identifying name or number, to tie the statements to the same access list. You can have as many criteria statements as you want, limited only by the available memory. Of course, as you add more statements, comprehension and management of your access lists becomes more difficult.

Router as a Closed System: The Implied Deny All Traffic

At the end of every access list is an implied "deny all traffic" criteria statement. When a packet does not match any of your criteria statements, the router will block the packet by default.

Caution: For most protocols, if you define an inbound access list for traffic filtering, you should include explicit access list criteria statements to permit routing updates. If you do not, you might effectively lose communication from the interface when the router blocks routing updates with the implicit "deny all traffic" statement at the end of the access list.

Interestingly enough, your router comes with access-list 0, which allows all traffic. So, Cisco ships your router as an open system — everything is allowed unless denied. The removal of this access list effectively turns on packet filtering.

Bringing Order to Chaos

When you enter additional criteria, the router appends the new statements to the end of the existing access list statements. Unfortunately, you cannot delete individual statements after you create them. You can only delete an entire access list. Then, you can re-enter the commands you just deleted, but not the ones you intended to delete.

If the router did a sort on some criteria before packet processing, then this would not affect you. Or, it also would make a difference should the router process all statements looking for a match before making a decision on blocking any packet. But it does not. Thus, the order of access list statements is important. When the router is deciding whether to forward or block a packet, the Cisco IOS software tests the packet against each criteria statement in the order you created them. Should the router detect a match, the router will not check any further criteria statements. If you explicitly permit all traffic, the router will never check statements you add later.

If you need additional statements, you must delete the access list and retype it with the new entries, unless the statements make sense added to the end of the existing access list.

Exhibit 3 graphically shows the philosophy of access list creation. When writing permit statements, start specifically. When writing deny statements, start generically. In addition to helping you create the correct rules, these simple axioms reduce the amount of router rule processing and make the list more efficient.

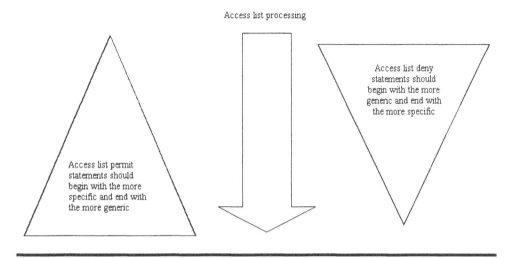

Access list processing

Access list permit statements should begin with the more specific and end with the more generic

Access list deny statements should begin with the more generic and end with the more specific

Exhibit 3   Access List Processing

To summarize these rules: every access list has an implicit "deny everything else" statement at the end of the list to ensure that attributes that you do not expressly permit are, in fact, denied. It also is important to remember that:

- Checking stops after the first match.
- When no match is found, the packet is dropped; that is, it goes into the bit bucket.

Comparing Basic and Advanced Access Lists

This chapter describes how to use standard and static extended access lists, which are the basic types of access lists. Subsequent chapters will introduce advanced access list concepts. You should use some type of basic access list with each routed protocol that you have configured for your router interfaces.

Standard access lists deny or permit packets traversing a router interface based solely on the source address or address range of the packet. You can use standard access lists as a tool to restrict access to specific users and allow access to others. You apply the access lists to the interface of a router where you want to filter traffic. Typically, you use standard access lists to implement your policy for:

- Access to router resources
- Route distribution
- Packets passing through a router

One problem with standard access lists is the lack of granularity: it is an all-or-nothing proposition. You permit traffic to the network or you do not. You might want to control the traffic flow a little better. Extended access lists provide the above controls but also allow you to control the flow of packets through the router. Perhaps you want to restrict the packets to a particular host to only HTTP or SSL HTTP ports. You cannot do this with standard access lists because they deal only with addresses, not services or applications; so you must use the extended access list format. In addition, there is no way to specify the protocol — ICMP, TCP, or UDP — in the standard access list.

Besides the basic types of access lists described in this chapter, there are also more advanced access lists available that provide additional security features and greater control over packets. These advanced access lists and features are described in Chapters 16 through 18.

Specifying Standard IP Access Lists

One of the first things you need to know is that there is one predefined access list — access-list 0 — that permits any access. Removing access-list 0 permits you to start filtering.

All access lists are similar in syntax, but we will look at standard and extended access lists in this chapter. Following is the syntax for a standard access list:

```
2501-1(config)#access-list access-list-number {permit |
    deny} address [wildcard-mask] [log]
```

where `access-list-number` is an integer from 1 to 99. Exhibit 2 showed you the list numbers for the various types of access lists you can create. In this case, you select a number from 1 to 99 as you are creating a standard IP access list. You can have more than one access list statement in an access list. Your access list number identifies an individual access group that can consist of multiple access list entries. `address` and `wildcard-mask` are 32-bit values for IP addresses. The optional `wildcard-mask` is a bit mask. The router interprets a 1 to signify any value, so 0 or 1 is valid. A 0 indicates an exact match. Making any octet all 1s (255) means match anything. Thus, if you specify the last octet as all 1s, you are really specifying all hosts in that network.

You can use the `host`, `any`, and `log` keywords, which you will learn about when you get to the extended IP access list syntax. `log` became available as an option for standard access lists with IOS version 11.3.

Using the Standard Access List

The following access-list entries demonstrate a simple security policy. Exhibit 4 shows the logical flow of the standard access list. You can trace packets through the router using this flowchart.

The first command permits access for all hosts on the Class C network 192.168.180.0 and the second permits access for all hosts on Class B network 172.16.0.0

```
2501-1(config)#access-list 1 permit 192.168.180.0 0.0.0.255
2501-1(config)#access-list 1 permit 172.16.0.0 0.0.255.255
```

The router will deny any packets from network 192.168.181.0 and any packets from 172.17.0.0, but it will allow all traffic from hosts 192.168.180.1 and 172.16.1.1.

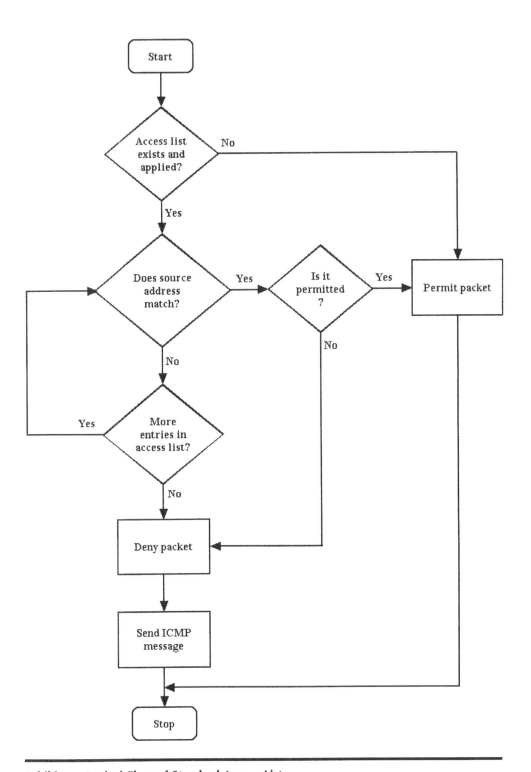

Exhibit 4   Logical Flow of Standard Access Lists

As you probably observed from this access list, you do not have a lot of granularity. Depending on the interface, you can filter inbound and outbound traffic but you cannot specify source and destination addresses. You also cannot filter on applications or source ports.

The previous is an example of controlling access to resources. You can also create access lists for route acceptance and distribution. You want a policy that restricts your router from forwarding any traffic not destined for your subnetworks. So, assuming your subnetworks are 10.30 and 10.33, the following rules would apply:

```
2501-1(config)#access-list 3 permit 10.30.0.0
2501-1(config)#access-list 3 permit 10.33.0.0
```

It is important to distinguish between hosts in a subnetwork and the subnetwork itself. For example, look at the following access list for a Class C address:

```
2501-1(config)#access-list 3 permit 192.168.24.0
```

This entry specifies the host 192.168.24.0. This is a strange address because Class C addresses do not typically end in a zero, whereas network addresses do. The following entry is very different because it includes all hosts in subnet 192.168.24.

```
2501-1(config)#access-list 3 permit 192.168.24.0 0.0.0.255
```

The first entry does not include all hosts in network 192.168.24.0/24. So, although it is a strange entry, you might use it to build an access list for routing as follows:

```
2501-1(config)#router eigrp 100
2501-1(config)#distribute-list 3 in Serial0
```

This entry allows only the route to network 192.168.24.0 into the routing table using the EIGRP protocol. Thus, it is important to remind yourself of your policy and what you hope to accomplish with each entry when trying to implement your policy.

If you have read and understood Appendix G, "Determining Wildcard Mask Ranges," then you know that ip access-list 3 permit 192.168.24.0 0.0.0.255 not only includes network 192.168.24.0/24, but also includes networks 192.168.24.0/25, 192.168.24.128/25, and 192.168.24.192/26. It includes these networks, and others, which have different mask lengths. So it is best when writing rules to be very specific; otherwise, you might get unexpected results and allow or disallow some traffic.

Netmasks and Wildcard Masks

Perhaps at this point you are somewhat confused between netmask and wildcard mask. If you are unsure of netmasks, refer to Appendix B, "Subnetting," for a thorough discussion. In the example just used, the netmask for 192.168.24.0/24 is 255.255.255.0 (or the 24 bits specified). The 1s specify the network portion of the address. The access list wildcard mask for the network is 0.0.0.255, or the remaining 8 bits because they refer to the host portion of the address. You can generalize this and say that the access list wildcard mask that matches all addresses in a network will have 1s in the 32-n rightmost bits and 0 in the leftmost n bits. For the network 192.168.24.0/26, the access list wildcard mask that matches all hosts is 0.0.0.63. This is equivalent to 6 bits in the rightmost column. It is 6 bits because the network borrowed 2 bits for the subnet mask. And the network mask on the interface is 255.255.255.192. You can test your numbers because they must total 255.

For a supernet such as 192.168.24.0/22, the access list wildcard mask matching all hosts is 0.0.3.255 and the network mask is 255.255.252.0. If you find this math a little fuzzy, review Appendix B again (or for the first time).

Implicit Wildcard Masks

A very useful IP address and wildcard mask is 0.0.0.0 and 255.255.255.255. This combination translates into all possible addresses. Because each bit in the wildcard mask is 1, any value (0 or 1) will match.

You saw the use of the implicit wildcard mask in the following:

```
2501-1(config)#access-list 3 permit 10.30.0.0
```

This is functionally equivalent to:

```
2501-1(config)#access-list 3 permit 10.30.0.0 0.0.0.0
```

A zero means that only the absolute value is allowed. So, if you apply this on a bit-by-bit basis, you will end with the same address you started with. This is an important concept as well. Implicit wildcard masks are a handy concept because they save typing, but make sure you know what the rule really does and that you have not given or taken away access.

Understanding Sequential Rule Processing

As previously stated, the router processes the rules in sequence. It takes the first rule, and when there is a match, the router either permits or denies. When there is no match, the router processes the next rule, and so on, until it finishes the rules and then blocks everything. So the order of the rules or entries is extremely important when you are trying to implement your organization's policy. Take the following simple security policy for a company:

Rule 1: Block all traffic to subnet 0.23.0.0 for Class A network 10.0.0.0
Rule 2: Except allow traffic to host 10.23.2.5
Rule 3: Allow traffic for all other subnets of 10.0.0.0

If you did the rules in the order shown, you would have a problem. You would not allow traffic to host 10.24.2.5 because you blocked all traffic to subnet 24 in Rule 1. So your rules should look something like the following:

```
2501-1(config)#access-list 2 permit 10.23.2.5 0.0.0.0
2501-1(config)#access-list 2 deny 10.23.0.0 0.0.255.255
2501-1(config)#access-list 2 permit 10.0.0.0 0.255.255.255
```

First you let in the allowed host in the subnet and then block the remainder of the subnet. You could have written the rules as follows:

```
2501-1(config)#access-list 2 deny 10.23.0.0 0.0.255.255
2501-1(config)#access-list 2 permit 10.23.2.5 0.0.0.0
2501-1(config)#access-list 2 permit 10.0.0.0 0.255.255.255
```

Had you written the above rules, you would have blocked access to host 10.23.2.5 in the first statement, which is contrary to the policy statements for the company. Thus, order is important!

Specifying Extended IP Access Lists

Standard access lists just do not provide the granularity in rule writing you might require. Conceivably, you want to allow access to only one service or application on a host or you do not want people on the outside pinging hosts. This is where you use the extensions to the standard access list. You can extend it to specify protocol type, protocol port, and destination in a certain direction. For example, you can filter out selected types of connections by denying packets that are attempting to use that service. You also can use IP extended access lists (range 100 to 199) and Transmission Control Protocol (TCP) or User Datagram Protocol (UDP) port numbers to filter traffic. When a client attempts to establish a connection for e-mail, Telnet, FTP, etc., the connection will attempt to open a service on a specified port number. You can, therefore, filter out selected types of connections by denying packets that are attempting to use that service. For a list of well-known services and ports, see Appendix D, "Well-Known Ports and Services."

Following is the syntax for the extended access list:

```
access-list access-list-number {permit | deny} {protocol |
   protocol-keyword} {source source-mask | any} [operator
   port [port]] {destination destination-mask | any}
   [operator port [port]] [options]
```

where

- access-list-number is an integer from 100 to 199.
- protocol corresponds to the protocol name or number. Acceptable keywords are:

```
ahp       Authentication Header Protocol
eigrp     Cisco's EIGRP routing protocol
esp       Encapsulation Security Payload
```

```
gre     Cisco's GRE tunneling
icmp    Internet Control Message Protocol
igmp    Internet Gateway Message Protocol
igrp    Cisco's IGRP routing protocol
ip      Any Internet Protocol
ipinip  IP in IP tunneling
nos     KA9Q NOS compatible IP over IP tunneling
ospf    OSPF routing protocol
pcp     Payload Compression Protocol
pim     Protocol Independent Multicast
tcp     Transmission Control Protocol
udp     User Datagram Protocol
```

Refer to Appendix C, "IP Protocol Numbers," for a list of possible numbers for this keyword.

- source and source-mask are 32-bit values for source IP addresses.
- destination and destination-mask are 32-bit values for destination IP addresses.
- operator and port are used to compare port numbers, service access points, or contact names.
  - *operator* can be *lt* or < (less than), *eq* or = (equal to), *gt* or > (greater than), and *neq* (not equal to). Range is a valid operator as well.
  - *port* is the decimal value of destination port for the specified protocol. Again, refer to Appendix D, "Well-Known Ports and Services," for the possible values for this keyword.
- options include established, icmp-type, log, and remark. Established indicates an established connection. icmp-type is used for filtering ICMP message type. You can also specify the ICMP message code (0-255). log or logging causes an information logging entry. remark allows you to add text comments to an access list.

Some configurations are so common that Cisco has provided some text substitutes for ports or address pairs. For example, you remember the useful IP address and wildcard mask of 0.0.0.0 and 255.255.255.255. This combination matched any host or network address. You can replace this combination with the keyword any.

You also can replace <IP address> 0.0.0.0 with the form host <IP address>. Notice the host keyword, which basically takes the place of a mask of 0.0.0.0.

In addition, you can replace well-known ports with their protocol acronyms. For example, the following two commands are functionally equivalent.

```
2501-1(config)#access-list 100 permit 6 0.0.0.0
   255.255.255.255 172.16.10.1 0.0.0.0 eq 80
2501-1(config)#access-list 100 permit tcp any host
   172.16.10.1 eq www
```

Exhibit 5   CERT Advisory on TCP and UDP Services

Service	Protocol	Port Number
DNS zone transfers	TCP	53
TFTP daemon (tftpd)	UDP	69
link	TCP	87
Sun RPC	TCP/UDP	111[a]
BSD UNIX r-commands (rsh, rlogin, etc.)	TCP	512–514
line printer daemon (lpd)	TCP	515
UNIX-to-UNIX Copy Program daemon (uucpd)	TCP	540
Open Windows	TCP/UDP	2000
NFS	UDP	2049
X Windows	TCP/UDP	6000+

[a] Port 111 is only a directory service. If you can guess the ports where the actual data services are provided, you can access them. Most RPC services do not have fixed port numbers. You should find the port where these services can be found and block them. Unfortunately, because you can bind ports anywhere, Cisco recommends blocking all UDP ports except DNS where practical.

Obviously, the first command is more cryptic. Using text shortens the access list and also generally makes them more readable and hence more understandable.

So now you are probably thinking to yourself: What ports do I filter or block? As a result of the Robert Morris Internet Worm of 1988, ARPA funds helped set up the Computer Emergency Response Team/Coordination Center at the Software Engineering Institute of Carnegie-Mellon University in Pittsburgh, Pennsylvania. The CERT/CC (http://www.cert.org) provides a valuable resource for all users of the Internet, and recommends filtering the services listed in Exhibit 5.

The Systems Administration, Networking and Security (SANS) Institute (http://www.sans.org) recommends that you block the ports in Exhibit 6. It also recommends that you block incoming ICMP echo request (ping and traceroute), and outgoing echo replies, time exceeded, and destination unreachable messages except "packet too big" messages (type 3, code 4).

Finally, the book in the bibliography by Cheswick and Bellovin (Addison-Wesley, 1994) is also an excellent source.

SANS experts are quick to point out that filtering on any list of ports is not an adequate substitute for the development of a comprehensive security solution. You may block and still be at risk because those individuals who have gained access to your network can exploit these ports when you do not properly secure them on every host system in your organization.

There are a number of nonstandard services available from the Internet that provide value-added services when connecting to the outside world. In the case of a connection to the Internet, these services can be very elaborate and complex. Examples of these services are Gnutella, World Wide Web (WWW), Wide Area Information Service (WAIS), gopher, and Mosaic. These systems provide a wealth of information to the user in some organized fashion and allow structured browsing and searching. Most of these systems have their own defined protocol. Some, such as Mosaic, use several different protocols to obtain the information in

Exhibit 6   SANS Advice on TCP and UDP Services

Service	Protocol	Port Number
Log-in services		
FTP	TCP	21
SSH	TCP	22
Telnet	TCP	23
NetBIOS	TCP	139
rlogin et al.	TCP	512–514
RPC and NFS		
Portmap/rpcbind	TCP/UDP	111
NFS	TCP/UDP	2049
lockd	TCP/UDP	4045
NetBIOS in Windows NT (NBT)		
loc-srv	TCP/UDP	135
netbios-ns	UDP	137
netbios-dgm	UDP	138
netbios-ssn	TCP/UDP	139
microsoft-ds	TCP/UDP	445
X Windows	TCP	6000–6255
Naming services		
DNS to all machines that are not DNS servers	UDP	53
DNS zone transfers except from external secondaries	TCP	53
LDAP	TCP/UDP	389
Mail		
SMTP to all machines except external mail relays	TCP	25
POP	TCP	109–110
IMAP	TCP	143
World Wide Web		
HTTP except to external Web servers	TCP	80
SSL except to external Web servers	TCP	443
Common high-order HTTP ports	TCP	8000, 8080, 8888
Small Services		
Ports below 20	TCP/UDP	<20
time	TCP/UDP	37
Miscellaneous		
TFTP	UDP	69
Finger	TCP	79
NNTP	TCP	119
NTP	TCP	123
SNMP	TCP/UDP	161–162
BGP	TCP	179
Syslog	UDP	514
LPD	TCP	515
SOCKS	TCP	1080

Exhibit 7   Bit Patterns

Third Octet Decimal Value	Binary Equivalent
8	00001000
9	00001001
10	00001010
11	00001011

question. Use caution when designing access lists applicable to each of these services. In many cases, the access lists will become interrelated as these services become interrelated. Gnutella is a good example.

The source and destination masks also deserve a little more discussion at this point. They are bit masks that apply to the corresponding bit in the source or destination address. A 1 in the mask is a wildcard in that it matches anything. It is a match no matter what value is the corresponding bit in the address. A 0 in the mask indicates that the corresponding bit must match the bit in the IP address exactly, or the absolute value. So far, you have seen only masks with 0 or 255, but you can use other masks as well. Let us look at four networks and see whether one entry might provide the same results. Look at the following access list entries:

```
2501-1(config)#access-list 100 ip permit 172.16.8.0
    0.0.0.255 any
2501-1(config)#access-list 100 ip permit 172.16.9.0
    0.0.0.255 any
2501-1(config)#access-list 100 ip permit 172.16.10.0
    0.0.0.255 any
2501-1(config)#access-list 100 ip permit 172.16.11.0
    0.0.0.255 any
```

Start by looking at the network numbers and seeing whether the networks have anything in common. Clearly, the first two octets or bytes are the same (172.16). So, let us write out the next octet in binary as shown in Exhibit 7.

Looking at the binary equivalent, you can see that the first 6 bits are the same: 000010. The last 2 bits vary from 00 to 11, all the possible values for the 2 bits. Any bit pattern in those 2 bits will match, whereas the first 6 bits must be the real value. Therefore, you can consider the last 2 bits as wildcard, so the pattern for the third octet is 00000011, or 3 in decimal. Now you can write one access list to replace the previous four as follows:

```
2501-1(config)#access-list 100 permit ip 172.16.8.0
    0.0.3.255 any
```

In fact, any one of the following satisfies the same goal:

```
2501-1(config)#access-list 100 permit ip 172.16.9.0
    0.0.3.255 any
```

Exhibit 8   Bit Patterns

Third Octet Decimal Value	Binary Equivalent
10	00001010
11	00001011
12	00001100
13	00001101

```
2501-1(config)#access-list 100 permit ip 172.16.10.0
  0.0.3.255 any
2501-1(config)#access-list 100 permit ip 172.16.11.0
  0.0.3.255 any
```

You should probably stick with the first access list, as it is more intuitive. Think of it as starting at network 8 and you have three more networks. This is fairly illuminating but does not help us write any rules for masking yet. Let us look at four more access list entries:

```
2501-1(config)#access-list 100 ip permit 172.16.10.0
  0.0.0.255 any
2501-1(config)#access-list 100 ip permit 172.16.11.0
  0.0.0.255 any
2501-1(config)#access-list 100 ip permit 172.16.12.0
  0.0.0.255 any
2501-1(config)#access-list 100 ip permit 172.16.13.0
  0.0.0.255 any
```

Again, write out the next octet in binary as shown in Exhibit 8.

The first 6 bits are not the same anymore. The last 3 bits are different and have the values 010, 011, 100, and 101. So, if you apply what you just saw, you might create the following:

```
2501-1(config)#access-list 100 ip permit 172.16.10.0
  0.0.7.255 any
```

However, this is wrong because it includes networks from 8 (1000) to 15 (1111). Look at the examples and you can conclude two things:

- The number of values you match is a power of 2. There are 2, 4, 8, 16, 32, 64, 128, or 256 values that you can match together.
- The starting address matched is a multiple of the number of values you match. If you match two addresses, then the first address you match is a multiple of 2 (even). If you match four addresses, then the starting address is a multiple of 4, etc.

Exhibit 9   Bit Patterns

Third Octet Decimal Value	Binary Equivalent
217	11011001
221	11011101

So if you try the address and mask pair 172.16.10.0 0.0.3.255, you violate Rule 1. You need to match a power of 2, in this case 4, because you are trying to match four networks. The second rule specifies that the values matched must start on a multiple of 4, and 10 obviously is not. Because the closest multiple of 4 is 8, that is why network 172.16.8.0 worked. Because 10 is not a multiple of 4, you cannot use a single mask to match the four networks. You can, however, use more than one set of masks. Although 10 is not divisible by 4, it is still an even number. This means that a mask of 1 with 10 would cover networks 10 and 11 and a mask of 1 with 12 would cover networks 12 and 13 as shown following:

```
2501-1(config)#access-list 100 ip permit 172.16.10.0
   0.0.1.255 any
2501-1(config)#access-list 100 ip permit 172.16.12.0
   0.0.1.255 any
```

Thus, you can add some additional rules to ones you just saw:

- The wildcard mask is always one less than the group size. If you have a group of 8, the wildcard mask is 7. A group of 64 has a wildcard mask of 63.
- Your matching rules should always give the base address of a range, followed by the mask. While any address within the range will work, to eliminate future headaches, start with the base value.
- If you want to match some number of addresses that is not a power of 2 or does not start at a multiple of a power of 2, you have to write two or more access lists, each covering part of the range. You could, of course, include more addresses in your range. This may or may not cause problems.

You can condense access lists whenever bits match, which can happen in the middle of the octet and not just at the end. Consider the following:

```
2501-1(config)#access-list 100 ip permit 172.16.217.0
   0.0.0.255 any
2501-1(config)#access-list 100 ip permit 172.16.221.0
   0.0.0.255 any
```

Write out the next octet in binary as shown in Exhibit 9.
   Using the pattern from Exhibit 9, you can combine the two into one:

```
2501-1(config)#access-list 100 ip permit 172.16.217.0
   0.0.4.255 any
```

While you can combine access lists, you may not want to. The access list you created is not exactly intuitive. So unless there are compelling reasons otherwise, such as a resource constraint, you might want to leave the two access lists for, if for no other reason, documentation purposes. To help you with your calculations, you will find the Binary/Decimal Conversion Chart found in Appendix A helpful. Finally, to really make things easy for you, Exhibit 10 provides common access wildcard masks for networks.

The command syntax revolves around the access list number. As with addressing itself, prudent use of access list numbers may save you time and effort. Remember that you are going to write rules and group them and apply the group to an interface. Also remember that you are limited in the amount of access lists you can write; for example, 100 to 199 for extended IP access lists.

Finally, you should refer to the extended IP access format as static; that is, the port is open and the rules do not change until you go into the router and physically modify it. It really is static because the router makes its decision to drop a packet strictly on the packet it is looking at. In Chapter 17, you will learn about dynamic access lists.

Creating Access Lists

Let us create an organization that wants to implement packet filtering. This example organization has the following security policy:

- The organization permits incoming e-mail and news for a few hosts.
- The organization permits FTP, Telnet, and rlogin services only to hosts on the firewall subnet.

This example assumes that the organization uses IP addresses 172.16.0.0/16.

Before network loading the access control definition, the organization would remove any previous definition of this access list with the following command:

```
2501-1(config)#no access-list 100
```

> **Note:** If you delete an access list using the `no access-list` command, the router will default to all packets allowed. So, you have a small window of vulnerability after the execution of this command and the moment you enter the new access list statement. Once you enter the first access list entry, the router falls back to explicit denial. The risk that this window of opportunity may cause you grief is small, but it is possible. There is a simple way around this. Build a new list with a new access list number. Apply this new one by changing the access-group statement. Then you can use the previous list to make changes and then apply it in the same fashion.
>
> You will see in Chapter 16 that using named access lists also helps.

Exhibit 10 Wildcard Masks for Prefix Lengths

Prefix Length	Subnet Mask	Wildcard Mask Matching All Hosts	Valid Networks with the Prefix
/8	255.0.0.0	0.255.255.255	{1-126,128-223}.0.0.0
/9	255.128.0.0	0.127.255.255	{1-126,128-223}.{0-128}.0.0
/10	255.192.0.0	0.63.255.255	{1-126,128-223}.{0,64,128,192}.0.0
/11	255.224.0.0	0.31.255.255	{1-126,128-223}.{0,32,64,128,192,224}.0.0
/12	255.240.0.0	0.15.255.255	{1-126,128-223}.{0,16,32,48,64,80,96,102}.0.0
			{1-126,128-223}.{128,144,160,176,192,208,224,240}.0.0
/13	255.248.0.0	0.7.255.255	{1-126,128-223}.{0,8,16,24,32,40,48,56}.0.0
			{1-126,128-223}.{64,72,80,88,96,104,112,120}.0.0
			{1-126,128-223}.{128,136,144,152,160,168,176,184}.0.0
			{1-126,128-223}.{192,200,208,216,224,232,240,248}.0.0
/14	255.252.0.0	0.3.255.255	{1-126,128-223}.{0,4,8,…248,252}.0.0
/15	255.254.0.0	0.1.255.255	{1-126,128-223}.{0,2,4…252,254}.0.0
/16	255.255.0.0	0.0.255.255	{1-126,128-223}.{0-255}.0.0
/17	255.255.128.0	0.0.127.255	{1-126,128-223}.{0-255}.{0,128}.0
/18	255.255.192.0	0.0.63.255	{1-126,128-223}.{0-255}.{0,64,128,192}.0
/19	255.255.224.0	0.0.31.255	{1-126,128-223}.{0-255}.{0,32,64,96}.0
			{1-126,128-223}.{0-255}.{128,160,192,224}.0
/20	255.255.240.0	0.0.15.255	{1-126,128-223}.{0-255}.{0,16,32,48}.0
			{1-126,128-223}.{0-255}.{64,80,96,102}.0
			{1-126,128-223}.{0-255}.{128,144,160,176}.0
			{1-126,128-223}.{0-255}.{192,208,224,240}.0
/21	255.255.248.0	0.0.7.255	{1-126,128-223}.{0-255}.{0,8,16,24}.0
			{1-126,128-223}.{0-255}.{32,40,48,56}.0
			{1-126,128-223}.{0-255}.{64,73,80,88}.0
			{1-126,128-223}.{0-255}.{96,104,112,120}.0
			{1-126,128-223}.{0-255}.{128,136,144,152}.0
			{1-126,128-223}.{0-255}.{192,200,208,216}.0
			{1-126,128-223}.{0-255}.{224,232,240,248}.0
/22	255.255.252.0	0.0.3.255	{1-126,128-223}.{0-255}.{0,4,8…248,252}.0
/23	255.255.254.0	0.0.1.255	{1-126,128-223}.{0-255}.{0,2,4…252,254}.0
/24	255.255.255.0	0.0.0.255	{1-126,128-223}.{0-255}.{0-255}.0
/25	255.255.255.128	0.0.0.127	{1-126,128-223}.{0-255}.{0-255}.{0,128}
/26	255.255.255.192	0.0.0.63	{1-126,128-223}.{0-255}.{0-255}.{0,64,128,192}
/27	255.255.255.224	0.0.0.31	{1-126,128-223}.{0-255}.{0-255}.{0,32,64,96}
			{1-126,128-223}.{0-255}.{0-255}.{128,160,192,224}
/28	255.255.255.240	0.0.0.15	{1-126,128-223}.{0-255}.{0-255}.{0,16,32,48}.
			{1-126,128-223}.{0-255}.{0-255}.{64,80,96,102}
			{1-126,128-223}.{0-255}.{0-255}.{128,144,160,176}
			{1-126,128-223}.{0-255}.{0-255}.{192,208,224,240}
/29	255.255.255.248	0.0.0.7	{1-126,128-223}.{0-255}.{0-255}.{0,8,16,24}
			{1-126,128-223}.{0-255}.{0-255}.{32,40,48,56}
			{1-126,128-223}.{0-255}.{0-255}.{64,73,80,88}
			{1-126,128-223}.{0-255}.{0-255}.{96,104,112,120}
			{1-126,128-223}.{0-255}.{0-255}.{128,136,144,152}
			{1-126,128-223}.{0-255}.{0-255}.{192,200,208,216}
			{1-126,128-223}.{0-255}.{0-255}.{224,232,240,248}
/30	255.255.255.252	0.0.0.3	{1-126,128-223}.{0-255}.{0-255}.{0,4,8…248,252}
/31	255.255.255.254	0.0.0.1	{1-126,128-223}.{0-255}.{0-255}.{0,2,4…252,254}
/32	255.255.255.255	0.0.0.0	{1-126,128-223}.{0-255}.{0-255}.{0-254}

The organization can now use the `access-list` command to permit any packets returning to machines from already established connections. With the `established` keyword, a match occurs when the TCP datagram has the acknowledgment (ACK) or reset (RST) bits set.

```
2501-1(config)#access-list 100 permit tcp 0.0.0.0
   255.255.255.255 172.16.0.0 0.0.255.255 established
```

If any firewall routers share a common network with an outside provider, the organization may want to allow access from those hosts to its network. In this example, the outside provider has a serial port that uses the firewall router Class B address (172.16.14.2) as a source address as follows:

```
2501-1(config)#access-list 100 permit ip 172.16.14.2 0.0.0.0
   0.0.0.0 255.255.255.255
```

Unfortunately, it is not practical to give a simple list of commands that will provide appropriate spoofing protection; access list configuration depends too much on the individual network. However, the basic goal is simple: to discard packets that arrive on interfaces that are not viable paths from the supposed source addresses of those packets. For example, on a two-interface router connecting a corporate network to the Internet, any datagram that arrives on the Internet interface, but whose source address field claims that it came from a machine on the corporate network, should be discarded. Similarly, any datagram arriving on the interface connected to the corporate network, but whose source address field claims that it came from a machine outside the corporate network, should be discarded. Following are some simple rules you should consider implementing:

1. Any incoming packet must not have a source address for your internal network.
2. Any incoming packet must have a destination address for your internal network.
3. Any outgoing packet must have a source address for your internal network.
4. Any outgoing packet must not have a destination address for your internal network.
5. Any incoming or outgoing packet must not have a source or destination address of a private address or an address listed in the RFC1918 reserved space. These include the private network addresses (10.0.0.0/8, 172.16.0.0/12, or 192.168.0.0/16) and the loopback network (127.0.0.0/8).
6. Block any source routed packets or any packets with the IP options field set.

If CPU resources allow, you should apply anti-spoofing techniques on any interface where it is feasible to determine what traffic may legitimately arrive. Some appropriate commands include:

```
2501-1(config)#access-list 100 deny icmp any any redirect
2501-1(config)#access-list 100 deny ip host 127.0.0.0
   0.255.255.255 any
```

```
2501-1(config)#access-list 100 deny ip 224.0.0.0
   31.255.255.255 any
2501-1(config)#access-list 100 deny ip host 0.0.0.0 any
```

The first access list denies ICMP traffic from any host to any other host when it is a redirect. The `redirect` is a keyword. The second access list denies any traffic (i.e., ICMP, TCP, and UDP) to the reserved network 127 from anywhere. The address 127.0.0.1 is a special address, sometimes called the loopback address, that designates the localhost. You should see an entry in the host file on your system (look in /etc/hosts on UNIX systems and \windows\hosts on Windows 95, 98, and Me) for localhost. The third denies any traffic to the multicast addresses. The last denies traffic from a host address of 0.0.0.0 to anywhere (this may help stop you from becoming someone's zombie or agent in a denial-of-service attack).

The following example illustrates how this example organization might deny traffic from a user attempting to spoof any of the private addresses from both the inside and the outside:

```
2501-1(config)#access-list 100 deny ip any 10.0.0.0
   0.255.255.255
2501-1(config)#access-list 100 deny ip 10.0.0.0
   0.255.255.255 any
2501-1(config)#access-list 100 deny ip any 172.16.0.0
   0.15.255.255
2501-1(config)#access-list 100 deny ip 172.16.0.0
   0.15.255.255 any
2501-1(config)#access-list 100 deny ip any 192.168.0.0
   0.0.255.255
2501-1(config)#access-list 100 deny ip 192.168.0.0
   0.0.255.255 any
```

You might also want to include an entry to log when there is some evidence someone is port scanning your network or router. Pick a known cracker target, such as chargen (character generator on port 19), and monitor attempted access. You might consider these attempts as indicative of cracker activity.

```
2501-1(config)#access-list 100 deny tcp any any eq 19 log
```

The following commands allow Domain Name System (DNS) and Network Time Protocol (NTP) requests and replies:

```
2501-1(config)#access-list 100 permit udp 0.0.0.0
   255.255.255.255 0.0.0.0 255.255.255.255 eq 53
2501-1(config)#access-list 100 permit udp 0.0.0.0
   255.255.255.255 0.0.0.0 255.255.255.255 eq 123
```

The second command accepts time updates from any source. This could lead to fraudulent updates or spoofed packets. Up to this point, where there are specified ports, they have only been destination ports — not source. You might want to match on the source port as well as the destination. NTP uses port 123 for both source and destination. Should you find a packet destined for port 123 with a source of something other than 123, then chances are that it is something other than NTP packets. So let us fine-tune the last statement.

```
2501-1(config)#access-list 100 permit udp 172.16.0.0
   0.0.255.255 eq 123 172.16.0.0 0.0.255.255 eq 123
```

You might want to allow Traceroute packets. If you do, you will need to allow UDP out of your network and ICMP into your network. Th default port that Traceroute starts with is generally 33434, and some implementations increment the port with each set of probes. The following two commands should allow Traceroute to work:

```
2501-1(config)#access-list 100 permit udp host 172.16.0.0
   0.0.255.255 eq 33434 any
2501-1(config)#access-list 100 permit icmp any 172.16.0.0
   0.0.255.255 ttl-exceeded
```

The following command denies the network file server (NFS) User Datagram Protocol (UDP) port:

```
2501-1(config)#access-list 100 deny udp 0.0.0.0
   255.255.255.255 0.0.0.0 255.255.255.255 eq 2049
```

The following commands deny OpenWindows on ports 2001 and 2002, and deny X11 on ports 6001 and 6002. This protects the first two screens on any host. If you have any machine that uses more than the first two screens, be sure to block the appropriate ports.

```
2501-1(config)#access-list 100 deny tcp 0.0.0.0
   255.255.255.255 0.0.0.0 255.255.255.255 eq 6001
2501-1(config)#access-list 100 deny tcp 0.0.0.0
   255.255.255.255 0.0.0.0 255.255.255.255 eq 6002
2501-1(config)#access-list 100 deny tcp 0.0.0.0
   255.255.255.255 0.0.0.0 255.255.255.255 eq 2001
2501-1(config)#access-list 100 deny tcp 0.0.0.0
   255.255.255.255 0.0.0.0 255.255.255.255 eq 2002
```

You will need also to create access list entries for ports 6003 through 6255 to cover XWindows correctly. That is a lot of access list entries, but there is a simpler way and the access list entries are not necessarily all required. You can use the range keyword to get rid of most of the entries as follows:

```
2501-1(config)#access-list 100 deny tcp 0.0.0.0
   255.255.255.255 0.0.0.0 255.255.255.255 range 6000 6255
2501-1(config)#access-list 100 deny tcp 0.0.0.0
   255.255.255.255 0.0.0.0 255.255.255.255 range 2001 2002
```

The following command permits Telnet access to the communication server (172.16.13.2):

```
2501-1(config)#access-list 100 permit tcp 0.0.0.0
   255.255.255.255 172.16.13.2 0.0.0.0 eq 23
```

The following commands permit FTP access to the host on subnet 13:

```
2501-1(config)#access-list 100 permit tcp 0.0.0.0
   255.255.255.255 172.16.13.100 0.0.0.0 eq 21
2501-1(config)#access-list 100 permit tcp 0.0.0.0
   255.255.255.255 172.16.13.100 0.0.0.0 eq 20
```

If you wanted to improve your rules, you could match on the source port for the preceding command and use the following instead:

```
2501-1(config)#access-list 100 permit tcp 0.0.0.0
   255.255.255.255 gt 1023 172.16.13.100 0.0.0.0 eq 20
```

You know that the source will open an ephemeral port (greater than 1023), so you can specify those ports as the source.

For the following examples, network 172.16.1.0 is on the internal network. The following commands permit TCP' and UDP connections for port numbers greater than 1023 to a very limited set of hosts. Make sure no communication servers or protocol translators are in this list.

```
2501-1(config)#access-list 100 permit tcp 0.0.0.0
   255.255.255.255 172.16.13.100 0.0.0.0 gt 1023
2501-1(config)#access-list 100 permit tcp 0.0.0.0
   255.255.255.255 172.16.1.100 0.0.0.0 gt 1023
2501-1(config)#access-list 100 permit tcp 0.0.0.0
   255.255.255.255 172.16.1.101 0.0.0.0 gt 1023
2501-1(config)#access-list 100 permit udp 0.0.0.0
   255.255.255.255 172.16.13.100 0.0.0.0 gt 1023
2501-1(config)#access-list 100 permit udp 0.0.0.0
   255.255.255.255 172.16.1.100 0.0.0.0 gt 1023
2501-1(config)#access-list 100 permit udp 0.0.0.0
   255.255.255.255 172.16.1.101 0.0.0.0 gt 1023
```

Standard FTP uses ports above 1023 for its data connections; therefore, for standard FTP operation, ports above 1023 must all be open.

Many sites today choose to block incoming TCP sessions from the outside world while allowing outgoing connections. The trouble with this is that blocking incoming connections kills traditional FTP client programs because these programs use the port command to tell the server where to connect to send the file. The client opens a control connection to the server, but the server then opens a data connection to an effectively arbitrarily chosen (> 1023) port number on the client.

Fortunately, there is an alternative to this behavior that allows the client to open the data socket and allows you to have the router and FTP also. The client sends a `pasv` command to the server, receives back a port number for the data socket, opens the data socket to the indicated port, and finally sends the transfer.

To implement this method, you must replace the standard FTP client program with a modified one that supports the `pasv` command. Most recent implementations of the FTP server already support the `pasv` command. The only trouble with this idea is that it breaks down when the server site has also blocked arbitrary incoming connections.

Care should be taken in providing anonymous FTP service on the host system. Anonymous FTP service allows anyone to access the hosts, without requiring an account on the host system. Also, be careful in the implementation and setup of the anonymous FTP service to prevent any obvious access violations. Unless you have a compelling reason not to, you should disable anonymous FTP service.

The following commands permit DNS access to the DNS server(s) listed by the Network Information Center (NIC):

```
2501-1(config)#access-list 100 permit udp 0.0.0.0
   255.255.255.255 gt 1023 172.16.13.100 0.0.0.0 eq 53
2501-1(config)#access-list 100 permit udp 0.0.0.0
   255.255.255.255 gt 1023 172.16.13.101 0.0.0.0 eq 53
2501-1(config)#access-list 100 permit tcp 172.16.13.101
   255.255.255.255 gt 53 172.16.13.100 0.0.0.0 eq 53
```

The last command allows a zone transfer between the primary and secondary domain name systems. Be vigilant when you use TCP and DNS together!

The following commands permit incoming Simple Mail Transfer Protocol (SMTP) e-mail to only a few machines:

```
2501-1(config)#access-list 101 permit tcp 0.0.0.0
   255.255.255.255 172.16.13.100 0.0.0.0 eq 25
2501-1(config)#access-list 101 permit tcp 0.0.0.0
   255.255.255.255 172.16.13.101 0.0.0.0 eq 25
```

The following commands allow internal Network News Transfer Protocol (NNTP) servers to receive NNTP connections from a list of authorized peers:

```
2501-1(config)#access-list 100 permit tcp host 10.10.10.1
   host 172.16.1.100 eq 119
2501-1(config)#access-list 100 permit tcp host 10.10.10.2
   host 172.16.1.100 eq 119
```

ICMP does not use ports but, instead, you can filter on packet type, with the most common packet type being echo and echo-reply. The following command permits Internet Control Message Protocol (ICMP), specifically message type echo:

```
2501-1(config)#access-list 100 permit icmp 0.0.0.0
   255.255.255.255 0.0.0.0 255.255.255.255 echo
```

You can find the various ICMP types listed in Appendix F, "ICMP Types and Codes." Using this appendix, you can see that you also could use the following command to accomplish the same thing:

```
2501-1(config)#access-list 100 permit icmp any any eq 8
```

The following command denies General Routing Encapsulation (GRE) protocol:

```
2501-1(config)#access-list 100 permit 47 0.0.0.0
   255.255.255.255 0.0.0.0 255.255.255.255
```

GRE is used for tunneling non-IP protocols such as Novell IPX and AppleTalk through IP and by the PPTP protocol.

Applying Access Lists to Interfaces

After you load your access list onto the router and store it into nonvolatile random-access memory (NVRAM), you must assign it to the appropriate interface. As an example, you can do this with the following configuration commands:

```
2501-1(config)#int e0
2501-1(config-if)#ip access-group access-list-number [in |
   out]
```

The above applies to an Ethernet segment, but you could apply it to lines as well. The in | out keywords indicate whether you intend to filter inbound or outbound traffic on the interface.

The example organization wanted to filter traffic coming from the outside world via serial 0 before the router switches it to subnet 13 (Ethernet 0). Therefore, you must assign to Ethernet 0 the access-group command, which assigns an access list to filter incoming connections as follows:

```
2501-1#config t
Enter configuration commands, one per line. End with CNTL/Z.
2501-1(config)#interface ethernet 0
2501-1(config-if)#ip access-group 2 out
2501-1(config-if)#exit
2501-1(config)#interface ethernet 1
2501-1(config-if)#ip access-group 100 in
```

To control outgoing access to the Internet from the network, define an access list and apply it to the outgoing packets on serial 0 of the firewall router. To do this, returning packets from hosts using Telnet or FTP must be allowed to access the firewall subnetwork 172.16.13.0. A very simple rule might look similar to the following:

```
2501-1(config)#access-list 2 permit 172.16.0.0
```

For some protocols, you can apply up to two access lists to an interface: one inbound access list and one outbound access list. With other protocols, you apply only one access list that checks both inbound and outbound packets.

Caution: You can only apply one IP access list for each direction — inbound and outbound — at any time.

If the access list is inbound, when the router receives a packet, the Cisco IOS software checks the access list's criteria statements for a match. If the router permits the packet, the software continues to process the packet. If the router denies the packet, the software discards the packet.

If the access list is outbound, after receiving and routing a packet to the outbound interface, the software checks the access list's criteria statements for a match. If the router permits the packet, the software transmits the packet. If the router denies the packet, the software discards the packet.

Creating and Editing Access List Statements on a TFTP Server

Because the order of access list criteria statements is important, and because you cannot reorder or delete criteria statements on your router, Cisco recommends that you create all access list statements on a TFTP server and then download the entire access list to your router.

To use a TFTP server, create the access list statements using any text editor and save the access list in ASCII format to a TFTP server that your router can access. Then, from your router, use the `copy tftp running-config file_id` command to copy the access list to your router. Substitute the name of your file with the access list statements for `file_id`. Finally, perform the `copy running-config startup-config` command to save the access list to your router's NVRAM. Then, should you ever want to make changes to an access list, you can make them to the text file on the TFTP server and copy the edited file to your router as before.

Note: The first command of an edited access list file should delete the previous access list (e.g., type a `no access-list` command at the beginning of the file). If you do not first delete the previous version of the access list, then when you copy the edited file to your router, you will merely append the additional criteria statements to the end of the existing access list.

Practice Session

In this Practice Session, you will practice the following:

- Logging in
- Saving log data
- Switching modes
- Entering configuration mode
- Creating access lists for spoofing attempts
- Enabling and saving syslog data
- Logging out

Note: You might want to wait until the end of Chapter 16 before doing the Practice Session in this chapter.

---

1. Log in to the SimRouter Web page.
2. Double-click on router 2501-1 to telnet to that router. This will open a console session.
3. Enter your **Username** and **Password** at the applicable prompt. These are the ones you set up in Chapter 2. You will need to hit the Enter key twice to get to the > prompt.
4. Again, save the log for your session. To do this, select | Terminal | Start Logging | from the menu bar in the Telnet window. The Telnet client will ask you where you wish to store the log and with what name. Your choice. You are going to save the log so that when you build this configuration file, you can cut-and-paste it into the next as a starting point, rather than having to enter the same information each Practice Session.
5. Enter the enable mode:

   `2501-1#`**`enable`**

6. When prompted to put in the enable secret password, enter **oscar**.
7. Type **terminal length 0**. This command instructs the router to scroll through long command output without pausing (the —More— message).
8. You will paste the running-config that you saved from the Chapter 14 log. At the 2501-2# prompt, type **config t**.
9. If you did not do this, open your log file with the text editor of your choice (e.g., use | Start | Programs | Accessories | Notepad |). Do a find on sh running-config and copy from the first "!" to "end." At the 2501-2(config)# prompt, paste this configuration.
10. Type **access-list 100 deny icmp any any redirect** and press Enter.
11. Type **access-list 100 deny ip host 127.0.0.0 0.255.255.255 any** and press Enter.
12. Type **access-list 100 deny ip 224.0.0.0 31.255.255.255 any** and press Enter.
13. Type **access-list 100 deny ip host 0.0.0.0 any** and press Enter.
14. Type **access-list 100 deny ip any 10.0.0.0 0.255.255.255** and press Enter.

15. Type **access-list 100 deny ip 10.0.0.0 0.255.255.255 any** and press Enter.
16. Type **access-list 100 deny ip any 172.16.0.0 0.15.255.255** and press Enter.
17. Type **access-list 100 deny ip 172.16.0.0 0.15.255.255 any** and press Enter.
18. Type **access-list 100 deny ip any 192.168.0.0 0.0.255.255** and press Enter.
19. Type **access-list 100 deny ip 192.168.0.0 0.0.255.255 any** and press Enter.
20. Type **sh running-config** and press Enter. You will use this new configuration to start the next Practice Session.
21. Type **quit** to log out from router 2501-1. Close the Telnet window and return to the SimRouter Topology Map.
22. Click on Log Out on the SimRouter Web page.

Security and Audit Checklist

1. Does your organization have a security architecture that details the security policy for packet filtering?
   - Yes
   - No
2. Have you reviewed the recommendations from CERT, SANS, and other sources for packet filtering?
   - Yes
   - No
3. Does your policy seem reasonable?
   - Yes
   - No
4. Do you use access lists in your organization?
   - Yes
   - No
5. Do you use access lists on the following segments?
   - Ethernet
   - Token Ring
   - ISDN
   - Serial
6. Do you use access lists in your organization for:
   - AppleTalk?
   - Apollo Domain?
   - DECnet?
   - Ethernet address?
   - Ethernet type code?
   - IP?
   - IPX?
   - IPX SAP?

- ISO CLNS?
- NetBIOS IPX?
- Source-route bridging?
- Transparent bridging?
- VINES?
- XNS?

7. Do you filter TCP traffic?
   - Yes
   - No
8. Do you filter UDP traffic?
   - Yes
   - No
9. Do you filter ICMP traffic?
   - Yes
   - No
10. Do you filter any other IP traffic?
    - Yes
    - No
11. Do you use standard access lists?
    - Yes
    - No
12. Do you use static extended IP access lists?
    - Yes
    - No
13. Do you use the log keyword?
    - Yes
    - No
14. Do you have a procedure in place to review access lists for currency?
    - Yes
    - No
15. Is someone tasked with reviewing access list counters?
    - Yes
    - No
16. Do you have a formal procedure for creating, updating, and deleting access lists?
    - Yes
    - No
17. Does someone other than the implementers authorize all access list changes?
    - Yes
    - No

Conclusion

In this chapter, you learned about packet filtering to prevent unauthorized access to your network. You saw the syntax for standard and extended IP access lists, and you learned how to apply those that you created.

There are many reasons to configure access lists. For example, you can use access lists to restrict contents of routing updates or to provide traffic flow control. However, one of the most important reasons to configure access lists is to provide security for your network; this is the primary thrust of this chapter.

You should use access lists to provide a basic level of security for accessing your network. If you do not configure access lists on your router, you are allowing all packets to pass through the router and into your network. Moreover, you can use access lists to decide what types of traffic your router will forward or block at its interfaces. For example, you can permit your router to route e-mail traffic, but at the same time block all Telnet traffic.

The most important thing to remember is that your organization needs to do the tough stuff, which is to do the work and develop a security policy. Once you have a security policy, almost anyone can implement it. (Especially after they read this book.)

Chapter 16 continues with access lists and looks at some additional keywords, named access lists, and route filtering before moving on to the advanced packet filtering topics.

Chapter 16

Basic Traffic Filtering, Part 2

In this chapter, you will learn about:

- Access lists redux
- Named access lists
- Prefix lists
- AS-path lists
- Community lists
- Monitoring and verifying access and prefix lists

In Chapter 15, you started exploring the concept of access lists. Access lists in all their forms are a key control for regulating access to your network. You learned strictly about standard and static extended access lists. Implicit in the discussion in the chapter were the following principles:

1. Access lists usually deny everything by default, that nothing specifically allowed is denied.
2. Access lists control traffic in one direction — in or out — on an interface.
3. The router examines every packet against an applied access list in the direction of the packet.
4. The router compares packets with the access list, starting at the top of the access list and continuing until a match happens. The implied deny statement is a match for all packets.
5. The router routes outbound packets to the appropriate interface before applying an access list.
6. The router compares inbound packets to the access list and, when permitted, routes the packets to the correct interface.
7. Any interface can have a maximum of one access list applied to both the inbound traffic and outbound traffic.

These principles apply, regardless of the protocol or interface.

Chapter 15 touched on static extended access lists. Let us now review the extended access list syntax and introduce some new keywords and concepts, such as named access lists.

Extended IP Access Lists

You can filter out selected types of connections by denying packets that are attempting to use that service. Use IP extended access lists (range 100 to 199 and 2000 to 2699) to filter traffic based on Transmission Control Protocol (TCP) or User Datagram Protocol (UDP) port numbers. When session initiation begins for e-mail, Telnet, FTP, etc., the connection will attempt to open a service on a specified port number. You can therefore filter out selected types of connections by denying packets that are attempting to use that service. Following is a more complete syntax for the extended access list:

```
2501-1(config)#access-list access-list-number [dynamic
   dynamic-name [timeout minutes]] {deny | permit} protocol
   source source-wildcard destination destination-wildcard
   [precedence precedence] [tos tos] [log] [time-range time-
   range-name]
```

To remove any access list, use the no form of this command:

```
2501-1(config)#no access-list access-list-number
```

Exhibits 1 through 7 provide descriptions of the keywords used with the `access-list` command.

The preceding syntax remains very generic, so take a look at a few examples to see how you would use it with various protocols. For Internet Control Message Protocol (ICMP), you can use the following syntax:

```
2501-1(config)#access-list access-list-number [dynamic
   dynamic-name [timeout minutes]] {deny | permit} icmp
   source source-wildcard destination destination-wildcard
   [icmp-type [icmp-code] | icmp-message] [precedence
   precedence] [tos tos] [log] [time-range time-range-name]
```

For Internet Group Management Protocol (IGMP), you can use the following syntax:

```
2501-1(config)#access-list access-list-number [dynamic
   dynamic-name [timeout minutes]] {deny | permit} igmp
   source source-wildcard destination destination-wildcard
   [igmp-type] [precedence precedence] [tos tos] [log] [time-
   range time-range-name]
```

Exhibit 1   Syntax Description

Keyword	Description
access-list- number	Number of an access list. This is a decimal number from 100 to 199 or 2000 to 2699. Generally, one uses the lower set of numbers or names the access list. You will learn about named access lists later in the chapter.
dynamic dynamic-name	You can designate this access list as a dynamic access list. Refer to Chapter 17 for dynamic or lock-and-key access list information. The dynamic keyword is optional.
timeout minutes	You can specify the absolute length of time (in minutes) that a temporary access list entry can remain in a dynamic access list. The default is an infinite length of time and allows an entry to remain permanently. Refer to Chapter 16 for lock-and-key access lists. The timeout keyword is optional.
deny	Denies access when the packet matches the conditions.
permit	Permits access when the packet matches the conditions.
protocol	Name or number of an IP protocol. You can specify one of the keywords eigrp, gre, icmp, igmp, igrp, ip, ipinip, nos, ospf, tcp, or udp, or an integer in the range 0 to 255 representing an IP protocol number. To match any Internet protocol (including ICMP, TCP, and UDP), use the keyword ip. Refer to Appendix C, "IP Protocol Numbers," for a list of protocols and their decimal values.
source	Number of the network or host where the packet came from. There are three ways to specify the source: Use a 32-bit quantity in four-part, dotted-decimal format. Use the keyword any as an abbreviation for a source and source-wildcard of 0.0.0.0 255.255.255.255. Use host source as an abbreviation for a source and source-wildcard of source 0.0.0.0.
source- wildcard	Wildcard bits to apply to the source address. There are three ways to specify the source-wild card: Use a 32-bit quantity in four-part, dotted-decimal format. Place ones in the bit positions you want to ignore. Use the keyword any as an abbreviation for a source and source-wildcard of 0.0.0.0 255.255.255.255. Use host source as an abbreviation for a source and source-wildcard of source 0.0.0.0.
destination	Number of the network or host where the packet is being sent. There are three ways to specify the destination: Use a 32-bit quantity in four-part, dotted-decimal format. Use the keyword any as an abbreviation for a source and source-wildcard of 0.0.0.0 255.255.255.255. Use host source as an abbreviation for a source and source-wildcard of source 0.0.0.0.
destination- wildcard	Wildcard bits to apply to the destination. There are three ways to specify the destination: Use a 32-bit quantity in four-part, dotted-decimal format. Use the keyword any as an abbreviation for a source and source-wildcard of 0.0.0.0 255.255.255.255. Use host source as an abbreviation for a source and source-wildcard of source 0.0.0.0.

Exhibit 1   Syntax Description (Continued)

Keyword	*Description*
precedence precedence	Optionally, the router can filter packets by precedence level, as specified by a number from 0 to 7, or by name as listed in Exhibit 2.
tos tos	Optionally, the router can filter packets by type of service level, as specified by a number from 0 to 15, or by name as listed in Exhibit 3.
icmp-type	Optionally, the router can filter ICMP packets by ICMP message type. The type is a number from 0 to 255. Refer to Exhibit 4 for ICMP types.
icmp-code	Optionally, the router can filter ICMP packets by ICMP message type and can also be filtered by the ICMP message code. The code is a number from 0 to 255. Refer to Exhibit 4 for ICMP codes.
icmp-message	Optionally, the router can filter ICMP packets by an ICMP message type name or ICMP message type and code name. The possible names are listed in Exhibit 4.
igmp-type	Optionally, the router can filter IGMP packets by IGMP message type or message name. A message type is a number from 0 to 15. IGMP message names are listed in Exhibit 5.
operator	You can optionally compare source or destination ports. Possible operands include lt (less than), gt (greater than), eq (equal), neq (not equal), and range (inclusive range). If you position the operator after the source and source-wildcard, it must match the source port. If you position the operator after the destination and destination-wildcard, it must match the destination port. The range operator requires two port numbers. All other operators require one port number.
port	(Optional) The decimal number or name of a TCP or UDP port. A port number is a number from 0 to 65535. TCP port names are listed in Exhibit 6. You can only use TCP port names when filtering TCP. UDP port names are listed in Exhibit 7. You can only use UDP port names when filtering UDP.
established	(Optional) For the TCP protocol, you can indicate an established connection. The rule matches when the TCP datagram has the ACK or RST bits set. A non-matching case is that of the initial TCP datagram to form a connection.
log	(Optional) Causes an informational logging message about the packet that matches the entry to be sent to the console. (The level of messages logged to the console is controlled by the logging console command.) The message includes the access list number, whether the packet was permitted or denied; the protocol, whether it was TCP, UDP, ICMP, or a number; and, when appropriate, the source and destination addresses and source and destination port numbers. The IOS generates the message for the first packet that matches, and then at 5-minute intervals, including the number of packets permitted or denied in the prior 5-minute interval.
time-range time-range-name	(Optional) Name of the time range that applies to this statement. You specify the name of the time range and its restrictions by the time-range command. You cover time-range in Chapter 17.

Exhibit 2   Precedence Names

```
critical
flash
flash-override
immediate
internet
network
priority
routine
```

Exhibit 3   Type of Service (ToS) Names

```
max-reliability
max-throughput
min-delay
min-monetary-cost
normal
```

Now take a look at some examples of the use of these new keywords. In the following example, serial interface 0 is part of a Class B network with the address 172.16.0.0, and the mail host's address is 172.16.1.1. Use the keyword established for TCP to indicate an established connection. A match occurs when the TCP datagram has the ACK or RST bits set, which indicates that the packet belongs to an existing connection.

```
2501-1(config)#access-list 199 permit tcp 0.0.0.0
  255.255.255.255 172.16.0.0 0.0.255.255 established
2501-1(config)#access-list 199 permit tcp 0.0.0.0
  255.255.255.255 172.16.1.1 0.0.0.0 eq 25
2501-1(config)#interface serial 0
2501-1(config-if)#ip access-group 199 in
```

The following example also permits ICMP echo and echo-reply packets:

```
2501-1(config)#access-list 199 permit icmp any any echo
2501-1(config)#access-list 199 permit icmp any any echo-
  reply
```

You will study the access-list command in more detail in the next two chapters. Right now, it is appropriate to look at named access lists, which helps remove one of the resource constraints when using standard and extended access lists.

**Exhibit 4   ICMP Message Type Names
and ICMP Message Type and Code Names**

```
administratively-prohibited
alternate-address
conversion-error
dod-host-prohibited
dod-net-prohibited
echo
echo-reply
general-parameter-problem
host-isolated
host-precedence-unreachable
host-redirect
host-tos-redirect
host-tos-unreachable
host-unknown
host-unreachable
information-reply
information-request
mask-reply
mask-request
mobile-redirect
net-redirect
net-tos-redirect
net-tos-unreachable
net-unreachable
network-unknown
no-room-for-option
option-missing
packet-too-big
parameter-problem
port-unreachable
precedence-unreachable
protocol-unreachable
reassembly-timeout
redirect
router-advertisement
router-solicitation
source-quench
source-route-failed
time-exceeded
timestamp-reply
timestamp-request
traceroute
ttl-exceeded
unreachable
```

Exhibit 5   IGMP Message Names

```
dvmrp
host-query
host-report
Pim
trace
```

Exhibit 6   TCP Port Names

```
bgp
chargen
daytime
discard
domain
echo
finger
ftp
ftp-data
gopher
hostname
irc
klogin
kshell
lpd
nntp
pop2
pop3
sunrpc
Syslog
tacacs-ds
talk
telnet
time
uucp
whois
www
```

Named Access Lists

Cisco first introduced named access lists in IOS version 11.0. Named access lists allow you to use a character string instead of an access list number. If you use named access lists, you are no longer limited to the 99 standard access lists (1–99) or the 100 extended access lists (100–199). (Of course, Cisco expanded the number of standard access lists to 798 (1–99 and 1300–1999) and extended access lists to

Exhibit 7   UDP Port Names

```
biff
bootpc
bootps
discard
dns
dnsix
echo
mobile-ip
nameserver
netbios-dgm
netbios-ns
ntp
rip
snmp
snmptrap
sunrpc
syslog
tacacs-ds
talk
tftp
time
who
xdmcp
```

798 (100–199 and 2000–2699).) You can also use meaningful names to apply to your access lists. For example, you could create an access list for the interface to the Internet and name it "from-internet." This may make troubleshooting easier down the road long after you originally create the access list. Named access lists might also help with changes to the list. Named access lists allow you to delete one entry or statement from the access list. (You will find in Chapter 18 that reflexive access lists require a name.)

You are limited to 100 characters for the name of your access list, but that should be sufficient to name the list in a consequential fashion. Named access lists must start with a standard alphabetic ASCII character. Names are case-sensitive, so "INTERNET" is not the same as "internet." You can create standard and extended access lists, and they can even have the same name should that prove useful.

When using named standard access lists, first define the name of the access list using the following command:

```
2501-1(config-if)#ip access-list standard access-list-name
```

As previously stated, the name is any string of up to 100 characters. The command for extended access lists is almost identical. You just substitute the keyword standard for the keyword extended as follows:

```
2501-1(config-if)#ip access-list extended access-list-name
```

To set conditions for a named IP access list, use the {deny | permit} access-list configuration command. To remove a deny condition from an access list, use the no form of this command. Following are examples of the various forms of these commands.

2501-1(config-std-nacl)#**{deny | permit}** *source* **[***source-wildcard***]**

2501-1(config-std-nacl)#**no {deny | permit}** *source* **[***source-wildcard***]**

2501-1(config-ext-nacl)#**{deny | permit} protocol source source-wildcard destination destination-wildcard [precedence precedence] [tos tos] [log] [time-range time-range-name]**

2501-1(config-ext-nacl)#**no {deny | permit} protocol source source-wildcard destination destination-wildcard**

For TCP, use the following syntax:

2501-1(config-ext-nacl)#**{deny | permit} tcp** *source source-wildcard* **[***operator port* **[***port***]]** *destination destination-wildcard* **[***operator port* **[***port***]] [established] [precedence** *precedence***] [tos** *tos***] [log] [time-range** *time-range-name***]**

For UDP, use the following syntax:

2501-1(config-ext-nacl)#**{deny | permit} udp source source-wildcard [operator port [port]] destination destination-wildcard [operator port [port]] [precedence precedence] [tos tos] [log] [time-range time-range-name]**

For ICMP, use the following syntax:

2501-1(config-ext-nacl)#**{deny | permit} icmp source source-wildcard destination destination-wildcard [icmp-type [icmp-code] | icmp-message] [precedence precedence] [tos tos] [log] [time-range time-range-name]**

For IGMP, use the following syntax:

2501-1(config-ext-nacl)#**{deny | permit} igmp** *source source-wildcard destination destination-wildcard* **[***igmp-type***] [precedence** *precedence***] [tos** *tos***] [log] [time-range** *time-range-name***]**

The following example sets a deny condition for a standard access list named "from-internet":

```
2501-1(config)#ip access-list standard from-internet
2501-1(config-std-nacl)#deny 192.168.155.0 0.0.0.255
2501-1(config-std-nacl)#permit 172.16.0.0 0.0.255.255
2501-1(config-std-nacl)#permit 10.0.0.0 0.255.255.255
2501-1(config-std-nacl)#! Note: all other access implicitly
   denied
```

To write a comment about an entry in a named IP access list, use the following commands in the order shown. The first command you perform once; but you can perform the second command multiple times in the access list, before or after any permit or deny command.

```
2501-1(config)#ip access-list standard access-list-name
2501-1(config-std-nacl)#remark remark
```

or

```
2501-1(config)#ip access-list extended access-list-name
2501-1(config-ext-nacl)#remark remark
```

You can use the remark keyword to indicate the purpose of the permit or deny statement. This is good documentation and may help someone else debug the access list in the future.

For completeness, you should know how to add a remark to a numbered access list. To write a comment about an entry in a numbered IP access list, use the following command before or after any access-list permit or access-list deny command:

```
2501-1(config)#access-list access-list-number remark
```

Now look at situations where you might choose to use named access lists with remarks. In the first example of a named access list, you disallow the Cracker subnet access:

```
2501-1(config-if)#ip access-list standard prevention
2501-1(config-std-nacl)#remark Do not allow the Cracker in
   subnet
2501-1(config-std-nacl)#deny 172.16.0.0 0.0.255.255
```

In the succeeding named access list example, you do not allow the Human Resources host to use outbound Telnet:

```
2501-1(config-if)#ip access-list extended telnetting
2501-1(config-ext-nacl)#remark Do not allow the HR host to
   telnet out
2501-1(config-ext-nacl)#deny tcp host 172.16.1.200 any eq
   telnet
```

Implementing Routing Policies

In Chapter 15, you read that you can use standard access lists for controlling routes accepted and distributed. Chapter 3, "Routed and Routing Protocols," went into great detail on routing protocols, hops, and other metrics. Routers receive packets from other routers and make decisions on routes based on this information. You want to route packets correctly because doing so affects security, application performance, and cost.

As a security or network administrator you can use access lists to do route filtering and you can do filtering based on characteristics of routes.

Refer to Exhibit 8 for the purposes of the following illustrative scenario. Suppose an administrator makes a mistake when typing a network address in the router. Instead of address 19.0.0.0/8, the administrator types 10.0.0.0/8. Looking at your keyboard, you can see that this is a simple mistake because the 0 and 9 keys are positioned next to each other. Thus, one's hand can slip and type the wrong entry.

The administrator has a problem. The networks 10.0.0.0/8, 11.0.0.0/8, and 12.0.0.0/8 have no routes for network 19.0.0.0/8 and networks 11.0.0.0/8 and 12.0.0.0/8 have two routes for network 10.0.0.0/8. This is problematic because no one has a route for 19.0.0.0/8 and the other networks can no longer reach that network. In addition, anyone in network 19.0.0.0/8 cannot use the services of any other network because the other networks cannot resolve the path for the return packets. To makes things worse, the Router 1–Router 2 link is a high-speed one, whereas the Router 2–Router 4 link is not; so this may make Router 1 more favorable when Router 2 wishes to route a packet to 10.0.0.0/8.

You could minimize the impact of typographical errors. You know what routes each router should advertise. If you enforce a security policy that says you will only accept routes from known sites, then your router should neither accept any mistakenly advertised routes nor propagate them. To implement this with access lists, you first build a policy set for network 19.0.0.0/8 as follows:

```
2501-1(config)#access-list 1 permit 19.0.0.0
```

You would then apply this access list to the serial interfaces of Routers 2 and 3. So, if you used EIGRP as a routing protocol, you might use this:

```
2501-1(config)#router eigrp 1000
2501-1(config-router)#distribute-list 1 in Serial 1
```

The first command states that you want to modify the EIGRP routing protocol for Autonomous System 1000. The second command says that you only permit routes defined in access-list 1. So, when Router 1 tried to propagate the route to network 10.0.0.0/8 to Routers 2 and 3, they would deny the route based on the access-list, which states only network 19.0.0.0/8. This will still cause problems for network 19.0.0.0/8 but will isolate the problem to Router 1, which has the incorrect route. To ensure that bad routes do not propagate, you would need the following commands as well:

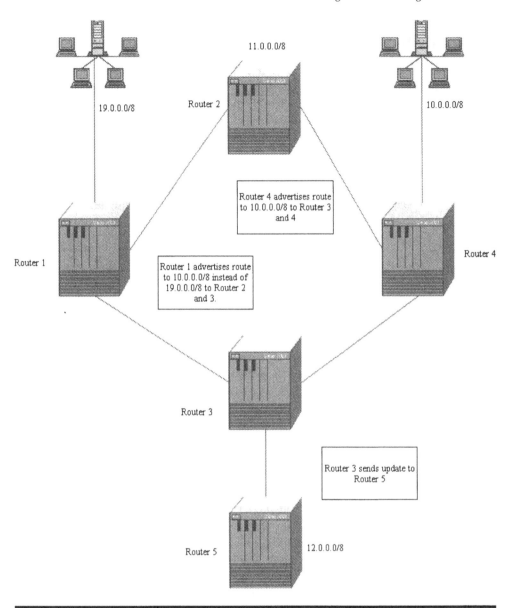

Exhibit 8   Routing Example

```
2501-1(config)#access-list 2 permit 19.0.0.0
2501-1(config)#router eigrp 1000
2501-1(config-router)#distribute-list 2 out Ethernet 0
```

You would then apply these commands list to the Ethernet interfaces of Routers 2 and 3.

You just saw the use of the distribute-list command. The syntax of the distribute-list command is:

```
distribute-list distribute-list-number {in | out} protocol
```

You can choose one of the following for protocol:

- bgp: Border Gateway Protocol (BGP)
- connected: Connected
- egp: Exterior Gateway Protocol (EGP)
- eigrp: Enhanced Interior Gateway Routing Protocol (EIGRP)
- ethernet: IEEE 802.3
- igrp: Interior Gateway Routing Protocol (IGRP)
- null: Null interface
- ospf: Open Shortest Path First protocol
- rip: Routing Information Protocol
- serial: Serial
- static: Static routes

When one router passes routing information (e.g., RIP) to another router with a different routing protocol (e.g., IGRP), you want to ensure that the latter router ignores the RIP information. To do this, use the following commands:

```
2501-1(config)#access-list 1 deny any
2501-1(config)#router rip
2501-1(config-router)#network 192.168.0.0
2501-1(config-router)#redistribute igrp 10
2501-1(config-router)#distribute-list 1 in
```

The deny statement gives us an empty policy set. The network statement says broadcast RIP information on all interfaces connected to network 192.168.0.0/16. The fourth statement says the router will redistribute all routes learned from IGRP process 10 into RIP. The final statement restricts the information that the router accepts. So, the deny access list overrides and denies all routes, and thus the router will ignore all routes advertised by RIP. Hopefully, you can understand the value of these statements on a border router.

Prefix Lists

In most circumstances, the standard and extended access lists provide enough flexibility to specify sets of IP addresses or networks. However, when you want to set policies for networks based on their network mask, they fall short.

When working with networks of varying prefix lengths, there are situations where the standard access lists just do not work. For example, you want to configure an access list that includes network 172.30.0.0/16 but does not include network 172.30.0.0/24. Using the information you have seen thus far, you might try:

```
2501-1(config)#access-list 1 permit 172.30.0.0 0.0.0.0
2501-1(config)#access-list 1 deny 172.30.0.0 0.0.0.255
```

Hopefully, you recognize by now that 172.30.0.0/24 succeeds on the first rule.

Standard access lists do not work or are not practical when you want to include and exclude networks based on their netmask. The prefix-list access list makes it much easier to implement your policy when using netmasks. To handle the simple example above, you would write the following:

```
2501-1(config)#ip prefix-list Class-B-Only seq 5 permit
    172.30.0.0/16
2501-1(config)#ip prefix-list Class-B-Only seq 10 deny
    172.30.0.0/24
```

As with the standard and extended access lists, the router matches entries in sequence and stops processing entries on a match. The sequence number in the prefix-list determines the order of matching, starting with the entry with the lowest number. You can select any number from 1 to 4,294,967,294 for the sequence number. Where there is no match, there is an implicit deny. So for the example above, you could eliminate the second entry and achieve the same policy.

If you want to permit network 192.168.32.0/19 and all possible prefixes part of that CIDR address (i.e., all prefixes starting with 192.168.32.0/19 equal to and greater in length), you could try implementing this policy with standard access lists such as:

```
2501-1(config)#access-list 1 deny 192.168.64.0 0.0.192.0
2501-1(config)#access-list 1 permit 192.168.32.0 0.0.31.255
```

The first command denies the shorter length prefixes, while the second permits everything else. My head hurts just looking at these two commands! You can achieve the same goal with the following command:

```
2501-1(config)#ip prefix-list Slash19-and-Longer seq 15
    permit 192.168.32.0/19 ge 19
```

Somehow, a keyword and value appeared at the end of the command. Perhaps you should look at the syntax for the command. The structure of the `ip prefix-list` command is:

```
ip prefix-list prefix-list-name [seq sequence-number]
    {permit | deny} prefix/prefix-length [ge greater-equal-
    to-value] [le less-equal-to-value]
```

You can create a prefix-list-name of letters, numbers, and special characters, such as the dash. You can optionally specify a sequence number. If you do not specify a sequence number, the IOS will generate one starting with 5 and increment the value by 5. Remember that the router processes the lists in the order of the sequence numbers, so they are crucial. Using numbers wisely allows you to change a line or add another entry without having to delete the entire list. You can insert numbers in between existing numbers; so if you have entries 5 and 10, you can create entry 7 that the IOS will process after 5 but before 10. The next keyword you specify is either `permit` or `deny`: your choice. Yes, you choose the one that best implements your policy. And remember that there is an implicit deny at the end of the prefix-list. You follow the action with a CIDR-style address; that is, the prefix and prefix length separated by a slash. Use the last optional keywords to specify the length of the prefixes. If you do not use them, the route must match exactly on the address and the netmask length. In the example, you include the ge 19 keywords to show that you want those prefixes with a netmask greater than or equal to 19.

If you do not want the IOS to generate the next sequence number automatically, use this command:

```
2501-1(config)#ip prefix-list sequence-number
```

As usual, you can use the no ip prefix-list command to remove a prefix-list.

```
no ip prefix-list prefix-list-name [seq sequence-number]
```

This is a useful feature because you can delete specific entries rather than having to delete a complete access list as you had to do with standard and extended access lists. Should you delete the seq keyword, the IOS will delete the entire prefix-list.

One last point on prefix-lists. You can use them in BGP routing statements in the same manner you use standard access lists. The following commands show this:

```
2501-1(config)#ip prefix-list Class-B-only seq 25 permit
   172.28.0.0/16
2501-1(config)#router bgp 65350
2501-1(config-router)#neighbor 192.168.32.1 remote-as 65351
2501-1(config-router)#neighbor 192.168.32.1 prefix-list
  Class-B-only in
```

The example uses the prefix-list keyword instead of the distribute-list keyword, otherwise, it works the same as previous examples.

Finally, you can also use the following access lists with BGP:

```
as-path access-list name {permit | deny} {regular
   expression}
ip community-list community-list-number {permit | deny}
   string1 [string2]...[stringN]
```

You select any number or name for the keyword name. Exhibit 9 shows the characters you can use for the regular expression.

For example, to include the routes with an AS path of 1, use the following:

```
2501-1(config-router)#as-path access-list 5 permit ^1$
```

An example of the community access list is:

```
2501-1(config-router)#ip community-list 100 permit 65000:1
   65000:2 65000:3
```

Exhibit 9   Regular Expression Characters

Character	Description
.	Match individual character
*	Match any number of the preceding expression
+	Match at least one of the preceding expression
^	Beginning of line
$	End of line
(	Start including next expression as one unit until a matching parenthesis is reached
)	Include previous expressions, starting with a (as a single unit
–	Beginning of line, end of line, left or right parenthesis, left or right bracket, or whitespace

These last two access lists are advanced subjects and only someone with thorough knowledge of the BGP routing protocol should write them. They are included here so you know that these lists are available for filtering BGP information.

Monitoring and Verifying Access and Prefix Lists

Periodically, you may need to view the contents of access lists configured on your router. Most likely, this is your first step after creating some new access lists. Very early on you learned one simple tool for viewing access lists — show running-config. This command will show all interfaces and access lists. Of course, it may take the router a while to spit out the output and you may miss a rule due to the sheer volume of data.

So you may want to narrow your scope. To determine what access lists your organization has applied to a specific interface, use the following user command:

```
2501-1#show ip interface
```

To look at access lists in more detail, use the following user command:

```
2501-1>show access-lists
Standard IP access list 2
permit 172.16.13.0, wildcard bits 0.0.0.255
deny 172.16.12.5, wildcard bits 0.0.0.0
permit 172.16.12.0, wildcard bits 0.0.0.255
Extended IP access list 102
permit tcp 172.16.13.0 0.0.0.255 172.16.4.0 eq 23
permit udp host 172.16.13.2 172.16.4.4 eq 69
permit tcp host 172.16.13.3 any any
deny 0.0.0.0 255.255.255.255
2501-1>
```

This command shows you all the access lists on the router, both simple and extended. If you want to see only a specific access list, just append the access list number to the end of the command as follows:

```
2501-1>show access-lists 2
```

Unfortunately, the output format you see with this command is not the same as the input format for the commands, so you cannot cut-and-paste these rules directly into another router. In addition, this command does not show any comments you may have added for readability or troubleshooting.

Tip: You may find that your access lists just do not work, even when there is no obvious reason. You have used the `show access-lists` and `route` commands and cannot discern a problem with the statements. Perhaps your access lists are completely ignored and stop traffic despite your permit statement. Should you find this to be the case, the problem may rest with the IOS. There are known problems with some versions of Cisco's IOS. You can use the Cisco Bug Navigator™ to point out those versions. This program requires that you have a support contract, which is probably not a problem.

Viewing Access List Counters

When the router filters traffic using an access list, it keeps track of the access list entries it is using as well as how many times it uses the access list entries. To see what access list entries packets are using, try:

```
2501-1#sh ip access-list 102
Extended IP access list 102
deny tcp any any telnet log-input (3 matches)
deny tcp any any smtp log-input
permit ip any any (166 matches)
```

This command shows you how many packets are hitting each line of a given access list. In the example above, you can see that most packets are getting through (166 out of a possible 169). You also should notice the new keyword `log-input` in the two deny statements. The difference between `log-input` and the plain old `log` keyword is that `log-input` would record the interface the packet came through as well as the normal log data. In Chapter 5 you learned about logging and, at the time, you saw that it was a good idea to set up a syslog server when you want to do logging; otherwise, the data goes to the console.

Viewing IP Accounting

You also can use the router's IP accounting facility to check whether or not your extended access list entries are correct. IP accounting lets you keep track of the source and destination addresses of transit packets, that is, packets that come in and go out on an interface. In addition, the IP accounting feature allows you to track the source and destination addresses of packets that the router does not pass — those denied by explicit or implicit filtering — so you can see those packets that made it through or those that the router has blocked.

Caution: IP accounting does not work with some switching modes. In fact, it is even worse than that. With some versions of the IOS on certain hardware platforms, turning on IP accounting may disable packet forwarding. Be aware and RTFM before using this feature.

To use this facility, you must first turn on IP accounting using the following commands:

```
2501-1#config t
2501-1(config)#int e0
2501-1(config-if)#ip accounting output-packets
2501-1(config-if)#ip accounting access-violations
```

If you use just the ip accounting command without a keyword, you will turn on accounting for transit packets only. Like outgoing access lists, IP accounting will not capture any information on packets generated by the router, such as NTP requests or Telnet sessions originating from the router.

Once you have activated accounting on an interface, you can view the contents of the accounting database using the following enable command.

```
2501-1#show ip accounting
```

You should see a table similar to the following:

```
Source          Destination       Packets        Bytes
10.8.0.1        10.16.0.1               9        18964
10.16.0.1       10.8.0.1               14       847642
10.8.0.1        10.24.0.1               7        12478
Accounting data age is 1
```

Here you see some packets being passed by the router to servers on the inside. Every entry in the table shows the source and destination address, as well as the number of packets and bytes sent from one IP address to another. The final entry in the accounting table tells you how many minutes have passed since the router either started or cleared the accounting table.

If you had used the ip accounting access-violations command, then you could see the results using the show ip accounting access-violations command. Here is some sample output from the latter command:

```
Source              Destination      Packets        Bytes      ACL
172.16.0.1          10.16.0.1             42        24768      101
192.168.200.1       10.8.0.1              24        12245      101
192.168.201.1       10.16.0.1              7        12478      101
Accounting data age is 2
```

You can see three attempts to access the internal network that the router denied.

Your router uses one database for storing the transit accounting and access list violation records. It is, of course, limited in size and you will lose accounting information when the database is full. When the database is full, the router does not overwrite existing records; instead, it writes no new entries. If the database is full, then the IOS will write a message at the end of the show ip accounting output such as:

```
Accounting threshold exceeded for 13475 packets(s) violating
    access list(s)
```

Obviously, your organization needs to have a plan and a procedure for dealing with this situation. You can increase the size of the buffer for the accounting table using the ip accounting-threshold configuration command. The default is 512 entries. Although you can increase the table size, realize that the accounting table takes up memory. So, when memory is an issue, be prepared to fight this objection.

Although the router stores access list violations and transit information in the same database, you can decide how many entries you will keep for each. For example, you can use the ip accounting transits command followed by number of entries.

Another way to manage the database is to selectively write records. You can limit what entries the router writes to the accounting table using the ip account-ing-list command. So, if you want to only write accounting records for packets coming from or going to network 10.0.0.0/8 or host 192.168.155.155, you would use the following commands:

```
2501-1(config-if)#ip accounting-list 10.0.0.0 0.255.255.255
2501-1(config-if)#ip accounting-list 192.168.155.155
```

The final accounting command you should know is the following:

```
2501-1#clear ip accounting
```

This command will clear the accounting database. It makes sense to run this command after you change an access list so that you see the statistics for the new access list and not the old one.

Viewing Access List Counters

You can use the show ip prefix-list command to view prefix lists. Should you use the command without an argument, the IOS will show all prefix lists.

Should you use the name of a prefix list, the IOS will only show you that prefix list. You can also use the keyword detail to get more detailed information and use the keyword summary to get less. An example follows:

2501-1#**show ip prefix-list detail**

This will provide you with detailed information on the prefix lists. Detail provides the number of entries (or count), the number of entries with range statements, the range of sequence numbers (or sequences), the number of times you use the list in policy settings (or refcount), and matches (or hit count) for each entry. To reset the hit counts for Slash19-and-Longer, use the following command:

2501-1#**clear ip prefix-list Slash19-and-Longer**

Practice Session

In this Practice Session, you will practice the following:

- Logging in
- Saving log data
- Switching modes
- Entering configuration mode
- Creating access lists
- Applying access lists to an interface
- Debugging access lists with Ping and Telnet
- Enabling and saving syslog data
- Logging out

1. Log in to the SimRouter Web page.
2. Double-click on router 2501-1 to telnet to that router. This will open a console session.
3. Enter your **Username** and **Password** at the applicable prompt. These are the ones you set up in Chapter 2. You will need to hit the Enter key twice to get to the > prompt.
4. Again, save the log for your session. To do this, select | Terminal | Start Logging | from the menu bar in the Telnet window. The Telnet client will ask you where you wish to store the log and with what name. Your choice. You are going to save the log so that when you build this configuration file, you can cut-and-paste this in Chapter 17 as a starting point, rather than having to enter the same information each Practice Session.
5. Enter the enable mode:

   2501-1#**enable**

6. When prompted to put in the enable secret password, enter **oscar**.
7. Type **terminal length 0**. This command instructs the route to scroll through long command output without pausing (the —More— message).
8. You will paste the running-config that you saved from the Chapter 15 log. At the 2501-2# prompt, type **config t**.

9. If you did not do this, open your log file with the text editor of your choice (e.g., use | Start | Programs | Accessories | Notepad |). Do a find on `sh running-config` and copy from the first "!" to "end." At the `2501-2(config)#` prompt, paste this configuration.

10. Type **int e0** and press Enter.

11. Type **network 10.8.0.0 0.255.255.2555** and press Enter.

12. Double-click on router 2524-1 to telnet to that router. This will open a console session.

13. Enter your **Username** and **Password** at the applicable prompt. These are the ones you set up in Chapter 2. You will need to hit the Enter key twice to get to the > prompt.

14. Enter the enable mode:

    `2501-1#`**enable**

15. When prompted to put in the enable secret password, enter **oscar**.

16. At the `2501-2#` prompt, type **config t**.

17. Type **int e0** and press Enter.

18. Type **network 10.16.0.0 0.255.255.2555** and press Enter.

19. To verify your routers are setup correctly, type **ping 11.8.0.1** and press Enter.

20. Type **traceroute 11.8.0.1** and press Enter.

21. Type **no access-list 100** and press Enter. This command removes any access list you may have already created. If you did the Practice Session in Chapter 15, then you definitely need this command; otherwise, the router will just append the statements you add from now on to the end of the list.

22. Type **access-list 100 permit tcp 0.0.0.0 255.255.255.255 11.8.0.0 0.0.255.255 established** and press Enter.

23. Type **access-list 100 permit ip 11.8.0.0 255.255.0.0 0.0.0.0 255.255.255.255** and press Enter.

24. Type **access-list 100 deny icmp any any redirect** and press Enter.

25. Type **access-list 100 permit icmp any any 0.0.0.0 echo** and press Enter.

26. Type **access-list 100 deny ip host 127.0.0.0 0.255.255.255** any and press Enter.

27. Type **access-list 100 deny ip 224.0.0.0 31.255.255.255 any** and press Enter.

28. Type **access-list 100 deny ip host 0.0.0.0 any** and press Enter.

29. Type **access-list 100 deny ip any 10.0.0.0 0.255.255.255** and press Enter.

30. Type **access-list 100 deny ip 10.0.0.0 0.255.255.255** any and press Enter.

31. Type **access-list 100 deny ip any 172.16.0.0 0.15.255.255** and press Enter.

32. Type **access-list 100 deny ip 172.16.0.0 0.15.255.255 any** and press Enter.

33. Type **access-list 100 deny ip any 192.168.0.0 0.0.255.255** and press Enter.
34. Type **access-list 100 deny ip 192.168.0.0 0.0.255.255 any** and press Enter.
35. Type **access-list 100 deny tcp any any eq 19 log** and press Enter.
36. Type **access-list 100 permit udp 0.0.0.0 255.255.255.255 0.0.0.0 255.255.255.255 eq 53** and press Enter.
37. Type **access-list 100 permit udp 0.0.0.0 255.255.255.255 0.0.0.0 255.255.255.255 eq 123** and press Enter.
38. Type **access-list 100 permit udp 11.16.0.0 0.0.255.255 eq 123 172.16.0.0 0.0.255.255 eq 123** and press Enter.
39. Type **access-list 100 deny udp 0.0.0.0 255.255.255.255 0.0.0.0 255.255.255.255 eq 2049** and press Enter.
40. Type **access-list 100 deny tcp 0.0.0.0 255.255.255.255 0.0.0.0 255.255.255.255 range 6000 6255** and press Enter.
41. Type **access-list 100 deny tcp 0.0.0.0 255.255.255.255 0.0.0.0 255.255.255.255 range 2001 2002** and press Enter.
42. Type **access-list 100 permit tcp 0.0.0.0 255.255.255.255 11.8.0.2 0.0.0.0 eq 23** and press Enter.
43. Type **access-list 100 permit tcp 0.0.0.0 255.255.255.255 11.8.0.100 0.0.0.0 eq 21** and press Enter.
44. Type **access-list 100 permit tcp 0.0.0.0 255.255.255.255 11.8.0.100 0.0.0.0 eq 20** and press Enter.
45. Type **access-list 100 permit tcp 0.0.0.0 255.255.255.255 gt 1023 11.8.0.100 0.0.0.0 eq 20** and press Enter.
46. Type **access-list 100 permit tcp 0.0.0.0 255.255.255.255 11.8.0.100 0.0.0.0 gt 1023** and press Enter.
47. Type **access-list 100 permit tcp 0.0.0.0 255.255.255.255 11.8.0.100 0.0.0.0 gt 1023** and press Enter.
48. Type **access-list 100 permit tcp 0.0.0.0 255.255.255.255 11.8.0.101 0.0.0.0 gt 1023** and press Enter.
49. Type **access-list 100 permit udp 0.0.0.0 255.255.255.255 11.8.0.100 0.0.0.0 gt 1023** and press Enter.
50. Type **access-list 100 permit udp 0.0.0.0 255.255.255.255 11.8.0.100 0.0.0.0 gt 102**3 and press Enter.
51. Type **access-list 100 permit udp 0.0.0.0 255.255.255.255 11.8.0.101 0.0.0.0 gt 1023** and press Enter.
52. Type **access-list 100 permit udp 0.0.0.0 255.255.255.255 gt 1023 11.8.0.100 0.0.0.0 eq 53** and press Enter.
53. Type **access-list 100 permit udp 0.0.0.0 255.255.255.255 gt 1023 11.8.0.101 0.0.0.0 eq 53** and press Enter.
54. Type **access-list 100 permit tcp 11.8.0.101 255.255.255.255 gt 53 11.8.0.100 0.0.0.0 eq 53** and press Enter.
55. Type **access-list 101 permit tcp 0.0.0.0 255.255.255.255 11.8.0.100 0.0.0.0 eq 25** and press Enter.
56. Type **access-list 101 permit tcp 0.0.0.0 255.255.255.255 host 11.8.0.101 eq 25** and press Enter.

57. Type **access-list 100 deny 47 0.0.0.0 255.255.255.255 0.0.0.0 255.255.255.255** and press Enter.
58. Type **access-list 2 permit 10.8.0.0** and press Enter.
59. Type **int e0** and press Enter.
60. Type **interface ethernet 0** and press Enter.
61. Type **ip access-group 100 in** and press Enter.
62. Type **ip access-group 2 out** and press Enter.
63. Type **ip accounting output-packets** and press Enter.
64. Type **ip accounting access-violations** and press Enter.
65. Type **exit** and press Enter.
66. Go to router 2524-1.
67. Type **access-list 2 permit 10.16.0.0** and press Enter.
68. Type **interface ethernet 0** and press Enter.
69. Type **ip access-group 2 out** and press Enter.
70. Type **ip accounting output-packets** and press Enter.
71. Type **ip accounting access-violations** and press Enter.
72. To verify your routers are set up correctly, type **ping 11.8.0.1** and press Enter.
73. From the command prompt, type **telnet 11.8.0.100** and press Enter.
74. Type **quit** to log out from router 2524-1. Close the Telnet window and return to the Telnet window for 2501-1 session.
75. Type **show ip interface** and press Enter.
76. Type **show access-lists** and press Enter.
77. Type **show access-lists 2** and press Enter.
78. Type **show access-lists 100** and press Enter.
79. Type **show ip accounting output-packets** and press Enter.
80. Type **show ip accounting access-violations** and press Enter.
81. Type **sh running-config** and press Enter. You will use this new configuration to start the next Practice Session.
82. Type **quit** to log out from router 2501-1. Close the Telnet window and return to the SimRouter Topology Map.
83. Click on Log Out on the SimRouter Web page.

Security and Audit Checklist

1. Do you use standard named access lists in your organization?
   - Yes
   - No
2. Do you use extended named access lists in your organization?
   - Yes
   - No
3. Do you have a standard for naming access lists in your organization?
   - Yes
   - No
4. Do you use remarks in your access lists to document the access list?
   - Yes
   - No

5. Do you use access lists to control routing updates?
    - ■ Yes
    - ■ No
6. Do you use prefix lists in your organization?
    - ■ Yes
    - ■ No
7. Do you use as-path access lists in your organization?
    - ■ Yes
    - ■ No
8. Do you use community lists in your organization?
    - ■ Yes
    - ■ No
9. Does someone in your organization have responsibility for verifying that access lists work as planned?
    - ■ Yes
    - ■ No
10. Is there a procedure for verifying access lists in your organization?
    - ■ Yes
    - ■ No
11. Do you use access lists logging?
    - ■ Yes
    - ■ No
12. Do you log to syslog?
    - ■ Yes
    - ■ No
13. Does someone in your organization have responsibility for reviewing access list violations?
    - ■ Yes
    - ■ No
14. Do you use IP accounting access lists in your organization?
    - ■ Yes
    - ■ No
15. Does someone in your organization have responsibility for reviewing accounting data?
    - ■ Yes
    - ■ No
16. Do you have a procedure for analyzing accounting data?
    - ■ Yes
    - ■ No
17. Do you have a procedure for clearing the accounting database?
    - ■ Yes
    - ■ No

Conclusion

In this chapter, you learned more about the static extended access list. You saw how to use more of the keywords with the `access-list` command. Chapter 17 looks at another keyword when you deal with time-based access lists.

In the previous chapter, you learned that you could use access lists to restrict contents of routing updates. In this chapter, you learned how to filter routes. The penultimate chapter will introduce you to neighbor authentication. The judicious use of these concepts will help reduce the risk that you not update your router with fraudulent routes. Using access lists for route filtering is CPU-intensive. Overuse of route filtering can slow the flow of packets. If you make mistakes, the router might drop packets. Typically, your router uses "netflow" or fast switching, which is optimum switching. The router has a number of specialized processors for fast switching. When you use router filtering, you use the slowest mode or process switching. The router usually has but one processor available for process switching. Process switching also handles interactive log-ins, SNMP requests, and access control. So, when using router filtering look at:

- Access list length
- Number of routes received in an update
- Number of updates received

Reduce any of these and you will reduce the processing impact on your router.

You learned how to configure prefix list, community lists, and as-path access lists. Finally, you saw how to view access lists, access list counters, and prefix lists.

Chapter 17 continues on with methods for protecting your network. Specifically, you will learn about time-based access lists and dynamic access lists. So be a dynamo; do not waste any time and get right at them.

Chapter 17

Advanced Traffic Filtering, Part 1

In this chapter, you will learn about:

- Using time ranges
- Configuring time-based access lists
- Using lock-and-key
- Configuring lock-and-key

This chapter describes how to configure time-based access lists and lock-and-key security at your router. Time-based access lists allow you to implement access lists based on the time of day and the day of the week. Lock-and-key is a traffic filtering security feature available for IP (internet Protocol).

Using Time Ranges

You can create access lists that control access based on the time of day and the day of the week. To do so, you create a time range that defines specific times of the day and week. You identify the time range by a name and then reference it by a function so that the router imposes those time restrictions on the function.

You might wonder whether this is a useful feature. Perhaps a real-world case will help to illustrate. One day, I was at a client's site when the gentleman I was with suddenly looked at his watch and without warning reached out and threw me against the wall. Before I could ask what was happening, the doors flew open and about 30 people came charging out like someone had shot them from a gun. It was quitting time! Had my client not pushed me out of the way, I may have been trampled to death. So you can venture to guess that these people were not using the system or network after quitting hours. Why not set up an access list that prevents them from using the network after, say, 4 PM? Because, if someone is using the network, it is not these people because they are already at home with their feet up. The time range allows the security or network administrator to define when the permit or deny statements in the access list are in effect.

Currently, Cisco only allows the use of time ranges with IP and IPX extended access lists. Both named and numbered access lists can reference a time range. This book only covers IP timed-based access lists, but the IPX ones work much the same. Prior to this feature, access list statements were always in effect until you removed them. Later in the chapter, you will see how lock-and-key further limits the time access lists are effective.

The Benefits of Time-Based Access Lists

You are probably wondering what are the benefits of time-based access lists beyond the simple story given above. Well, there are many possible benefits of time ranges, but here are a few motivators:

- An administrator has more control over permitting or denying a user access to resources, such as an application or an on-demand link.
- The administrator can set time-based security policy, including:
  - Perimeter security using the Cisco IOS Firewall feature set or access lists
  - Data confidentiality with Cisco Encryption Technology or IPSec
- The administrator can enhance policy-based routing and queuing functions.
- You can automatically reroute traffic cost effectively when provider access rates vary by time of day. You might decide to use different interfaces at different times of the day due to provider tariffs.
- Service providers can dynamically change a committed access rate (CAR) configuration to support the Quality-of-Service (QOS) service level agreements (SLAs) that they negotiate for certain times of the day.
- Network administrators can control logging messages. Access list entries can log traffic at certain times of the day, but not continuously. Therefore, administrators can simply deny access without having to analyze many logs generated during peak hours.

Configuring Time-Based Access

Creating a time-based access list requires two steps:

1. Define a time range.
2. Reference the time range with an access-list function.

First take a look at defining a time range, which is a relatively simple task.

Defining a Time Range

To define a time range, complete the following steps.

Step 1. Identify the Time Range

You identify the time range by a meaningful name. To specify when an access list or other feature is in effect, use the time-range global configuration command.

```
router(config)#time-range time-range-name
```

To remove the time limitation, use the no form of this command.

```
router(config)#no time-range time-range-name
```

You identify time-range entries by a name, which is referred to by one or more other configuration commands. The time-range name cannot contain a space or quotation mark, and must start with an alphabetic character.

Currently, only IPX and IP extended access lists use the time-range feature. Multiple time ranges can occur in a single access list or other feature.

After the time-range command, use the periodic command, the absolute command, or some combination of them to define when the feature is in effect. Cisco allows multiple periodic commands in a time range, but allow only one absolute command.

Note: Note that the names for time-range entries and named access lists are different names. To avoid confusion, do not use the same name for both.

The following example denies Web (HTTP) traffic on Monday through Friday between the hours of 8:00 AM and 6:00 PM, but allows UDP traffic on Saturday and Sunday from noon to midnight only.

```
router(config)#time-range no-http
router(config)#periodic weekdays 8:00 to 18:00
router(config)#time-range udp-yes
router(config)#periodic weekend 12:00 to 24:00
router(config)#ip access-list extended strict
router(config)#deny tcp any any eq http time-range no-http
router(config)#permit udp any any time-range udp-yes
router(config)#interface ethernet 0
router(config)#ip access-group strict in
```

Step 2. Specify the Time Range

The next step furnishes the syntax for the absolute and periodic commands. The next chapter section provides information on how to apply these statements to an interface as shown in this example.

You can specify absolute, periodic, or a combination of both as time ranges. To specify an absolute time when a time range is in effect, use the `absolute` configuration command.

```
router(config)#absolute [start time date] [end time date]
```

To remove the time limitation, use the no form of this command:

```
router(config)#no absolute
```

The `absolute` command sets the absolute time and date that the associated permit or deny statement goes into effect. The time is expressed in a 24-hour clock, in the form of hours:minutes. For example, 8:00 is 8:00 AM and 20:00 is 8:00 PM. The date is expressed in the format day month year. The minimum start is 00:00 1 January 1993. If you do not specify a start time and date, the permit or deny statement takes effect immediately.

Note: Please take note that the format for date is day month year. If you live in the United States, you are more familiar with the month day year format. So be careful and do not set up the date incorrectly or it may not work the way you intended.

You can specify the time and date that the associated permit or deny statement is no longer in effect. Use the same time and date format as described for the start time and date. The end time and date must be a time in the future and after the start time and date. The maximum end time is 23:59 31 December 2035. If you do not specify an end time and date, the permit or deny statement is in effect indefinitely.

The following example configures an access list named northeast, which references a time range named new-app. You have a new application that the developers are putting into production at the beginning of the year. You can create an access list and time range that together permit traffic on Ethernet interface 0 starting at 12:00 noon on January 1, 2002, and going forever.

```
router(config)#time-range new-app
router(config)#absolute start 12:00 1 January 2002
router(config)#ip access-list extended northeast
router(config)#permit ip any any time-range new-app
router(config)#interface ethernet 0
router(config)#ip access-group northeast in
```

The following example permits UDP traffic until noon on December 31, 2001. After that time, the router will deny all UDP traffic egress from Ethernet interface 0.

```
router(config)#time-range old-app
router(config)#absolute end 12:00 31 December 2001
```

Exhibit 1   Periodic Arguments

Argument	Description
daily	Monday through Sunday
weekdays	Monday through Friday
weekend	Saturday and Sunday

```
router(config)#ip access-list extended northeast
router(config)#permit udp any any time-range old-app
router(config)#interface ethernet 0
router(config)#ip access-group northeast out
```

The absolute command is one way to specify when a time range is in effect. Another way is to specify a periodic length of time with the periodic command. Use either of these commands after the time-range command, which identifies the name of the time range. Only one absolute entry is allowed per time-range command, but you may have multiple periodic statements.

If a time-range command has both absolute and periodic values specified, then the IOS evaluates the periodic items only after the absolute start time is reached, and are not further evaluated after the absolute end time is reached.

Note: All time specifications are taken as local time. To ensure that the time range entries take effect at the desired times, you must synchronize the system clock. Use NTP or the hardware calendar to synchronize the clock.

To specify when a time range is in effect, use the periodic time-range configuration command. To remove the time limitation, use the no form of this command.

```
router(config)#periodic days-of-the-week hh:mm to [days-of-
    the-week] hh:mm
router(config)#no periodic days-of-the-week hh:mm to [days-
    of-the-week] hh:mm
```

The first keyword of this command is the starting day or days that the associated time range is in effect. The second keyword is the ending day or days the associated statement is in effect. You can use any single day or combinations of days: Monday, Tuesday, Wednesday, Thursday, Friday, Saturday, or Sunday. So, you could substitute **Monday Tuesday Wednesday** for days-of-the-week. Other possible values are shown in Exhibit 1. If the ending days of the week are the same as the starting days of the week, you can omit them.

The first occurrence of the hh:mm keyword is the starting hours:minutes that the associated time range is in effect. The second occurrence is the ending

Exhibit 2   Typical Settings

Policy Requirement	Command
Monday through Friday, 8:00 AM to 6:00 PM only	`periodic weekday 8:00 to 18:00`
Every day of the week, from 8:00 AM to 6:00 PM only	`periodic daily 8:00 to 18:00`
Every minute from Monday 8:00 AM to Friday 8:00 PM	`periodic monday 8:00 to friday 20:00`
All weekend, from Saturday morning through Sunday night	`periodic weekend 00:00 to 23:59`
Saturdays and Sundays, from noon to midnight	`periodic weekend 12:00 to 23:59`

hours:minutes the associated statement is in effect. The hours:minutes are expressed in a 24-hour clock. For example, 8:00 is 8:00 AM and 20:00 is 8:00 PM.

Unlike the `absolute` command, multiple periodic entries are allowed per `time-range` command.

Note: The IOS assumes that all time specifications are local time. To ensure that the time range entries take effect at the desired times, you should synchronize the system clock, using NTP or the hardware calendar.

Exhibit 2 provides some typical settings for your convenience.

The following example permits Telnet traffic on Mondays, Tuesdays, and Fridays between the hours of 9:00 AM and 5:00 PM.

```
router(config)#time-range testing
router(config)#periodic Monday Tuesday Friday 9:00 to 17:00
router(config)#ip access-list extended developers
router(config)#permit tcp any any eq telnet time-range
   testing
router(config)#interface ethernet 0
router(config)#ip access-group developers in
```

In time-range configuration mode, specify when you wish the function to apply or be in effect. Specify some combination of `absolute` and `periodic` commands; multiple periodic statements are allowed; only one absolute statement is allowed.

Note: The time range relies on the system clock of the router, so you need a reliable clock source. Therefore, you should use the Network Time Protocol (NTP) to synchronize the router clock. NTP is a TCP application that assures accurate local timekeeping with reference to radio and atomic clocks located on the Internet. This protocol can help synchronize distributed clocks within milliseconds over long time periods.

Repeat these tasks if you have multiple items you want in effect at different times. For example, repeat the steps to include multiple permit or deny statements in an access list in effect at different times.

The following example permits UDP traffic out Ethernet interface 0 on weekends only, from 8:00 AM on January 1, 2002, to 6:00 PM on December 31, 2003.

```
router(config)#time-range testing
router(config)#absolute start 8:00 1 January 2002 end 18:00
  31 December 2003
router(config)#periodic weekends 00:00 to 23:59
router(config)#ip access-list extended northeast
router(config)#permit udp any any time-range testing
router(config)#interface ethernet 0
router(config)#ip access-group northeast out
```

Note: If you use absolute and periodic time ranges together, you should know that the router will only evaluate the periodic value statements after the absolute time starts.

Referencing the Time Range

For the router to apply a time range, you must reference it by name in a feature that can implement time ranges. To reference the time range, create an IP extended access list.

To reference the time range with an access-list function, you use the keyword time-range with the access-list command. To create an IP named extended access list, use the following commands beginning in global configuration mode:

```
router(config)#ip access-list extended name
router(config)#{deny | permit} protocol source source-
  wildcard destination destination-wildcard [precedence
  precedence] [tos tos] [established] [log] [time-range
  time-range-name]
```

The first command defines an extended IP access list using a name. In access-list configuration mode, specify the conditions allowed or denied. You do this with the second command above. Use the log keyword to get access list logging messages, including violations.

When you already have a permit or deny statement in effect, use the following command to specify a time range to restrict time of access.

```
router(config)#{deny | permit} protocol any any [log] [time-
  range time-range-name]
```

For more information about configuring IP extended access lists, see the Chapters 15 and 16. Later in this chapter, you will see the syntax for the dynamic access list, which also supports time ranges.

Take a look at an example that pulls everything together. The following example denies HTTP traffic on Monday through Friday between the hours of 8:00 AM and 6:00 PM. The example allows UDP traffic on Saturday and Sunday from noon to 8:00 PM only.

```
router(config)#time-range no-http
router(config)#periodic weekdays 8:00 to 18:00
router(config)#time-range udp-yes
router(config)#periodic weekend 12:00 to 20:00
router(config)#ip access-list extended strict
router(config)#deny tcp any any eq http time-range no-http
router(config)#permit udp any any time-range udp-yes
router(config)#interface ethernet 0
router(config-if)#ip access-group strict in
```

There you have time-based access lists. As previously mentioned, you can use time restrictions with the next topic — lock-and-key.

Using Lock-and-Key

Companies trying to maintain security these days generally disallow remote access across the Internet because of the possibility of snoopers watching for passwords or other valuable information. Some companies require that all remote access be via direct dial-up, with PPP and CHAP, and possibly callback providing security. This is fine for local access; but for traveling or remote employees, the long-distance bill adds up quickly. Telecommuting and remote access by mobile, outbound staff is on the rise. Serious numbers of remote users using multiple access servers can burden the network staff.

Meanwhile, as Internet service provider (ISP) networks grow, local access points make Internet access financially attractive. Not only does using an ISP save the cost of phone calls, but it allows an organization to outsource the task of managing the network access servers and modems to the service provider.

Your organization needs a solution to secure these users coming in via the Internet. Cisco provides a facility called lock-and-key that can help. Lock-and-key is a traffic filtering security feature that dynamically filters IP traffic. You configure lock-and-key using IP dynamic extended access lists. Static access lists cannot create lock-and-key access list entries. However, you can use lock-and-key with other standard access lists and static extended access lists. When triggered, lock-and-key reconfigures the interface's existing IP access list to permit designated users to reach their designated host(s). Afterward, lock-and-key reconfigures the interface back to its original state.

When you configure lock-and-key, designated users whose IP traffic is normally blocked at a router can gain temporary access through the router. For a user to gain access to a host through a router with lock-and-key configured, the user must first telnet to the router. When a user initiates a standard Telnet session to the router, lock-and-key automatically attempts to authenticate the user. If users are authenticated, they will then gain temporary access through the router and can reach their destination host.

Once an entry is added to a traditional access list, it remains there until it is removed manually. With lock-and-key, you can create a temporary opening in an access list by using a response to a user authentication procedure. The idea is to give temporary access, after proper authentication, to pre-authorized users whose traffic the router would normally block. Lock-and-key reconfigures the interface's existing IP access list to permit these designated users to reach their destination. When the connection is terminated, the interface is configured back to its original state.

Benefits of Lock-and-Key

Lock-and-key provides the same benefits as standard and static extended access lists. Refer to Chapter 15, "Basic Traffic Filtering, Part 1" for a discussion of these benefits. Dynamic packet filtering offers a major improvement over static packet filtering. Lock-and-key also has the following security benefits over standard and static extended access lists:

- Lock-and-key uses a challenge mechanism to authenticate individual users.
- Lock-and-key provides simpler management in large internetworks. Before, when a user needed access to internal resources, you had to punch a hole through the firewall. If you had lots of users, you had to do this on a regular basis. Thus, you have punched lots of holes in your firewall.
- In many cases, lock-and-key reduces the amount of router processing required for access lists. Dynamic packet filters use state tables that allow the router to make decisions based not only on the present packet, but also on previous traffic. However, a dynamic packet filter is more resource intensive because it has to create and maintain a state table in memory.
- Lock-and-key reduces the opportunity for network break-ins by network hackers. A dynamic packet filter creates a state table, which contains information about all established connections. A FIN=1 ACK=1 scan packet will not get through because the filter will receive the packet and not see an entry for that communication session. Because there is no communication session, there is no reason an outside host should try to tear down a session, so the filter will drop the packet.

Caution: Lock-and-key access allows an external event, such as a Telnet session, to place an opening in the firewall by temporarily reconfiguring an interface to allow user access. Lock-and-key does not prevent someone from discovering the source IP, but it does reduce the window of opportunity to exploit the open port. While this opening exists, another host might spoof the authenticated user's address to gain access behind the firewall, so the router is susceptible to source address spoofing. Lock-and-key does not cause the address-spoofing problem; rather, this is an inherent problem of the TCP/IP protocol suite. Spoofing is a problem built in to all access lists, and lock-and-key does not specifically address this problem.

To prevent spoofing, you could configure network data encryption as described in Chapter 19, "Using Cisco Encryption Technology." Configure encryption so that a secured remote router encrypts traffic from the remote host and that the router's interface providing lock-and-key decrypts it locally. You want to ensure that the router encrypts all traffic using lock-and-key when entering the router; this way, hackers cannot spoof the source address because they cannot duplicate the encryption or authenticate as required as part of the encryption setup process.

- With lock-and-key, you can specify users permitted access to various source and destination hosts. These users must pass a user authentication process before they are permitted access to their designated host(s).
- Lock-and-key creates dynamic user access through a firewall, without compromising other configured security restrictions.

An organization will benefit from the use of lock-and-key access in the following scenarios:

- When you want a specific remote user (or group of remote users) to access a host within your network, connecting from a remote host via the Internet, lock-and-key authenticates the user, and then permits limited access through your firewall router for the individual's host or subnet, for a period of time.
- When you want a subset of hosts on a local network to access a host on a remote network protected by a firewall, lock-and-key will allow access to the remote host only for the desired set of local users' hosts. Lock-and-key requires the users to authenticate through a TACACS+ server (or other security server) before allowing their hosts to access the remote hosts.

Activating Lock-and-Key

The following process describes the lock-and-key access operation:

1. A user opens a Telnet session to an access server, a border router, or firewall router configured for lock-and-key. The user connects via the virtual terminal port on the router.
2. The Cisco IOS software receives the Telnet packet, opens a Telnet session, prompts for a password, and performs a user authentication process. The user must pass authentication before the router allows access. The router or a central access security server, such as a TACACS+ or RADIUS server, can perform the authentication.
3. User authentication takes place. When the user passes authentication, the IOS software creates a temporary entry in the dynamic access list. The router terminates the user Telnet session at this time.
4. The user exchanges data through the firewall.
5. The software deletes the temporary access list entry when a configured timeout (idle or absolute) is reached, or when the security or network administrator manually clears it. The temporary entry can persist well after the user is finished. You can configure an idle timeout or an absolute timeout. Should the absolute timeout kick in while the user is still active, the user must re-authenticate via another short-lived Telnet session.

Note: The router does not automatically delete the temporary access list entry when the user terminates a session. The temporary access list entry remains until a configured timeout is reached or until it is cleared by the system administrator.

Router Performance Impacts with Lock-and-Key

When lock-and-key is configured, router performance can be affected in the following ways:

- When lock-and-key is triggered, the dynamic access list forces an access list rebuild on the silicon switching engine (SSE). This causes the SSE switching path to slow down at this time.
- Dynamic access lists require the idle timeout facility (even when you leave the timeout to default) and therefore cannot be SSE switched. The router must handle these entries in the protocol fast-switching path.
- When remote users trigger lock-and-key at a border router, the router must create additional access list entries on the border router interface. The interface's access list will grow and dwindle dynamically. The IOS will dynamically remove entries from the list after either the idle timeout or absolute timeout period expires. Large access lists can degrade packet switching performance, so if you notice performance problems, you should look at the border router configuration to see whether you should remove temporary access list entries generated by lock-and-key.

Prerequisites for Configuring Lock-and-Key

Lock-and-key uses IP extended access lists. You must have a solid understanding of how access lists are used to filter traffic before you attempt to configure lock-and-key. Access lists were described in Chapters 15 and 16.

Lock-and-key employs user authentication and authorization as implemented by Cisco's Authentication, Authorization, and Accounting (AAA) model. You must understand how to configure AAA user authentication and authorization before you configure lock-and-key. User authentication and authorization is explained in Chapter 7, "Implementing AAA Security Services."

Lock-and-key uses the `autocommand` command, which you should also understand.

Configuring Lock-and-Key

The most significant (dare I say "key"?) component of lock-and-key is dynamic access lists. These are access lists that are temporary, active only after user authentication, and eventually go inactive, either after an idle period or when you wish to force the user to re-authenticate.

This section deals with the steps to take when configuring lock-and-key security. While completing these steps, be sure to follow the guidelines listed in the section "Lock-and-Key Configuration Tips."

There are several steps to setting up lock-and-key access; here is a checklist.

1. [Preparation] Set up and test authentication methodology (see Chapters 6 and 12).
2. [Preparation] Set up encryption (see Chapter 19).
3. Configure a dynamic access list.
4. Apply it to an interface, using the usual command:

   ```
   2501-1(config)#ip access-group access-list-number
   ```

5. In line configuration mode, specify authentication method for the full range of VTY ports:

   ```
   2501-1(config)#line vty 0 4
   2501-1(config-line)#login tacacs
   ```

   or perhaps:

   ```
   2501-1(config)#line vty 0 4
   2501-1(config-line)#login local
   2501-1(config)#username ptdavis password secret
   ```

   or even:

   ```
   2501-1(config)#line vty 0 4
   2501-1(config-line)#login
   ```

```
2501-1(config-line)#password cisco
```

6. Enable the creation of temporary dynamic access list entries. If you do not specify the host argument, you allow all hosts on the entire network to set up a temporary access list entry.

```
2501-1(config-line)#autocommand access-enable [host]
   [timeout minutes]
```

The timeout option here is an idle timeout, defaulting to no timeout. This command is applied to the VTY ports.

Start by configuring an access list. To configure lock-and-key, perform the following task in global configuration mode.

```
2501-1(config)#access-list access-list-number dynamic
   dynamic-name [timeout minutes] {deny | permit} protocol
   source source-wildcard destination destination-wildcard
   [precedence precedence] [tos tos] [established] [log]
   [log-input]
```

You use access list numbers ranging from 100 to 199. Pick any name as long as it starts with an alphabetic character. The timeout keyword is optional, but it allows you to specify an absolute timeout for dynamic entries. You can select any value from 1 to 9999. Should you not specify absolute, by default the entry never times out, or in other words, it is available for an infinite time period. You can replace the protocol keyword with IP, TCP, and UDP. You can specify a real host or specify any for the source and destination address. Usually, you will specify the any keyword because the router will replace the source IP address with that of the authenticating host. The router uses precedence to filter on the precedence level name or number. ToS defines filtering by service level specified by a name or number from 0 to 15. Use the other keywords in the same manner as before. For example, you want to create a dynamic access list named open_sesame with an absolute timeout of 5 minutes.

```
2501-1(config)#access-list 101 dynamic open_sesame timeout 5
   permit ip any any log
```

At activation time, when the user telnets into the NAS or router from, say 172.16.1.1, this effectively creates the following rule.

```
access-list 101 permit ip host 172.16.1.1 any log
```

In general, the router substitutes the IP address of the Telnet source for the source address or the destination address in the dynamic statements, depending on whether the access list is inbound or outbound. For inbound access lists, the Telnet source is the source in the access list statement. For outbound access lists, the Telnet source becomes the destination of the dynamic access list. Therefore, the intent is for the router to apply the dynamic access list to the interface connecting to the Internet, to the authenticating user.

The access list can also have non-dynamic statements in it, which act as they normally would. In general, you need to allow Telnet into the router so that the user can authenticate. You would typically stop other access, so you need lock-and-key access to pass other types of traffic through the gateway router.

Configure a dynamic access list, which serves as a template and placeholder for temporary access list entries. The following command configures an interface.

`2501-1(config)#`**`interface type number`**

In interface configuration mode, apply the access list to the interface.

`2501-1(config-if)#`**`ip access-group access-list-number {in |`**
   `out}`

In global configuration mode, define one or more virtual terminal (VTY) ports. If you specify multiple VTY ports, you must configure them all identically because the software hunts for available VTY ports on a round-robin basis. If you do want to configure all your VTY ports for lock-and-key access, you can specify a group of VTY ports for just lock-and-key support.

`2501-1(config)#`**`line vty line-number [ending-line-number]`**

Use one of the following commands to configure user authentication.

`2501-1(config-line)#`**`login tacacs`**

or

`2501-1(config-line)#`**`username name password secret`**
`2501-1(config-line)#`**`login local`**

or

`2501-1(config-line)#`**`password password`**

Next, create the temporary access list entries.

`2501-1(config)#`**`autocommand access-enable host [timeout`**
   `minutes]`

This command enables the creation of temporary access list entries. If you do not specify the `host` keyword, the router will allow all hosts on the entire network to set up a temporary access list entry (which would sort of make your dynamic access list useless). The dynamic access list contains the network mask to enable the new network connection. If you do not specify a timeout, the router will not remove the entry until you reboot the router. If you use both the absolute and idle timers, make sure you make the idle timer less than the absolute timer. Following is an example in which three VTY ports are configured:

```
2501-1(config)#line vty 0 2
2501-1(config-line)#login local
2501-1(config)#autocommand access-enable host timeout 10
```

One other thing you should consider for the additional VTY lines. Should you take no additional steps, the router will treat every Telnet session as an attempt to open a dynamic entry. Because the router closes the Telnet session after authenticating the user, you cannot open a Telnet session to the router to do routine maintenance. You must specify another command in your router. Enter the rotary 1 command after the other commands. This command enables normal Telnet access to the router on port 3001. Thus, the commands to use are:

```
2501-1(config)#line vty 3 4
2501-1(config-line)#login local
2501-1(config-line)#rotary 1
```

Tip: Remember to write an access list that allows the administrator's workstation access to port 3001 on the router. More importantly, block access from all other locations.

Make sure you do this correctly; otherwise, you may disable all Telnet to the router. If your router is remote and you do not have remote access via the auxiliary port, you may find yourself on a plane going to visit your router.

When starting the session, the administrator will need to specify the port; for example, telnet 172.16.0.1 3001.

Caution: Although you could use the local database for Telnet, it is not recommended because the Telnet protocol sends the userid and the associated password across the network in cleartext. Also, although you can use a line password, this likewise is not recommended. Even if you could pick a password that is sufficiently robust, you will lose individual accountability. Anyone with knowledge of the password can log in.

Lock-and-Key Configuration Tips

You should understand the tips in this section before attempting to configure lock-and-key.

Tips for Configuring Dynamic Access Lists

Here are a few tips from Cisco when configuring dynamic access lists:

1. Turn on logging and review the logs for suspicious activity.
2. Do not create more than one dynamic access list name for any one access list. The router will only use the first one.
3. Do not re-use a dynamic-name on another access list. You must make all named entries globally unique within the configuration. The software just re-uses the entry for that name that it already has.
4. Limit the dynamic access list entries, when possible, to specific protocols and specific destination addresses.
5. Assign attributes to the dynamic access list in the same way you assign attributes to a static access list. The temporary access list entries inherit the attributes assigned to this list.
6. Configure Telnet as the protocol so that the user must telnet into the router for authentication before they can gain access through the router.
7. Either define an idle timeout now with the `timeout` keyword in the `access-enable` command in the `autocommand` command, or define an absolute timeout value later with the `access-list` command. You must define either an idle timeout or an absolute timeout; otherwise, the temporary access list entry will remain configured indefinitely on the interface (long after session termination) until you remove the entry manually. (You can configure both idle and absolute timeouts if you desire.)
8. If you configure an idle timeout, make the idle timeout value equal to the WAN idle timeout value.
9. If you configure both idle and absolute timeouts, make the idle timeout value less than the absolute timeout value.
10. The only values replaced in the temporary entry are the source or destination address, depending on whether the access list was in the input access list or output access list. The temporary rule inherits all other attributes, such as port, from the main dynamic access list.
11. Deploy dynamic access lists together with the time-based access lists you saw earlier in the chapter. This way, you limit the periods when users can create dynamic entries. If you see repeated attempts outside the authorized hours, this might indicate cracker activity. Hopefully, your staff is aware of the hours when access is permitted.
12. The IOS always puts each addition to the dynamic list at the beginning of the dynamic list.
13. If multiple users cause temporary entries to a dynamic access list, they go at the beginning of the list. You cannot specify the order of temporary access list entries, but this does not matter because they are host-specific entries.
14. Change user passwords frequently.
15. The IOS never writes temporary access list entries to NVRAM. The IOS saves the dynamic list but it does not save temporary entries.
16. To manually clear or to display dynamic access lists, refer to the section "Maintaining Lock-and-Key" later in this chapter.

Tips for Configuring Lock-and-Key Authentication

These tips correspond to lock-and-key authentication. There are three possible methods, as described in this section, for configuring an authentication query process.

Note: Cisco recommends that you use the TACACS+ server for authentication. TACACS+ provides authentication, authorization, and accounting services. It also provides protocol support, protocol specification, and a centralized security database. You can get more information on TACACS+ in Chapter 12, "Configuring TACACS+."

Method 1: Configuring a Security Server

Use a network access security server such as a TACACS+ server. This method requires additional configuration steps on the TACACS+ server but allows for stricter authentication queries and more sophisticated tracking capabilities.

```
2501-1(config-line)#login tacacs
```

The following example shows how to configure lock-and-key access, with authentication on a TACACS+ server. Lock-and-key access is configured on the BRI0 interface. Four VTY ports are defined with the password "quebec."

```
aaa authentication login default tacacs+ enable
aaa accounting exec stop-only tacacs+
aaa accounting network stop-only tacacs+
enable password papa
!
isdn switch-type basic-dms100
!
interface ethernet0
ip address 172.18.23.9 255.255.255.0
!!
interface BRI0
ip address 172.18.21.1 255.255.255.0
encapsulation ppp
dialer idle-timeout 3600
dialer wait-for-carrier-time 100
dialer map ip 172.18.21.2 name janet
dialer-group 1
isdn spid1 2036333715291
isdn spid2 2036339371566
ppp authentication chap
```

```
ip access-group 102 in
!
access-list 102 permit tcp any host 172.18.21.2 eq telnet
access-list 102 dynamic testlist timeout 5 permit ip any any
!
!
ip route 172.18.250.0 255.255.255.0 172.18.21.2
priority-list 1 interface BRI0 high
tacacs-server host 172.18.23.21
tacacs-server host 172.18.23.14
tacacs-server key test1
tftp-server rom alias all
!
dialer-list 1 protocol ip permit
!
line con 0
password quebec
line aux 0
line VTY 0 4
autocommand access-enable timeout 5
password quebec
!
```

Method 2: Configuring the username Command

Use the username command. This method is more effective than line protection
because the router determines authentication on a user basis.

```
2501-1(config-line)#username name password password
2501-1(config-line)#login local
```

The first access list entry allows only Telnet into the router. The second access-
list entry is always ignored until lock-and-key is triggered.

The next example shows how to configure lock-and-key access with authentication occurring locally at the router. Lock-and-key is configured on the Ethernet
0 interface.

```
username name password romeo
interface ethernet0
ip address 172.18.23.9 255.255.255.0
ip access-group 101 in
access-list 101 permit tcp any host 172.18.23.2 eq telnet
access-list 101 dynamic test timeout 120 permit ip any any
line vty 0
login local
autocommand access-enable timeout 5
```

After a user telnets into the router, the router will attempt to authenticate the user. When authentication is successful, the autocommand executes and the Telnet session terminates. The `autocommand` creates a temporary inbound access list entry at the Ethernet 0 interface, based on the second access list entry (i.e., `test`). This temporary entry will expire after 5 minutes, as specified by the timeout.

Method 3: Configuring the `password` and `login` Commands

Use the `password` and `login` commands. This method is less effective because you configure the password for the port, not for the user. Therefore, any user who knows the password can authenticate successfully.

```
2501-1(config-line)#password password
2501-1(config-line)#login
```

Using only a password is not the best way to go and, as such, you will not find an example in this chapter.

Tips for Configuring the `autocommand` Command

These tips deal with configuring the `autocommand` command.

1. If you use a TACACS+ server to authenticate the user, you should configure the `autocommand` command on the TACACS+ server as a per-user auto-command. If you use local authentication, use the autocommand on the line.
2. Configure all virtual terminal (VTY) ports with the same `autocommand` command. Omitting an `autocommand` command on a VTY port allows a random host to gain EXEC mode access to the router and does not create a temporary access list entry in the dynamic access list.
3. If you did not previously define an idle timeout with the `autocommand` `access-enable` command, you must define an absolute timeout now with the `access-list` command. You must define either an idle timeout or an absolute timeout; otherwise, the temporary access list entry will remain configured indefinitely on the interface (even after the user has terminated their session) until the entry is removed manually by an administrator. (You could configure both idle and absolute timeouts if you wish.)
4. If you configure both idle and absolute timeouts, the absolute timeout value must be greater than the idle timeout value.

Verifying and Maintaining Lock-and-Key Configuration

You can verify that you successfully configured lock-and-key on the router by asking a user to test the connection. The user should log in from a host that you permitted in the dynamic access list and the user should have AAA authentication and authorization configured for them.

To test the connection, the user should telnet to the router, allow the Telnet session to close, and then attempt to access a host on the other side of the router. This host must be one that you permitted by the dynamic access list. The user should access the host with an application that uses the IP, such as SMTP, HTTP, or Telnet.

Maintaining Lock-and-Key

When your organization uses lock-and-key, dynamic access lists will dynamically grow and dwindle as you add and delete entries. You need to ensure that you delete entries in a timely way because, while entries exist, the risk of a spoofing attack is present. Also, the more entries, the greater the hit on router performance.

If you have not configured an idle or absolute timeout, entries will remain in the dynamic access list until you manually remove them. If this is the case, make sure that you are extremely vigilant about removing entries. Develop a routine for removing entries.

Displaying Dynamic Access List Entries

You can display temporary access list entries when they are in use. After you clear a temporary access list entry or the router clears it because of the absolute or idle timeout parameter, the IOS can no longer display it. The number of matches displayed indicates the number of times the access list entry was hit.

To view dynamic access lists and any temporary access list entries currently established, perform the following task in privileged EXEC mode:

```
2501-1#show access-lists [access-list-name]
```

You saw this command used in Chapter 15 should you want to refresh your memory.

Deleting Dynamic Access List Entries

To manually delete a temporary access list entry, perform the following task in privileged EXEC mode:

```
2501-1#clear access-template [access-list-number | name]
   [dynamic-name] [source] [destination]
```

Now that you know how to set them up and knock them down, let us practice.

Practice Session

In this Practice Session, you will practice the following:

- Logging in
- Saving log data

- Switching modes
- Entering configuration mode
- Creating dynamic access lists
- Applying access lists to an interface
- Enabling and saving syslog data
- Logging out

1. Log in to the SimRouter Web page.
2. Double-click on router 2501-1 to telnet to that router. This will open a console session.
3. Enter your **Username** and **Password** at the applicable prompt. These are the ones you set up in Chapter 2. You will need to hit the Enter key twice to get to the > prompt.
4. Again, save the log for your session. To do this, select | Terminal | Start Logging | from the menu bar in the Telnet window. The Telnet client will ask you where you wish to store the log and with what name. Your choice. You are going to save the log so that when you build this configuration file, you can cut-and-paste this in Chapter 18 as a starting point, rather than having to enter the same information each Practice Session.
5. Enter the enable mode:

   `2501-1#`**`enable`**

6. When prompted to put in the enable secret password, enter **oscar**.
7. Type **terminal length 0**. This command instructs the router to scroll through long command output without pausing (the —More— message).
8. You will paste the `running-config` that you saved from the Chapter 16 log. At the 2501-1# prompt, type **config t**.
9. If you did not do this, open your log file with the text editor of your choice (e.g., use | Start | Programs | Accessories | Notepad |). Do a find on sh running-config and copy from the first "!" to "end." At the 2501-1(config)# prompt, paste this configuration.
10. Type **no access-list 100** and press Enter. This command removes any access list you may have already created. If you did the Practice Session in Chapter 16, then you definitely need this command; otherwise, the router will just append the statements you add from now on to the end of the list.
11. Type **access-list 100 dynamic open_temp permit ip any any log** and press Enter.
12. Type **interface ethernet 0** and press Enter.
13. Type **ip access-group northeast in** and press Enter.
14. Type **ip access-group 100 in** and press Enter.
15. Type **ip access-group northeast in** and press Enter.
16. Type **line vty 0 2** and press Enter.
17. Type **username peter password secret** and press Enter.
18. Type **login local** and press Enter.
19. Type **autocommand access-enable host timeout 10** and press Enter.
20. Type **line vty 3 4** and press Enter.

21. Type **username peter password secret** and press Enter.
22. Type **login local** and press Enter.
23. Type **rotary 1** and press Enter.
24. Type **exit** and press Enter.
25. Type **quit** to log out from router 2501-1. Close the Telnet window and return to the SimRouter Topology Map.
26. Click on Log Out on the SimRouter Web page.

Security and Audit Checklist

1. Do you use time-based access lists in your organization?
   - Yes
   - No
2. Has your organization assigned meaningful names to the time-based access lists?
   - Yes
   - No
3. Has your organization evaluated required times for the time-based access lists?
   - Yes
   - No
4. Do these times seem reasonable?
   - Yes
   - No
5. Are time-based access lists used to control inbound traffic?
   - Yes
   - No
6. Are time-based access lists used to control outbound traffic?
   - Yes
   - No
7. Does your organization use absolute times for access lists?
   - Yes
   - No
8. Does your organization use periodic times for access lists?
   - Yes
   - No
9. Has your organization evaluated the use of lock-and-key control?
   - Yes
   - No
10. Do you use dynamic access lists in your organization?
    - Yes
    - No
11. What do use for authentication?
    - TACACS+
    - RADIUS
    - Local database
    - Line password

12. Have you made arrangements to ensure that the administrator can telnet to the router?
    - ■ Yes
    - ■ No
13. Does the `autocommand` command include the `host` keyword?
    - ■ Yes
    - ■ No
14. Does the `autocommand` command include the `timeout` keyword?
    - ■ Yes
    - ■ No
15. Is the timeout period appropriate?
    - ■ Yes
    - ■ No
16. Does someone have responsibility for reviewing the logs for suspicious activity?
    - ■ Yes
    - ■ No
17. Did you create more than one dynamic access list for any one access list?
    - ■ Yes
    - ■ No
18. Do you use dynamic access lists with time-based access lists?
    - ■ Yes
    - ■ No
19. Do you manually clear dynamic entries from the access lists?
    - ■ Yes
    - ■ No
20. Does someone have the responsibility to clear dynamic entries?
    - ■ Yes
    - ■ No
21. If you answered Yes to the previous question, does your organization have a procedure in place to ensure that this is done?
    - ■ Yes
    - ■ No

Conclusion

In this chapter, you learned about time-based access lists. This is a useful feature to limit the time that someone can connect to a particular port. You can configure an absolute time range or a periodic one. With absolute, you can specify when an access list starts for example. With periodic, you can set the time and day that someone can upload a file.

You also learned about dynamic access lists in this chapter. Why use this feature? Suppose you dial into your ISP, you identify yourself, and you try to connect to your company only to run smack into an access list on a packet-filtering router. Access denied! Drat! This is where Cisco's lock-and-key feature enters the picture. You connect to your ISP, you telnet to a border router or access server, you authenticate yourself to it, and then it punches a temporary hole in the firewall that lets you in.

Using lock-and-key, you allow selected users (and the hosts they are on) through a firewall into a secured internal or external network. While still fraught with risks, this is better than standard and extended access lists because static access lists:

- Leave permanent openings that hackers might find and exploit
- Are difficult to manage in a large network
- Can require the router to do excessive processing, depending on what is in the list
- Do not offer a mechanism to authenticate individual users

Remember to authenticate all VTY ports (remote connections) or you have left an open door. And remember to define either an idle timeout or an absolute timeout value, or your temporary access list entries will not go away.

Chapter 18 takes a look at the final topics for preventing unauthorized access to a network—reflexive access lists and context-based access control. When you finish that chapter, you should have many good ideas for keeping out unwanted packets and perpetrators.

Chapter 18

Advanced Traffic Filtering, Part 2

In this chapter, you will learn about:

- Using reflexive access lists
- Configuring reflexive access lists
- Using context-based access control
- Configuring context-based access control

This chapter describes how to configure reflexive access lists and context-based access control (CBAC) on your router. Reflexive access lists provide the ability to filter network traffic at a router, based on IP upper-layer protocol session information. Similarly, CBAC allows you to filter on applications, content, and protocols.

Reflexive access lists and CBAC have something else in common. You need to determine where to apply your list. You ordinarily use reflexive access lists and CBAC in one of two basic ways. In the first way, you want to prevent IP traffic from entering the router and the internal network, unless the traffic is part of a session already established from within the internal network, so you configure reflexive access lists or CBAC for the external interface.

In the second way, you want to allow external traffic to access the services in your organization's demilitarized zone (DMZ) or screened subnet, such as DNS or WWW, but you want to prevent IP traffic from entering your internal network unless you can associate that traffic with an established session from within your internal network. Thus, you configure reflexive access lists or CBAC for the internal interface. Keep these thoughts about interfaces in mind when applying a list to an interface. This is getting ahead of the subject, so let us start by reflecting on reflexive access lists.

About Reflexive Access Lists

Previous chapters have examined standard and extended access lists as well as some enhanced capability such as time-based and dynamic access lists. While these access lists are an enhancement to traditional access lists, they still have limitations, including the opening of access from the untrusted side to the trusted side without control and the inability to provide different clients with different kinds of access. Reflexive access lists, introduced in IOS Version 11.3, allow filtering of IP packets based on upper-layer session information. You can use reflexive access lists to permit IP traffic for sessions originating from within your network but deny IP traffic for sessions originating from outside your network. You do this with reflexive filtering, a kind of session filtering.

Reflexive access lists allow you to dynamically open your filtering router to allow reply packets back through, in response to an outbound TCP connection or UDP session initiated from within your network. This feature reduces an organization's exposure to spoofing and denial-of-service because desirable inbound flows are mostly in response to outbound traffic.

To use this feature, you first create a temporary named access list. The special new access list commands for named access lists then allow the router to dynamically add and remove entries from the temporary access list. The router, in effect, spies on your outbound traffic; and when it sees the initiation of a new connection, it adds an entry to the temporary access list to allow replies back in.

More specifically, the IOS uses an access list to filter traffic leaving your network. One or more statements in the access lists with the `reflect` keyword cause the addition of a permit entry to the temporary named access list whenever it sees new outbound traffic. The IOS uses a corresponding access list to filter traffic coming into your network. Every time the IOS processes a line containing the keyword `evaluate` and the name of a temporary access list, it checks the inbound packet against the permit statements in the temporary access list. That is, it answers the question: is it in response to something that originated with your network? When the inbound packet matches a permit statement, the router allows the traffic into the network.

The temporary permit entries match the TCP or UDP with source and destination addresses swapped, and source and destination ports swapped. That is, take what goes out, flip the source and destination information, and allow that back in. Other IP protocols such as ICMP and IGMP behave appropriately (no port numbers).

The software removes temporary access list entries at the end of the session. For TCP, the IOS removes the entry five seconds after it detects two set FIN bits, or immediately after a TCP packet with the RST bit set. (If you are not sure what these bits are, refer to Chapter 2, "Understanding OSI and TCP/IP.") Two set FIN bits means that the session is terminating, and the five-second window allows the session to shut down gracefully. A set RST bit indicates an abrupt session closure. The IOS also removes the temporary entry at the point when the IOS has not seen any packets for the session for a configurable timeout period. This is necessary to support connectionless protocols such as UDP, and presumably also as a failsafe measure in the event the software somehow misses the FIN or RST.

For UDP and other protocols, the IOS determines the end of the session differently than for TCP. Because UDP services and other protocols are connectionless (or sessionless), there is no session tracking information embedded in packets. Therefore, the IOS considers the end of a session as a predetermined, configurable length of time (known as the timeout period) when it has not detected packets for the session.

You define reflexive access lists with extended named IP access lists only. You cannot define reflexive access lists with numbered or standard named IP access lists, or with other protocol access lists such as IPX. Use reflexive access lists in conjunction with other standard access lists and static extended access lists.

Reflexive access lists are similar in many ways to other access lists. They contain condition statements or entries that define criteria for permitting IP packets. The IOS evaluates these entries in order, and when a match occurs, examines no more entries.

However, reflexive access lists have significant differences from other types of access lists. They contain only temporary entries that the IOS automatically creates when a new IP session begins, for example, with an outbound packet, and removes the entries when the session ends. The IOS does not apply the reflexive access lists directly to an interface, but instead nests them within an extended named IP access list that the IOS applies to the interface. Also, because of the nesting, reflexive access lists do not have the usual implicit "deny all traffic" statement at the end of the list.

Configure reflexive access lists on border routers — routers that pass traffic between an internal and external network. These are often firewall routers.

Session Filtering

You are perhaps muttering, "Didn't this idiot already cover this? I just use the `established` keyword in my extended access list to allow replies back through." Well, yes and no (about the just use it part, anyway.) With basic standard and static extended access lists, you can approximate session filtering using the `established` keyword with the `permit` command. The `established` keyword filters TCP packets based on whether or not the ACK or RST bits are set. Set ACK or RST bits indicate that the packet is not the first in the session, so the packet belongs to an established session. You could permanently apply an access list with this filter criterion to any interface.

You also can filter by allowing only ports greater than 1023 into your network. Again, this filter criterion is part of an access list that you could apply permanently to an interface.

Reflexive access lists, however, provide a truer form of session filtering, which is much more difficult to spoof because the IOS must match more filter criteria before permitting a packet through. For example, the IOS will check the source and destination addresses and the source and destination port numbers, not just ACK and RST bits. Also, session filtering uses temporary filters that the IOS will remove when the session ends. This presents a smaller window of opportunity to an attacker.

Moreover, the previous method of using the `established` keyword was available only for the TCP upper-layer protocol. Reflexive access lists do work with UDP or ICMP, and with different internal port numbers. So, for the other upper-layer protocols, such as UDP, ICMP, etc., you would have to either permit all incoming traffic or define all possible permissible source and destination address and port pairs for each protocol. In addition to being an unmanageable task, you would exhaust NVRAM space.

Reflexive access lists just increase the capabilities of extended access lists; so while they are powerful, they are not too radical a change from what you are already doing.

How Reflexive Access Lists Work

When someone initiates a new IP upper-layer session, such as TCP or UDP, from inside your network with a packet traveling to the external network, it triggers a reflexive access list. When triggered, the reflexive access list generates a new, temporary entry. This entry will permit traffic to enter your network when the traffic is part of the session, but will not permit traffic to enter your network when the traffic is not part of the session.

For example, should a host forward a TCP packet outside your network, and this packet is the first packet of a TCP session, then the IOS will create a new, temporary reflexive access list entry for this connection. It adds this entry to the reflexive access list, which it applies to inbound traffic. The temporary entry has the following characteristics:

- The entry is always a permit entry.
- The entry specifies the same protocol as the original outbound packet.
- The entry specifies the same source and destination addresses as the original outbound TCP packet, except the IOS naturally swaps the addresses. This entry characteristic applies only for TCP and UDP packets. Other protocols, such as ICMP and IGMP, do not have port numbers, and the IOS specifies other criteria. For example, for ICMP, it uses type numbers instead.
- The IOS will evaluate inbound TCP traffic against the entry until the entry expires. If an inbound TCP packet matches the entry, the router will forward the inbound packet into the network.
- The entry will expire and the IOS will remove it after the last packet of the session passes through the interface.
- If the IOS does not detect packets belonging to the session for a predetermined, configurable length of time (i.e., the timeout period), the entry will expire.

Restrictions on Using Reflexive Access Lists

Reflexive access lists do not work with some applications that use port numbers that change during a session. For example, when the port numbers for a return packet are different from the originating packet, the IOS will deny the return packet, although the packet is actually part of the same session.

FTP is a good example of an application with changing port numbers. You initiate the session on port 21, while the daemon sends data on port 20. With reflexive access lists, if you start an FTP request from within your network, the request will not complete. Instead, you must use Passive or PAS-V FTP when originating requests from within your network. This form of FTP allows you to set up both connections rather than having the server set up the data channel.

Configuring Reflexive Access Lists

You should ensure that you have a basic understanding of IP and access lists; specifically, you should know how to configure extended named IP access lists. To learn about configuring IP extended access lists, refer to Chapter 15, "Basic Traffic Filtering, Part 1"; and to learn about named access lists, refer to Chapter 16, "Basic Traffic Filtering, Part 2."

Configuring the Interface

Before you configure reflexive access lists, you must decide whether to configure reflexive access lists on an internal or external interface. Think back to the discussion at the beginning of the chapter and decide whether you will apply it on the internal or external interface. The simplest use of reflexive access lists is to put both access control lists on the same interface, applied in opposite directions.

To configure reflexive access lists for an outbound interface, perform these tasks:

1. Define the reflexive access list in an outbound IP extended named access list.
2. Nest the reflexive access list in an inbound IP extended named access list.
3. Optionally, set a global timeout value.

Note: The defined outbound reflexive access list evaluates traffic traveling out of the network: when the IOS matches the defined reflexive access list, it creates temporary entries in the nested inbound reflexive access list. The IOS will then apply these temporary entries to traffic traveling into the network.

You do the opposite to configure an internal interface.

Note: The IOS uses the defined inbound reflexive access list to evaluate traffic traveling out of the network: when the IOS matches the defined reflexive access list, it creates temporary entries in the nested outbound reflexive access list. The IOS applies these temporary entries to traffic traveling into the network.

Defining the Reflexive Access List

To define a reflexive access list, you use an entry in an extended named IP access list. This entry must use the `reflect` keyword. The rules for the entry are:

- If you are configuring reflexive access lists for an external interface, you should apply the extended named IP access list to the outbound traffic.
- If you are configuring reflexive access lists for an internal interface, you should apply the extended named IP access list to the inbound traffic.

To define reflexive access lists, perform the following tasks, starting in global configuration mode:

2501-1(config)#**ip access-list extended {*access-list-number* | *name*}**

To create a reflexive access list that enables the IOS to generate automatically its temporary entries, use the `permit (reflexive) access-list` configuration command. For the external interface, specify the outbound access list. For the internal interface, specify the inbound access list.

2501-1(config-ext-nacl)#**permit *protocol* any any reflect *name* [timeout *seconds*]**

This command defines the reflexive access list using the reflexive permit entry. The `protocol` keyword is either the name or number of an IP protocol. You can use one of the keywords `gre`, `icmp`, `ip`, `ipinip`, `nos`, `tcp`, or `udp`, or an integer in the range 0 to 255 representing the IP protocol number. Appendix C provides a list of these IP protocol numbers. To match any Internet protocol (including ICMP, TCP, and UDP), use the keyword `ip`.

The `name` keyword specifies the name of the reflexive access list. Names cannot contain a space or quotation mark, and must begin with an alphabetic character to prevent ambiguity with numbered access lists. You can use up to 64 characters for the name.

Optionally, you can specify the timeout and the number of seconds to wait (when the IOS does not detect session traffic) before entries expire in this reflexive access list. Use a positive integer from 0 to $2^{32} - 1$ (i.e., 4,294,967,296 − 1 or approximately 136 years). If you do not specify this option, the number of seconds defaults to the global timeout value.

Repeat this step for every IP upper-layer protocol. For example, you can define reflexive filtering for TCP sessions and also for UDP sessions. You can use the same name for multiple protocols.

Use the no form of this command to delete the reflexive access list, where you only defined one protocol, or to delete protocol entries from the reflexive access list, where you defined multiple protocols.

2501-1(config-ext-nacl)#**no permit *protocol* any any reflect *name***

If you never applied the extended named IP access list you just specified to an interface, you must also do this. For the external interface, apply the extended access list to the interface's outbound traffic.

```
2501-1(config-if)#ip access-group name out
```

For the internal interface, apply the extended access list to the interface's inbound traffic.

```
2501-1(config-if)#ip access-group name in
```

These commands apply the extended named IP access list to the interface, in interface configuration mode.

Mixing Reflexive Access List Statements with Other Permit and Deny Entries

The extended IP access list that contains the reflexive access list permit statement can also contain other normal permit and deny statements. However, as you have seen with other access lists, the order of entries is important.

If you configure reflexive access lists for an external interface, then when an outbound IP packet reaches the interface, the IOS will sequentially evaluate the packet against each entry in the outbound access list until a match occurs. If the packet matches an entry prior to the reflexive permit entry, the IOS will not evaluate the packet against the reflexive permit entry, and it will not create a temporary entry for the reflexive access list; that is, the IOS will not trigger reflexive filtering.

The IOS will evaluate the outbound packet by the reflexive permit entry only when no other match occurs first. Then, should the packet match the protocol specified in the reflexive permit entry, the router will forward the packet out the interface and create a corresponding temporary entry in the inbound reflexive access list, unless the corresponding entry already exists, indicating the outbound packet belongs to a session in progress. The temporary entry specifies criteria that permit inbound traffic only for the same session.

Nesting the Reflexive Access List

After you define a reflexive access list in one IP extended access list, you must nest the reflexive access list within a different extended named IP access list. Nest the entries according to these rules:

- If you are configuring reflexive access lists for an external interface, nest the reflexive access list within an extended named IP access list applied to inbound traffic.
- If you are configuring reflexive access lists for an internal interface, nest the reflexive access list within an extended named IP access list applied to outbound traffic.

After you nest a reflexive access list, the IOS will evaluate any packets heading into your internal network against any reflexive access list temporary entries, along with the other entries in the extended named IP access list. To nest reflexive access lists, perform the following tasks, starting in global configuration mode.

`2501-1(config)#`**`ip access-list extended name`**

You now need to add an entry for each reflexive access list name that points to the previously defined access list. To nest a reflexive access list within an access list, use the `evaluate access-list` configuration command.

`2501-1(config-ext-nacl)#`**`evaluate name`**

You specify the name of the reflexive access list that you want evaluated for IP traffic entering your internal network. This is the name defined in the `permit reflexive` command. The `evaluate` command terminates an extended IP named access list that included one or more reflexive entries.

Use the no form of this command to remove a nested reflexive access list from the access list.

Again, the order of entries is important. Normally, when the IOS evaluates a packet against entries in an access list, it evaluates the entries in sequential order; and when a match occurs, it does not evaluate any more entries.

With a reflexive access list nested in an extended access list, the IOS evaluates the extended access list entries sequentially up to the nested entry, then it evaluates the reflexive access list entries sequentially, and then it evaluates the remaining entries in the extended access list sequentially. As usual, after a packet matches any of these entries, the software will not evaluate any more entries.

If you have never applied the extended named IP access list you just specified to an interface, you must also complete this task. Apply the extended named IP access list to an interface, in interface configuration mode. For an external interface, apply the extended access list to the interface's inbound traffic.

`2501-1(config-if)#`**`ip access-group name in`**

For an internal interface, apply the extended access list to the interface's outbound traffic.

`2501-1(config-if)#`**`ip access-group name out`**

Setting a Global Timeout Value (Optional)

Reflexive access list entries expire when the IOS does not detect packets for the session for a certain length of time (the timeout period). You can specify the timeout for a particular reflexive access list when you define the reflexive access list. But if you do not specify the timeout for a given reflexive access list, the list will use the global timeout value instead.

To specify the length of time that reflexive access list entries will continue to exist when no packets in the session are detected, use the `ip reflexive-list` `timeout` global configuration command. This command applies only to reflexive access lists that do not already have a specified timeout. To change the global timeout value, perform the following task in global configuration mode:

`2501-1(config)#`**`ip reflexive-list timeout `**`seconds`

The global timeout value is 300 seconds by default, but you can change the global timeout to a different value at any time. Use any positive integer from 0 to $2^{32} - 1$. (Again, that is a lot of time: an eternity in the computer world.)

Use this command to specify the number of seconds to wait (when no session traffic is being detected) before temporary access list entries expire. To observe this in action, use `show access-list`. Before someone sends traffic, you will just see the inbound and outbound named extended access control list. After firing off some traffic, you will see the temporary access list and its entries, along with number of matches and time left before expiration.

Use the no form to reset the timeout period to the default timeout of 300 seconds.

`2501-1(config)#`**`no ip reflexive-list timeout`**

Example Reflexive Access Lists Configurations

Now that you have seen all the commands, take a look at two examples. The first is an external interface configuration example and the second is an internal interface configuration example. In the first example, the policy permits both inbound and outbound TCP traffic at interface Serial 1, but only when the first packet in any given session originates from inside the network. The interface Serial 1 connects to the Internet. The first thing to do is to define the interface where you wish to apply the session filtering configuration:

`2501-1(config)#`**`interface serial 1`**

Then apply access lists to the interface, for both inbound traffic and for outbound traffic:

`2501-1(config-if)#`**`ip access-group infilter in`**
`2501-1(config-if)#`**`ip access-group outfilter out`**

Next, define the outbound access list that evaluates all outbound traffic on interface Serial 1:

`2501-1(config-if)#`**`ip access-list extended outfilter`**

Tip: Use meaningful names for all the named access lists involved. Later, it will make troubleshooting a whole lot simpler.

You must define a reflexive access list, say tcpapps, that permits all outbound TCP traffic and creates a new access list named tcpapps. Also, when an outbound TCP packet is the first in a new session, the IOS will automatically create a corresponding temporary entry in the reflexive access list tcpapps.

2501-1(config-if)#**permit tcp any any reflect tcpapps**

Define the inbound access list to evaluate all inbound traffic on interface Serial 1.

2501-1(config-if)#**ip access-list extended infilter**

Define inbound access list entries. This example permits BGP and Enhanced IGRP traffic and restricts ICMP packets. You must create an entry that points to the reflexive access list. If a packet does not match the first three entries, the IOS will evaluate the packet against all the entries in the reflexive access list tcpapps.

2501-1(config-if)#**permit bgp any any**
2501-1(config-if)#**permit eigrp any any**
2501-1(config-if)#**deny icmp any any**
2501-1(config-if)#**evaluate tcpapps**

The last step is to define the global idle timeout value for all reflexive access lists. In this example, when you defined the reflexive access list tcpapps, you did not specify a timeout value, so tcpapps uses the global timeout. Accordingly, let us create an entry that will remove the corresponding reflexive access list entry when there is no TCP traffic for an established session for 120 seconds (or 2 minutes).

2501-1(config-if)#**ip reflexive-list timeout 120**

Enter the show interface serial 1 command and you should see the following:

```
interface Serial 1
ip access-group infilter in
ip access-group outfilter out
!
ip reflexive-list timeout 120
!
ip access-list extended outfilter
permit tcp any any reflect tcpapps
!
ip access-list extended infilter
permit bgp any any
permit eigrp any any
deny icmp any any
evaluate tcpapps
```

The second example is similar to the previous example, the only difference being that you swap the entries for the outbound and inbound access lists. Refer to the previous example for details.

```
interface Ethernet 0
ip access-group infilter in
ip access-group outfilter out
!
ip reflexive-list timeout 120
!
ip access-list extended outfilter
permit bgp any any
permit eigrp any any
deny icmp any any
evaluate tcpapps
!
ip access-list extended infilter
permit tcp any any reflect tcpapps
```

Reflexive access lists solve some of our filtering problems, and, in the right context, CBAC solves some others.

About Context-based Access Control (CBAC)

Reflexive access lists allow the creation of dynamic openings in an outbound access list in response to an outbound data connection. This allows traffic from untrusted networks to your trusted networks only when someone in the trusted network initiates the connection. While a great enhancement, it does not help you deal with multi-channel applications such as FTP and CU-SeeMe. This is where context-based access control (CBAC) comes in. CBAC intelligently filters TCP and UDP packets based on application-layer protocol session information. Without CBAC, Cisco limits traffic filtering to access list implementations that examine packets at the network layer, or at most, the transport layer. CBAC inspects traffic traveling through your firewall to discover and manage state information for TCP and UDP applications. The IOS uses this state information to create temporary openings in the firewall router's access lists to allow return traffic and additional data connections for permissible sessions; that is, sessions originating from within the protected internal network.

In general, when you configure inspection for a protocol, the router will only permit return traffic entering the internal network when the packets are part of a valid, pre-existing session that is currently maintaining state information.

CBAC, introduced in IOS Version 11.2P, works to provide the following network controls:

1. Traffic filtering
2. Traffic inspection
3. Alerts and audit trails
4. Intrusion detection

Traffic Filtering

Without CBAC, you are limited to traffic filtering that examines packets at the network layer, or at most, the transport layer. However, CBAC examines not only network layer and transport layer information, but also the application-layer protocol information, such as FTP connection information, to learn about the state of the session. So, you can support protocols involving multiple channels created as a result of negotiations in the control channel. Most of the multimedia protocols, as well as FTP, RPC, and SQL*Net, involve multiple channels.

Perhaps your clients are out there browsing on the Internet. They are going to sites with active or mobile code, such as Java. With Java, you must protect against the risk of users inadvertently downloading destructive applets into your network. To protect against this risk, you could require all users to disable Java in their browsers. This is not likely to happen so it is not an acceptable solution. However, you can create a CBAC inspection rule to filter Java applets at the firewall, which allows users to download only trusted applets from outside the router.

CBAC does not provide intelligent filtering for all protocols; it only works for the protocols that you specify. If you do not specify a certain protocol for CBAC, the existing access lists will determine how to filter that protocol. The IOS will not create temporary openings for protocols that you have not specified for CBAC inspection.

Traffic Inspection

CBAC inspects traffic that travels through the firewall to discover and manage state information for TCP and UDP sessions. As mentioned, the IOS uses this state information to create temporary openings in the firewall's access lists to allow return traffic and additional data connections for permissible sessions.

Inspecting packets at the application layer and maintaining TCP and UDP session information provide CBAC with the ability to detect and prevent certain types of network attacks, such as SYN flooding. A SYN flood attack occurs when a network attacker floods a server with a barrage of requests for connection and does not complete the connection. The resulting volume of half-open connections can overwhelm the server, causing it to deny service to valid requests.

CBAC helps to protect against denial-of-service (DoS) attacks in other ways. CBAC inspects packet sequence numbers in TCP connections to see whether they are within expected ranges, and then drops any suspicious packets. You also can configure CBAC to drop half-open connections, which require router processing and memory resources to maintain. Additionally, CBAC can detect unusually high rates of new connections and issue alert messages.

In addition, CBAC can help by protecting against certain DoS attacks involving fragmented IP packets. Although the firewall prevents an attacker from making actual connections to a given host, the attacker can disrupt services provided by that host. This is done by sending many non-initial IP fragments or by sending complete fragmented packets through a router with an access control list that only filters the first fragment of a fragmented packet. These fragments can tie up resources on the target host as it tries to reassemble the incomplete packets.

You can configure CBAC to inspect the following types of sessions:

- All TCP sessions, regardless of the application (sometimes called "single-channel" or "generic" TCP inspection)
- All UDP sessions, regardless of the application (sometimes called "single-channel" or "generic" UDP inspection)

You can also configure CBAC to specifically inspect certain applications. You can configure CBAC for the following application-layer protocols:

- CU-SeeMe (only the White Pine version)
- FTP
- H.323 (such as NetMeeting, ProShare)
- HTTP (Java blocking)
- Microsoft NetShow
- RealAudio
- RTSP (Real-Time Streaming Protocol)
- RPC (Sun RPC, not DCE RPC)
- SMTP
- SQL*Net
- StreamWorks
- TFTP
- Trusted UNIX R-commands (such as `rlogin`, `rexec`, and `rsh`)
- VDOLive

Alerts and Audit Trails

CBAC further generates real-time alerts and audit trails. Enhanced audit trail features use syslog to track all network transactions: recording timestamps, source host, destination host, ports used, and the total number of transmitted bytes for advanced, session-based reporting. Real-time alerts send syslog error messages to central management consoles upon detecting suspicious activity. Using CBAC inspection rules, you can configure alerts and audit trail information on a per-application basis. For example, if you want to generate audit trail information for HTTP traffic, you can specify that in the CBAC rule covering HTTP inspection.

Intrusion Detection

CBAC provides a limited amount of intrusion detection to protect against specific SMTP attacks. With intrusion detection, the software reviews and monitors syslog messages for specific attack signatures. Certain types of network attacks have specific characteristics (or signatures). When CBAC detects an attack signature, it resets the offending connections and sends syslog information to the syslog server.

Understanding Context-Based Access Control (CBAC)

You should understand the material in this section before configuring CBAC. If you do not understand how CBAC works, you might inadvertently introduce security risks by configuring CBAC inappropriately.

CBAC creates temporary openings in access lists at firewall interfaces. The IOS creates these openings when specified traffic exits your internal network through the firewall. The openings allow returning traffic (which would normally be blocked) and additional data channels to enter your internal network back through the firewall. The IOS allows the traffic back through the firewall only when it is part of the same session as the original traffic that triggered CBAC when exiting through the firewall.

Throughout this material, the terms "inbound" and "outbound" describe the direction of traffic relative to the router interface where you apply CBAC. For example, when you apply a CBAC rule inbound on interface E0, then the IOS will inspect packets entering interface E0 from the network. If you apply a CBAC rule outbound on interface E0, then the IOS will inspect packets leaving interface E0 to the network. This is similar to the way ACLs work. For example, consider a CBAC inspection rule named hqusers, and suppose that you apply the rule inbound at interface E0:

```
2501-1(config-if)#ip inspect hqusers in
```

This command causes CBAC to inspect the packets coming into this interface from the network. If a packet is attempting to initiate a session, CBAC will then determine whether it allows this protocol, create a CBAC session, add the appropriate ACLs to allow return traffic, and do any needed content inspection on any future packets for this session.

The terms "input" and "output" are used to describe the interfaces where network traffic enters or exits the firewall router. A packet enters the firewall router via the input interface, where the firewall software inspects it, and then exits the router via the output interface.

Inspecting Packets

With CBAC, you specify what protocols you want the router to inspect, and you specify an interface and interface direction (in or out) where inspection originates. CBAC will inspect only specified protocols.

CBAC only inspects packets entering the firewall when they first pass the inbound access list at the input interface and outbound access list at the output interface. When the access list denies a packet, the router simply drops the packet and CBAC will not inspect it.

CBAC inspection tracks sequence numbers in all TCP packets, and drops those packets with sequence numbers that are not within expected ranges.

CBAC inspection recognizes application-specific commands (such as an illegal SMTP commands) in the control channel, and detects and prevents certain application-level attacks.

When CBAC suspects an attack, the DoS feature can take several actions:

- Generate alert messages
- Protect system resources
- Block packets from suspected attackers

CBAC uses timeout and threshold values to manage session state information, helping to determine when to drop sessions that do not become fully established. Setting timeout values for network sessions helps prevent DoS attacks by freeing up system resources, dropping sessions after a specified amount of time. Setting threshold values for network sessions helps prevent DoS attacks by controlling the number of half-open sessions, which limits the amount of system resources applied to half-open sessions. When dropping a session, CBAC sends a reset message to the devices at both endpoints (source and destination) of the session. When the system under DoS attack receives a `reset` command, it releases (or frees up) processes and resources related to that incomplete session.

CBAC provides three thresholds against DoS attacks:

- The total number of half-open TCP or UDP sessions
- The number of half-open sessions based on time
- The number of half-open TCP-only sessions per host

If a threshold is exceeded, CBAC has two options:

- Send a reset message to the endpoints of the oldest half-open session, making resources available to service newly arriving SYN packets.
- In the case of half-open TCP-only sessions, CBAC temporarily blocks all SYN packets for the duration you configured with the threshold value. When the router blocks a SYN packet, it never initiates the TCP three-way handshake, which prevents the router from using memory and processing resources needed for valid connections.

For detailed information about setting timeout and threshold values in CBAC to detect and prevent DoS attacks, refer to the Configuring Global Timeouts and Thresholds section.

Maintaining Session State Information

Whenever the router inspects a packet, it updates a state table to include information about the state of the session. The router will only permit return traffic back through the firewall when the state table contains information indicating that the packet belongs to a permissible session. CBAC controls the traffic that belongs to a valid session. When it inspects return traffic, it updates the state table information as necessary.

CBAC dynamically creates and deletes access list entries at the router's interfaces, according to the information the IOS maintains in the state tables. You apply these access list entries to the interfaces to examine traffic flowing back into the internal network. These entries create temporary openings in the firewall to permit only traffic that is part of a permissible session.

The IOS never saves the temporary access list entries to NVRAM.

Handling UDP

Because UDP is a connectionless protocol, there are no actual sessions, and thus the software approximates sessions by examining the information in the packet and determining whether the packet is similar to other UDP packets (e.g., same source/destination addresses and port numbers) and whether it detected the packet within the configurable UDP idle timeout period.

How Context-Based Access Control (CBAC) Works

This section describes a sample sequence of events that occurs when you configure CBAC at an external interface that connects to an external network such as the Internet. In this example, a TCP packet exits the internal network through the router's external interface. The TCP packet is the first packet of an FTP session and you configured TCP for CBAC inspection.

1. The packet reaches the firewall's external interface.
2. The IOS evaluates the packet against the interface's existing outbound access list and permits the packet. (The software would simply drop a denied packet at this point.)
3. CBAC inspects the packet to determine and record information about the state of the packet's connection. The router records this information in a new state table entry created for the new connection. (If you had not configured the packet's application for CBAC inspection, the router would simply forward the packet out the interface at this point without CBAC inspection.)
4. Based on the obtained state information, CBAC creates a temporary access list entry that it inserts at the beginning of the external interface's inbound extended access list. This temporary access list entry permits inbound packets that are part of the same connection as the outbound packet just inspected.
5. The router forwards the outbound packet out the interface.
6. At some point, an inbound packet reaches the interface. This packet is part of the same FTP connection previously established with the outbound packet. The IOS evaluates the inbound packet against the inbound access list and permits it because of the previously created temporary access list entry.
7. CBAC inspects the permitted inbound packet and updates the connection's state table entry as necessary. Based on the updated state information, the IOS might modify the inbound extended access list temporary entries to permit only valid packets for the current state of the connection.
8. CBAC inspects any additional inbound or outbound packets belonging to the connection to update the state table entry and to modify the temporary inbound access list entries as required, and the router forwards the packets through the interface.
9. When the connection terminates or times out, the IOS deletes the connection's state table entry and the connection's temporary inbound access list entries.

In the sample process just described, you would configure the router's access lists as follows:

■ You apply an outbound IP access list to the external interface. This access list permits all packets that you want to allow to exit the network, including packets you want CBAC to inspect. In this case, you permit FTP packets.

■ You apply an inbound extended IP access list to the external interface. This access list denies any traffic inspected by CBAC, including FTP packets. When CBAC is triggered with an outbound packet, CBAC creates a temporary opening in the inbound access list to permit only traffic that is part of a valid, existing session.

If you had configured the inbound access list to permit all traffic, CBAC would create pointless openings in the firewall for packets that you permit anyway.

Restrictions on Using CBAC

CBAC has the following restrictions:

■ CBAC is available only for IP protocol traffic. CBAC only inspects TCP and UDP packets. (CBAC cannot inspect other IP traffic, such as ICMP, and you should filter it with basic access lists instead.)

■ If you reconfigure your access lists when you configure CBAC, be aware that when your access lists block TFTP traffic into an interface, you cannot remotely reboot the router over that interface. (This is not a CBAC-specific limitation, but is part of existing access list functionality.)

■ CBAC does not inspect packets with the router as the source or destination address.

■ CBAC ignores ICMP Unreachable messages.

■ H.323 V2 and RTSP protocol inspection supports only the following multimedia client/server applications: Cisco IP/TV, RealNetworks RealAudio G2 Player, Apple QuickTime 4.

■ With FTP, CBAC does not allow third-party connections (three-way FTP transfer).

■ When CBAC inspects FTP traffic, it only allows data channels with the destination port in the range of 1024 to 65535.

■ CBAC will not open a data channel when the FTP client/server authentication fails.

Configuring Context-Based Access Control (CBAC)

This section describes how to configure context-based access control (CBAC). To apply a set of inspection rules to an interface, use the `ip inspect` interface configuration command.

```
2501-1#conf t
2501-1(config)#ip inspect inspection-name {in | out}
```

The `inspection-name` keyword identifies which set of inspection rules to apply. You must also apply the inspection rules to either inbound or outbound traffic.

Use the `no` form of this command to remove the set of rules from the interface.

```
2501-1#no ip inspect inspection-name {in | out}
```

If you do not apply a set of inspection rules to an interface, CBAC will not inspect any traffic. Inspection rules are not defined until you define them using this command. To define a set of inspection rules, enter this command for each protocol that you want CBAC to inspect, using the same inspection-name. Give each set of inspection rules a unique inspection-name. Define either one or two sets of rules per interface; you can define one set to examine both inbound and outbound traffic, or you can define two sets: one for outbound traffic and one for inbound traffic.

To define a single set of inspection rules, configure inspection for all the desired application-layer protocols, and for TCP or UDP as desired. This combination of TCP, UDP, and application-layer protocols join together to form a single set of inspection rules with a unique name.

In general, when you configure inspection for a protocol, the router will permit return traffic entering the internal network only when the packets are part of a valid, existing session for which it is maintaining state information.

Use this command to apply a set of inspection rules to an interface. Typically, when the interface connects to the external network, you apply the inspection rules to outbound traffic; alternately, when the interface connects to the internal network, you apply the inspection rules to inbound traffic.

If you apply the rules to outbound traffic, then the router will only allow return inbound packets when they belong to a valid connection with existing state information. Someone must initiate this connection with an outbound packet. If you apply the rules to inbound traffic, then the router will only permit return outbound packets when they belong to a valid connection with existing state information. Someone must initiate this connection with an inbound packet.

CBAC Configuration Task List

To configure CBAC, perform the tasks described in the following chapter sections:

1. Choosing an internal or external interface (required)
2. Configuring IP access lists at the interface (required)
3. Configuring global timeouts and thresholds (required)
4. Defining an inspection rule (required)
5. Applying the inspection rule to an interface (required)
6. Configuring logging and audit trail (required)
7. Verifying CBAC (optional)

Following CBAC configuration, you can monitor and maintain CBAC.

Note: If you try to configure CBAC but do not have a good understanding of how CBAC works, you might inadvertently introduce security risks to the firewall and to the protected network. Make sure you understand what CBAC does before you attempt to configure CBAC.

Choosing an Internal or External Interface

You must decide whether to configure CBAC on an internal or external interface of your firewall. "Internal" refers to the side where sessions must originate for their traffic to be permitted through the firewall. "External" refers to the side where sessions cannot originate (the IOS will block sessions originating from the external side).

If you intend to configure CBAC in two directions, you should configure CBAC in one direction first, using the appropriate internal and external interface designations. When you configure CBAC in the other direction, the IOS will swap interface designations. (You can configure CBAC in two directions at one or more interfaces. Configure CBAC in two directions when the networks on both sides of the firewall require protection, such as with extranet or intranet configurations, and for protection against DoS attacks.)

Configuring IP Access Lists at the Interface

For CBAC to work properly, you need to make sure that you have IP access lists configured appropriately at the interface. Follow these three general rules when evaluating your IP access lists at the firewall.

- Start with a basic configuration. If you try to configure access lists without a good understanding of how access lists work, you might inadvertently introduce security risks to the firewall and to the protected network. Again, make sure you understand what access lists do before you configure your router. A basic initial configuration allows all network traffic to flow from the protected networks to the unprotected networks, while blocking network traffic from any unprotected networks.
- Permit CBAC traffic to leave the network through the router. All access lists that evaluate traffic leaving the protected network should permit traffic that CBAC will inspect. For example, when CBAC will inspect Telnet, then you should permit Telnet traffic on all access lists that apply to traffic leaving the network.
- Use extended access lists to deny CBAC return traffic entering the network through the firewall. For the IOS to create temporary openings in an access list, you must use an extended access list. So wherever you have access lists that you will apply to returning traffic, you must use extended access lists. The access lists should deny CBAC return traffic because CBAC will open up temporary holes in the access lists. (You want traffic normally blocked when it enters your network.)

Note: If your firewall only has two connections — one to the internal network and one to the external network — using all inbound access lists works well because the IOS will stop all packets before they get a chance to affect the router itself.

Configuring the External Interface

Here are some tips for your access lists when configuring CBAC on an external interface.

1. If you have an outbound IP access list at the external interface, you can use either a standard or extended access list. This outbound access list should permit traffic that you want CBAC to inspect. If you do not permit traffic, CBAC cannot inspect it and the router will simply drop it.
2. Use an extended access list for the inbound IP access list at the external interface. This inbound access list should deny traffic that you want CBAC to inspect. (CBAC will create temporary openings in this inbound access list, as appropriate, to permit only return traffic that is part of a valid, existing session.)

Configuring the Internal Interface

Here are some tips for your access lists when configuring CBAC on an internal interface.

1. If you have an inbound IP access list at the internal interface or an outbound IP access list at external interface(s), you can use either a standard or extended access list. These access lists should permit traffic that you want CBAC to inspect. If the router does not permit traffic, CBAC cannot inspect it and the router will simply drop it.
2. Use an extended access list for the outbound IP access list at the internal interface and the inbound IP access list at the external interface. These outbound access lists should deny traffic that you want CBAC to inspect. You do not necessarily need to configure an extended access list at both the outbound internal interface and the inbound external interface, but at least one is necessary to restrict traffic flowing through the firewall into the internal protected network.

Configuring Global Timeouts and Thresholds

CBAC uses timeouts and thresholds to determine how long to manage state information for a session, and to determine when to drop sessions that do not become fully established. These timeouts and thresholds apply globally to all sessions.

You can use the default timeout and threshold values, or you can pick values more suited to your security policy. You should make any changes to the timeout and threshold values before you continue configuring CBAC.

Note: If you want to enable the more aggressive TCP host-specific denial-of-service prevention that includes the blocking of connection initiation to a host, you must set the block-time specified in the `ip inspect tcp max-incomplete host` command (see the last row in Exhibit 1).

Exhibit 1 Timeout and Threshold Values

Command	Description	Default
`ip inspect tcp synwait-time seconds`	Use this command to define how long software will wait for a TCP session to reach the established state before dropping the session.[a] The session is in established state after detection of the session's first SYN bit.	30 seconds
`ip inspect tcp finwait-time seconds`	Use this command to define how long the router will maintain TCP session state information after detecting a FIN-exchange for the session. The FIN-exchange occurs when the TCP session is ready to close.[a] The timeout set with this command is referred to as the "finwait" timeout.	5 seconds
`ip inspect tcp idle-time seconds`	The length of time a TCP session will still be managed after no activity (the TCP idle timeout).[a] When the software detects a valid TCP packet that is the first in a session, the software establishes state information for the new session. If the software detects no packets for the session for a time period defined by the TCP idle timeout, the software will not continue to manage state information for the session. This command does not affect any of the currently defined inspection rules that have explicitly defined timeouts. If you change the TCP idle timeout with this command, the new timeout will apply to any new inspection rules you define or to any existing inspection rules that do not have an explicitly defined timeout.	3600 seconds (1 hour)
`ip inspect udp idle-time seconds`	The length of time a UDP session will still be managed after no activity (the UDP idle timeout). If the software detects no UDP packets for the UDP session for the a period of time defined by the UDP idle timeout, the software will not continue to manage state information for the session. The global value specified for this timeout applies to all UDP sessions inspected by CBAC. You can override this global value for specific interfaces when you define a set of inspection rules with the `ip inspect name` command. This command does not affect any of the currently defined inspection rules that have explicitly defined timeouts. If you change the UDP idle timeout with this command, the new timeout will apply to any new inspection rules you define or to any existing inspection rules that do not have an explicitly defined timeout.	30 seconds

Exhibit 1   Timeout and Threshold Values (Continued)

Command	Description	Default
ip inspect dns- timeout seconds	The length of time the router will manage a DNS name lookup session after no activity. When the software detects a valid UDP packet for a new DNS name lookup session, the software establishes state information for the new DNS session. If the software detects no packets for the DNS session for a time period defined by the DNS idle timeout, the software will not continue to manage state information for the session. The DNS idle timeout applies to all DNS name lookup sessions inspected by CBAC. The DNS idle timeout value overrides the global UDP timeout. The DNS idle timeout value also enters aggressive mode and overrides any timeouts specified for specific interfaces when you define a set of inspection rules with the ip inspect name (global configuration) command.	5 seconds
ip inspect max- incomplete high number	The number of existing half-open sessions that will cause the software to start deleting half-open sessions.[a] For TCP, "half-open" means that the session has not reached the established state. For UDP, "half-open" means that the firewall has detected traffic from one direction only. Context-based access control (CBAC) measures both the total number of existing half-open sessions and the rate of session establishment attempts. Both TCP and UDP half-open sessions are counted in the total number and rate measurements. Measurements are made once a minute. When the number of existing half-open sessions rises above a threshold (the max-incomplete high number), the software will delete half-open sessions as required to accommodate new connection requests. The software will continue to delete half-open requests as necessary, until the number of existing half-open sessions drops below another threshold (the max-incomplete low number).	500 existing half-open sessions
ip inspect max- incomplete low number	The number of existing half-open sessions that will cause the software to stop deleting half-open sessions.[a]	400 existing half-open sessions

Exhibit 1   Timeout and Threshold Values (Continued)

Command	Description	Default
ip inspect one-minute high number	The rate of new sessions that will cause the software to start deleting half-open sessions.[a] The software will continue to delete half-open sessions, as necessary, until the rate of new connection attempts drops below another threshold (the one-minute low number). The rate thresholds are measured as the number of new session connection attempts detected in the last one-minute sample period. (The rate is calculated as an exponentially decayed rate.)	500 half-open sessions per minute
ip inspect one-minute low number	The rate of new sessions that will cause the software to stop deleting half-open sessions.[a]	400 half-open sessions per minute
ip inspect tcp max-incomplete host number block-time minutes	The number of existing half-open TCP sessions with the same destination host address that will cause the software to start dropping half-open sessions to the same destination host address.[a] Whenever the number of half-open sessions with the same destination host address rises above a threshold (the max-incomplete host number), the software will delete half-open sessions according to one of the following methods: If the block-time seconds timeout is 0 (the default), the software will delete the oldest existing half-open session for the host for every new connection request to the host. This ensures that the number of half-open sessions to a given host will never exceed the threshold. If the block-time seconds timeout is greater than 0, the software will delete all existing half-open sessions for the host, and then block all new connection requests to the host. The software will continue to block all new connection requests until the block-time expires. The software also sends syslog messages whenever the max-incomplete host number is exceeded, and when blocking of connection initiations to a host starts or ends.	50 existing half-open TCP sessions; 0 minutes

[a] The global value specified for this threshold applies to all TCP and UDP connections inspected by CBAC.

All the available CBAC timeouts and thresholds are listed in Exhibit 1, along with the corresponding command and default value. To change a global timeout or threshold, use the `global configuration` command in the Command column.

An unusually high number of half-open sessions (either absolute or measured as the arrival rate) could indicate that a DoS attack is occurring. For TCP, "half-open" means that the session has not reached the established state — the participants have not completed the TCP three-way handshake. For UDP, "half-open" means that the firewall has not detected return traffic.

CBAC measures both the total number of existing half-open sessions and the rate of session establishment attempts. Both TCP and UDP half-open sessions count in the total number and rate measurements. The IOS makes rate measurements several times per minute.

When the number of existing half-open sessions rises above a threshold (the max-incomplete high number), the software will delete half-open sessions as required to accommodate new connection requests. The software will continue to delete half-open requests, as necessary, until the number of existing half-open sessions drops below another threshold (the max-incomplete low number).

When the rate of new connection attempts rises above a threshold (the one-minute high number), the software will delete half-open sessions as required to accommodate new connection attempts. The software will continue to delete half-open sessions, as necessary, until the rate of new connection attempts drops below another threshold (the one-minute low number). The IOS measures rate thresholds as the number of new session connection attempts detected in the last one-minute sample period.

There is a lot of data in the preceding discussion and Exhibit 1, so perhaps a few examples are in order. The following example changes the synwait timeout to 20 seconds:

```
2501-1(config)#ip inspect tcp synwait-time 20
```

The following example sets the global UDP idle timeout to 120 seconds (2 minutes):

```
2501-1(config)#ip inspect udp idle-time 120
```

The following example sets the DNS idle timeout to 30 seconds:

```
2501-1(config)#ip inspect dns-timeout 30
```

To reset any threshold or timeout to the default value, use the no form of the command in Exhibit 1. The following example sets the DNS idle timeout back to the default (5 seconds):

```
2501-1(config)#no ip inspect dns-timeout
```

The following example sets the global TCP idle timeout to 1800 seconds (30 minutes)

```
2501-1(config)#ip inspect tcp idle-time 1800
```

The following example changes the finwait timeout to 10 seconds:

```
2501-1(config)#ip inspect tcp finwait-time 10
```

The following example changes the finwait timeout back to the default (5 seconds):

```
2501-1(config)#no ip inspect tcp finwait-time
```

The following example causes the software to start deleting half-open sessions when the number of existing half-open sessions rises above 900, and to stop deleting half-open sessions when the number drops below 800:

```
2501-1(config)#ip inspect max-incomplete high 900
2501-1(config)#ip inspect max-incomplete low 800
```

The following example causes the software to start deleting half-open sessions when more than 1000 session establishment attempts have been detected in the last minute, and to stop deleting half-open sessions when fewer than 950 session establishment attempts have been detected in the last minute:

```
2501-1(config)#ip inspect one-minute high 1000
2501-1(config)#ip inspect one-minute low 950
```

The following example changes the max-incomplete host number to 40 half-open sessions, and changes the block-time timeout to 2 minutes (120 seconds):

```
2501-1(config)#ip inspect tcp max-incomplete host 40 block-
   time 120
```

Whenever the session exceeds the max-incomplete host threshold, the software will drop half-open sessions differently, depending on whether the block-time timeout is zero or a positive non-zero number. When the block-time timeout is zero, the software will delete the oldest existing half-open session for the host for every new connection request to the host and will let the SYN packet through. When the block-time timeout is greater than zero, the software will delete all existing half-open sessions for the host and then block all new connection requests to the host. The software will continue to block all new connection requests until the block-time expires.

Defining an Inspection Rule

After you configure global timeouts and thresholds, you must define an inspection rule. This rule specifies what IP traffic (which application-layer protocols) CBAC will inspect at an interface. Normally, you define only one inspection rule. The only exception might occur when you want to enable CBAC in two directions, as described earlier.

An inspection rule should specify each desired application-layer protocol as well as generic TCP or generic UDP if desired. The inspection rule consists of a series of statements each listing a protocol and specifying the same inspection rule name. Inspection rules include options for controlling alert and audit trail messages and for checking IP packet fragmentation.

To define an inspection rule, follow the instructions in the following sections:

1. Configuring application-layer protocol inspection
2. Configuring generic TCP and UDP inspection

Configuring Application-Layer Protocol Inspection

This section provides instructions for configuring CBAC with the following inspection information:

- Configuring application-layer protocols
- Configuring Java blocking
- Configuring IP packet fragmentation inspection

Configuring Application-Layer Protocols

In general, if you configure inspection for an application-layer protocol, the IOS will permit packets for that protocol to exit the firewall and only allow packets for that protocol back in when they belong to a valid, existing session. CBAC inspects each protocol to maintain information about the session state and to determine whether that packet belongs to a valid existing session.

To configure CBAC inspection for an application-layer protocol, use one or both of the following commands in global configuration mode:

```
2501-1(config)#ip inspect name inspection-name protocol
  [alert {on | off}] [audit-trail {on | off}] [timeout
  seconds]
```

This command configures CBAC inspection for an application-layer protocol (except for RPC and Java). Use one of the protocol keywords shown in Exhibit 2.

Repeat this command for each desired protocol. Use the same inspection-name to create a single inspection rule. For example, you can use the following command to monitor SMTP and to send an alert when CBAC detects an illegal command:

```
2501-1(config)#ip inspect name firewall ftp audit-trail on
  timeout 60
```

The following command enables CBAC inspection for the RPC application-layer protocol.

```
2501-1(config)#ip inspect name inspection-name rpc program-
  number number [wait-time minutes] [alert {on | off}]
  [audit-trail {on | off}] [timeout seconds]
```

Exhibit 2 **Application Protocol Keywords for the** `ip inspect name` **Command**

Application Protocol	Protocol Keyword
CU-SeeMe	`cuseeme`
FTP	`ftp`
H.323	`h323`
Microsoft NetShow	`netshow`
UNIX R commands (`rlogin, rexec, rsh`)	`rcmd`
RealAudio	`realaudio`
SMTP	`smtp`
SQL*Net	`sqlnet`
StreamWorks	`streamworks`
TFTP	`tftp`
VDOLive	`vdolive`

You can specify multiple RPC program numbers by repeating this command for each program number. Use the same inspection-name to create a single inspection rule. Should you want to inspect an RPC program, you would use:

```
2501-1(config)#ip inspect name firewall rpc program-number
   10001
```

Exhibit 2 identifies application protocol keywords for the `ip inspect name` command.

> **Note:** For CBAC inspection to work with NetMeeting 2.0 traffic (an H.323 application-layer protocol), you must also configure inspection for TCP, as described later in the "Configuring Generic TCP and UDP Inspection" section. This requirement exists because NetMeeting 2.0 uses an additional TCP channel not defined in the H.323 specification.

Configuring Java Blocking

With Java, you must protect against the risk of users inadvertently downloading destructive applets into your network. To protect against this risk, you could require all users to disable Java in their browser. If this is not an agreeable solution, you can use CBAC to filter Java applets at the firewall, which allows users to download only applets residing within the firewall and trusted applets from outside the firewall.

Java inspection enables Java applet filtering at the firewall. Java applet filtering distinguishes between trusted and untrusted applets by relying on a list of external sites that you designate as acceptable. If an applet is from one of these sites, the firewall allows the applet through. If the applet is not from a friendly site, the router will block the applet. Alternately, you could permit applets from all sites except for sites specifically designated as "hostile."

Note: Before you configure Java inspection, you must configure a standard access list that defines "friendly" and "hostile" external sites. You configure this access list to permit traffic from friendly sites, and to deny traffic from hostile sites. If you do not configure an access list, but use a "placeholder" access list in the `ip inspect name inspection-name` http command, the router will block all Java applets.

Java applet filtering distinguishes between trusted and untrusted applets by relying on a list of external sites that you designate as "friendly." If an applet is from a friendly site, the firewall allows the applet through. If the applet is not from a friendly site, the IOS will block the applet. Alternately, you could permit applets from all external sites except for those you specifically designate as hostile. To block all Java applets except for applets from friendly locations, use the following commands in global configuration mode:

```
2501-1(config)#ip access-list standard name permit ... deny ...
```

or

```
2501-1(config)#access-list access-list-number {deny |
   permit} protocol source [source-wildcard] eq www
   destination [destination-wildcard]
```

Use the any keyword for the destination as appropriate, but ensure not to misuse it and inadvertently allow all applets through.

```
2501-1(config)#ip inspect name inspection-name http [java-
   list access-list] [alert {on | off}] [audit-trail {on |
   off}] [timeout seconds]
```

The above command blocks all Java applets except for applets from the friendly sites defined previously in the access list. Java blocking only works with standard access lists. Use the same inspection-name as specified for other protocols to create a single inspection rule. As an example, look at these commands:

```
2501-1(config)#access-list 1 permit 10.0.0.0 0.255.255.255
2501-1(config)#ip inspect name firewall http java-list 1
   audit-trail on
```

Caution: CBAC does not detect or block encapsulated Java applets. Therefore, the IOS will not block wrapped or encapsulated Java applets, such as applets in .zip or .jar format, at the firewall. CBAC also does not detect or block applets loaded via FTP, gopher, or HTTP on a nonstandard port.

Configuring IP Packet Fragmentation Inspection

CBAC inspection rules can help protect hosts against certain DoS attacks involving fragmented IP packets. Using fragmentation inspection, the firewall maintains an interfragment state for IP traffic. The software will discard non-initial fragments unless your rules permit the corresponding initial fragment to pass through the firewall. The IOS will discard non-initial fragments received before the corresponding initial fragments.

Note: Fragmentation inspection can have undesirable effects in certain cases because it can result in the firewall discarding any packet whose fragments arrive out of order. There are many circumstances that can cause out-of-order delivery of legitimate fragments. Applying fragmentation inspection in situations where legitimate fragments, which are likely to arrive out of order, might have a severe performance impact.

Cisco disabled the fragmentation inspection feature by default. You must explicitly enable fragmentation detection for an inspection rule using the `ip inspect name` command.

Configuring Generic TCP and UDP Inspection

You can configure TCP and UDP inspection to permit TCP and UDP packets to enter the internal network through the firewall, even when you have not configured the application-layer protocol for inspection. However, TCP and UDP inspection do not recognize application-specific commands and therefore might not permit all return packets for an application, particularly when the return packets have a different port number than the previous exiting packet. Any application-layer protocol that the CBAC inspects will take precedence over the TCP or UDP packet inspection. For example, when you configure inspection for FTP, the IOS will record all control channel information in the state table, and will permit all FTP traffic back through the firewall when the control channel information is valid for the state of the FTP session. The fact that you configured TCP inspection is irrelevant to the FTP state information.

With TCP and UDP inspection, packets entering the network must exactly match the corresponding packet that previously exited the network. The entering packets must have the same source/destination addresses and source/destination port numbers as the exiting packet (but reversed); otherwise, the IOS will block entering packets at the interface. Also, the software will drop all TCP packets with a sequence number outside the window. With UDP inspection configured, the IOS will only permit replies back in through the firewall when it receives the packet within a configurable time after the last request was sent out. (You can configure this time with the `ip inspect udp idle-time` command.)

To configure CBAC inspection for TCP or UDP packets, use one or both of the following commands in global configuration mode:

```
2501-1(config)#ip inspect name inspection-name tcp [alert
   {on | off}] [audit-trail {on | off}] [timeout seconds]
```

which enables CBAC inspection for TCP packets. Use the same inspection-name as specified for other protocols to create a single inspection rule.

```
Router(config)#ip inspect name inspection-name udp [alert
   {on | off}] [audit-trail {on | off}] [timeout seconds]
```

The above command enables CBAC inspection for UDP packets. Use the same inspection-name as specified for the other protocols to create a single inspection rule.

Applying the Inspection Rule to an Interface

After you define an inspection rule, you apply this rule to an interface. Normally, you apply only one inspection rule to one interface. The only exception might occur if you want to enable CBAC in two directions, as described earlier. For CBAC configured in both directions at a single firewall interface, you should apply two rules, one for each direction. If you are configuring CBAC on an external interface, apply the rule to outbound traffic. If you are configuring CBAC on an internal interface, apply the rule to inbound traffic.

To apply an inspection rule to an interface, use the following command in interface configuration mode:

```
2501-1(config-if)#ip inspect inspection-name {in | out}
```

This command applies an inspection rule to an interface.

Configuring Logging and Audit Trail

Turn on logging and audit trail to provide a record of network access through the firewall, including illegitimate access attempts and inbound and outbound services. To configure logging and audit trail functions, enter the following commands in global configuration mode:

```
2501-1(config)#service timestamps log datetime
```

This command adds the date and time to syslog and audit trail messages. Do not forget to configure the router's clock; otherwise, the timestamp is useless.

```
2501-1(config)#logging host
```

This command specifies the host name or IP address of the host where you want to send syslog messages.

```
2501-1(config)#logging facility facility-type
```

This command configures the syslog facility where error messages are sent.

```
2501-1(config)#logging trap level
```

This optional command limits messages logged to the syslog servers based on severity. The default is level 7 (informational).

```
2501-1(config)#ip inspect audit-trail
```

This command turns on CBAC audit trail messages. To turn on CBAC audit trail messages for display on the console after each CBAC session closes, use the `ip inspect audit trail` global configuration command. Use the `no` form of this command to turn off CBAC audit trail messages. By default, the IOS will not display audit trail messages.

Verifying CBAC

You can view and verify CBAC configuration, status, statistics, and session information using one or more of the following commands in EXEC mode.

```
2501-1#show ip access-lists
```

This command displays the contents of all current IP access lists.

```
2501-1#show ip inspect name
```

This command shows a particular configured inspection-name inspection rule.

```
2501-1#show ip inspect config
```

This command shows the complete CBAC inspection configuration.

```
2501-1#show ip inspect interfaces
```

This command shows interface configuration with regard to applied inspection rules and access lists.

```
2501-1#show ip inspect session [detail]
```

This command shows existing sessions that are currently being tracked and inspected by CBAC. The detail keyword is optional. You will see information from the CBAC state table.

```
2501-1#show ip inspect all
```

This command shows all CBAC configuration and all existing sessions that CBAC is currently tracking and inspecting.

In most cases, you can tell whether CBAC is inspecting network traffic properly because network applications are working as expected. In some cases, however, you might want to verify CBAC operation. For example, to verify RTSP or H.323 inspection, initiate an RTSP- or H.323-based application through the firewall. Use the show ip inspect session and show ip access lists commands to verify CBAC operation. These commands display the dynamic ACL entries and the established connections for a multimedia session.

Monitoring and Maintaining CBAC

You can watch for network attacks and investigate network problems using debug commands and system messages. This section has the following sections:

1. Debugging CBAC
2. Turning off CBAC

Debugging CBAC

To assist CBAC debugging, you can turn on audit trail messages that will display on the console after each CBAC session closes. You also can configure audit trail information on a per-application basis using the CBAC inspection rules.

To turn on audit trail messages, use the following command in global configuration mode:

```
2501-1(config)#ip inspect audit-trail
```

This command turns on CBAC audit trail messages.

If required, you also can use the CBAC debug commands listed in this section. (You can turn off debugging for each of the commands in this section using the no form of the command. To disable all debugging, use the privileged EXEC commands no debug all or undebug all.)

The following debug commands are available:

- Generic debug commands
- Transport-level debug commands
- Application-protocol debug commands

Generic Debug Commands

You can use the following generic debug commands, entered in privileged EXEC mode:

```
2501-1#debug ip inspect function-trace
```

This command displays messages about software functions called by CBAC.

```
2501-1#debug ip inspect object-creation
```

This command displays messages about software objects being created by CBAC. Object creation corresponds to the beginning of CBAC-inspected sessions.

```
2501-1#debug ip inspect object-deletion
```

This command displays messages about software objects being deleted by CBAC. Object deletion corresponds to the closing of CBAC-inspected sessions.

```
2501-1#debug ip inspect events
```

This command displays messages about CBAC software events, including information about CBAC packet processing.

```
2501-1#debug ip inspect timers
```

This command displays messages about CBAC timer events such as when a session reaches a CBAC idle timeout.

```
2501-1#debug ip inspect detail
```

This command enables the detailed option, which you can use in combination with other options to get additional information.

Transport-Level Debug Commands

You can use the following transport-level debug commands, entered in privileged EXEC mode:

```
2501-1#debug ip inspect tcp
```

This command displays messages about CBAC-inspected TCP events, including details about TCP packets.

```
2501-1#debug ip inspect udp
```

This command displays messages about CBAC-inspected UDP events, including details about UDP packets.

Application-Protocol Debug Commands

You can use the following application-protocol debug command, entered in privileged EXEC mode:

```
2501-1#debug ip inspect protocol
```

This command displays messages about CBAC-inspected protocol events, including details about the protocol's packets. Refer to Exhibit 2 to determine the protocol keyword.

Turning Off CBAC

You can turn off CBAC using the no ip inspect global configuration command.

Note: The no ip inspect command removes all CBAC configuration entries and resets all CBAC global timeouts and thresholds to the defaults. The IOS deletes all existing sessions and removes their associated access lists.

In most situations, turning off CBAC has no negative security impact because CBAC creates "permit" access lists. Without CBAC configured, the IOS does not maintain any "permit" access lists . Therefore, no derived traffic (returning traffic or traffic from the data channels) can go through the firewall. The exceptions are SMTP and Java blocking. With CBAC turned off, unacceptable SMTP commands or Java applets may go through the firewall.

Practice Session

In this Practice Session, you will practice the following:

- Logging in
- Saving log data
- Switching modes
- Entering configuration mode
- Creating reflexive and CBAC access lists
- Applying access lists to an interface
- Enabling and saving syslog data
- Logging out

1. Log in to the SimRouter Web page.
2. Double-click on router 2501-1 to telnet to that router. This will open a console session.
3. Enter your **Username** and **Password** at the applicable prompt. These are the ones you set up in Chapter 2. You will need to hit the Enter key twice to get to the > prompt.

4. Again, save the log for your session. To do this, select | Terminal | Start Logging | from the menu bar in the Telnet window. The Telnet client will ask you where you wish to store the log and with what name. Your choice. You are going to save the log so that when you build this configuration file, you can cut-and-paste this in Chapter 19 as a starting point, rather than having to enter the same information each Practice Session.

5. Enter the enable mode:

   `2501-1#`**`enable`**

6. When prompted to put in the enable secret password, enter **oscar**.

7. Type **terminal length 0**. This command instructs the router to scroll through long command output without pausing (the —More— message).

8. You will paste the running-config that you saved from the Chapter 17 log. At the 2501-1# prompt, type **config t**.

9. If you did not do this, open your log file with the text editor of your choice (e.g., use | Start | Programs | Accessories | Notepad |). Do a find on sh running-config and copy from the first "!" to "end." At the 2501-1(config)# prompt, paste this configuration.

10. To deny TCP and UDP traffic from any source or destination while permitting specific ICMP protocol traffic, use the following commands.

    `2501-1(config)#`**`access-list 100 deny tcp any any`**
    `2501-1(config)#`**`access-list 100 deny udp any any`**
    `2501-1(config)#`**`access-list 100 permit icmp any any`**
    `echo-reply`
    `2501-1(config)#`**`access-list 100 permit icmp any any`**
    `time-exceeded`
    `2501-1(config)#`**`access-list 100 permit icmp any any`**
    `big-packet`
    `2501-1(config)#`**`access-list 100 permit icmp any any`**
    `traceroute`
    `2501-1(config)#`**`access-list 100 permit icmp any any`**
    `unreachable`
    `2501-1(config)#`**`access-list 100 deny ip any any`**

11. You need to apply the access list 100 inbound at interface Ethernet1/1 to block all access from the unprotected network to the protected network. Type **interface Ethernet1/1** and press Enter. Type **ip access-group 100 in** and press Enter.

12. Next, to create an inspection rule named "hqusers" for RTSP and H.323, type **ip inspect name hqusers rtsp** and press Enter. Type **ip inspect name hqusers h323** and press Enter.

13. To apply this inspection rule inbound at interface Ethernet1/0 to inspect traffic from users on the protected network, type **interface Ethernet1/0** and press Enter. Type **ip inspect hqusers in** and press Enter. When CBAC detects multimedia traffic from the protected network, CBAC creates dynamic entries in access list 100 to allow return traffic for multimedia sessions.

14. Type **exit** and press Enter.

15. Type **sh running-config** and press Enter. You will use this new configuration to start the next Practice Session.
16. Type **quit** to log out from router 2501-1. Close the Telnet window and return to the SimRouter Topology Map.
17. Click on Log Out on the SimRouter Web page.

Security and Audit Checklist

1. Do you use reflexive access lists in your organization?
   - Yes
   - No
2. Do you have a policy on the use of reflexive access lists in your organization?
   - Yes
   - No
3. Do you mix reflexive access lists statements with other permit or deny statements?
   - Yes
   - No
4. Have you applied the access lists for an external interface to the inbound traffic?
   - Yes
   - No
5. Have you applied the access lists for an internal interface to the outbound traffic?
   - Yes
   - No
6. Do you use reflexive access lists for the following applications?
   - CU-SeeMe
   - FTP
   - NetMeeting
7. Do you use a global timeout for the reflexive access lists?
   - Yes
   - No
8. Is the timeout value reasonable?
   - Yes
   - No
9. Do you use the timeout on the permit statement access?
   - Yes
   - No
10. Is this timeout value reasonable?
    - Yes
    - No
11. Do you use context-based access control in your organization?
    - Yes
    - No
12. Do you have a policy for the use of CBAC in your organization?
    - Yes
    - No

13. Do you use CBAC for:
     - Traffic filtering?
     - Traffic inspection?
     - Alerts and audit trails?
     - Intrusion detection?
14. Do you use a global timeout for the CBAC?
     - Yes
     - No
15. Is the timeout value reasonable?
     - Yes
     - No
16. Do you use the following thresholds?
     - tcp synwait-time
     - tcp finwait-time
     - tcp idle-time
     - udp idle-time
     - dns-timeout
     - max-incomplete high
     - max-incomplete low
     - one-minute high
     - one-minute-low
     - tcp max-incomplete host
17. Are the threshold values reasonable?
     - Yes
     - No
18. Do you use CBAC for?
     - Application-layer traffic
     - Java blocking
     - TCP traffic
     - UDP traffic
     - IP packet fragments
19. Does your organization use logging?
     - Yes
     - No
20. Does someone have responsibility for monitoring CBAC?
     - Yes
     - No
21. Does someone have responsibility for maintaining CBAC?
     - Yes
     - No

Conclusion

In this chapter, you first learned about reflexive access lists. Reflexive access lists are an important part of securing your network against network hackers, as part of your firewall defense. Set up an extended named access list that filters the traffic leaving the trusted network. It should contain at least one reflect command referencing a temporary named access list.

Reflexive access lists provide a level of security against spoofing and certain denial-of-service attacks. Reflexive access lists are simple to use and, compared to basic access lists, provide greater control over packets entering your network.

On the other hand, CBAC protects against certain types of attacks, but not every type of attack. You should not consider CBAC a silver bullet, the panacea, or as a perfect impenetrable defense. Determined or skilled attackers could still successfully launch effective attacks. While there is no such thing as a perfect defense, CBAC detects and prevents most of the popular attacks on your network. So, it is an enhancement over simple packet filtering.

However, CBAC uses about 600 bytes of memory per connection. Because of this memory usage, you should use CBAC only when you really need it. There also is additional processing that occurs whenever the IOS inspects packets.

Use reflexive access lists and CBAC to limit spoofing and denial-of-service attacks from the outside. They are not that difficult to understand and provide enhanced functionality over standard and extended access lists.

This concludes all the chapters on filtering. You learned about standard access lists, extended access lists, named access lists, prefix lists, AS-path lists, community lists, time-based access lists, lock-and-key, reflexive access lists, and context-based access control.

Now you can turn your attention to preventing network data interception, starting with information on using Cisco Encryption Technology.

PREVENTING NETWORK DATA INTERCEPTION

Chapter 19

Using Encryption and IKE

In this chapter, you will learn about:

- Cisco Encryption Technology (CET)
- Configuring Certification Authority interoperability
- Configuring Internet Key Exchange Security Protocol

Code Wars

The Soviet Union does it. The Mossad does it. The Central Intelligence Agency does it. Gangsters and industrial spies do it. Terrorists do it as well. Your employees might even do it! There are so many people doing it that it is amazing they are not interfering with each other. What is it? Eavesdropping. National security is not the only area targeted for monitoring.

The bad guys target medical and financial records for their confidential information. Other corporate information is of interest and open to compromise. Protecting information has existed for a long time. Evidence shows that Julius Caesar, Chaucer, and Thomas Jefferson encoded data.

With the advent of personal computer and telecommunications technologies, such as LANs, society is generating and storing more information than at any other time. The need for message encoding or cryptography has never been greater.

Cryptography is a major communication security measure. Encryption is the transformation of plaintext into coded form (encryption) or from coded form into plaintext (decryption). It usually consists of a step-by-step procedure, usually mathematical, for completing a specific function; for example, a personal identification number (PIN) verification algorithm. Simply, it is a process in which the algorithm scrambles data in its readable form into an unreadable form. It is the transformation performed using an algorithm. Passing the cleartext through an algorithm along with a variable piece of data, or key, does this. You reverse the process by passing the ciphertext through the algorithm with the same or related key to decrypt or recover the cleartext.

Transmitted information is susceptible to being read when unencrypted. In fact, this is what makes eavesdropping so easy. For Ethernet segments, all you need to do is put your network interface card in promiscuous mode and get yourself sniffer software or a packet analyzer, and away you go. Getting the software is the easiest part. Many operating systems come with it bundled: to wit, IPFilter with AIX, Nettladm with HP-UX, Network Monitor with Windows NT/2000 Server, and Snoop with SunOS and Solaris. You can find ones that run on the DOS/Windows platform: ethereal, ethdump/ethload, fergie, gobbler, and tcpdump, to name a few. Or you can use those that run on Linux/UNIX; for example, ethereal, hunt, juggernaut, sniffit, and tcdump. These lists are not exhaustive, so obviously getting the software is a non-starter. Thus, you must assume that anyone who wants to is reading your unencrypted data at this precise moment as you read this chapter.

But it gets worse. Someone could tamper with packets and cause damage by delaying, overloading, or denying network communications within your organization. Attackers can get active packet analyzers, which would let them take a packet out of the stream, manipulate it, and reinsert it back into the stream.

You should encrypt communication channels when shielding is inadequate and your data is sensitive. And, router updates are sensitive. Encryption is the only practical means for protecting information transmitted across the network. Recent interest in encryption has increased as technological advances have decreased costs while increasing the amount of information exchanged electronically.

This chapter goes hand in glove with Chapter 20. In this chapter, you will learn how to set up a key exchange protocol and Certification Authority interoperability. These two features are prerequisites (but not required) for IPSec, which is discussed in Chapter 20. Your journey into Cisco encryption technologies starts with an older encryption technology — Cisco Encryption Technology (CET).

Cisco Encryption Technology

Cisco Encryption Technology (CET) is a proprietary security solution introduced in Cisco IOS Release 11.2. It provides network data encryption at the IP packet level and implements the following standards:

- Digital Signature Standard (DSS)
- Diffie-Hellman (DH) public key algorithm
- Data Encryption Standard (DES)

To configure CET, you complete the following tasks:

1. Generate DSS public and private keys using the `crypto key generate dss` *key-name* `[slot]` command.
2. Exchange DSS public keys using either the `crypto key exchange dss passive` `[`*tcp-port*`]` command or the `crypto key exchange dss` *ip-address key-name* `[`*tcp-port*`]` command.

3. Enable DES encryption algorithms using either the `crypto cisco algorithm des [cfb-8 | cfb-64]` command or the `crypto cisco algorithm 40-bit-des [cfb-8 | cfb-64]` command.
4. Define crypto maps and assign them to interfaces using a dynamic or named access list.
5. Back up your configuration and restrict access to the configuration.

Finally, if you decide to use CET, you will find the following commands helpful for diagnosing encryption problems:

```
router#sh crypto card [slot | vip]
router#sh crypto engine connections active
router#sh crypto engine connections dropped packets
router#sh crypto Cisco algorithms
router#sh crypto Cisco connections
```

The first command provides the status of an ESA, so it is only available on Cisco 7200, RSP7000, or 7500 series routers with an ESA card installed. Use the second command to view current active encrypted session connections for all crypto engines. The third command shows you information about packets dropped during encrypted sessions for all router crypto engines. Use the fourth command to view what DES algorithms you enabled on the router. The final command lets you view current and pending encrypted session connections. There are several other commands, so remember that you can always find out about them using the `show crypto ?` command.

You might have heard of IPSec, an IETF standard. IPSec shares the same benefits as CET: both technologies protect sensitive data traveling across unprotected networks and, like CET, IPSec provides its security services at the network layer so that you do not have to configure individual servers, workstations, or applications. This benefit can provide great cost savings. Instead of providing the security services you do not need to deploy and coordinate security on a per-application, per-computer basis, you can simply change the network infrastructure to provide the needed security services. IPSec also provides the following additional benefits not present in CET:

- *Multi-vendor interoperability.* Because IPSec is standards-based, Cisco devices can interoperate with other IPSec-compliant networking devices to provide the IPSec security services. IPSec-compliant devices could include both Cisco devices and non-Cisco devices such as workstations, servers, and other devices.
- *Host implementations.* A mobile user could establish a secure connection back to his office. For example, the user can establish an IPSec "tunnel" with a corporate firewall requesting authentication services to gain access to the corporate network; then the router could authenticate all of the traffic between the user and the firewall. The user can then establish an additional IPSec tunnel requesting data privacy services with an internal router or end system. However, CET supports only router-to-router implementations.

- *Scalability.* IPSec provides support for the Internet Key Exchange (IKE) protocol and for digital certificates. IKE provides negotiation services and key derivation services for IPSec. Digital certificates allow automatic authentication of devices between peers without the need for manual key exchanges required by Cisco Encryption Technology. This support allows IPSec solutions to scale better than CET solutions, making IPSec preferable for use with medium-sized, large-sized, and growing networks, where you require secure connections between many devices.
- *Data authentication.* IPSec provides authentication and encryption, whereas CET provides only encryption.
- *Anti-replay.* CET does not prevent the replay of messages and therefore is susceptible to this form of attack.
- *Stronger encryption.* CET supports only 40- and 56-bit DES, which the U.S. Department of Commerce has decertified for financial transactions because of concern for the short keys and the successful brute-force attacks on the algorithm with these key lengths.

However, CET does provide one distinct advantage over IPSec. CET is faster, partly because it is now only offered in hardware and partly because it is not as thorough. For example, CET does not offer per-packet data authentication or packet expansion.

Differences between IPSec and Cisco Encryption Technology

Should you implement CET or IPSec network security in your network? The answer depends on your requirements. If you require only Cisco router-to-Cisco router encryption, then you could run CET, which is a more mature, higher-speed solution; however, it is limited to several hardware platforms. (Refer to Exhibit 1.)

If you require a standards-based solution that provides multi-vendor interoperability or remote client connections, you should implement IPSec. Also, if you want to implement data authentication with or without encryption, IPSec is the right choice.

Should you desire, you could configure both CET and IPSec simultaneously in your network, even simultaneously on the same device. A Cisco device can simultaneously have CET secure sessions and IPSec secure sessions, with multiple peers.

Before going further, it is a good idea to compare CET and IPSec so that you can get the lay of the land. Exhibit 1 compares Cisco Encryption Technology to IPSec. To summarize, CET supports 40- and 56-bit encryption algorithms. You can only use CET between two Cisco routers. You should know that with the exception of the acceleration card within the 7200 and 7500 series routers, Cisco is discontinuing CET after IOS version 12.1. Consequently, you will only learn about IKE and IPSec in this book.

If you currently deploy CET, you should consider upgrading your software before you must. Cisco recommends that you use IPSec with Internet Key Exchange (IKE) security protocol. The IKE security protocol is a key management protocol standard used with the IPSec standard. You can configure IPSec without IKE, but IKE enhances IPSec by providing additional features, flexibility, and ease of configuration for the IPSec standard.

Exhibit 1   Cisco Encryption Technology versus IPSec

Feature	Cisco Encryption Technology	IPSec
Availability	Cisco IOS Release11.2 and later	Cisco IOS Release 11.3(3)T and later
Hardware support	Encryption Service Adapter (ESA) for the Cisco 7200/7500	Integrated Services Adapter (ISA) for the Cisco 7100/7200
Standards	Pre-IETF standards; so CET is only interoperable Cisco router-to-router	IETF standard, so IPSec works with all IPSec-compliant implementations
Protected traffic	Software encrypts selected IP traffic based on extended access lists you define	Software encrypts and/or authenticates selected IP traffic based on extended access lists; additionally, you can use different keys or different algorithms to protect different traffic
Device authentication	Manual between each peer at installation	IKE uses digital certificates as a type of "digital ID card" when you configure Certification Authority support; also supports manually configured authentication shared secrets and public keys
Certificate support	No	X509.V3 support; will support public key infrastructure standard when completed
Encryption	IP and ULP headers remain in the clear	In tunnel mode, the software encrypts the IP and ULP headers; in transport mode, IP headers remain in the clear but the software encrypts ULP headers; in tunnel mode, the software also encrypts the inner IP header
Data authentication with or without encryption	Encryption only	Can configure data authentication and encryption together, or can configure AH header to provide data authentication without encryption
Redundancy support	Concurrent redundant CET peers not supported	Concurrent redundant IPSec peers supported
Remote access solution	No	Client encryption using Cisco Secure VPN client that supports Windows 99/98/Me/XP/NT/2K; Cisco intends to release a Unified VPN client labeled simply Cisco Client
Packet expansion	None	Tunnel mode adds a new IP and IPSec header to the packet; transport mode adds a new IPSec header

Before configuring IPSec or IKE, you should set up your certification authorities with the correct information.

Certification Authority (CA) Interoperability Overview

Cisco provides Certification Authority (CA) interoperability in support of the IPSec standard. Cisco does not provide a CA itself, but CA interoperability permits Cisco IOS devices and CAs to communicate so that your Cisco IOS device can obtain and use digital certificates from the CA. Without CA interoperability, Cisco IOS devices could not use CAs when deploying IPSec. Although you can implement IPSec in your network without the use of a CA, using a CA provides manageability and scalability for IPSec. This feature is useful and you should configure it only when you also configure both IPSec and IKE in your network.

Cisco supports the following standards with CA interoperability:

- *IPSec (IP Security Protocol):* a framework of open standards providing data confidentiality, integrity, and authentication between participating peers. IPSec provides these security services at the IP layer; it uses IKE to handle negotiation of protocols and algorithms based on local policy and to generate the encryption and authentication keys for IPSec use. You can use IPSec to protect one or more data flows between a pair of hosts, between a pair of security gateways, or between a security gateway and a host.

- *IKE (Internet Key Exchange):* a hybrid protocol that implements Oakley and Skeme key exchanges inside the ISAKMP framework. While you can use IKE with other protocols, its initial implementation is with the IPSec protocol. IKE provides authentication of IPSec peers, negotiates IPSec keys, and negotiates IPSec security associations.

- *PKCS #7 (Public-Key Cryptography Standard #7):* a standard from RSA Data Security, Inc., used to encrypt and sign certificate enrollment messages.

- *PKCS #10 (Public-Key Cryptography Standard #10):* a standard syntax from RSA Data Security, Inc., for certificate requests.

- *RSA Keys:* Ron Rivest, Adi Shamir, and Leonard Adleman developed the public key RSA algorithms. RSA keys come in pairs: one public key and one private key.

- *X.509v3 certificates:* certificate support that allows the IPSec-protected network to scale by providing the equivalent of a digital ID card to every device. When two devices wish to communicate, they exchange digital certificates to prove their identity, thus removing the need to manually exchange public keys with each peer or to manually specify a shared key at each peer. Your organization can obtain certificates from a Certification Authority (CA). X.509 is part of the X.500 standard from the ITU.

Overview of Certification Authorities

This section provides background information on Certification Authorities (CAs), including the following:

1. Purpose of CAs
2. Implementing IPSec without CAs
3. Implementing IPSec with CAs
4. About Registration Authorities

Note: You need a Certification Authority (CA) available to your network before you can configure this interoperability feature. Your CA must support Cisco's PKI protocol, the Certificate Enrollment Protocol (CEP). Cisco and VeriSign co-developed CEP, an early implementation of the IETF standard: Certificate Request Syntax (CRS). CEP specifies how a device communicates with a CA, including the methods for retrieving the CA's public key, retrieving a CRL, and enrolling a device. CEP uses the PKCS #7 and #10 standards.

Purpose of CAs

CAs have responsibility for managing certificate requests and issuing certificates to participating IPSec network devices. These services provide centralized key management for the participating devices. CAs simplify the administration of IPSec network devices. You can use a CA with a network containing multiple IPSec-compliant devices such as routers or servers.

How are certificates used to authenticate parties to a conversation? Digital signatures, enabled by public key cryptography, provide a means to digitally authenticate devices and individual users. In public key cryptography, such as the RSA encryption system, each user has a key-pair containing both a public and a private key. The keys act as complements and anything encrypted with one of the keys can be decrypted with the other. In simple terms, a signature is formed when the device encrypts data with a user's private key. The receiver verifies the signature by decrypting the message with the sender's public key. The fact that the receiver could decrypt the message using the sender's public key indicates that the holder of the private key, the sender, must have created the message. This process relies on the receiver having a copy of the sender's public key and knowing with a high degree of certainty that it really does belong to the sender, and not to someone pretending to be the sender.

Digital certificates provide this link. A digital certificate contains information to identify a user or device, such as the name, serial number, company, department, or IP address. It also contains a copy of the entity's public key. A Certification Authority (CA), a third party that is explicitly trusted by the receiver to validate identities and to create digital certificates, signs the certificate itself.

To validate the CA's signature, the receiver must first know the CA's public key. Normally, you will handle this out-of-band or through an operation done at installation. For example, software developers configure most Web browsers with the public keys of several CAs by default. The Internet Key Exchange (IKE), a key component of IPSec, can use digital signatures to authenticate peer devices before setting up security associations.

Without digital signatures, one must manually exchange public keys or secrets between each pair of devices using IPSec to protect their communications. Without certificates, every new device you add to the network will require a configuration change on every other device with which it securely communicates. However, using digital certificates, the CA enrolls each device. When two devices wish to communicate, they exchange certificates and digitally sign data to authenticate each other. When you add a new device to the network, one simply enrolls that device with a CA, and none of the other devices need modification. When the new device attempts an IPSec connection, the devices automatically exchange certificates and the router can authenticate the device.

Implementing IPSec without CAs

Without a CA, should you want to enable IPSec services (e.g., encryption) between two Cisco routers, you must first ensure that each router has the other router's key, such as an RSA public key or a shared key. Thus, you must manually perform one of the following:

- At each router, enter the other router's RSA public key
- At each router, specify a shared key for use between the routers

Each router uses the other router's key to authenticate the identity of the other router; this authentication always occurs whenever the two routers exchange IPSec traffic.

If you have multiple Cisco routers in a mesh topology and want to exchange IPSec traffic passing between all of those routers, then you must first configure shared keys or RSA public keys between all of those routers. This could turn into a big job.

Every time a new router is added to the IPSec network, you must configure keys between the new router and each of the existing routers. Consequently, the more devices requiring IPSec services, the more involved the key administration becomes. Obviously, this approach does not scale well for larger, more complex networks requiring encryption.

Implementing IPSec with CAs

With a CA, you do not need to configure keys between all of the encrypting routers. Instead, you individually enroll each participating router with the CA, requesting a certificate for that router. After you do this, each participating router can dynamically authenticate all other participating routers.

To add a new IPSec router to the network, you only need to configure that new router to request a certificate from the CA, instead of making multiple key configurations with all the other existing IPSec routers.

About Registration Authorities

Some CAs have a Registration Authority (RA) as part of their implementation. An RA is essentially a server acting as a proxy for the CA so that CA functions can continue when the CA is offline. Some of the configuration tasks described in this document differ slightly, depending on whether or not your CA supports an RA.

Configuring Certification Authority Interoperability

To enable your Cisco device to interoperate with a CA, complete the following required and optional tasks:

1. Manage NVRAM memory usage.
2. Configure the router's host name and IP domain name.
3. Generate an RSA key-pair.
4. Declare a Certification Authority.
5. Authenticate the CA.
6. Request your certificate.
7. Save your configuration.
8. Monitor and maintain Certification Authority interoperability.

Managing NVRAM Memory Usage

Your router uses certificates and Certificate Revocation Lists (CRLs) when it uses a CA. Normally, it stores certain of these certificates and all CRLs locally in the router's NVRAM, and each certificate and CRL uses a moderate amount of memory. Your router normally stores its certificate, the CA's certificate, and maybe two Registration Authority (RA) certificates (when the CA supports an RA). In addition, the router normally stores one CRL at your router unless your CA supports an RA; then you can store multiple CRLs at your router.

In general, storing these certificates and CRLs locally will not present a problem. However, memory might sometimes become an issue, particularly when your CA supports an RA and you end up storing a large number of CRLs on your router.

To save NVRAM space, you can specify that the router should not store certificates and CRLs locally, but should retrieve them from the CA when needed. To specify this, turn on query mode by using the following command in global configuration mode:

```
4500(config)#crypto ca certificate query
```

Note: You will use router 4500 for this chapter, rather than 2501-1.

Turning on query mode causes the router to not store certificates and CRLs locally. This is an optional step.

Note: Query mode may affect availability when the CA is down. Also, this mode will save NVRAM space but could result in a slight performance impact.

If you do not turn on query mode at this time, but later decide that you should, you can turn on query mode at that time even when your router has already stored certificates and CRLs. In this case, when you turn on query mode, the router will delete stored certificates and CRLs after you save your configuration.

Note: Should you copy your configuration to a TFTP site prior to turning on query mode, you will save any stored certificates and CRLs at the TFTP site.

If you turn on query mode now, you can turn off query mode later should you wish. If you turn off query mode later, you also should perform the `copy system:running-config nvram:startup-config` command at that time to save all current certificates and CRLs to NVRAM; otherwise, you might lose them during a reboot and you would need to retrieve them the next time your router needed them.

Configuring the Router's Host Name and IP Domain Name

You must configure the router's host name and IP domain name unless you have already done so. The router assigns a fully qualified domain name (FQDN) to the keys and certificates IPSec uses, and it bases the FQDN on the host name and IP domain name you assign to the router. For example, the router would name a certificate "4500.pdaconsulting.com" based on a router host name of "4500" and a router IP domain name of ".pdaconsulting.com." To configure the router's host name and IP domain name, use the following commands in global configuration mode:

```
4500(config)#hostname 4500
```

This command configures the router's host name.

```
4500(config)#ip domain-name pdaconsulting.com
```

Generating an RSA Key-Pair

The router uses RSA key-pairs to sign and encrypt IKE key management messages; thus, you need a key-pair before you can obtain a certificate for your router. To generate an RSA key-pair, use the following command in global configuration mode:

```
4500(config)#crypto key generate rsa [usage-keys]
```

This command generates RSA key-pairs: one encryption pair and one signature pair. Use the `usage-keys` keywords to specify special-usage keys instead of general-purpose keys.

> **Note:** If you already have RSA key-pairs when you issue this command, the IOS will warn you and prompt you to replace the existing keys with the new keys.

If you generate special-usage keys, the IOS will generate two pairs of RSA keys. The software will use one pair with any IKE policy specifying RSA signatures as the authentication method and the other pair with any IKE policy specifying RSA encrypted nonces as the authentication method. If you plan to use both RSA authentication methods in your IKE policies, you might prefer to generate special-usage keys.

> **Note:** You cannot generate special-usage and general-purpose key-pairs: one or the other.

If you generate general-purpose keys, the IOS will generate only one pair of RSA keys. The software will use the pair with IKE policies specifying either RSA signatures or RSA encrypted nonces. So, your general-purpose key-pair gets used more frequently than a special-usage pair. This is not a problem if you change your keys often enough.

When you generate RSA keys, the IOS will prompt you to enter a modulus length as follows.

```
The name for the keys will be: 4500.pdaconsulting.com
Choose the size of the key modulus in the range of 360 to
    2048 for your General Purpose Keys. Choosing a key modulus
    greater than 512 may take a few minutes.

How many bits in the modulus [512]: 1024
Generating RSA keys …
[OK]
```

A longer modulus offers better security, but takes longer to generate. You can use any value from 360 to 2048. You should avoid anything less than 512 bits and Cisco recommends you use 1024.

Declaring a CA

You should declare one Certification Authority (CA) for use by your router. To declare a CA, use the following commands starting in global configuration mode:

```
4500(config)#crypto ca identity name
```

Use the CA's domain name for the name keyword; otherwise, your router does not know about any CA. You must declare one with this statement. This command puts you into the ca-identity configuration mode. Next, you use the following command to specify the URL of the CA.

```
4500(ca-identity)#enrollment url url
```

You must specify this URL in the form of http://CA_name where CA_name is the CA's host DNS name or IP address. The URL should include any non-standard cgi-bin script location; for example, http://CA_name/script_location, where script_location is the full path to the CA scripts. You router does not use the CA URL until you specify it.

If your CA system provides a Registration Authority (RA), then specify RA mode.

```
4500(ca-identity)#enrollment mode ra
```

If your CA system provides an RA and supports LDAP (Lightweight Directory Access Protocol), you must specify the location of the LDAP server.

```
4500(ca-identity)#query url url
```

You must specify this URL in the format ldap://server_name, where server_name is the host DNS name or IP address of the LDAP server. This command is only valid when you use the enrollment mode ra command.

Optionally, you can specify a retry period.

```
4500(ca-identity)#enrollment retry period minutes
```

After requesting a certificate, the router waits to receive a certificate from the CA. Should the router not receive a certificate within a period of time (the retry period), the router will send another certificate request. By default, the router will keep sending these requests forever unless you use the enrollment retry count command. You can change the retry period from the default of 1 minute. Your choice for the keyword minutes is a value from 1 to 60.

As well, you can optionally specify how many times the router will continue to send unsuccessful certificate requests before giving up.

```
4500(ca-identity)#enrollment retry count count
```

By default, the router will never give up trying (the default retry count of zero). You can specify any value from 1 to 100.

Optionally, you can specify that your router still can accept other peers' certificates even when the appropriate CRL is not accessible to your router.

```
4500(ca-identity)#crl optional
```

The default is that the router must have and check the appropriate CRL before accepting another IPSec peer's certificate. If your router does not have the applicable CRL and cannot obtain one, it will reject the peer's certificate unless you use the

Exhibit 2   Security and CA Availability

	Query — Yes	Query — No
CRL Optional — Yes	Sessions will go through even when the CA is not available, but the CA might have revoked the certificate.	Sessions will go through even when the CA is not available, but the CA might have revoked the certificate.
CRL Optional — No	The router will not accept certificates when the CA is not available.	Sessions will go through and the router will verify them against the CRL stored locally.

`crl optional` command. If you use this command, your router will still try to obtain a CRL; but when it cannot, it will accept the peer's certificate anyway.

You should exit ca-identity configuration mode with the following command.

```
4500(ca-identity)#exit
```

You can determine the trade-off between security and availability with the `query url` and `crl optional` commands, as shown in Exhibit 2.

Authenticating the CA

The router needs to authenticate the CA. It does this by obtaining the CA's self-signed certificate containing the CA's public key. Because the CA's certificate is self-signed (the CA signs its own certificate), you should manually authenticate the CA's public key by contacting the CA administrator to compare the CA certificate's fingerprint when you perform this step. You need to authenticate the CA when you initially configure CA support at your router.

To get the CA's public key, use the following command in global configuration mode:

```
4500(config)#crypto ca authenticate name
```

This command will retrieve the CA's public key. Use the same name that you used when declaring the CA with the `crypto ca identity` command.

Requesting Your Own Certificate(s)

You need to obtain a signed certificate from the CA for each of your router's RSA key-pairs. If you generated general-purpose RSA keys, your router only has one RSA key-pair and needs only one certificate. If you previously generated special-usage RSA keys, your router has two RSA key-pairs and needs two certificates. To request signed certificates from the CA, use the following command in global configuration mode:

```
4500(config)#crypto ca enroll name
```

This command causes your router to request as many certificates as there are RSA key-pairs, so you only need to perform this command once, even when you have special-usage RSA key-pairs. You are, in effect, enrolling your router when you obtain your certificates.

When you enter this command, the IOS prompts you for a password. You can create a password of up to 80 characters. You need this password to revoke your certificate. When you ask the CA administrator to revoke a certificate, the administrator can use this password as a challenge against fraudulent or mistaken revocation requests.

Note: This command requires you to create a challenge password that the IOS will not save with the configuration. You need this password in the event you want to revoke your certificate; thus, you must remember this password.

Note: If your router reboots after you issue the `crypto ca enroll` command but before you receive the certificate(s), you must reissue the command and notify the CA administrator.

Saving Your Configuration

Always remember to save your work when you make configuration changes. Perform the `copy system:running-config nvram:startup-config` command to save your configuration. This command includes saving RSA keys to private NVRAM. The IOS does not save RSA keys with your configuration when you perform a `copy system:running-config rcp:` or `copy system:running-config tftp:` command.

Monitoring and Maintaining CA Interoperability

The following tasks are optional, depending on your particular requirements:

1. Request a Certificate Revocation List
2. Delete your router's RSA keys
3. Delete peer's public keys
4. Delete certificates from the configuration
5. View keys and certificates

Requesting a Certificate Revocation List

You can request a Certificate Revocation List (CRL) only when your CA does not support a Registration Authority (RA). When your router receives a certificate from a peer, your router will download a CRL from the CA. Your router then checks the CRL to make sure the CA has not revoked the certificate the peer sent. Should the certificate appear on the CRL, your router will not accept the certificate and will not authenticate the peer.

Your router can reuse a CRL with subsequent certificates until the CRL expires when query mode is off. If your router receives a peer's certificate after the applicable CRL expires, the router will download the new CRL.

If your router has a CRL that has not yet expired but you suspect that the CRL's contents are out-of-date, you can request that the router immediately download the latest CRL to replace the old CRL. To request immediate download of the latest CRL, use the following command in global configuration mode:

```
4500(config)#crypto ca crl request name
```

This command replaces the currently stored CRL at your router with the newest version of the CRL.

Deleting Your Router's RSA Keys

For whatever reason, you might want to delete your router's RSA keys. For example, if you believe someone or something has compromised the RSA keys in some way and you should no longer use them, delete the keys. To delete all of your router's RSA keys, use the following command in global configuration mode:

```
4500(config)#crypto key zeroize rsa
```

After deleting a router's RSA keys, you should also complete these two additional tasks:

- Ask the CA administrator to revoke your router's certificates at the CA; you must supply the challenge password you created when you originally obtained the router's certificates with the `crypto ca enroll` command.
- Manually remove the router's certificates from the router configuration as described in the section Deleting Certificates from the Configuration.

Warning: You cannot undo this command after you save your configuration. After you delete RSA keys, you cannot use certificates or the CA or participate in certificate exchanges with other IPSec peers unless you reconfigure CA interoperability by regenerating keys, getting the CA's certificate, and requesting your certificate again.

Deleting Peer's Public Keys

Circumstances might dictate that you delete other peers' RSA public keys from your router's configuration. For example, you no longer trust the integrity of a peer's public key, so you should delete the key. To delete a peer's RSA public key, use the following commands starting in global configuration mode:

```
4500(config)#crypto key pubkey-chain rsa
```

This command places you in public key configuration mode.

```
4500(config-pubkey-chain)#no named-key key-name [encryption
  | signature]
```

This command deletes a remote peer's RSA public key. You must specify the peer's fully qualified domain name. It you want to specify the remote peer's IP address, you could use the following commands.

```
4500(config-pubkey-chain)#no addressed-key key-address
  [encryption | signature]
4500(config-pubkey-chain)#exit
```

These commands return you to global configuration mode.

Deleting Certificates from the Configuration

Should the need arise, you can delete certificates saved by your router. Your router saves its certificate, the CA's certificate, and any RA certificates (unless you put the router into query mode per the Managing NVRAM Memory Usage section).

To delete your router's certificate or RA certificates from your router's configuration, use the following commands in EXEC mode:

```
4500#show crypto ca certificates
```

First you view the certificates stored on your router and then note or write down the serial number of the certificate you wish to delete. Next, enter certificate chain configuration mode.

```
4500#config t
4500(config)#crypto ca certificate chain name
4500(config-cert-chain)#no certificate certificate-serial-
  number
```

The IOS will prompt you to remove the certificate. This deletes the certificate.

To completely delete the CA's certificate, you must remove the entire CA identity, which also removes all certificates associated with the CA: your router's certificate, the CA certificate, and any RA certificates. To remove a CA identity, use the following command in global configuration mode:

```
4500(config)#no crypto ca identity name
```

That is CA interoperability. After you finish configuring this feature, you next should configure IKE and IPSec. IKE configuration follows. You will learn about IPSec configuration in Chapter 20.

Understanding Internet Key Exchange (IKE)

Internet Key Exchange (IKE) defined in RFC 2409, is a key management protocol standard used with the IPSec standard. Cisco has implemented IKE as per the latest version of the "The Internet Key Exchange," Internet Draft (draft-ietf-ipsec-isakmp-oakley-xx.txt). While you can use IKE with other protocols, its initial implementation is with the IPSec protocol. IKE provides authentication of the IPSec peers, negotiates IPSec keys, and negotiates IPSec security associations. The last process requires that the two entities authenticate themselves to each other and exchange the required key material. IPSec assumes a security association is in place but does not have an automatic mechanism itself to create or maintain security associations.

IP Security (IPSec) protocol is an IP security feature that provides robust authentication and encryption of IP packets. IPSec is a framework of open standards that provides data confidentiality, data integrity, and data authentication between participating peers. IPSec provides these security services at the IP layer; it uses IKE to handle the negotiation of protocols and algorithms based on local policy and to generate the encryption and authentication keys. You can use IPSec to protect one or more data flows between a pair of hosts, between a pair of security gateways, or between a security gateway and a host. You can configure IPSec without IKE, but IKE enhances IPSec by providing additional features, flexibility, and ease of configuration for the IPSec standard. For more information on IPSec, see Chapter 20.

IKE is a hybrid protocol that implements the Oakley key exchange and Skeme key exchange inside the Internet Security Association and Key Management Protocol (ISAKMP) framework. That is, IKE implements the ISAKMP, Oakley, and Skeme security protocols. ISAKMP, defined in RFC 2408, is a protocol framework that defines payload formats, the mechanics of implementing a key exchange protocol, and the negotiation of a security association. Cisco implemented ISAKMP per the latest version of the "Internet Security Association and Key Management Protocol (ISAKMP)" Internet Draft (draft-ietf-ipsec-isakmp-xx.txt).

Oakley is a key exchange protocol that defines how to derive authenticated keying material. Skeme is a key exchange protocol that defines how to derive authenticated keying material, with rapid key refreshment.

IKE automatically negotiates IPSec security associations (SAs) and enables IPSec secure communications without costly manual configuration. There are two phases to IKE negotiation:

1. Peers mutually authenticate and negotiate to set up a bi-directional ISAKMP SA. This security association provides a secure communication channel for the second phase. One ISAKMP SA shared by peers can handle negotiations for multiple IPSec SAs.

2. Using the previous negotiated ISAKMP SA, the peers negotiate IPSec AH (Authentication Header) and ESP (Encapsulating Security Payload), as required. IPSec SAs are unidirectional; that is, the peers use a different key for each direction and thus the peers negotiate a pair to handle two-way traffic. Peers may define more than one pair.

Note: Seems like a lot of SAs going around causing confusion. Well, do not confuse IKE SAs with IPSec SAs; they are not the same. The software uses IKE SAs to negotiate the parameters for the IPSec SAs. There is one and only one IKE SA between peers, but peers can have multiple IPSec SAs for the same IKE SA.

Specifically, IKE provides several benefits over manually defined keys:

- Eliminates manual configuration of IPSec security parameters in the crypto maps at both peers
- Allows you to specify a lifetime for the IPSec security association
- Allows automatic change of encryption keys during IPSec sessions
- Allows IPSec to provide anti-replay services
- Allows the use of public key-based authentication and provides Certification Authority (CA) support for a manageable, scalable IPSec implementation
- Allows dynamic authentication of peers

IKE Supported Standards

The component technologies that IKE supports include:

- *DES (Data Encryption Standard).* DES is used to encrypt packet data. IKE implements the 56-bit DES-CBC with Explicit IV standard. Cipher Block Chaining (CBC) requires an initialization vector (IV) to start encryption. The IV is explicitly given in the IPSec packet.
- *3DES (Triple DES).* 3DES is used to encrypt data.
- *Diffie-Hellman.* A public-key cryptography protocol that allows two parties to establish a shared secret over an unsecured communications channel. IKE uses the Diffie-Hellman protocol to establish session keys. IKE supports 768-bit and 1024-bit Diffie-Hellman groups.
- *MD5 (Message Digest 5) HMAC variant.* MD5 is a hash algorithm used to authenticate packet data. HMAC is a variant that provides an additional level of hashing.
- *SHA (Secure Hash Algorithm) HMAC variant.* SHA is a hash algorithm used to authenticate packet data. HMAC is a variant that provides an additional level of hashing.
- *RSA signatures and RSA encrypted nonces.* RSA is the public key crypto-graphic system developed by Ron Rivest, Adi Shamir, and Leonard Adleman. RSA signatures provide non-repudiation, while RSA encrypted nonces allow repudiation.

Even when you use IKE, you will find management of the keys for IPSec for a large network difficult. This is where certificates and the aforementioned Certification Authorities come into play. Digital certificates together with trusted third-party CAs offer the mechanism to scale IPSec to the Internet and other large networks. IKE interoperates with the ITU's X.509v3 standard for certificates. This standard works with the IKE protocol when authentication requires public keys. This certificate support allows the protected network to scale by providing the equivalent of a digital ID card to each device. These digital ID cards become the basis for CAs authenticating IPSec connections.

When two devices wish to communicate, they exchange digital certificates to prove their identity, thus removing the need to manually exchange public keys with each peer or to manually specify a shared key at each peer.

Configuring Internet Key Exchange (IKE)

To configure IKE, perform the following tasks:

1. Enable or disable IKE.
2. Ensure access lists are compatible with IKE.
3. Create IKE policies.
4. Manually configure RSA keys.
5. Configure pre-shared keys.
6. Clear IKE connections.
7. Troubleshoot IKE.

You *must* complete the first three tasks; the remaining four are optional, depending on what parameters you configure.

Enabling or Disabling IKE

Cisco enables IKE by default. You do not need to enable IKE for individual interfaces, but you enable it globally for all interfaces on the router.

If you do not want to use IKE with your IPSec implementation, you can disable it at all IPSec peers. Should you disable IKE, you will have to make the following concessions at the peers:

- You must manually specify all the IPSec security associations in the crypto maps at all peers. (You will find a description of crypto map configuration in Chapter 20.)
- The peers' IPSec security associations will never time out for a given IPSec session.
- During IPSec sessions between the peers, the encryption keys will never change.
- Anti-replay services are not available between the peers.
- You cannot use Certification Authority (CA) support.

To disable or enable IKE, use one of the following commands in global configuration mode:

```
4500(config)#no crypto isakmp enable
```

This command disables IKE. Should you want to re-enable IKE, use the following command in global configuration mode.

```
4500(config)#crypto isakmp enable
```

If you disable IKE, you can skip the remainder of the tasks in this chapter and go directly to IPSec configuration in Chapter 20.

Ensuring that Access Lists Are Compatible with IKE

IKE negotiation uses UDP port 500. Confirm that you configure your access lists so that the router does not block UDP port 500 traffic at interfaces used by IKE and IPSec. In some cases, you might need to add a statement to your access lists to explicitly permit UDP port 500 traffic.

Creating IKE Policies

You must create IKE policies at each peer. An IKE policy defines a combination of security parameters for use during the IKE negotiation. To create an IKE policy, follow the guidelines in the following sections.

Understanding Security Associations

It is necessary to protect IKE negotiations, so each IKE negotiation begins by each peer agreeing on a common or shared IKE policy. This policy states what security parameters the router will use to protect subsequent IKE negotiations.

After the two peers agree on a policy, the router identifies the security parameters of the policy by a security association established at each peer, and these security associations apply to all subsequent IKE traffic during the negotiation. You can create multiple, prioritized policies at each peer to ensure that at least one policy will match a remote peer's policy.

Defining Policy Parameters

There are five parameters to define in each IKE policy, as shown in Exhibit 3. These parameters apply to the IKE negotiations when you establish the IKE security association.

Authentication Methods

IPSec peers mutually authenticate. They must agree on a common authentication protocol during the negotiation process. You saw that IKE supports the following authentication methods:

Exhibit 3 IKE Policy Parameters

Parameter	Accepted Values	Keyword	Default Value
Encryption algorithm	56-bit DES-CBC 168-bit 3DES	des 3des	56-bit DES-CBC
Hash algorithm	SHA-1 (HMAC variant) MD5 (HMAC variant)	sha md5	SHA-1
Authentication method	RSA signatures RSA encrypted nonces Pre-shared keys	rsa-sig rsa-encr pre-share	RSA signatures
Diffie-Hellman group identifier	768-bit Diffie-Hellman 1024-bit Diffie-Hellman	1 2	768-bit Diffie-Hellman
Security association's lifetime	Can specify any number of seconds		86,400 seconds (one day)

- *RSA signatures.* This method uses digital signatures. Each device digitally signs a data set and sends it to the other party. RSA signatures provide non-repudiation. This is the default method.
- *RSA encrypted nonces.* This method uses public key encryption. Each party generates a pseudo-random number or nonce, encrypts it with the public key of the other party, and sends it to them. The parties then authenticate each other by computing a keyed hash value containing the other peer's nonce, decrypting it with the local private key as well as other publicly and privately available information.
- *Pre-shared keys.* You configure each peer with the same-shared key. The peers authenticate each other by computing and sending a keyed hash of data including the shared key. If the receiving peer can independently recreate the same hash using the pre-shared key, it knows that both parties must share the same key.

IKE Matching Peer Policy

When IKE negotiation begins, IKE looks for an IKE policy that is the same on both peers. The peer that initiates the negotiation will send all its policies to the remote peer, and the remote peer will try to find a match. The remote peer looks for a match by comparing its highest priority policy against the other peer's received policies. The remote peer checks its policies in order of its priority — highest priority first — until it finds a match.

A match is made when both policies from the two peers contain the same encryption, hash, authentication, and Diffie-Hellman parameter values, and when the remote peer's policy specifies a lifetime less than or equal to the lifetime in the compared policy. If the lifetimes are not identical, IKE will use the shorter lifetime from the remote peer's policy.

When IKE cannot find an acceptable match, IKE refuses negotiation and the devices will not establish IPSec. When IKE finds a match, IKE will complete negotiation and the devices will create IPSec security associations.

> **Note:** Depending on the authentication method you specify in a policy, IKE might require additional configuration. If a peer's policy does not have the required companion configuration, the peer will not submit the policy when attempting to find a matching policy with the remote peer.

Selecting Parameter Values

You can select certain values for each parameter, per the IKE standard. But why choose one value over another?

If you are using a device that supports only one of the values for a parameter, the other device's supported value limits your choice. Aside from this, there is often a trade-off between security and performance, and many of these parameter values represent such a trade-off. (There is that risk assessment rearing its ugly head again!) You should evaluate the level of your network's security risks and your tolerance for these risks. Then the following tips might help you select the value to specify for each parameter.

1. The encryption algorithm currently has two options: 56-bit DES-CBC and 168-bit 3DES. DES is quicker but not as secure as 3DES.
2. The hash algorithm has two options: SHA-1 and MD5. MD5 has a smaller digest and is considered slightly faster than SHA-1. Individuals have demonstrated a successful (but extremely difficult) attack against MD5; however, the HMAC variant used by IKE prevents this attack.
3. The authentication method has three options: RSA signatures, RSA encrypted nonces, or pre-shared keys.
4. RSA signatures provide non-repudiation for the IKE negotiation (you can prove to a third party after the fact that you did indeed have an IKE negotiation with the remote peer). RSA signatures require use of a Certification Authority (CA). Using a CA can dramatically improve the manageability and scalability of your IPSec network.
5. RSA encrypted nonces provide repudiation for the IKE negotiation (you cannot prove to a third party that you had an IKE negotiation with the remote peer). Use this to prevent a third party from knowing about your activity over the network. RSA encrypted nonces require that peers possess each other's public keys but do not use a Certification Authority. Instead, there are two ways for peers to get each others' public keys:
   a. During configuration, you manually configure RSA keys (as described in the section "Manually Configuring RSA Keys").
   b. If your local peer has previously used RSA signatures during a successful IKE negotiation with a remote peer, your local peer already possesses the remote peer's public key. The peers exchange public keys during the RSA-signatures-based IKE negotiations.
6. Pre-shared keys are clumsy to use when your secured network is large, and do not scale well with a growing network. However, they do not require use of a Certification Authority, as do RSA signatures, and you may find them easier to set up in a small network with fewer than ten nodes.

7. The Diffie-Hellman group identifier has two options: 768-bit or 1024-bit Diffie-Hellman. The 1024-bit Diffie-Hellman is more difficult to crack, but requires more CPU time to execute.
8. The security association's lifetime is set to any value. As a general rule, the shorter the lifetime (up to a point), the more secure your IKE negotiations. However, with longer lifetimes, you can set up future IPSec security associations more quickly.

Creating Policies

You can create multiple IKE policies, each with a different combination of parameter values. For each policy that you create, you assign a unique priority (1 through 10,000, with 1 being the highest priority).

You can configure multiple policies on each peer, but at least one of these policies must contain exactly the same encryption, hash, authentication, and Diffie-Hellman parameter values as one of the policies on the remote peer. You need not make the lifetime parameter the same.

If you do not configure any policies, your router will use the default policy, which is always set to the lowest priority, and which contains each parameter's default value.

To configure a policy, use the following commands starting in global configuration mode:

```
4500(config)#crypto isakmp policy priority
```

This command identifies the policy to create. The priority number you assign uniquely identifies each policy. There is a default policy, which is always the lowest priority. This command puts you into the config-isakmp mode.

```
4500(config-isakmp)#encryption {des | 3des}
```

The preceding command specifies the encryption algorithm.

Next, you specify the hash algorithm. You have two choices. SHA-1 is the default.

```
4500(config-isakmp)#hash {sha | md5}
```

Specify one of the three authentication methods. An RSA signature is the default.

```
4500(config-isakmp)#authentication {rsa-sig | rsa-encr |
   pre-share}
```

Specify the Diffie-Hellman group identifier: 1 for 768-bit or 2 for 1024-bit keys; 1 is the default.

```
4500(config-isakmp)#group {1 | 2}
```

Specify the security association's lifetime in seconds. The default is 86,400 seconds (1 day).

```
4500(config-isakmp)#lifetime seconds
```

Exit the config-isakmp command mode.

```
4500(config-isakmp)#exit
```

Exit to EXEC mode.

```
4500(config)#exit
```

When you finish, you can view all existing IKE policies. Use this command in EXEC mode.

```
4500#show crypto isakmp policy
Protection suite of priority 1
    encryption algorithm:    DES-Data Encryption Standard
                             (56 bit keys).
    hash algorithm:          Message Digest 5
    authentication method:   Pre-Shared Key
    Diffie-Hellman group:    #2 (1024 bit)
    lifetime:                86400 seconds, no volume limit
Default protection suite
    encryption algorithm:    DES-Data Encryption Standard
                             (56 bit keys).
    hash algorithm:          Secure Hash Standard
    authentication method:   Rivest-Shamir-Adleman Signature
    Diffie-Hellman group:    #1 (768 bit)
    lifetime:                86400 seconds, no volume limit
```

Should you not specify a value for a parameter, the software will assign the default value.

Note: The default policy and the default values for configured policies do not show up in the configuration when you issue a `show running` command. Instead, to see the default policy and any default values within configured policies, use the `show crypto isakmp policy` command.

For example, you could configure the following:

```
4500(config)#crypto isakmp policy 10
4500(config-isakmp)#encryption des
4500(config-isakmp)#hash md5
4500(config-isakmp)#authentication rsa-sig
4500(config-isakmp)#group 2
4500(config-isakmp)#lifetime 5400
```

```
4500(config-isakmp)#exit
4500(config)#crypto isakmp policy 20
4500(config-isakmp)#authentication pre-share
4500(config-isakmp)#lifetime 10800
4500(config-isakmp)#exit
```

This example shows the default values for each parameter:

```
4500(config)#crypto isakmp policy 1
4500(config-isakmp)#encryption des
4500(config-isakmp)#hash sha
4500(config-isakmp)#authentication rsa-sig
4500(config-isakmp)#group 1
4500(config-isakmp)#lifetime 86400
4500(config-isakmp)#exit
4500(config)#exit
```

The above configuration would result in the following policies:

```
4500#show crypto isakmp policy
Protection suite of priority 10
   encryption algorithm:     DES–Data Encryption Standard
                             (56 bit keys).
   hash algorithm:           Message Digest 5
   authentication method:    Rivest-Shamir-Adleman Signature
   Diffie-Hellman group:     #2 (1024 bit)
   lifetime:                 5400 seconds, no volume limit
Protection suite of priority 20
   encryption algorithm:     DES–Data Encryption Standard
                             (56 bit keys).
   hash algorithm:           Secure Hash Standard
   authentication method:    Pre-Shared Key
   Diffie-Hellman group:     #1 (768 bit)
   lifetime:                 10800 seconds, no volume limit
Default protection suite
   encryption algorithm:     DES–Data Encryption Standard
                             (56 bit keys).
   hash algorithm:           Secure Hash Standard
   authentication method:    Rivest-Shamir-Adleman Signature
   Diffie-Hellman group:     #1 (768 bit)
```

Additional Configuration Required for IKE Policies

Depending on the authentication method you specify in your IKE policies, you need to do certain additional configuration before IKE and IPSec can successfully use the IKE policies.

Each authentication method requires additional companion configuration as follows:

- *RSA signatures method.* If you specify RSA signatures as the authentication method in a policy, you must configure the peers to obtain certificates from a Certification Authority (CA). Of course, you must properly configure the CA to issue the certificates. Configure this certificate support as previously described in this chapter. Each peer uses the certificates to securely exchange public keys. RSA signatures require that each peer have the remote peer's public signature key. When both peers have valid certificates, they will automatically exchange public keys with each other as part of any IKE negotiation using RSA signatures.

- *RSA encrypted nonces method.* If you specify RSA encrypted nonces as the authentication method in a policy, you need to ensure that each peer has the other peers' public keys. Unlike RSA signatures, the RSA encrypted nonces method does not use certificates to exchange public keys. Instead, you must ensure that each peer has the others' public keys as follows:
  - Either manually configure RSA keys as described in the section "Manually Configuring RSA Keys," or
  - Ensure that an IKE exchange using RSA signatures has already occurred between the peers. The peers' public keys are exchanged during the RSA-signatures-based IKE negotiations. To make this happen, specify two policies: a higher-priority policy with RSA encrypted nonces and a lower-priority policy with RSA signatures. When IKE negotiations occur, the router will use RSA signatures the first time because the peers do not yet have each other's public keys. Then, future IKE negotiations can use RSA encrypted nonces because the peers will have exchanged public keys. Of course, this alternative requires that you have configured Certification Authority support.

- *Pre-shared keys authentication method.* If you specify pre-shared keys as the authentication method in a policy, you must configure these pre-shared keys. If you configure RSA encryption and the peers negotiate signature mode, the peer will request both signature and encryption keys. Basically, the router will request as many keys as the configuration will support. If you do not configure RSA encryption, it will just request a signature key.

Manually Configuring RSA Keys

You must manually configure RSA keys when you specify RSA encrypted nonces as the authentication method in an IKE policy and you are not using a Certification Authority (CA).

To manually configure RSA keys, perform these tasks at each IPSec peer that uses RSA encrypted nonces in an IKE policy:

1. Generate RSA keys.
2. Set ISAKMP identity.
3. Specify all the other peers' RSA public keys.

Generating RSA Keys

To generate RSA keys, use the following commands starting in global configuration mode:

```
4500(config)#crypto key generate rsa [usage-keys]
4500(config)#exit
```

Refer to the discussion on the use of the usage-keys keywords earlier in this chapter.

To view the generated RSA public key (in EXEC mode), use this command.

```
4500#show crypto key mypubkey rsa
% Key pair was generated at: 15:37:25 UTC Nov 16 2001
Key name: 4500.pdaconsulting.com
Usage: General Purpose Key
Key Data:
30819F30 0D06092A 864886F7 0D010101 05000381 8D003081 89028181 00D4D768
CDC0F217 91FB333B 70E42C9E 2259EB0F 7B10C338 ECBB4D79 44F8B1BE 1F04F81B
0638786E F562AC95 FA2A1F9B 40CB724E 8B8C82D7 1F40BD7D E4C331D7 991EB7E3
5335BE5B 7EBDFF8C 9C568BF9 D38509E2 19578047 E51AD0EA 8C6017D7 C0B0AEEE
0F730A3D 931F171D 401211E7 221BE324 7BD65E90 6660C90D E910B5F7 E7020301 0001
```

Remember to repeat these tasks at every peer (without CA support) that uses RSA encrypted nonces in an IKE policy.

Setting ISAKMP Identity

You should set the ISAKMP identity for each peer that uses pre-shared keys in an IKE policy. When two peers use IKE to establish IPSec security associations, each peer sends its identity to the remote peer. Each peer sends either its host name or its IP address, depending on how you have the router's ISAKMP identity set.

By default, a peer's ISAKMP identity is the peer's IP address. If appropriate, you could change the identity to be the peer's host name instead. As a general rule, set all peers' identities the same way: either all peers should use their IP address or all peers should use their host name. When some peers use their host names and some peers use their IP addresses to identify themselves to each other, IKE negotiations could fail if the router does not recognize a remote peer's identity and cannot perform a DNS lookup to resolve the address.

To set a peer's ISAKMP identity, use the following commands in global configuration mode:

```
4500(config)#crypto isakmp identity {address | hostname}
```

At the local peer, specify the peer's ISAKMP identity by IP address or by host name. You can specify up to eight addresses.

```
4500(config)#ip host hostname address1 [address2…address8]
```

At all remote peers, if you specify the local peer's ISAKMP identity using a host name, map the peer's host name to its IP address(es) at all the remote peers. You might find this step unnecessary if you have already mapped the host name/address in a DNS server.

Remember to repeat these tasks at each peer that uses pre-shared keys in an IKE policy.

Specifying All the Other Peers' RSA Public Keys

At each peer, specify all the other peers' RSA public keys using the following commands starting in global configuration mode:

```
4500(config)#crypto key pubkey-chain rsa
```

Enter public key configuration mode. Indicate the remote peer's RSA public key you intend to specify. If the remote peer uses its host name as its ISAKMP identity, use the named-key command and specify the remote peer's fully qualified domain (such as 4500.pdaconsulting.com) as the key-name.

```
4500(config-pubkey-chain)#named-key key-name [encryption |
  signature]
```

Alternately, when the remote peer uses its IP address as its ISAKMP identity, you can use the addressed-key command and specify the remote peer's IP address as the key-address.

```
4500(config-pubkey-chain)#addressed-key key-address
  [encryption name | signature]
```

If you used a fully qualified domain name to name the remote peer above (using the named-key command), you can optionally specify the remote peer's IP address. Only use this command when the router has a single interface that processes IPSec.

```
4500(config-pubkey-key)#address ip-address
```

Specify the remote peer's RSA public key. This is the key viewed by the remote peer's administrator previously when he generated his router's RSA keys.

```
4500(config-pubkey-key)#key-string
4500(config-pubkey)#key-string
4500(config-pubkey)#quit
```

Repeat the step to specify the RSA public keys of all the other IPSec peers that use RSA encrypted nonces in an IKE policy. Then return to global configuration mode:

```
4500(config-pubkey-key)#exit
```

Remember to repeat these tasks at each peer that uses RSA encrypted nonces in an IKE policy.

In the following example, you manually configure the RSA public key of the two IPSec peers. The peer at 10.10.10.1 uses general-purpose keys, while the other peer at 10.10.10.2 uses special-usage keys.

```
4500(config)#crypto key pubkey-chain rsa
4500(config-pubkey-chain)#named-key
  peerone.pdaconsulting.com
4500(config-pubkey-key)#address 10.10.10.1
4500(config-pubkey-key)#key-string
4500(config-pubkey)#key-string
4500(config-pubkey)#quit
4500(config-pubkey-key)#exit
4500(config-pubkey-chain)#addressed-key 10.10.10.2
  encryption
4500(config-pubkey-key)#key-string
4500(config-pubkey)#key-string
4500(config-pubkey)#quit
4500(config-pubkey-key)#exit
4500(config-pubkey-chain)#addressed-key 10.10.10.2
  signature
4500(config-pubkey-key)#key-string
4500(config-pubkey)#key-string
4500(config-pubkey)#quit
4500(config-pubkey-key)#exit
4500(config-pubkey-chain)#exit
4500(config)#exit
4500#
```

To view RSA public keys while or after you configure them, use the following command in EXEC mode:

```
4500#show crypto key pubkey-chain rsa {name key-name |
  address key-address}
Codes: M-Manually configured, C-Extracted from certificate
Code  Usage      IP-Address    Name
M     General    10.10.10.1    X.500 DN name:
M     Encrypt    10.10.10.2
M     Signing    10.10.10.2
```

Use this command to view a list of all the RSA public keys stored on your router or view details of a particular RSA public key stored on your router.

Configuring Pre-Shared Keys

To configure pre-shared keys, perform the following tasks at each peer using pre-shared keys in an IKE policy.

1. First, set each peer's ISAKMP identity. You should set each peer's identity to either its host name or its IP address. By default, the IOS sets a peer's identity to its IP address. Setting ISAKMP identities was previously described in the section Setting ISAKMP Identity.
2. Next, specify the shared keys at each peer. Note that two peers share a given pre-shared key. At a given peer you could specify the same key to share with multiple remote peers; however, a more secure approach is to specify different keys to share between different pairs of peers.

To specify pre-shared keys at a peer, use the following commands starting in global configuration mode.

- At the local peer, specify the shared key to be used with a particular remote peer. If the remote peer has specified its ISAKMP identity with an address, use the address keyword in this step; otherwise, use the hostname keyword in this step.

```
4500(config)#crypto isakmp key keystring address peer-
    address
4500(config)#crypto isakmp key keystring hostname peer-
    hostname
```

- At the remote peer, specify the shared key for use by the remote peer. This is the same key you just specified at the local peer. If the local peer specified its ISAKMP identity with an address, use the address keyword in this step; otherwise, use the hostname keyword in this step.

```
4500(config)#crypto isakmp key keystring address peer-
    address
4500(config)#crypto isakmp key keystring hostname peer-
    hostname
```

Remember to repeat these tasks at each peer that uses pre-shared keys in an IKE policy.

Clearing IKE Connections

If desired, you can clear existing IKE connections. To clear IKE connections, use the following commands in EXEC mode:

```
4500#show crypto isakmp sa
```

This command allows you to view existing IKE connections so that you can note the connection identifiers for the connections you wish to clear.

```
4500(config)#clear crypto isakmp [connection-id]
```

If you do not use the `connection-id` keywords, the router will clear all existing connections. The connection-id has a value from 0 to 299.

Troubleshooting Certification Authority (CA) Interoperability and IKE

When troubleshooting, it is often necessary and useful to view keys and certificates. You use these commands in EXEC mode. To view your router's RSA public keys, use the following command.

```
4500#show crypto key mypubkey rsa
```

The next command allows you to view a list of all the RSA public keys your router stores. These include the public keys of peers that have sent your router their certificates during peer authentication for IPSec.

```
4500#show crypto key pubkey-chain rsa
```

This next command allows you to view details of a particular RSA public key stored on your router.

```
4500#show crypto key pubkey-chain rsa [name key-name |
  address key-address]
```

Use the `name` or `address` keywords to display details about a particular RSA public key stored on your router.

Finally, use the following command to view information about your certificate, the CA's certificate, and any RA certificates.

```
4500#show crypto ca certificates
```

To view the parameters for each configured IKE policy, use this command:

```
4500#show crypto isakmp policy
```

To view all current IKE security associations, use this command:

```
4500#show crypto isakmp sa
```

Exhibit 4 shows the various states you may see displayed in the output of this command. When an ISAKMP SA exists, most likely you will see it in its quiescent state (OAK_QM_IDLE). For long exchanges, you may observe some of the OAK_MM states.

Exhibit 4   States in Mode Exchange

State	Mode	Explanation
OAK_MM_NO_STATE	Main	The peers have created the ISAKMP SA, but nothing else has happened. There is no state.
OAK_MM_SA_SETUP	Main	The peers have agreed on parameters for the ISAKMP SA.
OAK_MM_KEY_FETCH	Main	The peers have exchanged Diffie-Hellman public keys and generated a shared secret. The ISAKMP SA remains unauthenticated.
OAK_MM_KEY_AUTH	Main	The peers have authenticated the ISAKMP SA. If the router initiated this exchange, this state transitions immediately to OAK_QM_IDLE and a quick mode exchange begins.
OAK_AG_NO_STATE	Aggressive	The peers have created the ISAKMP SA but nothing else has happened. There is no state.
OAK_AG_INIT_EXCH	Aggressive	The peers have done the first exchange in aggressive mode but have not authenticated the SA.
OAK_AG_AUTH		The peers have authenticated the ISAKMP SA. If the router initiated this exchange, this state transitions immediately to OAK_QM_IDLE and a quick mode exchange begins.
OAK_QM_IDLE	Quick	The ISAKMP SA is idle. The peer remains authenticate with its peer, and the peer may use the ISAKMP SA for subsequent quick mode exchanges. It is in a quiescent state.

Note: As mentioned, ISAKMP/Oakley has two phases: main mode and quick mode. An Oakley exchange starts with a main mode exchange and continues with a quick mode exchange. The main mode establishes the Oakley SA and the quick mode establishes the IPSec SA. You can have many quick mode exchanges per main mode exchange because the Oakley SA can have a longer lifetime than the IPSec SA. The combination of the main mode and quick mode produces a very powerful secure session key exchange mechanism through use of finite key lifetimes.

And finally, you can display debug messages about IKE events with the following command:

```
4500#debug crypto isakmp
```

To turn debug mode off, use the following command:

```
4500#no debug crypto isakmp
```

After you complete IKE configuration, you can configure IPSec, as discussed in Chapter 20.

Practice Session

In this Practice Session, you will practice the following:

- Logging in
- Saving log data
- Switching modes
- Entering configuration mode
- Configuring CA interoperability
- Configuring IKE
- Enabling and saving syslog data
- Logging out

1. Log in to the SimRouter Web page.
2. Double-click on router 4500 to telnet to that router. This will open a console session.
3. Enter your **Username** and **Password** at the applicable prompt. These are the ones you set up in Chapter 2. You will need to hit the Enter key twice to get to the > prompt.
4. Again, save the log for your session. To do this, select | Terminal | Start Logging | from the menu bar in the Telnet window. The Telnet client will ask you where you wish to store the log and with what name. Your choice. You are going to save the log so that when you build this configuration file, you can cut-and-paste this in Chapter 20 as a starting point, rather than having to enter the same information each Practice Session.
5. Enter the enable mode:

   `4500#`**`enable`**

6. When prompted to put in the enable secret password, enter **oscar**.
7. Type **terminal length 0**. This command instructs the router to scroll through long command output without pausing (the —More— message).
8. You will paste the `running-config` that you saved from yesterday's log. At the 4500# prompt, type **config t**.
9. If you did not do this, open your log file with the text editor of your choice (e.g., use | Start | Programs | Accessories | Notepad |). Do a find on sh `running-config` and copy from the first "!" to "end." At the 4500(config)# prompt, paste this configuration.
10. This practice session creates two IKE policies, with policy 15 as the highest priority, policy 20 as the next priority, and the existing default priority as the lowest priority. It also creates a pre-shared key for policy 20 with the remote peer whose IP address is 192.168.224.33. Type **crypto isakmp policy 15** and press Enter.
11. Type **encryption des** and press Enter.
12. Type **hash md5** and press Enter.
13. Type **authentication rsa-sig** and press Enter.

14. Type **group 2** and press Enter.
15. Type **lifetime 5000** and press Enter.
16. Type **crypto isakmp policy 20** and press Enter.
17. Type **authentication pre-share** and press Enter.
18. Type **lifetime 10000** and press Enter.
19. Type **crypto isakmp key 1234567890 address 192.168.224.33** and press Enter.
20. Type **exit** and press Enter.
21. Type **show crypto isakmp policy** and press Enter.
22. Type **sh running-config** and press Enter. You will use this new configuration to start the next Practice Session.
23. Type **quit** to log out from router 4500. Close the Telnet window and return to the SimRouter Topology Map.
24. Click on Log Out on the SimRouter Web page.

Security and Audit Checklist

1. Do you use encryption in your organization?
   - ■ Yes
   - ■ No
2. Do you use Cisco Encryption Technology (CET) in your organization?
   - ■ Yes
   - ■ No
3. Is CET implemented in hardware?
   - ■ Yes
   - ■ No
4. Is CET implemented in software?
   - ■ Yes
   - ■ No
5. Do you use a Certification Authority (CA) within your organization?
   - ■ Yes
   - ■ No
6. Do you use a Registration Authority (RA) within your organization?
   - ■ Yes
   - ■ No
7. Do you use the crl optional command?
   - ■ Yes
   - ■ No
8. Do you have a procedure for authenticating the Certification Authority's certificate?
   - ■ Yes
   - ■ No
9. Do you have a procedure for obtaining a certificate from the Certification Authority?
   - ■ Yes
   - ■ No

10. Do you have a procedure for saving your configuration changes?
    - Yes
    - No
11. Does someone in your organization have responsibility for monitoring and maintaining Certification Authority interoperability?
    - Yes
    - No
12. Does your organization use certificate revocation lists?
    - Yes
    - No
13. Do you have a procedure for requesting CRLs?
    - Yes
    - No
14. Do you have a procedure for deleting unwanted or compromised keys in your organization?
    - Yes
    - No
15. Do you have a procedure for deleting unwanted or compromised certificates in your organization?
    - Yes
    - No
16. Does your organization support IKE?
    - Yes
    - No
17. Does your firewall allow UDP port 500?
    - Yes
    - No
18. Which encryption algorithm does your organization support?
    - DES
    - 3DES
19. Which hash algorithm does your organization support?
    - SHA-1
    - MD5
20. Which authentication method does your organization support?
    - RSA signatures
    - RSA encrypted nonces
    - Pre-shared keys
21. Which Diffie-Hellman group does your organization support?
    - 768-bit
    - 1024-bit
22. Does your organization support multiple IKE policies?
    - Yes
    - No
23. Is the use of these IKE policies appropriate?
    - Yes
    - No

24. Does your organization use pre-shared keys?
    - ■ Yes
    - ■ No

25. If you use manually configured RSA keys, does your organization have a procedure?
    - ■ Yes
    - ■ No

Conclusion

In this chapter, you first learned about Cisco Encryption Technology. Because CET is proprietary technology, Cisco is attempting to phase it out. You should use IPSec, an open standard, which you will learn about in Chapter 20.

If you decide to use IPSec, there are two complementary technologies that you need to preconfigure. When you use one, you need to ensure that your Certification Authority works with your router. You learned that in this chapter.

You will learn in Chapter 20 that you can manually configure keys, but it is a lot of work. You learned about IKE in this chapter; IKE is a key management protocol used with IPSec. Using IKE saves you a lot of time and effort.

Now that you have participated in the preliminaries, it is time to turn your attention to the main event — IPSec. You will learn how to configure IPSec in Chapter 20.

Chapter 20

Configuring IPSec

In this chapter, you will learn about:

- Creating crypto access lists
- Defining transform sets
- Creating crypto map entries
- Applying crypto map sets to interfaces
- Monitoring and maintaining IPSec

IPSec Network Security

The previous chapter provided a teaser on IPSec. This chapter expands on that information to allow you to configure IPSec on your interface. It is thus helpful to look at IPSec again.

IPSec (IP Security protocol) is a framework of open standards developed by the Internet Engineering Task Force (IETF) that provides security for transmission of sensitive information over untrusted networks such as the Internet. With IPSec, you can transmit data across a public network without fear of observation, modification, replay, or spoofing. Using IPSec, you can create virtual private networks (VPNs), including intranets, extranets, and remote user access. Organizations can create private communities of interest without regard for the specifics of the involved networks.

IPSec is not a single protocol, but a suite of specifications that together make up the encryption standard. There are so many different RFCs relating to IPSec, each covering the areas just mentioned and others. However, you will find RFC 2411, the IPSec document road map, a good reference starting point. Start your IPSec research with that RFC.

IPSec acts at the network layer, protecting and authenticating IP packets between participating IPSec devices (or peers), such as Cisco routers, and implements the following standards:

- *IP Security (IPSec) protocol.* IPSec provides data confidentiality, data integrity, and data authentication between participating peers. IPSec uses IKE to handle negotiation of protocols and algorithms based on local policy and to generate the encryption and authentication keys. You can use IPSec to protect one or more data flows between a pair of hosts, between a pair of security gateways, or between a security gateway and a host. You can find IPSec documentation at http://www.ietf.org/html.charters/ipsec-charter.html. Cisco's overall IPSec implementation is per the latest version of the "Security Architecture for the Internet Protocol" Internet Draft (draft-ietf-arch-sec-xx.txt). The IETF described an earlier version of IPSec in RFCs 1825 through 1829. While Internet Drafts supersede these RFCs, Cisco IOS IPSec implements RFC 1828 (IP Authentication using Keyed MD5) and RFC 1829 (ESP DES-CBC Transform) for backward compatibility.

- *Internet Key Exchange (IKE).* IKE is a hybrid protocol that implements Oakley and Skeme key exchanges inside the ISAKMP framework. While you can use IKE with other protocols, its initial implementation is with the IPSec protocol. IKE provides authentication of the IPSec peers, negotiates IPSec security associations, and establishes IPSec keys. For more information on IKE, see Chapter 19.

- *Data Encryption Standard (DES).* You use DES to encrypt packet data. Cisco IOS implements the mandatory 56-bit DES-CBC with Explicit IV. Cipher Block Chaining (CBC) requires an initialization vector (IV) to start encryption. The IV is explicitly given in the IPSec packet. For backward compatibility, Cisco IOS IPSec also implements the RFC 1829 version of ESP DES-CBC. Cisco offers DES mainly to accommodate an international market, where export restrictions might limit the availability of strong encryption.

- *3DES.* Triple DES, with a key length of 168 bits, is an algorithm that you can use instead of DES to encrypt packet data.

- *MD5 (Message Digest 5) HMAC variant.* MD5 is a hash algorithm. HMAC is a keyed hash variant used to authenticate data. Refer to RFC 1321.

- *SHA (Secure Hash Algorithm) HMAC variant.* SHA is a hash algorithm. HMAC is a keyed hash variant used to authenticate data. Refer to FIPS 180-1.

HMAC is a secret key authentication algorithm. You can find a description of HMAC in RFC 2104 (Keyed-Hashing for Message Authentication Codes).

IPSec as implemented in Cisco IOS software supports the following additional standards:

- *Authentication Header (AH).* AH is a security protocol that provides data authentication and optional anti-replay services. IPSec embeds the AH in the protected data (a full IP datagram). Cisco implements both the older RFC 1828 AH and the updated AH protocol. The updated AH protocol is per the latest version of the "IP Authentication Header" Internet Draft (draft-ietf-ipsec-auth-header-xx.txt). RFC 1828 specifies the Keyed MD5 authentication algorithm; it does not provide anti-replay services. The updated AH protocol allows for the use of various authentication algorithms. Cisco IOS has implemented the mandatory MD5 and SHA (HMAC variants) authentication algorithms. The updated AH protocol provides anti-replay services.

- *Encapsulating Security Payload (ESP)*. ESP is a security protocol that provides data privacy services, optional data authentication, and anti-replay services. ESP encapsulates the data for protection. Cisco implements both the older RFC 1829 ESP and the updated ESP protocol. The updated ESP protocol is per the latest version of the "IP Encapsulating Security Payload" Internet Draft (draft-ietf-ipsec-esp-v2-xx.txt). RFC 1829 specifies DES-CBC as the encryption algorithm; it does not provide data authentication or anti-replay services. The updated ESP protocol allows for the use of various cipher algorithms and (optionally) various authentication algorithms. Cisco IOS implements the mandatory 56-bit DES-CBC with Explicit IV and Triple DES as the encryption algorithms, and MD5 or SHA (HMAC variants) as the authentication algorithms. The updated ESP protocol does provide anti-replay services.

IPSec services are similar to those provided by Cisco Encryption Technology (CET), a proprietary security solution introduced in Cisco IOS Software Release 11.2. The IPSec standard was not available when Release 11.2 came out. However, IPSec provides a more robust security solution and is standards based. IPSec also provides data authentication and anti-replay services in addition to data confidentiality services, while CET only provides data confidentiality. For a comparison of IPSec and CET, refer to the previous chapter.

IPSec provides the following network security services. These services are optional. In general, your security policy will dictate the use of one or more of these services:

- *Data confidentiality*. The IPSec sender can encrypt packets before transmitting them across a network. This ensures that unauthorized individuals cannot read packets in transit. This assurance comes through encrypting packets before placing them on the wire (or over the ether). By encrypting the packet, you are ensuring that only authorized people can decipher the contents of the packets.
- *Data integrity*. The IPSec receiver can authenticate packets sent by the IPSec sender to ensure that no one altered the data during transmission. You can achieve this by doing a MAC of the message. This is sometimes called *connectionless integrity*.
- *Data origin authentication*. The IPSec receiver can authenticate the source of the IPSec sent packets. This service depends on the data integrity service. By authenticating the sender, you can prevent spoofing attacks.
- *Anti-replay*. An attacker might capture legitimate packets and resend them. The IPSec receiver can detect and reject replayed packets.

The current IP header cannot give you any of these services. Many attacks rely on the fact that IPv4 cannot give you these services. Although the IETF developed IPSec for IPv6, Cisco and other vendors have retrofitted IPSec to work with IPv4.

IPSec Compatibility

You can use Cisco Encryption Technology (CET) and IPSec together; the encryption technologies can coexist in your network. Any router may support concurrent encryption links using either IPSec or CET. A single interface can even support the use of IPSec or CET for protecting different data flows.

Cisco does not support IPSec on VIP2 interfaces (VIP2-40 or above) or the Encryption Service Adapter (ESA) card. Like CET, there is currently one hardware accelerator for IPSec. It is the Integrated Services Adapter (ISA) available with the Cisco 7100 and 7200 Series VPN routers.

IPSec works with process and fast switching, but not with optimum or flow switching. IPSec works with the following serial encapsulations: High-Level Data-Links Control (HDLC), Point-to-Point Protocol (PPP), and Frame Relay. IPSec also works with the GRE and IPinIP Layer 3, L2F, L2TP, DLSw+, and SRB tunneling protocols; however, IPSec does not support multi-point tunnels. Thus, you could use IPSec over a GRE Tunnel to encrypt non-IP based traffic, such as Novel's IPX. IPSec may not support other Layer 3 tunneling protocols.

Because the IPSec Working Group has not yet addressed the issue of group key distribution, you cannot currently use IPSec to protect group traffic (such as broadcast or multicast traffic). At this time, you only can apply IPSec to unicast IP datagrams.

If you use Network Address Translation (NAT), you should configure static NAT translations so that IPSec will work properly. In general, NAT translation should occur before the router performs IPSec encapsulation; that is, you should have IPSec working with global addresses.

Understanding IPSec

In simple terms, IPSec provides secure tunnels between two peers, such as two routers. You define what packets you consider sensitive and want sent through these secure tunnels, and you define the parameters to protect these sensitive packets by specifying the characteristics of these tunnels. Then, when the IPSec peer sees such a sensitive packet, it sets up the appropriate secure tunnel and sends the packet through the tunnel to the remote peer.

More accurately, these tunnels are sets of security associations established between two IPSec peers. The security associations define the protocols and algorithms you want applied to sensitive packets, and also specify the keying material for the two peers. Security associations are unidirectional and are established per security protocol (AH or ESP).

With IPSec, you define the traffic to protect between two IPSec peers by configuring access lists and applying these access lists to interfaces by way of crypto map sets. Therefore, you can select traffic based on source and destination address, and optionally Layer 4 protocol and port. Similar to CET, you use access lists for IPSec to designate protected traffic, not traffic to block or permit through the interface. Separate access lists define blocking and permitting at the interface.

A crypto map set can contain multiple entries, each with a different access list. The IOS searches the crypto map entries in order and the router attempts to match the packet to the access list specified in that entry.

When a packet matches a permit entry in a particular access list, and you have tagged the corresponding crypto map entry as cisco, the IOS triggers CET and will establish connections when necessary. When you tag the crypto map entry as ipsec-isakmp, the IOS triggers IPSec. When no security association exists that

IPSec can use to protect this traffic to the peer, IPSec uses IKE to negotiate with the remote peer to set up the necessary IPSec security associations on behalf of the data flow. The negotiation uses information specified in the crypto map entry as well as the data flow information from the specific access list entry.

When you tag the crypto map entry as ipsec-manual, IOS also triggers IPSec. When no security association exists that IPSec can use to protect this traffic to the peer, the router drops the traffic. In this case, you create the security associations via the configuration, without the intervention of IKE. If the security associations do not exist, you did not configure IPSec correctly.

Once established, the IOS applies the set of security associations (outbound, to the peer) to the triggering packet as well as to subsequent applicable packets as those packets exit the router. Applicable packets are packets that match the same access list criteria that the original packet matched. For example, you could encrypt all applicable packets before forwarding them to the remote peer. The router uses the corresponding inbound security associations when processing the incoming traffic from that peer.

If you use IKE to establish security associations, the security associations will have lifetimes so that they will periodically expire and require renegotiation. This provides an additional level of security.

Multiple IPSec tunnels can exist between two peers to secure different data streams, with each tunnel using a separate set of security associations. For example, the router might just authenticate some data streams while encrypting and authenticating other data streams.

Access lists associated with IPSec crypto map entries also specify traffic requiring protection by IPSec. The router processes inbound traffic against the crypto map entries. If the IOS matches an unprotected packet with a permit entry in a particular access list associated with an IPSec crypto map entry, then the router will drop that packet because it was not sent as an IPSec-protected packet.

Crypto map entries also include transform sets. A transform set is an acceptable combination of security protocols, algorithms, and other settings to apply to IPSec-protected traffic. During the IPSec security association negotiation, the peers agree to use a particular transform set when protecting a particular data flow.

When two IPSec routers want to exchange IPSec-protected traffic, they must first authenticate each other; otherwise, IPSec protection cannot occur. IKE (see Chatper 19) provides the authentication.

Without a Certification Authority (CA), a router authenticates itself to the remote router using either RSA encrypted nonces or pre-shared keys. Both methods require that you previously configured keys between the two routers.

With a CA, a router authenticates itself to the remote router by sending a certificate to the remote router and performing some public key cryptography. The routers must send their unique certificate that the CA issued and validated. This process works because each router's certificate encapsulates the router's public key, the CA authenticates each certificate, and all participating routers recognize the CA as an authenticating authority. This is IKE with an RSA signature.

Your router can continue sending its own certificate for multiple IPSec sessions, and to multiple IPSec peers, until the certificate expires. When its certificate expires, the router administrator must obtain a new one from the CA.

CAs can also revoke certificates for devices. Other IPSec devices do not recognize revoked certificates as valid. The CA lists revoked certificates in a

Certificate Revocation List (CRL), which each peer may check before accepting another peer's certificate.

IPSec, RFC 1825, provides IP network-layer encryption and defines a new set of headers to add to IP datagrams. IPSec places these new headers after the IP header and before the Layer 4 protocol (typically TCP or UDP). They provide information for securing the payload of the IP packet, as described below.

You can use the Authentication Header (AH) and Encapsulating Security Payload (ESP) independently or together, although for most applications one method suffices. For both of these protocols, IPSec does not define the specific security algorithms to use; rather, it provides an open framework for implementing industry-standard algorithms. Initially, most implementations of IPSec will support MD5 from RSA Data Security or the Secure Hash Algorithm (SHA) as defined by the U.S. Government for integrity and authentication. The Data Encryption Standard (DES) is currently the most commonly offered bulk encryption algorithm, although RFCs are available that define how to use many other encryption systems, including Blowfish, CAST, IDEA, and RC4.

Understanding AH

The AH, defined in RFC 1826, is a mechanism for providing strong integrity and authentication for IP datagrams. It can also provide non-repudiation, depending on the cryptographic algorithm you use and how you perform keying. For example, use of an asymmetric digital signature algorithm such as RSA could provide non-repudiation services.

AH does not provide data confidentiality and protection from traffic analysis. If you need confidentiality, you should consider using IP ESP, either in lieu of or with AH. The AH may appear after any other headers examined at each hop, and before any other headers not examined at an intermediate hop.

Exhibit 1 illustrates the AH header format. The fields of the AH header include:

- *Next Header:* 8-bit field that identifies the type of header following this header, typically either IP when in tunnel mode or TCP or UDP when in transport mode. The IPv4 or IPv6 header immediately preceding the AH will contain the value 51 in its Next Header (or Protocol) field.
- *Payload Length:* 8-bit field representing the length of the AH in 32-bit words minus 2. The default length of the AH data field is 96 bits, which is three 32-bit words. The fixed portion of the AH is three 32-bit words, for a total of six 32-bit words. This gives a payload length of $6 - 2 = 4$.
- *Security Parameter Index (SPI):* 32-bit field that identifies each security association (SA).
- *Sequence Number:* 32-bit field used as a counter value to prevent anti-replay attacks. The counter increases with each new packet in an SA sent, up to a maximum value of $2^{32} - 1$. Once the IOS reaches the maximum value, the peers will negotiate another SA and the IOS will reset the counter.
- *Authentication Data:* a variable-length field that contains the message authentication code (MAC) for the packet. A MAC is very similar to a digital signature. The algorithm creates a hash value from the original packet and then encrypts it using a shared key.

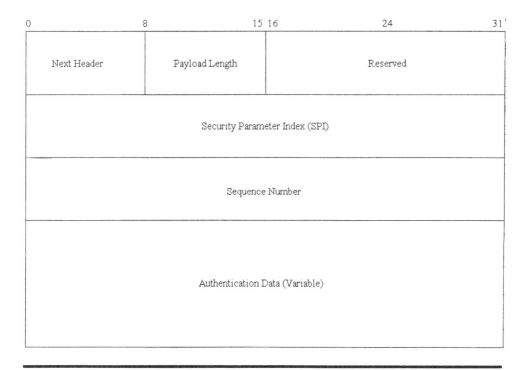

Exhibit 1 AH Header Format

Understanding ESP

ESP (Encapsulating Security Payload), defined in RFC 1827, can appear anywhere after the IP header and before the final transport-layer protocol. The Internet Assigned Numbers Authority (IANA) has assigned Protocol Number 50 to ESP. The header immediately preceding an ESP header will always contain the value 50 in its Next Header (IPv6) or Protocol (IPv4) field. ESP consists of an unencrypted header followed by encrypted data. The encrypted data includes both the protected ESP header fields and the protected user data, which is either an entire IP datagram or an upper-layer protocol frame (such as TCP or UDP). Exhibit 2 illustrates the ESP header format. The fields of the ESP header include:

- *Security Parameter Index (SPI):* 32-bit field that identifies each security association (SA).
- *Sequence Number:* 32-bit field used as a counter value to prevent anti-replay attacks. The counter increases with each new packet in an SA sent up to a maximum value of $2^{32} - 1$. Once the IOS reaches the maximum value, the peers will negotiate another SA and the IOS will reset the counter.
- *Payload Data:* a variable-length field that contains the encrypted original upper-layer information when in transport mode or the encrypted entire original IP packet when in tunnel mode.
- *Padding:* 0 to 255-byte field. Padding serves three purposes:
  - Some algorithms require that the plaintext is a multiple of a certain number of bytes.

0	8	15 16	24	31

Security Parameter Index (SPI)
Sequence Number
Payload Data (variable)

Payload Data (continued)	Padding (0-255 Bytes)

Padding (continued)	Pad Length	Next Header

Authentication Data (variable)

Exhibit 2   ESP Header Format

- The ESP format requires that the pad length and the next header fields align within a 32-bit word, so the padding ensures this.
- Padding allows the masking of the real length of the upper-layer information or IP packet. This prevents an attacker from performing traffic analysis based on the size of the packets. This feature is *traffic flow confidentiality.*
- *Pad Length:* 8-bit field that specifies the number of pad bytes.
- *Next Header:* 8-bit field that identifies the type of header following this header, typically either IP when in tunnel mode, or TCP or UDP when in transport mode.
- *Authentication Data:* a variable-length field that contains the message authentication code (MAC) for the packet. However, the AH field in an ESP header does not include any portion of the IP header in its hash calculation. When in transport mode, it does not include fields in the original IP header; when in tunnel mode, it does not include fields in the new IP header.

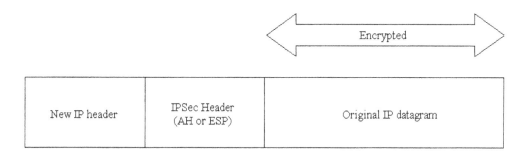

Exhibit 3 Encapsulation in Tunnel Mode

IP ESP seeks to provide confidentiality and integrity by encrypting data requiring protection and placing the encrypted data in the data portion of the IP ESP. Depending on the user's security requirements, you can use this mechanism to encrypt either a transport-layer segment (such as TCP, UDP, ICMP, or IGMP) or an entire IP datagram. Encapsulating the protected data is necessary to provide confidentiality for the entire original datagram. Use of this specification will increase the IP protocol processing costs in participating systems and will also increase the communications latency. The increased latency is primarily due to the encryption and decryption required for each IP datagram containing an ESP.

In tunnel mode ESP, the software places the original IP datagram in the encrypted portion of the ESP and then places that entire ESP frame within a datagram having unencrypted IP headers. Exhibit 3 illustrates the header in tunnel mode. The router uses the information in the unencrypted IP headers to route the secure datagram from origin to destination. You might see an unencrypted IP Routing header included between the IP header and the ESP.

The IETF developed tunnel mode for use by gateways. This mode allows a network device, such as a router, to act as an IPSec proxy. That is, the router performs encryption on behalf of the hosts. The source's router encrypts packets and forwards them along the IPSec tunnel. The destination's router decrypts the original IP datagram and forwards it on to the destination system. The major advantage of tunnel mode is that the end systems do not need modification to enjoy the benefits of IPSec. Tunnel mode also protects against traffic analysis: with tunnel mode an attacker can only determine the tunnel endpoints and not the true source and destination of the tunneled packets, even when they are the same as the tunnel endpoints. As defined by the IETF, you can only use IPSec transport mode when both the source and the destination systems understand IPSec. In most cases, you deploy IPSec with tunnel mode. Doing so allows you to implement IPSec in the network architecture without modifying the operating system or any applications on your PCs, servers, and hosts.

In transport mode ESP, the software inserts an ESP header into the IP datagram immediately prior to the transport-layer protocol header (such as TCP, UDP, or ICMP). Exhibit 4 illustrates the header in transport mode. In this mode, one conserves bandwidth because there are no encrypted IP headers or IP options.

The software encrypts only the IP payload and leaves the original IP headers intact. This mode has the advantage of adding only a few bytes to each packet. It also allows devices on the public network to see the final source and destination of the packet. This capability allows you to enable special processing (e.g., quality

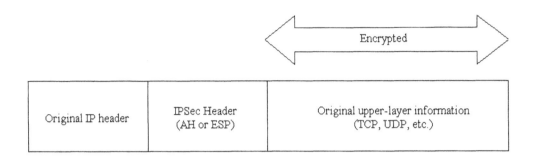

Exhibit 4   Encapsulation in Transport Mode

Exhibit 5   Features of the IPSec Security Headers

Feature	AH	ESP
Data confidentiality		X
Traffic flow confidentiality		X
Data integrity	X	X
Data origin authentication	X	X
Anti-replay	X	X

of service) in the intermediate network based on the information on the IP header. However, the software will encrypt the Layer 4 header, limiting the examination of the packet. Unfortunately, by passing the IP header in the clear, transport mode allows an attacker to perform some traffic analysis. For example, an attacker could see when one CEO sent a lot of packets to another CEO. This might indicate a possible merger. However, the attacker would only know that IP packets were sent; the attacker could not determine the application.

Exhibit 5 summarizes the security features of AH and ESP.

Security Association

Security association (SA) is another key IPSec concept. Think of an SA as a security tunnel between two IPSec peers. You can create a separate SA for different types of traffic flows. For example, you could have an SA between two hosts for TCP traffic and a separate SA between the same two hosts for UDP traffic. You could have separate SAs for each TCP or UDP port you use. IPSec uniquely identifies each SA with the following parameters:

- *Security parameter index (SPI).* The software assigns a simple bit string or SPI to each SA. IPSec inserts an SPI into the AH or ESP header. The SPI allows the receiving IPSec peer to assign a packet to an SA.
- *IP destination address.* The destination of the IPSec datagram.
- *Security protocol identifier.* Whether the IPSec header is AH or ESP.

IPSec uses this information to uniquely identify each SA connection between communicating peers. As stated, two devices may have more than one SA between them, and the SPI uniquely identifies them because you can have the same destination address and security protocol, but not the same SPI. Each SA can have a different security protocol. You may have some traffic between two peers that you only want to use the AH header for authentication purposes and other traffic that you want encrypted. IPSec is sufficiently flexible to permit these various configurations.

Security Protocol Database

IPSec uses a database called the *security protocol database* (SPD) to determine what IPSec parameters to apply to a particular class of IP traffic. The SPD defines what types of IP traffic will require processing by IPSec and what types will not. For those IP packets that require processing by IPSec, the SPD defines whether the packets will use an AH or ESP header and also defines what algorithms IPSec will use for the different types of packets. It is through the SPD that an IPSec device creates SAs. An IPSec device consults its SPD for each IP packet to determine whether IPSec will process the packet and, if so, where the packet belongs.

In the IPSec implementation, extended access lists perform most of the functions of the SPD to classify the various kinds of packets that IPSec will process. The crypto map performs the match between traffic classified by an access list and the type of security protocol and algorithms for use. Also, you can use several different algorithms with the AH and ESP security protocols, so you must specify the algorithms that you will use.

Internet Security Association and Key Management Protocol

While IPSec protocols provide the actual protection for the IP datagrams, it is ISAKMP (Internet Security Association and Key Management Protocol) that negotiates policy and provides a common framework for generating keys that the IPSec peers share. IPSec security protocols deal with the algorithms used and the security protocol header formats. Key management focuses on how you can exchange keys for use by the IPSec algorithms across an untrusted network. Typically, each SA will require at least two keys, one for the transmission of data in each direction. If you plan on using AH and ESP headers for an SA, you will need four keys: two for each SA for each security protocol header.

Because these keys are secret keys, you cannot just send them unencrypted across an untrusted network. You need a secure method for exchanging these keys among peers. You could set up the keys manually, but this would be cumbersome and would not allow the flexibility required for the Internet. Thus, you need an automated process. This process is IKE (see Chapter 19). IKE handles the exchange of keys. In some Cisco literature you get the impression that ISAKMP and IKE are the same protocol. ISAKMP facilitates the exchange of secret-session keys across an untrusted network. Both parties share session keys to encrypt the ISAKMP/Oakley tunnel. When the two sides have agreed on the algorithms to use, they must derive key material to use for IPSec with AH, ESP, or both. AH and ESP use these keys for authentication and encryption.

Exhibit 6   IPSec Traffic Characteristics

Protocol Name	Protocol Type	Protocol Number
ESP	IP	50
AH	IP	51
IKE	UDP	500

Configuring IPSec

You need to configure IKE as described in Chapter 19. If you decide not to use IKE, you still need to disable it.

After you have completed IKE configuration, configure IPSec. Simplistically, you configure IPSec by:

- Creating a security association (either manually or with IKE)
- Defining the SPD (i.e., access lists specifying what traffic to secure)
- Defining the transform set, which is the cryptographic algorithms and IPSec mode
- Applying the SPD and transform set access lists to an interface using crypto map sets

Now that you have the 25,000-foot view of configuring IPSec, you can zero in on the details. To configure IPSec, complete the tasks in the following sections *at each participating IPSec peer*:

1. Ensure access lists compatibility with IPSec.
2. Set global lifetimes for IPSec security associations.
3. Create crypto access lists.
4. Define transform sets.
5. Create crypto map entries.
6. Apply crypto map sets to interfaces.
7. Monitor and maintain IPSec.

Ensuring Access Lists Compatibility with IPSec

IKE uses UDP port 500; the IPSec ESP and AH protocols use protocol numbers 50 and 51. Ensure that you configure your access lists so you do not block protocol numbers 50 and 51 and UDP port 500 traffic at the interfaces IPSec uses. In some cases, you might need to add a statement to your access lists to explicitly permit this traffic. Exhibit 6 summarizes the characteristics of IPSec traffic.

Setting Global Lifetimes for IPSec Security Associations

Assume that the particular crypto map entry does not have lifetime values configured; when the router requests new security associations (SAs) it will specify its global lifetime values in the request to the peer. It will use this value as the lifetime of the new SAs. When the router receives a negotiation request from the peer, it will use the smaller of either the lifetime value proposed by the peer or the locally configured lifetime value as the lifetime of the new SAs.

The security association (and corresponding keys) will expire according to whichever comes sooner, either after the number of seconds has passed (specified by the seconds keyword) or after the amount of traffic in kilobytes is passed (specified by the kilobytes keyword). SAs that you establish manually (via a crypto map entry marked as ipsec-manual) have an infinite lifetime.

Peers negotiate a new SA before reaching the lifetime threshold of the existing SA to ensure that a new SA is ready for use when the old one expires. They negotiate the new SA either 30 seconds before the seconds lifetime expires or when the volume of traffic through the tunnel reaches 256 kilobytes less than the kilobytes lifetime (whichever comes first).

If no traffic has passed through the tunnel during the entire life of the SA, peers do not negotiate a new SA when the lifetime expires. Instead, the peers will negotiate a new SA only when IPSec sees another packet requiring protection.

You can change the global lifetime values that the IOS uses when negotiating new IPSec security associations. IPSec security associations use shared keys. These keys and their SAs time out together. You can override these global lifetime values for a particular crypto map entry. These lifetimes only apply to SAs established via IKE. Manually established SAs do not expire.

There are two lifetimes: a timed lifetime and a traffic-volume lifetime. A security association expires after reaching the first of these lifetimes. The default lifetimes are 3600 seconds (1 hour) and 4,608,000 kilobytes (10 megabytes per second for 1 hour).

If you change a global lifetime, the IOS will not apply the new lifetime value to currently existing SAs, but will use it in the negotiation of subsequently established SAs. If you want to use the new values immediately, you can clear all or part of the security association database.

Note: IPSec ignores the lifetime values for manually established security associations, that is, security associations you establish using the ipsec-manual crypto map entry.

To change a global lifetime for IPSec security associations, use one or more of the following commands in global configuration mode:

```
4500(config)#crypto ipsec security-association lifetime
seconds seconds
```

Note: You will use router 4500 for this chapter, rather than router 2501-1.

This command causes the security association to time out after the specified number of seconds has passed. You can select any value from 120 to 86,400. Again, the default is 3600 seconds (1 hour).

To change the global traffic-volume lifetime for IPSec SAs, use the following commands starting in global configuration mode:

```
4500(config)#crypto ipsec security-association lifetime
   kilobytes kilobytes
```

This command causes the security association to time out after the specified amount of traffic (in kilobytes) has passed through the IPSec tunnel using the security association. You can select any value from 2560 to 536,870,912. Again, the default is 4,608,000 kilobytes. The default is equivalent to 10 megabytes per second for 1 hour.

You have four choices for clearing existing security associations, as follows:

```
4500#clear crypto sa
4500#clear crypto sa peer {ip-address | peer-name}
4500#clear crypto sa map map-name
4500#clear crypto sa spi destination-address protocol spi
```

This causes any existing SAs to expire immediately; future SAs will use the new lifetimes. Otherwise, any existing SAs will expire according to the previously configured lifetimes. You substitute either ah or esp for the protocol keyword in the last command.

Warning: Using the clear crypto sa command without parameters will clear out the full SA database, which will clear out active security sessions. You can also specify the peer, map, or entry keywords to clear out only a subset of the SA database.

Creating Crypto Access Lists

You use crypto access lists to define what IP traffic you want or do not want to protect by cryptography. These access lists are not the same as regular access lists, which determine what traffic to forward or block at an interface.

The access lists themselves are not specific to IPSec; they are no different from what you would use for CET. It is the crypto map entry referencing the specific access list that defines whether the IOS applies IPSec or CET processing to the traffic matching a permit in the access list.

Crypto access lists associated with IPSec crypto map entries have four primary functions:

- Select outbound traffic for IPSec protection (permit = protect).
- Indicate the data flow for protection by the new security associations (specified by a single permit entry) when initiating negotiations for IPSec security associations.

- Process inbound traffic in order to filter out and discard traffic that should have been protected by IPSec.
- Determine whether or not to accept requests for IPSec security associations on behalf of the requested data flows when processing IKE negotiation from the IPSec peer. (Negotiation is only done for ipsec-isakmp crypto map entries.) For acceptance, when the peer initiates the IPSec negotiation, it must specify a data flow "permitted" by a crypto access list associated with an ipsec-isakmp crypto map entry.

If you want certain traffic to receive one combination of IPSec protection (e.g., authentication only) and other traffic to receive a different combination of IPSec protection (e.g., both authentication and encryption), you need to create two different crypto access lists to define the two different types of traffic. Then you use these different access lists in different crypto map entries that specify different IPSec policies.

Later, you will associate the crypto access lists to particular interfaces when you configure and apply crypto map sets to the interfaces (following instructions in the sections Creating Crypto Map Entries and Applying Crypto Map Sets to Interfaces).

To create crypto access lists, use one of the following commands in global configuration mode:

```
4500(config)#access-list access-list-number {deny | permit}
   protocol source source-wildcard destination destination-
   wildcard [precedence precedence] [tos tos] [log]
4500(config)#ip access-list extended name
```

Specify conditions to determine what IP packets you want to protect by enabling or disabling cryptography for traffic that matches these conditions. You specify conditions using an IP access list designated by either a number or a name. The `access-list` command designates a numbered extended access list; the `ip access-list extended` command designates a named access list.

Cisco recommends that you configure *mirror image* crypto access lists for use by IPSec as appropriate. Follow with permit and deny statements and avoid using the any keyword, as described in the sections Defining Mirror Image Crypto Access Lists at Each IPSec Peer. Also see the next section, Crypto Access List Tips.

Crypto Access List Tips

Using the `permit` keyword causes crypto protection for all IP traffic matching the specified conditions, using the policy described by the corresponding crypto map entry. Using the `deny` keyword prevents traffic from being protected by crypto in the context of that particular crypto map entry. That is, it does not allow the router to apply the policy as specified in this crypto map entry to this traffic. If you deny this traffic in all of the crypto map entries for that interface, then you have not protected the traffic by either CET or IPSec crypto.

The IOS will apply the crypto access list you define to an interface after you define the corresponding crypto map entry and apply the crypto map set to the interface. You must define different access lists in different entries of the same crypto map set. However, the router will evaluate both inbound and outbound traffic against the same "outbound" IPSec access list. Therefore, you apply the access list's criteria in the forward direction to traffic exiting your router, and in the reverse direction to traffic entering your router.

If you configure multiple statements for a given crypto access list used for IPSec, in general the first permit statement that the router matches is the statement it will use to determine the scope of the IPSec security association. That is, the router will set up the IPSec security association to protect traffic that meets the criteria of the matched statement only. Later, should traffic match a different permit statement of the crypto access list, the router will negotiate a new separate IPSec security association to protect traffic matching the newly matched access list statement.

Note: The IOS restricts access lists for crypto map entries tagged as ipsec-manual to a single permit entry and the router will ignore subsequent entries. That is, the security associations established by that particular crypto map entry are only for a single data flow. To support multiple manually established security associations for different kinds of traffic, you should define multiple crypto access lists and then apply each one to a separate ipsec-manual crypto map entry. Each access list should include one permit statement defining what traffic to protect.

The router will drop any unprotected inbound traffic that matches a permit entry in the crypto access list for a crypto map entry flagged as IPSec because it expected this traffic to be IPSec protected.

Note: If you view your router's access lists using a command such as `show ip access-lists`, you will see all extended IP access lists in the command output. This includes extended IP access lists used for traffic filtering purposes as well as those used for crypto. The `show` command output does not differentiate between the different uses of the extended access lists.

Defining Mirror Image Crypto Access Lists at Each IPSec Peer

Cisco recommends that for every crypto access list specified for a static crypto map entry you define at the local peer, that you also define a *mirror image* crypto access list at the remote peer. This ensures that the router can correctly process traffic that has IPSec protection applied locally at the remote peer. The crypto map entries themselves must also support common transforms and must refer to the other system as a peer.

You can establish IPSec security associations (SAs), as expected, whenever the two peers' crypto access lists are mirror images of each other. However, you can only establish an IPSec SA some of the time when the access lists are not mirror images of each other. This can happen in the case where an entry in one peer's access list is a subset of an entry in the other peer's access list. IPSec SA establishment is critical to IPSec; without SAs, IPSec does not work, causing the router to drop silently any packets matching the crypto access list criteria instead of forwarding them with IPSec security.

Because of the complexities introduced when you do not configure crypto access lists as mirror images at peer IPSec devices, Cisco strongly encourages you to use mirror image crypto access lists.

Using the any Keyword in Crypto Access Lists

When you create crypto access lists, using the any keyword might cause problems. Cisco discourages the use of the any keyword to specify source or destination addresses. Likewise, do not use the any keyword in a permit statement when you have multicast traffic flowing through the IPSec interface; the any keyword can cause multicast traffic to fail.

Cisco strongly discourages the use of the permit any statement because this will cause the router to protect all outbound traffic (and all protected traffic sent to the peer specified in the corresponding crypto map entry) and all inbound traffic. Then, if you do not not specify IPSec protection for inbound packets, the router will silently drop them, including packets for routing protocols, NTP, echo, echo response, and others.

You need to make sure you define the packets to protect. If you must use the any keyword in a permit statement, then you must preface that statement with a series of deny statements to filter out any traffic that would otherwise fall within that permit statement, but that you do not want protected.

Defining Transform Sets

A transform set represents a certain combination of security protocols and algorithms. During the IPSec SA negotiation, the peers agree to use a particular transform set for protecting a particular data flow.

You can specify multiple transform sets and then specify one or more of these transform sets in a crypto map entry. The router will use the transform set defined in the crypto map entry in the IPSec SA negotiation to protect the data flows specified by that crypto map entry's access list.

During IPSec SA negotiations with IKE, the peers search for a common transform set. When they find such a transform set, the router will select it and apply it to the protected traffic as part of both peers' IPSec security associations.

With manually established security associations, there is no negotiation with the peer, so both sides must specify the same transform set.

Exhibit 7   Allowed Transform Combinations

AH Transform (pick no more than one)		ESP Encryption Transform (pick no more than one)		ESP Authentication Transform (pick no more than one only when you select esp-des transform)	
Transform	Description	Transform	Description	Transform	Description
ah-md5-hmac	AH with the MD5 (HMAC variant) authentication algorithm	esp-des	ESP with 56-bit DES encryption algorithm	esp-md5-hmac	ESP with the MD5 (HMAC variant) authentication algorithm
ah-sha-hmac	AH with the SHA (HMAC variant) authentication algorithm	esp-rfc1829	Older ESP protocol (per RFC 1829); does not allow an ESP authentication algorithm	esp-sha-hmac	ESP with the SHA (HMAC variant) authentication algorithm
ah-rfc1828	Older AH protocol (per RFC 1828)				

If you change a transform set definition, the router will only apply the change to crypto map entries that reference the transform set. It will not apply the change to existing security associations, but will use the changed transform set in subsequent negotiations when establishing new security associations. Should you want the new settings to take effect sooner, you can clear all or part of the security association database using the `clear crypto sa` command. (This command is discussed in several places in this chapter.)

To define a transform set, use the following commands starting in global configuration mode:

```
4500(config)#crypto ipsec transform-set transform-set-name
   transform1 [transform2 [transform3]]
```

This command defines a transform set. You can enter up to three transform sets. There are complex rules defining what entries you can use for the transform arguments. You can find an explanation of these rules in the command description for the `crypto ipsec transform-set` command; Exhibit 7 provides a list of allowed transform combinations. Simply put, acceptable transform combinations include:

- `ah-md5-hmac`
- `esp-des`
- `esp-des and esp-md5-hmac`
- `ah-sha-hmac and esp-des and esp-sha-hmac`
- `ah-rfc1828 and esp-rfc1829`

The following are some tips on selecting transforms:

1. If your router is establishing tunnels with a device that only supports older transforms, then you must select ah-rfc1828 or ah-rfc1828 and esp-rfc1829.
2. If you want to provide data confidentiality, include an ESP encryption transform. You have two choices.
3. If you want to ensure data authentication for the outer IP header as well as the data itself, include an AH transform. You have three choices.
4. If you use an ESP encryption transform, consider including an ESP authentication transform or an AH transform to provide authentication services for the transform set. You have two choices.
5. If you want data authentication using AH or ESP, you can choose from the MD5 or SHA authentication algorithms. Cryptographers consider SHA stronger, but it is slower.
6. If you choose to use a transform, you should check to see whether the IPSec peer supports it.

With that advice in mind, you might create the following transform set.

```
4500(config)#crypto ipsec transform-set myset esp-des ah-
sha-hmac esp-md5-hmac
```

With this command, you set up three transforms. This command puts you into the crypto transform configuration mode.

```
4500(cfg-crypto-trans)#initialization-vector size [4 | 8]
```

If you specified the esp-rfc1829 transform in the transform set, you can change the initialization vector size used with the esp-rfc1829 transform. The default is 8. The change will only affect the negotiation of subsequent IPSec SAs. Should you want to use the settings sooner, use the clear crypto sa command.

You can change the mode associated with the transform set.

```
4500(cfg-crypto-trans)#mode [tunnel | transport]
```

With tunnel mode, IPSec protects the entire original IP packet through encryption, authentication, or both. IPSec headers and trailers encapsulate the original IP packet. Then, IPSec pre-appends a new IP header to the packet, which specifies the IPSec endpoints as the source and destination addresses. With transport mode, IPSec protects only the payload (or data) of the original IP packet. IPSec headers and trailers encapsulate the payload. The original IP headers remain intact and IPSec does not protect them. The mode setting is only applicable to traffic whose source and destination addresses are the IPSec peer addresses; it is ignored for all other traffic. (All other traffic is in tunnel mode only.) The change will only affect the negotiation of subsequent IPSec SAs. Should you want to use the settings sooner, use the clear crypto sa command.

Exit the crypto transform configuration mode:

```
4500(cfg-crypto-trans)#exit
4500(config)#exit
```

To clear the crypto settings, use one of the following EXEC commands.

```
4500#clear crypto sa
```

Warning: Using the clear crypto sa command without a parameter will clear out the full SA database, which will clear out active security sessions.

```
4500#clear crypto sa peer {ip-address | peer-name}
4500#clear crypto sa map map-name
4500#clear crypto sa spi destination-address protocol spi
```

This step clears existing IPSec SAs so that any changes to a transform set will take effect on newly established SAs. The IOS immediately reestablishes manually established SAs. You can also specify the peer, map, or entry keywords to clear out only a subset of the SA database. Should you use the peer keyword, you must specify the peer's IP address or its fully qualified domain name, for example, peerone.pdaconsulting.com. Should you use the map keyword, you must specify the crypto map set. Should you use the entry keyword, you must specify the IP address of your peer or the remote peer, either the AH or ESP protocol, and the SPI, which you can find by displaying the SA database.

Look at an example that defines a transform set and changes the mode to transport.

```
4500(config)#crypto ipsec transform-set test esp-des esp-
   sha-hmac
4500(cfg-crypto-trans)#mode transport
4500(cfg-crypto-trans)#exit
4500(config)#
```

You configure transport mode in this example. Remember that transport mode only encrypts the data and leaves the addresses alone. Transport mode has less overhead than tunnel mode because it only needs to add a couple of bits to the header. Again, tunnel mode is the default.

Creating Crypto Map Entries

Cisco expanded crypto maps, used previously only with Cisco Encryption Technology (CET), to specify IPSec policy. Crypto map entries created for IPSec pull together the various parts for setting up IPSec SAs, including:

- The traffic for IPSec protection (per a crypto access list)
- A set of security associations to protect the granularity of the flow
- The remote IPSec peer (i.e., where to send the IPSec-protected traffic)
- The local address for the IPSec traffic
- The IPSec protection to apply to this traffic (selecting from a list of one or more transform sets)
- Manually established or IKE-established SAs
- Other parameters necessary to define an IPSec security association

You group crypto map entries with the same crypto map name (but different map sequence numbers) into a crypto map set. Later, you will apply these crypto map sets to interfaces; then, the router will evaluate all IP traffic passing through the interface against the applied crypto map set. When a crypto map entry sees outbound IP traffic requiring protection and the crypto map specifies the use of IKE, the local peer negotiates an SA with the remote peer according to the parameters included in the crypto map entry. Otherwise, when the crypto map entry specifies the use of manual SAs, you should have previously configured an SA. If a dynamic crypto map entry sees outbound traffic requiring protection and no SA exists, the router drops the packet.

The router uses the policy described in the crypto map entries during the negotiation of SAs. If the local router initiates the negotiation, it will use the policy specified in the static crypto map entries to create the offer to send to the specified IPSec peer. If the IPSec peer initiates the negotiation, the local router will check the policy from the static crypto map entries, as well as any referenced dynamic crypto map entries, to decide whether to accept or reject the peer's offer.

For IPSec to succeed between two IPSec peers, both peers' crypto map entries must contain compatible configuration statements. When two peers try to establish an SA, they must each have at least one crypto map entry that is compatible with one of the other peer's crypto map entries. For two crypto map entries to be compatible, they must at least meet the following criteria:

- The crypto map entries must contain compatible crypto access lists (e.g., mirror image access lists). Where the responding peer uses dynamic crypto maps, you must use the peer's crypto access list to permit the entries in the local crypto access list.
- The crypto map entries must each identify the other peer (unless the responding peer is using dynamic crypto maps).
- The crypto map entries must have at least one transform set in common.

Load Sharing

You can define multiple remote peers using crypto maps to allow for load sharing. When one peer fails, there is still a protected path. The router will send the packets to the last peer that it heard from (received either traffic or a negotiation request from) for a given data flow. If the attempt fails with the first peer, IKE tries the next peer on the crypto map list.

If you are not sure how to configure each crypto map parameter to guarantee compatibility with other peers, you might consider configuring dynamic crypto maps as described in the section Creating Dynamic Crypto Maps. Dynamic crypto maps are useful when the remote peer initiates the establishment of the IPSec tunnels (such as in the case of an IPSec router fronting a server). They are not useful when you locally initiate the establishment of the IPSec tunnels because the dynamic crypto maps are policy templates, not complete statements of policy.

To create crypto map entries, follow the guidelines and tasks listed and discussed below:

1. Determine your crypto maps.
2. Create crypto map entries for establishing manual SAs.
3. Create crypto map entries that use IKE to establish SAs.
4. Create dynamic crypto maps.

Determining Your Crypto Maps

You can apply only one crypto map set to a single interface. The crypto map set can include a combination of CET, IPSec/IKE, and IPSec/manual entries. Multiple interfaces can share the same crypto map set when you want to apply the same policy to multiple interfaces.

If you create more than one crypto map entry for a given interface, use the seq-num keyword of each map entry to rank the map entries: the lower the seq-num, the higher the priority. At the interface that has the crypto map set, the router evaluates traffic against higher-priority map entries first.

You must create multiple crypto map entries for a given interface when any of the following conditions exist:

- If separate IPSec peers handle different data flows.
- If you want to apply different IPSec security to different types of traffic (to the same or separate IPSec peers); for example, if you want to authenticate traffic between one set of subnets, and authenticate and encrypt traffic between another set of subnets. In this case, you should define the different types of traffic in two separate access lists, and you must create a separate crypto map entry for each crypto access list.
- If you are not using IKE to establish a particular set of SAs and want to specify multiple access list entries, you must create separate access lists (one per permit entry) and specify a separate crypto map entry for each access list.

Creating Crypto Map Entries for Establishing Manual Security Associations

Should you decide to use manual SAs, you will need to have a prior arrangement between you and the remote IPSec peer. You may wish to begin any new relationship with manual SAs, and then move to using SAs established via IKE, or the remote party's system may not support IKE. If you do not use IKE for establishing the SAs, there is no negotiation of SAs, so you must configure the information in both systems the same way so that the router can successfully process IPSec traffic.

The local router can simultaneously support manual and IKE-established security associations, even within a single crypto map set. There is very little reason to disable IKE on the local router (unless the router only supports manual SAs, which is unlikely).

To create crypto map entries to establish manual security associations (SAs), that is, when you do not use IKE to establish the SAs, use the following commands starting in global configuration mode:

```
4500(config)#crypto map map-name seq-num ipsec-manual
```

Use this command to specify the crypto map entry to create or modify. The sequence number is a value from 0 to 65,535. The following command puts you into the crypto map configuration mode.

```
4500(config-crypto-map)#match address [access-list-id |
  name]
```

The specified access list determines what traffic IPSec should protect and what traffic IPSec should not protect in the context of this crypto map entry. The `access-list-id` keyword is a value from 100 to 199. Your access list can specify only one permit entry when you do not use IKE. You specify the number or the name of the extended access list you want to match.

Next you specify the remote IPSec peer.

```
4500(config-crypto-map)#set peer {hostname | ip-address}
```

This is the peer where you want to forward IPSec-protected traffic. You can only specify one peer when you do not use IKE. You specify the IPSec peer by its host name or IP address.

Now specify the transform set to use.

```
4500(config-crypto-map)#set transform-set transform-set-name
```

You must use the same transform set that you specified in the remote peer's corresponding crypto map entry. Again, you can only specify one transform set when you do not use IKE. Next set the session keys.

```
4500(config-crypto-map)#set session-key [inbound | outbound]
  ah spi hex-key-data
4500(cfg-crypto-map)#set session-key [inbound | outbound]
  esp spi cipher hex-key-data [authenticator hex-key-data]
```

Note: Prior to IOS release 12.0, you would have used the crypto map statement `set security-association [inbound | outbound]` rather than the `set session-key [inbound | outbound]` command.

If the specified transform set includes the AH protocol, set the AH Security Parameter Indexes (SPIs) and keys to apply to inbound and outbound protected traffic. This manually specifies the AH security association for use with the protected traffic.

If the specified transform set includes the ESP protocol, set the ESP Security Parameter Indexes (SPIs) and keys to apply to inbound and outbound protected traffic. If the transform set includes an ESP cipher algorithm, specify the cipher keys. If the transform set includes an ESP authenticator algorithm, specify the authenticator keys. This manually specifies the ESP security association for use with the protected traffic. The spi keyword is a value from 256 to 4,294,967,295.

Exit crypto-map configuration mode and return to global configuration mode.

```
4500(config-crypto-map)#exit
```

Repeat these steps to create additional crypto map entries as required.

Creating Crypto Map Entries that Use IKE to Establish Security Associations

When you use IKE to establish SAs, the IPSec peers can negotiate the settings they will use for the new SAs. This means that you can specify lists, such as lists of acceptable transforms, within the crypto map entry. To create crypto map entries that will use IKE to establish the SAs, use the following commands starting in global configuration mode:

```
4500(config)#crypto map map-name seq-num ipsec-isakmp
```

Name the crypto map entry you wish to create or modify. The next command puts you into the crypto map configuration mode:

```
4500(config-crypto-map)#match address [access-list-id | name]
```

Name or enumerate an extended access list. The access-list-id keyword is a value from 100 to 199. This access list determines the traffic that IPSec will or will not protect in the context of this crypto map entry. Specify a remote IPSec peer:

```
4500(config-crypto-map)#set peer {hostname | ip-address}
```

This is the peer where you want the router to forward IPSec protected traffic. Repeat for multiple remote peers.

Now specify which transform sets you allow for this crypto map entry.

```
4500(config-crypto-map)#set transform-set transform-set-
    name1 [transform-set-name2…transform-set-name6]
```

List multiple transform sets in order of priority, with the highest priority first.

If you want the peers to negotiate the SAs for this crypto map entry using different IPSec SA lifetimes than the global lifetimes, specify an SA lifetime for the crypto map entry.

```
4500(config-crypto-map)#set security-association lifetime
   seconds seconds
4500(config-crypto-map)#set security-association lifetime
   kilobytes kilobytes
```

You can specify any value from 120 to 86,400 for seconds, and from 2560 to 536,870,912 for kilobytes. You can specify that the router should establish separate SAs for each source and destination host-pair.

```
4500(config-crypto-map)#set security-association level per-
   host
```

Without this command, a single IPSec "tunnel" could carry traffic for multiple source hosts and multiple destination hosts. With this command, when the router requests new SAs, it will establish one set for traffic between Host A and Host B, and a separate set for traffic between Host A and Host C. Use this command cautiously; multiple streams between given subnets can rapidly consume resources.

You can also specify that IPSec should ask for *perfect forward secrecy* (PFS) when requesting new SAs for this crypto map entry, or should demand PFS in requests received from the IPSec peer.

```
4500(config-crypto-map)#set pfs [group1 | group2]
```

The group1 keyword specifies that IPSec should use the 768-bit Diffie-Hellman prime modulus group when performing the new exchange, while the group2 keyword specifies that IPSec should use the 1024-bit Diffie-Hellman prime modulus group when performing the new exchange.

Exit crypto-map configuration mode and return to global configuration mode.

```
4500(config-crypto-map)#exit
```

Repeat these steps to create additional crypto map entries as required.

Creating Dynamic Crypto Maps

Dynamic crypto maps (which require IKE) can ease IPSec configuration, and Cisco recommends their use with networks where the peers are not always predetermined or known. For example, you may have mobile users who obtain dynamically assigned IP addresses. First, the mobile clients need to authenticate themselves to the local router's IKE by something other than an IP address; for example, by a fully qualified domain name. Once authenticated, the router can process the SA request against a dynamic crypto map set up to accept requests (matching the specified local policy) from previously unknown peers.

Note: Dynamic crypto maps are only available for use by IKE.

A dynamic crypto map entry is essentially a crypto map entry without all the parameters configured. It acts as a policy template where the router dynamically configures the missing parameters later (as the result of an IPSec negotiation) to match a remote peer's requirements. This allows remote peers to exchange IPSec traffic with the router even when the router does not have a crypto map entry specifically configured to meet all of the remote peer's requirements.

The router does not use dynamic crypto maps to initiate new IPSec SAs with remote peers. It uses dynamic crypto maps when a remote peer tries to initiate an IPSec SA with the router. The router also uses dynamic crypto maps for evaluating traffic.

You include a dynamic crypto map set by reference as part of a crypto map set. You should set any crypto map entries referencing dynamic crypto map sets to the lowest-priority crypto map entries in the crypto map set (i.e., have the highest sequence numbers) so that the router evaluates the other crypto map entries first. Thus, the router will examine the dynamic crypto map set only when it does not successfully match the other static map entries.

If the router accepts the peer's request, then at the point that it creates the new IPSec SAs, it also creates a temporary crypto map entry. The software fills in this entry with the results of the negotiation. At this point, the router performs normal processing using this temporary crypto map entry as a normal entry, even requesting new SAs when the current ones are expiring (based on the policy specified in the temporary crypto map entry). Once the flow expires (i.e., all of the corresponding SAs expire), the router removes the temporary crypto map entry.

For both static and dynamic crypto maps, when unprotected inbound traffic matches a permit statement in an access list and the router has tagged the corresponding crypto map entry as IPSec, the router will drop the traffic because it is not IPSec-protected. It does this because the security policy, as specified by the crypto map entry, states that this traffic must be IPSec-protected.

For static crypto map entries, when outbound traffic matches a permit statement in an access list and the router has not yet established the corresponding SA, the router will initiate new SAs with the remote peer. With dynamic crypto map entries, when no SA exists, the router would simply drop the traffic (because you cannot use dynamic crypto maps for initiating new SAs).

Warning: Be careful when using the any keyword in permit entries in dynamic crypto maps. Where it is possible that the traffic covered by such a permit entry includes multicast or broadcast traffic, the access list should include deny entries for the appropriate address range. Access lists should also include deny entries for network and subnet broadcast traffic, and for any other traffic that you do not want IPSec-protected.

To configure dynamic crypto maps, follow these instructions:

1. Create a dynamic crypto map set.
2. Add the dynamic crypto map set into a regular (static) crypto map set.

Creating a Dynamic Crypto Map Set

You group dynamic crypto map entries, like regular static crypto map entries, into sets. A set is a group of dynamic crypto map entries, all with the same dynamic-map-name but each with a different dynamic-seq-num. To create a dynamic crypto map entry, use the following commands starting in global configuration mode:

```
4500(config)#crypto dynamic-map dynamic-map-name dynamic-
    seq-num
```

With this command, you specify the name of the dynamic crypto map set and the number of the crypto map entry.

Specify what transform sets you allow for the crypto map entry:

```
4500(config-crypto-map)#set transform-set transform-set-
    name1 [transform-set-name2...transform-set-name6]
```

List multiple transform sets in order of priority, starting with the highest priority first. This is the only configuration statement required in dynamic crypto map entries.

Now name an extended access list:

```
4500(config-crypto-map)#match address [access-list-id |
    name]
```

This access list determines the traffic IPSec should protect and the traffic IPSec should not protect. The `access-list-id` keyword has a value from 100 to 199. If you configure this, the data flow identity proposed by the IPSec peer must fall within a permit statement for this crypto access list. If you do not configure this, the router will accept any data flow identity proposed by the IPSec peer. However, if you configure this and the specified access list does not exist or is empty, the router will drop all packets. This is similar to static crypto maps because they also require that you specify an access list. Care must be taken when using the any keyword in the access list because the router uses the access list for packet filtering as well as for negotiation.

Specify a remote IPSec peer:

```
4500(config-crypto-map)#set peer {hostname | ip-address}
```

Repeat for multiple remote peers. You rarely configure this for dynamic crypto map entries because you often use dynamic crypto map entries for unknown remote peers.

If you want the router to negotiate security associations for this crypto map using shorter IPSec security association lifetimes than the globally specified lifetimes, specify a key lifetime for the crypto map entry:

```
4500(config-crypto-map)#set security-association lifetime
    seconds seconds
```

```
4500(config-crypto-map)#set security-association lifetime
  kilobytes kilobytes
```

As an option, you can specify that IPSec should ask for perfect forward secrecy (PFS) when requesting new SAs for this crypto map entry or should demand PFS in requests received from the IPSec peer.

```
4500(config-crypto-map)#set pfs [group1 | group2]
```

Now exit crypto-map configuration mode and return to global configuration mode:

```
4500(config-crypto-map)#exit
```

Dynamic crypto map entries specify crypto access lists that limit traffic where peers can establish IPSec SAs. When filtering traffic, the router will ignore a dynamic crypto map entry that does not specify an access list. A dynamic crypto map entry with an empty access list causes the router to drop traffic. When there is only one dynamic crypto map entry in the crypto map set, you must specify acceptable transform sets.

Adding the Dynamic Crypto Map Set into a Static Crypto Map Set

You can add one or more dynamic crypto map sets into a crypto map set via crypto map entries that reference the dynamic crypto map sets. You should set the crypto map entries referencing dynamic maps as the lowest-priority entries in a crypto map set; that is, those having the highest sequence numbers.

To add a dynamic crypto map set into a crypto map set, use the following command in global configuration mode:

```
4500(config)#crypto map map-name seq-num ipsec-isakmp
  dynamic dynamic-map-name
```

The dynamic keyword map-name specifies the name of the dynamic crypto map set to use as the policy template.

Applying Crypto Map Sets to Interfaces

You need to apply a crypto map set to each interface where IPSec traffic will flow through. Applying the crypto map set to an interface instructs the router to evaluate all the interface's traffic against the crypto map set and to use the specified policy during connection or SA negotiation on behalf of traffic protected by IPSec crypto.

To apply a crypto map set to an interface, use the following command in interface configuration mode:

```
4500(config)#interface s0
4500(config-if)#crypto map map-name
```

For redundancy, you could apply the same crypto map set to more than one interface. The default behavior is as follows:

- Each interface will have its own piece of the SA database.
- The router will use the IP address of the local interface as the local address for IPSec traffic originating from or destined to that interface.

If you apply the same crypto map set to multiple interfaces for redundancy purposes, you need to specify an identifying interface. This has the following effects:

- The router will establish the per-interface portion of the IPSec SA database one time and share it for traffic through all the interfaces that share the same crypto map.
- The router will use the IP address of the identifying interface as the local address for IPSec traffic originating from or destined to those interfaces sharing the same crypto map set.

You can use a loopback interface as the identifying interface.

To specify redundant interfaces and name an identifying interface, use the following command in global configuration mode:

```
4500(config-if)#crypto map map-name local-address interface-
   id
```

This command permits redundant interfaces to share the same crypto map, using the same local identity.

Monitoring and Maintaining IPSec

Certain configuration changes will only take effect when negotiating subsequent SAs. If you want the new settings to take effect immediately, you must clear the existing SAs so that the router will re-establish them with the changed configuration. For manually established SAs, you must clear and reinitialize the SAs or the changes will never take effect. If the router is actively processing IPSec traffic, it is desirable to clear only the portion of the SA database affected by the configuration changes; that is, clear only the SAs established by a given crypto map set. You should save clearing the full SA database for large-scale changes or when the router is processing very little other IPSec traffic.

To clear and reinitialize IPSec security associations, use one of the following commands in global configuration mode:

```
4500#clear crypto sa
```

Warning: Using the `clear crypto sa` command without parameters will clear out the full SA database, which will clear out active security sessions. You can also specify the `peer`, `map`, or `entry` keywords to clear out only a subset of the SA database.

```
4500#clear crypto sa peer {ip-address | peer-name}
4500#clear crypto sa map map-name
4500#clear crypto sa spi destination-address protocol spi
4500#clear crypto sa counters
```

Using the `counters` keyword clears the traffic counters maintained for each SA, but it does not reinitialize the SA itself.

To view information about your IPSec configuration, use one or more of the following commands in EXEC mode:

```
4500#show crypto ipsec transform-set [tag transform-set-
  name]
Transform set myset: { ah-sha-hmac }
will negotiate = { Tunnel, },
{ esp-des esp-md5-hmac }
will negotiate = { Tunnel, },

Transform set test: { esp-des esp-sha-hmac }
will negotiate = { Transport, },
```

The preceding command allows you to view your transform set configuration. Use the `tag` keyword to show only the transform set you specify; otherwise, you will see all transform sets configured at the router.

View your crypto map configuration with the following.

```
4500#show crypto map [interface interface | tag map-name]
```

Use the `interface` keyword to show only the crypto maps you applied to the specified interface. Similarly, use the `tag` keyword to show only the specified crypto map set.

To view information about IPSec SAs, use the following command.

```
4500#show crypto ipsec sa [map map-name | address | identity]
  [detail]
```

Use the `map` keyword to show any existing SAs created for the crypto map set. Alternately, use the `address` keyword to show all existing SAs sorted by AH or ESP protocol within the destination address. Or, use the `identity` keyword to show the flow information but no security association information. Finally, use the `detail` keyword to show detailed error counters. If you do not specify the any keyword, then the command shows all security associations sorted first by interface, then by traffic flow (e.g., source/destination address, mask, protocol, and port). Within a flow, show lists SAs by protocol (ESP/AH) and direction (inbound/outbound).

You can view information about dynamic crypto maps with the following command:

```
4500#show crypto dynamic-map [tag map-name]
```

Use the tag keyword to show only the crypto dynamic map set you specify.

To view global security lifetime association lifetime values, use the following EXEC command.

```
4500#show crypto ipsec security-association
Security association lifetime: 4608000 kilobytes/3600
   seconds
```

Now you will have the opportunity to try some of these cryptic commands.

Practice Session

In this Practice Session, you will practice the following:

- Logging in
- Saving log data
- Switching modes
- Entering configuration mode
- Configuring IPSec
- Enabling and saving syslog data
- Logging out

1. Log in to the SimRouter Web page.
2. Double-click on router 4500 to telnet to that router. This will open a console session.
3. Enter your **Username** and **Password** at the applicable prompt. These are the ones you set up in Chapter 2. You will need to hit the Enter key twice to get to the > prompt.
4. Again, save the log for your session. To do this, select | Terminal | Start Logging | from the menu bar in the Telnet window. The Telnet client will ask you where you wish to store the log and with what name. Your choice. You are going to save the log so that when you build this configuration file, you can cut-and-paste this in Chapter 21 as a starting point, rather than having to enter the same information each Practice Session.
5. Enter the enable mode:

   ```
   4500#enable
   ```

6. When prompted to put in the enable secret password, enter **oscar**.
7. Type **terminal length 0**. This command instructs the router to scroll through long command output without pausing (the —More— message).
8. You will paste the running-config that you saved from the Chapter 19 log. At the 4500# prompt, type config t.
9. If you did not do this, open your log file with the text editor of your choice (e.g., use | Start | Programs | Accessories | Notepad |). Do a find on sh running-config and copy from the first "!" to "end." At the 4500(config)# prompt, paste this configuration.

10. Type **access-list 101 permit ip 10.0.0.0 0.0.0.255 10.2.2.0 0.0.0.255** and press Enter. This configures the access list defining the traffic to protect.

11. Type `crypto inspect transform-set myset esp-des esp-sha` and press Enter. This configures the transform set that defines how the traffic is protected.

12. Type `crypto map mymap 10 ipsec-isakmp` and press Enter. This configures the crypto map that joins the IPSec access list and transform set, and specifies where to send protected traffic.

13. Type `match address 101` and press Enter. This tells the router to use access-list 101.

14. Type `set transform-set myset` and press Enter. This tells the router the transform set to use.

15. Type `set peer 10.10.1.1` and press Enter. This tells the router to use access-list 101.

16. Apply the crypto map to an interface. Type `interface s0` and press Enter.

17. Type `ip address 10.10.1.2` and press Enter.

18. Type `crypto map mymap` and press Enter. This tells the router to use access-list 101.

19. Type `exit` and press Enter. Type `exit` and press Enter.

20. Type `show crypto isakmp policy` and press Enter.

21. Type `sh running-config` and press Enter. You will use this new configuration to start the next Practice Session.

22. Type `quit` to log out from router 4500. Close the Telnet window and return to the SimRouter Topology Map.

23. Click on Log Out on the SimRouter Web page.

Security and Audit Checklist

1. Does your organization have a policy on the use of encryption?
   - Yes
   - No
2. Is the policy appropriate?
   - Yes
   - No
3. Does your organization have a policy on key management?
   - Yes
   - No
4. Does your organization have a policy on sharing keys?
   - Yes
   - No
5. Has your organization evaluated the following threats?
   - Data disclosure
   - Data modification
   - Spoofing
   - Repudiation
   - Replay

6. Do you use CET in your organization?
   - Yes
   - No
7. Is CET implemented in hardware?
   - Yes
   - No
8. Do you use IPSec in your organization?
   - Yes
   - No
9. Is IPSec implemented in hardware?
   - Yes
   - No
10. If your organization supports IPSec, does your firewall allow UDP port 500?
    - Yes
    - No
11. If your organization supports IPSec, does your firewall allow protocol Number 50?
    - Yes
    - No
12. If your organization supports IPSec, does your firewall allow protocol Number 51?
    - Yes
    - No
13. Do you use global lifetimes for SAs?
    - Yes
    - No
14. Is the lifetime for SAs appropriate?
    - Yes
    - No
15. Does your organization have a policy on issuing the `clear` command?
    - Yes
    - No
16. Do you use Authentication Header in your organization?
    - Yes
    - No
17. If yes, do you use:
    - `ah-md5-hmac`?
    - `ah-sha-hmac`?
    - `ah-rfc1828`?
18. Do you use Encapsulating Security Payload in your organization?
    - Yes
    - No
19. If yes, do you use:
    - Tunnel mode?
    - Transport mode?
20. If yes, do you use:
    - ESP encryption?
    - ESP authentication?

21. If ESP encryption, do you use:
    - esp-des?
    - esp-rc1829?
22. If ESP authentication, do you use:
    - esp-md5-hmac?
    - esp-sha-hmac?
23. Do you use manual crypto map entries?
    - Yes
    - No
24. Has someone been assigned responsibility for setting up these crypto maps?
    - Yes
    - No
25. Do you use IKE to establish security associations?
    - Yes
    - No
26. Do you use dynamic crypto maps?
    - Yes
    - No
27. Has someone been assigned responsibility for monitoring IPSec usage?
    - Yes
    - No

Conclusion

In this chapter, you learned about IPSec in more detail. You saw how to set up IPSec using manual configuration and IKE. IPSec addresses the concerns holding back large-scale VPN deployment. Using IPSec, you can protect the confidentiality of your data. Sometimes, the integrity of the information is more important than confidentiality. To ensure the identity of the originator and the integrity of the data, message authentication codes are a solution. Message authentication ensures the veracity and source of messages by processing the messages so additional information generated and transmitted with the message can be used for validation at the receiving node. You should use message authentication for those messages that need write protection as opposed to read protection. IPSec provides encryption and authentication.

Cisco is working continuously on improving its security offerings to gain a competitive edge. The new ISA hardware accelerator is just one such example. When you read this, Cisco might have newer technology, so consult with your subject expert.

Now turn your attention to preventing denial-of-service attacks such as SYN flooding and Smurf.

PREVENTING
DENIAL-OF-SERVICE

Chapter 21

Configuring Denial-of-Service Security Features

In this chapter, you will learn about:

- Configuring your router against common denial-of-service attacks
- Configuring TCP Intercept
- Enabling and setting TCP Intercept
- Monitoring and maintaining TCP Intercept
- Configuring NAT
- Verifying NAT operation
- Configuring traffic policing and queuing

This chapter describes how to protect your network against some of the well-known denial-of-service (DoS) attacks. You will learn how to configure your router to protect TCP servers from directed broadcasts; IP source routing; ICMP redirects; and TCP SYN-flooding attacks, a type of denial-of-service attack. Also, you will learn how to prevent packet flooding through queuing and traffic policing.

Understanding Denial-of-Service

You are watching the World Series and Matt Williams of the Diamondbacks is at bat. The count is 3-2, 2 out, and the bases are loaded. The phone rings and the ring indicates a long-distance call. Obviously, the caller is not watching the game. You answer the phone, only to find no one there. You curse and slam down the phone. Several seconds later, it happens again. You repeat the process. This series of events occurs several more times until, out of frustration, you turn off the ringer and let all the calls go to voicemail. At work the next morning, your buddy says, "Where were you? I tried to call last night to make sure you were watching the game." (If you are a Canadian, substitute Stanley Cup finals for World Series, Mats Sundin for Matt Williams, and Toronto Maple Leafs for Diamondbacks, etc. If you live anywhere else, substitute World Cup, Reynaldo, etc.) The point is that the unknown caller was tying up your phone line and denying your buddy access to you. It got so bad you had to take your phone off-line. You can see that it is very difficult to protect against this type of attack, save going off-line. Well, you could take this story and create a simple analogy using your router. Someone starts flooding your router or network with dubious packets. The packets cause the system to crash or consume all available resources. Your legitimate clients cannot get through or do anything. When someone hits your router with a denial-of-service attack, they hold up critical resources by blocking the door to lawful business activity. A denial-of-service (DoS) attack is an attack against your network availability.

Controlling the Hostile Environment

The attacks discussed in this chapter are relatively sophisticated ones, but they are by no means out of the reach of today's crackers. In fact, they can readily get scripts, programs, or code to launch attacks against you (refer to Chapter 1). You can often thwart these attacks when the public network providers involved have taken proper security measures. Thus, you should evaluate your level of trust in the security measures used by all the providers carrying your traffic. Ultimately, you cannot avoid some DoS attacks, no matter your diligence. In this case, you need to add vigilance to your arsenal. You must notice the attack and begin the process of tracking it back to its source, or find a way to stop it. Being aware is a good start, so take a look at some advice on protecting your organization against known DoS attacks.

Controlling Directed Broadcasts

Smurf, the extremely common and popular DoS attack, uses IP directed broadcasts as do related attacks. An IP directed broadcast is one in which a machine sends a datagram to the broadcast address of a subnetwork where it is not directly attached. In a Smurf attack, the attacker sends ICMP echo requests from a falsified source address to a directed broadcast address, causing all the hosts on the target subnet to send replies to the spoofed source. That is, instead of directing a Ping request to a single host as is normally done, the attacker sends the Ping to an address ending in either 0 or 255 (e.g., 10.1.2.0 or 10.1.2.255), which causes the Ping to go to all hosts in the network. So, when all the machines respond to the Ping, they send the response back to the falsified address, that is, the intended victim. By sending a continuous stream of such requests, the attacker can create a much larger stream of replies, which can completely inundate the host whose address the attacker is spoofing.

If you configure your router's interface with the `no ip directed-broadcast` command, the router will drop directed broadcasts that would otherwise have exploded into link-layer broadcasts at that interface.

```
2501-1(config-if)#no ip directed-broadcast
```

Do networks out there act in this manner? You bet. Visit http://www.netscan.org to view a list of what that site calls the "most egregious offenders," those sites that have failed to configure their routers and firewalls to disable IP directed broadcasts. This organization performs network scans to find those sites that could unintentionally act as a Smurf amplifier. You can find a similar list at http//www.pulltheplug.com/broadcasts.html. Make sure you configure your router so that you do not end up on their lists.

Cisco also recommends that you use the `ip verify unicast reverse-path` global configuration command to prevent DoS attacks such as Smurf. This forces a match of the routing entries in the Cisco Express Forwarding (CEF) table against the source IP address of the incoming packets. When there is no return route out of the interface, the router will drop the packet. You must enable CEF on your router as well.

To find out whether you are a potential Smurf amplifier, get yourself Fyodor's nmap program and run the following command:

```
nmap -n -sP -PI -o smurf.log
'209.12.*.0,63,64,127,128,191,192,255'
```

Controlling TCP and UDP Small Services

By default, Cisco devices up through IOS version 11.3 offer the small TCP and UDP services: echo, chargen, and discard. You will rarely use these services, especially the UDP versions, for legitimate purposes, but attackers will use them to launch DoS and other attacks that you could otherwise prevent by packet filtering. In fact, the notorious Fraggle denial-of-service attack exploits echo (port 7) over UDP.

Note: Perhaps you have not heard of Fraggle, Bonk, Boink, Land, Teardrop, Teardrop 2, New Teardrop, Bubonic, Smurf, Papa Smurf, Ping of Death, and the remainder of the gang. Well, mosey on over to http://www.rootshell.com. This Web site offers thousands of exploit scripts, code, and programs for your downloading pleasure. Makes gift-giving a lot easier this year.

For example, an attacker might send a DNS packet, falsifying the source address to a DNS server that is otherwise unreachable and falsifying the source port as the DNS service port (port 53). If the attacker sends such a packet to the Cisco's

UDP echo port, this is equivalent to the router sending a DNS packet to the server in question. So, the router would not apply any outgoing access list checks to this packet because the router would consider it locally generated by the router itself.

Although you can avoid most abuses of the small services or make them less dangerous by anti-spoofing access lists, you should disable the services in any router that is part of your firewall system or lies in a high-security portion of your organization. Because you rarely use the services, adopt the policy of disabling the services on all routers of any description.

Cisco disabled the small services by default in IOS 12.0 and later software. In earlier software, you can disable them using the following commands.

```
2501-1(config)#no service tcp-small-servers
2501-1(config)#no service udp-small-servers
```

Controlling IP Source Routing

The IP protocol supports source routing options that allow the sender of an IP datagram to control the route that datagram will take toward its ultimate destination, and generally the route that any reply will take. Network professionals rarely use these options for legitimate purposes in real networks. When an address uses source routing, it can send and receive traffic through the firewall router. You should use the following command unless you know that your network absolutely needs source routing.

```
2501-1(config)#no ip source-route
```

Controlling ICMP Redirects

Your anti-spoofing access list should filter out all ICMP redirects, regardless of source or destination address. An ICMP redirect message instructs an end node to use a specific router as its path to a particular destination. In a properly functioning IP network, a router will send redirects only to hosts on its own local subnets; no end node will ever send a redirect; and no redirect will ever traverse more than one network hop. However, an attacker might violate these rules; some attacks are based on this. So write the following rule to block redirects.

```
2501-1(config)#ip access-list access-list-number deny icmp
    any any redirect
```

Controlling Unreachable Messages

By default, when a router receives a non-broadcast packet with an unrecognized protocol whose destination address belongs to that router, it will send an ICMP Protocol Unreachable message back to the source. A router will also send back an ICMP Host Unreachable message should it receive a packet whose destination address is unknown. While seemingly reasonable, this opens the router up to

DoS attacks using ICMP. When a router spends all its time responding with ICMP messages, it cannot do much real processing.

You should prevent your router from sending out ICMP Host and Protocol Unreachable messages with the following interface command:

```
2501-1(config-if)#no ip unreachable
```

Controlling Proxy ARP

In Chapter 2, you learned about the Address Resolution Protocol (ARP) and the Reverse ARP. Well, there is also Proxy ARP. In this case, a device answers an ARP request destined for another device when that MAC address is known. When a proxy ARP device (e.g., a router) sees an ARP request for a host on a different network, the router responds to the ARP and then forwards the request to the remote network. Attackers have used Proxy ARP to launch a DoS attack that uses available bandwidth and router resources responding to repeated ARP requests. You can disable Proxy ARP with the following interface configuration command.

```
2501-1(config-if)#no ip proxy-arp
```

Managing the Floods

Locating your router in the fluvial floodplain of the Mississippi River is probably not a good idea; but a deluge of water is not the flood referenced here. Many DoS attacks rely on floods of useless packets. Recall Chapter 2, Exhibit 9; this diagram is shown here as Exhibit 1. The three-way handshake comes to a natural conclusion with each node setting the right acknowledgment numbers and code bits. But look at that diagram again. What do you suppose happens when the receiving Host B cannot send the acknowledgment packet back because the source address is unresolveable? Host B will start a process and eventually time it out. But if Host A is dastardly, it could send so many packets that the receiving system consumes all its resources. This may cause the system to crash, or it may just consume all the resources on the system so that legitimate clients cannot get in.

These floods congest network links, slow down hosts, and can also overload routers. Cisco provides the TCP Intercept feature specifically to reduce the impact of SYN-flooding attacks on hosts. The feature is available in certain software versions for many routers with model numbers of 4000 or greater. SYN-flood protection can be complex and results can vary, depending on flood rate, router speed and memory size, and the hosts you use.

About TCP Intercept

TCP Intercept tracks, intercepts, and validates TCP connection requests. This shields your host from direct contact by a nontrusted network or host. The TCP Intercept feature implements software to protect TCP servers from TCP SYN-flooding attacks, which are a type of denial-of-service attack. SYN-flooding occurs when a hacker floods a server with a barrage of requests for connection. Because

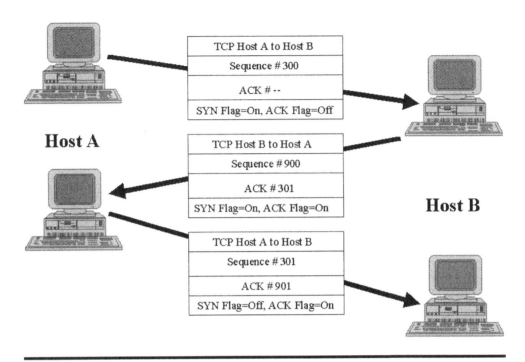

Exhibit 1   The TCP Three-Way Handshake

these messages have unreachable return addresses, the server cannot establish the connections. The resulting volume of unresolved open connections eventually overwhelms the server and can cause it to deny service to valid requests, thereby preventing legitimate users from connecting to your Web site, accessing e-mail, using FTP service, etc.

The TCP Intercept feature helps prevent SYN-flooding attacks by intercepting and validating TCP connection requests. TCP Intercept operates in one of two modes — intercept or watch mode — but the default is intercept. In intercept mode, the TCP Intercept software intercepts TCP synchronization (SYN) packets from clients to servers that match an extended access list. The software establishes a connection with the client on behalf of the destination server and, when successful, establishes the connection with the server on behalf of the client and knits the two half-connections together transparently. Thus, connection attempts from unreachable hosts will never reach the server. The software continues to intercept and forward packets throughout the duration of the connection.

In the case of illegitimate requests, the software's aggressive timeouts on half-open connections and its thresholds on TCP connection requests protect destination servers while still allowing valid requests.

When establishing your security policy using TCP Intercept, you can choose to intercept all requests or only those coming from specific networks or destined for specific servers. You can also configure the connection rate and threshold of outstanding connections.

You can choose to operate TCP Intercept in watch mode, as opposed to intercept mode. In watch mode, the software passively watches the connection requests flowing through the router. If a connection fails to get established in a configurable interval, the software intervenes and terminates the connection attempt.

The router cannot handle TCP options negotiated on handshake (such as RFC 1323 on window scaling) because the TCP Intercept software does not know what the server can do or will negotiate.

Exceeding preset thresholds in either mode causes aggressive behavior mode to start. During aggressive behavior mode, new connection attempts force a drop of an existing partial connection. Additionally, the retransmission and watch timeouts are cut in half. When the number of incomplete connections surpasses 1100, or it gets a surge of over 1100 connections in 60 seconds (by default), the router will delete the oldest connection request and then reduce retransmission time by 50 percent. Dropping back below another set of thresholds causes the router to revert back to normal.

Configuring TCP Intercept

Now that you know TCP Intercept concepts, it is time to configure the router. You perform the following tasks to configure TCP Intercept. You must perform the first task; the remaining are optional.

■ Enable TCP Intercept.
■ Set the TCP intercept mode.
■ Set the TCP Intercept drop mode.
■ Change the TCP intercept timers.
■ Change the TCP Intercept aggressive thresholds.
■ Monitor and maintain TCP Intercept.

Enabling TCP Intercept

To enable TCP intercept, you must perform these two steps:

1. Define an IP extended access list.
2. Enable the TCP Intercept.

This means that you perform the following tasks in global configuration mode:

```
4500(config)#access-list access-list-number {deny | permit}
  tcp any destination destination-wildcard
4500(config)#ip tcp intercept list {access-list-number | name}
```

You can define an access list to intercept all requests or only those coming from specific networks or destined for specific servers. The access-list-number is a value from 100 to 199. Typically, the access list will define the source as any and define specific destination networks or servers. That is, you do not attempt to filter on the source addresses because you do not necessarily know from where to intercept packets. You identify the destination to protect destination servers.

If the IOS finds no access list match, the router allows the request to pass with no further action.

Setting the TCP Intercept Mode

As mentioned, TCP Intercept can operate in either active intercept mode or passive watch mode. The default is intercept mode.

In intercept mode, the software actively intercepts each incoming connection request (SYN), responds on behalf of the server with an ACK and SYN, and then waits for an ACK of the SYN from the client. When the router receives that ACK, the original SYN is set to the server and the software performs a three-way handshake with the server. When this is complete, the router joins the two half-connections.

In watch mode, the router allows connection requests to pass through the router to the server but watches until they become established. If they fail to become established within 30 seconds (configurable with the `ip tcp intercept watch-timeout` command), the software sends a Reset to the server to clear up its state.

To set the TCP intercept mode, perform the following task in global configuration mode:

```
4500(config)#ip tcp intercept mode {intercept | watch}
```

Setting the TCP Intercept Drop Mode

When under attack, the TCP Intercept feature becomes more aggressive in its protective behavior. If the number of incomplete connections exceeds 1100 or the number of connections arriving in the last one minute exceeds 1100, each new arriving connection causes the router to delete the oldest partial connection. Also, the software reduces the initial retransmission timeout by half to 0.5 seconds (therefore, the total time trying to establish a connection is cut in half).

By default, the software drops the oldest partial connection. Alternatively, you can configure the software to drop a random connection. To set the drop mode, perform the following task in global configuration mode:

```
4500(config)#ip tcp intercept drop-mode {oldest | random}
```

Changing the TCP Intercept Timers

By default, the software waits for 30 seconds for a watched connection to reach established state before sending a Reset to the server. To change this value, perform the following task in global configuration mode:

```
4500(config)#ip tcp intercept watch-timeout seconds
```

By default, the software waits for 5 seconds from receipt of a reset or FIN-exchange before it ceases to manage the connection. To change this value, perform the following task in global configuration mode:

```
4500(config)#ip tcp intercept finrst-timeout seconds
```

By default, the software still manages a connection for 24 hours after no activity. To change this value, perform the following task in global configuration mode:

```
4500(config)#ip tcp intercept connection-timeout seconds
```

The value for the `seconds` keyword in all the commands above is a number from 1 to 2,147,483.

Changing the TCP Intercept Aggressive Thresholds

Two factors determine when aggressive behavior begins and ends: total incomplete connections and connection requests during the last one-minute sample period. Both thresholds have default values that you can reconfigure.

When activity exceeds a threshold, the TCP intercept assumes the server is under attack and goes into aggressive mode. When in aggressive mode, the following occurs:

- Each new arriving connection causes the oldest partial connection to be deleted. (You can change to a random drop mode.)
- The router reduces the initial retransmission timeout by half to 0.5 seconds, and so the total time trying to establish the connection is cut in half. When not in aggressive mode, the code does an exponential back-off on its retransmissions of SYN segments. The initial retransmission timeout is 1 second. The subsequent timeouts are 2 seconds, 4 seconds, 8 seconds, and 16 seconds. The code retransmits four times before giving up, so it gives up after 31 seconds without an acknowledgment.
- When in watch mode, the router reduces the watch timeout by half. If the default is in place, the watch timeout becomes 15 seconds.

You can change the drop strategy from the oldest connection to a random connection with the `ip tcp intercept drop-mode` command.

Note: The two factors determining aggressive behavior are related and work together. When either of the high values is exceeded, aggressive behavior begins. When both quantities fall below the low value, aggressive behavior ends.

You can change the threshold for triggering aggressive mode based on the total number of incomplete connections. The default values for low and high are 900 and 1100 incomplete connections, respectively. To change these values, perform the following tasks in global configuration mode:

```
4500(config)#ip tcp intercept max-incomplete low number
4500(config)#ip tcp intercept max-incomplete high number
```

You can also change the threshold for triggering aggressive mode based on the number of connection requests received in the last 1-minute sample period. The default values for low and high are 900 and 1100 connection requests, respectively. To change these values, perform the following tasks in global configuration mode:

```
4500(config)#ip tcp intercept one-minute low number
4500(config)#ip tcp intercept one-minute high number
```

The value for the number keyword in all of the commands above is a number from 1 to 2,147,483,647.

Now that you know all the commands, take a look at some simple examples. The following applies the TCP Intercept feature to access list 1 with the following features:

- Waits 30 seconds for connection to reach established state before sending a Reset.
- Waits 5 seconds from FIN or RST before ending connection management.
- Manages connection for 24 hours after inactivity.

```
4500(config)#ip tcp intercept list 1
4500(config)#ip tcp intercept watch-timeout 30
4500(config)#ip tcp intercept finrst-timeout 5
4500(config)#ip tcp intercept connection-timeout 86400
```

The following configuration defines extended IP access list 100, causing the software to intercept packets for all TCP servers on the 192.168.1.0/24 subnet:

```
4500(config)#ip tcp intercept list 100
4500(config)#access-list 100 permit tcp any 192.168.1.0
  0.0.0.255
```

Monitoring and Maintaining TCP Intercept

To display TCP intercept information, perform either of the following tasks in EXEC mode:

```
4500#show tcp intercept connections
```

This command displays incomplete connections and established connections.

```
4500#show tcp intercept statistics
```

This command displays TCP intercept statistics.

Another technique against DoS is network address translation (NAT).

About Network Address Translation

When you isolate your network from the outside world, you can use any address you choose. While it is prudent to use the private addresses specified in RFC 1918 (refer to http://www.normos.org/ietf/rfc/rfc1918.txt), nothing will happen if you do not. The problems occur when you connect your network to the outside world. Then you must use unique IP addresses. If you decide not to change your non-unique addresses or decide to use the private addresses specified in the RFC, you will need to do network address translation (NAT).

You can use NAT to translate the private address ranges dynamically to globally unique addresses. NAT allows you to translate these nonroutable addresses statically or dynamically to Internet-routable addresses. NAT sits between your network and the Internet, or between two organizations' networks, and translates IP addresses from private or illegal addressees to globally unique external addresses. The benefit of NAT for your organization is that you do not need to have a one-to-one relationship for your addresses. You can translate a large number of illegal addresses into a small number of legal ones.

You can also benefit from NAT by hiding your internal network. The attackers cannot see your internal network behind the router. If you use private addresses, the attackers cannot send packets to those addresses anyhow.

The concept behind NAT revolves around a few basic features:

- *Inside local addresses.* You can translate private Internet-illegal addresses to Internet-legal addresses.
- *Inside global addresses.* You can translate the Internet-legal addresses your organization uses for Internet access to inside local addresses.
- *Outside global addresses.* These are Internet-legal addresses used by hosts that are not part of your organization and that you are not translating.
- *Outside local addresses.* These are Internet-illegal addresses or private addresses that other organizations are using.

To facilitate simple Internet access, your organization need only translate inside local addresses to inside global addresses. Your router running the NAT service will change any source address in packets going out of your organization from an inside local to an inside global address. The router will maintain a dynamic table that associates these addresses to each other.

The Advantages and Disadvantages of NAT

Of course, NAT allows you to provide Internet access to a large number of clients when you only have a small number of legal addresses available, but NAT provides the following benefits as well:

- Because NAT provides translations from a single exit interface, it will hide your internal network structure from prying eyes. NAT does not replace a firewall system, but can improve your overall security posture. NAT performs a firewalling function, acting like a proxy server.

Caution: So as not to unnecessarily perpetuate the urban myth that NAT hides the internal network, some precautionary words. Your ISP may have helped you set up your network and addressing scheme and so has knowledge of that private network. Thus, they can insert a route to that network into their routing tables, thereby exposing your private network. NAT simply allows the router to translate private IP addresses into global IP addresses. That is all! No more, no less.

- You do not have to decide whether to use provider-assigned or provider-independent addresses for your internal network. You use private addresses for the internal network and provider-assigned addresses for the external address pool that NAT controls.
- NAT makes migration from one ISP to another relatively painless. Although your ISP owns your IP addresses, you can easily move from one ISP to another because all you have to do is update one entry in a DNS server somewhere. If you have a large number of static IP addresses, then moving from one ISP to another is a formidable task without NAT. You could use NAT to temporarily translate these static addresses to your new address range.
- You can use an internal address space as large as you want and need. In today's environment, you cannot not get your hands on a Class A or Class B network. You might get a few hundred, maybe a thousand or so. But using the Class A private addresses, you get 16,777,214 hosts!
- You can use the Easy IP feature of the IOS to assign IP addresses dynamically using PPP. Thus, you can subscribe to an ISP and get one dial-up account that provides only dynamic IP addresses and configure your router to translate that one address to a number of inside local addresses. The IOS will overload addresses to share that dial-up account among many users.
- You can use NAT to accomplish simple TCP load distribution because you can translate one IP address to many IP addresses to create a server farm. Just translate the external advertised address for your Web site on a round-robin basis to distribute the traffic across multiple hosts.

Not everything is perfect with NAT, as proven by the following disadvantages:

- If you use NAT, remember that the router becomes a stateful device that maintains the state of every connection requiring address translation. While beneficial, it also is your Achilles heel because your NAT device becomes a single point of failure.
- There are performance issues with NAT although the device basically acts like a proxy server. The IP has a header checksum (see Exhibit 5 in Chapter 2) that includes the source and destination addresses. The Internet layer must recalculate the checksum when the addresses change. This is not the problem because this happens every time the router changes any

value in the header. TCP and UDP also define checksums covering the packet's data and a pseudo-header containing the source and destination IP addresses. When you change these addresses, the router must update the checksum. While the IP header checksum typically only calculates about 20 bytes of header information, a TCP or UDP checksum calculates a value for all the data in the packet. Recomputing this checksum is a little more processor-intensive. You will most likely not have serious performance issues when you have no more than a T1 (or E1) line. But again, you need to do the tough stuff. You need to ensure that the benefits of using NAT outweigh the costs.

- Some application protocols that embed IP addresses inside the application will not work with NAT unless the protocol developer specifically supports NAT.
- Multi-channel applications such as FTP, H.323, SIP, and RTSP (discussed in Chapter 18) are problematic for NAT. NAT would treat the two channels as unrelated and fail.
- Access control based on source IP address is difficult when using NAT. This is especially true when using overloading because many hosts will share the same IP source address.
- You cannot use IPSec through NAT. The Authentication Protocol, by definition, detects alterations to an IP packet header. Thus, the receiving host will discard the packet because AH will show the packet as altered.

The next section explains how to configure network address translation (NAT) on a Cisco router for use in common network scenarios.

Configuring and Deploying NAT

The following steps guide you through defining what you want NAT to do and how to configure it.

1. Define NAT inside and outside interfaces. You need to establish which interfaces are inside and which are outside. Think of inside as referring to your internal network, and outside as referring to the Internet side of the router. Try to answer these questions about your interfaces:
   a. Do users exist off multiple interfaces?
   b. Are there multiple interfaces going to the Internet?
2. Define what you are trying to accomplish with NAT.
   a. Are you trying to allow internal users to access the Internet?
   b. Are you trying to allow the Internet to access internal devices (such as a mail server or Web server)?
   c. Are you trying to redirect TCP traffic to another TCP port or address?
   d. Are you using NAT during a network transition? For example, you changed a server's IP address and until you can update all the clients, you want the non-updated clients to access the server using the original IP address and you want the updated clients to access the same server using the new address.
   e. Are you using NAT to allow overlapping networks to communicate?

Exhibit 2   NAT Types and Features

NAT Types	Address Mapping	Public-to-Private Address Mapping	Required Public Addresses
Static NAT	Static	One-to-one	One public IP address per host
Traditional or dynamic NAT	Dynamic	One-to-one	One public IP address per host simultaneously accessing the external network
NAT or overloading	Dynamic	One-to-many	One public IP address per 64,000 simultaneous sessions

3. Configure NAT to accomplish what you defined above. Based on what you defined in Step 2, you need to determine what features to use. Exhibit 2 summarizes the following NAT features.

   a. *Static address translation:* a one-to-one mapping of an internal address to an external legal address. Use this in the case where you have systems, such as a Web server, accessible from the outside world. Thus, you could assign a private IP address to your Web server but you would need to translate the address to make it accessible to your clients.

   b. *Dynamic address translation:* translates local address to external address from a pool. You need to set up the pool of outside addresses for allocation equal to the number of addresses you need to translate. The router will create the translations as required.

   c. *Address overloading:* allows you to conserve IP addresses by allowing multiple addresses to translate to the same address. With overloading, you could make it look like all Internet traffic has the same source address. Address overloading uses TCP and UDP port numbers to track what traffic belongs to which internal host.

   e. Any combination of the above.

4. Cisco IOS 11.2 and above support these features. Some questions to reflect upon:

   a. What type of addressing scheme are you using on the inside network?

   b. How many inside devices do you need to statically translate?

   c. Should you use overloading only, or use it once the router exhausts all the addresses in the NAT pool?

5. Verify NAT operation.

Defining NAT Inside and Outside Interfaces

The first step in deploying NAT is to define NAT inside and outside interfaces. You may find it easy to define your internal network as inside and the external network as outside. However, the terms "internal" and "external" are subject to debate as well.

For example, you may want to allow internal users to access the Internet, but you may not have enough valid addresses to accommodate everyone. If all communication with devices in the Internet will originate from the internal devices, then you need a single valid address or a pool of valid addresses.

To configure network address translation, you use the `ip nat {inside |` `outside}` command as follows.

```
2501-1(config)#ip nat inside
2501-1(config)#ip nat outside
```

The first command translates:

- The source of IP packets traveling inside to outside
- The destination of the IP packets traveling outside to inside

The second command translates:

- The source of the IP packets traveling outside to inside
- The destination of the IP packets traveling inside to outside

For example, you want NAT to allow certain devices (the first 31 from each subnet) on the inside to originate communication with devices on the outside by translating their invalid address to a valid address or pool of addresses. You have defined the pool as the range of addresses 172.16.10.1 through 172.16.10.63. Now you are ready to configure NAT. To accomplish what was defined above, you need to use dynamic NAT. With dynamic NAT, the translation table in the router is initially empty and gets populated once traffic that needs translation passes through the router. (This is different from static NAT, where you statically configure a translation and place it in the translation table without the need for any traffic). The first thing you need to do is define the Ethernet segments 0 and 1 with an IP address and as a NAT inside interface.

```
2501-1(config)#interface ethernet 0
2501-1(config-if)#ip address 10.10.10.1 255.255.255.0
2501-1(config-if)#ip nat inside
2501-1(config-if)#exit
2501-1(config)#interface ethernet 1
2501-1(config-if)#ip address 10.10.20.1 255.255.255.0
2501-1(config-if)#ip nat inside
```

The next commands define serial 0 with an IP address and as a NAT outside interface.

```
2501-1(config-if)#interface serial 0
2501-1(config-if)#ip address 172.16.10.64 255.255.255.0
2501-1(config-if)#ip nat outside
2501-1(config-if)#exit
```

Next, you define a NAT pool named no-overload with a range of addresses from 172.16.10.1 to 172.16.10.63. This sets up the pool of addresses for dynamic address translation.

```
2501-1(config)#ip nat pool no-overload 172.16.10.1
  172.16.10.63 prefix 24
```

The format of this command is ip nat pool name *start-ip-address*
end-ip-address {netmask *netmask* | prefix-length *prefix-
length*} {*type rotary*]. Keywords type rotary specify that the range
of addresses in the address pool identify real inside hosts among which TCP load
distribution will occur.

Use the next command to indicate that the IOS will translate the source address
for any packets it receives on the inside interface permitted by access-list 1 to an
address out of the NAT pool "no-overload."

```
2501-1(config)#ip nat inside source list 1 pool no-overload
```

The format of this command is ip nat source {list {*access-list-
number* | *name*} pool name [overload] | static local-ip-
address global-ip-address].

You must now create access-list 1 and permit packets with source addresses
ranging from 10.10.10.0 through 10.10.10.31, and 10.10.20.0 through 10.10.20.31.

```
2501-1(config)#access-list 1 permit 10.10.10.0 0.0.0.31
2501-1(config)#access-list 1 permit 10.10.20.0 0.0.0.31
```

Caution: Do not configure access lists referenced by NAT commands
with permit any. Using permit any can result in NAT consuming too
many router resources, which can cause network problems.

Notice in the above configuration that only the first 32 addresses from subnet
10.10.10.0 and the first 32 addresses from subnet 10.10.20.0 are permitted by
access-list 1. Therefore, the IOS will translate only these source addresses. There
may be other devices with other addresses on the inside network, but the IOS
will not translate them.

Once you have set up the access list to define those addresses needing translation,
you should set up the translation parameters in global configuration mode:

```
2501-1(config)#ip nat translation timeout 3600
2501-1(config)#ip nat translation tcp-timeout 3600
2501-1(config)#ip nat translation udp-timeout 240
2501-1(config)#ip nat translation finrst-timeout 30
2501-1(config)#ip nat translation dns-timeout 45
```

The above commands solve one of the problems of using NAT. NAT has
trouble determining when a connection ends so that the IOS can free the allocated
IP addresses. For TCP, this is relatively simple but UDP is a little more difficult.
The first command sets the translation timeout to 3600 seconds (1 hour); the
default is 24 hours. The second line sets the TCP timeout to 3600 seconds (1 hour)
as well; the default is 24 hours. This keyword specifies when TCP port translations

will time out. The udp-timeout keyword works in the same way as the tcp-timeout keyword; however, the default timeout for UDP is 300 seconds (5 minutes). You set it to 240 seconds (4 minutes) with the command above. The finrst-timeout keyword specifies the timeout value that applies to the FIN and RST TCP packets used to terminate a connection. The default is 60 seconds and you have set it to 30 seconds. Finally, the dns-timeout keyword specifies how long it will take for connections to a DNS server to time out. The default value is 60 seconds but you lowered it to 45 seconds. If you want to use the defaults, you need do nothing. But you might want to change them because the defaults are very conservative. You should realize that the timeouts do not work with static or overload translation. More often than not, you will use overloading or static translations, so you usually do not need to worry about timeout values. But they do exist, and they are helpful for dynamic translations.

In the next example, you can configure NAT to translate each of the inside devices to the same valid address. This method is known as *overloading*. Again, you define Ethernet 0 and Ethernet 1 with an IP address and as a NAT inside interface:

```
2501-1(config)#interface ethernet 0
2501-1(config-if)#ip address 10.10.10.1 255.255.255.0
2501-1(config-if)#ip nat inside
2501-1(config-if)#exit
2501-1(config)#interface ethernet 1
2501-1(config-if)#ip address 10.10.20.1 255.255.255.0
2501-1(config-if)#ip nat inside
2501-1(config-if)#exit
```

Next, you define serial 0 with an IP address and as a NAT outside interface.

```
2501-1(config)#interface serial 0
2501-1(config-if)#ip address 172.16.10.64 255.255.255.0
2501-1(config-if)#ip nat outside
```

You must define a NAT pool with a range of a single IP address, 172.16.10.1. You must name the pool; here, it is ovrld.

```
2501-1(config-if)#ip nat pool ovrld 172.16.10.1 172.16.10.1
  prefix 24
```

Next, indicate that any packets received on the inside interface permitted by access-list 1 will have the source address translated to an address out of the NAT pool named ovrld. The IOS will overload translations allowing multiple inside hosts to share the same valid IP address.

```
2501-1(config-if)#ip nat inside source list 1 pool ovrld
  overload
```

Next, write the access lists to permits packets with source addresses ranging from 10.10.10.0 through 10.10.10.31, and 10.10.20.0 through 10.10.20.31.

```
2501-1(config-if)#access-list 1 permit 10.10.10.0 0.0.0.31
2501-1(config-if)#access-list 1 permit 10.10.20.0 0.0.0.31
```

Take note that the nat pool ovrld only has a range of one address. The keyword overload used in the ip nat inside source list 1 pool ovrld overload command allows NAT to translate multiple inside devices to the single address in the pool.

You could also use the ip nat inside source list 1 interface serial 0 overload command, which configures NAT to overload on the address you assigned to the serial 0 interface.

When you configure overloading, the router maintains enough information from higher-level protocols (e.g., TCP or UDP port numbers) to translate the global address back to the correct local address. When multiple local addresses map to one global address, the TCP or UDP port numbers of each inside host distinguish between the local addresses.

The final step is to verify that NAT is operating as intended.

Take a look at one more example in which you can redirect TCP traffic to another TCP port or address. You have a Web server on the internal network with which you want devices on the Internet to initiate communication. You could configure the internal Web server to listen for Web traffic on a TCP port other than port 80. For example, you could configure the internal Web server to listen on TCP port 8080. In this case, you could use NAT to redirect traffic destined to TCP port 80 to TCP port 8080.

You decide that you want NAT to redirect packets from the outside destined for 172.16.10.8:80 to 172.16.10.8:8080. You can achieve your goal using a static nat command to translate the TCP port number. A sample configuration follows. First, you must define Ethernet 0 with an IP address and as a NAT inside interface, and serial 0 with an IP address and as a NAT outside interface.

```
2501-1(config)#interface ethernet 0
2501-1(config-if)#ip address 172.16.10.1 255.255.255.0
2501-1(config-if)#ip nat inside
2501-1(config-if)#interface serial 0
2501-1(config-if)#ip address 200.200.200.5 255.255.255.252
2501-1(config-if)#ip nat outside
```

Now you use the static nat command to specify that the IOS will translate any packet received by the inside interface with a source address of 172.16.10.8:8080 to 172.16.10.8:80.

```
2501-1(config-if)#ip nat inside source static tcp
   172.16.10.8 8080 172.16.10.8 80
```

Note: The configuration description for the static nat command indicates the IOS will translate any packet received in the inside interface with a source address of 172.16.10.8:8080 to 172.16.10.8:80.

Exhibit 3   Show Commands

Command	Description
`show ip nat statistics`	Displays NAT statistics; you will see the active total translations, outside interfaces, inside interfaces, hits or translations, misses or creations, and expired translations
`show ip nat translations [verbose]`	Displays NAT translations; the `verbose` keyword optionally displays additional information for every table entry, including the age of the entry and the last time used

This also implies that the IOS will translate any packet received on the outside interface with a destination address of 172.16.10.8:80 to the destination 172.16.10.8:8080.

The final step is to verify that NAT is operating as intended.

Verifying NAT Operation

Once you have configured NAT, verify that it is operating as intended and expected. You can do this in a number of ways: using a network analyzer, debug commands, or show commands. You can use the show commands shown in Exhibit 3.

NAT often increases the complexity of debugging tasks because you will have translated addresses.

Queuing and Traffic Policing

Cisco provides other technologies that can help you battle denial-of-service (DoS) attacks and enhance performance. You can manage traffic flows in a network by enabling queuing and traffic policing methods to limit particular traffic. This section focuses on queuing and traffic policing.

Queuing

Collectively known as queuing technologies, these features can help manage congestion on a router interface by determining the order for transmitting packets out, based on the priorities you put on those packets. You can control the traffic allowed through a router interface in preference to other traffic. These technologies are useful when you have more data to send than the router can actually send, or when you have traffic congestion on an interface. When you have no congestion, using queuing techniques serves little purpose. There are four types of queues:

- First in, first out (FIFO)
- Weighted fair queuing (WFQ)
- Custom queuing (CQ)
- Priority queuing (PQ)

FIFO is the fastest queuing method and is the default for interfaces with speeds greater than 2.048 Mbps (E1 capacity). WFQ uses a scheduling method that provides a fair allocation of bandwidth to all network traffic. The method applies a priority to traffic so that it can classify traffic into conversations and determine traffic requirements for each conversation vis-à-vis other conversations. It uses a flow-based algorithm that moves interactive traffic (such as Telnet) to the front of the queues to reduce response time and fairly shares the remaining bandwidth among high-traffic flows.

There is one WFQ command you need.

```
2501-1(config)#fair-queue discard-threshold dynamic-queue-
   number reserved-conversations-number
```

The defaults for the parameters are 64, 256 and 0. Do not change the values unless you have a good reason.

CQ allows you to create up to 16 queues and to specify the number of bytes to forward from each queue. You can allocate resources to applications that require a certain fixed amount of bandwidth. Additionally, you can specify the maximum number of packets in each queue, further allowing you control the traffic available to each queue. CQ cycles through each queue in round-robin fashion. When a queue is empty, it moves to the next queue. When it is not, CQ services each queue until either the byte count limit for the queue is reached or the queue is empty. There are actually 17 queues, with Queue 0 reserved for the system.

There are four CQ commands you need.

```
2501-1(config)#queue-list list-number interface interface-
   type interface-number queue-number
```

This command assigns packets arriving on an interface to a queue.

```
2501-1(config)#queue-list list-number protocol protocol-name
   queue-number queue-keyword keyword-value
```

Possible values for queue-keyword are shown in Exhibit 4. Use this command to assign packets with a certain packet size to a queue.

```
2501-1(config)#queue-list list-number queue queue-number
   byte-count byte-count-number
```

You can use the above command to set the number of bytes that you allow each queue to transfer when the router services it.

Exhibit 4   Keywords

Keyword	Description
gt	Greater than a certain byte count
lt	Less than a certain byte count
tcp	TCP port to match (either source or destination)
udp	UDP port to match (either source or destination)
fragments	IP fragments

```
2501-1(config)#queue-list list-number queue queue-number
  limit limit-number
```

Finally, the previous command allows you to set the number of packets stored in a queue.

Note: When using custom queuing, do not forget to specify a default queue.

Once you create queues and assign appropriate byte-count and packet-limit sizes, you apply the queue to an interface using the following commands:

```
2501-1(config)#interface interface-type interface-number
2501-1(config-if)#custom-queue-list list-number
```

PQ is similar to CQ, except an individual queue can dominate other queues. You do not have 16 queues but rather high, medium, normal, and low. The router will service all the traffic in a higher-level queue before servicing a lower-level queue. You can classify how the router places traffic in a queue based on protocol, protocol access list, incoming interface, or packet size. The IOS always places interface keepalives in the high-priority queue. You must explicitly allocate all other traffic; otherwise, it ends up in the normal queue.

There are four priority queuing (PQ) commands you need.

```
2501-1(config)#priority-list list-number protocol protocol-
  name {high | medium | normal | low} queue-keyword keyword-
  value
```

This command allows you to assign a particular protocol (AppleTalk, IP, IPX, etc.) to one of the priority queues. You can optionally specify a keyword such as list to specify the use of an access list or one of the keywords in Exhibit 4.

```
2501-1(config)#priority-list list-number interface
  interface-name {high | medium | normal | low}
```

You can use this command to assign packets arriving on a particular router interface to a queue.

```
2501-1(config)#priority-list list-number default {high |
   medium | normal | low}
```

Use the previous command to set up a default queue where you do not have explicit queue statements.

```
2501-1(config)#priority-list list-number queue-limit [high-
   limit [medium-limit [normal-limit [low-limit]]]]
```

This command allows you to change the packet-limit counts for each of the queues. The limit is any value from 0 to 32,767. The default values for the queues are 20, 40, 60, and 80 datagrams, respectively.

Once you create queues and assign appropriate byte-count and packet-limit sizes, you apply the queue to an interface using the following commands:

```
2501-1(config)#interface interface-type interface-number
2501-1(config-if)#priority-group list-number
```

Note: When creating a priority list, do not forget to specify a default queue.

A complete discussion of queuing is beyond the scope of this book, but take a look at how you could use priority queuing. You want to ensure that your application running on TCP port 666 gets sufficient bandwidth.

```
2501-1(config)#interface serial0
2501-1(config-if)#priority-group 1
2501-1(config-if)#priority-list 1 protocol ip high tcp 666
2501-1(config-if)#priority-list 1 protocol ip normal
2501-1(config-if)#priority-list 1 queue-limit 40 40 60 80
```

This devilishly simple set of commands provides our application precedence over other applications. It also sets queue limits.

Use your imagination and you can see how you can limit the impact of denial-of-service attacks on your organization by placing them in low-priority queues.

Traffic Policing

Traffic policing refers to the features that allow a device to strictly limit the amount of traffic the router will send or receive on an interface. Cisco calls its traffic policing software Committed Access Rate (CAR). CAR services limit the input or output transmission rate on an interface based on various criteria. Typically, you would configure CAR at the edge of your network, such as the Internet connection between ISPs or between an ISP and a customer. Cisco recommends that you use CAR on your routers to limit inbound levels of ICMP traffic. You can also reduce the amount of SYN traffic to help against SYN-flooding and distributed DoS attacks.

CAR can limit traffic based on IP precedence, incoming interface, or an IP access list. You can configure the action that CAR takes when traffic exceeds its allocated limit, such as dropping the connection or resetting its precedence value.

Configuring CAR

When configuring CAR, you must first determine the average bits per second (bps) for normal traffic flow. Then you define a normal burst rate and an exceed burst rate. You allow traffic to burst above the normal rate up to the normal burst rate. The router may discard any traffic exceeding the normal rate plus the normal burst rate. The probability that it will discard the traffic increases until the traffic reaches the value of the normal rate plus the exceed burst rate. Once traffic exceeds the value of the normal rate plus the exceed burst rate, the router will discard all traffic. Wow! Maybe some numbers will help with that. The normal rate is 512,000 bps; the normal burst rate is 56,000 bps; and the exceed burst rate is 64,000 bps. Traffic up to 568,000 bps (i.e., 512,000 + 56,000) still meets the thresholds. Traffic between 568,001 and 576,000 bps exceeds the thresholds and the router may discard the traffic. The router will discard all traffic above 576,000 bps.

To configure CAR, you only need the following interface configuration command.

```
2501-1(config-if)#rate-limit {input | output} [access-group
   [rate-limit] acl-index] bps burst-normal burst-max
   conform-action action exceed-action action
```

The conform and exceed actions are one of the following:

- Continue; that is, continue with the next rate-limit command
- Drop
- Set-prec-continue; that is, set the IP precedence and continue with the next rate-limit command
- Set-prec-transmit; that is, set the IP precedence and transmit packet
- Transmit

Thus, if you want to apply the example you first saw in this section, you would use the following two commands starting in global configuration mode.

```
2501-1(config)#interface serial0
2501-1(config-if)#rate-limit input 512000 56000 64000
   conform-action transmit exceed-action drop
```

When you are defining CAR for multiple traffic classes, you also must define CAR access lists to classify the traffic you want CAR to police. Following are the command and an example.

```
2501-1(config-if)#access-list rate-limit acl-index
  {precedence | mac-address | mask prec-mask}
2501-1(config-if)#access-list rate-limit 100 4000.1e01.4337
```

If desired, you can use a standard or extended IP access list instead of the preceding rate-limit access list.

You have learned quite a few techniques for preventing in this chapter. You will try some of them in the Practice Section. But before you do, take a look at some more things you can do to improve network availability.

Detecting Unauthorized Configuration Changes

Are you prepared for a network outage caused by a router change? An authorized change that does not work is just as disastrous as an unauthorized change. Fortunately, there is third-party software that can help with this problem.

Tripwire for Routers and Switches can monitor your routers for changes. When Tripwire detects that a device is down or that someone changed a configuration file (whether intentionally or unintentionally; maliciously or accidentally), it will report in detail exactly what changed and when. You could configure Tripwire for Routers and Switches to respond to changes by sending e-mail alerts or restoring changed files to their trusted state.

Tripwire operation is pretty straightforward. After installation, Tripwire for Routers and Switches takes a snapshot of your trusted baseline configuration files. Then periodically, the software runs integrity checks on the routers to determine whether anyone made changes to the start-up or running configuration files. If it finds no changes, you do not need to take action.

However, when it detects changes, it sends an e-mail alert and generates a record describing the changes. It highlights changes in color so that you can examine them against the previous file, line by line in a side-by-side format.

If you approve the detected changes, Tripwire then updates the configuration baseline. If you do not approve the changes, authorized network managers can restore the router to its trusted configuration. You can complete restoration within minutes of an alert. A very nice tool indeed.

Resolving Names

Setting up name resolution properly might also aid in improving network availability. First, you can configure a host table into the router with the `ip host` command. This is a good idea even when you have an available domain name system (DNS) on your network segment. Murphy's law says it will disappear at some time and result in a network outage when your router cannot resolve addresses of the authentication server or other routers. In global configuration mode, use the following command.

```
2501-1(config)#ip host new_york_router 10.10.1.2
2501-1(config)#ip host washington_router 10.20.1.2
```

Put at least your major routers and servers into each router, and update this list as you add new devices. It is well worth the effort the day your network goes down.

In addition, you should configure the router with the local domain name, even if DNS is not yet available:

```
2501-1(config)#ip domain-name pdaconsulting.com
```

If one or more DNS servers are available, configure the router with their addresses:

```
2501-1(config)#ip name-server 10.10.2.1
2501-1(config)#ip name-server 10.20.2.1 172.16.3.2
  192.168.4.3
```

DNS resolution is on by default. If you do not have an available DNS server, it is useful to turn off DNS name resolution using the following command.

```
2501-1(config)#no ip domain-lookup
```

This speeds response in case you make router command entry errors. For example, if you enter an invalid command, the IOS parser makes some assumptions. If you enter a syntactically correct command, the router will execute it. If you do not enter a correct command, the parser assumes you want to start a Telnet session with a host named whatever you incorrectly entered.

Thus, these are just some other ways you can configure or use to ensure the availability of your networks. Now it is time to practice.

Practice Session

In this Practice Session, you will practice the following:

- Logging in
- Saving log data
- Switching modes
- Pasting configuration files
- Configuring denial-of-service controls
- Configuring TCP Intercept
- Configuring priority queuing
- Enabling and saving syslog data
- Logging out

1. Log in to the SimRouter Web page.
2. Double-click on router 2501-1 to telnet to that router. This will open a console session.
3. Enter your **Username** and **Password** at the applicable prompt. These are the ones you set up in Chapter 2. You will need to hit the Enter key twice to get to the > prompt.

4. Again, save the log for your session. To do this, select | Terminal | Start Logging | from the menu bar in the Telnet window. The Telnet client will ask you where you wish to store the log and with what name. Your choice. You are going to save the log so that when you build this configuration file, you can cut-and-paste it in Chapter 22 as a starting point, rather than having to enter the same information each day.

5. Enter the enable mode:

   `2501-1#`**`enable`**

6. When prompted to put in the enable secret password, enter **oscar**.

7. Type **terminal length 0**. This command instructs the router to scroll through long command output without pausing (the —More— message).

8. You will paste the running-config that you saved from yesterday's log. At the 2501-1# prompt, type **config t**.

9. If you did not do this, open your log file with the text editor of your choice (e.g., use | Start | Programs | Accessories | Notepad |). Do a find on sh running-config and copy from the first "!" to "end." At the 2501-1(config)# prompt, paste this configuration.

10. Type **no service tcp-small-servers** and press Enter. This will disable echo, chargen, and discard TCP services.

11. Do the same for the UDP services. Type **no service udp-small-servers** and press Enter.

12. Do not allow anyone to use source routing. Type **no ip source-route** and press Enter.

13. Disable proxy ARP by typing **no ip proxy-arp** and press Enter.

14. Turn on TCP watch mode. Type **ip tcp intercept mode watch** and press Enter.

15. Type **int s0** and press Enter.

16. Apply an access list to prevent SYN-flooding. Type **access-list 1 permit tcp any 10.0.0.0 0.255.255.255** and press Enter.

17. Type **ip tcp intercept list 1** and press Enter. This applies TCP intercept to access list 1.

18. Type **custom-queue-list 1** and press Enter.

19. Set up priority queuing for Lotus Notes traffic. Type **queue-list 1 protocol ip 1 tcp 1352** and press Enter.

20. Put FTP in another queue. Type **queue-list 1 protocol ip 3 tcp ftp** and press Enter.

21. Type **queue-list 1 protocol ip 3 tcp ftp-data** and press Enter.

22. Type **queue-list 1 protocol ip 2** and press Enter.

23. Type **queue-list 1 default 4** and press Enter.

24. Type **queue-list 1 queue 1 byte-count 4500** and press Enter.

25. Set up CAR. Type **rate-limit input 512000 56000 6400 conform-action transmit exceed-action drop** and press Enter.

26. Type **exit**, then **sh tcp intercept statistics** and press Enter.

27. Type **sh running-config** and press Enter. You will use this new configuration to start the next Practice Session.

28. Type **quit** to log out from router 2501-1. Close the Telnet window and return to the SimRouter Topology Map.

29. Click on Log Out on the SimRouter Web page. Edit and save your session log. If you have followed along in the Practice Sessions, you should have a pretty good base configuration. Good luck!

Security and Audit Checklist

1. Has your organization identified denial-of-service threats?
   - Yes
   - No
2. Has your organization quantified the organization's vulnerability to denial-of-service threats?
   - Yes
   - No
3. Has your organization identified controls to eliminate, mitigate, or accept denial-of-service threats?
   - Yes
   - No
4. Does someone in your organization have responsibility for monitoring TCP intercept information?
   - Yes
   - No
5. Is the assignment of this responsibility appropriate?
   - Yes
   - No
6. Does someone in your organization have responsibility for monitoring NAT information?
   - Yes
   - No
7. Is the assignment of this responsibility appropriate?
   - Yes
   - No
8. Do you control directed broadcasts?
   - Yes
   - No
9. Do you control TCP and UDP small services?
   - Yes
   - No
10. Do you control IP source routing?
    - Yes
    - No
11. Do you control ICMP redirects?
    - Yes
    - No
12. Do you control unreachable messages?
    - Yes
    - No

13. Do you control Proxy ARP?
    - Yes
    - No
14. Do you control SYN flooding?
    - Yes
    - No
15. Do you use TCP intercepts?
    - Yes
    - No
16. Have you applied TCP intercepts on all critical interfaces?
    - Yes
    - No
17. Which intercept mode does your organization use?
    - Intercept
    - Watch
18. Is your use of the TCP intercept mode appropriate?
    - Yes
    - No
19. Which intercept drop mode does your organization use?
    - Oldest
    - Random
20. Does your organization use TCP Intercept timers?
    - Yes
    - No
21. Is your use of the TCP intercept watch-timeout appropriate?
    - Yes
    - No
22. Is your use of the TCP intercept first-timeout appropriate?
    - Yes
    - No
23. Is your use of the TCP intercept connection-timeout appropriate?
    - Yes
    - No
24. Is your use of the TCP intercept max-complete low command appropriate?
    - Yes
    - No
25. Is your use of the TCP intercept max-complete high command appropriate?
    - Yes
    - No
26. Is your use of the TCP intercept one-minute low command appropriate?
    - Yes
    - No
27. Is your use of the TCP intercept one-minute low command appropriate?
    - Yes
    - No

28. Is your use of the TCP intercept one-minute low command appropriate?
    - Yes
    - No

29. Is your use of the TCP intercept one-minute high command appropriate?
    - Yes
    - No

30. Does your organization use network address translation (NAT)?
    - Yes
    - No

31. Does your organization have a policy for the use of network address translation?
    - Yes
    - No

32. Do users in your organization reside on multiple interfaces?
    - Yes
    - No

33. Are there multiple interfaces going to the Internet?
    - Yes
    - No

34. Is your organization trying to allow internal users to access the Internet?
    - Yes
    - No

35. Is your organization trying to allow the Internet to access internal devices?
    - Yes
    - No

36. Is your organization trying to redirect TCP traffic to another port, address, or protocol?
    - Yes
    - No

37. Is your organization using network address translation during a network transition?
    - Yes
    - No

38. Is your organization using network address translation to allow overlapping networks to communicate?
    - Yes
    - No

39. Do you know what type of addressing scheme you are using on the inside network?
    - Yes
    - No

40. Does your organization know how many devices need translation?
    - Yes
    - No

41. Is your organization using:
    - Static address translation?
    - Dynamic address translation?
    - Address overloading?
    - Combination of the above?

42. Is your use of the NAT global timeout appropriate?
    - Yes
    - No
43. Is your use of the NAT translation tcp-timeout appropriate?
    - Yes
    - No
44. Is your use of the NAT translation udp-timeout appropriate?
    - Yes
    - No
45. Is your use of the NAT translation finrst-timeout appropriate?
    - Yes
    - No
46. Is your use of the NAT translation dns-timeout appropriate?
    - Yes
    - No
47. Does your organization have a policy on queuing?
    - Yes
    - No
48. What queuing technology does your organization use?
    - FIFO
    - WFQ
    - CQ
    - PQ
49. If you use custom queuing, do the queues and the assigned traffic seem appropriate?
    - Yes
    - No
50. If you use priority queuing, does the traffic assigned to the high queue seem appropriate?
    - Yes
    - No
51. If you use priority queuing, does the traffic assigned to other queues seem appropriate?
    - Yes
    - No
52. Does your organization use CAR?
    - Yes
    - No
53. Does the bps value your organization selected for the normal traffic seem appropriate?
    - Yes
    - No
54. Does the bps value your organization selected for the normal burst rate seem appropriate?
    - Yes
    - No
55. Does the bps value your organization selected for the exceed burst rate seem appropriate?
    - Yes
    - No

56. Does the conform action your organization selected seem appropriate?
    ■ Yes
    ■ No
57. Does the exceed action your organization selected seem appropriate?
    ■ Yes
    ■ No
58. Does your router have appropriate host table entries?
    ■ Yes
    ■ No
59. Is your organization doing anything else to prevent denial-of-service attacks?
    ■ Yes
    ■ No

Conclusion

In this chapter, you learned how to protect your organization against directed broadcasts; echo-, chargen-, and discard-based attacks; attacks needing source routing; ICMP redirect and unreachable; Proxy ARP; and SYN-flooding.

You also saw how to configure NAT using the following steps:

1. Define NAT inside and outside interfaces.
2. Define what you are trying to accomplish with NAT.
3. Configure NAT to accomplish what you defined in Step 2.
4. Verify NAT operation.

Finally, you learned how queuing and traffic policing might help in your battle against those attackers bent on denying service to your legitimate clients.

Another feature Cisco introduced in IOS version is Hot Standby Router Protocol (HSRP). This protocol accommodates a circuit failure in your router. HSRP will allow you to take two or more routers and make them appear to the network as a single point or a "virtual router" to use as the default gateway. Use the `standby` command.

One final thought on denial-of-service attacks. There are things you can do to ensure that your organization does not become an unwitting accomplice to attacks on other networks. In Chapters 15 through 18, you learned quite a bit about traffic filtering. Set up egress filtering on your border or firewall routers to prevent suspicious traffic from leaving your network. A few simple commands to ensure that traffic leaving your network did truly originate in your network will severely hamper attackers abusing networks using your network without your knowledge. Be a considerate netizen.

You are rounding the bend and heading for home. In Chapter 22 you will learn about neighbor authentication and tie up some loose ends.

PREVENTING FRAUDULENT ROUTE UPDATES AND OTHER UNAUTHORIZED CHANGES

VI

Chapter 22

Configuring Neighbor Authentication and Other Security Features

---

In this chapter, you will learn about:

- Neighbor authentication
- Plaintext authentication
- MD5 authentication
- Key chains
- Removing unnecessary services
- Configuring Secure Shell

In Chapter 5, "Router Management," you learned about some tools to gather information about the routers directly connected to your router. You used Ping, Telnet, Traceroute, and the Cisco Discovery Protocol. You were gathering information about neighbors.

In Chapter 3, "Routed and Routing Protocols," you learned that routers move data between two networks or subnetworks, and that path determination is where the router must determine an appropriate path for the packets. Routers learn about the network topology by communicating with other routers. A router must know the interface to switch the message, and uses the routing tables to determine that interface. These routing tables have hardware interface information that provides the router with the beginning route (for the router) to move the packet to the destination address. Routers announce their presence, as well as the routes they provide, to the other routers on the network. Routing protocols, such as Routing Information Protocol, Open Shortest Path First, and Enhanced Interior Gateway Routing Protocol, provide the mechanisms for maintaining router routing tables. Such protocols share route information that the routers use to build and maintain routing tables. Messages providing route information on changes in the status of routers or links prompt the routing software algorithm to recalculate routes and update the router's routing tables accordingly. It is these messages that are problematic. You must ensure the integrity of these routing exchanges.

To understand why ensuring the integrity of these routing exchanges is important, consider what would happen if a malicious (or even careless) individual starts sending dynamic route updates with false information. The sender might send the erroneous information intentionally or unintentionally. At best, your network could have mysterious black holes or quagmires into which your valuable packets disappear or get bogged down instead of going on their way to the correct destinations. At worst, your routers might start sending packets for some or all of your machines to the attacker's machine or network, where she could analyze the packets at her leisure. She can use her packet analyzer and sit on the wire waiting for you to send your packets over her segment. *Neighbor authentication* or *route authentication* can help by allowing your routers to ensure that the routing updates they receive are legitimate.

You can prevent your router from receiving fraudulent route updates by configuring neighbor router authentication. If the routing protocol you select supports signed updates, then you should seriously consider using them. Configuration is simple. Simplistically, you give the router the authentication key for an interface or a neighbor, and the router takes it from there.

You should consider neighbor or route authentication as part of your total security plan. This chapter describes what neighbor router authentication is, how it works, and why you should use it to increase your overall network security. In addition, this chapter covers extra security measures to protect your routers and the applications behind them.

Using Neighbor Authentication

When configured, neighbor authentication occurs whenever routers exchange routing updates with neighboring routers. This authentication ensures that a router receives reliable routing information from a trusted source. The router exchanges secrets to ensure that it trusts the source. It is quite simple: when the router trusts the source, it trusts the updates.

Without neighbor authentication, individuals could send unauthorized or deliberately malicious routing updates that could compromise the security of your network traffic. A security compromise might occur when an unfriendly party diverts or analyzes your network traffic. For example, an unauthorized router could send a fictitious routing update to convince your router to send traffic to an incorrect destination. The cracker could analyze the diverted traffic to learn your confidential information, or merely use it to disrupt your organization's ability to communicate effectively. It was bad enough when crackers had packet analyzers that allowed passive wiretapping; that is, they could view the contents of any unencrypted packet. But now the crackers have access to active packet analyzers. These devices allow the cracker to take the packet out of the stream, manipulate it, and re-insert it into the stream. Neighbor authentication prevents any such fraudulent route updates from being received by your router.

Note: Be aware that should a trusted neighbor send fraudulent routes because, for example, someone compromised the router, there is not much you can do about it. Neighbor authentication will not help — for obvious reasons.

You can configure neighbor authentication for the following routing protocols:

- Border Gateway Protocol (BGP)
- DRP Server Agent
- Intermediate System-to-Intermediate System (IS-IS)
- IP Enhanced Interior Gateway Routing Protocol (IGRP)
- Open Shortest Path First (OSPF)
- Routing Information Protocol (RIP) version 2

You should configure your router for neighbor authentication when that router meets all of the following conditions:

- The router uses any of the routing protocols just mentioned.
- It is conceivable that the router might receive a false route update.
- If the router received a false route update, then it might compromise your network.
- You configured a router for neighbor authentication, so you also need to configure the neighbor router for neighbor authentication.

The answers to at least the first three questions require a risk analysis. For without a detailed risk analysis, it is difficult to predict threats and vulnerabilities. Again, there are many good tomes on risk analysis that can get you started on the process. If you have not done a risk analysis, get one and get started.

Understanding Neighbor Authentication

When you configure neighbor authentication on a router, the router authenticates the source of each routing update packet that it receives. The router accomplishes this by exchanging an authenticating key (sometimes referred to as a password) that is known to both the sending and receiving router.

There are two types of neighbor authentication used:

- Plaintext authentication
- Message Digest Algorithm version 5 (MD5) authentication

Both forms of neighbor authentication work similarly, except that MD5 sends a message digest instead of the authenticating key itself. The router creates the message digest using the key and a message, but the key itself is not sent, thereby preventing it from being read while in transmission. Plaintext authentication sends the authenticating key itself over the wire.

> **Note:** Only use plaintext authentication as a last resort. Do not use it as part of your security strategy. Its primary benefit is management — not security — because it can help you avoid accidental changes to the routing infrastructure. Use the recommended MD5 authentication instead.

> **Caution:** As with all keys, passwords, and other security secrets, it is imperative that you closely guard the authenticating keys used for neighbor authentication. The security benefits of neighbor authentication rely on your keeping all authenticating keys confidential.

Plaintext Authentication

Each participating neighbor router must share an authenticating key. You specify this key at each router during configuration. You can specify multiple keys with some protocols, but then you must identify each key by a key number.

In general, when a routing update is sent, the following authentication sequence occurs:

Step 1. A router sends a routing update with a key and the corresponding key number to the neighbor router. For those protocols that only support one key, the key number is always zero.

Step 2. The receiving neighbor router checks the received key against the key for that router that it stores in memory.

Step 3. When the two keys match, the receiving router accepts the routing update packet. If the two keys do not match, then the router rejects the routing update packet.

These following protocols use plaintext authentication:

- DRP Server Agent
- IS-IS
- OSPF
- RIP version 2

Take a look at some examples.

Configuring IS-IS Plaintext Authentication

By default, the router does not authenticate IS-IS packets. To configure the authentication password for an interface, use the `isis password` interface configuration command.

```
2501-1(config-if)#isis password password {level-1 | level-2}
```

The password keyword is the authentication password you assign to the interface. The routers exchange the password as plaintext and thus provide only limited security. You can assign different passwords for different routing levels using the level-1 and level-2 keyword arguments.

When you select the level-1 keyword, you independently configure the authentication password for Level 1. For Level 1 routing, the router acts as a station router only. When you select the level-2 keyword, you independently configure the authentication password for Level 2. For Level 2 routing, the router acts as an area router only. Specifying the level-1 or level-2 keywords disables the password only for Level 1 or Level 2 routing, respectively. When you do not specify a keyword, the default is level-1.

The above command enables you to prevent unauthorized routers from forming adjacencies with this router, and thus protects the network from intruders.

The following example configures a password mysecret for Ethernet interface 0 at Level 1:

```
2501-1(config)#interface ethernet 0
2501-1(config-if)#isis password mysecret level-1
```

To disable authentication for Intermediate System-to-Intermediate System (IS-IS), use the no isis password {level-1 | level-2} command.

Configuring OSPF Plaintext Authentication

By default, the router does not authenticate OSPF packets. For example, to use text authentication for OSPF, you add:

```
2501-1(config)#int e0
2501-1(config-if)#ip address 10.8.0.1 255.0.0.0
2501-1(config-if)#ip ospf authentication-key mysecret
2501-1(config-if)#router ospf 1
2501-1(config-router)#network 192.168.0.0 0.0.255.255 area 1
2501-1(config-router)#network 0.0.0.0 255.255.255.255 area 0
2501-1(config-router)#area 0 authentication
```

The first three commands define an interface Ethernet 0 with an authentication key. The next two commands tell the router to start an OSPF process, placing interfaces in 192.168.0.0/16 in area 0 and all others in area 1. The last command tells the router to use authentication in area 0. Because Ethernet 0 is in area 0, all of the router's updates to area 0 will use the authentication key mysecret. If an update arrives on interface e0 that does not authenticate with this key, the router will reject it. For this reason, all routers in an OSPF area must either use authentication keys or not use them. You cannot mix and match them.

MD5 Authentication

MD5 authentication works in a similar manner to plaintext authentication, except that the router never sends the key over the wire. Instead, the router uses the

MD5 algorithm to produce a message digest of the key (also called a "hash"). The MD5 hash algorithm with a secret key yields a 128-bit hash value.

Hash algorithms are checksum-like functions, except they are explicitly designed so that a cipherpunk cannot construct a forged message that yields the same result as a legitimate one. Like checksums, one-way hash functions take an arbitrarily long data sequence and compute a check value of a fixed size, called the hash value. Unlike checksums, one-way hash functions try to generate a unique fingerprint of the data. The cryptographers designed the algorithm to make it as difficult as possible to construct another data sequence that yields exactly the same result.

Hash functions are very sensitive to minor changes in the input text and thus provide the best protection for larger data items. Changing even a single bit will change the MD5 hash.

Attackers cannot generate the correct checksum value for a given message unless they have a copy of the secret key you used. The correct hash value depends on constructing the same input data, which includes both the data sent and the secret key. Also, attackers cannot construct a similar, beneficial message that yields the same hash value. Even if, by some remote coincidence, they happened to construct a message that yielded the same hash value, they have no way of verifying that fact before sending it. Given how difficult it is to construct a message that matches a given hash value, the chances are remote that any particular attempt would succeed.

The message digest is then sent instead of the key itself. This ensures that nobody can eavesdrop on the line and learn keys during transmission.

The following protocols use MD5 authentication:

- OSPF
- RIP version 2
- BGP
- IP Enhanced IGRP

Take a look at some examples.

Configuring OSPF MD5 Authentication

By default, the router does not authenticate OSPF packets. To enable authentication for an OSPF area, use the `area authentication` router configuration command.

```
2501-1(config-router)#area area-id authentication message-
    digest
```

Specify an `area-id` identifier where you want authentication enabled. You can specify the identifier as either a decimal value or an IP address.

You must use the same authentication type for all routers and access servers in an area. Thus, you cannot use plaintext with some and MD5 with others.

To remove an area's authentication specification or a specified area from the configuration, use the no form of the above command.

When you enable MD5 authentication with the `message-digest` keyword, you must enable OSPF MD5 authentication with the `ip ospf message-digest-key` interface configuration command.

```
2501-1(config-if)#ip ospf message-digest-key keyid md5 key
```

The `keyid` keyword is an identifier in the range 1 to 255. The key is an alphanumeric password of up to 16 bytes.

Caution: If you do not use the `service password-encryption` command when implementing OSPF MD5 authentication, the router stores the MD5 secret as plaintext in NVRAM.

Usually, you use one key per interface to generate authentication information when sending packets and to authenticate incoming packets. The neighbor router must have the same key value.

When you change keys, the router assumes its neighbors do not have the new key yet, so it begins a rollover process. It sends two copies of the same packet: one authenticated by the new key and the other by the old key. Rollover allows neighboring routers to continue communication while the network administrator is updating them with a new key. Rollover stops once the local router finds that all its neighbors know the new key. The router knows that a neighbor has the new key when it receives packets from the neighbor authenticated by the new key. After all neighbors have the new key, you should manually remove the old key with the `no ip ospf message-digest-key keyid` command.

Do not keep more than one key per interface. Every time you add a new key, you should remove the old key to prevent the local router from communicating with a weak or old key. Also, removing the old key reduces overhead during rollover.

The following example sets a new key 20 with the password mgb3p16:

```
2501-1(config)#interface serial 1
2501-1(config-if)#ip ospf message-digest-key 10 md5 rbpv294
2501-1(config-if)#ip ospf message-digest-key 20 md5 mgb3p16
```

Configuring RIP v2 MD5 Authentication

By default, the router does not authenticate RIP packets. To specify the type of authentication used in Routing Information Protocol (RIP) version 2 packets, use the `ip rip authentication mode` interface configuration command:

```
2501-1(config)#int e0
2501-1(config-if)#ip rip authentication mode {text | md5}
```

If you pick text, you will get cleartext authentication. Pick md5 and you get keyed MD5 authentication. So, if you want to configure the interface to use MD5 authentication:

```
2501-1(config-if)#ip rip authentication mode md5
```

Now you need to enable authentication for RIP version 2 packets and specify the set of keys to use on the interface. To enable authentication and to specify the set of keys to use on an interface, use the `ip rip authentication key-chain` interface configuration command:

```
2501-1(config-if)#ip rip authentication key-chain name-of-
    chain
```

The `name-of-chain` keywords enable authentication and specify the group of valid keys. If you do not configure a key chain with the `key-chain` command, the router will not perform any authentication on the interface (not even the default text authentication).

The following example configures the interface to accept and send any key belonging to the key chain named chain1.

```
2501-1(config-if)#ip rip authentication key-chain chain1
```

To restore cleartext authentication, use the no form of this command.

```
2501-1(config-if)#no ip rip authentication mode
```

Configuring BGP MD5 Authentication

You can invoke authentication between two BGP peers, causing the router to verify each segment sent on the TCP connection between them. Configuring authentication for BGP updates to neighbors is somewhat straightforward. To enable Message Digest 5 (MD5) authentication on a TCP connection between two Border Gateway Protocol (BGP) peers, use the `neighbor password` router configuration command:

```
2501-1(config-router)#neighbor {ip-address | peer-group-
    name} password string
```

Specify either the ip address of the BGP-speaking neighbor or the name of a BGP peer group. If you specify a BGP peer group by using the `peer-group-name` argument, all the members of the peer group will inherit the characteristic configured with this command. The `string` keyword is a case-sensitive password of up to 80 characters, and must start with an alphabetic character.

Caution: Do not specify a password in the format number-space-anything. The space after the number causes problems.

Thus, simply tell the BGP routing process what password to use for each neighbor:

```
2501-1(config)#router bgp 101
2501-1(config-router)#network 10.8.0.0
2501-1(config-router)#neighbor 10.16.0.1 remote-as 102
2501-1(config-router)#neighbor 10.16.0.1 password mysecret
2501-1(config-router)#neighbor 10.24.0.1 remote-as 103
2501-1(config-router)#neighbor 10.24.0.1 password
   theirsecret
```

You must use the same password on both BGP peers; otherwise, they cannot make the connection. The authentication feature uses the MD5 algorithm. Specifying this command causes the generation and checking of the MD5 digest on every segment sent on the TCP connection. Thus, there is some overhead.

Configuring a password for a neighbor will cause the router to tear down an existing session and establish a new one.

Each neighbor can use a different password, just as each interface could use a different authentication key in OSPF. You can also specify some neighbors that do not use passwords; so your router will authenticate exchanges with these routers.

Using Key Chains

You can configure key chains for the following routing protocols:

- RIP version 2
- IP Enhanced IGRP
- DRP Server Agent

These routing protocols offer the additional function of managing keys by using key chains. When you configure a key chain, you specify a series of keys with lifetimes, and the Cisco IOS software rotates through each of these keys. This decreases the likelihood that someone will compromise the keys.

Each key definition within the key chain must specify a time interval during which the key is active (its "lifetime"). Then, during a given key's lifetime, the router sends routing update packets with this activated key.

Your router cannot use keys during time periods when you have not activated them. Therefore, you should overlap key activation times for a given key chain to avoid any period of time when the router does not have an active key. If a time period occurs in which the router does not have an active key, neighbor authentication cannot occur, and therefore routine updates will fail. You can specify multiple key chains.

Key chains allow you to use a rotating series of keys to decrease the likelihood of compromise. The router needs to know the time to rotate through keys in synchronization with the other participating routers so that all routers use the correct key at the same moment in time. Because the lifetime of each key is time sensitive, you should enable the NTP (Network Time Protocol) before using key chains. Refer to the Network Time Protocol (NTP) commands in Chapter 5.

Finding Neighbor Authentication Configuration Information

To find complete configuration information for neighbor authentication, you should refer to the appropriate material on the routing protocol you intend to support. For example, you need to look up options for the neighbor command when working with BGP. For OSPF, review the interface and area parameters.

Preventing fraudulent router updates is an important security measure, so analyze your risks and determine if it is necessary for your network. However, there are other things you can do to further protect your network. The next chapter section looks at those measures.

Removing Unnecessary Services

As a general rule, you should disable any unnecessary service in any router that is reachable from a potentially hostile network. The services listed in this section are sometimes useful, but you should disable them if you do not have a compelling reason for their use. Again, this assumes that someone in your organization has performed a risk analysis.

TCP and UDP Small Services

In Chapter 21 you learned to use the no service tcp-small-servers and no service udp-small-servers commands to disable echo, chargen, and discard on TCP and UDP, respectively. Cisco disables these services by default in IOS v12 and greater, but it is good form to use this command anyway to show that you really intended to remove them. These services provide little benefit, except to crackers intent on denying service.

Finger

Cisco routers provide an implementation of the finger service that people can use to find out the users logged into a network device. Although this information is usually not tremendously sensitive, it is sometimes useful to an attacker. However, any information that an attacker gets is useful: who knows what the last piece of the puzzle is? You can disable the finger service with the command no service finger:

```
2501-1(config)#no service finger
```

Simple Network Management Protocol (SNMP)

In Chapter 5, you spent time learning about SNMP. As you know, you can use SNMP to monitor and manage your network devices. Unfortunately, the security with SNMP is weak, so you probably should not use SNMP over a public network. You can disable the SNMP service with the command no snmp-server:

```
2501-1(config)#no snmp-server
```

Hypertext Transfer Protocol (HTTP)

Cisco provides the capability to manage the router with your Web browser. If you decide to use this feature, you must take the same precautions as you would for remote log-in access. The simplest thing to do is to disable the Web server on the router using the following global configuration command.

```
2501-1(config)#no ip http server
```

If you decide that you cannot live without the Web interface, then you should take some steps to make its usage more secure. First, you can assign the HTTP service to a port other than port 80, just to fool those automated tools out there. Use the following global configuration command:

```
2501-1(config)#ip http port 1881
```

Now the cracker will see an application running on port 1881. Ensure that whatever port you select is not one known to have security vulnerabilities or one that the router routinely uses. You can also assign an access list to the HTTP server:

```
2501-1(config)#ip http access-class 50
```

This command uses the standard access list that you use to apply to VTY lines. The number value is one from 1 to 99. And you can raise the bar and require authentication for the service as follows:

```
2501-1(config)#ip http authentication tacacs
```

This command requires TACACS authentication for the router HTTP server. You can choose between enable passwords, local username and password, and TACACS.

Network Time Protocol (NTP)

The Network Time Protocol (NTP) is not particularly dangerous but any unneeded service may represent a path for penetration. If you actually use NTP, it is important to explicitly configure a trusted time source and to use proper authentication because corrupting the time base is a good way to subvert certain security protocols. If you are not using NTP on a particular router interface, you can disable it with the interface command no ntp enable.

```
2501-1(config-if)#no ntp enable
```

Cisco Discovery Protocol (CDP)

You can use Cisco Discovery Protocol (CDP) for some network management functions but CDP is dangerous in that it allows any system on a directly connected segment to learn that the router is a Cisco device and to determine the model number and the Cisco IOS software version being run. In addition, you saw in Chapter 1 that someone could use it to mount a denial-of-service attack.

A cracker may, in turn, use this information to design attacks against the router. The impact is lessened because CDP information is accessible only to directly connected systems. You can disable CDP with the global configuration command no cdp run. In addition, you can disable CDP on a particular interface with no cdp enable.

```
2501-1(config)#no cdp run
2501-1(config-if)#no cdp enable
```

Unused Addresses

When you are no longer using an interface, do not let it lay about; disable it. To remove an IP address from an Ethernet segment, you would use the following commands starting in global configuration mode:

```
2501-1(config)#interface e0
2501-1(config-if)#no ip address
```

Classless Addresses

When you are not using classless addressing, you should use the following command to specify this.

```
2501-1(config)#no ip classless
```

Although this is the default, it is good form (and good documentation) to include this statement.

You might want to specify the format of your network masks as well, as shown in the following:

```
2501-1(config)#ip netmask-format decimal
```

This means your addresses and netmasks are in the format 192.168.200.0 255.255.254.0.

On the other hand, you can get some unpredictable results when using classless notation and you do not specify the ip classless command. Routes advertised using classless IP address ranges are not properly treated by a router when you do not use the ip classless command. Take a look at a real-world example to explain. You have an ISP that provides access to certain networks that it advertises to you using BGP. Some of these addresses are portions of what was an old classful Class A network. Your ISP filters out any traffic coming from you that does not match that list of networks. If you do not specify classless routing, your router will think that it must route the entire Class A network. So your router will block any traffic between you and any address in that Class A block not passed through by your ISP.

So, determine whether you are using classless or classful addressing, and configure your router accordingly. It is very easy to misconfigure your router and a little more difficult to spot.

Configuring Secure Shell (SSH)

Just when you thought it was safe, encryption rears its ugly head once more. You should know how to configure Secure Shell, which requires the use of encryption. As you saw early on, service password-encryption mode provides weak password encryption because there are freely available programs that can crack your passwords in seconds. You should also know that there are strong rumors of an exhaustive attack program that can crack the stronger enable secret password in about 24 hours on a Pentium-based computer. Thus, you need a secure method to protect your passwords. Secure Shell (SSH) is one way. SSH lets you encrypt and protect passwords sent across the Internet. With SSH for PC clients, you can tunnel other protocols inside its encrypted Telnet-like session, so you can secure POP, SMTP, and FTP across the Internet. Secure Shell allows administrators secure encrypted access to remote routers. It encrypts the session traffic so that an observer cannot learn passwords from watching configuration commands or watching your session as you do a show run command.

Cisco added support for Secure Shell (version 1) to IOS Release 12.1(1) T, for the 1700, 2600, 3600, 7200, 7500, and ubr920 series routers. Cisco's implementation currently uses only user and password authentication, which you can do with TACACS+ or RADIUS. It supports DES and 3DES algorithms.

Before you can use SSH, you must configure the router with a host name and DNS domain name, which you did in Chapter 21. Next, generate an RSA key-pair for the router. This is done in global-configuration mode with the following command:

```
router(config)#crypto key generate rsa
```

Once you have an RSA key-pair, you can then enable the SSH server.

```
router(config)#ip ssh [timeout seconds] [authentication-
  retries number-of-retries]
```

The timeout default is 120 seconds and only applies to the SSH negotiation phase. Once the router starts the EXEC session, the standard vty idle timeout default of 10 minutes applies. The authentication-retries default is 3, but you can set it as high as 5. Every SSH session uses a virtual terminal, which normally numbers 0 to 4, so you can have a maximum of five simultaneous SSH sessions.

To check your work, and to show existing SSH sessions, use the show command.

```
router#show ip ssh
```

You have two choices to terminate an existing SSH session:

```
router#disconnect ssh session-number
```

or

```
router#clear line vty number
```

You can view the session number with the show ip ssh command. The number keyword is a number from 0 to 4, whichever one.

You can get debug support with the following command:

```
router#debug ip ssh
```

And finally, use the command crypto key zeroize rsa when you want to delete a key. However, this will disable the SSH server. When you do zeroize a key, you may need to re-enable SSH on the vty ports as follows:

```
router(config)#line vty 0 4
router(config-line)#transport input ssh
```

Setting up the Secure Shell server is only half the equation. You must do something on the client side. Using the SSH client requires no configuration. You initiate the client in EXEC mode with the following command syntax:

```
router#ssh [-l userid] [-c {des | 3des}] [-o
    numberofpasswdprompts n] [-p portnum] {ip-address |
    hostname} [command]
```

The optional userid keyword specifies the user log-in to use on the remote computer, where it is different from your present userid. The -c option selects the encryption technique (56i, or k2 DES, or 3DES image required). The portnum is the destination port (default 22). Use the optional -o- numberofpasswdprompts n number to set how many password prompts before session termination. Use the ip-address or hostname argument to specify the computer or router you want to connect. The optional keyword command that is a command that you want to send to the remote computer.

There you have it. Before looking at the Practice Session, you should refresh your memory by reviewing the next section.

Some Final Guidelines for Configuring a Router

As with all networking devices, you should always protect access by configuring passwords. You should consider configuring user authentication, authorization, and accounting as described in Section 2 of this book. You should also consider the following recommendations:

1. When setting passwords for privileged access to the router, use the enable secret command rather than the enable password command, which does not have as strong an encryption algorithm.

2. Password-protect the console port. In authentication, authorization, and accounting (AAA) environments, use the same authentication for the console as for elsewhere. In a non-AAA environment, at a minimum, configure the `login` and `password` *password* commands.

3. Avoid the use of default passwords. Technically, Cisco has no default passwords but you can find a list of common passwords at http://security.nerdnet.com/index.php or http://www.securityparadigm.com/dad.htm.

4. For AAA security services, use TACACS+ or RADIUS to provide authentication, authorization, and accounting. TACACS+ is Cisco's proprietary protocol and they recommend it. RADIUS is an open standard and supported by more vendors. There is that trade-off once again.

5. Think about access control before you connect a console port to the network in any way, including attaching a modem to the port. Be aware that a break on the console port might give total control of the router, even when you configure access control.

6. Apply access lists and password protection to all virtual terminal (VTY) ports. Use access lists to limit Telnet to your router. Use SSH when available.

7. Create a warning banner stating that only authorized users can access the system and that you will monitor the activity of all clients.

8. Do not enable any local service (such as CDP, finger, or NTP) that you do not use. Cisco Discovery Protocol (CDP) and Network Time Protocol (NTP) are on by default, and you should turn these off when you do not need them. Any enabled service could present a potential security risk. A determined, hostile party might find a way to misuse the enabled services to access the router or the network. For local services that you enable, protect them against misuse. Protect by configuring the services to communicate only with specific peers, and protect by configuring access lists to deny packets for the services at specific interfaces.

9. You should also disable minor services. For IP, enter the `no service tcp-small-servers` and `no service udp-small-servers` global configuration commands. In Cisco IOS Release 12.0 and later, you will find these services disabled by default.

10. If you decide not to disable the HTTP service, then use access lists and authentication to improve security.

11. If you decide to use FTP, configure CBAC to provide greater control over the traffic you allow or do not allow. You can also use passive-mode FTP.

12. Disable SNMP on all external interfaces.

13. If you insist on using TFTP to update your router, then you must ensure that only authorized workstations (read network administrator) can use the service. Also, you must protect the configuration files while they reside on the TFTP server or this will become your weakest link and the point of attack.

14. Prevent the router from being used as a relay by configuring access lists on any asynchronous Telnet ports.

15. Protect the networks on both sides of the router from spoofing from the other side. You can protect against spoofing by configuring input access lists at all interfaces to pass only traffic from expected source addresses, and to deny all other traffic.

16. You should also disable source routing. For IP, enter the `no ip source-route` global configuration command. Disabling source routing at all routers can also help prevent spoofing.

17. Normally, you should disable directed broadcasts for all applicable protocols on all your routers. For IP, use the `no ip directed-broadcast` command. On rare occasions, some IP networks require directed broadcasts; where this is the case, do not disable directed broadcasts. Attackers can misuse directed broadcasts to multiply the power of their denial-of-service attacks, by sending every denial-of-service packet to every host on a subnet. Furthermore, some hosts have other intrinsic security risks present when handling broadcasts.

18. Border routers connected to the Internet should deny any packet using a private source IP address. You must not route these packets to the Internet.

19. Configure neighbor authentication and only accept updates from trusted sources, such as your ISP.

20. Configure the `no proxy-arp` command to prevent internal addresses from being revealed. This is especially important when you do not already have NAT configured to prevent internal addresses from being revealed.

21. Use reflexive access lists to control those sessions originating from your network. After your client establishes a legitimate connection to the outside, you can allow the return traffic — and only the return traffic.

22. Configure an access list that includes entries permitting certain ICMP traffic from unprotected networks. While an access list that denies all IP traffic not part of a connection inspected by CBAC seems most secure, it is not practical for normal router operation. The router expects to see ICMP traffic from other routers in the network. Additionally, CBAC does not inspect ICMP traffic, meaning that you need specific entries in the access list to permit return traffic for ICMP commands. For example, a user on a protected network uses the `ping` command to get the status of a host on an unprotected network; without entries in the access list that permit echo reply messages, the user on the protected network gets no response to the `ping` command.

23. Include access list entries to permit the following ICMP messages:
    a. Echo reply
    b. Time-exceeded
    c. Packet-too-big
    d. Unreachable

24. Add an access list entry denying any network traffic from a source address matching an address on the protected network. This is known as anti-spoofing protection because it prevents traffic from an unprotected network from assuming the identity of a device on the protected network.

25. Add an entry denying broadcast messages with a source address of 255.255.255.255 or 0.0.0.0. This entry helps to prevent broadcast attacks.

26. By default, the last entry in an extended access list is an implicit denial of all IP traffic not specifically allowed by other entries in the access list. Although this is the default setting, the router will not display this final deny statement by default in an access list. So, you could add an entry to the access list denying IP traffic with any source or destination address with no undesired effects.

27. Use access lists to filter route updates. Accept only updates from trusted systems.
28. Instead of access lists, you can use the `ip route 192.168.100.0 255.255.255.0 null0` command as a replacement. This command would send all traffic for that network to a null device.
29. Use network address translation (NAT) to hide the addresses of your internal systems. If for no other reason, you will save IP addresses and will not need to manage static addresses.
30. Configure TCP intercepts to detect possible SYN-flooding.
31. Use IPSec to protect the data flowing from one router to another router when cost justified. Do not forget to allow UDP port 500 for IKE and protocols 50 for ESP and 51 for AH.
32. Set up a process to control all changes. Use software to determine when someone has changed the configuration.
33. Turn on logging and review the log content on a periodic basis. Use a log server and set up a routine to back up the log data. Follow up on any "unusual" activity.
34. Keep up-to-date on all patches. This will help you to prevent some of the known attacks.
35. Consider the use of Cisco's Secure Access Control Manager, Secure Policy Manager, Secure Security Manager, Secure Scanner, and Secure Intrusion Detection System if you have some loose coins.
36. Keep the router in a secure room.

Well, that is it; however, you still have a Practice Session to complete.

Practice Session

In this Practice Session, you will practice the following:

- Logging in
- Saving log data
- Switching modes
- Creating a base configuration
- Enabling and saving syslog data
- Logging out

1. Log in to the SimRouter Web page.
2. Double-click on router 2501-1 to telnet to that router. This will open a console session.
3. Enter your **Username** and **Password** at the applicable prompt. These are the ones you set up in Chapter 2. You will need to hit the Enter key twice to get to the > prompt.
4. Again, save the log for your session. To do this, select | Terminal | Start Logging | from the menu bar in the Telnet window. The Telnet client will ask you where you wish to store the log and with what name. Your choice. You are going to save the log so that when you build this configuration, you can cut-and-paste it in the future as a starting point, rather than having to enter the same information every time.

5. Enter the enable mode:

    2501-1#**enable**

6. When prompted to put in the enable secret password, enter **oscar**.
7. Type **terminal length 0**. This command instructs the router to scroll through long command output without pausing (the —More— message).
8. Rather than paste the configuration from yesterday, start anew. Because the router boots up as a new router, you will need to run setup. Type **setup** to launch setup mode.
9. When prompted to continue with the configuration dialog, enter **yes**.
10. Type **no** to Would you like to enter basic management setup.
11. When asked whether you want to see the current interface summary, enter **no**. You are more than welcome to look at it, but there is nothing of value. You are going to set these values.
12. At the enter host name (2501-1) prompt, type **2501-1**.
13. When prompted to put in the enable secret password, enter **alpha**.
14. When prompted to enter the enable password, enter **bravo**.
15. When prompted to enter the virtual terminal password, enter **charlie**.
16. When asked whether you want to Configure SNMP Network Management, enter **no**.
17. Setup will ask you whether you want, in turn, to configure DECnet, AppleTalk, IPX, IP, IGRP, RIP, and bridging. Enter **yes** to configure IP and RIP; **no** to the others.
18. Now you must configure the interfaces. The router will ask you whether you want to configure Ethernet 0. The default is no, but enter **yes**. Type **yes** to configure the IP address for the interface. Enter **10.8.0.1** for the IP address for the interface and **255.0.0.0** for the subnet mask.
19. Configure Serial 0 with **200.100.50.25 255.255.255.0** and Serial 1 with **201.100.50.25**.
20. Review the configuration and type **2** to save the new configuration. The IOS will automatically save the configuration to NVRAM.
21. Double-click on router 4500 to telnet to that router. This will open a console session.
22. Repeat Steps 3 through 17. Of course, you must substitute **4500** wherever you see **2501-1**.
23. Bypass the ISDN configuration parameters by typing **0** to Choose ISDN BRI Switch Type. Type **no** to Do you want to configure BRI0 (BRI d-channel) interface.
24. Now you must configure the other interfaces. The router will ask you whether you want to configure Ethernet 0. The default is no, but enter **yes**. Type **yes** to configure the IP address for the interface. Enter **220.100.50.25** for the IP address for the interface and **255.255.255.0** for the subnet mask. Enter **no** to bypass configuring Serial 0 and Serial 1.
25. Review the configuration and type **2** to save the new configuration. The IOS will automatically save the configuration to NVRAM.
26. To verify your work, type **ping 200.100.50.25**.
27. Also try **traceroute 200.100.50.25 or trace 200.100.50.25**.
28. You can also test router connectivity using Telnet. Type **telnet 200.100.50.25**.

29. Enter the enable mode by entering **enable** and pressing Enter.
30. When prompted to put in the enable secret password, enter **oscar** and press Enter.
31. Type **terminal length 0**. This command instructs the route to scroll through long command output without pausing (the —More— message).
32. At the 2501-1# prompt, type **config t**.
33. Because the Serial 0 is a connection to the public network, you will want to create an inbound filter. Let us configure some anti-spoofing entries:

```
access-list 100 deny ip 127.0.0.0 0.255.255.255 any
    log-input
access-list 100 deny ip 10.0.0.0 0.255.255.255 any log-
    input
access-list 100 deny ip 172.16.0.0 0.0.255.255 any log-
    input
access-list 100 deny ip 192.168.0.0 0.0.255.255 any
    log-input
access-list 100 deny ip 224.0.0.0 7.255.255.255 any
    log-input
access-list 100 deny ip host 0.0.0.0 any log-input
access-list 100 deny ip host 255.255.255.255 any log-
    input
```

34. Deny any services you do not want in:

```
access-list 100 deny icmp any any echo log-input
access-list 100 deny icmp any any redirect log-input
access-list 100 deny icmp any any time-exceeded log-
    input
access-list 100 deny udp any any eq snmp log-input
access-list 100 deny udp any any eq snmptrap log-input
access-list 100 deny igmp any any
access-list 100 deny tcp any any eq 22
access-list 100 deny tcp any any eq 69
access-list 100 deny tcp any any eq 123
```

35. Block those nasty Trin00 DDoS ports:

```
access-list 100 deny tcp any any eq 27665
access-list 100 deny udp any any eq 27444
access-list 100 deny udp any any eq 31335
```

36. You also want to block the Stacheldraht DDoS ports:

```
access-list 100 deny tcp any any eq 1660
access-list 100 deny tcp any any eq 65000
```

37. If you do not want MP3 and other files using gnutella, block them:

```
access-list 100 deny tcp any any eq 6346
```

38. Block the SubSeven Trojans.

```
access-list 100 deny tcp any any eq 1243
access-list 100 deny tcp any any eq 1245
access-list 100 deny tcp any any eq 2773
access-list 100 deny tcp any any eq 2774
access-list 100 deny tcp any any eq 6667
access-list 100 deny tcp any any eq 7000
access-list 100 deny tcp any any eq 7215
access-list 100 deny tcp any any eq 16959
access-list 100 deny tcp any any eq 27374
```

39. Block the BackOrifice Trojans:

```
access-list 100 deny tcp any any eq 79
access-list 100 deny udp any any eq 1349
access-list 100 deny tcp any any eq 8787
access-list 100 deny udp any any eq 8787
access-list 100 deny tcp any any eq 8879
access-list 100 deny udp any any eq 8879
access-list 100 deny tcp any any eq 31336
access-list 100 deny tcp any any eq 31337
access-list 100 deny udp any any eq 31337
access-list 100 deny udp any any eq 31338
access-list 100 deny tcp any any eq 54320
access-list 100 deny udp any any eq 54320
access-list 100 deny tcp any any eq 54321
access-list 100 deny udp any any eq 54321
```

40. Block the NetBus and Whack-a-Mole Trojans:

```
access-list 100 deny tcp any any eq 6666
access-list 100 deny tcp any any eq 12345
access-list 100 deny udp any any eq 12345
access-list 100 deny tcp any any eq 12346
access-list 100 deny tcp any any eq 12361
access-list 100 deny tcp any any eq 12362
access-list 100 deny tcp any any eq 12363
access-list 100 deny tcp any any eq 12456
access-list 100 deny tcp any any eq 20034
access-list 100 deny tcp any any eq 21554
```

41. Allow all other traffic in:

```
access-list 100 permit ip any any
```

42. Block Traceroute on serial 0 outbound:

```
access-list 101 deny icmp any any time-exceeded log
access-list 101 permit ip any any
```

43. Get rid of all unnecessary services:

```
no service tcp-small-servers
no service udp-small-servers
no ip source-route
no ip proxy-arp
no service finger
no snmp-server
no ip http server
no ntp enable
no cdp run
no ip classless
```

44. Enter the following commands to turn on TCP watch mode and apply it to an interface:

```
ip tcp intercept mode watch
int s0
access-list 1 permit tcp any 200.100.50.0 0.0.0.255
ip tcp intercept list 1
```

45. Apply the various access lists to this interface:

```
ip access-group 100 in
ip access-group 101 out
```

46. Turn off CDP on this interface:

```
no cdp enable
```

47. Remove any addresses from Serial 1 interface:

```
interface e0
no ip address
```

48. Type **exit** and press Enter. You want to configure Ethernet 0 inbound to stop Ping:

```
access-list 102 deny icmp any any echo
access-list 102 permit ip any any
```

49. Type **exit** and press Enter to disconnect from router 2501-1. You should see the 4500# prompt again.
50. Try the Ping command again by typing **ping 10.8.0.1**. What do you see?
51. Also, try **traceroute 10.8.0.1** or **trace 10.8.0.1**. What happened?
52. Finally, test router connectivity using Telnet. Type **telnet 10.8.0.1**. Now what happened?
53. In the Telnet window for router 4500, select | Terminal | Stop Capture | from the menu bar to stop capturing the Telnet output.
54. Type **sh running-config**. The IOS displays the current running configuration as it is captured to the log file.
55. Type **quit** to log out from router 4500. Close the Telnet window and return to the SimRouter Topology Map.

56. Select the Telnet window for the 2501-1 session.
57. In the Telnet window for router 2501-1, select | Terminal | Stop Capture | from the menu bar to stop capturing the Telnet output.
58. Type **sh running-config**. The IOS displays the current running configuration as it is captured to the log file.
59. Type **quit** to log out from router 2501-1. Close the Telnet window and return to the SimRouter Topology Map.
60. Click on Log Out on the SimRouter Web page.

Study this configuration. If you have faithfully completed all the Practice Sessions, then you should have the start of a good configuration. Use your favorite text editor and cut-and-paste it. Put in your network addresses and make all the other necessary changes. **But remember: this base configuration is not an adequate substitute for a risk analysis!**

Security and Audit Checklist

1. Do you use Neighbor Authentication in your organization?
   ■ Yes
   ■ No
2. What protocols are you supporting?
   ■ BGP
   ■ DRP Server Agent
   ■ Enhanced IGRP
   ■ IS-IS
   ■ OSPF
   ■ RIP version 2
3. If you are using RIP version 2, what form of neighbor authentication do you use?
   ■ Plaintext authentication
   ■ MD5 authentication
4. If you are using OSPF, what form of neighbor authentication do you use?
   ■ Plaintext authentication
   ■ MD5 authentication
5. Does your organization use key chains?
   ■ Yes
   ■ No
6. Does your organization use the Network Time Protocol (NTP)?
   ■ Yes
   ■ No
7. Does someone in your organization have responsibility for managing the key?
   ■ Yes
   ■ No
8. Is this assignment appropriate?
   ■ Yes
   ■ No

9. Do you have a documented procedure for generating MD5 keys?
   - Yes
   - No
10. Do you use the `service password-encryption` command?
    - Yes
    - No
11. Has your organization removed the following?
    - tcp-small-servers
    - udp-small-servers
    - finger
    - http
    - ntp
    - cdp
    - unused addresses
12. If your organization uses HTTP, have you done anything else to protect HTTP?
    - Yes
    - No
13. Does your organization use Secure Shell (SSH)?
    - Yes
    - No

Conclusion

In this chapter you learned how to establish the server host and how to enable neighbor authentication. Plaintext authentication sends a plaintext key with each message. This is vulnerable to snooping. MD5 authentication performs an MD5 hash using a shared secret key, which is less vulnerable to snooping.

Unfortunately, not all routing protocols support neighbor authentication. For those protocols that do not, you should:

- Configure your routers to exchange routing information only when you must, preferably only with machines under your direct control.
- Filter out unwanted routing exchanges with some neighbors using administrative distances.
- Filter updates received to ensure that they are reasonable.

For example, you know that your default router can only come from one of several routers, so filter the default route from any updates from any other router, even when the router is under your control.

In addition, you learned that there are some services you can safely remove from your router. Before removing any of them, determine if there is any need for the service in your organization. If there is no need, it is simple: remove it. But when there is a need, you must analyze the risk from using the service and then make your determination after you have the best information.

Well, that is it. If you made it this far, then you should have a good and thorough knowledge of the things you need to do to harden your router. This author does not mean to trivialize the book but, simplistically:

- Use AAA security services to prevent unauthorized access to the router itself.
- Use access lists to prevent unauthorized access to your network.
- Use encryption to prevent network data interception.
- Use the other IOS features, such as TCP intercepts, to prevent denial-of-service attacks.
- Use neighbor authentication to prevent fraudulent route updates.

Cisco has provided a rich feature set. Now the onus is on you and your organization to turn them on. Do not delay. Act now. Remember that the barbarians are at the gate; they are armed and they are coming after you. Good luck!

APPENDICES

Appendix A

IP Addressing

In any network, every destination must have a unique identifier that other machines can use to send information. This unique identifier is commonly referred to as an *address*. An IP (Internet Protocol) address is a unique identifier for a node or host connection on an IP network. In reality, on an IP network, an address identifies a network attachment point as opposed to a particular machine. Hence, single machines with multiple interfaces (i.e., network interface cards) will have multiple IP addresses — one for each interface. Machines with multiple addresses are called multi-homed machines because they live on more than one network. A router is a multi-homed device, but not all multi-homed devices are routers. You might have file servers and firewalls residing on more than one network.

If your computer connects to the Internet via a telephone modem, cable modem, DSL adapter, or other dial-up mechanism, your Internet service provider (ISP) probably assigns you a temporary or *dynamic IP address* every time you connect. When your computer disconnects from the Internet, you free up the address assigned to your connection and your ISP may later reassign it to another computer. If you have heard of DHCP (Dynamic Host Configuration Protocol), then you already know the software that assigns temporary IP addresses.

If your computer connects to a local area network (LAN), your LAN's DHCP server can assign a temporary IP address. Or, a system administrator may have assigned a permanent or *static IP address* to your computer. Now you know where you get an IP address from, but where does your ISP or network administrator get it?

At one time, the answer was simple. When there was little activity and the Internet was novel, all IP addresses came directly from the Internet Assigned Numbers Authority (IANA) (http://www.iana.org/). In a sense, the IANA owns all 4,294,967,296 (or 2^{32}) possible IP addresses. At one time, the IANA allocated blocks of consecutive IP addresses to the military, universities, government departments and agencies, and businesses. These organizations, in turn, assigned IP addresses to their computers from the blocks given them by the IANA. When the

Exhibit 1   Binary to Decimal Conversion

Binary	2^7	2^6	2^5	2^4	2^3	2^2	2^1	2^0
Decimal	128	64	32	16	8	4	2	1

organization grew and required more addresses, the IANA gave them additional blocks of IP addresses.

As Internet use grew, so did the demand for addresses. Eventually, the IANA thought enough was enough and delegated the bureaucratic job of allocating IP address to three regional organizations. The IANA allocated each of these Regional Internet Registries (RIRs) a large chunk of unused IP addresses to meet the demands of each of their regions.

Today, RIPE (http://www.ripe.net/), the Reseaux IP Europeens, handles requests for IP addresses from Europe, the Middle East, and North Africa. The APNIC (http://www.apnic.net/), or Asia Pacific Network Information Centre, allocates IP addresses to computers located in Asia and the Pacific. The remainder of the world, including North and South America, the Caribbean, and sub-Saharan Africa, obtain their IP addresses from ARIN (http://www.arin.net), the American Registry for Internet Numbers. In the summer of 2001, the Canadian Internet Registration Authority (CIRA) (http://www.cira.ca) was formed to register Canadian domains.

But if you are thinking about contacting one of these to obtain some IP addresses of your own, think not. Today, Regional Internet Registries only give ISPs blocks of IP addresses. ISPs are responsible for sub-allocation of their IP addresses — the assignment of IP addresses to customers — whether the customers are individuals, companies, government agencies, schools, or even smaller ISPs.

So what do these addresses look like? An IP address is a 32-bit binary number. Most humans are not very good at remembering very large binary numbers. You start to talk to people about numbers that large and their eyes glaze over. So, typically, you represent an IP address as four decimal values, each representing 8 bits, in the range 0 to 255 (known as octets) separated by decimal points. This is known as "dotted decimal" or "dotted quad" notation. Sometimes, you represent the 32-bit address in hexadecimal format.

Each bit in the octet or byte represents a value. Each binary value converts to a decimal value. To calculate the value for each bit, use Exhibit 1.

You add bit values together to determine a decimal equivalent number. For example:

$$11000000 \qquad 10101000 \qquad 11001000 \qquad 11001000$$

$$11000000 = 2^7 + 2^6 = 128 + 64 = 192$$
$$10101000 = 2^7 + 2^5 + 2^3 = 128 + 32 + 8 = 168$$
$$11001000 = 2^7 + 2^6 + 2^3 = 128 + 64 + 8 = 200$$
$$11001000 = 2^7 + 2^6 + 2^3 = 128 + 64 + 8 = 200$$

Thus, the binary address 11000000101010001100100011001000 equals 192.168.200.200. Exhibit 2 provides a conversion chart for values from 0 to 255.

Every IP address consists of two parts: one that identifies the network and one that identifies the node. The class of the address and the subnet mask determine what part refers to the network address and what part refers to the node address.

Exhibit 2   Binary/Decimal Conversion Chart

Decimal	Binary	Decimal	Binary	Decimal	Binary	Decimal	Binary
0	00000000	45	00101101	90	01011010	135	10000111
1	00000001	46	00101110	91	01011011	136	10001000
2	00000010	47	00101111	92	01011100	137	10001001
3	00000011	48	00110000	93	01011101	138	10001010
4	00000100	49	00110001	94	01011110	139	10001011
5	00000101	50	00110010	95	01011111	140	10001100
6	00000110	51	00110011	96	01100000	141	10001101
7	00000111	52	00110100	97	01100001	142	10001110
8	00001000	53	00110101	98	01100010	143	10001111
9	00001001	54	00110110	99	01100011	144	10010000
10	00001010	55	00110111	100	01100100	145	10010001
11	00001011	56	00111000	101	01100101	146	10010010
12	00001100	57	00111001	102	01100110	147	10010011
13	00001101	58	00111010	103	01100111	148	10010100
14	00001110	59	00111011	104	01101000	149	10010101
15	00001111	60	00111100	105	01101001	150	10010110
16	00010000	61	00111101	106	01101010	151	10010111
17	00010001	62	00111110	107	01101011	152	10011000
18	00010010	63	00111111	108	01101100	153	10011001
19	00010011	64	01000000	109	01101101	154	10011010
20	00010100	65	01000001	110	01101110	155	10011011
21	00010101	66	01000010	111	01101111	156	10011100
22	00010110	67	01000011	112	01110000	157	10011101
23	00010111	68	01000100	113	01110001	158	10011110
24	00011000	69	01000101	114	01110010	159	10011111
25	00011001	70	01000110	115	01110011	160	10100000
26	00011010	71	01000111	116	01110100	161	10100001
27	00011011	72	01001000	117	01110101	162	10100010
28	00011100	73	01001001	118	01110110	163	10100011
29	00011101	74	01001010	119	01110111	164	10100100
30	00011110	75	01001011	120	01111000	165	10100101
31	00011111	76	01001100	121	01111001	166	10100110
32	00100000	77	01001101	122	01111010	167	10100111
33	00100001	78	01001110	123	01111011	168	10101000
34	00100010	79	01001111	124	01111100	169	10101001
35	00100011	80	01010000	125	01111101	170	10101010
36	00100100	81	01010001	126	01111110	171	10101011
37	00100101	82	01010010	127	01111111	172	10101100
38	00100110	83	01010011	128	10000000	173	10101101
39	00100111	84	01010100	129	10000001	174	10101110
40	00101000	85	01010101	130	10000010	175	10101111
41	00101001	86	01010110	131	10000011	176	10110000
42	00101010	87	01010111	132	10000100	177	10110001
43	00101011	88	01011000	133	10000101	178	10110010
44	00101100	89	01011001	134	10000110	179	10110011

Exhibit 2   Binary/Decimal Conversion Chart (Continued)

Decimal	Binary	Decimal	Binary	Decimal	Binary	Decimal	Binary
180	10110100	199	11000111	218	11011010	237	11101101
181	10110101	200	11001000	219	11011011	238	11101110
182	10110110	201	11001001	220	11011100	239	11101111
183	10110111	202	11001010	221	11011101	240	11110000
184	10111000	203	11001011	222	11011110	241	11110001
185	10111001	204	11001100	223	11011111	242	11110010
186	10111010	205	11001101	224	11100000	243	11110011
187	10111011	206	11001110	225	11100001	244	11110100
188	10111100	207	11001111	226	11100010	245	11110101
189	10111101	208	11010000	227	11100011	246	11110110
190	10111110	209	11010001	228	11100100	247	11110111
191	10111111	210	11010010	229	11100101	248	11111000
192	11000000	211	11010011	230	11100110	249	11111001
193	11000001	212	11010100	231	11100111	250	11111010
194	11000010	213	11010101	232	11101000	251	11111011
195	11000011	214	11010110	233	11101001	252	11111100
196	11000100	215	11010111	234	11101010	253	11111101
197	11000101	216	11011000	235	11101011	254	11111110
198	11000110	217	11011001	236	11101100	255	11111111

Note: You can convert decimal to binary, and vice versa, using the Windows Calculator. Start the Calculator by selecting | Start | Programs | Accessories |. Select Scientific under the View menu. You should see the calculator in Exhibit 3.

The default setting is decimal. Type in a decimal number such as 200, and then click the radio button Bin (for binary). The Calculator converts the number to 11001000. To convert it back, just click on the Dec (for decimal) radio button. You can also use the Calculator to convert decimal and binary to hexadecimal.

Address Classes

The IANA originally grouped IP addresses in classes. There are five different address classes. You can determine what class any IP address is in by examining the first 4 bits of the high-order byte or octet of the IP address.

- Class A addresses begin with 0nnn, or 1 to 126 decimal.
- Class B addresses begin with 10nn, or 128 to 191 decimal.
- Class C addresses begin with 110n, or 192 to 223 decimal.
- Class D addresses begin with 1110, or 224 to 239 decimal.
- Class E addresses begin with 1111, or 240 to 254 decimal.

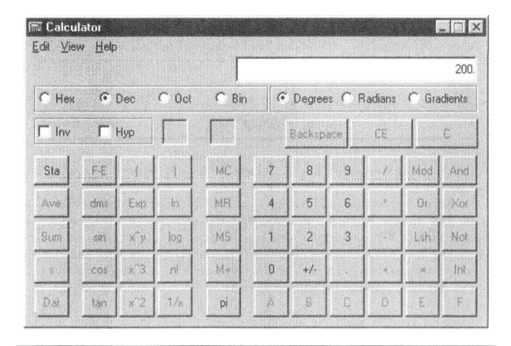

Exhibit 3   Windows Calculator in Scientific Mode

Addresses beginning with 01111111, or 127 decimal, are reserved for loopback and for internal testing on a local machine.

> **Note:** You can test this. You can try to ping 127.0.0.1, which is a reserved address for localhost — your machine.

Class D addresses are reserved for multicasting. Class E addresses are reserved for future use. Class E networks start with 11111. You should not use them for host addresses.

Although the IP address is a single 32-bit value, the set of all IP addresses is not a flat space. Instead, there is a two-level hierarchy of networks and hosts within the networks, each identified by a portion of the address. You can divide any address into a network number and a host number. In TCP/IP terminology, the network number identifies a set of machines that can communicate directly with each other at layer 2 of the OSI model. Now you can see how the class determines, by default, what part of the IP address belongs to the network (N) and what part belongs to the node (n).

- Class A: NNNNNNNN.nnnnnnnn.nnnnnnn.nnnnnnn
- Class B: NNNNNNNN.NNNNNNNN.nnnnnnnn.nnnnnnnn
- Class C: NNNNNNNN.NNNNNNNN.NNNNNNNN.nnnnnnnn

In our example, 192.168.220.200 is a Class C address; thus, by default, the network part of the address (also known as the network address) is defined by

Exhibit 4   Summary of Address Format

Class	High-Order Bits	Network Portion	Host Portion	Number of Addresses
A	0	7	24	16,777,214
B	10	14	16	65,534
C	110	21	8	254
D	1110	Multicast Group		268,435,456

the first three octets (192.168.200.n), and the node part is defined by the last octet (N.N.N.200).

To specify the network address for a given IP address, the node section is set to all "0"s. In our example, 192.168.200.0 specifies the network address for 192.168.200.200. When the node section is set to all "1"s, it specifies a broadcast that is sent to all hosts on the network. 192.168.200.255 specifies the example broadcast address. Note that this is true regardless of the length of the node section. Exhibit 4 summarizes address formats for the four major classes (A, B, C, and D).

There is a simple formula for figuring out how many hosts are in each network: $2^n - 2$. You can do the math; but for Class A, it is $2^{24} - 2$ or 16,777,214 hosts (or nodes more correctly). The formula for calculating how many networks you have is the same. So, for Class A networks, you have $2^7 - 2$ or 126. This means that you have 126 different Class A networks, each with 16,777,214 potential nodes.

Tip: You might wonder why you did not use 2^8 instead of 2^7, inasmuch as you use one octet or byte for the network portion of a Class A network. That is logical; but remember that the first bit was set to 1, so you really only had 7 bits to play with. You are correct if you think that means 2^{14} and 2^{21} networks for Class B and C, respectively.

Note: These formulae are extremely important in Appendix B, "Subnetting."

Private Networks

There are three IP network addresses reserved for private networks. The address used in an example above is one of them. The addresses are 10.0.0.0/8, 172.16.0.0/12, and 192.168.0.0/16. They can be used by anyone setting up internal IP networks, such as a lab or home LAN behind a NAT (network address translator), a proxy server, or a router. It is always safe to use these because routers on the Internet will never forward packets coming from these addresses. These addresses are defined in RFC 1918.

Exhibit 5   Addresses Reserved for Private Networks

Class	From IP Address	To IP Address	Classless Notation
A	10.0.0.0	10.255.255.255	10.0.0.0/8
B	172.16.0.0	172.31.255.255	172.16.0.0/12
C	192.168.0.0	192.168.255.255	192.168.0.0/16

Tip: If you do not know about subnetting and do not understand the notation 10.0.0.0/8, this covered in Appendix B, "Subnetting." If you think you understand subnetting and the notation, take a second to calculate the address range for the Class B private network before looking at Exhibit 5. You can calculate the Class C addresses as well, but it is a little easier.

Exhibit 5 summarizes the private addresses.

If you cannot remember the classless notation, refer to Appendix B, "Subnetting." There are some simple rules and guidelines specified for private addresses in RFC 1918:

- Routers must not propagate routing information about private networks on inter-enterprise links, such as a link to the Internet or a private link to another organization.
- Routers should not forward packets with private source or destination addresses across such links.
- You should contain indirect references, such as Domain Name System resource records, to such addresses within your organization.

Special Addresses

Before leaving the subject of addressing, there is one other thing you need to know. There are some special reserved addresses. You saw that there is a loopback network (network 127) and some private addresses (networks 10, 172.16–31, 192.168), but there are also some others. A general networking rule is that an address with all "0"s or all "1"s is reserved. All "0"s usually refers to the entire network or subnetwork. All "1"s usually refers to all hosts on the specified network or subnetwork. Exhibit 6 summarizes the special addresses.

To really understand classful and classless addressing, dive right into Appendix B.

Exhibit 6   Special Addresses

Dotted Decimal	Address Explanation
0.0.0.0	All hosts broadcast address for some Sun networks
nnn.nnn.nnn.0	Identifies entire network
nnn.nnn.nnn.255	All hosts on the specified network
10.0.0.0	Reserved Class A Proxy Server Address
127.0.0.1	Loopback address
172.16.0.0 to 172.31.0.0	Reserved Class B Proxy Server Address
192.168.nnn.0	Reserved Class C Proxy Server Address
255.255.255.255	All hosts broadcast for current networks

Appendix B

Subnetting

When the original people developed IP, there was no concept of local area networking. They had mainframes with terminals attached. This arrangement was hierarchical and the host mainframe was in charge and polled the terminals to see whether they had any data to send. On occasion, there was a need to transfer some data from their network to another network over a packet-switched network. This data flowed through the router.

Along came local area networks (LANs) based on broadcast technology rather than point-to-point technology. Users in a workgroup want to exchange information among themselves. The way IP worked, it would necessitate sending every packet to the router. On large networks, for example, a Class A network with a potential 16,777,214 endpoints, this resulted in a lot of unnecessary overhead. On top of that, it is unreasonable to assign a Class A or B network to an Ethernet network with a limit of 1200 attachments. Thus, *subnetting* was developed to divide physical networks into logical ones. Subnetting divides the network into a network portion and a subnet portion. Hosts whose addresses share a network number can send local broadcasts to one another and communicate without a router. Hosts with different network numbers can communicate only via an IP router.

When developing a subnet addressing scheme, it is important to ask yourself the following questions:

- How many networks does my organization currently need?
- How many hosts does my largest network currently need?
- How many networks will my organization need in the future?
- How many hosts will my largest network need in the future?

The answers to these questions will determine how you subnet your physical network. So, take a look at how to subnet your network.

In Appendix A, "IP Addressing," you saw that bits in the network portion of IP addresses identify the network; that is, the first byte in a Class A network, the

Exhibit 1   Default Network Masks

Class	Decimal Netmask	Binary Netmask
A	255.0.0.0	11111111000000000000000000000000
B	255.255.0.0	11111111111111110000000000000000
C	255.255.255.0	11111111111111111111111100000000

Exhibit 2   Setting the Netmask Output Format

Command	Resultant Output
terminal ip netmask-format bit-count	192.168.200.0/23
terminal ip netmask-format decimal	192.168.200.0 255.255.254.0
terminal ip netmask-format hexadecimal	192.168.200.0 0xFFFFFE00

first two bytes in a Class B network, and the first three bytes in a Class C network. As you can see, the division between the network number and host number differs for each network. To help router software distinguish between network and host portions, each address has an associated *network mask* (also known as a *mask, subnet mask,* or *netmask*). This network mask is a 32-bit number where the bits in the network portion are set to 1 and the bits in the host portion are set to 0. An IP address and its netmask go together like bacon and eggs. A mask of 11111111 11111111 00000000 00000000 indicates that the first 16 bits of the IP address represent the network portion and 16 bits represent the host portion. All bits in the network mask must be contiguous. Therefore, a network mask of 11111111 11111111 00000011 00000000 is not valid.

Note: Originally, the designers allowed discontiguous network masks, but this proved very difficult for the wetware — humans — to calculate.

Exhibit 1 provides the natural or default network masks.

Similar to IP addresses, a network mask is represented in dotted-decimal format. Thus, you might see a mask represented as 255.255.0.0 or 255.255.255.192. Because all the bits are contiguous, network professionals are using a different format for expressing the network mask. There is no longer a requirement for masks to fall on full-word or 8-bit boundaries. You may hear someone talking about a 23-bitmask, which means you have a mask with 23 1-bits, followed by 9 0-bits. This new notation is referred to as *base address/bit count notation.*

In the Cisco IOS, you can change the output format for network masks using the commands in Exhibit 2.

Subnetting is the first explicit use of network masks. Applying a network mask to an IP address allows you to identify the network and node parts of the address.

The big question is: how does a router use the subnet mask to determine what part of an IP address refers to the network address? Performing a bitwise logical AND operation between the IP address and the subnet mask results in the real *network address* or *number*. For example, using a test IP address and the default Class C subnet mask, we get:

```
11000000101010001100100011001000   192.168.200.200   Class C IP address
11111111111111111111111100000000   255.255.255.000   Default Class C netmask
11000000101010001100100000000000   192.168.200.0     Network address
```

More Restrictive Subnet Masks

You can add additional bits to the default subnet mask for a given class to further subnet, or break down, a network. That is, you can borrow some bits from the node bits and use them to create subnets. This results in a decrease in the possible number of node addresses because you are using some of the host bits to create subnets. With bits removed for subnets, you get fewer node addresses. Borrowing the bits will not only let you compute IP address ranges for each subnet, but it also lets you create a new subnet mask for the entire network. This new netmask will let routers and other network devices know that you have divided your network into subnets. The subnet mask will also tell these devices how many logical subnets you have created. When a bitwise logical AND operation is performed between the new subnet mask and IP address, the result defines the *subnet address*. There are some restrictions on the subnet address. Node addresses of all "0"s or all "1"s are reserved for specifying the local network (when a host does not know its network address) or all hosts on the network (broadcast address), respectively. This also applies to subnets; a subnet address cannot be all "0"s or all "1"s. This also implies that a 1-bit subnet mask is not allowed. This restriction is required because older standards enforced this restriction. Recent standards that allow the use of these subnets have superseded these standards, but many "legacy" devices do not support the newer standards. If you are operating in a controlled environment, such as a lab, you can safely use these restricted subnets.

To calculate the number of subnets or nodes, use the formula $(2^n - 2)$, where n is number of bits in either field. Multiplying the number of subnets by the number of nodes available per subnet yields the total number of nodes available for your class and subnet mask. Example:

```
11000000101010001100100011001000   192.168.200.200   Class C IP address
11111111111111111111111111100000   255.255.255.224   Class C netmask
11000000101010001100100011000000   192.168.200.192   Network address
```

In this example, a 3-bit subnet mask was used. There are six subnets $(2^3 - 2 = 6)$ available with this size mask (remember that subnets with all "0"s or all "1"s are not allowed). Each subnet has 30 nodes $(2^5 - 2 = 30)$. Each subnet can have nodes assigned to any address between the subnet address and the broadcast address. This gives a total of 180 nodes for the entire Class C address subnetted

Exhibit 3   Subnet Masks: Class A

Subnet Bits	Subnet Mask	Total Subnets	Total Hosts/Subnet
2	255.192.0.0	2	4,194,302
3	255.224.0.0	6	2,097,150
4	255.240.0.0	14	1,048,574
5	255.248.0.0	30	524,286
6	255.252.0.0	62	262,142
7	255.254.0.0	126	131,070
8	255.255.0.0	254	65,534
9	255.255.128.0	510	32,766
10	255.255.192.0	1,022	16,382
11	255.255.224.0	2,046	8,190
12	255.255.240.0	4,094	4,094
13	255.255.248.0	8,190	2,046
14	255.255.252.0	16,382	1,022
15	255.255.254.0	32,766	510
16	255.255.255.0	65,534	254
17	255.255.255.128	131,072	126
18	255.255.255.192	262,142	62
19	255.255.255.224	524,286	30
20	255.255.255.240	1,048,574	14
21	255.255.255.248	2,097,150	6
22	255.255.255.252	4,194,302	2

this way. Notice that this is less than the 254 nodes an unsubnetted Class C address would have.

Note: If you do not like the formula used above to calculate the number of nodes, you can add the low-order bits and subtract 1. This also works. So, using the example above, this would be 1 + 2 + 4 + 8 + 16 − 1 = 30.

Subnetting always reduces the number of possible nodes for a given network. There are complete subnet tables available for Class A (Exhibit 3), Class B (Exhibit 4), and Class C (Exhibit 5). These tables provide possible subnet masks for each class, along with calculations for the number of subnetworks and total hosts for each subnet.

Subnet examples

Here is another example. You have a Class C network address and you want to configure six networks of 30 hosts each. In this example, you would use the

Exhibit 4   Subnet Masks: Class B

Subnet Bits	Subnet Mask	Total Subnets	Total Hosts/Subnet
2	255.255.192.0	2	16,382
3	255.255.224.0	6	8,190
4	255.255.240.0	14	4,094
5	255.255.248.0	30	2,046
6	255.255.252.0	62	1,022
7	255.255.254.0	126	510
8	255.255.255.0	254	254
9	255.255.255.128	510	126
10	255.255.255.192	1,022	62
11	255.255.255.224	2,046	30
12	255.255.255.240	4,094	14
13	255.255.255.248	8,190	6
14	255.255.255.252	16,384	2

Exhibit 5   Subnet Masks: Class C

Subnet Bits	Subnet Mask	Total Subnets	Total Hosts/Subnet
2	255.255.255.192	2	62
3	255.255.255.224	6	30
4	255.255.255.240	14	14
5	255.255.255.248	30	6
6	255.255.255.252	62	2

subnet mask of 255.255.255.224. You start with 254 potential addresses but end up with 180. Why? First, Subnet 0, binary 000, is reserved to refer to "The Subnet." Second, Subnet 7, binary 111, is reserved for broadcast to all subnets within the network. This leaves only subnets 1 through 6 available. However, Host number 0, binary 00000, and host number 31, binary 11111, within each subnet are reserved, so only hosts with IDs 1 to 30 are available. So you have six subnets with 30 hosts in each, or 180 addresses.

Note: You can use the lost addresses or subnet 0 of a Class C network if you wish. You can configure the router to take advantage of the subnet 0 addresses using the following global configuration command:

router#**ip subnet-zero**

Using subnet 0 means your mask is 255.255.255.128.

Exhibit 6   Subnets and Addresses

#	Subnet	Broadcasts	Valid IP Addresses
1	219.129.44.32 (0s)	219.129.44.63 (1s)	219.129.44.33 to 219.129.44.62
2	219.129.44.64 (0s)	219.129.44.95 (1s)	219.129.44.65 to 219.129.44.94
3	219.129.44.96 (0s)	219.129.44.127 (1s)	219.129.44.97 to 219.129.44.126
4	219.129.44.128 (0s)	219.129.44.159 (1s)	219.129.44.129 to 219.129.44.158
5	219.129.44.160 (0s)	219.129.44.191 (1s)	219.129.44.161 to 219.129.44.190
6	219.129.44.192 (0s)	219.129.44.223 (1s)	219.129.44.193 to 219.129.44.222

Another detailed example may help. Your ISP assigns you a Class C network number of 219.129.44.0 (apologies to any one actual owner of this network address). If you use the subnet mask of 255.255.255.224, you end up with the addresses shown in Exhibit 6. Looking at this table, you can derive another rule for subnetting: a rule for calculating the subnet ranges. Take the lowest high-order bit you used to calculate the new subnet mask, or 32. This number becomes the incremental value used to create the IP address for the six subnets. Starting at 219.129.44.0 (an illegal address), the next address is 219.129.44.32, the next is 219.129.44.64, the next is 219.129.44.96, and so on, up to 219.129.44.192. The ending addresses are just 1 less than the beginning of the next subnet: 219.129.44.63, 219.129.44.95, 219.129.44.127, 219.129.44.159, 219.129.44.191, and 219.129.44.223. This makes our calculations much easier.

Take a look at another example of this easy calculation. You have a Class A network 10.0.0.0 that you want to break up in to a manageable 30 subnets. The subnet mask you will use is 255.248.0.0. So, using the rule above, the increment is the lowest high-order bit (or 8; i.e., 128, 64, 32, 16, and 8). You start with 10.8.0.1 and add 8. Exhibit 7 shows the IP address ranges for the 30 subnets.

Note: All these calculations might make your head hurt. Do not despair; there is help. Go to your favorite freeware/shareware site and download a subnet calculator. In Exhibit 8, you can see a utility called IP Subnet Calculator. There are plenty of them, so pick the one you like. If you have understood everything in this appendix, then this utility will be easy to use.

Finally, take a look at an example in a methodical way.

- All 4 bytes are written the same as when you are not subnetted.
- Write out the address in binary.
- Write out the subnet mask from the library.
- Logically AND the two.
- The bits of the outcome of the AND operation show the network and subnet.

Exhibit 7   IP Address Ranges for Subnets

Subnet #	Start Address	End Address
1	10.8.0.1	10.15.255.254
2	10.16.0.1	10.23.255.254
3	10.24.0.1	10.31.255.254
4	10.32.0.1	10.39.255.254
5	10.40.0.1	10.47.255.254
6	10.48.0.1	10.55.255.254
7	10.56.0.1	10.63.255.254
8	10.64.0.1	10.71.255.254
9	10.72.0.1	10.79.255.254
10	10.80.0.1	10.87.255.254
11	10.88.0.1	10.95.255.254
12	10.96.0.1	10.103.255.254
13	10.104.0.1	10.111.255.254
14	10.112.0.1	10.119.255.254
15	10.120.0.1	10.127.255.254
16	10.128.0.1	10.135.255.254
17	10.136.0.1	10.143.255.254
18	10.144.0.1	10.151.255.254
19	10.152.0.1	10.159.255.254
20	10.160.0.1	10.167.255.254
21	10.168.0.1	10.175.255.254
22	10.176.0.1	10.183.255.254
23	10.184.0.1	10.191.255.254
24	10.192.0.1	10.199.255.254
25	10.200.0.1	10.207.255.254
26	10.208.0.1	10.215.255.254
27	10.216.0.1	10.223.255.254
28	10.224.0.1	10.231.255.254
29	10.232.0.1	10.239.255.254
30	10.240.0.1	10.247.255.254

Operation:

```
10000001  00000001  00001001  00000001 — Address 129.1.9.1
11111111  11111111  11111000  00000000 — Mask 255.255.248.0
10000001  00000001  00001000  00000000 — Network 129.1, subnet 8
                                         True network 129.1.8.0
```

CIDR

There is another networking concept you must know. Now that you understand "classful" IP subnetting principles, you need to understand a complicating factor.

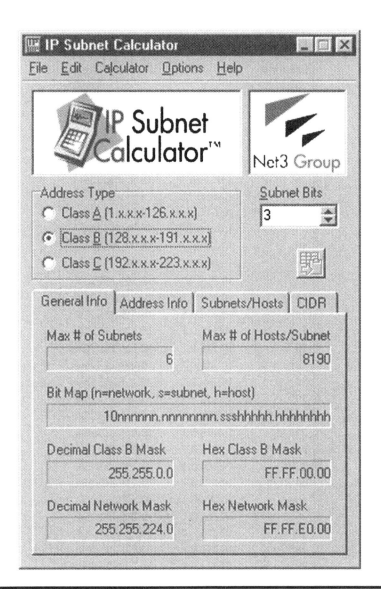

Exhibit 8   IP Subnet Calculator

The complicating factor is CIDR — Classless InterDomain Routing. The protocol designers invented CIDR several years ago to keep the Internet from running out of IP addresses. The "classful" system of allocating IP addresses was very wasteful; anyone who could reasonably show a need for more that 254 host addresses was given a Class B address block of 65,534 host addresses. Even more wasteful were companies and organizations that were allocated Class A networks, which contain over 16 million addresses! Only a tiny percentage of the allocated Class A address space actually has been assigned to a host computer on the Internet.

    People realized that they could conserve addresses if they could eliminate the class system. Removal of the class system was not for egalitarian or ideological reasons; the motivation was economy. By accurately allocating only the amount of address space actually needed by an organization, one could avoid the address space crisis for years. This was first proposed in 1992 as a scheme called *supernetting*. Under supernetting, the designers extended the classful subnet masks so that a network address and subnet mask could, for example, specify multiple Class C subnets with one address. For example, if you required approximately 1000 addresses, you could supernet four Class C networks together:

192.168.128.0   (11000000.10101000.10000000.00000000) Class C subnet address
192.168.129.0   (11000000.10101000.10000001.00000000) Class C subnet address
192.168.130.0   (11000000.10101000.10000010.00000000) Class C subnet address
192.168.131.0   (11000000.10101000.10000011.00000000) Class C subnet address
192.168.128.0   (11000000.10101000.10000000.00000000) Supernetted subnet
                                                           address

255.255.252.0   (11111111.11111111.11111100.00000000) Subnet mask
192.168.131.255 (11000000.10101000.10000011.11111111) Broadcast address

In this example, the subnet 192.168.128.0 includes all the addresses from 192.168.128.0 to 192.168.131.255. As you can see in the binary representation of the subnet mask, the network portion of the address is 22 bits long and the host portion is 10 bits long.

Under CIDR, the subnet mask notation is reduced to simplified shorthand, or base address/bit count notation. Instead of spelling out the bits of the subnet mask, it is simply listed as the number of 1s bits that start the mask. In the above example, instead of writing the address and subnet mask as:

192.168.128.0, Subnet mask 255.255.252.0

you could simply write the network address as:

192.168.128.0/22

This notation indicates the starting address of the network and the number of 1s bits (22) in the network portion of the address. If you look at the subnet mask in binary (11111111.11111111.11111100.00000000), you can easily see how this notation works.

The use of a CIDR notated address is the same as for a classful address. Classful addresses can be easily written in CIDR notation (Class A = /8, Class B = /16, and Class C = /24).

CIDR reduces the number of routing entries required through route aggregation, wherein a single routing entry represents IP address space across traditional classful bit boundaries. In this manner, Internet routers can summarize IP address space to other routers, thus minimizing the number of entries required.

It is expected that CIDR will provide the Internet with sufficient IP addresses for the next few years at least. After that, we will need IPv6, with its 128-bit addresses. This gives us 2^{128} addresses — an extremely large number. Under IPv6, even wasteful address allocation will comfortably allow a billion unique IP addresses for every person on Earth. This should suffice until the battle shown in the movie *Independence Day*. The complete details of CIDR are documented in RFC 1519.

Variable-Length Subnet Masking (VLSM)

Because of the aforementioned impending shortage of IP addresses, the designers also created *Variable-Length Subnet Masking (VLSM)*. VLSM allows you to use more than one subnet mask for the entire network. Newer routing protocols require that the router forward the number of bits used for subnetting with the route, so that packets do not get routed down the wrong path or start looping. Therefore, other routers can determine whether a packet is destined for a particular destination.

Local or Remote Destination

To send a message, the station must determine whether it should send that message to a device on its local network using its MAC address or send it to a default gateway (e.g., the router) for forwarding to another network. The station performs a logical AND on the destination address to determine whether the message is local or remote. If the station determines the message is local, then the station looks in its ARP cache for the corresponding MAC address for the destination address. If the MAC address is found, the station sends the message using the found MAC address. If the station does not find the MAC address, it performs an ARP broadcast to get the corresponding MAC address.

Finally, a station can send an ICMP message type 17 (Address Mask Request) to obtain the subnet mask of the network where they are attached. Stations submit this request to a known node (such as a gateway or router) or broadcast the request to the network. The node sends back an ICMP message type 18 (Address Mask Reply). Refer to Appendix F, "ICMP Types and Codes," for more information.

Appendix C

IP Protocol Numbers

In Chapter 2, "Understanding OSI and TCP/IP," you saw the IP header datagram format. An important field for filtering and blocking traffic within the IP header is the protocol field. The protocol field is 8 bits long. And because the field is 8 bits, it can accommodate 256 (or 2^8) different protocols.

The ICANN under the auspices of the IANA assigns and controls IP protocols. You can look in RFC 1700 for a current list of assigned numbers. Exhibit 1 shows the IP protocol numbers assigned.

Exhibit 1 IP Protocol Assignments

Value	Keyword	Description
0	HOPOPT	Hop-by-hop option (IP version 6)
1	ICMP	Internet Control Message Protocol
2	IGMP	Internet Group Management Protocol
3	GGP	Gateway-to-Gateway Protocol
4	IP	IP in IP (encapsulation)
5	ST	Stream
6	TCP	Transmission Control Protocol
7	CBT	CBT
8	EGP	Exterior Gateway Protocol
9	IGP	Any private interior gateway
10	BBN-RCC-MON	BBN (Bolt Beranek Newman) RCC Monitoring
11	NVP-II	Network Voice Protocol Version II
12	PUP	PUP
13	ARGUS	ARGUS
14	EMCON	EMCON
15	XNET	Cross Net Debugger
16	CHAOS	Chaos
17	UDP	User Datagram Protocol

Exhibit 1   IP Protocol Assignments (Continued)

Value	Keyword	Description
18	MUX	Multiplexing
19	DCN-MEAS	DCN Measurement subsystems
20	HMP	Host Monitoring Protocol
21	PRM	Packet Radio Measurement
22	XNS-IDP	XEROX NS IDP
23	TRUNK-1	Trunk-1
24	TRUNK-2	Trunk-2
25	LEAF-1	Leaf-1
26	LEAF-2	Leaf-2
27	RDP	Reliable Data Protocol
28	IRTP	Internet Reliable Transaction Protocol
29	ISO-TP4	ISO Transport Protocol Class 4
30	NETBLT	Bulk Data Transfer Protocol
31	MFE-NSP	MFE Network Services Protocol
32	MERIT-INP	MERIT Inter-Nodal Protocol
33	SEP	Sequential Exchange Protocol
34	3PC	Third Party Connect Protocol
35	IDPR	Inter-Domain Policy Routing protocol
36	XTP	XTP
37	DDP	Datagram Delivery Protocol
38	IDPR-CMTP	IDPR Control Message Transport Protocol
39	TP++	TP++ Transport Protocol
40	IL	IL Transport Protocol
41	IPv6	Internet Protocol version 6
42	SDRP	Source Demand Routing Protocol
43	IPv6-ROUTE	Routing Header (IP version 6)
44	IPv6-FRAG	Fragment Header (IP version 6)
45	IDRP	Inter-Domain Routing Protocol
46	RSVP	Reservation Protocol
47	GRE	General Routing Encapsulation
48	MHRP	Mobile Host Routing Protocol
49	BNA	BNA
50	ESP	Encapsulation Security Payload (IP version 6)
51	AH	Authentication Header (IP version 6)
52	I-NLSP	Integrated Net Layer Security Protocol
53	SWIPE	IP with Encryption
54	NARP	NBMA Address Resolution Protocol
55	MOBILE	IPO Mobility
56	TLSP	Transport Layer Security Protocol (Kryptonet Key Management)
57	SKIP	Skip
58	IPv6-ICMP	Internet Control Message Protocol (IP version 6)
59	IPv6-NoNxt	No Next Header (IP version 6)
60	IPv6-Opts	Destination Options (IP version 6)
61	HOST	Any host internal protocol

Exhibit 1   IP Protocol Assignments (Continued)

Value	Keyword	Description
62	CFTP	CFTP
63	Network	Any local network
64	SAT-EXPAK	SATNET and Backroom EXPAK
65	KRYPTOLAN	Kryptolan
66	RVD	MIT Remote Virtual Disk Protocol
67	IPPC	Internet Pluribus Packet Core
68	FILE	Any distributed file system
69	SAT-MON	SATNET Monitoring
70	VISA	VISA Protocol
71	IPCU	Internet Packet Core Utility
72	CPNX	Computer Protocol Network Executive
73	CPHB	Computer Protocol Heart Beat
74	WSN	Wang Span Network
75	PVP	Packet Video Protocol
76	BR-SAT-MON	Backroom SATNET Monitoring
77	SUN-ND	SUN ND PROTOCOL
78	WB-MON	Wideband Monitoring
79	WB-EXPAK	Wideband EXPAK
80	ISO-IP	ISO Internet Protocol
81	VMTP	VMTP
82	SECURE-VMTP	SECURE-VMTP
83	VINES	Banyan VINES
84	TTP	TTP
85	NSFNET-IGP	NSFNET Interior Gateway Protocol
86	DGP	Dissimilar Gateway Protocol
87	TCF	TCF
88	EIGRP	Enhanced Interior Gateway Routing Protocol
89	OSPFIGP	OSPF Interior Gateway Protocol
90	Sprite-RPC	Sprite RPC Protocol
91	LARP	Locus Address Resolution Protocol
92	MTP	Multicast Transport Protocol
93	AX.25	AX.25 Frames
94	IPIP	IP-within-IP Encapsulation Protocol
95	MICP	Mobile Internetworking Control Protocol
96	SCC-SP	Semaphore Communications Security Protocol
97	ETHERIP	Ethernet-within-IP Encapsulation
98	ENCAP	Encapsulation Header
99	ENCRYPT	Any private encryption scheme
100	GMTP	GMTP
101	IFMP	Ipsilon Flow Management Protocol
102	PNNI	PNNI over IP
103	PIM	Protocol Independent Multicast
104	ARIS	ARIS
105	SCPS	SCPS
106	QNX	QNX

Exhibit 1   IP Protocol Assignments (Continued)

Value	Keyword	Description
107	AN	Active Networks
108	IPPCP	IP Payload Compression Protocol
109	SNP	Sitara Network Protocol
110	COMPAQ-PEER	Compaq Peer-to-Peer Protocol
111	IPXIP	IPX in IP Encapsulation
112	VRRP	Virtual Router Redundancy Protocol
113	PGM	PGM Reliable Transport Protocol
114	NOHOP	Zero Hop Protocols
115	L2TP	Layer 2 Tunneling Protocol
116	DDX	D-II Transport Protocol
117-254	UNASSIGNED	Unassigned
255	RESERVED	Reserved

Appendix D

Well-Known Ports and Services

Formerly the IANA and now the ICANN assign and control "well-known ports." On most systems, system (or root) processes own and use the well-known ports and can only be used by programs executed by privileged users.

TCP ports name the ends of logical connections that carry long-term conversations or, alternatively, sessions. For the purpose of providing services to unknown callers, the system defines a service contact port. The list in this appendix specifies the ports used by the server process as its contact port. The contact port is sometimes called the "well-known port." Wherever possible, these same port assignments are used with the UDP.

The assigned ports use a small portion of the possible port numbers. There are 2^{16} (65,536) possible ports. For many years, the IANA assigned ports in the range 0 to 255. Recently, the IANA has expanded the range from 0 to 1023. The IANA does not control Registered Ports (the range 1024 to 65535) and, on most systems, ordinary user processes or programs executed by ordinary users can use these ports.

You can look in RFC 1700 for a current list of "Well Known and Registered Ports." Exhibit 1 shows these Well-Known Ports.

Exhibit 1   Well-Known Port Assignments

Keyword	Decimal/Protocol	Description
	0/tcp	Reserved
	0/udp	Reserved
tcpmux	1/tcp	TCP Port Service Multiplexer
tcpmux	1/udp	TCP Port Service Multiplexer
compressnet	2/tcp	Management Utility
compressnet	2/udp	Management Utility
compressnet	3/tcp	Compression Process
compressnet	3/udp	Compression Process
	4/tcp	Unassigned
	4/udp	Unassigned
rje	5/tcp	Remote Job Entry
rje	5/udp	Remote Job Entry
	6/tcp	Unassigned
	6/udp	Unassigned
echo	7/tcp	Echo
echo	7/udp	Echo
	8/tcp	Unassigned
	8/udp	Unassigned
discard	9/tcp	Discard
discard	9/udp	Discard
	10/tcp	Unassigned
	10/udp	Unassigned
systat	11/tcp	Active Users
systat	11/udp	Active Users
	12/tcp	Unassigned
	12/udp	Unassigned
daytime	13/tcp	Daytime
daytime	13/udp	Daytime
	14/tcp	Unassigned
	14/udp	Unassigned
	15/tcp	Unassigned [was netstat]
	15/udp	Unassigned
	16/tcp	Unassigned
	16/udp	Unassigned
qotd	17/tcp	Quote of the Day
qotd	17/udp	Quote of the Day
msp	18/tcp	Message Send Protocol
msp	18/udp	Message Send Protocol
chargen	19/tcp	Character Generator
chargen	19/udp	Character Generator
ftp-data	20/tcp	File Transfer [Default Data]
ftp-data	20/udp	File Transfer [Default Data]
ftp	21/tcp	File Transfer [Control]
ftp	21/udp	File Transfer [Control]
	22/tcp	Unassigned

Exhibit 1 Well-Known Port Assignments (Continued)

Keyword	Decimal/Protocol	Description
	22/udp	Unassigned
telnet	23/tcp	Telnet
telnet	23/udp	Telnet
	24/tcp	Any private mail system
	24/udp	Any private mail system
smtp	25/tcp	Simple Mail Transfer
smtp	25/udp	Simple Mail Transfer
	26/tcp	Unassigned
	26/udp	Unassigned
nsw-fe	27/tcp	NSW User System FE
nsw-fe	27/udp	NSW User System FE
	28/tcp	Unassigned
	28/udp	Unassigned
msg-icp	29/tcp	MSG ICP
msg-icp	29/udp	MSG ICP
	30/tcp	Unassigned
	30/udp	Unassigned
msg-auth	31/tcp	MSG Authentication
msg-auth	31/udp	MSG Authentication
	32/tcp	Unassigned
	32/udp	Unassigned
dsp	33/tcp	Display Support Protocol
dsp	33/udp	Display Support Protocol
	34/tcp	Unassigned
	34/udp	Unassigned
	35/tcp	Any private printer server
	35/udp	Any private printer server
	36/tcp	Unassigned
	36/udp	Unassigned
time	37/tcp	Time
time	37/udp	Time
rap	38/tcp	Route Access Protocol
rap	38/udp	Route Access Protocol
rlp	39/tcp	Resource Location Protocol
rlp	39/udp	Resource Location Protocol
	40/tcp	Unassigned
	40/udp	Unassigned
graphics	41/tcp	Graphics
graphics	41/udp	Graphics
nameserver	42/tcp	Host Name Server
nameserver	42/udp	Host Name Server
nicname	43/tcp	Who Is
nicname	43/udp	Who Is
mpm-flags	44/tcp	MPM FLAGS Protocol
mpm-flags	44/udp	MPM FLAGS Protocol

Exhibit 1   Well-Known Port Assignments (Continued)

Keyword	Decimal/Protocol	Description
mpm	45/tcp	Message Processing Module [recv]
mpm	45/udp	Message Processing Module [recv]
mpm-snd	46/tcp	MPM [default send]
mpm-snd	46/udp	MPM [default send]
ni-ftp	47/tcp	NI FTP
ni-ftp	47/udp	NI FTP
auditd	48/tcp	Digital Audit Daemon
auditd	48/udp	Digital Audit Daemon
login	49/tcp	Login Host Protocol
login	49/udp	Login Host Protocol
re-mail-ck	50/tcp	Remote Mail Checking Protocol
re-mail-ck	50/udp	Remote Mail Checking Protocol
la-maint	51/tcp	IMP Logical Address Maintenance
la-maint	51/udp	IMP Logical Address Maintenance
xns-time	52/tcp	XNS Time Protocol
xns-time	52/udp	XNS Time Protocol
domain	53/tcp	Domain Name Server
domain	53/udp	Domain Name Server
xns-ch	54/tcp	XNS Clearinghouse
xns-ch	54/udp	XNS Clearinghouse
isi-gl	55/tcp	ISI Graphics Language
isi-gl	55/udp	ISI Graphics Language
xns-auth	56/tcp	XNS Authentication
xns-auth	56/udp	XNS Authentication
	57/tcp	Any private terminal access
	57/udp	Any private terminal access
xns-mail	58/tcp	XNS Mail
xns-mail	58/udp	XNS Mail
	59/tcp	Any private file service
	59/udp	Any private file service
	60/tcp	Unassigned
	60/udp	Unassigned
ni-mail	61/tcp	NI MAIL
ni-mail	61/udp	NI MAIL
acas	62/tcp	ACA Services
acas	62/udp	ACA Services
	63/tcp	Unassigned
	63/udp	Unassigned
covia	64/tcp	Communications Integrator (CI)
covia	64/udp	Communications Integrator (CI)
tacacs-ds	65/tcp	TACACS-Database Service
tacacs-ds	65/udp	TACACS-Database Service
sql*net	66/tcp	Oracle SQL*NET
sql*net	66/udp	Oracle SQL*NET
bootps	67/tcp	Bootstrap Protocol Server

Exhibit 1 Well-Known Port Assignments (Continued)

Keyword	Decimal/Protocol	Description
bootps	67/udp	Bootstrap Protocol Server
bootpc	68/tcp	Bootstrap Protocol Client
bootpc	68/udp	Bootstrap Protocol Client
tftp	69/tcp	Trivial File Transfer
tftp	69/udp	Trivial File Transfer
gopher	70/tcp	Gopher
gopher	70/udp	Gopher
netrjs-1	71/tcp	Remote Job Service
netrjs-1	71/udp	Remote Job Service
netrjs-2	72/tcp	Remote Job Service
netrjs-2	72/udp	Remote Job Service
netrjs-3	73/tcp	Remote Job Service
netrjs-3	73/udp	Remote Job Service
netrjs-4	74/tcp	Remote Job Service
netrjs-4	74/udp	Remote Job Service
	75/tcp	Any private dial-out service
	75/udp	Any private dial-out service
deos	76/tcp	Distributed External Object Store
deos	76/udp	Distributed External Object Store
	77/tcp	Any private RJE service
	77/udp	Any private RJE service
vettcp	78/tcp	vettcp
vettcp	78/udp	vettcp
finger	79/tcp	Finger
finger	79/udp	Finger
www-http	80/tcp	World Wide Web HTTP
www-http	80/udp	World Wide Web HTTP
hosts2-ns	81/tcp	HOSTS2 Name Server
hosts2-ns	81/udp	HOSTS2 Name Server
xfer	82/tcp	XFER Utility
xfer	82/udp	XFER Utility
mit-ml-dev	83/tcp	MIT ML Device
mit-ml-dev	83/udp	MIT ML Device
ctf	84/tcp	Common Trace Facility
ctf	84/udp	Common Trace Facility
mit-ml-dev	85/tcp	MIT ML Device
mit-ml-dev	85/udp	MIT ML Device
mfcobol	86/tcp	Micro Focus Cobol
mfcobol	86/udp	Micro Focus Cobol
	87/tcp	Any private terminal link
	87/udp	Any private terminal link
kerberos	88/tcp	Kerberos
kerberos	88/udp	Kerberos
su-mit-tg	89/tcp	SU/MIT Telnet Gateway
su-mit-tg	89/udp	SU/MIT Telnet Gateway

Exhibit 1   Well-Known Port Assignments (Continued)

Keyword	Decimal/Protocol	Description
dnsix	90/tcp	DNSIX Securit Attribute Token Map
dnsix	90/udp	DNSIX Securit Attribute Token Map
mit-dov	91/tcp	MIT Dover Spooler
mit-dov	91/udp	MIT Dover Spooler
npp	92/tcp	Network Printing Protocol
npp	92/udp	Network Printing Protocol
dcp	93/tcp	Device Control Protocol
dcp	93/udp	Device Control Protocol
objcall	94/tcp	Tivoli Object Dispatcher
objcall	94/udp	Tivoli Object Dispatcher
supdup	95/tcp	SUPDUP
supdup	95/udp	SUPDUP
dixie	96/tcp	DIXIE Protocol Specification
dixie	96/udp	DIXIE Protocol Specification
swift-rvf	97/tcp	Swift Remote Virtual File Protocol
swift-rvf	97/udp	Swift Remote Virtual File Protocol
tacnews	98/tcp	TAC News
tacnews	98/udp	TAC News
metagram	99/tcp	Metagram Relay
metagram	99/udp	Metagram Relay
newacct	100/tcp	[unauthorized use]
hostname	101/tcp	NIC Host Name Server
hostname	101/udp	NIC Host Name Server
iso-tsap	102/tcp	ISO-TSAP
iso-tsap	102/udp	ISO-TSAP
gppitnp	103/tcp	Genesis Point-to-Point Trans Net
gppitnp	103/udp	Genesis Point-to-Point Trans Net
acr-nema	104/tcp	ACR-NEMA Digital Imag. & Comm. 300
acr-nema	104/udp	ACR-NEMA Digital Imag. & Comm. 300
csnet-ns	105/tcp	Mailbox Name Nameserver
csnet-ns	105/udp	Mailbox Name Nameserver
3com-tsmux	106/tcp	3COM-TSMUX
3com-tsmux	106/udp	3COM-TSMUX
rtelnet	107/tcp	Remote Telnet Service
rtelnet	107/udp	Remote Telnet Service
snagas	108/tcp	SNA Gateway Access Server
snagas	108/udp	SNA Gateway Access Server
pop2	109/tcp	Post Office Protocol — Version 2
pop2	109/udp	Post Office Protocol — Version 2
pop3	110/tcp	Post Office Protocol — Version 3
pop3	110/udp	Post Office Protocol — Version 3
sunrpc	111/tcp	SUN Remote Procedure Call
sunrpc	111/udp	SUN Remote Procedure Call
mcidas	112/tcp	McIDAS Data Transmission Protocol
mcidas	112/udp	McIDAS Data Transmission Protocol

Exhibit 1   Well-Known Port Assignments (Continued)

Keyword	Decimal/Protocol	Description
auth	113/tcp	Authentication Service
auth	113/udp	Authentication Service
audionews	114/tcp	Audio News Multicast
audionews	114/udp	Audio News Multicast
sftp	115/tcp	Simple File Transfer Protocol
sftp	115/udp	Simple File Transfer Protocol
ansanotify	116/tcp	ANSA REX Notify
ansanotify	116/udp	ANSA REX Notify
uucp-path	117/tcp	UUCP Path Service
uucp-path	117/udp	UUCP Path Service
sqlserv	118/tcp	SQL Services
sqlserv	118/udp	SQL Services
nntp	119/tcp	Network News Transfer Protocol
nntp	119/udp	Network News Transfer Protocol
cfdptkt	120/tcp	CFDPTKT
cfdptkt	120/udp	CFDPTKT
erpc	121/tcp	Encore Expedited Remote Procedure Call
erpc	121/udp	Encore Expedited Remote Procedure Call
smakynet	122/tcp	SMAKYNET
smakynet	122/udp	SMAKYNET
ntp	123/tcp	Network Time Protocol
ntp	123/udp	Network Time Protocol
ansatrader	124/tcp	ANSA REX Trader
ansatrader	124/udp	ANSA REX Trader
locus-map	125/tcp	Locus PC-Interface Net Map Ser
locus-map	125/udp	Locus PC-Interface Net Map Ser
unitary	126/tcp	Unisys Unitary Login
unitary	126/udp	Unisys Unitary Login
locus-con	127/tcp	Locus PC-Interface Conn Server
locus-con	127/udp	Locus PC-Interface Conn Server
gss-xlicen	128/tcp	GSS X License Verification
gss-xlicen	128/udp	GSS X License Verification
pwdgen	129/tcp	Password Generator Protocol
pwdgen	129/udp	Password Generator Protocol
cisco-fna	130/tcp	Cisco FNATIVE
cisco-fna	130/udp	Cisco FNATIVE
cisco-tna	131/tcp	Cisco TNATIVE
cisco-tna	131/udp	Cisco TNATIVE
cisco-sys	132/tcp	Cisco SYSMAINT
cisco-sys	132/udp	Cisco SYSMAINT
statsrv	133/tcp	Statistics Service
statsrv	133/udp	Statistics Service
ingres-net	134/tcp	INGRES-NET Service
ingres-net	134/udp	INGRES-NET Service
loc-srv	135/tcp	Location Service

Exhibit 1   Well-Known Port Assignments (Continued)

Keyword	Decimal/Protocol	Description
loc-srv	135/udp	Location Service
profile	136/tcp	PROFILE Naming System
profile	136/udp	PROFILE Naming System
netbios-ns	137/tcp	NETBIOS Name Service
netbios-ns	137/udp	NETBIOS Name Service
netbios-dgm	138/tcp	NETBIOS Datagram Service
netbios-dgm	138/udp	NETBIOS Datagram Service
netbios-ssn	139/tcp	NETBIOS Session Service
netbios-ssn	139/udp	NETBIOS Session Service
emfis-data	140/tcp	EMFIS Data Service
emfis-data	140/udp	EMFIS Data Service
emfis-cntl	141/tcp	EMFIS Control Service
emfis-cntl	141/udp	EMFIS Control Service
bl-idm	142/tcp	Britton-Lee IDM
bl-idm	142/udp	Britton-Lee IDM
imap2	143/tcp	Interim Mail Access Protocol v2
imap2	143/udp	Interim Mail Access Protocol v2
news	144/tcp	NewS
news	144/udp	NewS
uaac	145/tcp	UAAC Protocol
uaac	145/udp	UAAC Protocol
iso-tp0	146/tcp	ISO-IP0
iso-tp0	146/udp	ISO-IP0
iso-ip	147/tcp	ISO-IP
iso-ip	147/udp	ISO-IP
cronus	148/tcp	CRONUS-SUPPORT
cronus	148/udp	CRONUS-SUPPORT
aed-512	149/tcp	AED 512 Emulation Service
aed-512	149/udp	AED 512 Emulation Service
sql-net	150/tcp	SQL-NET
sql-net	150/udp	SQL-NET
hems	151/tcp	HEMS
hems	151/udp	HEMS
bftp	152/tcp	Background File Transfer Program
bftp	152/udp	Background File Transfer Program
sgmp	153/tcp	SGMP
sgmp	153/udp	SGMP
netsc-prod	154/tcp	NETSC
netsc-prod	154/udp	NETSC
netsc-dev	155/tcp	NETSC
netsc-dev	155/udp	NETSC
sqlsrv	156/tcp	SQL Service
sqlsrv	156/udp	SQL Service
knet-cmp	157/tcp	KNET/VM Command/Message Protocol
knet-cmp	157/udp	KNET/VM Command/Message Protocol

Exhibit 1   Well-Known Port Assignments (Continued)

Keyword	Decimal/Protocol	Description
pcmail-srv	158/tcp	PCMail Server
pcmail-srv	158/udp	PCMail Server
nss-routing	159/tcp	NSS-Routing
nss-routing	159/udp	NSS-Routing
sgmp-traps	160/tcp	SGMP-TRAPS
sgmp-traps	160/udp	SGMP-TRAPS
snmp	161/tcp	SNMP
snmp	161/udp	SNMP
snmptrap	162/tcp	SNMPTRAP
snmptrap	162/udp	SNMPTRAP
cmip-man	163/tcp	CMIP/TCP Manager
cmip-man	163/udp	CMIP/TCP Manager
cmip-agent	164/tcp	CMIP/TCP Agent
cmip-agent	164/udp	CMIP/TCP Agent
xns-courier	165/tcp	Xerox
xns-courier	165/udp	Xerox
s-net	166/tcp	Sirius Systems
s-net	166/udp	Sirius Systems
namp	167/tcp	NAMP
namp	167/udp	NAMP
rsvd	168/tcp	RSVD
rsvd	168/udp	RSVD
send	169/tcp	SEND
send	169/udp	SEND
print-srv	170/tcp	Network PostScript
print-srv	170/udp	Network PostScript
multiplex	171/tcp	Network Innovations Multiplex
multiplex	171/udp	Network Innovations Multiplex
cl/1	172/tcp	Network Innovations CL/1
cl/1	172/udp	Network Innovations CL/1
xyplex-mux	173/tcp	Xyplex
xyplex-mux	173/udp	Xyplex
mailq	174/tcp	MAILQ
mailq	174/udp	MAILQ
vmnet	175/tcp	VMNET
vmnet	175/udp	VMNET
genrad-mux	176/tcp	GENRAD-MUX
genrad-mux	176/udp	GENRAD-MUX
xdmcp	177/tcp	X Display Manager Control Protocol
xdmcp	177/udp	X Display Manager Control Protocol
nextstep	178/tcp	NextStep Window Server
nextstep	178/udp	NextStep Window Server
bgp	179/tcp	Border Gateway Protocol
bgp	179/udp	Border Gateway Protocol
ris	180/tcp	Intergraph

Exhibit 1   Well-Known Port Assignments (Continued)

Keyword	Decimal/Protocol	Description
ris	180/udp	Intergraph
unify	181/tcp	Unify
unify	181/udp	Unify
audit	182/tcp	Unisys Audit SITP
audit	182/udp	Unisys Audit SITP
ocbinder	183/tcp	OCBinder
ocbinder	183/udp	OCBinder
ocserver	184/tcp	OCServer
ocserver	184/udp	OCServer
remote-kis	185/tcp	Remote-KIS
remote-kis	185/udp	Remote-KIS
kis	186/tcp	KIS Protocol
kis	186/udp	KIS Protocol
aci	187/tcp	Application Communication Interface
aci	187/udp	Application Communication Interface
mumps	188/tcp	Plus Five's MUMPS
mumps	188/udp	Plus Five's MUMPS
qft	189/tcp	Queued File Transport
qft	189/udp	Queued File Transport
gacp	190/tcp	Gateway Access Control Protocol
gacp	190/udp	Gateway Access Control Protocol
prospero	191/tcp	Prospero Directory Service
prospero	191/udp	Prospero Directory Service
osu-nms	192/tcp	OSU Network Monitoring System
osu-nms	192/udp	OSU Network Monitoring System
srmp	193/tcp	Spider Remote Monitoring Protocol
srmp	193/udp	Spider Remote Monitoring Protocol
irc	194/tcp	Internet Relay Chat Protocol
irc	194/udp	Internet Relay Chat Protocol
dn6-nlm-aud	195/tcp	DNSIX Network Level Module Audit
dn6-nlm-aud	195/udp	DNSIX Network Level Module Audit
dn6-smm-red	196/tcp	DNSIX Session Mgt Module Audit Redir
dn6-smm-red	196/udp	DNSIX Session Mgt Module Audit Redir
dls	197/tcp	Directory Location Service
dls	197/udp	Directory Location Service
dls-mon	198/tcp	Directory Location Service Monitor
dls-mon	198/udp	Directory Location Service Monitor
smux	199/tcp	SMUX
smux	199/udp	SMUX
src	200/tcp	IBM System Resource Controller
src	200/udp	IBM System Resource Controller
at-rtmp	201/tcp	AppleTalk Routing Maintenance
at-rtmp	201/udp	AppleTalk Routing Maintenance
at-nbp	202/tcp	AppleTalk Name Binding
at-nbp	202/udp	AppleTalk Name Binding

Exhibit 1   Well-Known Port Assignments (Continued)

Keyword	Decimal/Protocol	Description
at-3	203/tcp	AppleTalk Unused
at-3	203/udp	AppleTalk Unused
at-echo	204/tcp	AppleTalk Echo
at-echo	204/udp	AppleTalk Echo
at-5	205/tcp	AppleTalk Unused
at-5	205/udp	AppleTalk Unused
at-zis	206/tcp	AppleTalk Zone Information
at-zis	206/udp	AppleTalk Zone Information
at-7	207/tcp	AppleTalk Unused
at-7	207/udp	AppleTalk Unused
at-8	208/tcp	AppleTalk Unused
at-8	208/udp	AppleTalk Unused
tam	209/tcp	Trivial Authenticated Mail Protocol
tam	209/udp	Trivial Authenticated Mail Protocol
z39.50	210/tcp	ANSI Z39.50
z39.50	210/udp	ANSI Z39.50
914c/g	211/tcp	Texas Instruments 914C/G Terminal
914c/g	211/udp	Texas Instruments 914C/G Terminal
anet	212/tcp	ATEXSSTR
anet	212/udp	ATEXSSTR
ipx	213/tcp	IPX
ipx	213/udp	IPX
vmpwscs	214/tcp	VM PWSCS
vmpwscs	214/udp	VM PWSCS
softpc	215/tcp	Insignia Solutions
softpc	215/udp	Insignia Solutions
atls	216/tcp	Access Technology License Server
atls	216/udp	Access Technology License Server
dbase	217/tcp	dBASE UNIX
dbase	217/udp	dBASE UNIX
mpp	218/tcp	Netix Message Posting Protocol
mpp	218/udp	Netix Message Posting Protocol
uarps	219/tcp	Unisys ARPs
uarps	219/udp	Unisys ARPs
imap3	220/tcp	Interactive Mail Access Protocol v3
imap3	220/udp	Interactive Mail Access Protocol v3
fln-spx	221/tcp	Berkeley rlogind with SPX auth
fln-spx	221/udp	Berkeley rlogind with SPX auth
rsh-spx	222/tcp	Berkeley rshd with SPX auth
rsh-spx	222/udp	Berkeley rshd with SPX auth
cdc	223/tcp	Certificate Distribution Center
cdc	223/udp	Certificate Distribution Center
	224–241	Reserved
	242/tcp	Unassigned
	242/udp	Unassigned

Exhibit 1   Well-Known Port Assignments (Continued)

Keyword	Decimal/Protocol	Description
sur-meas	243/tcp	Survey Measurement
sur-meas	243/udp	Survey Measurement
	244/tcp	Unassigned
	244/udp	Unassigned
link	245/tcp	LINK
link	245/udp	LINK
dsp3270	246/tcp	Display Systems Protocol
dsp3270	246/udp	Display Systems Protocol
	247–255	Reserved
	256–343	Unassigned
pdap	344/tcp	Prospero Data Access Protocol
pdap	344/udp	Prospero Data Access Protocol
pawserv	345/tcp	Perf Analysis Workbench
pawserv	345/udp	Perf Analysis Workbench
zserv	346/tcp	Zebra server
zserv	346/udp	Zebra server
fatserv	347/tcp	Fatmen Server
fatserv	347/udp	Fatmen Server
csi-sgwp	348/tcp	Cabletron Management Protocol
csi-sgwp	348/udp	Cabletron Management Protocol
	349–370	Unassigned
clearcase	371/tcp	Clearcase
clearcase	371/udp	Clearcase
ulistserv	372/tcp	UNIX Listserv
ulistserv	372/udp	UNIX Listserv
legent-1	373/tcp	Legent Corporation
legent-1	373/udp	Legent Corporation
legent-2	374/tcp	Legent Corporation
legent-2	374/udp	Legent Corporation
hassle	375/tcp	Hassle
hassle	375/udp	Hassle
nip	376/tcp	Amiga Envoy Network Inquiry Protocol
nip	376/udp	Amiga Envoy Network Inquiry Protocol
tnETOS	377/tcp	NEC Corporation
tnETOS	377/udp	NEC Corporation
dsETOS	378/tcp	NEC Corporation
dsETOS	378/udp	NEC Corporation
is99c	379/tcp	TIA/EIA/IS-99 modem client
is99c	379/udp	TIA/EIA/IS-99 modem client
is99s	380/tcp	TIA/EIA/IS-99 modem server
is99s	380/udp	TIA/EIA/IS-99 modem server
hp-collector	381/tcp	HP performance data collector
hp-collector	381/udp	HP performance data collector
hp-managed-node	382/tcp	HP performance data managed node
hp-managed-node	382/udp	HP performance data managed node

Exhibit 1   Well-Known Port Assignments (Continued)

Keyword	*Decimal/Protocol*	*Description*
hp-alarm-mgr	383/tcp	HP performance data alarm manager
hp-alarm-mgr	383/udp	HP performance data alarm manager
arns	384/tcp	A Remote Network Server System
arns	384/udp	A Remote Network Server System
ibm-app	385/tcp	IBM Application
ibm-app	385/tcp	IBM Application
asa	386/tcp	ASA Message Router Object Def.
asa	386/udp	ASA Message Router Object Def.
aurp	387/tcp	Appletalk Update-Based Routing Protocol
aurp	387/udp	Appletalk Update-Based Routing Protocol
unidata-ldm	388/tcp	Unidata LDM Version 4
unidata-ldm	388/udp	Unidata LDM Version 4
ldap	389/tcp	Lightweight Directory Access Protocol
ldap	389/udp	Lightweight Directory Access Protocol
uis	390/tcp	UIS
uis	390/udp	UIS
synotics-relay	391/tcp	SynOptics SNMP Relay Port
synotics-relay	391/udp	SynOptics SNMP Relay Port
synotics-broker	392/tcp	SynOptics Port Broker Port
synotics-broker	392/udp	SynOptics Port Broker Port
dis	393/tcp	Data Interpretation System
dis	393/udp	Data Interpretation System
embl-ndt	394/tcp	EMBL Nucleic Data Transfer
embl-ndt	394/udp	EMBL Nucleic Data Transfer
netcp	395/tcp	NETscout Control Protocol
netcp	395/udp	NETscout Control Protocol
netware-ip	396/tcp	Novell Netware over IP
netware-ip	396/udp	Novell Netware over IP
mptn	397/tcp	Multi Protocol Trans. Net.
mptn	397/udp	Multi Protocol Trans. Net.
kryptolan	398/tcp	Kryptolan
kryptolan	398/udp	Kryptolan
	399/tcp	Unassigned
	399/udp	Unassigned
work-sol	400/tcp	Workstation Solutions
work-sol	400/udp	Workstation Solutions
ups	401/tcp	Uninterruptible Power Supply
ups	401/udp	Uninterruptible Power Supply
genie	402/tcp	Genie Protocol
genie	402/udp	Genie Protocol
decap	403/tcp	decap
decap	403/udp	decap
nced	404/tcp	nced
nced	404/udp	nced
ncld	405/tcp	ncld

Exhibit 1   Well-Known Port Assignments (Continued)

Keyword	Decimal/Protocol	Description
ncld	405/udp	ncld
imsp	406/tcp	Interactive Mail Support Protocol
imsp	406/udp	Interactive Mail Support Protocol
timbuktu	407/tcp	Timbuktu
timbuktu	407/udp	Timbuktu
prm-sm	408/tcp	Prospero Resource Manager System Management
prm-sm	408/udp	Prospero Resource Manager System Management
prm-nm	409/tcp	Prospero Resource Manager Node Management
prm-nm	409/udp	Prospero Resource Manager Node Management
decladebug	410/tcp	DECLadebug Remote Debug Protocol
decladebug	410/udp	DECLadebug Remote Debug Protocol
rmt	411/tcp	Remote MT Protocol
rmt	411/udp	Remote MT Protocol
synoptics-trap	412/tcp	Trap Convention Port
synoptics-trap	412/udp	Trap Convention Port
smsp	413/tcp	SMSP
smsp	413/udp	SMSP
infoseek	414/tcp	InfoSeek
infoseek	414/udp	InfoSeek
bnet	415/tcp	BNet
bnet	415/udp	BNet
silverplatter	416/tcp	Silverplatter
silverplatter	416/udp	Silverplatter
onmux	417/tcp	Onmux
onmux	417/udp	Onmux
hyper-g	418/tcp	Hyper-G
hyper-g	418/udp	Hyper-G
ariel1	419/tcp	Ariel
ariel1	419/udp	Ariel
smpte	420/tcp	SMPTE
smpte	420/udp	SMPTE
ariel2	421/tcp	Ariel
ariel2	421/udp	Ariel
ariel3	422/tcp	Ariel
ariel3	422/udp	Ariel
opc-job-start	423/tcp	IBM Operations Planning and Control Start
opc-job-start	423/udp	IBM Operations Planning and Control Start
opc-job-track	424/tcp	IBM Operations Planning and Control Track
opc-job-track	424/udp	IBM Operations Planning and Control Track
icad-el	425/tcp	ICAD
icad-el	425/udp	ICAD
smartsdp	426/tcp	smartsdp

Exhibit 1   Well-Known Port Assignments (Continued)

Keyword	Decimal/Protocol	Description
smartsdp	426/udp	smartsdp
svrloc	427/tcp	Server Location
svrloc	427/udp	Server Location
ocs_cmu	428/tcp	OCS_CMU
ocs_cmu	428/udp	OCS_CMU
ocs_amu	429/tcp	OCS_AMU
ocs_amu	429/udp	OCS_AMU
utmpsd	430/tcp	UTMPSD
utmpsd	430/udp	UTMPSD
utmpcd	431/tcp	UTMPCD
utmpcd	431/udp	UTMPCD
iasd	432/tcp	IASD
iasd	432/udp	IASD
nnsp	433/tcp	NNSP
nnsp	433/udp	NNSP
mobileip-agent	434/tcp	MobileIP-Agent
mobileip-agent	434/udp	MobileIP-Agent
mobilip-mn	435/tcp	MobilIP-MN
mobilip-mn	435/udp	MobilIP-MN
dna-cml	436/tcp	DNA-CML
dna-cml	436/udp	DNA-CML
comscm	437/tcp	comscm
comscm	437/udp	comscm
dsfgw	438/tcp	dsfgw
dsfgw	438/udp	dsfgw
dasp	439/tcp	dasp
dasp	439/udp	dasp
sgcp	440/tcp	sgcp
sgcp	440/udp	sgcp
decvms-sysmgt	441/tcp	decvms-sysmgt
decvms-sysmgt	441/udp	decvms-sysmgt
cvc_hostd	442/tcp	cvc_hostd
cvc_hostd	442/udp	cvc_hostd
https	443/tcp	https Mcom (SSL)
https	443/udp	https Mcom (SSL)
snpp	444/tcp	Simple Network Paging Protocol
snpp	444/udp	Simple Network Paging Protocol
microsoft-ds	445/tcp	Microsoft-DS
microsoft-ds	445/udp	Microsoft-DS
ddm-rdb	446/tcp	DDM-RDB
ddm-rdb	446/udp	DDM-RDB
ddm-dfm	447/tcp	DDM-RFM
ddm-dfm	447/udp	DDM-RFM
ddm-byte	448/tcp	DDM-BYTE
ddm-byte	448/udp	DDM-BYTE

Exhibit 1   Well-Known Port Assignments (Continued)

Keyword	Decimal/Protocol	Description
as-servermap	449/tcp	AS Server Mapper
as-servermap	449/udp	AS Server Mapper
tserver	450/tcp	TServer
tserver	450/udp	TServer
	451–511	Unassigned
exec	512/tcp	Remote process execution; authentication performed using passwords and UNIX loppgin names
biff	512/udp	Used by mail system to notify users of new mail received; currently receives messages only from processes on the same machine
login	513/tcp	Remote log-in à la Telnet; automatic authentication performed based on privileged port numbers and distributed databases that identify "authentication domains"
who	513/udp	Maintains databases showing who is logged in to machines on a local net and the load average of the machine
cmd	514/tcp	Like exec, but automatic authentication is performed as for log-in server
syslog	514/udp	Syslog daemon
printer	515/tcp	Spooler
printer	515/udp	Spooler
	516/tcp	Unassigned
	516/udp	Unassigned
talk	517/tcp	Like tenex link, but across machine — unfortunately, does not use link protocol (this is actually just a rendezvous port from which a tcp connection is established)
talk	517/udp	Like tenex link, but across machine — unfortunately, does not use link protocol (this is actually just a rendezvous port from which a tcp connection is established)
ntalk	518/tcp	
ntalk	518/udp	
utime	519/tcp	unixtime
utime	519/udp	unixtime
efs	520/tcp	Extended file name server
router	520/udp	Local routing process (on site); uses variant of Xerox NS routing information protocol
	521–524	Unassigned
timed	525/tcp	timeserver
timed	525/udp	timeserver
tempo	526/tcp	newdate
tempo	526/udp	newdate
	527–529	Unassigned

Exhibit 1   Well-Known Port Assignments (Continued)

Keyword	Decimal/Protocol	Description
courier	530/tcp	rpc
courier	530/udp	rpc
conference	531/tcp	chat
conference	531/udp	chat
netnews	532/tcp	readnews
netnews	532/udp	readnews
netwall	533/tcp	For emergency broadcasts
netwall	533/udp	For emergency broadcasts
	534–538	Unassigned
apertus-ldp	539/tcp	Apertus Technologies Load Determination
apertus-ldp	539/udp	Apertus Technologies Load Determination
uucp	540/tcp	uucpd
uucp	540/udp	uucpd
uucp-rlogin	541/tcp	uucp-rlogin
uucp-rlogin	541/udp	uucp-rlogin
	542/tcp	Unassigned
	542/udp	Unassigned
klogin	543/tcp	
klogin	543/udp	
kshell	544/tcp	krcmd
kshell	544/udp	krcmd
	545–549	Unassigned
new-rwho	550/tcp	new-who
new-rwho	550/udp	new-who
	551–554	Unassigned
dsf	555/tcp	
dsf	555/udp	
remotefs	556/tcp	rfs server
remotefs	556/udp	rfs server
	557–559	Unassigned
rmonitor	560/tcp	rmonitord
rmonitor	560/udp	rmonitord
monitor	561/tcp	
monitor	561/udp	
chshell	562/tcp	chcmd
chshell	562/udp	chcmd
	563/tcp	Unassigned
	563/udp	Unassigned
9pfs	564/tcp	plan 9 file service
9pfs	564/udp	plan 9 file service
whoami	565/tcp	whoami
whoami	565/udp	whoami
	566–569	Unassigned
meter	570/tcp	demon
meter	570/udp	demon

Exhibit 1   Well-Known Port Assignments (Continued)

Keyword	Decimal/Protocol	Description
meter	571/tcp	udemon
meter	571/udp	udemon
	572–599	Unassigned
ipcserver	600/tcp	Sun IPC server
ipcserver	600/udp	Sun IPC server
	601–605	Unassigned
urm	606/tcp	Cray Unified Resource Manager
urm	606/udp	Cray Unified Resource Manager
nqs	607/tcp	nqs
nqs	607/udp	nqs
sift-uft	608/tcp	Sender-Initiated/Unsolicited File Transfer
sift-uft	608/udp	Sender-Initiated/Unsolicited File Transfer
npmp-trap	609/tcp	npmp-trap
npmp-trap	609/udp	npmp-trap
npmp-local	610/tcp	npmp-local
npmp-local	610/udp	npmp-local
npmp-gui	611/tcp	npmp-gui
npmp-gui	611/udp	npmp-gui
	612–633	Unassigned
ginad	634/tcp	ginad
ginad	634/udp	ginad
	635–665	Unassigned
mdqs	666/tcp	
mdqs	666/udp	
doom	666/tcp	doom Id Software
doom	666/tcp	doom Id Software
	667–703	Unassigned
elcsd	704/tcp	errlog copy/server daemon
elcsd	704/udp	errlog copy/server daemon
	705–708	Unassigned
entrustmanager	709/tcp	EntrustManager
entrustmanager	709/udp	EntrustManager
	710–728	Unassigned
netviewdm1	729/tcp	IBM NetView DM/6000 Server/Client
netviewdm1	729/udp	IBM NetView DM/6000 Server/Client
netviewdm2	730/tcp	IBM NetView DM/6000 send/tcp
netviewdm2	730/udp	IBM NetView DM/6000 send/tcp
netviewdm3	731/tcp	IBM NetView DM/6000 receive/tcp
netviewdm3	731/udp	IBM NetView DM/6000 receive/tcp
	732–740	Unassigned
netgw	741/tcp	netGW
netgw	741/udp	netGW
netrcs	742/tcp	Network based Rev. Cont. Sys.
netrcs	742/udp	Network based Rev. Cont. Sys.
	743	Unassigned

Exhibit 1   Well-Known Port Assignments (Continued)

Keyword	Decimal/Protocol	Description
flexlm	744/tcp	Flexible License Manager
flexlm	744/udp	Flexible License Manager
	745–746	Unassigned
fujitsu-dev	747/tcp	Fujitsu Device Control
fujitsu-dev	747/udp	Fujitsu Device Control
ris-cm	748/tcp	Russell Info Sci Calendar Manager
ris-cm	748/udp	Russell Info Sci Calendar Manager
kerberos-adm	749/tcp	kerberos administration
kerberos-adm	749/udp	kerberos administration
rfile	750/tcp	
loadav	750/udp	
pump	751/tcp	
pump	751/udp	
qrh	752/tcp	
qrh	752/udp	
rrh	753/tcp	
rrh	753/udp	
tell	754/tcp	send
tell	754/udp	send
	755–757	Unassigned
nlogin	758/tcp	
nlogin	758/udp	
con	759/tcp	
con	759/udp	
ns	760/tcp	
ns	760/udp	
rxe	761/tcp	
rxe	761/udp	
quotad	762/tcp	
quotad	762/udp	
cycleserv	763/tcp	
cycleserv	763/udp	
omserv	764/tcp	
omserv	764/udp	
webster	765/tcp	
webster	765/udp	
phonebook	767/tcp	Phone
phonebook	767/udp	Phone
	768	Unassigned
vid	769/tcp	
vid	769/udp	
cadlock	770/tcp	
cadlock	770/udp	
rtip	771/tcp	
rtip	771/udp	

Exhibit 1   Well-Known Port Assignments (Continued)

Keyword	Decimal/Protocol	Description
cycleserv2	772/tcp	
cycleserv2	772/udp	
submit	773/tcp	
notify	773/udp	
rpasswd	774/tcp	
acmaint_dbd	774/udp	
entomb	775/tcp	
acmaint_transd	775/udp	
wpages	776/tcp	
wpages	776/udp	
	777–779	Unassigned
wpgs	780/tcp	
wpgs	780/udp	
	781–785	Unassigned
concert	786/tcp	Concert
concert	786/udp	Concert
	787–799	Unassigned
mdbs_daemon	800/tcp	
mdbs_daemon	800/udp	
device	801/tcp	
device	801/udp	
	802–995	Unassigned
xtreelic	996/tcp	Central Point Software
xtreelic	996/udp	Central Point Software
maitrd	997/tcp	
maitrd	997/udp	
busboy	998/tcp	
puparp	998/udp	
garcon	999/tcp	
applix	999/udp	Applix ac
puprouter	999/tcp	
puprouter	999/udp	
cadlock	1000/tcp	
ock	1000/udp	
	1001–1022	Unassigned
	1023/tcp	Reserved
	1024/udp	Reserved

Appendix E

Hacker, Cracker, Malware, and Trojan Horse Ports

Exhibit 1 provides a list of some port numbers that you must watch carefully. They are often associated with lax security and security breaches. If you find any of these ports open on your router, you should identify the application using the port. If you know the application and you trust it, then you can breathe a sigh of relief. If, on the other hand, you cannot identify the application, then you may have a serious problem.

Crackers and others who intend to harm you are scanning systems looking for these open ports. If they see them, their eyes light up like it is Christmas and they just received the present they asked for. Be vigilant and scan from outside your router looking for any of these ports.

Note: One day as I sat writing this book, I noticed hundreds of attempts to connect to port 6346 on my machine originating from different remote systems on various ports. If you look in Exhibit 1, you will notice that 6346 is the port for Gnutella, a file sharing peer-to-peer application as opposed to a client/server application (à la Napster). Gnutella is not limited to MP3 files (i.e., music); you can download any file using it. You can find Gnutella-compliant programs for most operating systems. A couple of other fascinating facts about Gnutella:

- Provides push function where the firewall blocks downloads
- Broadcasts PINGs to other clients on the network
- Home Web site provides tips on bypassing network security http://gnutella.wego.com)

Using the `netstat` command, I determined that I did not have any applications (services) running on port 6346. And by the way, I knew about the attempts because I had a firewall running on my system and it was blocking all attempts on that port.

Caution: The newer Trojans run on any port the cracker decides to run it on, so you must enumerate and identify all ports on your system. If there is a port you cannot identify, then you must take action. Block the port until you can identify it.

Exhibit 1   Problematic Ports

Port #	Protocol	General Description
0	ICMP	Click attack
1	TCP	Sockets des Troie
2	TCP	Death
5	TCP	Midnight Commander
8	ICMP	Ping Attack
9	UDP	Chargen
19	UDP	Chargen
20	TCP	Senna Spy FTP Server
21	TCP	Back Construction, Blade Runner, Cattivik FTP Server, CC Invader, Dark FTP, Dolly Trojan, Fore, FTP service, Invisible FTP, Juggernaut 42, Larva, Motlv FTP, Net Administrator, Ramen, Senna Spy FTP, server, The Flu, Traitor 21, WebEx, WinCrash
22	TCP	Shaft
23	TCP	Fire HecKer, Tiny Telnet Server, Truva Atl
25	TCP	Ajan, AntiGen, Barok, Email Password Sender (EPS), EPS II, Gip, Gris, Haebu Coceda (= Naebi), Happy 99, Hpteam mail, Hybris, I Love You, Kuang2, Magic Horse, Mail Bombing Trojan (MBT), Moscow Email Trojan, NewApt worm, ProMail Trojan, Shtrilitz, Stealth, Tapiras, Terminator, WinPC, WinSpy
30	TCP	Agent 40421
31	TCP	Agent 31, Hacker's Paradise, Master's Paradise
41	TCP	Deep Throat 1.0–3.1 + Mod (Foreplay)
48	TCP	DRAT v1.0–3.0b
50	TCP	DRAT
53	TCP	DNS
58	TCP	DMSetup
59	TCP	DMSetup
79	TCP	CDK, Firehotcker

Exhibit 1   Problematic Ports (Continued)

Port #	Protocol	General Description
80	TCP	711 Trojan, AckCmd, Back End, Back Orifice 2000 Plug-Ins, Cafeini, CGI Backdoor, Executor, God Message, God Message Creator, Hooker, IISworm, MTX, NCX, Reverse WWW Tunnel Backdoor, RingZero, Seeker, WAN Remote, Web Server CT, WebDownloader
81	TCP	RemoConChubo
90	TCP	Hidden Port 2.o
99	TCP	Hidden Port, NCX
109	TCP	b00ger, Sekure SDI
110	TCP	ProMail Trojan
113	TCP	Invisible Identd Daemon, Kazimas
119	TCP	Happy 99
121	TCP	Attack Bot, God Message, JammerKillah
123	TCP	Net Controller
129	TCP	Password Generator Protocol
133	TCP	Farnaz
135	TCP/UDP	NetBIOS Remote procedure call, Winnuke
137	TCP	Chode
137	UDP	Msinit
138	TCP	Chode
139	TCP	Chode, God Message worm, Msinit, Netlog, Network, Qaz
142	TCP	NetTaxi
146	TCP/UDP	Infector 1.3
170	TCP	A-Trojan
334	TCP	Backage
411	TCP	Backage
420	TCP	Breach, Incognito
421	TCP	TCP Wrappers Trojan
455	TCP	Fatal Connections
456	TCP	Hacker's Paradise
513	TCP	Grlogin
514	TCP	RPC Backdoor
531	TCP	Net666, Rasmin
555	TCP	Phase Zero
555	TCP	711 Trojan, Ini-Killer, NeT Administrator, phAse zero, Phase-0, Stealth Spy
605	TCP	Secret Service
666	TCP	Attack FTP, Back Construction, Backdoor, BLA Trojan, Cain & Abel, NokNok, Satans Back Door, Satanz, ServeU, Shadow Phyre, th3ripperz
667	TCP	SniperNet
669	TCP	DP trojan
692	TCP	GayOL
777	TCP	AIM Spy Application, Undetected
808	TCP	WinHole
911	TCP	Dark Shadow

Exhibit 1   Problematic Ports (Continued)

Port #	Protocol	General Description
999	TCP	DeepThroat, Foreplay, WinSATAN
1000	TCP	Der Spaeher, Direct Connection
1001	TCP	Der Spaeher, Le Guardien, Silencer, SK Silencer, WebEx
1010	TCP	Doly Trojan 1.1–1.7 (SE)
1011	TCP	Doly Trojan
1012	TCP	Doly Trojan
1015	TCP	Doly Trojan 1.5
1016	TCP	Doly Trojan
1020	TCP	Vampire
1024	TCP	Jade, Latinus, NetSpy 1.0–2.0
1025	TCP	Remote Storm
1025	UDP	Maverick's Matrix 1.2–2.0, Remote Storm
1027	TCP	ICQ
1029	TCP	ICQ
1032	TCP	ICQ
1033	TCP	NetSpy
1035	TCP	Multidropper
1042	TCP	Bla 1.0–2.0
1045	TCP	Rasmin
1049	TCP	/sbin/initd
1050	TCP	MiniCommand
1053	TCP	The Thief
1054	TCP	AckCmd
1080	TCP	Socks/Wingate, WinHole
1081	TCP	WinHole
1082	TCP	WinHole
1083	TCP	WinHole
1090	TCP	Xtreme
1095	TCP	Remote Administration Tool (RAT)
1097	TCP	Rat
1098	TCP	Rat
1099	TCP	Blood Fest Evolution, Rat
1150	TCP	Orion
1151	TCP	Orion
1170	TCP	Psyber Stream Server, Streaming Audio Server, Voice
1200	UDP	NoBackO
1201	UDP	NoBackO
1207	TCP	SoftWar
1212	TCP	Kaos
1214	TCP	KaZaa File Sharing (not a Trojan)
1234	TCP	Sub Seven Java Client, Ultors Trojan
1243	TCP	BackDoor-G, Psyber Stream Server, SubSeven, SubSeven Apocalypse, Tiles
1245	UDP	SubSeven Default Port, VooDoo Doll
1255	TCP	Scarab

Exhibit 1   Problematic Ports (Continued)

Port #	Protocol	General Description
1256	TCP	Project nEXT
1269	TCP	Maverick's Matrix
1272	TCP	The Matrix
1313	TCP	NETrojan
1338	TCP	Millenium Worm
1349	UDP	BackOrifice DLL Comm
1394	TCP	GoFriller, Backdoor G-1
1492	TCP	FTP99CMP
1505	TCP/UDP	FunkProxy
1509	TCP	Psyber Streaming Server (PSS)
1524	TCP	Trinoo
1568	TCP	Remote Hack
1600	TCP	Direct Connection, Shivka-Burka
1604	TCP/UDP	ICA Browser
1703	TCP	Exploiter
1777	TCP	Scarab
1807	TCP	SpySender
1966	TCP	Fake FTP
1967	TCP	WM FTP Server
1969	TCP	OpC BO
1981	TCP	ShockRave
1999	TCP	BackDoor 2.00–2.03, Sub Seven, TransScout
2000	TCP	Der Spaher, Der Spaeher, Insane Network, Last 2000, Remote Explorer 2000, Senna Spy Trojan Generator, TransScout
2001	TCP	Der Spaeher 3 Der Spaeher v3.0, TransScout Transmission Scout v1.1–1.2, Trojan Cow 1.0
2002	TCP	TransScout
2003	TCP	TransScout
2004	TCP	TransScout
2005	TCP	TransScout
2023	TCP	HackCity, Pass Ripper, Ripper Pro
2080	TCP	WinHole
2086	TCP	Netscape/CORBA exploit
2115	TCP	Bugs
2130	UDP	Mini Backlash
2140	TCP	Deep Throat, The Invasor
2140	UDP	Deep Throat v1.3 server, Deep Throat 1.3 KeyLogger
2155	TCP	Illusion Mailer
2283	TCP	HLV Rat 5.30
2311	TCP	Studio 54
2330	TCP	Contact
2331	TCP	Contact
2332	TCP	Contact
2333	TCP	Contact
2334	TCP	Contact

Exhibit 1   Problematic Ports (Continued)

Port #	Protocol	General Description
2335	TCP	Contact
2336	TCP	Contact
2337	TCP	Contact
2338	TCP	Contact
2339	TCP	Contact, Voice Spy
2339	UDP	Voice Spy
2345	TCP	Doly Trojan
2400	TCP	PortD
2565	TCP	Striker
2583	TCP	WinCrash2
2600	TCP	Digital RootBear
2716	TCP	The Prayer 1.2–1.3
2721	TCP	Phase Zero
2773	TCP	SubSeven, SubSeven 2.1 Gold
2774	TCP	SubSeven, SubSeven 2.1 Gold
2801	TCP	Phineas Phucker
2989	UDP	Rat
3000	TCP	Remote Shut
3024	TCP	WinCrash 1.03
3028	TCP	Ring Zero
3031	TCP	Microspy
3128	TCP	Reverse WWW Tunnel Backdoor, RingZero
3129	TCP	Master's Paradise 9.x
3149	UDP	Master's Paradise
3150	TCP	Deep Throat, The Invasor
3150	UDP	Deep Throat, Foreplay, Mini Backlash
3332	TCP	Q0 BackDoor
3456	TCP	Terror
3459	TCP	Eclipse 2000, Sanctuary
3700	TCP	Portal of Doom
3777	TCP	PsychWard
3791	TCP	Total Solar Eclypse
3801	UDP	Eclypse 1.0
4000	TCP	SkyDance
4092	TCP	WinCrash-alt
4100	TCP	Watchguard Firebox admin DoS Expl
4242	TCP	Virtual Hacking Machine (VHM)
4321	TCP	BoBo 1.0–2.0
4444	TCP	Prosiak, Swift Remote
4567	TCP	File Nail
4590	TCP	ICQ Trojan
4950	TCP	ICQ Trojan
5000	TCP	Back Door Setup, Blazer5, Bubbel, ICKiller, Ra1d, Sockets de Troie/socket23
5000	UDP	Sockets de Trois v1./Bubbel

Exhibit 1   Problematic Ports (Continued)

Port #	Protocol	General Description
5001	TCP	Sockets de Trois v1./Bubbel
5001	UDP	Back Door Setup, Sockets de Troie/socket23
5002	TCP	cd00r, Shaft
5010	TCP	Solo
5011	TCP	One of the Last Trojans (OOTLT)
5025	TCP	WM Remote KeyLogger
5031	TCP	Net Metropolitan 1.0
5032	TCP	Net Metropolitan 1.04
5321	TCP	Firehotcker, BackDoorz
5321	UDP	Firehotcker
5333	TCP	Backage, NetDemon
5343	TCP	WC Remote Administration Tool (wCrat)
5400	TCP	Back Construction 1.2, Blade Runner
5401	TCP	Back Construction, Blade Runner
5402	TCP	Back Construction, Blade Runner
5512	TCP	Illusion Mailer, Xtcp
5521	TCP	Illusion Mailer
5550	TCP	Xtcp 2.0–2.1, X-Tcp Trojan
5555	TCP	ServeMe
5556	TCP	BO Facil
5557	TCP	BO Facil
5568	TCP	Robo-Hack
5569	TCP	Robo-Hack
5637	TCP	PC Crasher
5638	TCP	PC Crasher
5714	TCP	WinCrash
5741	TCP	WinCrash
5742	TCP	WinCrash
5760	TCP	Portmap Remote Root Linux Exploit
5880	TCP	Y3K RAT
5882	TCP/UDP	Y3K RAT
5888	TCP/UDP	Y3K RAT
5889	TCP	Y3K RAT
6000	TCP	The Thing 1.6
6006	TCP	Bad Blood
6112	TCP/UDP	Battle.net Game (not a Trojan)
6346	TCP	Gnutella clone (not a Trojan). See Note following.
6400	TCP	tHe tHing
6661	TCP	TEMan, Weia-Meia
6666	TCP	Dark Connection Inside, NetBus worm
6667	TCP	Dark FTP, ScheduleAgent, SubSeven, Sub-7 Trojan (new icq notification), Trinity, Win Satan
6669	TCP	Host Control, Vampyre 1.0–1.2
6670	TCP	BackWeb Server, Deep Throat, Foreplay, WinNuke eXtreame
6671	TCP	Deep Throat

Exhibit 1   Problematic Ports (Continued)

Port #	Protocol	General Description
6674	TCP	Deep Throat
6711	TCP	BackDoor-G, Deep Throat, Sub Seven, VP Killer
6712	TCP	Funny, Sub Seven
6713	TCP	Sub Seven
6723	TCP	Mstream attack-handler
6771	TCP	Deep Throat, Foreplay
6776	TCP	2000 Cracks, Back Door-G, Sub Seven, VP Killer
6838	UDP	Mstream Agent-handler
6883	UDP	DeltaSource
6912	TCP	ShitHeap
6939	TCP	Indoctrination 0.1–0.11
6969	TCP	GateCrasher, IRC 3, Net Controller, Priority
6970	TCP	GateCrasher 1.0–1.2
7000	TCP	Exploit Translation Server, Kazimas, Remote Grab, Sub Seven, SubSeven 2.1 Gold
7001	TCP	Freak88, Freak2k
7028	TCP	Unknown Trojan
7028	UDP	Unknown Trojan
7215	TCP	SubSeven, SubSeven 2.1 Gold
7300	TCP	Net Monitor
7301	TCP	Net Monitor
7306	TCP	Net Monitor
7307	TCP	Net Monitor
7308	TCP	Net Monitor
7424	TCP/UDP	Host Control
7597	TCP	QaZ (Remote Access Trojan)
7626	TCP	Glacier
7777	TCP	God Message, Tini
7789	TCP	Back Door Setup, ICKiller
7891	TCP	The ReVeNgEr
7983	UDP	MStream handler-agent
8080	TCP	Brown Orifice, RemoConChubo, Reverse WWW Tunnel Backdoor, RingZero
8787	TCP/UDP	BackOrifice 2000
8879	TCP/UDP	BackOrifice 2000
8988	TCP	BacHack
8989	TCP	Recon, recon2, xcon
9000	TCP	Netministrator
9090	TCP	Tst2, tiny telnet server
9325	UDP	MStream Agent-handler
9400	TCP	InCommand 1.0–1.4
9999	TCP	The prayer 1.2–1.3
9872	TCP	Portal of Doom
9873	TCP	Portal of Doom
9874	TCP	Portal of Doom

Exhibit 1   Problematic Ports (Continued)

Port #	Protocol	General Description
9875	TCP	Portal of Doom
9876	TCP	Cyber Attacker
9878	TCP	TransScout
9989	TCP	iNi-Killer
9999	TCP	The Prayer
10000	TCP	OpwinTRojan
10005	TCP	OpwinTRojan
10008	TCP	Cheese worm
10067	TCP	Portal of Doom
10067	UDP	Portal of Doom
10085	TCP	Syphillis
10086	TCP	Syphillis
10100	TCP	Control Total, Gift trojan
10101	TCP	BrainSpy Vbeta, Silencer
10167	TCP	Portal of Doom
10167	UDP	Portal of Doom
10498	UDP	Mstream handler-agent
10520	TCP	Acid Shivers + LMacid
10528	TCP	Host Control
10529	TCP	Acid Shivers
10607	TCP	Coma 1.09
10666	TCP	Ambush
10666	UDP	Ambush
11000	TCP	Senna Spy
11050	TCP	Host Control
11051	TCP	Host Control
11223	TCP	Progenic Trojan 1.0–1.3, Secret Agent
11831	TCP	Latinus Server
12076	TCP	Gjamer
12223	TCP	Hack'99
12223	UDP	Hack'99 KeyLogger
12345	TCP	Ashley, cron/crontab, Fat Bitch Trojan, GabanBus, GirlFriend, icmp_client.c, icmp_pipe.c, Mypic, NetBus, NetBus Toy, NetBus worm, Pie Bill Gates, Ultor's Trojan, Whack Job, X-bill
12345	UDP	GabanBus, NetBus, Pie Bill Gates, X-bill
12346	TCP	Fat Bitch Trojan, GabanBus, NetBus, X-bil
12349	TCP	BioNet
12456	TCP	NetBus
12361	TCP	Whack-a-Mole
12362	TCP	Whack-a-Mole
12363	TCP	Whack-a-Mole
12623	UDP	DUN Control
12624	TCP	ButtMan
12631	TCP	Whack Job
12701	TCP	Eclypse 2000

Exhibit 1   Problematic Ports (Continued)

Port #	Protocol	General Description
12754	TCP	Mstream attack-handler
13000	TCP	Senna Spy Trojans
13010	TCP	Hacker Brasil (HBR)
13013	TCP	PsychWard
13014	TCP	PsychWard
13223	TCP	Hack'99 KeyLogger
13473	TCP	Chupacabra
13700	TCP	Kuang2 the Virus
14500	TCP	PC Invader
14501	TCP	PC Invader
14502	TCP	PC Invader
14503	TCP	PC Invader
15000	TCP	NetDemon
15092	TCP	Host Control
15104	TCP	Mstream attack-handler
15382	TCP	SubZero
15858	TCP	CDK
16484	TCP	Mosucker
16660	TCP	stacheldraht
16772	TCP	ICQ Revenge
16959	TCP	SubSeven DEFCON8 2.1 Backdoor
16969	TCP	Priority
17166	TCP	Mosaic
17300	TCP	Kuang2 The Virus
17449	TCP	CrazzyNet, Kid Terror
17500	TCP	CrazzyNet
17569	TCP	Infector
17593	TCP	Audiodoor
17777	TCP	Nephron
18753	UDP	Shaft handler to Agent
19864	TCP	ICQ Revenge
19932	TCP	DropChute
20000	UDP	Millennium 1.0–2.0
20001	UDP	Millennium
20002	TCP	AcidkoR
20005	TCP	Mosucker
20023	TCP	VP Killer
20034	TCP	NetBus 2 Pro, NetRex, Whack Job
20203	TCP	Chupacabra, Logged!
20331	TCP	Bla Trojan
20432	TCP	Shaft Client to handlers
20433	UDP	Shaft Agent to handlers
21554	TCP	Exploiter, GirlFriend 1.3x (including Patch 1 and 2), Kid Terror, NetBus, Schwindler 1.82, Winsp00fer
21554	UDP	GirlFriend

Exhibit 1   Problematic Ports (Continued)

Port #	Protocol	General Description
22222	TCP	Prosiak
23005	TCP	NetTrash
23006	TCP	NetTrash
23023	TCP	Logged
23032	TCP	Amanda
23432	TCP	Asylum
23456	TCP	EvilFTP, UglyFTP, Whack Job
23476	UDP	Donald Dick
23477	TCP	Donald Dick
23777	TCP	InetSpy
24000	TCP	Infector
25685	TCP	Moonpie
25686	TCP	Moonpie
25982	TCP	Moonpie
26274	TCP	Delta Source
26274	UDP	Delta Source
26681	TCP	Voice Spy
27374	TCP	Bad Blood, Ramen, Seeker, SubSeven, SubSeven 2.1 Gold, SubSeven 2.1.4 DefCon 8, SubSeven Muie, Ttfloader
27374	UDP	Sub-7 2.1
27444	UDP	Trin00/TFN2K
27573	UDP	Sub-7 2.1
27573	TCP	Sub-7 2.1
27665	TCP	Trin00 DoS Attack
28678	TCP	Exploiter
29104	TCP	NetTrojan
29369	TCP	ovasOn
29559	TCP	Latinus Server
29891	TCP/UDP	The Unexplained
30000	TCP	Infector
30001	TCP	ErrOr32
30003	TCP	Lamers Death
30029	TCP	AOL Trojan
30100	TCP	NetSphere 1.0–1.31337
30101	TCP	NetSphere 1.0–1.31337
30102	TCP	NetSphere 1.0–1.31337
30103	UDP	NetSphere 1.31
30133	TCP	NetSphere Final
30303	TCP	Socket25, Sockets des Troie
30947	TCP	Intruse
30999	TCP	Kuang2
31335	UDP	Trin00 DoS Attack
31336	TCP	BO-Whack, Butt Funnel
31337	TCP	BackFire, Back Orifice Client, Baron Night, Beeone, BO2, BO Facil, BO Spy, cron/crontab, Freak88, Freak2k, icmp_pipe.c, Netpatch, Sockdmini

Exhibit 1   Problematic Ports (Continued)

Port #	Protocol	General Description
31337	UDP	Back Orifice (BO), DeepBO
31338	TCP	NetSpy DK
31338	UDP	Back Orifice, Deep BO
31339	TCP	NetSpy
31339	UDP	NetSpy DK
31554	TCP	Schwindler
31666	TCP	BOWhack
31780	TCP	Hack'a'Tack
31785	TCP	Hack'a'Tack
31787	TCP	Hack'a'Tack
31788	TCP	Hack'a'Tack
31789	UDP	Hack'a'Tack
31790	TCP	Hack'a'Tack
31791	UDP	Hack'a'Tack
31792	TCP	Hack'a'Tack
32001	TCP	Donald Dick
32100	TCP	Peanut Brittle, Project nEXT
32418	TCP	Acid Battery
33270	TCP	Trinity Trojan
33333	TCP	Blakharaz, Prosiak
33390	UDP	Unknown Trojan
33577	TCP	Son of Psych Ward
33777	TCP	Son of Psych Ward
33911	TCP	Spirit 2000 and 2001
34324	TCP	BigGluck, Tiny Telnet Server, TN
34444	TCP	Donald Dick
34555	UDP	Trinoo for Windows
35555	UDP	Trinoo for Windows
37237	TCP	Mantis
37651	TCP	Yet Another Trojan (YAT)
40412	TCP	The Spy
40421	TCP	Agent 40421, Master's of Paradise
40422	TCP	Master's Paradise
40423	TCP	Master's Paradise
40425	TCP	Master's Paradise
40426	TCP	Master's Paradise
41337	TCP	Storm
41666	TCP	Remote Boot Tool (RBT)
43210	TCP	Master's Paradise
44444	TCP	Prosiak
44575	TCP	Exploiter
47252	TCP	Delta Source
47262	UDP	Delta Source
49301	UDP	OnLine keyLogger
50130	TCP	Enterprise

Exhibit 1   Problematic Ports (Continued)

Port #	Protocol	General Description
50505	TCP	Sockets de Troie v2.
50776	TCP	Fore
50776	UDP	Schwindler 1.82
51966	TCP	Cafeini
52317	TCP	Acid Battery 2000
53001	TCP	Remote Windows Shutdown
54283	TCP	SubSeven, SubSeven 2.1 Gold
54320	TCP	Back Orifice 2000
54320	UDP	Back Orifice
54321	TCP	Back Orifice, School Bus
54321	UDP	Back Orifice 2000
55165	TCP	File Manager Trojan, WM Trojan Generator
55166	TCP	WM Trojan Generator
57341	UDP	NetRaider Trojan
57341	TCP	NetRaider Trojan
58339	TCP	ButtFunnel
60000	TCP	Deep Throat, Foreplay, Sockets des Troie
60001	TCP	Trinity
60068	TCP	Xzip 6000068
60411	TCP	Connection
61348	TCP	Bunker-Hill Trojan
61466	TCP	Telecommando
61348	TCP	Bunker-Hill Trojan
61603	TCP	Bunker-Hill Trojan
63485	TCP	Bunker-Hill Trojan
64101	TCP	Taskman
65000	TCP	Devil, Sockets des Troie, Stacheldraht
65000	TCP	Devil v1.3
65390	TCP	Eclypse
65421	TCP	Jade
65432	TCP/UDP	The Traitor (thetr41t0r)
65534	TCP	/sbin/initd
65535	TCP	ICE, RC1 Trojan

Appendix F

ICMP Types and Codes

ICMP provides useful and valuable information about the state of a network. Unfortunately, crackers can use the features of ICMP to mount an attack against an organization. For example, someone could send an ICMP Destination Unreachable packet. When a device cannot find a service, network, or host, it can respond to a request with a Destination Unreachable packet. The Destination Unreachable message will cause the sender to tear down the connection — in effect, a denial-of-service. Or, someone might send redirect messages to have you redirect traffic to a segment where they are running a packet analyzer or "sniffer." You will need to look for specific types of ICMP traffic.

To properly filter ICMP traffic, you need to know the various ICMP type and code combinations. You should study RFC 792 for a thorough understanding of ICMP types and codes. Exhibit 1 provides a list of possible ICMP type and code combinations that you might find and might want to filter or block.

Exhibit 1   ICMP Types and Codes

Type	Code	Name
0		Echo reply
1		Unassigned
2		Unassigned
3		Destination unreachable
3	0	Net unreachable
3	1	Host unreachable
3	2	Protocol unreachable
3	3	Port unreachable
3	4	Fragmentation needed and none set
3	5	Source route failed
3	6	Destination network unknown
3	7	Destination host unknown
3	8	Source host isolated
3	9	Communication with destination network administratively prohibited
3	10	Communication with destination host administratively prohibited
3	11	Destination network unreachable for type of service
3	12	Destination host unreachable for type of service
3	13	Communication administratively prohibited
3	14	Host precedence violation
3	15	Precedence cutoff in effect
4		Source quench
5		Redirect
5	0	Redirect datagram for the network
5	1	Redirect datagram for the host
5	2	Redirect datagram for the type of service and network
5	3	Redirect datagram for the type of service and host
6		Alternate host address
7		Unassigned
8		Echo
9		Router advertisement
10		Router selection
11		Time exceeded
11	0	Time to live exceeded in transit
11	1	Fragment reassembly (time exceeded)
12		Parameter problem
12	0	Pointer indicates the error
12	1	Missing a required option
12	2	Bad length
13		Timestamp request
14		Timestamp reply
15		Information request
16		Information reply
17		Address mask request
18		Address mask reply

Exhibit 1   ICMP Types and Codes (Continued)

Type	Code	Name
19		Reserved (security)
20–29		Reserved
30		Traceroute
31		Datagram conversion error
32		Mobile host redirector
33		Ipv6 where-are-you
34		Ipv6 i-am-here
35		Mobile register request
36		Mobile register reply
37		Domain name request
38		Domain name reply
39		Skip
40		Photuris
40	0	Reserved
40	1	Unknown security parameter index
40	2	Valid security parameters, but authentication failed
40	3	Valid security parameters, but decryption failed
41–255		Reserved

Appendix G

Determining Wildcard Mask Ranges

This appendix describes how to calculate the correct wildcard mask range when attempting to summarize an arbitrary range of IP addresses. Refer to Appendix A, "IP Addressing," for a comprehensive discussion of IP addressing and Appendix B, "Subnetting," for a thorough discussion of masks and subnetting.

Note: This appendix is not for the mathematically challenged. If you understand the concepts introduced here, you can always get yourself a gadget from the Internet to do the actual calculations. However, an understanding of the underlying theory is essential to your networking education.

To calculate the wildcard mask, it is helpful to have an example: you will summarize the range of IP addresses between 192.168.50.0/24 and 192.168.116.0/24. Because the first two octets are the same, they do not concern you. Also, the last byte (or octet) represents hosts, so disregard that octet. Thus, you will focus only on the third octet (50 and 116).

To calculate the correct wildcard mask, perform the following steps:

1. Write the octet in binary:

$$50 = 00110010$$
$$116 = 01110100$$

2. Find the lowest value in the first address (192.168.50.0) that is 1. Going from left to right, the bit position 2 is 1.

3. Check to see whether there are any high-order bits in the second address (192.168.116.0) that are greater than the high-order bit in the first address. Because there is one (bit 7 compared to bit 5), all bits to the right of the first bit in address 1 are included.

4. Set the mask equal to the value of the range found. Therefore, you include only the bits in position 1 in the range, and the value of the mask is 2^0, or 1. In binary, the value of each bit is 2 raised to the power $n - 1$, where n is the bit position.

5. Calculate the contiguous range using the beginning address and the mask as follows:

```
access-list 100 permit ip 192.168.50.0 0.0.1.255
```

6. Calculate the new beginning address as original plus 1 plus the mask, or $50 + 1 + 1 = 52$.

7. Write the octet in binary:

$$52 = 00110100$$
$$116 = 01110100$$

8. Find the lowest value in the first address (192.168.52.0) that is 1. Going from right to left, the bit position 3 is 1.

9. Check to see whether there are any high-order bits in the second address (192.168.116.0) that are greater than the high-order bit in the first address. Because there is one (bit 7 compared to bit 6), all bits to the right of the first bit in address 1 are included.

10. Set the mask equal to the value of the range found. Therefore, you include the bits in position 1–2 in the range, and the value of the mask is $2^0 + 2^1$, or 3. In binary, the value of each bit is 2 raised to the power $n - 1$, where n is the bit position.

11. Calculate the contiguous range using the beginning address and the mask as follows:

```
access-list 100 permit ip 192.168.52.0 0.0.3.255
```

12. Calculate the new beginning address as original plus 1 plus the mask, or $52 + 3 + 1 = 56$.

13. Write the octet in binary:

$$56 = 00111000$$
$$116 = 01110100$$

14. Find the lowest value in the first address (192.168.56.0) that is 1. Going from right to left, the bit position 4 is 1.

15. Check to see whether there are any high-order bits in the second address (192.168.116.0) that are greater than the high-order bit in the first address. Because there is one (bit 7 compared to bit 6), all bits to the right of the first bit in address 1 are included.

16. Set the mask equal to the value of the range found. Therefore, you include the bits in position 1–3 in the range, and the value of the mask is $2^0 + 2^1 + 2^2$, or 7. In binary, the value of each bit is 2 raised to the power n – 1, where n is the bit position.

17. Calculate the contiguous range using the beginning address and the mask as follows:

```
access-list 100 permit ip 192.168.56.0 0.0.7.255
```

18. Calculate the new beginning address as original plus 1 plus the mask, or 56 + 7 + 1 = 64.

19. Write the octet in binary:

$$64 = 01000000$$
$$116 = 01110100$$

20. Find the lowest value in the first address (192.168.64.0) that is 1. Going from right to left, the bit position 7 is 1.

21. Check to see whether there are any high-order bits in the second address (192.168.116.0) that are greater than the high-order bit in the first address. Because there are none (both are bit 7), find the high-order bit in the end address less than 7. This is 6.

22. If all the bits after the 6 are 1, then we are finished. But because they are not, you continue. You include all bits to the right of the first bit in address 2.

23. Set the mask equal to the value of the range found. Therefore, you include the bits in position 1–5 in the range, and the value of the mask is $2^0 + 2^1 + 2^2 + 2^3 + 2^4$, or 31. In binary, the value of each bit is 2 raised to the power n – 1, where n is the bit position.

24. Calculate the contiguous range using the beginning address and the mask as follows:

```
access-list 100 permit ip 192.168.64.0 0.0.31.255
```

25. Calculate the new beginning address as original plus 1 plus the mask, or 64 + 31 + 1 = 96.

26. Write the octet in binary:

$$96 = 01100000$$
$$116 = 01110100$$

27. Find the lowest value in the first address (192.168.96.0) that is 1. Going from right to left, the bit position 6 is 1.

28. Check to see whether there are any high-order bits in the second address (192.168.116.0) that are greater than the high-order bit in the first address. Because there are none (both are bit 7), find the high-order bit in the end address less than the next high-order bit in first address. This is 5.

29. If all the bits after the 5 are 1, then we are finished. Because they are not, you continue. You include all bits to the right of the first bit in address 2.

30. Set the mask equal to the value of the range found. Therefore, you include the bits in position 1–5 in the range, so the value of the mask is $2^0 + 2^1 + 2^2 + 2^3$, or 15. In binary, the value of each bit is 2 raised to the power $n - 1$, where n is the bit position.

31. Calculate the contiguous range using the beginning address and the mask as follows:

```
access-list 100 permit ip 192.168.96.0 0.0.15.255
```

32. Calculate the new beginning address as original plus 1 plus the mask, or 96 + 15 + 1 = 112.

33. Write the octet in binary:

$$112 = 01110000$$
$$116 = 01110100$$

34. Find the lowest value in the first address (192.168.64.0) that is 1. Going from right to left, the bit position 5 is 1.

35. Check to see whether there are any high-order bits in the second address (192.168.116.0) that are greater than the high-order bit in the first address. Because there are none (both are bit 7), find the high-order bit in the end address less than 7. This is 6.

36. If all the bits after the 5 are 1, then you are finished. Because they are not, you continue. You include all bits to the right of the first bit in address 2.

37. Set the mask equal to the value of the range found. Therefore, you include the bits in position 1–5 in the range, and the value of the mask is $2^0 + 2^1$, or 3. In binary, the value of each bit is 2 raised to the power $n - 1$, where n is the bit position.

38. Calculate the contiguous range using the beginning address and the mask as follows:

```
access-list 100 permit ip 192.168.112.0 0.0.3.255
```

39. Calculate the new beginning address as original plus 1 plus the mask, or 112 + 3 + 1 = 116.

40. Write the octet in binary:

$$116 = 01110100$$
$$116 = 01110100$$

Because the beginning address is equal to the ending address, you are finished. However, you must add the last entry to cover the network 192.168.116.0/24:

```
access-list 100 permit ip 192.168.116.0 0.0.0.255
```

You have completed the summarization process, and have all the required access lists. The complete set of access lists is shown following:

```
access-list 100 permit ip 192.168.50.0 0.0.1.255
access-list 100 permit ip 192.168.52.0 0.0.3.255
access-list 100 permit ip 192.168.56.0 0.0.7.255
access-list 100 permit ip 192.168.64.0 0.0.31.255
access-list 100 permit ip 192.168.96.0 0.0.15.255
access-list 100 permit ip 192.168.112.0 0.0.3.255
access-list 100 permit ip 192.168.116.0 0.0.0.255
```

Appendix H

Logical Operations

When dealing with IP addressing, you need to have a basic knowledge of binary mathematics. For example, to calculate subnet masks, you need to know how to do a logical AND. This appendix provides a cursory review and explanation of the common bitwise operations AND, OR, XOR, and NOT. In general, you perform logical operations between two data bits. The exception is the NOT command. Bits or binary digits are either 0 or 1 (off or on).

AND

The logical AND operation compares two bits and when both are "1," the result is "1"; otherwise, the result is "0." Exhibit 1 is a truth table showing how AND works. The input bits are **bold type** and the results are regular type.

You will need to use a logical AND when calculating real network addresses from a host address and subnet mask. Refer to Appendix C, "Subnetting," for a practical example of the use of the AND operation.

OR

The logical OR operation compares two bits and when either or both are "1," the result is "1"; otherwise, the result is "0." Exhibit 2 shows the logical OR command. The input bits are **bold type** and the results are regular type.

You use logical OR when calculating the range of addresses in an access list. You OR the wildcard mask to the source or destination address. Check out Chapters 15 and 16 for examples of the use of logical OR.

Exhibit 1　Logical AND

	0	1
0	0	0
1	0	1

Exhibit 2　Logical OR

	0	1
0	0	1
1	1	1

Exhibit 3　Logical XOR

	0	1
0	0	1
1	1	0

Exhibit 4　Logical NOT

0	1
1	0

XOR

The logical XOR — exclusive OR — operation compares two bits and when exactly one of them is "1," the result is "1"; otherwise, when the bits are the same, the result is "0." Exhibit 3 shows the logical XOR command. The input bits are **bold type** and the results are regular type.

NOT

The logical NOT operation simply changes the value of a single bit. When the bit is a "0," the operation changes it to "1." Conversely, when the bit is a "1," the operation changes it to a "0." Exhibit 4 reveals the logical NOT command. The input bits are **bold type** and the results are regular type.

Appendix I

Helpful Resources

This appendix provides a compendium of helpful resources that should make securing and controlling your router an easier task.

Mailing Lists

1. bugtraq@securityfocus.com
2. cisco@spot.colorado.edu
3. cisco-nsp@puck.nether.net
4. cisco-request@spot.colorado.edu
5. cust-security-announce@cisco.com
6. firewalls@lists.gnac.net
7. first-info@first.org
8. first-teams@first.org (which includes the CERT/CC)
9. nanog@merit.edu

Note: Use http://www.nexial.com/mailinglists/ to search the Cisco mailing list by year.

Tip: To subscribe to most mailing lists, send e-mail to any address above with no Subject and the following command in the body of the message:

Subscribe yourname@yourdomain.xx Yourname

Tip: You can enroll online to most of these mailing lists and more by filling out the subscription form at http://www.securityfocus.com.

Usenet Newsgroups

1. alt.certification.cisco
2. alt.fan.cisco
3. comp.dcom.sys.cisco
4. fido7.ru.cisco

World Wide Web URLs

1. *report.htm* — http://sentry-labs.com/report.htm
2. *Access Control Lists: Overview and Guidelines* — http://www.cisco.com/univercd/cc/td/doc/product/software/ios113ed/113ed_cr/secur_c/scprt3/scacls.htm
3. *accesslist1* — http://www.kcar.net/accesslist1.htm
4. *accesslist2* — http://www.kcar.net/accesslist2.htm
5. *Cisco 600 CBOS* — http://www.theregister.co.uk/content/5/19148.html
6. *Cisco IOS Release 12.0 Security Configuration Guide* — http://www.cisco.com/univercd/cc/td/doc/product/software/ios120/12cgcr/secur_c/index.htm
7. *Cisco Improving Security on Cisco Routers* — http://www.ieng.com/warp/public/707/21.html#snmp
8. *Cisco Simple Password Decryption* — http://www.neotech.demon.co.uk/ciscopwd.htm
9. *Cisco: CCNA Essentials (CCNAE)* — http://www.cisco.com/warp/public/10/wwtraining/cust/classes/C-TRNW-CCNAE.html
10. *Cisco: Cisco Secure Policy Manager* — http://www.cisco.com/warp/public/cc/pd/sqsw/sqppmn/
11. *Cisco: Context-based Access Control: Introduction and Configuration* — http://www.cisco.com/warp/public/110/32.html
12. *Cisco: Internet Security Advisories* — http://www.ieng.com/warp/public/707/advisory.html
13. *Cisco: Pass the Password* — http://www.alcrypto.co.uk/cisco/
14. *Cisco: Security Advisory: More Multiple Vulnerabilities in CBOS* — http://www.cisco.com/warp/public/707/CBOS-multiple2-pub.html
15. *Configuring Context-Based Access Control* — http://www.ieng.com/univercd/cc/td/doc/product/software/ios121/121cgc/secur_c/scprt3/scdcbac.htm
16. *Configuring IP Session Filtering (Reflexive Access Lists)* — http://www.cisco.com/univercd/cc/td/doc/product/software/ios113ed/113ed_cr/secur_c/scprt3/screflex.htm

17. *Configuring Lock-and-Key Security (Dynamic Access Lists)* — http://www.cisco.com/univercd/cc/td/doc/product/software/ios113ed/113ed_cr/secur_c/scprt3/sclock.htm

18. *Configuring TCP Intercept (Prevent Denial-of-Service Attacks)* — http://www.cisco.com/univercd/cc/td/doc/product/software/ios113ed/113ed_cr/secur_c/scprt3/scdenial.htm

19. *Context-Based Access Control Commands* — http://www.cisco.com/univercd/cc/td/doc/product/software/ios120/12cgcr/secur_r/srprt3/srcbac.htm

20. *Global Incident Analysis Center: Special Notice: Egress Filtering* — http://www.sans.org/y2k/egress.htm

21. *IOS Reference* — http://home.sc.rr.com/montuori/iosref.htm

22. *ITPRC: The Information Technology Professional's Resource Center* — http://www.itprc.com/

23. *Links, Links and More Links!* — http://cns.senecac.on.ca/~kansari/dcn586links.htm

24. *Looking Into Lock-and-Key* — http://www.mentortech.com/learn/welcher/papers/lockkey.htm

25. *Modesto Cisco Users Group: Resources* — http://cisco.artoo.net/resources.html

26. *Network Universe: The Online Networking Resource* — http://www.dtool.com/ccoconf.html

27. *Protection Against The Lion Worm: Investigative Research for Infrastructure Assurance (IRIA)* — investigation of criminal and terrorist activities that involve or target computer networks — http://www.ists.dartmouth.edu/IRIA/knowledge_base/tools/lionprotection.htm

28. *Reflexive Access List Commands* — http://akson.sgh.waw.pl/~chopin/ios120/12supdoc/12cmdsum/12cssec/csreflex.htm

29. *Reflexive Access Lists* — http://www.mentortech.com/learn/welcher/papers/reflexiveacl.html

30. *Rob's links* — http://rob.ossifrage.net/links/index.pl?11

31. *SecurityPortal: Cisco Security Resources* — http://www.securityportal.com/research/research.cisco.html

32. *Simple Network Management Protocol (SNMP)* — http://www.sce.carleton.ca/netmanage/snmp/cisco-intro.html

33. *Time-Based Access Lists Using Time Ranges* — http://www.cisco.com/univercd/cc/td/doc/product/software/ios120/120newft/120t/120t1/timerang.htm

34. *Top Ten Blocking Recommendations Using Cisco ACLs* — http://www.sans.org/infosecFAQ/firewall/blocking_cisco.htm

35. *Tripwire: Tripwire for Routers Assures Integrity of Networking Infrastructures* — http://www.tripwire.com/press/press_release/pr.cfml?prid=74&

36. *Welcome to www.certsolutions.com* — http://www.ciscocertified.com/

37. *ZDNet: eWEEK: Cisco fixes flaw in IOS software* — http://www.zdnet.com/eweek/stories/general/0,11011,2691594,00.html

38. *ZDNet: eWEEK: Flaws leave Cisco's IOS vulnerable* — http://www.zdnet.com/eweek/stories/general/0,11011,2780976,00.html

39. *ZDNet: PC Week: Cisco brings management suite to small business —*
    http://www.zdnet.com/pcweek/stories/news/0,4153,2420814,00.html

Request Comments

1. RFC0792 — Internet Control Message Protocol
2. RFC0814 — Name, addresses, ports, and routes
3. RFC0903 — Reverse Address Resolution Protocol
4. RFC0936 — Another Internet subnet addressing scheme
5. RFC0925 — Multi-LAN address resolution
6. RFC0932 — Subnetwork addressing scheme
7. RFC0950 — Internet Standard Subnetting Procedure
8. RFC1038 — Draft Revised IP security option
9. RFC1281 — Guidelines for the Secure Operation of the Internet
10. RFC1365 — An IP Address Extension Proposal
11. RFC1375 — Suggestion for New Classes of IP Addresses
12. RFC1334 — PPP Authentication Protocols
13. RFC1352 — SNMP Security Protocols
14. RFC1411 — Telnet Authentication: Kerberos Version 4
15. RFC1446 — Security Protocols for Version 2 of the Simple Network Management Protocol (SNMPv2)
16. RFC1466 — Guidelines for Management of IP Address Space
17. RFC1467 — Status of CIDR Deployment in the Internet
18. RFC1492 — An Access Control Protocol, Sometimes Called TACACS
19. RFC1510 — The Kerberos Network Authentication Service (V5)
20. RFC1517 — Applicability Statement for the Implementation of Classless Inter-Domain Routing (CIDR)
21. RFC1518 — An Architecture for IP Address Allocation with CIDR
22. RFC1519 — Classless Inter-Domain Routing (CIDR): An Address Assignment and Aggregation Strategy
23. RFC1631 — The IP Network Address Translator (NAT)
24. RFC1675 — Security Concerns for IPng
25. RFC1681 — On Many Addresses per Host
26. RFC1700 — Assigned Numbers
27. RFC1704 — On Internet Authentication
28. RFC1744 — Observations on the Management of the Internet Address Space
29. RFC1776 — The Address is the Message
30. RFC1810 — Report on MD5 Performance
31. RFC1814 — Unique Addresses are Good
32. RFC1825 — Security Architecture for the Internet Protocol
33. RFC1826 — IP Authentication Header
34. RFC1827 — IP Encapsulating Security Payload
35. RFC1828 — IP Authentication Using Keyed MD5
36. RFC1829 — The ESP DES-CBC Transform
37. RFC1851 — The ESP Triple DES Transform
38. RFC1852 — IP Authentication Using Keyed SHA
39. RFC1853 — IP in IP Tunneling

40. RFC1858 — Security Considerations for IP Fragment Filtering
41. RFC1900 — Renumbering Needs Work
42. RFC1917 — An Appeal to the Internet Community to Return Unused IP Networks (Prefixes) to the IANA
43. RFC1910 — User-based Security Model for SNMPv2
44. RFC1918 — Address Allocation for Private Internets
45. RFC1948 — Defending Against Sequence Number Attacks
46. RFC2008 — Implications of Various Address Allocation Policies for Internet Routing
47. RFC2036 — Observations on the Use of Components of the Class A Address Space within the Internet
48. RFC2050 — Internet Registry IP Allocation Guidelines
49. RFC2101 — IPv4 Address Behaviour Today
50. RFC2104 — Keyed-Hashing for Message Authentication Codes
51. RFC2196 — Site Security Handbook
52. RFC2350 — Expectations for Computer Security Incident Response
53. RFC2401 — Security Architecture for the Internet Protocol
54. RFC2411 — IP Security Document Roadmap
55. RFC2504 — Users' Security Handbook
56. RFC2519 — A Framework for Inter-Domain Route Aggregation
57. RFC2577 — FTP Security Considerations
58. RFC2588 — IP Multicast and Firewalls
59. RFC2663 — IP Network Address Translator (NAT) Terminology and Considerations
60. RFC2709 — Security Model with Tunnel-mode IPSec for NAT Domains
61. RFC2828 — Internet Security Glossary
62. RFC2827 — Network Ingress Filtering: Defeating Denial-of-Service Attacks which employ IP Source Address Spoofing
63. RFC2979 — Behavior of and Requirements for Internet Firewalls

You can find the above RFCs by searching by title or number at http://www.rfc-editor.org/rfcsearch.html.

Appendix J

Bibliography

Cryptography

1. Bamford, James. 1983. *The Puzzle Palace*. Penguin Books: New York.
2. Kippenhahn, Rudolf. 1999. *Code Breaking: A History and Exploration*. Overlook Press: Woodstock, NY.
3. Schneier, Bruce. 1994. *Applied Cryptography*. John Wiley & Sons: New York.
4. Singh, Simon. 1999. *The Code Book*. Fourth Estate: London.
5. Smith, Richard E. 1997. *Internet Cryptography*. Addison-Wesley: Reading, MA.

Firewalls

1. Amoroso, Edward and Ronald Sharp. 1996. *Intranet and Internet Firewall Strategies*. Ziff-Davis Press: Emeryville, CA.
2. Chapman, D. Brent and Elizabeth D. Zwicky. 1995. *Building Internet Firewalls*. O'Reilly & Associates: Sebastopol, CA.
3. Cheswick, William R. and Steven M. Bellovin. 1994. *Firewalls and Internet Security*. Addison-Wesley: Reading, MA.
4. Fuller, Scott and Kevin Pagan. 1997. *Intranet Firewalls*. Ventana Communications Group: Research Triangle Park, NC.
5. Goncalves, Marcus. 1997. *Firewalls Complete*. McGraw-Hill: New York.
6. Goncalves, Marcus. 1997. *Protecting Your Web Site with Firewalls*. Prentice-Hall PTR: Upper Saddle River, NJ.
7. Schuler, Kevin. 1998. *Microsoft Proxy Server 2 on Site*. Coriolis: Scottsdale, AZ.
8. Siyan, Karanjit S. and Chris Hare. 1995. *Internet Firewalls and Network Security*. New Riders Publishing: Indianapolis, IN.

General Security

1. ARCA, edited by. 1993. *INFOSEC Handbook*. ARCA: San Jose, CA.
2. Davis, Peter T. and Barry D. Lewis. 1996. *Computer Security for Dummies*. IDG Books: Foster City, CA.
3. Flynn, Nancy. 2001. *The E-Policy Handbook*. AMACOM: New York.
4. Icove, David, Karl Seger, and William VonStorch. 1995. *Computer Crime: A Crimefighter's Handbook*. O'Reilly & Associates, Inc.: Sebastopol, CA.
5. Kovacich, Dr. Gerald L. 1998. *Information Systems Security Officer's Guide*. Butterworth-Heinemann: Woburn, MA.
6. Pipkin, Donald L. 2000. *Information Security*. Hewlett-Packard Professional Books: Upper Saddle River, NJ.
7. Schneier, Bruce. 2000. *Secrets and Lies*. John Wiley & Sons: New York.

Hacking

1. Chirillo, John. 2001. *Hack Attacks Denied*. John Wiley & Sons: New York.
2. Chirillo, John. 2001. *Hack Attacks Revealed*. John Wiley & Sons: New York.
3. Cornwall, Hugo. 1990. *Data Theft*. Mandarin Paperbacks: London.
4. Cornwall, Hugo. 1988. *Hacker's Handbook III*. Random Century Ltd.: London.
5. Cornwall, Hugo. 1991. *The Industrial Espionage Book*. Random Century Ltd.: London.
6. Denning, Dorothy E. 1999. *Information Warfare and Security*. Addison-Wesley: Reading, MA.
7. Dr. K. 2000. *A Complete H@cker's Handbook*. Carlton Books: London.
8. Goodell, Jeff. 1996. *The Cyberthief and the Samurai*. Dell: New York.
9. Hafner, Katie and John Markoff. 1991. *Cyberpunk: Outlaws and Hackers on the Computer Frontier*. Simon & Schuster: New York.
10. Landreth, Bill. 1989. *Out of the Inner Circle*. Tempus Books: Redmond, WA.
11. Littman, Jonathan. 1996. *The Fugitive Game*. Little, Brown & Company: Boston, MA.
12. Littman, Jonathan. 1997. *The Watchman*. Little, Brown & Company: Boston, MA.
13. McClure, Stuart, Joel Scambray, and George Kurtz. 1999. *Hacking Exposed*. Osborne/McGraw-Hill: Berkeley, CA.
14. Russell, Ryan and Stace Cunningham. 2000. *Hack Proofing Your Network: Internet Tradecraft*. Syngress: Rockland, MA.
15. Schwartau, Winn. 2000. *Cybershock: Surviving Hackers, Phreakers, Identity Thieves, Internet Terrorists and Weapons of Mass Disruption*. Thunder's Mouth Press: New York.
16. Schwartau, Winn. 1994. *Information Warfare*. Thunder's Mouth Press: New York.
17. Shimomura, Tsutomu and John Markoff. 1996. *Takedown*. Hyperion: New York.
18. Slatalla, Michelle and Joshua Quittner. 1995. *Masters of Deception: The Gang that Ruled Cyberspace*. Harper Collins Publishers: New York.

19. Sterling, Bruce. 1992. *The Hacker Crackdown*. Bantam Books: New York.
20. Stoll, Clifford. 1989. *The Cuckoo's Egg*. Doubleday: New York.
21. The Knightmare. 1994. *Secrets of a Super Hacker*. Loompanics Unlimited: Port Townsend, WA.
22. Wang, Wallace. 2001. *Steal This Computer Book 2*. No Starch Press: San Francisco.
23. Winkler, Ira. 1997. *Corporate Espionage*. Prima Publishing: Rocklin, CA.

Internet/Intranet Security

1. Ahuja, Vijay. 1996. *Network and Internet Security*. Academic Press: Boston.
2. Ahuja, Vijay. 1997. *Secure Commerce on the Internet*. Academic Press Professional: Boston.
3. Atkins, Derek, Paul Buis, et al. 1996. *Internet Security: Professional Reference*. New Riders: Indianapolis, IN.
4. Barrett, Daniel J. 1996. *Bandits on the Information Superhighway*. O'Reilly & Associates: Sebastopol, CA.
5. Bernstein, Terry, Anish B. Bhimani, Eugene Schultz, and Carol A. Siegel. 1996. *Internet Security for Business*. John Wiley & Sons: New York.
6. Brenton, Chris with Cameron Hunt. 2001. *Active Defense*. Sybex: San Francisco.
7. Cohen, Frederick B. 1995. *Protection and Security on the Information Superhighway*. John Wiley & Sons: New York.
8. Cole, Eric. 2001. *Hackers Beware*. New Riders: Indianapolis, IN.
9. Cooper, Frederic J., et al. 1995. *Implementing Internet Security*. New Riders: Indianapolis, IN.
10. Crume, Jeff. 2000. *Inside Internet Security*. Addison-Wesley: Harlow, GB.
11. Dahl, Andrew and Leslie Lesnick. 1996. *Internet Commerce*. New Riders: Indianapolis, IN.
12. Edwards, Mark Joseph. 1998. *Internet Security with Windows NT*. Duke Press: Loveland, CO.
13. Freiss, Martin. 1997. *Protecting Networks with SATAN*. O'Reilly & Associates: Sebastopol, CA.
14. Hare, Chris and Karanjit Siyan. 1996. *Internet Firewalls and Network Security*. New Riders: Indianapolis, IN.
15. Howard, Garry S. 1995. *Introduction to Internet Security: From Basics to Beyond*. Prima Online: Rocklin, CA.
16. Hughes Jr., Larry J. 1995. *Actually Useful Internet Security Techniques*. New Riders: Indianapolis, IN.
17. Kyas, Othmar. 1997. *Internet Security*. International Thomson Computer Press: London.
18. Lynch, Daniel C. and Leslie Lundquist. 1996. *Digital Money: The New Era of Internet Commerce*. John Wiley & Sons: New York.
19. McCarthy, Linda. 1998. *Intranet Security: Stories from the Trenches*. Sun Microsystems Press: Mountain View, CA.
20. McMahon, David. 2000. *Cyber Threat: Internet Security for Home and Business*. Warwick Publishing: Toronto.

21. Pabrai, Uday O. and Vijay K. Gurbani. 1996. *Internet & TCP/IP Network Security*. McGraw-Hill: New York.
22. Randall, Neil. 1995. *Teach Yourself the Internet in a Week*. Sams.Net: Indianapolis, IN.
23. Schwartau, Winn and Chris Goggans. 1996. *The Complete Internet Business Toolkit*. Van Nostrand Reinhold: New York.
24. Stallings, William. 1995. *Internet Security Handbook*. IDG Books: Foster City, CA.
25. Stallings, William, Peter Stephenson, et al. 1995. *Implementing Internet Security*. New Riders: Indianapolis, IN.
26. Vacca, John. 1996. *Internet Security Secrets*. IDG Books: Foster City, CA.
27. Vacca, John. 1997. *Intranet Security*. Charles River Media, Inc.: Rockland, MA.
28. Weiss, Aaron. 1995. *The Complete Idiot's Guide to Protecting Yourself on the Internet*. Que: Indianapolis, IN.

Intrusion Detection

1. Amoroso, Edward. 1999. *Intrusion Detection: An Introduction to Internet Surveillance, Correlation, Trace Back, Traps, and Repsonse*. Intrusion.Net Books: Sparta, NJ.
2. Bace, Rebecca Gurley. 2000. *Intrusion Detection*. Macmillan Technical Publishing: Indianapolis, IN.
3. Escamilla, Terry. 1998. *Intrusion Detection*. John Wiley & Sons: New York.
4. Murray, James D. 1998. *Windows NT Event Logging*. O'Reilly: Sebastopol, CA.
5. Northcutt, Stephen. 1999. *Network Intrusion Detection: An Analyst's Handbook*. New Riders: Indianapolis, IN.
6. Northcutt, Stephen, Mark Cooper, Matt Fearnow, and Karen Frederick. 2001. *Intrusion Signatures and Analysis*. New Riders: Indianapolis, IN.
7. Proctor, Paul E. 2001. *The Practical Intrusion Detection Handbook*. PH PTR: Upper Saddle River, NJ.

Legal

1. Johnston, David, Sunny Handa, and Charles Morgan. 1997. *Cyberlaw*. Stoddart Publishing: Toronto.
2. Overly, Michael R. 1999. *e-policy: How to Develop Computer, E-mail, and Internet Guidelines to Protect Your Company and Its Assets*. AMACOM: New York.
3. Rose, Lance. 1995. *NetLaw: Your Rights in the Online World*. McGraw-Hill: New York.
4. Schelling, Jeffrey M. 1998. *Cyberlaw Canada*. Self-Counsel Press: North Vancouver, British Columbia.

Network Security

1. Alexander, Michael. 1997. *Net Security: Your Digital Doberman.* Ventana Communications Group: Research Triangle Park, NC.
2. Anonymous. 1997. *Maximum Security: A Hacker's Guide to Protecting Your Internet Site and Network.* Sams Publishing: Indianapolis, IN.
3. Benton, Chris with Cameron Hunt. 2001. *Active Defense: A Comprehensive Guide to Network Security.* Sybex: San Francisco.
4. Davis, Peter T., Editor. 1996. *Securing Client/Server Computer Networks.* McGraw-Hill: New York.
5. Hu, Wei. 1995. *DCE Security Programming.* O'Reilly & Associates: Sebastopol, CA.
6. Hunt, Craig. 1992. *TCP/IP Network Administration.* O'Reilly & Associates: Sebastopol, CA.
7. Klander, Lars. 1997. *Hacker Proof: The Ultimate Guide to Network Security.* Jamsa Press: Las Vegas, NV.
8. Kosiur, Dave. 1998. *Building and Managing Virtual Private Networks.* John Wiley & Sons: New York.
9. Murhammer, Martin W., Tim A. Bourne, Tamas Gaidosch, Charles Kunzinger, Laura Rademacher, and Andreas Weinfurter. 1998. *A Guide to Virtual Private Networks.* PH PTR: Upper Saddle River, NJ.
10. Simonds, Fred. 1996. *Network Security: Data and Voice Communications.* McGraw-Hill: New York.
11. Stallings, William. 1995. *Network and Internetwork Security.* Prentice-Hall: Englewood Cliffs, NJ.
12. Stang, David J. and Sylvia Moon. 1993. *Network Security Secrets.* IDG Books: San Mateo, CA.

Privacy

1. A Michael Wolff Book. 1996. *How You Can Access the Facts and Cover Your Tracks.* Wolff New Media: New York.
2. Bacard, Andre. 1995. *The Computer Privacy Handbook.* Peachpit Press: Berkeley, CA.
3. Banks, Michael A. 1997. *Web Psychos and Stalkers and Pranksters.* Coriolis Group Books: Albany, NY.
4. Cavoukian, Ann and Don Tapscott. 1995. *Who Knows: Safeguarding Your Privacy in a Networked World.* Random House of Canada: Toronto.
5. Goncalves, Marcus et al. 1997. *Internet Privacy Kit.* Que: Indianapolis, IN.
6. Pfaffenberger, Bryan. 1997. *Protect Your Privacy on the Internet.* John Wiley & Sons: New York.

Routers

1. Ballew, Scott M. 1997. *Managing IP Networks with Cisco Routers.* O'Reilly & Associates: Sebastopol, CA.

2. Chappell, Laura A. 2000. *Basic TCP/IP LAN Configurations*. podbooks.com: San Jose, CA.
3. Ciccarelli, Patrick and Christina Faulkner. 1999. *CCNA Jumpstart*. Sybex: San Francisco.
4. Cisco Documentation. 1999. *Cisco IOS 12.0 Network Security*. Cisco Press: Indianapolis, IN.
5. Hamilton, Andrew, John Mistichelli, with Bryant G. Tow. 2000. *Cisco Routers 24seven*. Sybex: San Francisco.
6. Held, Gil and Kent Hundley. 2000. *Cisco Access Lists Field Guide*. McGraw-Hill: New York.
7. Held, Gil and Kent Hundley. 1999. *Cisco Security Architectures*. McGraw-Hill: New York.
8. Lammle, Todd and William Tedder. 2000. *CCNA Virtual Lab e-trainer*. Sybex: San Francisco.
9. Lewis, Chris. 1997. *Cisco TCP/IP Routing Professional Reference*. McGraw-Hill: New York.
10. Lusignan, Russell, Olivier Steudler, and Jacques Allison. 2000. *Managing Cisco Network Security*. Syngress: Rockland, MA.
11. Mason, Andrew G. and Mark J. Newcomb. 2001. *Cisco Secure Internet Security Solutions*. Cisco Press: Indianapolis, IN.
12. Odom, Wendell. 1999. *CCNA Exam Certification Guide*. Cisco Press: Indianapolis, IN.
13. Rees, Matthew J. and Jeffrey T. Coe. 1999. *Routing and Switching*. Coriolis: Scottsdale, AZ.
14. Sedayao, Jeff. 2001. *Cisco IOS Access Lists*. O'Reilly & Associates: Sebastopol, CA.
15. Shaughnessy, Tom. 2000. *Cisco: A Beginner's Guide*. Osborne/McGraw-Hill: Berkeley, CA.
16. Syngress Media, Inc. 1999. *Cisco CCNA Test Yourself Practice Exams*. Osborne/McGraw-Hill: Berkeley, CA.

Appendix K

Acronyms and Abbreviations

AAA   Authentication, authorization, and accounting
AAI   Administration authority identifier
ABR   Area Border Routers
ACE   Access control entry
ACK   Positive acknowledgment
ACL   Access control list
ACP   Access control point
ACS   Access control server
ADS   Active Directory Service
ADSL   Asymmetrical Digital Subscriber Line
AES   Advanced Encryption Standard
AH   Authentication Header
ALG   Application level gateway
AM   Amplitude modulation
ANSI   American National Standards Institute
API   Application Programming Interface
ARA   AppleTalk Remote Access
ARAP   AppleTalk Remote Access Protocol
ARP   Address Resolution Protocol
ARPA   Advanced Research Projects Agency
AS   Autonomous system; authentication server
ASA   Adaptive security algorithm
ASBR   Autonomous System Border Router
ASCII   American Standard Code for Information Interchange
ATM   Asynchronous Transfer Mode
AR   Access rate
AV   Attribute value
BDR   Backup designated router
BECN   Backward explicit congestion notification
BER   Bit error rate

BGP	Border Gateway Protocol
BIA	Burnt-in address
BIOS	Basic input/output system
BOC	Bell Operating Company
Bps	Bytes per second
bps	Bits per second
BRI	Basic Rate Interface
BTE	Broadband terminal equipment
BTR	Bit transfer rate
BTU	Basic transmission unit
C-CRT	Cisco Countermeasure Research Team
CA	Certification Authority
CAM	Content-addressable memory
CAN	Campus area network
CAR	Committed access rate
CAU	Controlled access unit
CBAC	Context-based access control
CBC	Cipher block chaining
CBR	Constant bit rate
CCO	Cisco Connection Online
CCR	Current cell rate
CDDI	Copper Distributed Data Interface
CDP	Cisco Discovery Protocol
CEF	Cisco Express Forwarding
CEP	Certificate Enrollment Protocol
CERT	Computer Emergency Response Team
CET	Cisco Encryption Technology; computer-enhanced telephony
CHAP	Challenge Handshake Authentication Protocol
CIAC	Computer Incident Advisory Capability
CIDR	Classless Interdomain Routing
CIR	Committed information rate
CLI	Command line interface
CLNS	Connectionless network service
CPE	Customer premises equipment
CPU	Central processing unit
CRC	Cyclical redundancy check
CRL	Certificate revocation list
CRTC	Canadian Radio-television and Telecommunications Commission
CSMA/CA	Carrier sense multiple access/collision avoidance
CSMA/CD	Carrier sense multiple access/collision detection
CSMA/CP	Carrier sense multiple access/collision prevention
CSU	Channel service unit
CTSS	Compatible Time-Sharing System
DAP	Directory Access Protocol
DARPA	Defense Advanced Research Projects Agency
DAT	Dynamic address translation; digital audio tape
DCE	Data communications (circuit-terminating) equipment; distributed computing environment
DDR	Dial-on-demand routing

DES	Data Encryption Standard
DHCP	Dynamic Host Configuration Protocol
DIG	Domain Internet Groper
DLCI	Data link connection identifier
DLL	Dynamic Link Library
DMZ	Demilitarized zone
DNS	Domain Name System
DOI	Domain of interpretation (pronounced "doey")
DoS	Denial-of-service
DRAM	Dynamic random access memory
DS	Directory service
DSA	Digital Signature Algorithm
DSL	Digital subscriber line
DSS	Digital Signature Standard
DSU	Digital service unit
DTE	Data terminating (terminal) equipment
DUAL	Diffusing Update Algorithm
EBCDIC	Extended Binary Coded Decimal Interchange Code
ECC	Elliptic curve cryptosystem
ECMA	European Computer Manufacturers Association
EDI	Electronic data interchange
EGP	Exterior Gateway Protocol
EIA	Electronics Industries Alliance
EIGRP	Enhanced Interior Gateway Routing Protocol
EMI	Electromagnetic interference
ES-ES	End-system to end-system
ES-IS	End-system to intermediate-system
ESP	Encapsulating security payload
FAQ	Frequently asked question
FCC	Federal Communications Commission
FDDI	Fiber Distributed Data Interface
FDX	Full duplex
FECN	Forward explicit congestion notification
FIFO	First in, first out
FIRST	Forum of Incidence Response and Security Teams
FM	Frequency modulation
FTP	File Transfer Protocol
FQDN	Fully qualified domain name
GAP	Gateway Access Protocol
Gb	Gigabit
GB	Gigabyte
Gbps	Gigabits per second
GBps	Gigabytes per second
GGP	Gateway-to-gateway protocol
GID	Group ID
GNS	Get nearest server
GRE	Generic routing encapsulation
GSM	Global System for Mobile Communication
GUI	Graphical user interface

HAND	Have a nice day
HDLC	High-Level Data Link Control
HDX	Half duplex
HMAC	Hash message authentication code
HSRP	Hot Standby Router Protocol
HTML	Hypertext Markup Language
HTTP	Hypertext Transfer Protocol
Hz	Hertz
IAB	Internet Advisory Board
IC	Integrated circuit
ICMP	Internet Control Message Protocol
ICP	Internet Control Protocol
ID	Identifier, identification
IDEA	International Data Encryption Algorithm
IDF	Intermediate Distribution Facility
IDP	Internet Datagram Protocol
IDS	Intrusion detection system
IEEE	Institute of Electrical and Electronic Engineers
IETF	Internet Engineering Task Force
IGMP	Internet Gateway Management Protocol
IGP	Interior Gateway Protocol
IGRP	Interior Gateway Routing Protocol
IIS	Internet Information Server
IKE	Internet Key Exchange
IMAP	Interactive Mail Access Protocol; Interim Mail Access Protocol
I/O	Input/output
IOS	Internetworking operating system
IP	Internet protocol
IPng	Internet Protocol next-generation
IPSec	Internet Protocol Security protocol
IPX	Internetwork packet exchange
IR	Infrared
IRC	Internet relay chat
IRQ	Interrupt request
IS-IS	Intermediate System to Intermediate System protocol
ISAKMP	Internet Security Association and Key Management Protocol
ISA	Industry Standard Architecture
ISDN	Integrated Services Digital Network; it still does nothing
ISO	International Organization for Standardization
ISOC	Internet Society
ISN	Initial sequence number
ISP	Internet service provider
IT	Information technology
ITU	International Telecommunications Union
JEIDA	Japan Electronic Industry Development Association
kb	Kilobit
KB	Kilobyte
kbps	Kilobits per second
KBps	Kilobytes per second

KDC   Key distribution center
L2F   Layer 2 Forwarding
L2TP   Layer 2 Tunneling Protocol
LAA   Locally administered addresses
LAN   Local area network
LCD   Liquid crystal display
LDAP   Lightweight Directory Access Protocol
LEC   Local exchange carrier
LED   Light-emitting diode
LIFO   Last in, first out
LLC   Logical link control
LMI   Local management interface
lpd   Line printer daemon
MAC   Media Access Control
MAN   Metropolitan area network
MAU   Media attachment unit
Mb   Megabit
MB   Megabyte
Mbps   Megabits per second
MBps   Megabytes per second
MBZ   Must be zero
MDF   Main distribution facility
MIB   Management information base
MIME   Multipurpose Internet Mail Extensions
Modem   Modulator/demodulator
MS-CHAP   Microsoft Challenge Handshake Authentication Protocol
MSAU   Multi-station access unit
MTA   Mail transfer agent
MTU   Maximum transmission unit
MUA   Mail user agent
NADN   Nearest downstream neighbor
NAPT   Network address port translation
NAS   Network access server
NASI   NetWare Asynchronous Services Interface
NAT   Network address translation
NAUN   Nearest upstream neighbor
NBMA   Non-broadcast multi-access
NBP   Name Binding Protocol
NBT   NetBIOS over TCP/IP
NCP   Network control program
NCSA   National Center for Supercomputing Applications
NCSC   National Computer Security Center
NDIS   Network Driver Interface Specification
NDS   NetWare Directory Service
NetBEUI   NetBIOS Extended User Interface
NetBIOS   Network Basic Input/Output System
NFS   Network file system
NIC   Network interface card
NIS   Network Information Service

NIST   National Institute of Standards and Technology
NMS   Network management system
NNTP   Network News Transfer Protocol
NOC   Network operations center (or centre)
NOS   Network operating system
NNTP   Network News Transfer Protocol
NPDU   Network protocol data unit
NTP   Network Time Protocol
NVRAM   Non-volatile random access memory
ODBC   Open Database Connectivity
ODI   Open Data Link Interface
OOB   Out-of-band
OOUI   Object-oriented user interface
OS   Operating system
OSI   Open Systems Interconnection model
OSPF   Open Shortest Path First protocol
OTP   One-time password
OU   Organizational unit
OUI   Organizational unit identifier
P2P   Peer-to-peer
PAD   Packet assembler/disassembler
PAM   Port-to-application mapping
PAP   Password Authentication Protocol; Packet Access Protocol
PAT   Port address translation
PBX   Private branch exchange
PCI   Peripheral component interconnect
PCMCIA   Personal Computer Memory Card International Association
PDN   Public data network
PDU   Protocol data unit
Perl   Practical Extraction and Reporting Language
PFS   Perfect forward secrecy
PGP   Pretty good privacy
PING   Packet Internet Groper
PKCS   Public Key Cryptography Standards
PKI   Public key infrastructure
POE   Point of entry
POP   Post Office Protocol; point of presence
POS   Point-of-sale
POST   Power-on self test
POTS   Plain old telephone system
PPP   Point-to-Point Protocol
PPTP   Point-to-Point Tunneling Protocol
PRI   Primary rate interface
PSIRT   Cisco's Product Security Incident Response Team
PSTN   Public switched telephone network
PVC   Permanent virtual circuit
QoS   Quality of service
RA   Registration Authority
RADIUS   Remote Authentication Dial-In User Service

RAID	Redundant array of inexpensive disks; redundant array of independent disks
RAM	Random access memory
RARP	Reverse Address Resolution Protocol
RAS	Remote access server; reliability, availability, and serviceability
RBOC	Regional Bell Operating Company
RDBMS	Relational database management system
RF	Radio frequency
RFC	Request for Comments
RFI	Request for Proposal; radio frequency interference
RID	Router identification
RIF	Route information field
RIP	Routing Information Protocol
RISC	Reduced instruction set computer
ROM	Read-only memory
RPC	Remote procedure call
RRAS	Routing and remote access service
RSA	Rivest, Shamir, and Adleman
RTFM	Read the Flight Manual, or something like that!
RTMP	Routing Table Maintenance Protocol
SA	Security association
SAINT	Security Administrator's Integrated Network Tool
SATAN	Security Administrator's Tool for Analyzing Networks
SCSI	Small Computer System Interface
SET	Secure electronic transaction
SGMP	Simple Gateway Management Protocol
SHA	Secure hash algorithm
SKIP	Simple Key Management for Internet Protocols
SLIP	Serial Line Internet (Interface) Protocol
SMTP	Simple Mail Transport (Transfer) Protocol
SNAP	Subnetwork Access Protocol
SNMP	Simple Network Management Protocol
SOHO	Small office/home office
SONET	Synchronous optical network
SPAN	Switched port analyzer
SPD	Security protocol database
SPF	Shortest path first
SPX	Sequenced packet exchange
SQL	Structured Query Language
SRB	Source route bridging
SSE	Silicon switching engine
SSH	Secure shell
SSL	Secure Sockets Layer
SSP	Silicon switch processor
STLP	Secure Transport Layer Protocol
STP	Shielded twisted pair
SVC	Switched virtual circuit
TA	Terminal adapter
TACACS	Terminal Access Controller Access Control System

TACACS+ Terminal Access Controller Access Control System Plus
Tb   Terabit
TB   Terabyte
Tbps   Terabits per second
TBps   Terabytes per second
TCP   Transmission control protocol
TCP/IP   Transmission control protocol/Internet protocol
TCSEC   The Trusted Computer System Evaluation Criteria
TFTP   Trivial File Transfer Protocol
TGS   Ticket granting server
TGT   Ticket granting ticket
TIA   Telecommunications Industry Association
TLI   Transport Layer Interface
TLS   Transport layer security
TTL   Time-to-Live
UAA   Universally administered addresses
UDP   User Datagram Protocol
UID   User ID
UL   Underwriters Laboratories
ULP   Upper-layer protocol
UPS   Uninterruptible power supply
URL   Uniform resource locator
UTP   Unshielded twisted pair
UUCP   UNIX-to-UNIX Copy Program
VAN   Value-added network
vBNS   Very high performance Backbone Network Service
VC   Virtual circuit
VLAN   Virtual local area network
VLSM   Variable-length subnet masking
VPN   Virtual private network
VRML   Virtual Reality Markup Language
VSA   Vendor-specific attribute
VTY   Virtual terminal
WAN   Wide area network
WML   Wireless Markup Language
WWW   World Wide Web
XTACACS   Extended Terminal Access Controller Access Control System
ZIP   Zone Information Protocol

Appendix L

Glossary

Access: The ability and the means necessary to approach, to store in or retrieve data from, to communicate with, and to make use of any computer system resource.

Access category: One of the classes to which a user, a program, or a process in a system can be assigned because of the resources or groups of resources that each user, program, or process is authorized to use.

Access control entry (ACE): An entry in an access control list (ACL). The entry contains a security ID (SID) and a set of access rights. A process with a matching security ID is allowed access rights, denied rights, or allowed rights with auditing.

Access control list (ACL): The part of a security descriptor that enumerates the protection (i.e., permission) given to an object.

Access control mechanisms: Hardware or software features, operating procedures, management procedures, and various combinations of these designed to detect and prevent unauthorized access and to permit authorized access to a system.

Access guidelines: Used here in the sense of guidelines for the modification of specific access rights. A general framework drawn up by the owner or custodian to instruct the data set security administrator on the degree of latitude that exists for the modification of rights of access to a file without the specific authority of the owner or custodian.

Access layer: The layer where network devices act as an intermediary connection point between the end systems and the distribution layer.

Access list: A catalog of users, programs, or processes and the specifications of access categories to which each is assigned.

Access period: A segment of time, generally expressed daily or weekly, when access rights prevail.

Access right: A permission granted to a process to manipulate a particular object in a particular manner (e.g., calling a service). Different object types support different access rights, which are stored in the object's access control list (ACL).

Access token: An object uniquely identifying a user who has logged on.

Access type: An access right to a particular device, program, or file; for example, read, write, execute, append, allocate, modify, delete, create.

Access validation: Checking a user's account information to determine when the subject should be granted the right to perform the requested operation.

Accessibility: The ease with which information can be obtained.

Accidental: Outcome from the lack of care or any situation in which the result is negatively different from that intended; for example, poor program design is a result of poor planning.

Accountability: The quality or state that enables violations or attempted violations of a system security to be traced to individuals who can then be held responsible.

Acknowledgment (ACK): A positive response message to a request for synchronization when establishing a communication session between two devices.

Adapter: A term for a network interface card. See *network interface card.*

Adaptive Security Algorithm (ASA): A Cisco proprietary method for ensuring security.

Address: A number or group of numbers uniquely identifying a network node within its network (or internetwork).

Administrator: The person responsible for the operation of the network. The administrator maintains the network, reconfiguring and updating it as the need arises.

Agents: Software watchdogs used by SNMP to monitor network processes. See *SNMP.*

Alert: (1) An audible or visual alarm that signals an error or serves as a warning of some sort. (2) An asynchronous notification that one thread sends to another.

Algorithm: A step-by-step procedure, usually mathematical, for doing a specific function; for example, a PIN verification algorithm or an encryption algorithm.

Analog: A system based on a continuous ratio, such as voltage or current values.

Analog transmission: A communications scheme using a continuous signal, varied by amplification. Broadband networks use analog transmissions.

Analytical attack: An attempt to break a code or cipher key by discovering flaws in its encryption algorithm.

ANDing: Uses binary math AND to compare an IP address with its subnet mask to determine the network address.

ANSI: The acronym for American National Standards Institute, which sets standards for many technical fields.

Anti-replay: A security service in which the receiver can reject old or duplicate packets to protect itself against replay attacks. IPSec provides optional anti-replay services using a sequence number combined with the use of authentication.

AppleTalk: Macintosh native protocol.

Application: The user's communication with the installation. A software program or program package enabling a user to perform a specific job, such as word processing or electronic mail.

Application layer: The highest layer in the OSI model. The application layer formats data for a particular function such as printing, e-mail, or Web browsing.

Application program/software: A program written for or by a user that applies to the user's work.

Application Programming Interface (API): A set of routines that an application program uses to request and carry out lower-level services performed by the operating system.

Application server: Provides resources directly or indirectly for clients. Services can include file, print, Web, fax, communications, workflow, and security.

Application system: A collection of programs and documentation used for an application.

Architecture: The general design of hardware or software, including how they fit together.

ARP (Address Resolution Protocol): A TCP/IP protocol used to map IP addresses to node hardware addresses.

ASCII: The acronym for American Standard Code for Information Interchange pronounced "ASK-ee."

Asynchronous: A methods of data communications in which transmissions are not synchronized with a signal. Local area networks transmit asynchronously.

Attacks: The methods used to commit security violations, such as masquerading and modification.

Attenuation: The difference in amplitude between a signal at transmission and at reception.

Audit policy: Defines the type of security events logged for a domain or for an individual computer; determines what NT will do when the security log becomes full.

Audit trail: A chronological record of system activities sufficient to enable the reconstruction, review, and examination of the sequence of environments and activities surrounding or leading to each event in the path of a transaction from its inception to the output of results.

Auditability: The physical or mental power to perform an examination or verification of financial records or accounts.

Auditing: The ability to detect and record security-related events, particularly any attempt to create, access, or delete objects.

Authenticate: (1) To confirm that the object is what it purports to be. To verify the identity of a person (or other agent external to the protection system) making a request. (2) To identify or verify the eligibility of a station, an originator, or an individual to access specific categories of information.

Authentication: A process by which a user or service identifies itself to another service. For example, a client can authenticate to a router or a router can authenticate to another router.

Authorization: The process that grants the necessary and sufficient permissions for the intended purpose. A means by which the router determines what privileges you have in a network.

Authorize: To grant the necessary and sufficient permissions for the intended purpose.

Automated security monitoring: The use of automated procedures to ensure that the security controls implemented within a system are not circumvented.

Autonomous switching: Feature on Cisco routers that provides faster packet processing by allowing the ciscoBus to switch packets independently without interrupting the system processor.

B Channel (Bearer channel): A 64-kbps ISDN channel providing full-duplex communications.

Back up: To make a spare copy of a disk, directory, or file to another storage device such as a disk or tape drive.

Backbone: A central network cable system that connects other networks.

Background processing: The action of completing tasks in the background.

Backoff: After a collision, all Ethernet devices will wait a random amount of time before attempting re-transmission.

Backup: A copy of a disk or of a file on a disk.

Backup procedures: The provisions made for the recovery of data files and program libraries, and for restart or replacement of equipment after the occurrence of a system failure or disaster.

Bandwidth: The range of frequencies available for signaling; the difference, expressed in hertz, between the lowest and highest frequencies of a band. Or simplistically, the rate that a network can transfer data.

Batch: The processing of a group of related transactions or other items at planned intervals.

Baud: A unit of signaling speed. The speed in baud is the number of discrete conditions or events per second.

BGP (Border Gateway Protocol): A commonly used routing protocol for inter-domain routing. It is the standard EGP for the Internet. BGP handles the routing between two or more routers that serve as the border routers for particular autonomous systems.

Binary: A number system where information is represented as either on (a "1") or off (a "0").

Bit: A contraction of the words *binary digit*. The smallest unit of information a computer can hold. The value of a bit (1 or 0) represents a simple two-way choice, such as yes or no, on or off, positive or negative, or something or nothing.

Board: A term primarily used for the flat circuit board that holds chip sets and other electronic components, and printed conductive paths between the components.

Boot: (*v*) To start by loading the operating system into the computer. Starting is often accomplished by first loading a small program, which then reads a larger program into memory. The program is said to "pull itself up by its own bootstraps"[md]hence the term "bootstrapping," or "booting." Also means to start a computer or initial program load. (*n*) The process of starting or resetting a computer.

Boot Protocol (BOOTP): A protocol used for remotely booting systems on the network.

Border router: A high-end router used to connect autonomous systems. Also known as core routers.

Bottleneck: A device on the network that is slow in transmitting data, causing delays in the delivery of data.

bps (bits per second): A unit of data transmission rate.

Breach: A break in system security that results in admittance of a person or program to an object.

Bridge: A device used to connect LANs by forwarding packets addressed to other similar networks across connections at the Media Access Control data-link level. Routers, which operate at the protocol level, are also called bridges.

Broadband: A transmission system in which signals are encoded and modulated into different frequencies and then transmitted simultaneously with other signals.

Broadcast: A LAN data transmission scheme in which data packets are heard by all stations on the network.

Brouter: A hybrid device that bridges nonroutable layer 2 protocols and routes routable layer 3 protocols.

Browser: A program used to view information on the World Wide Web.

Brute-force attack: A computerized trial-and-error attempt to decode a cipher or password by trying every possible combination. Also known as an *exhaustive attack*.

Buffer: A temporary holding area of the computer's memory where information can be stored by one program or device and then read at a different rate by another, for example, a print buffer. Also, the printer's random access memory (RAM), measured in kilobytes. Because computer chips can transfer data much faster than mechanical printer mechanisms can reproduce it, small buffers are generally inserted between the two to keep the data flow in check.

Bug: An error in a program that prevents it from working as intended. The expression reportedly comes from the early days of computing when an itinerant moth shorted a connection and caused a breakdown in a room-sized computer.

Bus: A common connection. Networks that broadcast signals to all stations, such as Ethernet and ARCnet, are considered bus networks.

Byte: A unit of information having eight bits.

Cabling system: The wiring used to connect networked computers together.

Card: Another name for board.

CDP (Cisco Discovery Protocol): Media- and protocol-independent device-discovery protocol that runs on all Cisco-manufactured equipment, including routers, access servers, bridges, and switches. Using CDP, a device can advertise its existence to other devices and receive information about other devices on the same LAN or on the remote side of a WAN. Runs on all media that support SNAP, including LANs, Frame Relay, and ATM media.

Cells: Packets of fixed size used by Asynchronous Transfer Mode (ATM).

Central processing unit (CPU): The "brain" of the computer; the microprocessor performing the actual computations in machine language.

Certification: The technical evaluation, made as part of and in support of the accreditation process, establishing the extent that a particular computer system or network design and implementation meet a specified set of security requirements.

Channel: An information transfer path within a system. Can also refer to the mechanism by which the path is effected.

Character: Letter, numerical, punctuation, or any other symbol contained in a message.

Checksum: A way of providing error checking by calculating a value for a data packet that the destination device uses upon recalculation to determine whether it received the packet intact.

Chip: Slang for a silicon wafer imprinted with integrated circuits.

Circuit switching: A connectivity strategy in which a dedicated connection is established between the sender and receiver on a switched network. Data moves from the source to the destination along the circuit (the lines) that has been established for the particular session.

CiscoFusion: Cisco internetworking architecture that "fuses" together the scalability, stability, and security advantages of the latest routing technologies with the performance benefits of ATM and LAN switching, and the management benefits of VLANs.

CiscoView: GUI-based device-management software application that provides dynamic status, statistics, and comprehensive configuration information for Cisco internetworking devices. In addition to displaying a physical view of Cisco device chassis, CiscoView also provides device monitoring functions and basic troubleshooting capabilities, and can be integrated with several leading SNMP-based network management platforms.

Cisco IOS: Cisco system software that provides common functionality, scalability, and security for all products under the CiscoFusion architecture. Cisco IOS allows centralized, integrated, and automated installation and management of internetworks, while ensuring support for a wide variety of protocols, media, services, and platforms. See also *CiscoFusion*.

Classified: Subject to prescribed asset protection controls, including controls associated with classifications.

Classify: To assign a level of sensitivity and priority and, hence, security control to data.

Cleartext: Information that is in its readable state (before encryption and after decryption).

Click: As used in this book, to quickly press and release the mouse button. For example, you often click an icon to start an application.

Client: A computer that accesses shared network resources provided by another computer (a server). In a client/server database system, this is the computer (usually a workstation) that makes service requests.

Client/server: A network system design in which a processor or computer designated as a server (file server, database server, etc.) provides services to other client processors or computers.

Coax: Also known as coaxial, this is a cable that consists of two wires running inside a plastic sheath, insulated from each other.

Collision: A garbled transmission resulting from simultaneous transmissions by two or more workstations on the same network cable.

Commit bytes: The actual amount of memory that all the applications need at any given moment.

Communication link: An electrical and logical connection between two devices. On a local area network, a communication link is the point-to-point path between sender and recipient.

Communication program: A program that enables the computer to transmit data to and receive data from distant computers through the telephone system or some other communication system.

Compartmentalization: The breaking down of sensitive data into small, isolated blocks for reducing the risk to the data.

Completeness: Having all or necessary parts.

Compromise: The loss, misuse, or unauthorized disclosure of a data asset.

Condition: An operating situation when a threat arises. The condition is necessary and desirable for operations.

Confidential: A protection classification. Loss, misuse, or unauthorized disclosure of data with this protection classification could at most have a major negative impact. Such an incident would be harmful to the organization.

Confidentiality: A parameter showing the privacy of the information (used particularly in costing functions involving information that has a security classification or is considered proprietary or sensitive).

Configuration: (1) The total combination of hardware components — central processing unit, video display device, keyboard, and peripheral devices — forming a computer system. (2) The software settings allowing various hardware components of a computer system to communicate with each other.

Configuration register: In Cisco routers, a 16-bit, user-configurable value that determines how the router functions during initialization. The configuration register can be stored in hardware or software. In hardware, the bit position is set using a jumper. In software, the bit position is set by specifying a hexadecimal value using configuration commands.

Connect time: The amount of time a user connects to the file server.

Connection oriented: During communication between two devices, the receiving device will acknowledge to the sender that is has received the data. When part of the data is not received, the sender will retransmit the data.

Connectionless: During communication between two devices, there is no acknowledgment that the destination received the data.

Control program: A program designed to schedule and supervise the performance of data processing work by a computing system.

Cracker: Someone who breaks into systems for fun or profit.

Crash: (n) A malfunction caused by hardware failure or an error in the program. (v) To fail suddenly.

Credential: A general term that refers to authentication tickets, such as ticket granting tickets (TGTs) and service credentials. Kerberos credentials verify the identity of a user or service. If a network service decides to trust the Kerberos server that issued a ticket, it can be used in place of retyping in a username and password. Credentials have a default lifespan of eight hours.

Critical: Data with this preservation classification is essential to the organization's continued existence. The loss of such data would cause a serious disruption of the organization's operation.

Criticality: A parameter indicating dependence of the organization on the information.

Cryptoanalysis: The steps and operations performed in converting messages (cipher) into plaintext (clear) without initial knowledge of the key employed in the encryption algorithm.

Cryptographic system: The documents, devices, equipment, and associated techniques that are used as a unit to provide a single means of encryption (enciphering or encoding).

Cryptography: The transformation of plaintext into coded form (encryption), or from coded form into plaintext (decryption).

Cryptology: The field that includes both cryptoanalysis and cryptography.

Customer related: Identifying or relating specifically to a customer of the organization.

D channel (Data channel): A 16-kbps (BRI) or 64-kbps (PRI) full-duplex ISDN channel.

Damage: Impairment of the worth or usefulness of the information.

Data: Processable information with the associated documentation. The input that a program and its instructions perform on and that determines the results of processing.

Data contamination: A deliberate or accidental process or act that results in a change in the integrity of the original data.

Data-dependent protection: Protection of data at a level commensurate with the sensitivity level of the individual data elements, rather than with the sensitivity of the entire file that includes the data elements.

Data diddling: Unauthorized alteration of data as it is entered or stored in a computer.

Data integrity: Verified correspondence between the computer representation of information and the real-world events that the information represents. The condition of being whole, complete, accurate, and timely.

Data leakage: The theft of data or software.

Data-link layer: Layer 2 of the OSI model. The data-link layer receives data from the network layer and packages it as frames for the physical layer.

Data protection: Measures to safeguard data from undesired occurrences that intentionally or unintentionally lead to modification, destruction, or disclosure of data.

Data security: The result achieved through implementing measures to protect data against unauthorized events leading to unintentional or intentional modification, destruction, or disclosure of data.

Data storage: The preservation of data in various data media for direct use by the system.

Database: A collection of information organized in a form that can be readily manipulated and sorted by a computer user.

Database management system: A software system for organizing, storing, retrieving, analyzing, and modifying information in a database.

Database server: The "back end" processor that manages the database and fulfills database requests in a client/server database system.

Datagrams: Grouping of information in the data bit stream; datagrams are also referred to as packets or frames.

Debug: A colloquial term that means to find and correct an error or the cause of a problem or malfunction in a computer program. Usually synonymous with troubleshoot.

Debugger: A utility program that allows a programmer to see what is happening in the microprocessor and in memory while another program is running.

Decipher: To convert, by use of the appropriate key, ciphertext (encoded, encrypted) into its equivalent plaintext (clear).

Decimal: A numbering system that uses base 10.

Deliberate: Intended to harm. The results of deliberate actions might well be different from those expected by perpetrators or victims; for example, arson and vandalism.

Destruction: The act of rendering an asset ineffective or useless. It is a recognizable loss in which the file must be recovered from backup or reconstituted.

Device: A generic term for a computer subsystem, such as a printer, serial port, or disk drive. A device frequently requires its own controlling software, called a device driver.

Device driver: A software component that enables a computer system to communicate with a device. For example, a printer driver is a device driver that translates computer data into a form understood by the intended printer. In most cases, the driver also manipulates the hardware to transmit the data to the device.

DHCP (Dynamic Host Configuration Protocol): This is a tool that allows dynamic IP address allocation, simplifying machine configuration in your network.

Digital: A system based on discrete states, typically the binary conditions of on or off.

Digital transmission: A communications system that passes information encoded as pulses. Baseband networks use digital transmissions, as do microcomputers.

Directory: Pictorial, alphabetical, or chronological representation of the contents of a disk. Used to organize or group files on a disk. A directory is sometimes called a catalog or folder. The operating system uses a directory to keep track of the contents of the disk.

Disclosure: The act or an instance of revelation or exposure. A disclosure can be obvious, such as the removal of a tape from a library; or it can be concealed, such as the retrieval of a discarded report by an outsider or a disgruntled employee.

Discretionary access control (DAC): The protection that the owner of an object applies to the object by assigning various access rights to various users or groups of users.

Disk: A data storage device on which data is recorded on concentric circular tracks on a magnetic medium.

Disk drive: An electromechanical device that reads from and writes to disks. Two types of disk drives are in common use: floppy disk drives and hard disk drives.

Disk mirroring: The procedure of duplicating a disk partition on two or more disks, preferably on disks attached to separate disk controllers so that data remains accessible when either a disk or a disk controller fails. Disk mirroring provides a measure of fault tolerance.

Disk partition: A logical compartment on a physical disk drive. A single disk might have two or more logical disk partitions, each of which would be referenced with a different disk drive name.

Disk striping: The procedure of combining a set of same-sized disk partitions residing on separate disks into a single volume, forming a virtual "stripe" across the disks. This fault-tolerance technique enables multiple I/O operations in the same volume to proceed concurrently.

Documentation: A complete and accurate description and authorization of a transaction and each operation a transaction passes through. The written (can be automated) description of a system or program and how it operates.

Domain: A collection of computers that share a common domain database and security policy. Each domain has a unique name.

Domain controller: The server that authenticates domain log-ons and maintains the security policy and master database for a domain.

Domain name: A name assigned to a domain.

Double-click: As used in this book, to quickly press and release the mouse button twice without moving the mouse. Double-clicking is a means of rapidly selecting and activating a program or program feature.

Download: To transfer a file from a large computer or BBS to a personal computer. To *upload* is to perform the opposite operation.

Driver: A hardware device or a program that controls or regulates another device.

Duplexing: The concept of using two disk drives and two disk controllers to store data, one serving as primary and the other for backup purposes.

Dynamic Host Configuration Protocol (DHCP): The protocol used by a server to dynamically allocate IP addresses on a network. Designed to allow networked hosts to access configuration information across the network, instead of having to be configured by hand directly.

Dynamic routing: Internetwork routing that adjusts automatically to network topology or traffic changes based on information it receives from other routers.

Eavesdropping: Unauthorized interception of data transmissions.

Embarrassment: A parameter indicating the sensitivity of an organization to public knowledge of the information.

Employee related: Identifying or relating specifically to an employee of the organization.

Emulation: The imitation of a computer system, performed by a combination of hardware and software, that allows programs to run between incompatible systems.

Encapsulation: The process of adding protocol information to data from higher layers.

Encipher: To convert plaintext (clear) into unintelligible form by a cipher system.

Encryption: The process of converting data into a random set of characters unrecognizable to anyone except the intended recipient.

Enhanced IGRP (Enhanced Interior Gateway Routing Protocol, EIGRP): Advanced version of IGRP developed by Cisco. Provides superior convergence properties and operating efficiency, and combines the advantages of link state protocols with those of distance vector protocols. Compare with IGRP. See also *IGP, OSPF,* and *RIP.*

Enterprise network: A network bringing all sites together through a communications medium.

Error log: An audit trail of system warning messages displayed for the file server.

Ethernet: A local area network protocol developed by Xerox in 1973 and formalized in 1980. It is the most widely used network protocol.

Event: Any significant occurrence in the system or in an application that requires users to be notified, or an entry to be added to a log.

EXEC: Interactive command processor of Cisco IOS.

Expected lifetime: A parameter indicating the length of time the information is operative or has value to its owners.

Exposure: A quantitative rating (in dollars per year) expressing the organization's vulnerability to a given risk.

Extended partition: Free space on a hard disk that is used to allow the disk to be further partitioned into logical partitions or drives.

Fail safe: The automatic termination and protection of programs or other processing operations when a hardware or software failure is detected in a system.

Fail soft: The selective termination of affected nonessential processing when a hardware or software failure is detected in a system.

Fast switching: Cisco feature in which a route cache is used to expedite packet switching through a router. Contrast with *process switching.*

Fault tolerance: A computer and operating system's capability to respond gracefully to catastrophic events, such as a power outage or hardware failure. Usually, fault tolerance implies the capability either to continue the system's operation without loss of data or to shut down the system and restart it, recovering all processing in progress when the fault occurred.

Fiber-optic cable: A cable constructed using a thin glass core that conducts light rather than electrical signals.

Field: A particular type or category of information in a database management program (e.g., a variable). A location in a record where a particular type of data is stored. That is, a field is a single unit of data such as a name or address.

File: A single, named collection of related information stored on a magnetic medium.

File attribute: A restrictive label attached to a file that describes and regulates its use (e.g., archive, hidden, read-only, and system).

File server: A computer that shares files with other computers. Also, a computer that provides network stations with controlled access to shareable resources.

File size: The length of a file, typically given in bytes.

File system: In an operating system, the overall structure by which files are named, stored, and organized.

Firewall: One or more security devices with specialized software used to filter or block traffic from a less secure network to a more secure network.

Flash RAM: A special kind of ROM that you can erase and reprogram. Flash is used to store the Cisco IOS running on the router.

Format: The process of setting up a drive space to allow an operating system to use the space. Each operating system, such as MAC, DOS, and NT, uses distinct file system formats, and a drive must be formatted for the system to be able to use it.

Frequency: Number of cycles completed in one second.

FTP (File Transfer Protocol): A program that enables clients to transfer files between computers.

Full-duplex: Data can travel in both directions simultaneously.

Fully qualified domain name (FQDN): The complete host name and domain name of a network host.

Gateway: A device that provides routing and protocol conversion among physically dissimilar networks and computers (e.g., LAN to host, LAN to LAN, X.25, and SNA gateways). That is, a multi-homed host used to route network traffic from one network to another. Also used to pass network traffic from one protocol to another.

Gateway Discovery Protocol (CDP): Cisco protocol that allows hosts to dynamically detect the arrival of new routers as well as determine when a router goes down. Based on UDP. See also *UDP.*

Generic routing encapsulation (GRE): Tunneling protocol developed by Cisco that can encapsulate a wide variety of protocol packet types inside IP tunnels, creating a virtual point-to-point link to Cisco routers at remote points over an IP internetwork. By connecting multi-protocol subnetworks in a single-protocol backbone environment, IP tunneling using GRE allows network expansion across a single-protocol backbone environment.

Grant: To authorize.

GUI: Graphical user interface.

Hacker: A computer enthusiast. As used in the popular press, one who seeks to gain unauthorized access to computer systems.

Half-duplex: Data travels in either direction but not at the same time.

Handshaking: A dialog between a user and a computer, a computer and another computer, or one program and another program for identifying a user and authenticating his identity, through a sequence of questions and answers based on information either previously stored in the computer or supplied to the computer by the initiator of the dialog. Also, when used in context, it refers to the controlled movement of bits between a computer and a printer.

Hardware: In computer terminology, the machinery that forms a computer system.

Hardware address: The term used to describe the MAC address on a Macintosh address.

Helper address: Address configured on an interface to which broadcasts received on that interface will be sent.

Hertz (Hz): A measure of frequency or bandwidth. The same as cycles per second.

Hexadecimal: A numbering system that uses base 16.

Hierarchical database: A database organized in a tree-like structure.

Host computer: The computer that receives information from and sends data to terminals over telecommunication lines. It is also the computer that is in control in a data communications network. The host computer can be a mainframe computer, minicomputer, or microcomputer.

Host name resolution: The process of determining a network address when presented with a network host name and domain name, usually by consulting the Domain Name System.

Hot Standby Router Protocol (HSRP): Provides high network availability and transparent network topology changes. HSRP creates a Hot Standby router group with a lead router that services all packets sent to the Hot Standby address. The lead router is monitored by other routers in the group; and if it fails, one of these standby routers inherits the lead position and the Hot Standby group address.

Hub: (1) A device used on certain network topologies that modifies transmission signals, allowing the network to be lengthened or expanded with additional workstations. The hub is the central device in a star topology. (2) A computer that receives messages from other computers, stores them, and routes them to other computer destinations.

Hybrid: (1) On a local area network, the use of both peer-to-peer and client/server network architectures. (2) With respect to physical topology, the use of one or more physical topologies, including bus, ring, and star. (3) With respect to routing protocols, the use of both static and dynamic routes. (4) With respect to dynamic routing protocols, the use of features from both distance-vector and link-state algorithms.

I/O device (input/output device): A device that transfers information into or out of a computer.

Icon: In graphical environments, a small graphics image displayed on-screen to represent an object that can be manipulated by the user; for example, a recycle bin can represent a command for deleting unwanted text or files.

Identification: The process that enables, generally using unique machine-readable names, recognition of users or resources as identical with those previously described to a system.

IEEE (Institute of Electrical and Electronic Engineers): One of several groups whose members are drawn from industry and who attempt to establish industry standards. The IEEE 802 Committee has published numerous definitive documents on local area network standards.

Information: Includes input, output, software, data, and all related documentation.

Information pool: Consists of data designated as accessible by authorized individuals.

Initialize: (1) To set to an initial state or value in preparation for some computation. (2) To prepare a blank disk to receive information by organizing its surface into tracks and sectors; same as format.

Input/output (I/O): The process by which information is transferred between the computer's memory and its keyboard or peripheral devices.

Instance: An authorization level label for Kerberos principals. Most Kerberos principals are of the form user@REALM (e.g., ptdavis@pdaconsulting.COM). A Kerberos principal with a Kerberos instance has the form user/instance@REALM (e.g., ptdavis/admin@pdaconsulting.COM). The Kerberos instance can be used to specify the authorization level for the user if authentication is successful. It is up to the server of each network service to implement and enforce the authorization mappings of Kerberos instances. Note that the Kerberos realm name must be in uppercase characters.

Integrity: Freedom from errors.

Interior Gateway Routing Protocol (IGRP): IGP developed by Cisco to address the issues associated with routing in large, heterogeneous networks. Compare with *Enhanced IGRP.* See also *IGP, OSPF,* and *RIP.*

Interface: A device or program that allows two systems or devices to communicate with each other. An interface provides a common boundary between the two systems, devices, or programs. Also, the cables, connectors, and electrical circuits allowing communication between computers and printers.

Interface processor: Any of a number of processor modules used in the Cisco 7000 series routers.

Internetwork: Two or more connected networks or similar or different communication types.

Interrupt request lines (IRQ): Hardware lines over which devices can send signals to get the attention of the processor when the device is ready to accept or send information. Typically, each device connected to the computer uses a separate IRQ.

Intruder: A user or another agent attempting to gain unauthorized access to the file server.

IP address: A 32-bit network address that uniquely locates a host or network within its internetwork.

ISDN (Integrated Services Digital Network): A digital phone line that allows faster transmission speeds (128 kbps) than analog phone lines (56 kbps).

ISP (Internet service provider): A firm that offers connections to the Internet for a fee.

Jitter: Instability of a signal for a brief period.

Job: A combined run of one or more application programs that are automatically processed in sequence in the computer.

K56flex: A Rockwell International technology for the transmission of data over telephone lines with a capacity of 56Kbps.

Keep-alive message: A data packet sent between Session layers to keep inactivity from causing the connection to close down.

Kerberized: Applications and services that have been modified to support the Kerberos credential infrastructure.

Kerberos realm: A domain consisting of users, hosts, and network services that are registered to a Kerberos server. The Kerberos server is trusted to verify the identity of a user or network service to another user or network service. Kerberos realms must always be in uppercase characters.

Kerberos server: A daemon running on a network host. Users and network services register their identity with the Kerberos server. Network services query the Kerberos server to authenticate to other network services.

Kernel: The core of an operating system. The portion of the system that manages memory, files, and peripheral devices; maintains the time and date; launches applications; and allocates system resources.

Key distribution center (KDC): A Kerberos server and database program running on a network host.

Least privilege: A principle that users should be assigned only the access needed to perform their business functions.

Local area network (LAN): A communications system that uses directly connected computers, printers, and hard disks, allowing shared access to all resources on the network.

Logic bomb: Malicious action, initiated by software, that inhibits the normal system functions; a logic bomb takes effect only when specified conditions occur.

Logical access: Access to the information content of a record or field.

Logical file: Refers to the data that a file contains.

Logical partition: A subpartition of an extended partition on a drive, commonly called a logical drive. See *extended partition.*

Log-in: The process of accessing a file server or computer after physical connection has been established.

Log-on: The process of identifying oneself to a computer after connecting to it over a communications line. During a log-on procedure, the computer usually requests the user's name and a password. Also called log-in.

Mainframe: The term used for very large computers that support thousands of users and huge databases.

Map: (1) To assign a workstation drive letter to a server directory. (2) To translate a virtual address into a physical address.

Media Access Control (MAC): Part of the physical layer of a network that identifies the actual physical link between two nodes.

Media Access Control address: The address of the device that is found on the NIC. Also known as the physical address.

Menu: A list of options from which users select.

Menu option: An option on a menu that performs some action, prompts the user for additional information, or leads to another menu.

Microcomputer: A general term referring to a small computer having a micro-processor.

Mirroring: A method of ensuring data replication using two hard drives that are connected to the same disk controller. Less robust than duplexing because of the shared controller. Otherwise, duplexing and mirroring can be considered to be essentially the same.

Modem: A modulator-demodulator. A device that lets computers communicate over telephone lines by converting digital signals into the phone system's analog signals, and vice versa.

Modification: The partial alteration of an asset such that the form or quality of it has been changed somewhat. A file can appear intact and can be perfectly usable, but it may contain erroneous information.

Monitoring: The use of automated procedures to ensure that the controls implemented within a system are not circumvented.

Multi-homed: A computer that has more than one network card, either physically or logically. Often used as a router for connecting two networks.

Need-to-know: The necessity for access to, knowledge of, or possession of sensitive information to fulfill official duties. Responsibility for determining whether a person's duties require that he have access to certain information, and whether he is authorized to receive it, rests on the owner of the information involved and not on the prospective recipient.

NetBIOS Extended User Interface (NetBEUI): A small, fast protocol that requires little memory but is not routable.

NETscout: Cisco network management application that provides an easy-to-use GUI for monitoring RMON statistics and protocol analysis information. NETscout also provides extensive tools that simplify data collection, analysis, and reporting. These tools allow system administrators to monitor traffic, set thresholds, and capture data on any set of network traffic for any segment.

Network: A collection of interconnected, individually controlled computers, printers, and hard disks, along with the hardware and software used to connect them.

Network adapter: A circuit board that plugs into a slot in a PC and has one or more sockets to which you attach cables. Provides the physical link between the PC and the network cable. Also called network adapter card, network card, and network interface card (NIC).

Network address: A unique identifier of an entity on a network, usually represented as a number or series of numbers.

Network Basic Input/Output Operating System (NetBIOS): A network file-sharing application designed for use with PC DOS personal computers, usually implemented under TCP/IP at the application layer.

Network drive: An online storage device available to network users.

Network interface card (NIC): See *network adapter*.

Network operating system: An operating system installed on a server in a local area network that coordinates the activities of providing services to the computers and other devices attached to the network.

Network segment: The area of the network bound by bridges or switches where collisions are propagated, or the area bound by a router to prevent the propagation of broadcasts.

Network station: Any PC or other device connected to a network by means of a network interface board and some communications medium. A network station can be a workstation, bridge, or server.

Node: A point of interconnection to a network. Normally, a point at which a number of terminals are located.

Object: A passive entity that contains or receives data. Access to an object potentially implies access to the information it contains.

Offline: State in which the printer or some other device is not ready to receive data.

Operating system: Software that controls the internal operations (housekeeping chores) of a computer system. Operating systems are specific to the type of computer used.

Owner: An employee or agent of the client who is assigned responsibility for making and communicating certain judgments and decisions regarding business control and selective protection of assets, and for monitoring compliance with specified controls.

Package: A generic term referring to any group of detailed computer programs necessary to achieve a general objective. For example, an accounts receivable package would include all programs necessary to record transactions in customer accounts, produce customer statements, etc.

Packet: A group of bits transmitted as a whole on a network.

Pad: The shortened term for packet assembler-dissembler used in X.25 technologies.

Paging: The act of moving data to disk when physical memory is full. A component of virtual memory.

Parallel interface: A printer interface that handles data in parallel fashion, 8 bits (1 byte) at a time.

Parity bit: A way of marking the eighth bit in a data byte so that 7-bit ASCII characters between 0 and 127 are sent and received correctly. There are three kinds of parity: odd, even, and none.

Partition: A portion of a physical disk that functions as if it were a separate unit.

Password: Privileged information given to, or created by, the user, which is entered into a system for authentication purposes. A protected word or secret character string used to authenticate the claimed identity of an individual, a resource, or an access type.

Peer: In the context of encryption, a peer refers to a router or other device that participates in IPSec and IKE.

PCI: A 32-bit data transfer bus used in newer machines and generally faster than the older EISA bus. Most Intel-based machines built today support this standard.

Penetration: A successful unauthorized access to a system.

Perfect forward secrecy (PFS): A cryptographic characteristic associated with a derived shared secret value. With PFS, when someone compromises one key, he does not compromise previous and subsequent keys as well because the algorithm does not derive subsequent keys from previous keys.

Peripheral: Any device used for input/output operations with the computer's central processing unit (CPU). Peripheral devices are typically connected to the microcomputer with special cabling and include such devices as modems and printers.

Permission: (1) A particular form of allowed access; for example, permission to read as contrasted with permission to write. (2) A rule associated with an object (usually a directory, file, or printer) to regulate which users can access the object and in what manner.

Physical drive: The actual hardware that is set in the computer and used to store information. Often called the hard drive, C drive, or D drive after the letter assigned to it by the system.

Physical layer: The bottom layer of the OSI model, the physical layer specifies the type of media for use, the transmission format, and the topology of the network.

Physical security: Physical protection of assets achieved through implementing security measures.

PING: A network application that uses ICMP to verify reachability of another host on any internetwork.

Plaintext: Intelligible text or signals that have meaning and that can be read or acted on without the application of any decryption.

Polling: A means of controlling devices on a line.

Port: (1) A connection or socket used to connect a device to a computer, such as a printer, monitor, or modem. Information is sent from the computer to the device through a cable. (2) A communications channel through which a client process communicates with a protected subsystem.

Presentation layer: Layer 6 of the OSI model, the presentation layer manages the conversion from data structures used by the computer to a form necessary for communication over the network.

Principal: (1) The entity in a computer system to which authorizations are granted; thus, the unit of accountability in a computer system. (2) Also known as a Kerberos identity, this is who you are or what a service is according to the Kerberos server.

Privileges: A means of protecting the use of certain system functions that can affect system resources and integrity. System managers grant privileges according to the user's needs and deny them to restrict the user's access to the system. See *need-to-know*.

Process switching: Operation that provides full route evaluation and per-packet load balancing across parallel WAN links. Involves the transmission of entire frames to the router CPU, where they are repackaged for delivery to or from a WAN interface, with the router making a route selection for each packet. Process switching is the most resource-intensive switching operation that the CPU can perform. Contrast with *fast switching*.

Processing: A systematic sequence of operations performed on data.

Promiscuous mode: Collecting all data from the network, regardless of the ultimate physical address.

Protocol: (1) A set of characters at the beginning and end of a message that enables two computers to communicate with each other. (2) In networking, procedures or rules that control the way information is sent or received over the network.

Queue: A first-in/first-out data structure used for managing requests to process data; for example, files to be printed.

RAS (Remote Access Services): This is the NT 3.x version of Dial-Up Networking; it is used to connect machines together via telephone or other means.

Read: A fundamental operation that results only in the flow of information from an object to a subject.

Read access: Permission to read data.

Read-only: A term used to describe information stored in such a way that it can be played back (read) but not changed (written).

Record: A collection of related information (fields) that is treated as one unit within a file.

Redirector: Networking software that accepts I/O requests for remote files, named pipes, or mail slots and then sends (redirects) them to a network server on another machine.

Remote administration: Administration of one computer by an administrator located at another computer and connected to the first computer across the network.

Repeater: A device that extends the range of a network cable segment. A hub is really just a multi-port repeater.

Repudiation: A quality that prevents a third party from proving that a communication between two other parties ever took place. This is a desirable quality when you do not want your communications traced. Non-repudiation is the opposite quality: a third party can prove that a communication between two other parties took place. Non-repudiation is desirable if you want to trace your communications and prove that they occurred.

Request for Comments (RFC): The official designation of the Internet standards documents.

Resource: In a system, any function, device, or data collection that can be allocated to users or programs.

Resource sharing: The concurrent use of a resource by more than one user, job, or program.

Revoke: To take away previously authorized access from some principal.

Rights: User capabilities given for accessing files and directories on a file server.

Ring: A network topology that connects each workstation in a circular fashion and sends the network signal in a unidirectional manner through the circle.

RISC: Reduced Instruction Set Computer.

Risk: The potential that a given threat will occur within a specific period. The potential for realization of unwanted, negative consequences of an event.

Risk analysis: An analysis of system assets and vulnerabilities to establish an expected loss from certain events based on estimated probabilities of the occurrence of those events.

Routed protocol: A protocol transmittable to other networks by way of a router; examples include AppleTalk, DECnet, IP, and IPX.

Router: A layer 3 device that connects two or more networks together. A router reads packets sent along the network and determines their correct destination.

Routing protocol: A protocol that uses a specific algorithm to route data across a network.

Routing table: A table for keeping track of the routes to networks and the metrics associated with those networks.

Sag: A reduction in electrical signal to 80 percent of the normal voltage. Also known as a brownout.

Scavenging: Randomly searching for valuable data in a computer's memory or in discarded or incompletely erased magnetic media.

SCSI: The acronym for Small Computer System Interface. Originally designed for the UNIX world, it is designed to handle high speeds and multiple devices, such as disk and tape drives.

Security: Protection of all those resources that the client uses to complete its mission.

Security association (SA): Describes how two or more entities will utilize security services to communicate securely. For example, an IPSec SA defines the encryption algorithm (if used), the authentication algorithm, and the shared session key to be used during the IPSec connection.

Security descriptor: A data structure attached to an object that protects the object from unauthorized access. It contains an access control list (ACL) and controls auditing on the object.

Security policy: The set of laws, rules, and practices that regulate how an organization manages, protects, and distributes sensitive information.

Security policy database (SPD): Defines the traffic using IPSec security services. Cisco uses access lists to define the SPD.

Sensitive: A data classification category. Loss, misuse, or unauthorized disclosure of data with this protection classification would have a serious negative impact. Such an incident would be very harmful to the organization.

Sensitive program: An application program whose misuse through unauthorized activity could lead to serious misappropriation or loss of assets.

Sensitivity: The characteristic of a resource that implies its value or importance and can include its vulnerability.

Serial interface: An interface that handles data in serial fashion, one bit at a time.

Server: A computer that shares its resources (e.g., files and printers) with other computers on a network.

Server Manager: An application used to view and administer domains, workgroups, and computers.

Service credential: A credential for a network service. When issued from the KDC, this credential is encrypted with the password shared by the network service and the KDC, and with the user's TGT.

Session layer: Layer 5 of the OSI model, the session layer creates, maintains, and terminates communication between devices on a network.

Shared directory: A directory where network users can connect.

Shielding: Protective covering that eliminates electromagnetic and radio frequency interference.

Silicon switching: Switching based on the SSE, which allows the processing of packets independent of the SSP (Silicon Switch Processor) system processor. Silicon switching provides high-speed, dedicated packet switching. See also *silicon switching engine* and *Silicon Switch Processor.*

Silicon switching engine (SSE): Routing and switching mechanism that compares the data-link or network layer header of an incoming packet with a silicon-switching cache, determines the appropriate action (routing or bridging), and forwards the packet to the proper interface. The SSE is directly encoded in the hardware of the SSP (Silicon Switch Processor) of a Cisco 7000 series router. It can therefore perform switching independently of the system processor, making the execution of routing decisions much quicker than if they were encoded in software. See also *silicon switching* and *Silicon Switch Processor.*

Silicon Switch Processor (SSP): High-performance silicon switch for Cisco 7000 series routers that provides distributed processing and control for interface processors. The SSP leverages the high-speed switching and routing capabilities of the SSE to dramatically increase aggregate router performance, minimizing performance bottlenecks at the interface points between the router and a high-speed backbone. See also *silicon switching* and *silicon switching engine.*

Simplex: A transmission flow that only allows communication in one direction.

Small computer system interface (SCSI): A standard used for connecting microcomputers to peripheral devices, such as hard disks and printers, and to other computers and local area networks.

Sneaker: A computer professional who seeks to test security by attempting to gain unauthorized access to computer systems.

Software: Programs and routines to be loaded temporarily into a computer system, for example, compilers, utilities, and operating system and application programs.

SRVTAB: A password that a network service shares with the KDC. The network service authenticates an encrypted service credential by using the SRVTAB (also known as a KEYTAB) to decrypt it.

Stack: As used in this book, a synonym for protocol.

Star: A topology in which each node is connected to a central hub.

Subject: The combination of the user's access token and the program acting on the user's behalf.

Submenu: A menu below the main menu.

Subnet: A physical or logical subdivision of a TCP/IP network; usually a separate physical segment that uses a division of the site's IP network address to route traffic within the organizational internetwork.

Switched Port Analyzer (SPAN): Feature of the Catalyst 5000 switch that extends the monitoring abilities of existing network analyzers into a switched Ethernet environment. SPAN mirrors the traffic at one switched segment onto a pre-defined SPAN port. A network analyzer attached to the SPAN port can monitor traffic from any of the other Catalyst switched ports.

TACACS+ (Terminal Access Controller Access Control System Plus): Proprietary Cisco enhancement to Terminal Access Controller Access Control System (TACACS). Provides additional support for authentication, authorization, and accounting.

TCP/IP (Transmission Control Protocol/Internet Protocol): This is the protocol suite that drives the Internet. Very basically, TCP handles the message details and IP manages the addressing. It is probably the most widely used network protocol in the world today.

TCSEC: The Trusted Computer System Evaluation Criteria.

Telecommunication: The electronic transfer of information via telephone lines from computer to computer. See *bulletin board system, modem.*

Telnet: A program that allows terminal emulation for communicating between machines via TCP/IP.

TFTP (Trivial File Transfer Protocol): A simpler version of the FTP program that operates using UDP/IP services.

Threat: One or more events that can lead to either intentional or unintentional modification, destruction, or disclosure of data. If this eventuality were to occur, it would lead to an undesirable effect on the environment.

Ticket granting ticket (TGT): A credential that the key distribution center (KDC) issues to authenticated users. When users receive a TGT, they can authenticate to network services within the Kerberos realm represented by the KDC.

Token Ring: A network topology regulated by the passing of a token that governs the right to transmit.

Topology: The physical layout of the network cabling.

Transaction: A set of operations that completes a unified task.

Transient: An abrupt change in voltage, of short duration.

transmission-on/transmission-off (X-ON/X-OFF): A type of software handshaking.

Trapdoor: A set of special instructions, originally created for testing and troubleshooting, that bypasses security procedures and allows direct access to a computer's operating system or to other software.

Trojan horse: A program, purporting to do useful work, that conceals instructions to breach security whenever the software is invoked.

Trust relationship: Links between domains that enable passthrough authentication, in which a user only has one user account in one domain yet can access the entire network. A trusting domain honors the log-on authentications of a trusted domain.

Twisted pair: A common type of wiring that uses wires twisted together yet insulated from each other. Can be purchased shielded or unshielded.

UDP (User Datagram Protocol): An older protocol that does not offer good error detection or recovery. It is used by SNMP and TFTP, as well as the Network File System (NFS).

Unbounded media: Media that use radio frequencies, microwaves, or other media to transmit data.

User: Used imprecisely to refer to the individual who is accountable for some identifiable set of activities in a computer system.

User group: A computer club in which computer users exchange tips and information, publish a newsletter, support a local BBS, and listen to sales pitches from vendors at meetings. A meeting of like-minded individuals who practice information sharing, for example, GUIDE, SHARE, DECUS, ISSA, and EDPAA.

Utilities: Useful programs with which you can rename, copy, format, delete, and otherwise manipulate files and volumes.

V.90: An ITU-T standard for the transmission of data at a capacity of 56 kpbs over voice-grade lines.

Verification: Confirmation that the object is what it purports to be. Also, confirmation of the identity of a person (or other agent external to the protection system) making a request.

Virtual memory: Combines the physical RAM available in the machine with disk space to simulate an environment in which you have more memory than you physically have in RAM.

Virus: A program, usually a Trojan horse, that copies itself into new databases and computers whenever the infected parent program is invoked.

Volume: A storage device, such as a disk pack, mass storage system cartridge, or magnetic tape. For our purposes, diskettes, cassettes, mag cards, and the like are treated as volumes.

Volume set: A collection of partitions possibly spread over several disk drives that has been formatted for use as if it were a single drive.

Vulnerability: The cost that an organization would incur if an event were to happen.

Wideband: A communications channel that has greater bandwidth than voice-grade lines.

Wiretapping: Monitoring or recording data as it moves across a communications link; also known as traffic analysis.

Workgroup: In peer-to-peer networks, a workgroup is a name used on a network to represent a logical grouping of users organized by job type.

Workstation: In general, a powerful computer having considerable calculating and graphics capability.

Worm: A program that deletes data from a computer's memory.

Write: A fundamental operation that results only in the flow of data from a subject to an object.

Write access: Permission to write an object.

X.25: A protocol that allows you to route information through a packet-switching public data network, such as Datapac. An older technology, it operates at a top speed of 64 kbps and was designed for earlier days when telephone networks were less reliable than today.

About the Author

Peter T. Davis has 27 years of experience with information systems in large-scale installations in the financial and government sectors. He is now principal of Peter Davis & Associates, a training and consulting firm specializing in the security, audit, and control of information systems.

Davis is the author or co-author of eight other books, including *Computer Security for Dummies, Securing Client/Server Networks, Teach Yourself Windows NT Server 4 in 21 Days,* and *Teach Yourself Windows 2000 Server in 21 Days.* He is also an internationally known speaker on quality, security, audit, and control, and frequently speaks at user and professional conferences and meetings.

He received his Bachelor of Commerce (B. Comm) degree from Carleton University and holds several certifications, including Certified Management Accountant (CMA), Certified Information Systems Auditor (CISA), Information Systems Professional (ISP), Certified Information Systems Security Professional (CISSP), Certified Novell Administrator v3.11 (CNA), Certified Management Consultant (CMC), and Cisco Certified Network Administrator (CCNA). He is listed in the *International Who's Who of Professionals.*

Davis currently lives in Toronto, Ontario, Canada, with his wife and daughter. You can contact him via e-mail at ptdavis@pdaconsulting.com or by visiting www.pdaconsulting.com.

Index

9 780849 312908

Printed and bound by CPI Group (UK) Ltd, Croydon, CR0 4YY

22/10/2024

01777636-0020